The ultimate stats and facts guide to English Cup Football

Steve Pearce

BOXTREE

Thanks

SHOOT would like to thank Final Score RSL for their editorial and technical expertise in putting this publication together and Ian Cruise, Tim Barnett, Ian Piercy, David Prole, Tony Brown, Chris Peck, Tony Grimsey and Emma Mann for their invaluable assistance to the editor.

First published in 1997 by Boxtree, an imprint of Macmillan Publishers Ltd, 25 Eccleston Place, London SW1W 9NF and Basingstoke

Associated companies throughout the world

ISBN 0 7522 2234 1

Design by Colin Halliday.
All photographs by Professional Sport.
Statistics supplied by Final Score RSL. Tel 01277 632070. Fax 01277 632080

9 8 7 6 5 4 3 2 1

A CIP catalogue record for this book is available from the British Library

Printed by Mackays of Chatham plc, Kent

SHOOT magazine is published weekly by IPC Magazines Ltd, King's Reach Tower, Stamford St, London SE1 9LS. Subscription enquiries: Quadrant Subscription Services, FREEPOST CY1061, Haywards Heath, West Sussex RH16 3ZA. Tel: 01444 445555.

* Every effort has been made to ensure that the statistics in this book are correct at the time of going to press. Any omissions are entirely unintentional.

Contents

History of the League Cup

For the record

Introduction

The FA Cup is the oldest and most famous Cup competition in the world and the Final played at Wembley is watched each year by millions of soccer fans around the globe.

Every football mad schoolboy and every professional footballer dreams of coming out of the tunnel at the Twin Towers and walking on to the lush green turf to play in the FA Cup Final.

SHOOT, Britain's most famous football magazine, looks back over the years to the players who have realised that dream, the stars who have graced the competition, the clubs that have tasted glory, the moments that have made history and the heroes and villains of the greatest soccer tournament in the game.

Our *Ultimate Stats and Facts Guide to English Cup Football* is packed with information, giving a detailed and unrivalled history of the FA Cup, including EVERY match result from the First Round onwards.

There's also an extensive look at the League Cup, taking in EVERY result there has ever been in that competition as well, plus spotlights on the stars of the tournaments and amazing facts and feats surrounding the games and goals.

Included in both sections are special profiles on some of the greatest players who have graced the English Cup scene, top stars such as Bryan Robson, Mark Hughes, Ian Wright and Steve McManaman and a look at the teams that have tasted glory in both the major English Cup competitions down the years.

And that's not all. In typical SHOOT style, we've added that touch of humour that proves football really is a funny old game with loads of wild and wacky Cup tales.

If it's facts and stats you want, this is the book for you. Enjoy.

DAVE SMITH
SHOOT SPECIAL PROJECTS EDITOR

CHAPTER 1 History of the FA Cup

1872-1899

THE BIRTH OF THE FA CUP

The FA Cup was originally conceived at a meeting of the Football Association in London on July 20th, 1871, when the idea of a challenge competition was first aired.

Three months later, on October 16th, the rules were drafted and the first entries were received. But the originators didn't realise quite what an extraordinary competition their vision had created - the FA Cup was to become the greatest knock-out tournament in the world.

The first Cup - a stubby, heavily embossed silver trophy - was purchased for the princely sum of £20 and 15 teams entered that original competition: Barnes, Civil Service, Clapham Rovers, Crystal Palace (no connection with the present-day club), Hampstead Heathens, Harrow Chequers, Hitchin, Maidenhead, Marlow, Reigate Priory, Royal Engineers, Upton Park, The Wanderers, Queens' Park of Glasgow and Donnington School in south Lincolnshire.

After a patchy and erratic tournament - from which three clubs withdrew and Queen's Park were exempted until the Semi-Finals because of cost and distance - the Final at The Oval on March 16th, 1872, was between The Wanderers and Royal Engineers, watched by a crowd of 2,000.

The Engineers were firm favourites but, in the first of the great and romantic giantkilling acts which have helped give the FA Cup its very own place in footballing folklore, Wanderers snatched the trophy 1-0, with a goal from the wonderfully named Morton Peto Betts.

So the Cup had been born and The Wanderers would return a year later to retain the trophy with a 2-1 victory over Oxford University. Indeed, The Wanderers - the Manchester United of their day - would go on to take the trophy five times in the first seven years of the competition, with only Oxford University (1874) and Royal Engineers (1875) challenging their supremacy.

The only other side to enjoy a run of success like that in the early days were Blackburn Rovers, who won the trophy five times in nine years between 1883 and 1891.

Name Game

Morton Peto Betts, scorer of the first FA Cup Final goal, for Wanderers in 1872, was named after Samuel Morton Peto, an engineer who built Nelson's Column.

Split Personality

Francis Marindin could have played for either team in the 1875 Final - he was both an Old Etonian and a major in the Royal Engineers. He decided not to play for either.

KEY
a = abandoned
b = bye
B = both teams went through
d = disqualified
D = home team disqualified
d (end of line) = away team disqualified
e = extra-time
E = both teams were disqualified
N = neutral ground
nr = home team bye to next round
nrd = away team bye to next round
P = home team won on penalties
q = away team won on penalties
r = replay
s = scratched
s (end of line) =2nd-leg (1946)
T = home team went through on a toss of a coin
v = void game
w = walkover

1872

FIRST ROUND				
Barnes	2	Civil Ser	0	
Hampstead	b	Bye	-	
Hitchin	0	C.Palace	0	B
Maidenhd	2	Marlow	0	
Queens Pk	d	Donintn S	d	B
Royal Eng	w	Reigate P	s	
Upton Pk	0	Clapham R	3	
Wander's	w	Harrow Cq	s	
SECOND ROUND				
Barnes	1	Hampstead	1	
C.Palace	3	Maidenhd	0	
Hitchin	0	Royal Eng	5	
Queens Pk	w	Donintn S	s	
Wanderers	3	Clapham R	1	
Hampstead	1	Barnes	0	r
THIRD ROUND				
Queens Pk	b	Bye	-	
Royal Eng	3	Hampstead	0	
Wanderers	0	C.Palace	0	B
SEMI-FINAL				
Royal Eng	0	C.Palace	0	N
Wanderers	0	Queens Pk	0	N
Royal Eng	3	C.Palace	0	rN
Wanderers	w	Queens Pk	s	r
FINAL				
Wanderers	1	Royal Eng	0	N

1873

FIRST ROUND				
Barnes	0	S.Norwood	1	
Civil Ser	0	Royal Eng	3	
Clapham R	w	Hitchin	s	
C.Palace	2	Oxford U	3	
Maidenhd	1	Marlow	0	
Queens Pk	b	Bye	-	
Reigate P	2	Windsor H	4	
Upton Pk	0	1 Surrey R	2	
Wanderers	b	Bye	-	
SECOND ROUND				
1 Surrey R	0	Maidenhd	3	
Clapham R	0	Oxford U	3	
Queens Pk	b	Bye	-	
Royal Eng	b	Bye	-	
S.Norwood	1	Windsor H	0	v
Wanderers	b	Bye	-	
Windsor H	3	S.Norwood	0	r
THIRD ROUND				
Maidenhd	1	Windsor H	0	
Oxford U	1	Royal Eng	0	
Queens Pk	b	Bye	-	
Wanderers	b	Bye	-	
FOURTH ROUND				
Oxford U	4	Maidenhd	0	
Queens Pk	b	Bye	-	
Wanderers	b	Bye	-	
SEMI-FINAL				
Oxford U	w	Queens Pk	s	
Wanderers	b	Bye	-	
FINAL				
Wanderers	2	Oxford U	0	N

1874

FIRST ROUND				
1 Surrey R	0	Barnes	0	
Cambs Uv	1	S.Norwood	0	
Clapham R	w	Am.Ath.Cb	s	
C.Palace	0	Swifts	1	
H.Wycomb	w	O.Etonian	s	
Maidenhd	w	Civil Ser	s	
Marlow	0	Pilgrims	1	
Royal Eng	5	Brondsby	0	
Shrops Wa	0	Sheffield	0	
Trojans	w	Farninghm	s	
Upton Pk	0	Oxford U	4	
Uxbridge	3	Gitanos	0	
Wander's	w	Southl Pk	s	
Woodfd W	3	Reigate P	2	
Barnes	1	1 Surrey R	0	r
Sheffield	0	Shrops Wa	0	rT
SECOND ROUND				
Clapham R	1	Cambs Uv	1	
Maidenhd	1	H.Wycomb	0	
Oxford U	2	Barnes	0	
Royal Eng	2	Uxbridge	1	
Sheffield	1	Pilgrims	0	
Swifts	2	Woodfd W	1	
Wander's	w	Trojans	s	
Clapham R	1	Cambs Uv	1	r
Clapham R	4	Cambs Uv	1	r2
THIRD ROUND				
Clapham R	2	Sheffield	1	N
Royal Eng	7	Maidenhd	0	
Swifts	b	Bye	-	
Wanderers	1	Oxford U	1	
Oxford U	1	Wanderers	0	r
SEMI-FINAL				
Oxford U	1	Clapham R	0	N
Royal Eng	2	Swifts	0	N
FINAL				
Oxford U	2	Royal Eng	0	N

1875

FIRST ROUND				
Cambs Uv	0	C.Palace	0	
Civil Ser	w	Harrow Cq	s	
Clapham R	3	Panthers	0	
Hitchin	0	Maidenhd	1	
O.Etonian	0	Swifts	0	
Oxford U	6	Brondsby	0	
Pilgrims	3	S.Norwood	1	
Reigate P	b	Bye	-	
Royal Eng	3	Marlow	0	
Shrops Wa	w	Sheffield	s	
Southl Pk	0	Leyton	0	
Upton Pk	0	Barnes	3	
Wanderers	16	Farninghm	0	
Windsor H	w	Uxbridge	s	
Woodfd W	1	H.Wycomb	0	
Cambs Uv	2	C.Palace	1	r
Leyton	0	Southl Pk	5	r
Swifts	1	O.Etonian	1	r
O.Etonian	3	Swifts	0	r2
SECOND ROUND				
Clapham R	2	Pilgrims	0	
Maidenhd	2	Reigate P	1	
O.Etonian	b	Bye	-	
Oxford U	w	Windsor H	s	
Royal Eng	5	Cambs Uv	0	
Shrops Wa	1	Civil Ser	0	
Wanderers	5	Barnes	0	
Woodfd W	3	Southl Pk	0	
THIRD ROUND				
O.Etonian	1	Maidenhd	0	
Royal Eng	3	Clapham R	2	
Shrops Wa	1	Woodfd W	1	e
Wanderers	1	Oxford U	2	
Woodfd W	0	Shrops Wa	2	r
SEMI-FINAL				
O.Etonian	1	Shrops Wa	0	N
Royal Eng	1	Oxford U	1	N
Royal Eng	1	Oxford U	0	reN
FINAL				
Royal Eng	1	O.Etonian	1	eN
Royal Eng	2	O.Etonian	0	rN

1876

FIRST ROUND				
105 Rgmt	0	C.Palace	0	
Cambs Uv	w	Civil Ser	s	
Clapham R	w	Hitchin	s	
Herts Rng	4	Rochester	0	
Leyton	w	Harrow Cq	s	
Maidenhd	2	Ramblers	0	
O.Etonian	4	Pilgrims	1	
Oxford U	6	Forest Sh	0	
Panthers	1	Woodfd W	0	
Reigate P	1	Barnes	0	
Royal Eng	15	H.Wycomb	0	
S.Norwo'd	w	Clydesdle	s	
Sheffield	w	Shrops Wa	s	
Swifts	2	Marlow	0	

Doctor, Doctor

Robert Mills-Roberts, Preston goalkeeper in the 1888 and 1889 Finals, helped to treat injured players in both matches. He was a qualified doctor.

WHAT A STAR ★ ARTHUR KINNAIRD

The Honourable Arthur Kinnaird was 'without doubt the best player of the day' in soccer's early period. He won the FA Cup three times with Wanderers, scoring in all three Finals, then won two, drew two and lost four with Old Etonians, earning a reputation for vigour - "Let us have hacking," he cried - as well as devising ready tactics. When his mother said she feared he would come home with a broken leg, a friend replied: "If he does, madam, it will not be his own!" Kinnaird served as President of the FA for 33 years, but ironically died a few months before the FA Cup Final was played for the first time at Wembley.

Upton Pk	1	Southl Pk	0	
Wanderers	5	1 Surrey R	0	
C.Palace	3	105 Rgmt	0	r

SECOND ROUND

Clapham R	12	Leyton	0	
O.Etonian	8	Maidenhd	0	
Oxford U	8	Herts Rng	2	
Reigate P	0	Cambs Uv	8	
Royal Eng	w	Panthers	s	
S.Norwood	0	Swifts	5	
Sheffield	w	Upton Pk	s	
Wanderers	3	C.Palace	0	

THIRD ROUND

Cambs Uv	0	Oxford U	4	
O.Etonian	1	Clapham R	0	
Royal Eng	1	Swifts	3	
Wanderers	2	Sheffield	0	

SEMI-FINAL

Oxford U	0	O.Etonian	1	N
Wanderers	2	Swifts	1	N

FINAL

Wanderers	1	O.Etonian	1	N
Wanderers	3	O.Etonian	0	rN

1877

FIRST ROUND

105 Rgmt	3	1 Surrey R	0	
Barnes	w	O.Etonian	s	
Cambs Uv	w	H.Wycomb	s	
Clapham R	5	Reigate P	0	
Forest Sh	4	Gresham	1	
Herts Rng	1	Marlow	2	
Oxford U	w	O.Salopns	s	
Panthers	3	Wood Grg	0	
Pilgrims	4	Ramblers	1	
Queens Pk	b	Bye	-	
Rochester	5	Highbury	0	
Royal Eng	2	O.Harrovn	1	
S.Norwood	4	Saxons	1	
Sheffield	w	Trojans	s	
Shrops Wa	w	Druids	s	
Southl Pk	w	O.Wykemst	s	
Swifts	2	Reading H	0	
Upton Pk	7	Leyton	0	
Wanderer	w	Saffron W	s	

SECOND ROUND

Cambs Uv	2	Clapham R	1	
Marlow	1	Forest Sh	0	
Oxford U	6	105 Rgmt	1	
Pilgrims	1	Panthers	0	
Queens Pk	b	Bye	-	
Rochester	1	Swifts	0	
Royal Eng	3	Shrops Wa	0	
S.Norwood	0	Sheffield	7	
Upton Pk	1	Barnes	0	
Wanderers	6	Southl Pk	0	

THIRD ROUND

Cambs Uv	4	Rochester	0	
Oxford U	w	Queens Pk	s	
Royal Eng	1	Sheffield	0	
Upton Pk	2	Marlow	2	
Wanderers	3	Pilgrims	0	
Upton Pk	1	Marlow	0	r

FOURTH ROUND

Cambs Uv	1	Royal Eng	0	
Oxford U	0	Upton Pk	0	
Wanderers	b	Bye	-	
Oxford U	1	Upton Pk	0	r

SEMI-FINAL

Oxford U	b	Bye	-	
Wanderers	1	Cambs Uv	0	N

FINAL

Wanderers	2	Oxford U	1	eN

1878

FIRST ROUND

105 Rgmt	0	O.Harrovn	2	
1 Surrey R	1	Forest Sh	0	
Barnes	w	St Marks	s	
Cambs Uv	3	Southl Pk	1	
Darwen	3	Manchestr	0	
Druids	1	Shrops Wa	0	
Grantham	0	Clapham R	2	
Hawks	5	Minerva	2	
H.Wycomb	4	Wood Grg	0	
Maidenhd	10	Reading H	0	
Marlow	2	Hendon	0	
Notts Co	1	Sheffield	1	
O.Forests	w	O.Wykemst	s	
Oxford U	5	Herts Rng	2	
Pilgrims	0	Ramblers	0	
Queens Pk	b	Bye	-	
Reading	2	S.Norwood	0	
Remnants	4	St Stephns	0	
Royal Eng	w	Highbury	s	
Swifts	3	Leyton	2	
Upton Pk	3	Rochester	0	
Wanderers	9	Panthers	1	
Pilgrims	1	Ramblers	0	r
Sheffield	3	Notts Co	0	r

SECOND ROUND

Barnes	3	Marlow	1	
Cambs Uv	4	Maidenhd	2	e
Clapham R	4	Swifts	0	
Druids	w	Queens Pk	s	
H.Wycomb	0	Wanderers	9	
O.Harrovn	6	1 Surrey R	0	
Oxford U	1	O.Forests	0	
Remnants	2	Hawks	0	
Royal Eng	6	Pilgrims	0	
Sheffield	1	Darwen	0	
Upton Pk	1	Reading	0	

THIRD ROUND

O.Harrovn	2	Cambs Uv	2	
Oxford U	3	Clapham R	2	
Royal Eng	8	Druids	0	
Sheffield	b	Bye	-	
Upton Pk	3	Remnants	0	
Wanderers	1	Barnes	1	
O.Harrovn	2	Cambs Uv	2	re
Wanderers	4	Barnes	1	r
O.Harrovn	2	Cambs Uv	0	r2

FOURTH ROUND

O.Harrovn	3	Upton Pk	1	
Royal Eng	3	Oxford U	3	
Wanderers	3	Sheffield	0	
Royal Eng	2	Oxford U	2	re
Royal Eng	4	Oxford U	2	r2

SEMI-FINAL

Royal Eng	2	O.Harrovn	1	N
Wanderers	b	Bye	-	

FINAL

Wanderers	3	Royal Eng	1	N

1879

FIRST ROUND

Barnes	1	Maidenhd	1	
Brentwood	1	Pilgrims	3	
Cambs Uv	2	Herts Rng	0	
Clapham R	w	Finchley	s	
Darwen	w	Birch	s	
Eagley	b	Bye	-	
Forest Sh	7	Rochester	2	
Grey Fri	2	Marlow	1	

Minerva	w	105 Rgmt	s	
Notts Co	1	Nottm For	3	e
O.Harrovn	8	Southl Pk	0	
Oxford U	7	Wednew S	0	
Panthers	w	Runnymed	s	
Reading	1	Hendon	0	
Remnants	w	Unity	s	
Romford	3	Ramblers	1	
Royal Eng	3	O.Forests	0	
S.Norwo'd	w	Leyton	s	
Sheffield	1	Grantham	1	
Swifts	2	Hawks	1	
Upton Pk	5	Saffron W	0	
Wanderers	2	O.Etonian	7	
Grantham	1	Sheffield	3	r
Maidenhd	0	Barnes	4	r
SECOND ROUND				
Barnes	3	Upton Pk	2	e
Cambs Uv	3	S.Norwood	0	
Clapham R	10	Forest Sh	1	
Darwen	0	Eagley	0	
Grey Fri	0	Minerva	3	
Nottm For	2	Sheffield	0	
O.Harrovn	3	Panthers	0	
Oxford U	4	Royal Eng	0	
Reading	0	O.Etonian	1	
Remnants	6	Pilgrims	2	
Swifts	3	Romford	1	
Darwen	4	Eagley	1	r
THIRD ROUND				
Clapham R	1	Cambs Uv	0	e
O.Etonian	5	Minerva	2	
O.Harrovn	0	Nottm For	2	
Oxford U	2	Barnes	1	
Remnants	2	Darwen	3	e
Swifts	b	Bye	-	
FOURTH ROUND				
Clapham R	8	Swifts	1	
Nottm For	2	Oxford U	1	
O.Etonian	5	Darwen	5	
O.Etonian	2	Darwen	2	re
O.Etonian	6	Darwen	2	r2
SEMI-FINAL				
Clapham R	b	Bye	-	
O.Etonian	2	Nottm For	1	N
FINAL				
O.Etonian	1	Clapham R	0	N

1880

FIRST ROUND				
Acton	0	O.Carthus	4	
Aston V	b	Bye	-	
Birmingm	w	Panthers	s	
Blackburn	5	Tyne Assc	1	
Clapham R	7	Romford	0	
Eagley	0	Darwen	1	
Finchley	1	O.Harrovn	2	
Gresham	3	Kildare	0	
Grey Fri	2	Hanover U	1	
Hendon	1	O.Forests	1	
Henley	w	Reading	s	
Herts Rng	2	Minerva	1	
Hotspur	1	Argonauts	1	
Maidenhd	3	Calthorpe	1	
Mosquitos	3	St Peters	1	
Nottm For	4	Notts Co	0	
O.Etonian	w	Barnes	s	
Oxford U	1	Marlow	1	
Pilgrims	5	Clarence	2	
Remnants	1	Upton Pk	1	
Rochester	0	Wanderers	6	
Royal Eng	2	Cambs Uv	0	
S.Norwood	4	Brentwood	2	
Sheff Pro	b	Bye	-	
Sheffield	w	Queens Pk	s	
Staffd Rd	2	Wednew S	0	
Turton	7	Brigg	0	
West End	w	Swifts	s	
Argonauts	0	Hotspur	1	r
Marlow	0	Oxford U	1	r
O.Forests	2	Hendon	2	r
Upton Pk	5	Remnants	2	r
Hendon	3	O.Forests	1	r2
SECOND ROUND				
Blackburn	3	Darwen	1	
Clapham R	4	S.Norwood	1	
Grey Fri	9	Gresham	0	
Hendon	7	Mosquitos	1	
Henley	1	Maidenhd	3	
O.Etonian	b	Bye	-	
O.Harrovn	b	Bye	-	
Oxford U	6	Birmingm	0	
Pilgrims	w	Herts Rng	s	
Royal Eng	4	Upton Pk	1	
Sheffield	3	Sheff Pro	3	
Staffd Rd	1	Aston V	1	
Turton	0	Nottm For	6	
Wanderers	1	O.Carthus	0	
West End	1	Hotspur	0	
Aston V	3	Staffd Rd	1	r
Sheffield	3	Sheff Pro	0	r
THIRD ROUND				
Clapham R	7	Pilgrims	0	
Grey Fri	b	Bye	-	
Hendon	b	Bye	-	
Maidenhd	b	Bye	-	
Nottm For	6	Blackburn	0	
O.Etonian	3	Wanderers	1	
Oxford U	w	Aston V	s	
Royal Eng	2	O.Harrovn	0	
Sheffield	b	Bye	-	
West End	b	Bye	-	
FOURTH ROUND				
Clapham R	2	Hendon	0	
Maidenhd	0	Oxford U	1	
Nottm For	2	Sheffield	2	d
O.Etonian	5	West End	1	
Royal Eng	1	Grey Fri	0	
FIFTH ROUND				
Clapham R	1	O.Etonian	0	
Nottm For	b	Bye	-	
Oxford U	1	Royal Eng	1	e
Oxford U	1	Royal Eng	0	r
SEMI-FINAL				
Clapham R	b	Bye	-	
Oxford U	1	Nottm For	0	N
FINAL				
Clapham R	1	Oxford U	0	N

1881

FIRST ROUND				
Acton	1	Kildare	1	
Astley B	4	Eagley	0	
Aston V	5	Wednew S	3	
Blackburn	6	Sheff Pro	2	
Brentwo'd	0	O.Etonian	10	
Calthorpe	1	Grantham	2	
Clapham R	15	Finchley	0	
Darwen	8	Brigg	0	
Grey Fri	0	Windsor H	0	
Herts Rng	6	Barnes	0	
Maidenhd	1	O.Harrovn	1	
Marlow	6	clarence	0	
Nottm For	w	Caius Col	s	
Notts Co	4	Derbyshre	4	
O.Carthus	7	Saffron W	0	
Pilgrims	w	O.Philpds	s	
Rang Lon	w	Wanderers	s	
Reading	5	Hotspur	1	
Reading A	1	St Albans	0	

WHAT A STAR ✪ JIMMY FORREST

Blackburn were one of the dominant teams as professionalism grew in English soccer, and Jimmy Forrest was one of the dominant names. Although of average height he was a very powerful midfielder, with an ability to see gaps where others could not. He helped Rovers to win the Cup in three successive years: 1884, '85 and '86 and, although not a prolific scorer, he netted in the first two games. Forrest gained two further winners' medals, in 1890 and 1891, and was awarded 11 England caps at a time when international matches were few and far between.

Midland Treble

Aston Villa and neighbours West Brom are the only clubs to have met in three Finals. Villa won 2-0 in 1887 and 1-0 in 1895, but lost 0-3 in 1892.

Rochester	1	Dreadngt	2	
Romford	1	Reading M	1	
Royal Eng	0	Remnants	0	
Sheff Wed	w	Queens Pk	s	
Sheffield	5	Blkburn O	4	
St Peters	1	Hendon	8	
Staffd Rd	7	Spilsby	0	N
Swifts	1	O.Forests	1	
Turton	5	Brig Brit	0	
Upton Pk	8	Mosquitos	1	
West End	1	Hanover U	0	
Weybridge	3	Henley	1	
Derbyshre	2	Notts Co	4	re
Kildare	0	Acton	5	r
O.Forests	1	Swifts	2	r
O.Harrovn	0	Maidenhd	1	rN
Remnants	0	Royal Eng	1	r
Romford	w	Reading M	s	r
Windsor H	1	Grey Fri	3	r

SECOND ROUND

Astley B	0	Turton	3	
Blackburn	0	Sheff Wed	4	
Clapham R	b	Bye	-	
Grantham	1	Staffd Rd	1	
Grey Fri	1	Maidenhd	0	
Herts Rng	b	Bye	-	
Marlow	4	West End	0	
Nottm For	1	Aston V	2	
Notts Co	b	Bye	-	
O.Carthus	5	Dreadngt	1	
O.Etonian	2	Hendon	0	
Rang Lon	b	Bye	-	
Reading	0	Swifts	1	
Reading A	2	Acton	1	
Romford	b	Bye	-	
Royal Eng	1	Pilgrims	0	
Sheffield	1	Darwen	5	
Weybridg	0	Upton Pk	3	
Staffd Rd	7	Grantham	1	r

THIRD ROUND

Clapham R	2	Swifts	1	
Darwen	b	Bye	-	
Grey Fri	b	Bye	-	
Herts Rng	0	O.Etonian	3	
Marlow	b	Bye	-	
Notts Co	1	Aston V	3	
O.Carthus	b	Bye	-	
Romford	2	Reading A	0	
Royal Eng	6	Rang Lon	0	
Staffd Rd	b	Bye	-	
Turton	0	Sheff Wed	2	
Upton Pk	b	Bye	-	

FOURTH ROUND

Aston V	2	Staffd Rd	3	
Clapham R	5	Upton Pk	4	
Darwen	5	Sheff Wed	2	
O.Carthus	2	Royal Eng	0	
O.Etonian	4	Grey Fri	0	
Romford	2	Marlow	1	

FIFTH ROUND

Darwen	15	Romford	0	
O.Carthus	3	Clapham R	1	e
Staffd Rd	1	O.Etonian	2	

SEMI-FINAL

O.Carthus	4	Darwen	1	N
O.Etonian	b	Bye	-	

FINAL

O.Carthus	3	O.Etonian	0	N

1882

FIRST ROUND

Accringtn	w	Queens Pk	s	
Acton	0	Finchley	0	
Astley B	2	Turton	2	
Aston V	4	Nottm For	1	
Barnes	3	Rochester	1	
Blackburn	9	Blkburn P	1	
Bolton	5	Eagley	5	
Bootle	2	Blkburn L	1	
Darwen	3	Blkburn O	1	
Dreadngt	w	Caius Col	s	
Esher Leo	0	O.Carthus	5	
Grantham	6	Brigg	0	
Hanover U	b	Bye	-	
Henley	0	Maidenhd	2	
Herts Rng	0	Swifts	4	
Hotspur	1	Highbury	0	
Marlow	3	Brentwood	1	N
Mosquitos	1	Pilgrims	1	
Notts Co	w	Calthorpe	s	
O.Etonian	2	Clapham R	2	
O.Forests	3	Morton R	0	
Olympic	2	O.Harrovn	4	
Reading	5	Hendon	0	
Romford	w	Rang Lon	s	
Royal Eng	6	Kildare	0	
Sheff Hee	5	Lockwood	1	
Sheff Wed	2	Sheff Pro	0	
Sheffield	8	Brig Brit	0	
Sml Hth A	4	Derby T	1	
St Barts	w	Wanderers	s	
Staveley	5	Spilsby	1	
Upton Pk	3	St Albans	0	
Wednes O	9	Mitchells	1	
Wednew S	3	Staffd Rd	1	
West End	3	Remnants	2	
Windsor H	0	Reading M	1	
Woodfd Br	1	Reading A	1	
Acton	4	Finchley	0	r
Clapham R	0	O.Etonian	1	r
Eagley	0	Bolton	1	r
Pilgrims	5	Mosquitos	0	r
Reading A	2	Woodfd Br	1	r
Turton	1	Astley B	1	r
Astley B	3	Turton	3	r2N
Turton	2	Astley B	0	r3

SECOND ROUND

Aston V	b	Bye	-	
Blackburn	6	Bolton	2	
Darwen	3	Accringtn	1	
Dreadngt	b	Bye	-	
Hanover U	1	Upton Pk	3	
Maidenhd	2	Acton	1	e
Marlow	2	St Barts	0	
Notts Co	5	Wednew S	3	v
O.Carthus	7	Barnes	1	
O.Etonian	b	Bye	-	
O.Forests	3	Pilgrims	1	
Reading	1	West End	1	d
Reading A	1	Hotspur	4	
Reading M	3	Romford	1	
Royal Eng	b	Bye	-	
Sheff Wed	b	Bye	-	
Sheffield	0	Sheff Hee	4	
Staveley	3	Grantham	1	
Swifts	7	O.Harrovn	1	
Turton	4	Bootle	0	
Wednes O	6	Sml Hth A	0	
Notts Co	11	Wednew S	1	rN

THIRD ROUND

Aston V	2	Notts Co	2	e
Blackburn	b	Bye	-	
Darwen	4	Turton	1	
Dreadngt	1	Marlow	2	
Hotspur	0	Reading M	0	
Maidenhd	b	Bye	-	
O.Carthus	0	Royal Eng	2	
O.Etonian	3	Swifts	0	
O.Forests	b	Bye	-	
Reading	b	Bye	-	
Sheff Hee	b	Bye	-	
Sheff Wed	2	Staveley	2	
Upton Pk	b	Bye	-	
Wednes O	b	Bye	-	
Hotspur	2	Reading M	0	r
Notts Co	2	Aston V	2	re
Staveley	0	Sheff Wed	0	re
Aston V	4	Notts Co	1	r2
Sheff Wed	5	Staveley	1	r2N

FOURTH ROUND

Blackburn	5	Darwen	1	
Marlow	w	Reading	s	
O.Etonian	6	Maidenhd	3	
O.Forests	2	Royal Eng	1	
Sheff Wed	3	Sheff Hee	1	N
Upton Pk	5	Hotspur	0	
Wednes O	4	Aston V	2	

FIFTH ROUND

Blackburn	3	Wednes OA	1	
O.Etonian	b	Bye	-	
O.Forests	0	Marlow	0	
Sheff Wed	6	Upton Pk	0	
Marlow	1	O.Forests	0	r

SEMI-FINAL

Cup Nabbed!

The first of the four FA Cups was stolen in 1895 from a Birmingham shop, where it was on display. It was never recovered.

GIANTKILLERS

1883 Blackburn Olympic 2 Old Etonians 1

Old Etonians, one of the dominant clubs of the early days, were in their sixth Final in ten years when they were surprisingly beaten by the first northern winners. Olympic had had a comparatively easy path, beating Accrington, Lower Darwen, Darwen Ramblers, Church, Druids and Old Carthusians, but on the day they took two of their few chances. Etonians, the holders, took only one of many. Kinnaird had a goal disallowed and Dunn - founder of the Arthur Dunn Cup for public school old boys - missed all of extra-time through injury, but Olympic just about deserved their win.

Blackburn	0	Sheff Wed	0	N
O.Etonian	5	Marlow	0	N
Sheff Wed	1	Blackburn	5	rN
FINAL				
O.Etonian	1	Blackburn	0	N

1883

FIRST ROUND				
Aston U	b	Bye	-	
Aston V	4	Walsall	1	
Barnes	2	Brntwood	4	
Blkburn O	6	Accringtn	3	
Blackburn	11	Blkpool S	1	
Bolton Oy	4	Eagley	7	
Bolton	6	Bootle	1	
Chatham	b	Bye	-	
Church	5	Clitheroe	0	
Clapham R	3	Kildare	0	
Darwen	4	Blkburn P	1	
Darwen R	5	South Sh	2	
Dreadngt	1	S.Reading	2	v
Druids	1	Oswestry	1	
Etonian R	6	Romford	2	
Grimsby	w	Queens Pk	s	
Halliwell	3	G.Lever	2	
Hanover U	1	Mosquitos	0	
Haslingdn	b	Bye	-	
Hornchrch	0	Marlow	2	
Irwell Sp	2	L.Darwen	5	
Liverpl R	1	Southpt C	1	
Lockwood	4	Macclesfd	3	
Maidenhd	0	O.Westmst	2	
Mitchells	4	Calthorpe	1	
Northwich	3	Astley B	2	
Nottm For	w	Brig Brit	s	
Notts Co	6	Sheffield	1	
O.Carthus	6	Pilgrims	0	
O.Etonian	1	O.Forests	1	
Phoenix B	w	Grantham	s	
Reading	b	Bye	-	
Reading M	w	Remnants	s	
Rochester	2	Hotspur	0	
Royal Eng	3	Woodfd Br	1	
Sheff Hee	b	Bye	-	
Sheff Wed	12	Spilsby	2	
Sml Hth A	3	Staffd Rd	3	
Spital	1	Wednes OA	7	
Swifts	4	Highbury	1	
United Hp	3	London O	0	
Upton Pk	b	Bye	-	
Walsall	4	Staveley	1	
West End	1	Hendon	3	
Windsor H	3	Acton	0	
Dreadngt	1	S.Reading	2	r
O.Etonian	3	O.Forests	1	r
Oswestry	0	Druids	2	r
Southpt C	0	Liverpl R	4	r
Staffd Rd	6	Sml Hth A	2	r
SECOND ROUND				
Aston U	3	Mitchells	1	
Aston V	4	Wednes OA	1	
Blkburn O	8	L.Darwen	1	
Bolton	3	Liverpl R	0	
Church	b	Bye	-	
Clapham R	7	Hanover U	1	
Darwen	1	Blackburn	0	
Darwen R	3	Haslingden	2	
Druids	5	Northwich	0	
Eagley	3	Halliwell	1	
Grimsby	1	Phoenix B	9	
Hendon	2	Chatham	1	
Marlow	w	Reading M	s	
Nottm For	7	Sheff Hee	2	
Notts Co	b	Bye	-	
O.Carthus	7	Etonian R	0	
O.Etonian	2	Brentwood	1	
O.Westmst	b	Bye	-	
Rochester	b	Bye	-	

Preston Front

Preston's 26-0 win over Hyde on October 15th 1887 is still the biggest win ever recorded in the FA Cup...and there have been more than 50,000 ties contested in the competition's history!

Royal Eng	8	Reading	0	
S.Reading	b	Bye	-	
Sheff Wed	6	Lockwood	0	
Swifts	2	Upton Pk	2	
Walsall	4	Staffd Rd	1	
Windsor H	3	United Hp	1	
Swifts	3	Upton Pk	2	r
THIRD ROUND				
Aston V	3	Aston U	1	
Blkburn O	8	Darwen R	0	
Church	2	Darwen	2	
Clapham R	3	Windsor HP	0	
Druids	0	Bolton	0	
Eagley	b	Bye	-	
Hendon	11	S.Reading	1	
Marlow	b	Bye	-	
Nottm For	2	Sheff Wed	2	
Notts Co	4	Phoenix B	1	
O.Carthus	3	O.Westmst	2	
O.Etonian	7	Rochester	0	
Royal Eng	b	Bye	-	
Swifts	b	Bye	-	
Walsall	b	Bye	-	
Bolton	1	Druids	1	re
Darwen	0	Church	2	r
Sheff Wed	3	Nottm For	2	r
Druids	1	Bolton	0	r2N
FOURTH ROUND				
Aston V	2	Walsall	1	
Blkburn O	2	Church	0	
Clapham R	b	Bye	-	
Druids	2	Eagley	1	e
Marlow	0	Hendon	3	
O.Carthus	6	Royal Eng	2	
O.Etonian	2	Swifts	0	
Sheff Wed	1	Notts Co	4	
FIFTH ROUND				
Blkburn O	4	Druids	1	
Hendon	2	O.Etonian	4	
Notts Co	4	Aston V	3	
O.Carthus	5	Clapham R	3	
SEMI-FINAL				
Blkburn O	4	O.Carthus	0	N
O.Etonian	2	Notts Co	1	N
FINAL				
Blkburn O	2	O.Etonian	1	eN

1884

FIRST ROUND				
Accringtn	4	Blkpool S	0	
Acton	0	Upton Pk	2	
Blkburn O	5	Darwen R	1	
Blkburn P	6	Clithre L	0	
Blackburn	7	Southpt C	1	
Bolton As	5	Bradshaw	1	
Bolton	9	Bolton Oy	0	
Calthorpe	0	Walsall	9	
Clapham Rw		Kildare	s	
Clitheroe	3	South Sh	3	
Crewe	0	Queens P	10	
Darwen	2	Church	2	
Davenham	2	Macclesfd	0	
Derby Mid	b	Bye	-	
Druids	0	Northwich	1	
Grantham	3	Spilsby	2	
G.Lever	4	Astley B	1	
Halliwell	2	Eagley	5	
Hanover U	1	Brentwo'd	6	
Hendon	3	O.Etonian	2	
Hornchrch	0	Marlow	9	
Hull T	1	Grimsby	3	
Hurst	3	Turton	1	
Middlesbro	1	Staveley	5	
Mosquitos	3	Pilgrims	2	
Nottm For	w	Redcar	s	
Notts Co	3	Sheff Hee	1	
O.Forests	2	Dreadngt	1	
O.Westmst	3	Chatham	0	
Oswestry	2	Hartford	0	
Padiham	3	L.Darwen	1	
Preston NE	b	Bye	-	
Reading	2	S.Reading	2	
Reading M	1	O.Carthus	10	
Rochester	2	Uxbridge	1	
Romford	3	Woodfd Br	0	
Rossendle	6	Irwell Sp	2	D
Sheff Wed	b	Bye	-	
Sheffield	1	Lockwood	4	
Sml Hth A	1	Birm Excl	1	
Spital	1	Rotherhm	1	
Staffd Rd	5	Aston U	1	
Stoke	1	Manchestr	2	
Swifts	b	Bye	-	
Upton Rg	0	O.Wykemst	7	
Walsall	1	Aston V	5	
Wednes O	5	Mitchells	0	
West Brom	0	Wednew T	2	
West End	1	Maidenhd	0	
Windsor H	5	Royal Eng	3	
Wolves	4	Long Etn	1	
Wrexham Ow		Liverpl R	s	
Birm Excl	3	Sml Hth A	2	r
Church	0	Darwen	1	r
Rotherhm	7	Spital	2	r
S.Reading	0	Reading	4	r
South Sh	3	Clitheroe	2	r
SECOND ROUND				
Birm Excl	1	Derby Mid	1	
Blkburn P	2	Accringtn	3	d
Bolton	3	Bolton As	0	
Brentwood	b	Bye	-	
Clapham R	7	Rochester	0	
Darwen	1	Blkburn O	2	e
Eagley	b	Bye	-	
Grantham	4	Grimsby	0	
Hurst	3	Irwell Sp	2	v
Lockwood	3	Rotherhm	1	N
Northwich	5	Davenham	1	
Notts Co	3	Nottm For	0	
O.Carthus	2	O.Forests	7	
O.Westmst	2	Hendon	1	
Padiham	b	Bye	-	
Preston NE	4	G.Lever	1	
Queens P	15	Manchestr	0	
Reading	1	West End	0	
Romford	3	Mosquitos	1	
South Sh	0	Blackburn	7	
Staffd Rd	0	Aston V	5	
Staveley	3	Sheff Wed	1	
Swifts	2	Marlow	0	
Upton Pk	b	Bye	-	
Walsall	2	Wednew T	2	
Wednes O	4	Wolves	2	
Windsor H	0	O.Wykemst	1	
Wrexham O	3	Oswestry	4	
Derby Mid	2	Birm Excl	1	r
Irwell Sp	w	Hurst	s	r
Wednew T	6	Walsall	0	r
THIRD ROUND				
Blkburn O	b	Bye	-	
Blackburn	3	Padiham	0	
Bolton	8	Irwell Sp	1	
Clapham R	1	Swifts	2	
Grantham	1	Notts Co	4	
Northwich	b	Bye	-	
O.Forests	b	Bye	-	
O.Westmst	b	Bye	-	
O.Wykemst	b	Bye	-	
Oswestry	1	Queens Pk	7	
Preston NE	9	Eagley	1	
Reading	1	Upton Pk	6	
Romford	1	Brentwood	4	
Staveley	1	Lockwood	0	
Wednes O	4	Aston V	7	
Wednew T	1	Derby Mid	0	
FOURTH ROUND				
Blkburn O	6	O.Wykemst	0	
Blackburn	5	Staveley	1	
Northwich	3	Brntwood	0	
Notts Co	2	Bolton	2	e
O.Westmst	5	Wednew T	0	
Preston NE	1	Upton Pk	1	D
Queens Pk	6	Aston V	1	
Swifts	2	O.Forests	1	
Bolton	1	Notts Co	2	r
FIFTH ROUND				
Blkburn O	9	Northwich	1	
Notts Co	1	Swifts	1	
O.Westmst	0	Queens Pk	1	
Upton Pk	0	Blackburn	3	
Swifts	0	Notts Co	1	r
SEMI-FINAL				
Blackburn	1	Notts Co	0	N
Queens Pk	4	Blkburn O	1	N
FINAL				
Blackburn	2	Queens Pk	1	N

Goal-den boy

Bill Townley, the Blackburn outside-left, scored three goals in the 1890 Final and one in 1891. He scored three times in two games for England as well.

No arm done!

Lt Edmund Cresswell, of Royal Engineers, became the first player injured in a Cup Final when he fell in 1872 and broke his collar-bone. He stayed 'manfully at his post'.

1885

FIRST ROUND				
Accringtn	3	Southpt C	0	D
Acton	1	O.Carthus	7	
Aston U	0	Mitchells	5	
Aston V	4	Wednew T	1	
Birm Excl	2	Sml Hth A	0	
Blkburn O	12	Oswaldtw	0	
Blackburn	11	Rossendle	0	
Bolton As	w	Astley B	s	
Brentwood	2	Barnes	0	
Chatham	w	Windsor HP	s	
Chirk	4	Davenham	2	
Clapham R	3	Hendon	3	
Clithre L	w	Blkburn P	s	
Crewe	2	Oswestry	1	
Darwen	11	Bradshaw	0	
Darwen R	1	Fishwick	2	
Derby	0	Walsall	7	
Derby Juc	1	West Brom	7	
Derby Mid	1	Wednes OA	2	
Druids	6	Liverpl R	1	
Dulwich	3	Pilgrims	2	
Grantham	1	Grimsby	1	
Hanover U	1	Reading M	0	
Henley	b	Bye	-	
H.Walton	1	Darwen OW	1	
Hull T	1	Lincoln	5	
Hurst	2	Church	3	
Leek	4	Northwich	3	
Lockwood	0	Sheffield	3	
Long Etn	0	Sheff Wed	1	
L.Darwen	4	Halliwell	1	
Luton Wan	1	O.Etonian	3	
Macclesfd	9	Hartford	0	
Maidenhd	0	O.Wykemst	3	
Marlow	10	Royal Eng	1	
Middlesbr	w	Grimsby	s	
Newark	7	Spilsby	3	
Newtown	w	Staffd Rg	s	
Nottm For	5	Rotherhm	0	
Notts Co	2	Notts Oly	0	

55 Goals no glory

Preston scored 55 goals in seven FA Cup ties in 1887-88, including the record 26-0 defeat of Hyde...then lost the Final 1-2 to West Bromwich Albion.

O.Forests	8	Hoddesdon	0	
O.Westmst	6	Bourmth R	0	
Queens Pk	w	Stoke	s	
Reading	2	Rochester	0	
Redcar	3	Sunderld	1	
Romford	3	Clapton	2	
S.Reading	4	Casuals	1	
Sheff Hee	1	Notts Wan	0	
South Sh	w	Rawtenstl	s	
Spital	b	Bye	-	
Staveley	4	Notts Rng	1	
Swifts	3	O.Brightn	0	
Uxbridge	1	Hotspur	3	
Walsall	0	Staffd Rd	0	
West End	3	Upton Pk	3	
Witton	w	Clitheroe	s	
Wolves	0	Derby SL	0	
Wrexham O	1	Goldenhl	0	
Darwen O	4	H.Walton	1	r
Derby SL	4	Wolves	2	re
Grimsby	1	Grantham	0	r
Hendon	6	Clapham R	0	r
Upton Pk	w	West End	s	r
Walsall	2	Staffd Rd	1	r

SECOND ROUND

Blackburn	3	Blkburn O	2	
Brentwood	2	O.Etonian	2	
Chatham	1	Hendon	0	
Chirk	4	Wrexham O	1	
Darwen O	7	Bolton As	2	
Derby SL	0	Walsall	1	
Fishwick	0	Darwen	2	
Grimsby	3	Redcar	1	
Hanover U	2	O.Forests	1	
Hotspur	1	O.Wykemst	2	
Lincoln	b	Bye	-	
L.Darwen	b	Bye	-	
Macclesfd	1	Leek	5	
Middlesbro	4	Newark	1	
Mitchells	2	Birm Excl	2	
Newtown	1	Druids	1	
Nottm For	4	Sheff Hee	1	
O.Carthus	5	Marlow	3	
O.Westmst	7	Henley	0	
Queens Pk	2	Crewe	1	
Romford	3	Dulwich	0	
Sheff Wed	b	Bye	-	
Sheffield	4	Spital	1	
South Sh	2	Church	3	
Southpt C	3	Clithre L	1	
Staveley	0	Notts Co	2	
Swifts	3	S.Reading	2	
Upton Pk	3	Reading	1	
Walsall	0	Aston V	2	
West Brom	4	Wednes O	2	
Witton	b	Bye	-	
Druids	6	Newtown	0	r
Mitchells	2	Birm Excl	0	r
O.Etonian	6	Brentwood	1	r

THIRD ROUND

Aston V	0	West Brom	0	
Blackburn	5	Witton	0	
Church	10	Southpt C	0	
Darwen	b	Bye	-	
Druids	4	Chirk	1	
Grimsby	1	Lincoln	0	
Hanover U	0	Chatham	2	
Leek	2	Queens Pk	3	
L.Darwen	4	Darwen O	2	
Middlesbr	b	Bye	-	
Mitchells	2	Walsall	3	
Notts Co	5	Sheffield	0	
O.Carthus	b	Bye	-	
O.Etonian	b	Bye	-	
O.Wykemst	2	Upton Pk	1	
Romford	b	Bye	-	
Sheff Wed	1	Nottm For	2	
Swifts	1	O.Westmst	1	
O.Westmst	2	Swifts	2	r
West Brom	3	Aston V	0	r
Swifts	2	O.Westmst	1	r2

FOURTH ROUND

Blackburn	8	Romford	0	
Chatham	1	L.Darwen	0	
Church	3	Darwen	0	
O.Carthus	3	Grimsby	0	
O.Etonian	5	Middlesbr	2	e
Queens Pk	7	O.Wykems	0	
Swifts	0	Nottm For	1	
Walsall	1	Notts Co	4	
West Brom	1	Druids	0	

FIFTH ROUND

Blackburn	b	Bye	-	
Chatham	0	O.Carthus	3	
Church	b	Bye	-	
Nottm For	b	Bye	-	
Notts Co	b	Bye	-	
O.Etonian	b	Bye	-	
Queens Pk	b	Bye	-	
West Brom	b	Bye	-	

SIXTH ROUND

Church	0	O.Carthus	1	
Notts Co	2	Queens Pk	2	
O.Etonian	0	Nottm For	2	
West Brom	0	Blackburn	2	
Queens Pk	2	Notts Co	1	rN

SEMI-FINAL

Blackburn	5	O.Carthus	1	N
Nottm For	1	Queens Pk	1	N
Queens Pk	3	Nottm For	0	rN

FINAL

Blackburn	2	Queens Pk	0	N

1886

FIRST ROUND

Accringtn	5	Witton	4	
Astley B	3	Southpt C	2	
Barnes	1	Lancing O	7	
Blkburn O	4	Church	2	v
Bollingtn	0	Oswestry	5	
Bolton	6	Eagley	0	
Brentwood	3	Maidenhd	0	
Burslem P	3	Chirk	0	
Chatham	0	O.Carthus	2	
Clapham R	12	1 Surrey R	0	
Clitheroe	0	Blackburn	2	
Darlingtn	w	Walsall	s	
Darwen	2	Derby Juc	2	
Darwen O	11	Burnley	0	
Davenham	2	Goldenhl	1	
Derby	3	Mitchells	0	
Derby Mid	2	Birm Excl	1	
Dulwich	1	S.Reading	2	
Gainsbrgh	4	Grantham	1	
Halliwell	2	Fishwick	1	
Hanover U	1	Romford	1	
Hartford	1	Newtown	3	
Hendon	0	Clapton	4	
H.Walton	3	South Sh	4	
Hurst	2	Bradshaw	1	v
Leek	6	Wrexham O	3	
Lincoln	0	Grimsby	2	
Lincoln L	4	Grimsby	0	
Lockwood	2	Notts Rng	2	
Long Etn	2	Sheff Wed	0	
Luton Wan	3	Chesham	2	
Macclesfd	4	Northwich	1	
Marlow	3	Luton	0	
Middlesbr	w	Hornecstle	s	
Newark	0	Sheffield	3	
Nottm For	6	Mellors	2	
Notts Co	15	Rotherhm	0	
Notts Oly	2	Notts Wan	2	
O.Brightn	2	Acton	1	
O.Etonian	w	Bourmth R	s	
O.Harrovn	w	St James	s	
O.Westmst	3	Hotspur	1	
O.Wykemst	5	Uxbridge	0	
Oswaldtw	3	L.Darwen	1	
Padiham	w	Hearts	s	
Preston N	w	G.Lever	s	
Queens Pk	5	Partick T	1	
Rawtenstl	w	Rangers	s	
Redcar	3	Sunderld	0	
Rochester	6	Reading	1	
Rossendle	6	Clithre L	2	
Royal Eng	1	O.Forests	5	
Sheff Hee	2	Eckingt W	1	
Sml Hth A	9	Burton W	2	
Staffd Rd	7	Matlock	0	
Staffd Rg	1	Druids	4	
Staveley	1	Mexboro	1	

Round or oval?

Reg Birkett, who played for Clapham Rovers in the Finals of 1879 and 1880, had also scored England's first try in a Rugby Union international in 1871.

Stoke	2	Crewe	2	
Swifts	7	Casuals	1	
Third Lan	4	Blkburn P	2	
Upton Pk	4	Utd Lond	2	
Walsall	0	Aston V	5	
Wednes O	5	Burton S	1	
West Brom	4	Aston U	1	
Wolves	7	Derby SL	0	
Bradshaw	1	Hurst	1	rv
Church	2	Blkburn O		2r
Crewe	1	Stoke	0	re
Darwen	4	Derby Juc	0	r
Notts Oly	4	Notts Wan	1	r
Notts Rng	4	Lockwood	0	r
Romford	3	Hanover U	0	r
Staveley	w	Mexboro	s	r
Church	3	Blkburn O	1	r2
Hurst	3	Bradshaw	2	r2N

SECOND ROUND

Blackburn	1	Oswaldtw	0	
Brentwo'd	6	Lancing O	1	
Church	w	Third Lan	s	
Clapham R	b	Bye	-	
Darwen O	2	Accringtn	1	
Davenham	8	Macclesfd	1	
Derby	2	Aston V	0	
Derby Mid	1	Walsall	3	
Druids	2	Burslem P	2	e
Gainsbrgh	1	Middlesbro	2	
Grimsby	8	Darlingtn	0	
Hurst	3	Halliwell	1	v
Leek	w	Newtown	s	
Long Etn	1	Staveley	4	
Marlow	6	O.Etonian	1	
Nottm For	4	Notts Oly	1	
Notts Co	8	Sheffield	0	
O.Carthus	6	Upton Pk	0	
O.Harrovn	2	O.Forests	1	
O.Westmst	3	O.Brightn	0	
O.Wykems	10	Luton Wan	0	
Oswestry	1	Crewe	1	
Preston N	11	Astley B	3	
Rawtenstl	3	Bolton	3	D
Redcar	2	Lincoln L	0	
Romford	b	Bye	-	
Rossendle	9	Padiham	1	
S.Reading	1	Clapton	1	
Sheff Hee	1	Notts Rng	6	
Sml Hth A	3	Darwen	1	
South Sh	w	Queens Pk	s	
Swifts	5	Rochester	1	
West Brom	3	Wednes O	2	
Wolves	4	Staffd Rd	2	
Burslem P	5	Druids	1	r
Crewe	nr	Oswestry	d	r
Halliwell	w	Hurst	s	r
S.Reading	nr	Clapton	d	r

THIRD ROUND

Blackburn	6	Darwen O	1	
Bolton	2	Preston NE	3	d
Brentwood	b	Bye	-	
Church	5	Rossendle	1	
Davenham	2	Crewe	1	
Halliwell	1	South Sh	6	
Leek	2	Burslem P	3	ev
Marlow	s	O.Wykemstw		E
Middlesbro	2	Grimsby	1	
Notts Co	3	Notts Rng	0	
O.Carthus	b	Bye	-	
O.Westmst	5	Romford	1	
Redcar	b	Bye	-	
S.Reading	nr	Clapham R	d	
Sml Hth A	4	Derby	2	
Staveley	2	Nottm For	1	
Swifts	nr	O.Harrovn	d	
West Brom	b	Bye	-	
Wolves	2	Walsall	1	
Burslem P	w	Leek	s	r

FOURTH ROUND

Blackburn	b	Bye	-	
Bolton	b	Bye	-	
Burslem P	b	Bye	-	
Church	b	Bye	-	
Davenham	b	Bye	-	
Middlesbro	b	Bye	-	
Notts Co	b	Bye	-	
O.Carthus	b	Bye	-	
O.Westmst	b	Bye	-	
Redcar	b	Bye	-	
S.Reading	0	Brentwood	3	
Sml Hth A	b	Bye	-	
South Sh	b	Bye	-	
Staveley	b	Bye	-	
Swifts	b	Bye	-	
West Brom	3	Wolves	1	

FIFTH ROUND

Blackburn	7	Staveley	1	
Burslem P	2	Brentwood	1	v
Church	2	Swifts	6	
Davenham	1	Sml Hth A	2	
O.Westmst	r	Bolton	d	
Redcar	2	Middlesbro	1	
South Sh	2	Notts Co	1	
West Brom	1	O.Carthus	0	
Brentwo'd	4	Burslem P	4	reN
Brentwoo'd		Burslem P		sr2

SIXTH ROUND

Brentwood	1	Blackburn	3	
Sml Hth A	2	Redcar	0	
South Sh	1	Swifts	2	
West Brom	6	O.Westmst	0	

SEMI-FINAL

Blackburn	2	Swifts	1	N
West Brom	4	Sml Hth A	0	N

FINAL

Blackburn	0	West Brom	0	N
Blackburn	2	West Brom	0	rN

Ragged Rovers

Blackburn fans visiting London for the 1884 Final were described in one magazine as 'Northern barbarians...of uncouth garb and speech. A tribe of Arabs would not excite more amusement'. On the other hand, the Blackburn team that turned up for the 1890 Final against Sheffield Wednesday played the game in white evening dress, which they had bought on their arrival in London, because their kit clashed with Wednesday's colours!

1887

FIRST ROUND

Astley B	3	Burnley	3	
Aston U	1	Derby	4	
Aston V	13	Wednes O	0	
Birm Excl	3	Derby Mid	3	
Blkburn O	1	Partick T	3	
Blkburn P	2	Cliftonvl	2	
Blackburn	w	Halliwell	s	
Bollingtn	2	Oswestry	8	
Bolton	5	South Sh	3	
Bootle	2	G.Lever	4	
Bshp Ak C	0	Middlesbro	1	
Burslem P	1	Davenham	1	e
Burton S	0	Crosswl B	1	
Casuals	2	Dulwich	4	
Chatham	w	Bourmth R	s	
Chesham	4	Lyndhurst	2	
Chirk	8	Hartford	1	
Church	1	Rawtenstl	1	
Clapham R	0	O.Brightn	6	
Clapton	0	Crusaders	5	
Cleethps	2	Mellors	1	
Darwen	7	Hearts	1	
Darwen O	1	Cowlairs	4	
Derby SL	3	Walsall	3	
Fleetwd R	2	Newton Ht	2	d
Goldenhl	4	Macclesfd	2	v
Hendon	1	London C	2	
Hornecstle	2	Darlingtn	0	
Hotspur	3	Luton	1	
Leek	2	Druids	1	
Lincoln L	0	Grantham	1	
Lockwood	1	Long Etn	0	
Northwich	10	Furness	0	
Nottm For	3	Notts Oly	0	
Notts Co	13	Basford R	0	
O.Carthus	2	Reading	1	
O.Etonian	1	Royal Eng	0	
O.Forests	w	Cannon	s	
O.Harrovn	0	O.Westmst	4	
O.Wykemst	3	Hanover U	0	
Oswaldtw	2	Witton	3	
Queens Pk	0	Preston NE	3	
Rangers	w	Everton	s	
Redcar	4	Tyne Assc	0	
Renton	1	Accringtn	0	
Rochester	0	Marlow	2	
S.Reading	0	Maidenhd	2	
Sheff Hee	1	Grimsby	4	
Sheffield	0	Notts Rng	3	
Sml Hth A	1	Mitchells	3	

South Bk	0	Gainsbrgh	4	
Staveley	7	Atterclfe	0	
Stoke	10	Caernvn W	1	
Sunderld	2	Newcst WE	1	ev
Swifts	13	Luton Wan	0	
Swindon	1	Watford R	0	
Third Lan	5	H.Walton	0	
Upton Pk	9	1 Surrey R	0	
W'tn St G	0	Derby Juc	1	
West Brom	6	Burton W	0	
Wolves	6	Matlock	0	
Wrexham O	1	Crewe	4	
Burnley	2	Astley B	2	rD
Burslem P	3	Davenham	0	r
Cliftonvl	7	Blkburn P	2	r
Derby Mid	2	Birm Excl	1	r
Macclesfd	2	Goldenhl	3	r
Newcst WE	1	Sunderld	0	r
Rawtenstl	1	Church	7	r
Walsall	6	Derby SL	1	r

SECOND ROUND

Aston V	6	Derby Mid	1	
Burslem P	b	Bye	-	
Chatham	1	Hotspur	0	
Chesham	1	O.Etonian	7	
Chester	1	Goldenhl	0	D
Cleethps	1	Lockwood	4	
Crewe	6	Stoke	4	e
Darwen	w	Astley B	s	
Derby	1	Mitchells	2	
Grantham	3	Redcar	2	
G.Lever	1	Cliftonvl	3	
Hornecstle	b	Bye	-	
Leek	4	Oswestry	2	
Maidenhd	2	Dulwich	3	e
Marlow	4	Upton Pk	0	
Middlesbro	1	Lincoln	1	
Newcst WE	2	Gainsbrgh	6	
Northwich	0	Chirk	0	
Nottm For	2	Grimsby	2	
Notts Co	3	Notts Rng	3	
O.Brightn	1	O.Westmst	1	
O.Carthus	4	Crusaders	2	
O.Forests	b	Bye	-	
O.Wykems	0	London C	1	
Partick T	7	Fleetwd R	0	
Preston NE	6	Witton	0	
Rangers	2	Church	1	
Renton	2	Blackburn	2	e
Rossendle	2	Cowlairs	10	
Staveley	4	Rotherhm	0	
Swifts	7	Swindon	1	
Third Lan	2	Bolton	3	
Walsall	b	Bye	-	
West Brom	2	Derby Juc	1	
Wolves	14	Crosswl B	0	
Blackburn	0	Renton	2	r
Chirk	3	Northwich	0	r
Grimsby	0	Nottm For	1	r
Lincoln	2	Middlesbro	0	r
Notts Co	5	Notts Rng	0	r
O.Westmst	3	O.Brightn	0	r

THIRD ROUND

Aston V	2	Wolves	2	e
Chatham	1	O.Forests	4	
Chirk	0	Goldenhl	0	
Cliftonvl	0	Partick T	11	
Crewe	b	Bye	-	
Darwen	4	Bolton	3	
Gainsbrgh	2	Lincoln	2	e
Hornecstle	2	Grantham	0	
Leek	2	Burslem P	2	a
Lockwood	2	Nottm For	1	
Marlow	3	Dulwich	0	
O.Carthus	0	London C	0	
O.Etonian	0	O.Westmst	3	
Rangers	3	Cowlairs	2	
Renton	0	Preston NE	2	N
Staveley	0	Notts Co	3	
Swifts	b	Bye	-	
Walsall	2	Mitchells	7	
West Brom	b	Bye	-	
Burslem P	1	Leek	3	rN
Chirk	w	Goldenhl	s	r
Lincoln	1	Gainsbrgh	0	rN
O.Carthus	w	London C	s	r
Wolves	1	Aston V	1	re
Wolves	3	Aston V	3	r2e
Aston V	2	Wolves	0	r3

FOURTH ROUND

Aston V	b	Bye	-	
Chirk	b	Bye	-	
Crewe	0	Leek	1	
Darwen	b	Bye	-	
Hornecstle	b	Bye	-	
Lincoln	b	Bye	-	
Lockwood	b	Bye	-	
Marlow	b	Bye	-	
Mitchells	0	West Brom	1	N
Notts Co	b	Bye	-	
O.Carthus	b	Bye	-	
O.Westmst	b	Bye	-	
Partick T	b	Bye	-	
Preston NE	b	Bye	-	
Rangers	b	Bye	-	
Swifts	0	O.Forests	2	

FIFTH ROUND

Aston V	5	Hornecstle	0	
Chirk	1	Darwen	2	
Leek	0	O.Carthus	2	
Lockwood	0	West Brom	1	ev
Notts Co	5	Marlow	2	
O.Forests	0	Preston NE	3	
O.Westmst	1	Partick T	0	
Rangers	3	Lincoln	0	
West Brom	2	Lockwood	1	rN

SIXTH ROUND

Aston V	3	Darwen	2	
Notts Co	1	West Brom	4	
O.Carthus	1	Preston NE	2	e
Rangers	5	O.Westmst	1	

SEMI-FINAL

Aston V	3	Rangers	1	N
West Brom	3	Preston NE	1	N

FINAL

Aston V	2	West Brom	0	N

Early Promise

James Prinsep, youngest-ever FA Cup Finalist, played in the 1879 match at 17 years 245 days - and became England's most junior international when he won his only cap a week later.

1888

FIRST ROUND

Accringtn	11	Rossendle	0	
Aston K	2	Burton W	3	v
Basford R	3	Lincoln A	2	
Belper T	2	Sheff Wed	3	
Birm Excl	4	Warwick Co	1	v
Blkburn O	b	Bye	-	
Blkburn P	2	Distillry	1	D
Blackburn	w	Bury	s	
Bolton	1	Everton	0	v
Bootle	6	Workingtn	0	
Burnley	4	Darwen O	0	v
Burton S	7	Southfld	0	
Chatham	5	Luton	1	
Chesham	4	Watford R	2	v
Chester	2	Davenham	3	e
Chirk	4	Chester O	1	
Church	w	Cliftonvl	s	
Cleethps	0	Grimsby	4	
Crewe	5	Druids	0	
Crusaders	9	Lyndhurst	0	
Derby Juc	3	Derby SL	2	
Ecclesfd	4	Derby Mid	1	
Elswick R	3	Bshp Ak C	3	e
Fleetwd R	4	W.Manchst	1	
Gainsbrgh	7	Boston	0	
Gateshd A	0	Darlingtn	3	
Grantham	4	Lincoln L	0	
Hendon	2	O.Harrovn	4	
H.Walton	8	Heywood C	1	
Hitchin	2	O.Wykemst	5	
Hotspur	b	Bye	-	
Hurst	5	Astley B	3	v
Leek	2	Northwich	2	
Lincoln	4	Hornecstle	1	
Liverpl S	1	Halliwell	5	
Llangol'n	7	Oswestry	3	v
London C	1	O.Forests	6	
Long Etn	6	Pk Grange	3	
Macclesfd	1	Shrewsby	3	
Marlow	4	S.Reading	1	
Matlock	2	Rotherhm	3	
Middlesbro	4	Whitburn	0	
Millwall R	w	Casuals	s	
Newcst WE	5	Redcar	1	
Nottm For	2	Notts Swf	1	e
Notts Co	9	Lincoln R	0	
Notts Oly	3	Mellors	6	ev
Notts Rng	10	Jardines	1	
O.Brightn	1	Swindon	0	
O.Carthus	5	Hanover U	0	
O.Etonian	4	Lancing O	2	
O.St.Mark	7	East She'n	2	
O.Westmst	4	Clapton	1	
Oldbury T	0	Aston V	4	
Oswaldtw	3	Witton	4	v

GIANTKILLERS

1888 West Brom 2 Preston 1

Legend says that Preston asked for permission to be photographed with the Cup before the Final began, only to be told that they had better win it first. Their failure was perhaps the biggest surprise in soccer's brief history at that time, for they were the outstanding team of the period. Although the Football League did not come into existence until later that year, North End had been unbeaten in 44 consecutive matches in friendlies and various cups. The match drew what one Birmingham paper called 'an enormous crowd' of 19,000 to Kennington Oval.

Over Wan	3	W'tn St G	1	
Owlerton	2	Eckingt W	1	
Preston NE	26	Hyde	0	
Rawtenstl	1	Darwen	3	
Reading	0	Dulwich	2	v
Royal Eng	3	Rochester	0	v
Scarboro	3	Shankhse	5	
Sheff Hee	9	Attercife	0	
Sheffield	1	Lockwood	3	
Sml Hth A	6	Aston U	1	
South Bk	3	Newcst EE	2	e
South Sh	w	Denton	s	
Staffd Rd	2	G.Brdge U	1	v
Staveley	1	Derby	2	
Stoke	1	Burslem P	0	
Sunderld	4	Morpeth H	2	v
Swifts	3	Maidenhd	1	
Walsall	1	Wolves	2	
Walsall	1	Mitchells	2	
West Brom	7	Wednes O	1	
Wrexham O	b	Bye	-	
Astley B	w	Hurst	s	r
Aston K	w	Burton W	s	r
Bshp Ak C	0	Elswick R	2	r
Burnley	w	Darwen O	s	r
Dulwich	w	Reading	s	r
Everton	2	Bolton	2	r
G.Brdge U	1	Staffd Rd	1	r
Llangol'n	0	Oswestry	2	r
Morpeth H	2	Sunderld	3	r
Northwich	4	Leek	2	r
Notts Oly	1	Mellors	2	r
Oswaldtw	1	Witton	4	r
Royal Eng	w	Rochester	s	r
Warwick Co	0	Birm Excl	5	r
Watford R	3	Chesham	1	r
Bolton	1	Everton	1	r2
G.Brdge U	w	Staffd Rd	s	r2
Everton	2	Bolton	1	r3D
SECOND ROUND				
Accringtn	3	Burnley	2	
Astley B	0	Halliwell	4	
Birm Excl	b	Bye	-	
Blkburn O	1	Blackburn	5	
Bootle	1	South Sh	1	
Burton S	2	G.Brdge U	5	
Chatham	3	Royal Eng	1	
Chirk	10	Shrewsby	2	
Crusaders	3	O.Wykemst	2	
Darlingtn	4	Elswick R	3	e
Darwen	2	Church	0	
Derby	6	Ecclesfd	0	
Derby Juc	3	Rotherhm	2	
Distillry	2	Witton	4	
Dulwich	2	Hotspur	1	
Fleetwd R	1	H.Walton	3	
Grimsby	b	Bye	-	
Lincoln	2	Gainsbrgh	1	
Lockwood	b	Bye	-	
Long Etn	1	Sheff Wed	2	e
Marlow	2	O.Forests	3	e
Middlesbr	4	South Bk	1	
Mitchells	0	West Brom	1	
Northwich	0	Crewe	1	
Nottm For	2	Mellors	0	
Notts Co	w	Basford R	s	
Notts Rng	4	Grantham	0	
O.Etonian	3	O.St.Mark	2	
O.Harrovn	0	O.Brightn	4	
O.Westmst	8	Millwall R	1	
Oswestry	b	Bye	-	
Over Wan	0	Stoke	2	
Owlerton	1	Sheff Hee	0	
Preston NE	9	Bolton	1	
Preston NE	6	Everton	1	v
Shankhse	b	Bye	-	
Sml Hth A	0	Aston V	4	
Sunderld	3	Newcst WE	1	e
Swifts	b	Bye	-	
Watford R	1	O.Carthus	3	
Wolves	3	Aston K	0	
Wrexham O	1	Davenham	2	
South Sh	0	Bootle	3	r
THIRD ROUND				
Accringtn	1	Blackburn	3	
Aston V	b	Bye	-	
Crewe	b	Bye	-	
Crusaders	4	Chatham	0	
Darlingtn	0	Shankhse	2	
Darwen	1	Witton	1	
Davenham	2	Chirk	2	
Derby	6	Owlerton	2	
Derby Juc	2	Lockwood	1	
Dulwich	1	Swifts	3	
Grimsby	2	Lincoln	0	
G.Brdge U	2	Birm Excl	1	
H.Walton	1	Bootle	6	
Middlesbro	2	Sunderld	2	
Nottm For	2	Notts Co	1	
Notts Rng	b	Bye	-	
O.Carthus	5	O.Brightn	0	
O.Etonian	7	O.Westmst	2	
O.Forests	b	Bye	-	
Preston NE	4	Halliwell	0	
Sheff Wed	b	Bye	-	
Stoke	3	Oswestry	0	
West Brom	2	Wolves	0	
Chirk	6	Davenham	1	r
Sunderld	4	Middlesbro	2	rD
Witton	0	Darwen	2	rN
FOURTH ROUND				
Blackburn	b	Bye	-	
Chirk	b	Bye	-	
Crewe	2	Swifts	2	
Crusaders	0	Sheff Wed	1	
Darwen	3	Notts Rng	1	
Derby	b	Bye	-	
Derby Juc	b	Bye	-	
G.Brdge U	1	Bootle	2	
Middlesbr	b	Bye	-	
Nottm For	6	O.Etonian	0	
O.Carthus	b	Bye	-	
O.Forests	4	Grimsby	2	
Preston NE	b	Bye	-	

Easy Ride

In 1873 - the fledgling Cup's second year - Wanderers retained their trophy...but the feat was not quite as impressive as it seems. As holders, it was decided they should be exempt until the Final - the only time such a system has been in place.

Shankhse	0	Aston V	9	
Stoke	b	Bye	-	
West Brom	b	Bye	-	
Swifts	3	Crewe	2	rv
Crewe	2	Swifts	1	r2N

FIFTH ROUND

Aston V	1	Preston NE	3	
Chirk	0	Derby Juc	1	
Crewe	1	Derby	0	
Darwen	0	Blackburn	3	
Middlesbro	4	O.Forests	0	
Nottm For	2	Sheff Wed	4	
O.Carthus	2	Bootle	0	
West Brom	4	Stoke	1	

SIXTH ROUND

Derby Juc	2	Blackburn	1	
Middlesbro	0	Crewe	2	
Sheff Wed	1	Preston NE	3	
West Brom	4	O.Carthus	2	

SEMI-FINAL

Preston NE	4	Crewe	0	N
West Brom	3	Derby Juc	0	N

FINAL

West Brom	2	Preston NE	1	N

1889

FIRST ROUND

Accringtn	1	Blackburn	1	
Aston V	3	Witton	2	
Birm St.G	3	Long Etn	2	
Bootle	0	Preston NE	3	
Burnley	4	O.Westmst	3	
Chatham	2	South Sh	1	e
Derby	1	Derby Juc	0	
Grimsby	3	Sunder Ab	1	
Halliwell	2	Crewe	2	e
Nottm For	2	Linfield	2	e
Notts Co	2	O.Brightn	0	
Notts Rng	1	Sheff Wed	1	
Small Hth	2	West Brom	3	
Swifts	3	Wrexham	1	
Walsall	5	Sheff Hee	1	
Wolves	4	O.Carthus	3	
Blackburn	5	Accringtn	0	r
Crewe	1	Halliwell	5	r
Nottm For	w	Linfield	s	r
Sheff Wed	3	Notts Rng	0	r

SECOND ROUND

Aston V	5	Derby	3	
Blackburn	w	Swifts	s	
Chatham	1	Nottm For	1	e
Grimsby	0	Preston NE	2	
Halliwell	2	Birm St.G	3	
Sheff Wed	3	Notts Co	2	
West Brom	5	Burnley	1	
Wolves	6	Walsall	1	
Nottm For	2	Chatham	2	re
Chatham	3	Nottm For	2	r2N

THIRD ROUND

Blackburn	8	Aston V	1	
Chatham	1	West Brom	10	
Preston NE	2	Birm St.G	0	
Wolves	3	Sheff Wed	0	

SEMI-FINAL

Preston NE	1	West Brom	0	N
Wolves	1	Blackburn	1	N
Blackburn	1	Wolves	3	rN

FINAL

Preston NE	3	Wolves	0	N

1890

FIRST ROUND

Accringtn	3	West Brom	1	v
Birm St.G	4	Notts Co	4	e
Blackburn	4	Sunderld	2	e
Bolton	10	Distillry	2	
Bootle	1	Sunder Ab	3	d
Derby Mid	3	Nottm For	0	
Everton	11	Derby	2	
Lincoln	2	Chester	0	
Newcst WE	1	Grimsby	2	
Preston NE	6	Newton Ht	1	
Sheff Utd	2	Burnley	1	
Sheff Wed	6	Swifts	1	
Small Hth	3	Clapton	1	
South Sh	2	Aston V	4	
Stoke	3	O.Westmst	0	
Wolves	2	O.Carthus	0	
Accringtn	3	West Brom	0	r
Notts Co	6	Birm St.G	2	r

SECOND ROUND

Blackburn	3	Grimsby	0	
Bolton	13	Sheff Utd	0	
Bootle	2	Derby Mid	1	
Notts Co	4	Aston V	1	
Preston NE	4	Lincoln	0	
Sheff Wed	2	Accringtn	1	
Stoke	4	Everton	2	
Wolves	2	Small Hth	1	

THIRD ROUND

Bootle	0	Blackburn	7	
Preston NE	2	Bolton	3	
Sheff Wed	5	Notts Co	0	v
Wolves	4	Stoke	0	v
Sheff Wed	2	Notts Co	3	rv
Wolves	8	Stoke	0	r
Sheff Wed	2	Notts Co	1	r2N

SEMI-FINAL

Blackburn	1	Wolves	0	N
Sheff Wed	2	Bolton	1	N

FINAL

Blackburn	6	Sheff Wed	1	N

1891

FIRST ROUND

Accringtn	2	Bolton	2	
Aston V	13	Casuals	1	
Burnley	4	Crewe	2	
Chester	1	Lincoln	0	
Clapton	0	Nottm For	14	
Crusaders	0	Birm St.G	2	
Darwen	3	Kiddermst	1	v
Long Etn	1	Wolves	2	e
Midd Irn	1	Blackburn	2	v
R.Arsenal	1	Derby	2	
Sheff Utd	1	Notts Co	9	
Sheff Wed	12	Halliwell	0	
Stoke	3	Preston NE	0	
Sunderld	1	Everton	0	
Sunder Ab	2	93 Hghld R	0	
West Brom	w	O.Westmst	s	
Accringtn	5	Bolton	1	r
Darwen	13	Kiddermst	0	r
Midd Irn	0	Blackburn	3	r

SECOND ROUND

Accringtn	2	Wolves	3	e
Birm St.G	0	West Brom	3	
Blackburn	7	Chester	0	
Darwen	0	Sunderld	2	
Derby	2	Sheff Wed	3	
Notts Co	2	Burnley	1	
Stoke	3	Aston V	0	
Sunder Ab	1	Nottm For	1	
Nottm For	3	Sunder Ab	3	re
Nottm For	5	Sunder Ab	0	r2N

THIRD ROUND

Blackburn	2	Wolves	0	
Notts Co	1	Stoke	0	
Sheff Wed	0	West Brom	2	
Sunderld	4	Nottm For	0	

SEMI-FINAL

Blackburn	3	West Brom	2	N
Notts Co	3	Sunderld	3	N
Sunderld	0	Notts Co	2	rN

FINAL

Blackburn	3	Notts Co	1	N

1892

FIRST ROUND

Aston V	4	Heanor	1	
Blackburn	4	Derby	1	
Blackpool	0	Sheff Utd	3	
Bootle	0	Darwen	2	
Crusaders	1	Accringtn	4	
Everton	2	Burnley	4	v
Luton	0	Middlesbro	3	
Nottm For	2	Newcst EE	1	
O.Westmst	2	West Brom	3	

Unlucky Alex

A player named Alex Ferguson was in the Notts County team who lost the 1891 Final. He died aged 27 in the week before the 1894 match, which County went on to win.

Cash for Fergie

Fergie Suter, a stonemason who went on to appear in four Cup Finals with Blackburn, was widely considered to be one of the game's first professionals when he moved to the Darwen club from Scotland in 1879.

Preston NE	6	Midd Irn	0	
Sheff Wed	2	Bolton	1	v
Small Hth	5	Wool Ars	1	
Stoke	3	Casuals	0	v
Sunderld	3	Notts Co	0	v
Sunder Ab	1	Birm St.G	2	v
Wolves	2	Crewe	2	e
Crewe	1	Wolves	4	r
Everton	1	Burnley	3	r
Sheff Wed	4	Bolton	1	r
Stoke	3	Casuals	0	r
Sunderld	4	Notts Co	0	r
Sunder Ab	4	Birm St.G	0	r
SECOND ROUND				
Accringtn	1	Sunderld	0	v
Aston V	2	Darwen	0	
Burnley	1	Stoke	3	
Middlesbro	1	Preston NE	2	
Sheff Wed	2	Small Hth	0	
Sunder Ab	0	Nottm For	1	
West Brom	3	Blackburn	1	
Wolves	3	Sheff Utd	1	
Accringtn	1	Sunderld	3	r
THIRD ROUND				
Nottm For	2	Preston NE	0	
Stoke	2	Sunderld	2	e
West Brom	2	Sheff Wed	1	
Wolves	1	Aston V	3	
Sunderld	4	Stoke	0	r
SEMI-FINAL				
Aston V	4	Sunderld	1	N
West Brom	1	Nottm For	1	N
Nottm For	1	West Brom	1	rN
West Brom	6	Nottm For	2	r2N
FINAL				
West Brom	3	Aston V	0	N

1893

FIRST ROUND				
Accringtn	2	Stoke	1	
Blackburn	4	Newton Ht	0	
Blackpool	1	Sheff Utd	3	
Bolton	1	Wolves	1	e
Burnley	2	Small Hth	0	
Darwen	5	Aston V	4	
Everton	4	West Brom	1	
Grimsby	5	Stockton	0	
Loughbro	1	Northwich	2	
Marlow	1	Midd Irn	3	
Newcastle	2	Middlesbro	3	
Nottm For	4	Casuals	0	
Notts Co	4	Shankhse	0	
Preston NE	9	Burton S	2	
Sheff Wed	3	Derby	2	ev
Sunderld	6	Wool Ars	0	
Derby	1	Sheff Wed	0	rv
Wolves	2	Bolton	1	r
Sheff Wed	4	Derby	2	r2
SECOND ROUND				
Accringtn	1	Preston NE	4	
Blackburn	4	Northwich	1	
Darwen	2	Grimsby	0	
Everton	4	Nottm For	2	
Midd Irn	3	Notts Co	2	
Sheff Utd	1	Sunderld	3	
Sheff Wed	1	Burnley	0	
Wolves	2	Middlesbro	1	e
THIRD ROUND				
Blackburn	3	Sunderld	0	
Everton	3	Sheff Wed	0	
Preston NE	2	Midd Irn	2	
Wolves	5	Darwen	0	
Midd Irn	0	Preston NE	7	r
SEMI-FINAL				
Everton	2	Preston NE	2	N
Wolves	2	Blackburn	1	N
Preston NE	0	Everton	0	rN
Everton	2	Preston NE	1	r2N
FINAL				
Wolves	1	Everton	0	N

1894

FIRST ROUND				
Aston V	4	Wolves	2	
Derby	2	Darwen	0	
Leicester	2	South Sh	1	
Liverpool	3	Grimsby	0	
Midd Irn	2	Luton	1	
Newcastle	2	Sheff Utd	0	
Newton Ht	4	Middlesbro	0	
Nottm For	1	Heanor	0	e
Notts Co	1	Burnley	0	
Preston NE	18	Reading	0	
Small Hth	3	Bolton	4	
Stockport	0	Burton W	1	
Stoke	1	Everton	0	
Sunderld	3	Accringtn	0	
West Brom	2	Blackburn	3	
Wool Ars	1	Sheff Wed	2	
SECOND ROUND				
Burton W	1	Notts Co	2	
Leicester	0	Derby	0	e
Liverpool	3	Preston NE	2	
Newcastle	1	Bolton	2	
Newton Ht	0	Blackburn	0	e
Nottm For	2	Midd Irn	0	
Sheff Wed	1	Stoke	0	
Sunderld	2	Aston V	2	e
Aston V	3	Sunderld	1	r
Blackburn	5	Newton Ht	1	r
Derby	3	Leicester	0	r
THIRD ROUND				
Bolton	3	Liverpool	0	
Derby	1	Blackburn	4	
Nottm For	1	Notts Co	1	e
Sheff Wed	3	Aston V	2	e
Notts Co	4	Nottm For	1	r
SEMI-FINAL				
Bolton	2	Sheff Wed	1	N
Notts Co	1	Blackburn	0	N
FINAL				
Notts Co	4	Bolton	1	N

Net Profit

The 1892 Final was the first in which goal nets were used. They were invented by John Brodie, later chief engineer on the Mersey Tunnel.

1895

FIRST ROUND				
Aston V	2	Derby	1	
Barnsley	2	Liverpool	1	ev
Bolton	1	Wool Ars	0	
Burton W	1	Blackburn	2	
Bury	4	Leicester	1	
Darwen	0	Wolves	0	
Luton	0	Preston NE	2	
Middlesbro	4	Chestrfld	0	
Newcastle	2	Burnley	1	
Newton Ht	2	Stoke	3	
Sheff Utd	3	Millwall	1	
Sheff Wed	5	Notts Co	1	
Small Hth	1	West Brom	2	
Soton SM	1	Nottm For	4	
Southpt C	0	Everton	3	
Sunderld	11	Fairfield	1	
Liverpool	4	Barnsley	0	r
Wolves	2	Darwen	0	r
SECOND ROUND				
Aston V	7	Newcastle	1	
Bolton	1	Bury	0	
Everton	1	Blackburn	1	
Liverpool	0	Nottm For	2	
Sheff Utd	1	West Brom	1	
Sheff Wed	6	Middlesbro	1	
Sunderld	2	Preston NE	0	
Wolves	2	Stoke	0	
Blackburn	2	Everton	3	r
West Brom	2	Sheff Utd	1	r
THIRD ROUND				
Aston V	6	Nottm For	2	
Sheff Wed	2	Everton	0	
Sunderld	2	Bolton	1	
West Brom	1	Wolves	0	
SEMI-FINAL				
Aston V	2	Sunderld	1	N
West Brom	2	Sheff Wed	0	N
FINAL				
Aston V	1	West Brom	0	N

1896

FIRST ROUND				
Blackburn	1	West Brom	2	
Blackpool	4	Burton S	1	
Burnley	6	Wool Ars	1	
Burton W	1	Sheff Utd	1	
Chestrfld	0	Newcastle	4	
Crewe	0	Bolton	4	
Darwen	0	Grimsby	2	
Derby	4	Aston V	2	
Liverpool	4	Millwall	1	
Newton Ht	2	Kettering	1	
Nottm For	0	Everton	2	
Small Hth	1	Bury	4	
Soton SM	2	Sheff Wed	3	
Stoke	5	Tottenham	0	
Sunderld	4	Preston NE	1	
Wolves	2	Notts Co	2	
Notts Co	3	Wolves	4	r
Sheff Utd	1	Burton W	0	r
SECOND ROUND				
Blackpool	0	Bolton	2	

Burnley	1	Stoke	1	
Everton	3	Sheff Utd	0	
Grimsby	1	West Brom	1	
Newcastle	1	Bury	3	
Newton Ht	1	Derby	1	
Sheff Wed	2	Sunderld	1	
Wolves	2	Liverpool	0	
Derby	5	Newton Ht	1	r
Stoke	7	Burnley	1	r
West Brom	3	Grimsby	0	r
THIRD ROUND				
Bolton	2	Bury	0	
Derby	1	West Brom	0	
Sheff Wed	4	Everton	0	
Wolves	3	Stoke	0	
SEMI-FINAL				
Sheff Wed	1	Bolton	1	N
Wolves	2	Derby	1	N
Sheff Wed	3	Bolton	1	rN
FINAL				
Sheff Wed	2	Wolves	1	N

1897

FIRST ROUND				
Aston V	5	Newcastle	0	
Blackburn	2	Sheff Utd	1	
Derby	8	Barnsley	1	
Everton	5	Burton W	2	
Grimsby	0	Bolton	0	
Liverpool	4	Burton S	3	
Luton	0	West Brom	1	
Millwall	1	Wolves	2	
Newton Ht	5	Kettering	1	
Preston NE	6	Man City	0	
Sheff Wed	0	Nottm For	1	
Small Hth	1	Notts Co	2	
Soton SM	1	Heanor	1	
Stockton	0	Bury	0	
Stoke	5	Glossop N	2	
Sunderld	1	Burnley	0	
Bolton	3	Grimsby	3	re
Bury	12	Stockton	1	r
Heanor	0	Soton SM	1	r
Bolton	3	Grimsby	2	r2N
SECOND ROUND				
Aston V	2	Notts Co	1	
Blackburn	2	Wolves	1	
Derby	4	Bolton	1	
Everton	3	Bury	0	
Preston NE	2	Stoke	1	
Soton SM	1	Newton Ht	1	
Sunderld	1	Nottm For	3	
West Brom	1	Liverpool	2	
Newton Ht	3	Soton SM	1	r
THIRD ROUND				
Derby	2	Newton Ht	0	
Everton	2	Blackburn	0	
Liverpool	1	Nottm For	1	
Preston NE	1	Aston V	1	
Aston V	0	Preston NE	0	r
Nottm For	0	Liverpool	1	r
Aston V	3	Preston NE	2	r2N
SEMI-FINAL				
Aston V	3	Liverpool	0	N
Everton	3	Derby	2	N
FINAL				
Aston V	3	Everton	2	N

Scots Missed

After Rangers reached the Semi-Final in 1887 the Scottish FA banned its clubs from competing in the English Cup. The Irish followed suit, but Welsh clubs compete to this day.

1898

FIRST ROUND				
Burnley	3	Wool Ars	1	
Bury	1	Stoke	2	
Derby	1	Aston V	0	
Everton	1	Blackburn	0	
Liverpool	2	Hucknall	0	
Long Etn	0	Gainsbrgh	1	
Luton	0	Bolton	1	
Man City	1	Wigan Co	0	
Newton Ht	1	Walsall	0	
Nottm For	4	Grimsby	0	
Notts Co	0	Wolves	1	
Preston NE	1	Newcastle	2	
Sheff Utd	1	Burslem P	1	
Southmptn	2	Leicester	1	
Sunderld	0	Sheff Wed	1	
West Brom	2	N.Brig Tw	0	
Burslem P	2	Sheff Utd	1	re
SECOND ROUND				
Bolton	1	Man City	0	
Burnley	3	Burslem P	0	
Newton Ht	0	Liverpool	0	
Nottm For	4	Gainsbrgh	0	
Southmptn	1	Newcastle	0	
Stoke	0	Everton	0	
West Brom	1	Sheff Wed	0	
Wolves	0	Derby	1	
Everton	5	Stoke	1	r
Liverpool	2	Newton Ht	1	r
THIRD ROUND				
Bolton	0	Southmptn	0	
Burnley	1	Everton	3	
Derby	1	Liverpool	1	
West Brom	2	Nottm For	3	
Liverpool	1	Derby	5	r
Southmpt	4	Bolton	0	r
SEMI-FINAL				
Derby	3	Everton	1	N
Nottm For	1	Southmpt	1	N
Nottm For	2	Southmpt	0	rN
FINAL				
Nottm For	3	Derby	1	N

1899

FIRST ROUND				
Bristol C	2	Sunderld	4	
Burnley	2	Sheff Utd	2	
Everton	3	Jarrow	1	
Glossop	0	Newcastle	1	
Heanor	0	Bury	3	
Liverpool	2	Blackburn	0	
N.Bromptn	0	Southmptn	1	
Nottm For	2	Aston V	1	
Notts Co	2	Kettering	0	
Preston NE	7	Grimsby	0	
Sheff Wed	2	Stoke	2	
Small Hth	3	Man City	2	
Tottenham	1	Newton Ht	1	
West Brom	8	South Sh	0	
Wolves	0	Bolton	0	
Wool Ars	0	Derby	6	
Bolton	0	Wolves	1	r
Newton Ht	3	Tottenham	5	r
Sheff Utd	2	Burnley	1	r
Stoke	2	Sheff Wed	0	r
SECOND ROUND				
Derby	2	Wolves	1	
Everton	0	Nottm For	1	
Liverpool	3	Newcastle	1	
Notts Co	0	Southmptn	1	
Preston NE	2	Sheff Utd	2	
Stoke	2	Small Hth	2	
Tottenham	2	Sunderld	1	
West Brom	2	Bury	1	
Sheff Utd	2	Preston NE	1	r
Small Hth	1	Stoke	2	r
THIRD ROUND				
Nottm For	0	Sheff Utd	1	
Southmptn	1	Derby	2	
Stoke	4	Tottenham	1	
West Brom	0	Liverpool	2	
SEMI-FINAL				
Derby	3	Stoke	1	N
Sheff Utd	2	Liverpool	2	N
Sheff Utd	4	Liverpool	4	rN
Sheff Utd	1	Liverpool	0	r2N
FINAL				
Sheff Utd	4	Derby	1	N

Travel Club

Playing Old Etonians at The Oval in the Fourth Round in 1879, Darwen of Lancashire completed a remarkable comeback. 5-1 down with 15 minutes left they came back to draw 5-5! Darwen returned to London a few days later - after local fund-raising collected the £200 needed for the trip - and drew again, 2-2. A third long trip for Darwen (lost 6-2) prompted the FA to regionalise the early rounds in future years.

1900-1919

SOUTHERN COMFORT

The new century dawned with an historic achievement in the FA Cup, and one which will surely never be repeated.

In 1901, Tottenham Hotspur became the first southern club to win the trophy since the Old Etonians 18 years before and so ended a long run of northern dominance.

But Spurs' victory, over Sheffield United, was far more significant than that. Not only did it end that sorry southern sequence, but it was also the first time a non-League side had won the trophy since the formation of the Football League in 1888.

Jeepers Keepers

Bury won the Cup in 1903 by a record 6-0 margin, but Derby had to use three goalkeepers in the game because of injuries to the regular 'keeper and to his deputy.

That record still stands today and Tottenham are destined forever to be remembered as the only non-League side to win the FA Cup. The chances of it happening in the modern game are too remote to contemplate.

That remarkable victory was a wonderful achievement by the Londoners, even though it took them two attempts to clinch their place in the record books.

Bury the hatchet

In the 1900 competition Southampton became the first southern club to contest the FA Cup Final for 17 years, but they lost 4-0 to Bury.

The first match against the Sheffield club was watched by an astonishing crowd of 110,820 at the old Crystal Palace and ended in a 2-2 draw.

A replay was required, which took place at Burnden Park a week later and this time the non-Leaguers made no mistake, with goals from John Cameron, Tom Smith and Sandy Brown earning them a 3-1 win.

Perhaps it was fitting that Cameron should score the first goal as at the time he was Tottenham's player, manager and secretary!

But that shock victory for Spurs seemed to set the tone for the FA Cup in those early years of the 20th century.

No fewer than 12 different clubs lifted the trophy between Tottenham's win in 1901 and the interruption of the competition in 1915 due to the outbreak of World War I.

In that period, only Sheffield United and Aston Villa managed to win the Cup twice.

Fatty Foulke

William 'Fatty' Foulke, Sheff Utd's goalkeeper in the Finals of 1901 and 1902, weighed 22 stones at one stage of his career.

1900

FIRST ROUND				
Bristol C	2	Stalyb R	1	
Burnley	0	Bury	1	
Derby	2	Sunderld	2	
Jarrow	0	Millwall	2	
Man City	1	Aston V	1	
Newcastle	2	Reading	1	
Nottm For	3	Grimsby	0	
Notts Co	6	Chorley	0	
Portsmth	0	Blackburn	0	
Preston NE	1	Tottenham	0	
QPR	1	Wolves	1	
Sheff Utd	1	Leicester	0	
Sheff Wed	1	Bolton	0	
Southmptn	3	Everton	0	
Stoke	0	Liverpool	0	
Walsall	1	West Brom	1	
Aston V	3	Man City	0	r
Blackburn	1	Portsmth	1	re
Liverpool	1	Stoke	0	r
Sunderld	3	Derby	0	r
West Brom	6	Walsall	1	r
Wolves	0	QPR	1	re
Blackburn	5	Portsmth	0	r2
SECOND ROUND				
Aston V	5	Bristol C	1	
Liverpool	1	West Brom	1	
Nottm For	3	Sunderld	0	
Notts Co	0	Bury	0	
Preston NE	1	Blackburn	0	
QPR	0	Millwall	2	
Sheff Utd	1	Sheff Wed	1	
Southmptn	4	Newcastle	1	
Bury	2	Notts Co	0	r
Sheff Wed	0	Sheff Utd	2	r
West Brom	2	Liverpool	1	r
THIRD ROUND				
Millwall	1	Aston V	1	
Preston NE	0	Nottm For	0	
Sheff Utd	2	Bury	2	
Southmptn	2	West Brom	1	
Aston V	0	Millwall	0	re
Bury	2	Sheff Utd	0	r
Nottm For	1	Preston NE	0	r
Millwall	2	Aston V	1	r2N
SEMI-FINAL				
Bury	1	Nottm For	1	N
Southmptn	0	Millwall	0	N
Bury	3	Nottm For	2	reN
Southmptn	3	Millwall	0	rN
FINAL				
Bury	4	Southmptn	0	N

1901

FIRST ROUND				
Aston V	5	Millwall	0	
Bolton	1	Derby	0	
Kettering	1	Chestrfld	1	
Middlesbro	3	Newcastle	1	
Newton Ht	0	Burnley	0	
Nottm For	5	Leicester	1	
Notts Co	2	Liverpool	0	
Reading	2	Bristol R	0	
Sheff Wed	0	Bury	1	
Southmptn	1	Everton	3	
Stoke	1	Small Hth	1	
Sunderld	1	Sheff Utd	2	
Tottenham	1	Preston NE	1	
West Brom	1	Man City	0	
Wolves	5	N.Brig Tw	1	
Wool Ars	2	Blackburn	0	
Burnley	7	Newton Ht	1	r
Chestrfld	1	Kettering	2	re
Preston NE	2	Tottenham	4	r
Small Hth	2	Stoke	1	re
SECOND ROUND				
Aston V	0	Nottm For	0	
Bolton	0	Reading	1	
Middlesbr	5	Kettering	0	
Notts Co	2	Wolves	3	
Sheff Utd	2	Everton	0	
Small Hth	1	Burnley	0	
Tottenham	2	Bury	1	
Wool Ars	0	West Brom	1	
Nottm For	1	Aston V	3	re
THIRD ROUND				
Middlesbro	0	West Brom	1	
Reading	1	Tottenham	1	
Small Hth	0	Aston V	0	
Wolves	0	Sheff Utd	4	
Aston V	1	Small Hth	0	re
Tottenham	3	Reading	0	r
SEMI-FINAL				
Sheff Utd	2	Aston V	2	N
Tottenham	4	West Brom	0	N
Sheff Utd	3	Aston V	0	rN
FINAL				
Tottenham	2	Sheff Utd	2	N
Tottenham	3	Sheff Utd	1	rN

Spurs select

Tottenham, the first southern winners for 19 years in 1901 and members of the Southern League, didn't have a single player from south of Nottingham in their triumphant side. Spurs' historic winning team consisted of five Scots, two Welshmen, one Irishman and three northern English players!

1902

FIRST ROUND			
Blackburn	0	Derby	2
Bury	5	West Brom	1
Glossop	1	Nottm For	3
Grimsby	1	Portsmth	1
Liverpool	2	Everton	2
Man City	1	Preston NE	1
Middlesbro	1	Bristol R	1
N'hamptn	0	Sheff Utd	2
Notts Co	1	Reading	2
Oxford C	0	Lincoln	0
Sheff Wed	0	Sunderld	1
Stoke	2	Aston V	2
Tottenham	1	Southmptn	1
Walsall	1	Burnley	0

WHAT A STAR ✪ KENNETH HUNT

The Reverend Kenneth Reginald Gunnery Hunt is the only man to play for England - twice - after being ordained as a priest. He was a midfielder whose greatest day was in 1908, when he scored the first goal for Wolves (eighth in the Second Division) as they beat Newcastle (fourth in the First) to win the Cup 3-1. Several observers thought that Wolves were lucky to win, but Hunt maintained: "They played three-quarters of the football. We scored three-quarters of the goals." His plan to invite the team to tea at his vicarage the next afternoon had to be abandoned though, because the local lanes were crammed with fans.

Wolves	0	Bolton	2	
Wool Ars	0	Newcastle	2	
Aston V	1	Stoke	2	re
Bristol R	1	Middlesbro	0	re
Everton	0	Liverpool	2	r
Lincoln	4	Oxford C	0	r
Portsmth	2	Grimsby	0	r
Preston NE	0	Man City	0	re
Southmptn	2	Tottenham	2	re
Preston NE	2	Man City	4	r2e
Southmpt	2	Tottenham	1	r2N

SECOND ROUND				
Bristol R	0	Stoke	1	
Lincoln	1	Derby	3	
Man City	0	Nottm For	2	
Newcastle	1	Sunderld	0	
Reading	0	Portsmth	1	
Sheff Utd	2	Bolton	1	
Southmpt	4	Liverpool	1	
Walsall	0	Bury	5	

THIRD ROUND				
Bury	2	Southmpt	3	
Newcastle	1	Sheff Utd	1	
Nottm For	2	Stoke	0	
Portsmth	0	Derby	0	
Derby	6	Portsmth	3	r
Sheff Utd	2	Newcastle	1	r

SEMI-FINAL				
Sheff Utd	1	Derby	1	N
Southmpt	3	Nottm For	1	N
Sheff Utd	1	Derby	1	reN
Sheff Utd	1	Derby	0	r2N

FINAL				
Sheff Utd	1	Southmpt	1	N
Sheff Utd	2	Southmpt	1	rN

1903

FIRST ROUND				
Aston V	4	Sunderld	1	
Barnsley	2	Lincoln	0	
Blackburn	0	Sheff Wed	0	
Bolton	0	Bristol C	5	
Bury	1	Wolves	0	
Derby	2	Small Hth	1	
Everton	5	Portsmth	0	
Glossop	2	Stoke	3	
Grimsby	2	Newcastle	1	
Man Utd	2	Liverpool	1	
Millwall	3	Luton	0	
Nottm For	0	Reading	0	
Notts Co	0	Southmpt	0	
Preston NE	3	Man City	1	
Tottenham	0	West Brom	0	
Wool Ars	1	Sheff Utd	3	
Reading	3	Nottm For	6	re
Sheff Wed	0	Blackburn	1	r
Southmpt	2	Notts Co	2	re
West Brom	0	Tottenham	2	r
Notts Co	2	Soton	1	r2eN

SECOND ROUND				
Aston V	4	Barnsley	1	
Derby	2	Blackburn	0	
Everton	3	Man Utd	1	
Grimsby	0	Notts Co	2	
Millwall	4	Preston NE	1	
Nottm For	0	Stoke	0	
Sheff Utd	0	Bury	1	
Tottenham	1	Bristol C	0	
Stoke	2	Nottm For	0	r

THIRD ROUND				
Bury	1	Notts Co	0	
Derby	3	Stoke	0	
Millwall	1	Everton	0	
Tottenham	2	Aston V	3	

SEMI-FINAL				
Bury	3	Aston V	0	N
Derby	3	Millwall	0	N

FINAL				
Bury	6	Derby	0	N

Cup of change

After the 1910 Final, the original FA Cup trophy was presented to Lord Kinnaird to commemorate his first 21 years as president of the FA. A new cup design was chosen - and is still in use today.

1904

FIRST ROUND				
Blackburn	3	Liverpool	1	
Bristol C	1	Sheff Utd	3	
Bury	2	Newcastle	1	
Everton	1	Tottenham	2	
Man City	3	Sunderld	2	
Millwall	0	Middlesbro	2	
Notts Co	3	Man Utd	3	
Plymouth	2	Sheff Wed	2	
Portsmth	2	Derby	5	
Preston NE	1	Grimsby	0	
Reading	1	Bolton	1	
Southmpt	3	Burslem P	0	
Stockton	1	Wolves	4	
Stoke	2	Aston V	3	
West Brom	1	Nottm For	1	
Wool Ars	1	Fulham	0	
Bolton	3	Reading	2	r
Man Utd	2	Notts Co	1	r
Nottm For	3	West Brom	1	r
Sheff Wed	2	Plymouth	0	r

SECOND ROUND				
Aston V	0	Tottenham	1	
Blackburn	3	Nottm For	1	
Bolton	4	Southmpt	1	
Bury	1	Sheff Utd	2	
Derby	2	Wolves	2	
Preston NE	0	Middlesbro	3	
Sheff Wed	6	Man Utd	0	
Wool Ars	0	Man City	2	
Wolves	2	Derby	2	re
Derby	1	Wolves	0	r2N

THIRD ROUND				
Derby	2	Blackburn	1	
Man City	0	Middlebr	0	
Sheff Utd	0	Bolton	2	
Tottenham	1	Sheff Wed	1	
Middlebr	1	Man City	3	r
Sheff Wed	2	Tottenham	0	r

SEMI-FINAL				
Bolton	1	Derby	0	N
Man City	3	Sheff Wed	0	N

FINAL				
Man City	1	Bolton	0	N

Steve's Bloomer

The great Steve Bloomer scored 35 FA Cup goals during his career with Derby and Middlesbrough, including six in Semi-Finals and one in a Final, but never gained a winner's medal.

1905

FIRST ROUND				
Aston V	5	Leicester	1	
Blackburn	1	Sheff Wed	2	
Bolton	1	Bristol R	1	
Bury	1	Notts Co	0	
Derby	0	Preston NE	2	
Fulham	0	Reading	0	
Lincoln	1	Man City	2	
Liverpool	1	Everton	1	
Middlebr	1	Tottenham	1	
Newcastle	1	Plymouth	1	
Nottm For	2	Sheff Utd	0	
Small Hth	0	Portsmth	2	
Southmpt	3	Millwall	1	
Stoke	2	Grimsby	0	
Sunderld	1	Wolves	1	
Wool Ars	0	Bristol C	0	
Bristol C	1	Wool Ars	0	r
Bristol R	0	Bolton	3	r
Everton	2	Liverpool	1	r
Plymouth	1	Newcastle	1	r
Reading	0	Fulham	0	re
Tottenham	1	Middlebr	0	r
Wolves	1	Sunderld	0	r
Fulham	1	Reading	0	r2eN
Newcastle	2	Plymouth	0	r2N

SECOND ROUND				
Aston V	3	Bury	2	
Bristol C	0	Preston NE	0	
Fulham	1	Nottm For	0	
Man City	1	Bolton	2	
Sheff Wed	2	Portsmth	1	
Stoke	0	Everton	4	
Tottenham	1	Newcastle	1	
Wolves	2	Southmpt	3	
Newcastle	4	Tottenham	0	r
Preston NE	1	Bristol C	0	r

THIRD ROUND				
Aston V	5	Fulham	0	
Bolton	0	Newcastle	2	
Everton	4	Southmpt	0	

Home		Away		
Preston NE	1	Sheff Wed	1	
Sheff Wed	3	Preston NE	0	r

SEMI-FINAL

Home		Away		
Aston V	1	Everton	1	N
Newcastle	1	Sheff Wed	0	N
Aston V	2	Everton	1	rN

FINAL

Home		Away		
Aston V	2	Newcastle	0	N

1906

FIRST ROUND

Home		Away		
Aston V	11	King's Ln	0	
Birmghm C	1	Preston NE	0	
Blackpool	1	C.Palace	1	
Bradford	3	Barrow	2	
Brentford	2	Bristol C	1	
Brighton	3	Swindon	0	
Bshk Auck	0	Wolves	3	
Burslem P	0	Gainsbrgh	3	
Bury	1	Nottm For	1	
Clapton O	0	Chestrfld	0	
Crewe	1	Barnsley	1	
Derby	4	Kettering	0	
Everton	3	West Brom	1	
Fulham	1	QPR	0	
Hull	0	Reading	1	
Lincoln	4	Stockport	2	
Liverpool	2	Leicester	1	
Man Utd	7	Staple H	2	
Middlebr	3	Bolton	0	
Millwall	1	Burton U	0	
N.Bromptn	2	N'hamptn	1	
N.Crusader	3	Plymouth	6	
Newcastle	6	Grimsby	0	
Norwich	1	Tunbridge	1	
Sheff Utd	4	Man City	1	
Sheff Wed	1	Bristol R	0	
Southmpt	5	Portsmth	1	
Stoke	1	Blackburn	0	
Sunderld	1	Notts Co	0	
Tottenham	2	Burnley	0	
Wool Ars	1	West Ham	1	
Worcester	0	Watford	6	
Barnsley	4	Crewe	0	r
Chestrfld	3	Clapton O	0	r
C.Palace	1	Blackpool	1	re
Nottm For	6	Bury	2	r
Tunbridge	0	Norwich	5	r
West Ham	2	Wool Ars	3	r
Blackpool	1	C.Palace	0	r2N

SECOND ROUND

Home		Away		
Aston V	0	Plymouth	0	
Bradford	5	Wolves	0	
Brentford	3	Lincoln	0	
Brighton	1	Middlebr	1	
Derby	0	Newcastle	0	
Everton	3	Chestrfld	0	
Fulham	1	Nottm For	3	
Liverpool	1	Barnsley	0	
Man Utd	3	Norwich	0	
N.Bromptn	0	Southmpt	0	
Sheff Utd	1	Blackpool	2	
Sheff Wed	1	Millwall	1	
Stoke	0	Birmghm C	1	
Sunderld	1	Gainsbrgh	1	
Tottenham	3	Reading	2	
Wool Ars	3	Watford	0	
Middlebr	1	Brighton	1	re
Millwall	0	Sheff Wed	3	r
Newcastle	2	Derby	1	r
Plymouth	1	Aston V	5	r
Southmpt	1	N.Bromptn	0	r
Sunderld	3	Gainsbrgh	0	r
Brighton	1	Middlebro	3	r2N

THIRD ROUND

Home		Away		
Everton	1	Bradford	0	
Liverpool	2	Brentford	0	
Man Utd	5	Aston V	1	
Newcastle	5	Blackpool	0	
Sheff Wed	4	Nottm For	1	
Southmpt	6	Middlebr	1	
Tottenham	1	Birmghm C	1	
Wool Ars	5	Sunderld	0	
Birmghm C	2	Tottenham	0	re

FOURTH ROUND

Home		Away		
Birmghm C	2	Newcastle	2	
Everton	4	Sheff Wed	3	
Liverpool	3	Southmpt	0	
Man Utd	2	Wool Ars	3	
Newcastle	3	Birmghm C	0	re

SEMI-FINAL

Home		Away		
Everton	2	Liverpool	0	N
Newcastle	2	Wool Ars	0	N

FINAL

Home		Away		
Everton	1	Newcastle	0	N

1907

FIRST ROUND

Home		Away		
Blackburn	2	Man City	2	
Bolton	3	Brighton	1	
Bradford	2	Reading	0	
Brentford	2	Glossop	1	
Bristol C	4	Leeds C	1	
Bristol R	0	QPR	0	
Burnley	1	Aston V	3	
Burslem P	7	Irthlingb	1	
Burton U	0	N.Bromptn	0	
Crewe	1	Accringtn	1	
Derby	1	Chestrfld	1	
Everton	1	Sheff Utd	0	
Fulham	0	Stockport	0	
Gainsbrgh	0	Luton	0	
Grimsby	1	Wool Ars	1	
Lincoln	2	Chelsea	2	
Liverpool	2	Birmghm C	1	
Middlebr	4	N'hamptn	2	
Millwall	2	Plymouth	0	
Newcastle	0	C.Palace	1	
Norwich	3	Hastings	1	
Nottm For	1	Barnsley	1	
Notts Co	1	Preston NE	0	
Oldham	5	Kiddermst	0	
Oxford C	0	Bury	3	
Portsmth	2	Man Utd	2	
Sheff Wed	3	Wolves	2	
Southmpt	2	Watford	1	
Sunderld	4	Leicester	1	
Tottenham	0	Hull	0	
West Brom	1	Stoke	1	
West Ham	2	Blackpool	1	
Accringtn	1	Crewe	0	r
Barnsley	2	Nottm For	1	r
Chelsea	0	Lincoln	1	re
Chestrfld	1	Derby	1	ra
Fulham	2	Stockport	1	r
Hull	0	Tottenham	0	re
Luton	2	Gainsbrgh	1	r
Man City	0	Blackburn	1	r
Man Utd	1	Portsmth	2	r
N.Bromptn	0	Burton U	0	ra
QPR	0	Bristol R	1	r
Stoke	2	West Brom	2	re
Wool Ars	3	Grimsby	0	r
Chestrfld	0	Derby	4	r2N
N.Bromptn	2	Burton U	0	r2N
Tottenham	1	Hull	0	r2
West Brom	2	Stoke	0	r2N

SECOND ROUND

Home		Away		
Barnsley	1	Portsmth	0	
Blackburn	1	Tottenham	1	
Bolton	2	Aston V	0	
Bradford	1	Accringtn	0	
Brentford	1	Middlebr	0	
Bristol R	3	Millwall	0	
Burslem P	2	Notts Co	2	
Bury	1	N.Bromptn	0	
Derby	1	Lincoln	0	
Fulham	0	C.Palace	0	
Luton	0	Sunderld	0	
Oldham	0	Liverpool	1	
Southmpt	1	Sheff Wed	1	
West Brom	1	Norwich	0	
West Ham	1	Everton	2	
Wool Ars	2	Bristol C	1	
C.Palace	1	Fulham	0	r
Notts Co	5	Burslem P	0	r
Sheff Wed	3	Southmpt	1	r
Sunderld	1	Luton	0	r
Tottenham	1	Blackburn	1	re
Tottenham	2	Blackburn	1	r2N

THIRD ROUND

Home		Away		
Barnsley	1	Bury	0	
C.Palace	1	Brentford	1	
Everton	0	Bolton	0	
Liverpool	1	Bradford	0	
Notts Co	4	Tottenham	0	
Sheff Wed	0	Sunderld	0	
West Brom	2	Derby	0	
Wool Ars	1	Bristol R	0	
Bolton	0	Everton	3	r
Brentford	0	C.Palace	1	r
Sunderld	0	Sheff Wed	1	r

FOURTH ROUND

Home		Away		
Barnsley	1	Wool Ars	2	

Sporting Saint

C.B. Fry, a Southampton player in the 1902 Final, represented England at soccer and cricket, Oxford University at rugby and golf, and shared the world long-jump record.

WHAT A STAR ✪ SANDY BROWN

Tottenham Hotspur became the last non-League club, and the first London side, to win the Cup, when in the Southern League in 1901. Alexander Brown from Glenbuck - a town later to produce Liverpool legend Bill Shankly - was the man who did most towards that success. He scored 15 of Spurs' 20 goals, a record for any Cup-winning player in one season, and helped them to come from behind in five of their eight games. Yet Brown, who had been signed from Portsmouth, scored only ten times in League games that season, and a few months later he moved to Middlesbrough.

C.Palace	1	Everton	1	
Sheff Wed	1	Liverpool	0	
West Brom	3	Notts Co	1	
Everton	4	C.Palace	0	r
SEMI-FINAL				
Everton	2	West Brom	1	N
Sheff Wed	3	Wool Ars	1	N
FINAL				
Sheff Wed	2	Everton	1	N

1908

FIRST ROUND				
Aston V	3	Stockport	0	
Bolton	5	Woking	0	
Bradford	1	Wolves	1	
Brighton	1	Preston NE	1	
Bristol C	0	Grimsby	0	
Burnley	1	Southmpt	2	
Bury	2	Millwall	1	
Carlisle	2	Brentford	2	
Chelsea	9	Worksop	1	
Chestrfld	4	Stockton	0	
Coventry	2	C.Palace	4	
Everton	1	Tottenham	0	
Gainsbrgh	1	Watford	0	
Glossop	0	Man City	0	
Hastings	0	Portsmth	1	
Leicester	2	Blackburn	0	
Liverpool	4	Derby	2	
Luton	3	Fulham	8	
Man Utd	3	Blackpool	1	
N.Bromptn	3	Sunderld	1	
Newcastle	2	Nottm For	0	
N'hamptn	0	Bristol R	1	
Norwich	2	Sheff Wed	0	
Notts Co	2	Middlebr	0	
Oldham	2	Leeds C	1	
Plymouth	1	Barnsley	0	
QPR	1	Reading	0	
Stoke	5	Lincoln	0	
Swindon	0	Sheff Utd	0	
West Brom	1	Birmghm C	1	
West Ham	1	Rotherhm	0	
Wool Ars	0	Hull	0	
Birmghm C	1	West Brom	2	r
Brentford	1	Carlisle	3	re
Grimsby	2	Bristol C	1	r
Hull	4	Wool Ars	1	r
Man City	6	Glossop	0	r
Preston NE	1	Brighton	1	r
Sheff Utd	2	Swindon	3	re
Wolves	1	Bradford	0	r
Preston NE	0	Brighton	1	r2N
SECOND ROUND				
Aston V	3	Hull	0	
Bristol R	2	Chestrfld	0	
Fulham	2	Norwich	1	
Grimsby	6	Carlisle	2	
Liverpool	1	Brighton	1	
Man City	1	N.Bromptn	1	
Man Utd	1	Chelsea	0	
Newcastle	2	West Ham	0	
Notts Co	1	Bolton	1	
Oldham	0	Everton	0	
Plymouth	2	C.Palace	3	
Portsmth	1	Leicester	0	
Southmpt	1	West Brom	0	
Stoke	1	Gainsbrgh	1	
Swindon	2	QPR	1	
Wolves	2	Bury	0	
Bolton	2	Notts Co	1	re
Brighton	0	Liverpool	3	r
Everton	6	Oldham	1	r
Gainsbrgh	2	Stoke	2	re
N.Bromptn	1	Man City	2	r
Stoke	3	Gainsbrgh	1	r2N
THIRD ROUND				
Aston V	0	Man Utd	2	
Bolton	3	Everton	3	
Grimsby	1	C.Palace	0	
Man City	1	Fulham	1	
Newcastle	3	Liverpool	1	
Portsmth	0	Stoke	1	
Southmpt	2	Bristol R	0	
Wolves	2	Swindon	0	
Everton	3	Bolton	1	re
Fulham	3	Man City	1	r
FOURTH ROUND				
Everton	0	Southmpt	0	
Fulham	2	Man Utd	1	
Newcastle	5	Grimsby	1	
Stoke	0	Wolves	1	
Southmpt	3	Everton	2	r
SEMI-FINAL				
Newcastle	6	Fulham	0	N
Wolves	2	Southmpt	0	N
FINAL				
Wolves	3	Newcastle	1	N

1909

FIRST ROUND				
Birmghm C	2	Portsmth	5	
Blackpool	2	Hastings	0	
Bradford	2	Workingtn	0	
Brentford	2	Gainsbrgh	0	
Bristol C	1	Southmpt	1	
Bristol R	1	Burnley	4	
Bury	8	Kettering	0	
Chestrfld	0	Glossop	2	
Croydon C	1	Wool Ars	1	N
Everton	3	Barnsley	1	
Fulham	4	Carlisle	1	
Grimsby	0	Stockport	2	
Hull	1	Chelsea	1	
Liverpool	5	Lincoln	1	
Luton	1	Millwall	2	
Man City	3	Tottenham	4	
Man Utd	1	Brighton	0	
Newcastle	5	Clapton O	0	
N'hamptn	1	Derby	1	
Norwich	0	Reading	0	N
Nottm For	2	Aston V	0	
Notts Co	0	Blackburn	1	
Oldham	1	Leeds C	1	
Plymouth	1	Swindon	0	
Preston NE	1	Middlebr	0	
QPR	0	West Ham	0	
Sheff Utd	2	Sunderld	3	
Sheff Wed	5	Stoke	0	
Watford	1	Leicester	1	
West Brom	3	Bolton	1	
Wolves	2	C.Palace	2	
Wrexham	1	Exeter	1	
Chelsea	1	Hull	0	r

Palace Party

The attendance at Crystal Palace in 1905, when Aston Villa beat Newcastle 2-0, was 101,117 - the first six-figure soccer gate in the world.

C.Palace	4	Wolves	2	r
Derby	4	N'hamptn	2	r
Exeter	2	Wrexham	1	re
Leeds C	2	Oldham	0	r
Leicester	3	Watford	1	r
Reading	1	Norwich	1	re
Southmpt	0	Bristol C	2	r
West Ham	1	QPR	0	r
Wool Ars	2	Croydon C	0	r
Norwich	3	Reading	2	r2eN
SECOND ROUND				
Blackburn	2	Chelsea	1	
Bristol C	2	Bury	2	
C.Palace	0	Burnley	0	
Leeds C	1	West Ham	1	
Leicester	0	Derby	2	
Liverpool	2	Norwich	3	
Man Utd	1	Everton	0	
Newcastle	2	Blackpool	1	
Nottm For	1	Brentford	0	
Plymouth	2	Exeter	0	
Portsmth	2	Sheff Wed	2	
Preston NE	1	Sunderld	2	
Stockport	1	Glossop	1	
Tottenham	1	Fulham	0	
West Brom	1	Bradford	2	
Wool Ars	1	Millwall	1	
Burnley	9	C.Palace	0	r
Bury	0	Bristol C	1	r
Glossop	1	Stockport	0	re
Millwall	1	Wool Ars	0	r
Sheff Wed	3	Portsmth	0	r
West Ham	2	Leeds C	1	re
THIRD ROUND				
Bradford	0	Sunderld	1	
Bristol C	2	Norwich	0	
Derby	1	Plymouth	0	
Man Utd	6	Blackburn	1	
Nottm For	3	Millwall	1	
Sheff Wed	0	Glossop	1	
Tottenham	0	Burnley	0	
West Ham	0	Newcastle	0	
Burnley	3	Tottenham	1	r
Newcastle	2	West Ham	1	r
FOURTH ROUND				
Burnley	2	Man Utd	3	
Derby	3	Nottm For	0	
Glossop	0	Bristol C	0	
Newcastle	2	Sunderld	2	
Bristol C	1	Glossop	0	r
Sunderld	0	Newcastle	3	r
SEMI-FINAL				
Bristol C	1	Derby	1	N
Man Utd	1	Newcastle	0	N
Bristol C	2	Derby	1	rN
FINAL				
Man Utd	1	Bristol C	0	N

1910

FIRST ROUND				
Birmghm C	1	Leicester	4	
Blackburn	7	Accringtn	1	
Blackpool	1	Barnsley	1	
Bradford	4	Notts Co	2	
Bradfd PA	8	Bshk Auck	0	
Brighton	0	Southmpt	1	
Bristol C	2	Liverpool	0	
Burnley	2	Man Utd	0	
Bury	2	Glossop	1	
Chelsea	2	Hull	1	
Chestrfld	0	Fulham	0	
C.Palace	1	Swindon	3	
Derby	5	Millwall	0	
Gainsbrgh	1	Southend	1	
Grimsby	0	Bristol R	2	
Leyton	0	N.Bromptn	0	
Middlebr	1	Everton	1	
N'hamptn	0	Sheff Wed	0	
Norwich	0	QPR	0	
Nottm For	3	Sheff Utd	2	
Oldham	1	Aston V	2	
Plymouth	1	Tottenham	1	
Portsmth	3	Shrewsby	0	
Preston NE	1	Coventry	2	
Stockport	4	Bolton	1	
Stoke	1	Newcastle	1	
Sunderld	1	Leeds C	0	
West Brom	2	Clapton O	0	
West Ham	1	Carlisle	1	
Wolves	5	Reading	0	
Wool Ars	3	Watford	0	
Workingtn	1	Man City	2	
Barnsley	6	Blackpool	0	r
Everton	5	Middlebr	3	r
Fulham	2	Chestrfld	1	r
N.Bromptn	2	Leyton	2	re
Newcastle	2	Stoke	1	r
QPR	3	Norwich	0	r
Sheff Wed	0	N'hamptn	1	r
Southend	1	Gainsbrgh	0	r
Tottenham	7	Plymouth	1	r
West Ham	5	Carlisle	0	r
Leyton	1	N.Brompt	0	r2N
SECOND ROUND				
Aston V	6	Derby	1	
Barnsley	4	Bristol R	0	
Bradford	1	Blackburn	2	
Bristol C	1	West Brom	1	
Chelsea	0	Tottenham	1	
Everton	5	Wool Ars	0	
Leicester	3	Bury	2	
Newcastle	4	Fulham	0	
N'hamptn	0	Nottm For	0	
Portsmth	0	Coventry	1	
Southmpt	0	Man City	5	
Southend	0	QPR	0	
Stockport	0	Leyton	2	
Sunderld	3	Bradfd PA	1	
Swindon	2	Burnley	0	
Wolves	1	West Ham	5	
Nottm For	1	N'hamptn	0	r
QPR	3	Southend	2	r
West Brom	4	Bristol C	2	r
THIRD ROUND				
Aston V	1	Man City	2	
Barnsley	1	West Brom	0	
Coventry	3	Nottm For	1	
Everton	2	Sunderld	0	
Leyton	0	Leicester	1	
Newcastle	3	Blackburn	1	
QPR	1	West Ham	1	
Swindon	3	Tottenham	2	
West Ham	0	QPR	1	re
FOURTH ROUND				
Barnsley	1	QPR	0	
Coventry	0	Everton	2	
Newcastle	3	Leicester	0	
Swindon	2	Man City	0	
SEMI-FINAL				
Barnsley	0	Everton	0	N
Newcastle	2	Swindon	0	N
Barnsley	3	Everton	0	rN
FINAL				
Newcastle	1	Barnsley	1	N
Newcastle	2	Barnsley	0	rN

1911

FIRST ROUND				
Birmghm C	1	Oldham	1	
Blackburn	5	Southend	1	
Bolton	0	Chestrfld	2	
Bradfd PA	5	QPR	3	
Brentford	0	Preston NE	1	
Bristol C	0	Crewe	3	
Bristol R	0	Hull	0	
Burnley	2	Exeter	0	
Chelsea	0	Leyton	0	
Clapton O	1	Wool Ars	2	
C.Palace	0	Everton	4	
Derby	2	Plymouth	1	
Grimsby	3	Croydon C	0	v
Leeds C	1	Brighton	3	
Leicester	3	Southmpt	1	
Liverpool	3	Gainsbrgh	2	
Man Utd	2	Blackpool	1	

By Royal Appointment

King George V was the first member of the Royal family to see a Cup Final - when Burnley beat Liverpool 1-0 in 1914.

Penalty miss

Aston Villa star Charlie Wallace became the first player - and the last until Liverpool's John Aldridge in 1988 - to miss a penalty in an FA Cup Final when he failed to score with his spot-kick against Sunderland in the 1913 Final. Happilly for Wallace, Villa still won the Cup 1-0, thanks to a headed goal from Tommy Barber.

Middlebr	1	Glossop	0	
N.Bromptn	0	Bradford	1	
Newcastle	6	Bury	1	
N'hamptn	5	Luton	1	
Norwich	3	Sunderld	1	
Portsmth	1	Aston V	4	
Sheff Utd	0	Darlingtn	1	
Sheff Wed	1	Coventry	2	
Stoke	1	Man City	2	
Swindon	3	Notts Co	1	
Tottenham	2	Millwall	1	
Watford	0	Barnsley	2	
West Brom	4	Fulham	1	
West Ham	2	Nottm For	1	
Wolves	2	Accringtn	0	
Grimsby	8	Croydon C	1	r
Hull	1	Bristol R	0	re
Leyton	0	Chelsea	2	r
Oldham	2	Birmghm C	0	r

SECOND ROUND

Blackburn	0	Tottenham	0	
Bradford	2	Norwich	1	
Brighton	0	Coventry	0	
Burnley	2	Barnsley	0	
Chelsea	4	Chestrfld	1	
Crewe	1	Grimsby	5	
Darlingtn	2	Bradfd PA	1	
Derby	2	West Brom	0	
Everton	2	Liverpool	1	
Hull	1	Oldham	0	
Man Utd	2	Aston V	1	
Middlebr	0	Leicester	0	
Newcastle	1	N'hamptn	1	
Swindon	1	Wool Ars	0	
West Ham	3	Preston NE	0	
Wolves	1	Man City	0	
Coventry	2	Brighton	0	r
Leicester	1	Middlebr	2	re
Newcastle	1	N'hamptn	0	r
Tottenham	0	Blackburn	2	r

THIRD ROUND

Bradford	1	Grimsby	0	
Burnley	5	Coventry	0	
Darlingtn	0	Swindon	3	
Derby	5	Everton	0	
Middlebr	0	Blackburn	3	
Newcastle	3	Hull	2	
West Ham	2	Man Utd	1	
Wolves	0	Chelsea	2	

FOURTH ROUND

Bradford	1	Burnley	0	
Chelsea	3	Swindon	1	
Newcastle	4	Derby	0	
West Ham	2	Blackburn	3	

SEMI-FINAL

Bradford	3	Blackburn	0	N
Newcastle	3	Chelsea	0	N

FINAL

Bradford	0	Newcastle	0	N
Bradford	1	Newcastle	0	rN

1912

FIRST ROUND

Aston V	6	Walsall	0	
Birmghm C	0	Barnsley	0	
Blackburn	4	Norwich	1	
Bolton	1	Wool Ars	0	

Double Up

Like team-mate Billy Meredith, Sandy Turnbull appeared in a winning FA Cup Final side for both Manchester clubs. In 1904 he helped City to the trophy, while five years later he scored the goal that took United to victory against Bristol City.

Brentford	0	C.Palace	0	
Bristol R	1	Portsmth	2	
Bury	2	Millwall	1	
Chelsea	1	Sheff Utd	0	
Clapton O	1	Everton	2	
Crewe	1	Blackpool	1	
Croydon C	2	Leicester	2	
Darlingtn	2	Brighton	1	
Derby	3	Newcastle	0	
Fulham	2	Burnley	1	
Leeds C	1	Glossop	0	
Lincoln	2	Stockport	0	
Liverpool	1	Leyton	0	
Luton	2	Notts Co	4	
Man Utd	3	Huddersfld	1	
Middlebr	0	Sheff Wed	0	
N'hamptn	1	Bristol C	0	
Nottm For	0	Bradfd PA	1	
Oldham	1	Hull	1	
Preston NE	0	Man City	1	
QPR	0	Bradford	0	
Southmpt	0	Coventry	2	
Southpt C	0	Reading	2	
Sunderld	3	Plymouth	1	
Swindon	5	Sutton Jc	0	
Watford	0	Wolves	0	
West Brom	3	Tottenham	0	
West Ham	2	Gainsbrgh	1	
Barnsley	3	Birmghm C	0	r
Blackpool	2	Crewe	2	r
Bradford	4	QPR	0	r
C.Palace	4	Brentford	0	r
Hull	0	Oldham	1	r
Leicester	6	Croydon C	1	r
Sheff Wed	1	Middlebr	2	r
Wolves	10	Watford	0	r
Crewe	1	Blackpool	2	r2N

SECOND ROUND

Aston V	1	Reading	1	
Barnsley	1	Leicester	0	
Bolton	1	Blackpool	0	
Bradford	2	Chelsea	0	
Bradfd PA	2	Portsmth	0	
Coventry	1	Man Utd	5	
C.Palace	0	Sunderld	0	
Darlingtn	1	N'hamptn	1	
Derby	1	Blackburn	2	
Everton	1	Bury	1	
Fulham	3	Liverpool	0	
Leeds C	0	West Brom	1	
Man City	0	Oldham	1	
Middlebr	1	West Ham	1	
Swindon	2	Notts Co	0	
Wolves	2	Lincoln	1	
Everton	6	Bury	0	r
N'hamptn	2	Darlingtn	0	r
Reading	1	Aston V	0	r
Sunderld	1	C.Palace	0	re
West Ham	2	Middlebr	1	r

THIRD ROUND

Blackburn	3	Wolves	2	
Bolton	1	Barnsley	2	
Bradfd PA	0	Bradford	1	
Fulham	2	N'hamptn	1	
Oldham	0	Everton	2	
Reading	1	Man Utd	1	
Sunderld	1	West Brom	2	
West Ham	1	Swindon	1	
Man Utd	3	Reading	0	r
Swindon	4	West Ham	0	r

FOURTH ROUND

Barnsley	0	Bradford	0	
Man Utd	1	Blackburn	1	
Swindon	2	Everton	1	
West Brom	3	Fulham	0	
Blackburn	4	Man Utd	2	re
Bradford	0	Barnsley	0	re
Barnsley	0	Bradford	0	r2e
Barnsley	3	Bradford	2	r3eN

SEMI-FINAL

Barnsley	0	Swindon	0	N
West Brom	0	Blackburn	0	N
Barnsley	1	Swindon	0	rN
West Brom	1	Blackburn	0	reN

FINAL

Barnsley	0	West Brom	0	N
Barnsley	1	West Brom	0	reN

1913

FIRST ROUND

Blackburn	7	N'hamptn	2	
Bradfd PA	1	Barrow	1	
Bristol R	2	Notts Co	0	
Chelsea	5	Southend	2	
Chestrfld	1	Nottm For	4	
Croydon C	0	Wool Ars	0	
C.Palace	2	Glossop	0	
Derby	1	Aston V	3	
Everton	5	Stockport	1	
Fulham	0	Hull	2	

Bert on the spot

The first FA Cup Final penalty was scored by Albert Shepherd of Newcastle when they beat Barnsley 2-0 in a replay at Everton in 1910.

GIANTKILLERS

1909 Sheff Wed 0 Glossop 1

Glossop North End, from a small Derbyshire town - even now the population is only 25,000 - showed the modern lower league hopefuls the way by getting to the last eight of the Cup while a moderate Second Division side. And, ironically, 1996/97's FA Cup-fighters Chesterfield were their first victims, 2-0. They also knocked out Stockport County after extra-time in a replay before winning away to mighty Sheffield Wednesday, twice Champions and once Cup-winners in the previous five seasons. Glossop, who went on to lose to eventual finalists Bristol City, now play in the North-West Counties League.

Huddersfld	3	Sheff Utd	1	
Leeds C	2	Burnley	3	
Leicester	1	Norwich	4	
Liverpool	3	Bristol C	0	
Man City	4	Birmghm C	0	
Man Utd	1	Coventry	1	
Millwall	0	Middlebr	0	
N.Bromptn	0	Barnsley	0	
Newcastle	1	Bradford	0	
Oldham	2	Bolton	0	
Plymouth	2	Preston NE	0	
Portsmth	1	Brighton	2	
QPR	4	Halifax	2	
Rochdale	0	Swindon	2	
S.Shields	0	Gainsbrgh	1	
Sheff Wed	5	Grimsby	1	
Southmpt	1	Bury	1	
Stoke	2	Reading	2	
Sunderld	6	Clapton O	0	
Tottenham	1	Blackpool	1	
West Brom	1	West Ham	1	
Wolves	3	London C	1	
Barnsley	3	N.Bromptn	1	r
Bradfd PA	1	Barrow	0	r
Bury	2	Southmpt	1	r
Coventry	1	Man Utd	2	r
Middlebr	4	Millwall	1	r
Reading	3	Stoke	0	r
Tottenham	6	Blackpool	1	r
West Ham	2	West Brom	2	re
Wool Ars	2	Croydon C	1	r
West Ham	3	West Brom	0	r2N
SECOND ROUND				
Aston V	5	West Ham	0	
Barnsley	2	Blackburn	3	
Bradfd PA	3	Wolves	0	
Brighton	0	Everton	0	
Bristol R	1	Norwich	1	
Burnley	4	Gainsbrgh	1	
Chelsea	1	Sheff Wed	1	
C.Palace	2	Bury	0	
Huddersfld	1	Swindon	2	
Hull	0	Newcastle	0	
Middlebr	3	QPR	2	
Oldham	5	Nottm For	1	
Plymouth	0	Man Utd	2	
Reading	1	Tottenham	0	
Sunderld	2	Man City	0	
Wool Ars	1	Liverpool	4	
Everton	1	Brighton	0	re
Newcastle	3	Hull	0	r
Norwich	2	Bristol R	2	re
Sheff Wed	6	Chelsea	0	r
Bristol R	1	Norwich	0	r2N
THIRD ROUND				
Aston V	5	C.Palace	0	
Bradfd PA	2	Sheff Wed	1	
Bristol R	0	Everton	4	
Burnley	3	Middlebr	1	
Liverpool	1	Newcastle	1	
Oldham	0	Man Utd	0	
Reading	1	Blackburn	2	
Sunderld	4	Swindon	2	
Man Utd	1	Oldham	2	r
Newcastle	1	Liverpool	0	r
FOURTH ROUND				
Blackburn	0	Burnley	1	
Bradfd PA	0	Aston V	5	
Everton	0	Oldham	1	
Sunderld	0	Newcastle	0	
Newcastle	2	Sunderld	2	re
Newcastle	0	Sunderld	3	r2
SEMI-FINAL				
Aston V	1	Oldham	0	N
Sunderld	0	Burnley	0	N
Sunderld	3	Burnley	2	rN
FINAL				
Aston V	1	Sunderld	0	N

1914

FIRST ROUND				
Aston V	4	Stoke	0	
Birmghm C	2	Southend	1	
Blackburn	3	Middlebr	0	
Bolton	3	Port Vale	0	
Bradford	2	Wool Ars	0	
Bradfd PA	5	Reading	1	
Burnley	3	S.Shields	1	
Clapton O	2	Nottm For	2	
C.Palace	2	Norwich	1	
Derby	1	N'hamptn	0	
Gillinghm	1	Blackpool	0	
Glossop	2	Everton	1	
Huddersfld	3	London C	0	
Hull	0	Bury	0	
Leeds C	4	Gainsbrgh	2	
Leicester	5	Tottenham	5	
Liverpool	1	Barnsley	1	
Man City	2	Fulham	0	
Millwall	0	Chelsea	0	
Newcastle	0	Sheff Utd	5	
Oldham	1	Brighton	1	
Plymouth	4	Lincoln	1	
Portsmth	0	Exeter	4	
Preston NE	5	Bristol R	2	
QPR	2	Bristol C	2	
Sheff Wed	3	Notts Co	2	
Sunderld	9	Chatham	0	
Swansea	2	Merthyr T	0	
Swindon	1	Man Utd	0	
West Brom	2	Grimsby	0	
West Ham	8	Chestrfld	1	
Wolves	3	Southmpt	0	
Barnsley	0	Liverpool	1	r
Brighton	1	Oldham	0	re
Bristol C	0	QPR	2	re
Bury	2	Hull	1	r
Chelsea	0	Millwall	1	r
Nottm For	0	Clapton O	1	r
Tottenham	2	Leicester	0	r
SECOND ROUND				
Birmghm C	1	Huddersfld	0	
Blackburn	2	Bury	0	
Bolton	4	Swindon	2	

Blankety Blank

England full-back Jesse Pennington, who captained West Brom in the 1912 Final, played more than 500 games for the club without scoring a goal.

Brighton	3	Clapton O	1	
Burnley	3	Derby	2	
Exeter	1	Aston V	2	
Glossop	0	Preston NE	1	
Leeds C	0	West Brom	2	
Liverpool	2	Gillinghm	0	
Man City	2	Tottenham	1	
Millwall	1	Bradford	0	
Sheff Utd	3	Bradfd PA	1	
Sunderld	2	Plymouth	1	
Swansea	1	QPR	2	
West Ham	2	C.Palace	0	
Wolves	1	Sheff Wed	1	
Sheff Wed	1	Wolves	0	r

THIRD ROUND

Aston V	2	West Brom	1	
Birmghm C	1	QPR	2	
Blackburn	1	Man City	2	
Burnley	3	Bolton	0	
Millwall	0	Sheff Utd	4	
Sheff Wed	3	Brighton	0	
Sunderld	2	Preston NE	0	
West Ham	1	Liverpool	1	
Liverpool	5	West Ham	1	r

FOURTH ROUND

Liverpool	2	QPR	1	
Man City	0	Sheff Utd	0	
Sheff Wed	0	Aston V	1	
Sunderld	0	Burnley	0	
Burnley	2	Sunderld	1	r
Sheff Utd	0	Man City	0	re
Sheff Utd	1	Man City	0	r2N

SEMI-FINAL

Burnley	0	Sheff Utd	0	N
Liverpool	2	Aston V	0	N
Burnley	1	Sheff Utd	0	rN

FINAL

Burnley	1	Liverpool	0	N

1915

FIRST ROUND

Arsenal	3	Merthyr T	0	
Aston V	2	Exeter	0	
Birmghm C	2	C.Palace	2	
Blackpool	1	Sheff Utd	2	
Bolton	2	Notts Co	1	
Bradfd PA	1	Portsmth	0	
Brighton	2	Lincoln	1	
Bristol C	2	Cardiff	0	
Bristol R	0	Southend	0	
Burnley	3	Huddersfld	1	
Bury	1	Plymouth	1	
Chelsea	1	Swindon	1	
Croydon C	0	Oldham	3	
Darlingtn	0	Bradford	1	
Derby	1	Leeds C	2	
Everton	3	Barnsley	0	
Grimsby	0	N'hamptn	3	
Hull	1	West Brom	0	
Liverpool	3	Stockport	0	
Middlebr	9	Goole T	3	
Millwall	2	Clapton O	1	
Nottm For	1	Norwich	4	
Preston NE	0	Man City	0	
QPR	2	Glossop	1	
Reading	0	Wolves	1	
Rochdale	2	Gillinghm	0	
S.Shields	1	Fulham	2	
Sheff Wed	1	Man Utd	0	
Southmpt	3	Luton	0	
Swansea	1	Blackburn	0	
Tottenham	2	Sunderld	1	
West Ham	2	Newcastle	2	
Birmghm C	3	C.Palace	0	re
Chelsea	5	Swindon	2	re
Man City	3	Preston NE	0	r
Newcastle	3	West Ham	2	r
Plymouth	1	Bury	2	r
Southend	3	Bristol R	0	r

SECOND ROUND

Bolton	0	Millwall	0	e
Bradford	1	Middlebr	0	
Brighton	0	Birmghm C	0	e
Burnley	6	Southend	0	
Bury	0	Bradfd PA	1	
Chelsea	1	Arsenal	0	
Everton	4	Bristol C	0	
Fulham	2	Southmpt	3	e
Hull	2	N'hamptn	1	
Man City	1	Aston V	0	
Newcastle	1	Swansea	1	e
Norwich	3	Tottenham	2	
Oldham	3	Rochdale	0	
QPR	1	Leeds C	0	
Sheff Utd	1	Liverpool	0	
Sheff Wed	2	Wolves	0	
Birmghm C	3	Brighton	0	r
Millwall	2	Bolton	2	re
Swansea	0	Newcastle	2	r
Bolton	4	Millwall	1	r2

THIRD ROUND

Birmghm C	2	Oldham	3	
Bolton	2	Burnley	1	e
Bradford	1	Norwich	1	e
Man City	0	Chelsea	1	
QPR	1	Everton	2	N
Sheff Utd	1	Bradfd PA	0	e
Sheff Wed	1	Newcastle	2	
Southmpt	2	Hull	2	e
Hull	4	Southmpt	0	r
Norwich	0	Bradford	0	re
Bradford	2	Norwich	0	r2N

FOURTH ROUND

Bolton	4	Hull	2	
Bradford	0	Everton	2	
Chelsea	1	Newcastle	1	e
Oldham	0	Sheff Utd	0	e
Newcastle	0	Chelsea	1	re
Sheff Utd	3	Oldham	0	r

SEMI-FINAL

Chelsea	2	Everton	0	N
Sheff Utd	2	Bolton	1	N

FINAL

Sheff Utd	3	Chelsea	0	N

Golden Oldie

Billy Meredith, scorer of Manchester City's winner in the 1904 Final, played in a Semi-Final 20 years later, at 49-years-old!

GIANTKILLERS

1912 Barnsley 1 West Brom 0

Barnsley, beaten finalists in 1910 when ninth in the Second Division, finished 19th the following season, but a year after that they climbed to sixth in the table and won the FA Cup, with six survivors from two years earlier. They did so the hard way, knocking out three First Division opponents, playing 12 games and scoring only 11 goals, while conceding a mere three. West Brom, the overwhelming favourites, could not score against them at Crystal Palace or in the replay at Bramall Lane. The decider, a solo effort by Harry Tufnell, came after 1,168 of the 1,170 minutes that the Tykes slogged through to win the trophy.

1920-1939

WEMBLEY TAKES CENTRE STAGE

The 1920s staged arguably the most famous FA Cup Final of all time. Or perhaps that should be infamous.

The occasion was the 1923 Final between West Ham United and Bolton Wanderers - the first to be staged at the impressive new home of Wembley Stadium - and which subsequently became known as 'The White Horse Final'.

The FA had signed an agreement in 1921 to stage the Cup Final at Wembley for 21 years and that agreement made the construction of the stadium possible.

New Ground

Work on building Wembley Stadium, home to the FA Cup Final, began in January 1922 and was completed in April 1923. It was then the world's largest sporting arena.

The total cost of building the stadium was £750,000 and it was completed just four days before the Final. Controlled admission by ticket was not even considered: in a stadium of this size there was room for everyone. Or so they thought.

The date was Saturday, April 28th, 1923 and Wembley waited confidently to stage its first Final. Unfortunately for the organisers, enough people to fill the stadium twice over wanted to see the match - and its glamorous new surroundings.

By one o'clock the ground was full and by 1.45pm, when the gates were eventually shut, there were nearly 200,000 spectators squeezed inside Wembley's walls. King George V arrived at the ground at 2.45pm to be told by Frederick Wall, the secretary of the FA: "I fear, sir, that the match may not be played. The crowd has broken in and the ground is covered with people."

So entered Billy, a white police-horse ridden by Constable George Scorey, to assist with a good-natured clearance of the playing arena which finally allowed the game to go ahead, albeit 45 minutes later than scheduled.

For the record, the match ended 2-0 to Bolton with goals from David Jack and John Smith. Bolton won the Cup three times in the 20s, a decade also responsible for one of Cup Final day's great traditions, for it was before the 1927 Final between Cardiff and Arsenal that the hymn 'Abide With Me' was first sung.

Ernie A Baby

The first teenager to play in a Final at Wembley was Ernie Curtis, 19, with Cardiff in 1927 - not Cliff Bastin of Arsenal (18 in 1930) as many record books claim.

1920

FIRST ROUND

Arsenal	4	Rochdale	2	
Aston V	2	QPR	1	
Birmghm C	2	Everton	0	
Blackburn	2	Wolves	2	
Blackpool	0	Derby	0	
Bolton	0	Chelsea	1	
Bradford	2	Portsmth	0	
Bradfd PA	3	Nottm For	0	
Bristol R	1	Tottenham	4	
Bury	2	Stoke	0	
Cardiff	2	Oldham	0	
Castlefd	2	Hednesfd	0	
Darlingtn	0	Sheff Wed	0	
Fulham	1	Swindon	2	
Grimsby	1	Bristol C	2	
Huddersfd	5	Brentford	1	
Luton	2	Coventry	2	
Man City	4	Clapton O	1	
Middlesbr	4	Lincoln	1	
Newcastle	2	C.Palace	0	
Newport	0	Leicester	0	
Notts Co	2	Millwall	0	
Plymouth	2	Reading	0	
Port Vale	0	Man Utd	1	
Preston NE	3	Stockport	1	
S.Shields	1	Liverpool	1	
Sheff Utd	3	Southend	0	
Southmpt	0	West Ham	0	
Sunderld	6	Hull	2	
Thornycft	0	Burnley	0	N
W.Stanley	3	Gillinghm	1	
West Brom	0	Barnsley	1	
Burnley	5	Thornycft	0	r
Coventry	0	Luton	1	r
Derby	1	Blackpool	4	r
Leicester	2	Newport	0	r
Liverpool	2	S.Shields	0	r
Sheff Wed	0	Darlingtn	2	r
West Ham	3	Southmpt	1	r
Wolves	1	Blackburn	0	r

SECOND ROUND

Birmghm C	4	Darlingtn	0	
Bradford	2	Sheff Utd	1	
Bradfd PA	3	Castlefd	2	
Bristol C	1	Arsenal	0	
Burnley	1	Sunderld	1	
Chelsea	4	Swindon	0	
Leicester	3	Man City	0	
Luton	0	Liverpool	2	
Man Utd	1	Aston V	2	
Newcastle	0	Huddersfd	1	
Notts Co	1	Middlesbr	0	
Plymouth	4	Barnsley	1	
Preston NE	2	Blackpool	1	
Tottenham	4	W.Stanley	0	
West Ham	6	Bury	0	
Wolves	1	Cardiff	2	
Sunderld	2	Burnley	0	r

THIRD ROUND

Aston V	1	Sunderld	0	
Bristol C	2	Cardiff	1	
Chelsea	3	Leicester	0	
Huddersfd	3	Plymouth	1	
Liverpool	2	Birmghm C	0	
Notts Co	3	Bradfd PA	4	
Preston NE	0	Bradford	3	
Tottenham	3	West Ham	0	

FOURTH ROUND

Bristol C	2	Bradford	0	
Chelsea	4	Bradfd PA	1	
Huddersfd	2	Liverpool	1	
Tottenham	0	Aston V	1	

SEMI-FINAL

Aston V	3	Chelsea	1	N
Huddersfd	2	Bristol C	1	N

FINAL

Aston V	1	Huddersfd	0	eN

1921

FIRST ROUND

Aston V	2	Bristol C	0	
Blackburn	1	Fulham	1	
Bradford	3	Barnsley	1	
Bradfd PA	1	Clapton O	0	
Brentford	1	Huddersfd	2	
Brighton	4	Oldham	1	
C.Palace	2	Man City	0	
Darlingtn	2	Blackpool	2	
Derby	2	Middlesbr	0	
Everton	1	Stockport	0	
Grimsby	1	Norwich	0	
Hull	3	Bath C	0	
Leicester	3	Burnley	7	
Liverpool	1	Man Utd	1	
Luton	2	Birmghm C	1	
Millwall	0	Lincoln	3	
Newcastle	1	Nottm For	1	
N'hamptn	0	Southmpt	0	
Notts Co	3	West Brom	0	
Plymouth	2	Rochdale	0	
Preston NE	2	Bolton	0	
QPR	2	Arsenal	0	
Reading	0	Chelsea	0	
S.Shields	3	Portsmth	0	
Sheff Wed	1	West Ham	0	
Southend	5	Eccles U	1	
Sunderld	0	Cardiff	1	
Swansea	3	Bury	0	
Swindon	1	Sheff Utd	0	
Tottenham	6	Bristol R	2	
Watford	3	Exeter	0	
Wolves	3	Stoke	2	
Blackpool	2	Darlingtn	1	r
Chelsea	2	Reading	2	re
Fulham	1	Blackburn	0	r
Man Utd	1	Liverpool	2	r
Newcastle	2	Nottm For	0	r
Southmpt	4	N'hamptn	1	r
Chelsea	3	Reading	1	r2

SECOND ROUND

Bradfd PA	0	Huddersfd	1	
Brighton	0	Cardiff	0	
Burnley	4	QPR	2	
C.Palace	0	Hull	2	
Derby	1	Wolves	1	
Everton	1	Sheff Wed	1	
Grimsby	1	Southmpt	3	
Lincoln	0	Fulham	0	
Newcastle	1	Liverpool	0	
Notts Co	0	Aston V	0	
Preston NE	4	Watford	1	
S.Shields	0	Luton	4	
Southend	1	Blackpool	0	
Swansea	1	Plymouth	2	
Swindon	0	Chelsea	2	
Tottenham	4	Bradford	0	
Aston V	1	Notts Co	0	r
Cardiff	1	Brighton	0	r
Fulham	1	Lincoln	0	r
Sheff Wed	0	Everton	1	r
Wolves	1	Derby	0	r

THIRD ROUND

Aston V	2	Huddersfd	0	
Everton	3	Newcastle	0	
Fulham	0	Wolves	1	
Hull	3	Burnley	0	
Luton	2	Preston NE	3	
Plymouth	0	Chelsea	0	
Southmpt	0	Cardiff	1	
Southend	1	Tottenham	4	
Chelsea	0	Plymouth	0	re
Chelsea	2	Plymouth	1	r2N

FOURTH ROUND

Cardiff	1	Chelsea	0	
Everton	0	Wolves	1	
Hull	0	Preston NE	0	
Tottenham	1	Aston V	0	
Preston NE	1	Hull	0	r

SEMI-FINAL

Tottenham	2	Preston NE	1	N
Wolves	0	Cardiff	0	N
Wolves	3	Cardiff	1	rN

FINAL

Tottenham	1	Wolves	0	N

Early TV times

The first 'live' TV coverage of a Final was in 1938, with an estimated audience of 25,000.

1922

FIRST ROUND

Arsenal	0	QPR	0	
Aston V	6	Derby	1	
Barnsley	1	Norwich	1	
Blackburn	1	Southport	1	
Blackpool	1	Watford	2	
Bolton	1	Bury	0	
Bradfd PA	1	Sheff Wed	0	
Brentford	0	Tottenham	2	
Brighton	1	Sheff Utd	0	
Bristol C	0	Nottm For	0	
Burnley	2	Huddersfd	2	
Chelsea	2	West Brom	4	
Everton	0	C.Palace	6	
Gillinghm	1	Oldham	3	
Grimsby	1	Notts Co	1	
Hull	5	Middlesbr	0	
Leicester	2	Clapton O	0	
Man City	3	Darlingtn	1	
Man Utd	1	Cardiff	4	
Millwall	4	Ashington	2	
Newcastle	6	Newport	0	

N'hamptn	3	Reading	0	
Plymouth	1	Fulham	1	
Port Vale	2	Stoke	4	
Portsmth	1	Luton	1	
Preston NE	3	Wolves	0	
Southmpt	3	S.Shields	1	
Sunderld	1	Liverpool	1	
Swansea	0	West Ham	0	
Swindon	2	Leeds U	1	
Walsall	3	Bradford	3	
Worksop	1	Southend	2	
Bradford	4	Walsall	0	r
Fulham	1	Plymouth	0	r
Huddersfd	3	Burnley	2	r
Liverpool	5	Sunderld	0	r
Luton	2	Portsmth	1	r
Norwich	1	Barnsley	2	r
Nottm For	3	Bristol C	1	r
Notts Co	3	Grimsby	0	r
QPR	1	Arsenal	2	r
Southport	0	Blackburn	2	r
West Ham	1	Swansea	1	re
Swansea	1	West Ham	0	r2N

SECOND ROUND

Aston V	1	Luton	0	
Barnsley	3	Oldham	1	
Bolton	1	Man City	3	
Bradford	1	Notts Co	1	
Bradfd PA	2	Arsenal	3	
Brighton	0	Huddersfd	0	
C.Palace	0	Millwall	0	
Leicester	2	Fulham	0	
Liverpool	0	West Brom	1	
N'hamptn	2	Stoke	2	
Nottm For	3	Hull	0	
Preston NE	3	Newcastle	1	
Southmpt	1	Cardiff	1	
Southend	0	Swansea	1	
Swindon	0	Blackburn	1	
Tottenham	1	Watford	0	
Cardiff	2	Southmpt	0	r
Huddersfd	2	Brighton	0	r
Millwall	2	C.Palace	0	r
Notts Co	0	Bradford	0	re
Stoke	3	N'hamptn	0	r
Notts Co	1	Bradford	0	r2N

THIRD ROUND

Arsenal	3	Leicester	0	
Barnsley	1	Preston NE	1	
Blackburn	1	Huddersfd	1	
Cardiff	4	Nottm For	1	
Millwall	4	Swansea	0	
Stoke	0	Aston V	0	
Tottenham	2	Man City	1	
West Brom	1	Notts Co	1	
Aston V	4	Stoke	0	r
Huddersfd	5	Blackburn	0	r
Notts Co	2	West Brom	0	r
Preston NE	3	Barnsley	0	r

FOURTH ROUND

Arsenal	1	Preston NE	1	
Cardiff	1	Tottenham	1	
Huddersfd	3	Millwall	0	
Notts Co	2	Aston V	2	
Aston V	3	Notts Co	4	re
Preston NE	2	Arsenal	1	re
Tottenham	2	Cardiff	1	r

SEMI-FINAL

Huddersfd	3	Notts Co	1	N
Preston NE	2	Tottenham	1	N

FINAL

Huddersfd	1	Preston NE	0	N

1923

FIRST ROUND

Aberdare	1	Preston NE	3	
Aston V	0	Blackburn	1	
Blyth S	0	Stoke	3	
Bradford	1	Man Utd	1	
Brighton	1	Corinthns	1	
Bristol C	5	Wrexham	1	
Bury	2	Luton	1	
Cardiff	1	Watford	1	
Chelsea	1	Rotherm C	0	
Clapton O	0	Millwall	2	
Derby	2	Blackpool	0	
Everton	1	Bradfd PA	1	
Huddersfd	2	Birmghm C	1	
Hull	2	West Ham	3	
Leicester	4	Fulham	0	
Liverpool	0	Arsenal	0	
Man City	1	Charlton	2	
Merthyr T	0	Wolves	1	
Newcastle	0	Southmpt	0	
Norwich	0	Bolton	2	
Nottm For	0	Sheff Utd	0	
Oldham	0	Middlesbr	1	
Plymouth	0	Notts Co	0	
Portsmth	0	Leeds U	0	
QPR	1	C.Palace	0	
S.Shields	3	Halifax	1	
Sheff Wed	3	New Brig	0	
Sunderld	3	Burnley	1	
Swindon	0	Barnsley	0	
Tottenham	0	Worksop	0	
West Brom	0	Stalyb C	0	
Wigan Bor	4	Bath C	1	
Arsenal	1	Liverpool	4	r
Barnsley	2	Swindon	0	r
Bradfd PA	1	Everton	0	r
Corinthns	1	Brighton	1	reN
Leeds U	3	Portsmth	1	r
Man Utd	2	Bradford	0	r
Notts Co	0	Plymouth	1	r
Sheff Utd	0	Nottm For	0	re
Southmpt	3	Newcastle	1	r
Stalyb C	0	West Brom	2	r
Tottenham	9	Worksop	0	r
Watford	2	Cardiff	2	re
Brighton	1	Corinthns	0	r2N
Cardiff	2	Watford	1	r2N
Nottm For	1	Sheff Utd	1	r2eN
Sheff Utd	1	Nottm For	0	r3N

SECOND ROUND

Bolton	3	Leeds U	1	
Brighton	1	West Ham	1	
Bristol C	0	Derby	3	
Bury	3	Stoke	1	
Charlton	2	Preston NE	0	
Chelsea	0	Southmpt	0	
Leicester	0	Cardiff	1	
Middlesbr	1	Sheff Utd	1	
Millwall	0	Huddersfd	0	
Plymouth	4	Bradfd PA	1	
S.Shields	0	Blackburn	0	
Sheff Wed	2	Barnsley	1	
Tottenham	4	Man Utd	0	
West Brom	2	Sunderld	1	
Wigan Bor	2	QPR	4	
Wolves	0	Liverpool	2	
Blackburn	0	S.Shields	1	r
Huddersfd	3	Millwall	0	r
Sheff Utd	3	Middlesbr	0	r
Southmpt	1	Chelsea	0	r
West Ham	1	Brighton	0	r

THIRD ROUND

Bury	0	Southmpt	0	
Cardiff	2	Tottenham	3	
Charlton	1	West Brom	0	
Derby	1	Sheff Wed	0	

WHAT A STAR ✪ DAVID JACK

Scorer of the first goal at Wembley, the first man to play in four FA Cup Finals, and the first man to be transferred for a £10,000 fee. David Bone Nightingale Jack was a dominant force in soccer in the 20s and 30s, winning the Cup with Bolton in 1923 and 1926 and with Arsenal in 1930, before losing two years later. Jack - who later followed his father Bob into club management - was a very popular inside-forward, but was often ignored by England's selectors, and his nine caps were spread over almost as many years.

Huddersfd	1	Bolton	1	
Liverpool	1	Sheff Utd	2	
QPR	3	S.Shields	0	
West Ham	2	Plymouth	0	
Bolton	1	Huddersfd	0	r
Southmpt	1	Bury	0	r

FOURTH ROUND

Charlton	0	Bolton	1	
QPR	0	Sheff Utd	1	
Southmpt	1	West Ham	1	
Tottenham	0	Derby	1	
West Ham	1	Southmpt	1	re
West Ham	1	Southmpt	0	r2N

SEMI-FINAL

Bolton	1	Sheff Utd	0	N
West Ham	5	Derby	2	N

FINAL

Bolton	2	West Ham	0	N

1924

FIRST ROUND

Accringtn	0	Charlton	0	
Arsenal	4	Luton	1	
Ashington	1	Aston V	5	
Barnsley	0	Brighton	0	
Blackpool	1	Sheff Utd	0	
Burnley	3	S.Shields	2	
Cardiff	0	Gillinghm	0	
Chelsea	1	Southmpt	1	
Corinthns	1	Blackburn	0	
C.Palace	2	Tottenham	0	
Derby	2	Bury	1	
Everton	3	Preston NE	1	
Exeter	1	Grimsby	0	
Fulham	2	Llanelli	0	
Huddersfd	1	Birmghm C	0	
Hull	2	Bolton	2	
Leeds U	1	Stoke	0	
Liverpool	2	Bradford	1	
Man City	2	Nottm For	0	
Man Utd	1	Plymouth	0	
Middlesbr	0	Watford	1	
Millwall	0	West Brom	1	
N'hamptn	1	Halifax	1	
Norwich	0	Bristol C	1	
Oldham	2	Sunderld	1	
Portsmth	2	Newcastle	4	
QPR	1	Notts Co	2	
Sheff Wed	4	Leicester	1	
Swansea	1	Clapton O	1	
Swindon	4	Bradfd PA	0	
West Ham	5	Aberdare	0	
Wolves	3	Darlingtn	1	
Bolton	4	Hull	0	r
Brighton	1	Barnsley	0	r
Charlton	1	Accringtn	0	r
Clapton O	1	Swansea	1	re
Gillinghm	0	Cardiff	2	r
Halifax	1	N'hamptn	1	re
Southmpt	2	Chelsea	0	r
Halifax	4	N'hamptn	2	r2N
Swansea	2	Clapton O	1	r2N

SECOND ROUND

Bolton	1	Liverpool	4	
Brighton	5	Everton	2	
Burnley	0	Fulham	0	
Cardiff	1	Arsenal	0	
Charlton	0	Wolves	0	
C.Palace	0	Notts Co	0	
Derby	2	Newcastle	2	
Exeter	0	Watford	0	
Man City	2	Halifax	2	
Man Utd	0	Huddersfd	3	
Sheff Wed	1	Bristol C	1	
Southmpt	3	Blackpool	1	
Swansea	0	Aston V	2	
Swindon	2	Oldham	0	
West Brom	5	Corinthns	0	
West Ham	1	Leeds U	1	
Bristol C	2	Sheff Wed	0	r
Fulham	0	Burnley	1	re
Halifax	0	Man City	0	re
Leeds U	1	West Ham	0	r
Newcastle	2	Derby	2	re
Notts Co	0	C.Palace	0	re
Watford	1	Exeter	0	r
Wolves	1	Charlton	0	r
C.Palace	0	Notts Co	0	r2eN
Derby	2	Newcastle	2	r2eN
Man City	3	Halifax	0	r2N
C.Palace	2	Notts Co	1	r3N
Newcastle	5	Derby	3	r3

THIRD ROUND

Aston V	3	Leeds U	0	
Brighton	1	Man City	5	
Burnley	1	Huddersfd	0	
Cardiff	3	Bristol C	0	
C.Palace	1	Swindon	2	
Southmpt	0	Liverpool	0	
Watford	0	Newcastle	1	
West Brom	1	Wolves	1	
Liverpool	2	Southmpt	0	r
Wolves	0	West Brom	2	r

FOURTH ROUND

Man City	0	Cardiff	0	
Newcastle	1	Liverpool	0	
Swindon	1	Burnley	1	
West Brom	0	Aston V	2	
Burnley	3	Swindon	1	r
Cardiff	0	Man City	1	re

SEMI-FINAL

Aston V	3	Burnley	0	N
Newcastle	2	Man City	0	N

FINAL

Newcastle	2	Aston V	0	N

1925

FIRST ROUND

Accringtn	2	Portsmth	5	
Aston V	7	Port Vale	2	
Birmghm C	2	Chelsea	0	
Blackburn	1	Oldham	0	
Blackpool	0	Barrow	0	
Bolton	3	Huddersfd	0	
Bradfd PA	1	Middlesbr	0	
Bristol R	0	Bristol C	1	
Bury	0	Sunderld	3	
Cardiff	0	Darlingtn	0	
Coventry	0	Notts Co	2	
C.Palace	2	S.Shields	1	
Derby	0	Bradford	1	
Doncaster	1	Norwich	2	
Everton	2	Burnley	1	
Hull	1	Wolves	1	

Starling Effort

Ronnie Starling played in FA Cup Semi-Finals for four clubs in the 1930s - Hull, Newcastle, Sheffield Wednesday and Aston Villa. He lost three but was Wednesday's captain when they won the trophy in 1935.

Leicester	3	Stoke	0	
Liverpool	3	Leeds U	0	
Millwall	0	Barnsley	0	
Newcastle	4	Hartlepl	1	
Nottm For	1	Clapton O	0	
Preston NE	4	Man City	1	
QPR	1	Stockport	3	
Sheff Utd	5	Corinthns	0	
Sheff Wed	2	Man Utd	0	
Southmpt	3	Exeter	1	
Swansea	3	Plymouth	0	
Swindon	1	Fulham	2	
Tottenham	3	N'hamptn	0	
Watford	1	Brighton	1	
West Brom	4	Luton	0	
West Ham	0	Arsenal	0	
Arsenal	2	West Ham	2	re
Barnsley	2	Millwall	1	r
Barrow	0	Blackpool	2	r
Brighton	4	Watford	3	r
Darlingtn	0	Cardiff	0	re
Wolves	0	Hull	1	re
Cardiff	2	Darlingtn	0	r2N
West Ham	1	Arsenal	0	r2N

SECOND ROUND

Barnsley	0	Bradford	3	
Birmghm C	1	Stockport	0	
Blackburn	0	Portsmth	0	
Bradfd PA	1	Blackpool	1	
Bristol C	0	Liverpool	1	
Cardiff	1	Fulham	0	
Hull	3	C.Palace	2	
Newcastle	2	Leicester	2	
Nottm For	0	West Ham	2	
Notts Co	4	Norwich	0	
Sheff Utd	3	Sheff Wed	2	
Southmpt	1	Brighton	0	
Sunderld	0	Everton	0	
Swansea	1	Aston V	3	
Tottenham	1	Bolton	1	
West Brom	2	Preston NE	0	
Blackpool	2	Bradfd PA	1	r
Bolton	0	Tottenham	1	r
Everton	2	Sunderld	1	r
Leicester	1	Newcastle	0	r
Portsmth	0	Blackburn	0	re
Blackburn	1	Portsmth	0	r2N

THIRD ROUND

Hull	1	Leicester	1	

Liverpool	2	Birmghm C	1	
Notts Co	0	Cardiff	2	
Sheff Utd	1	Everton	0	
Southmpt	2	Bradford	0	
Tottenham	2	Blackburn	2	
West Brom	1	Aston V	1	
West Ham	1	Blackpool	1	
Aston V	1	West Brom	2	r
Blackburn	3	Tottenham	1	r
Blackpool	3	West Ham	0	r
Leicester	3	Hull	1	r

FOURTH ROUND

Blackburn	1	Blackpool	0	
Cardiff	2	Leicester	1	
Sheff Utd	2	West Brom	0	
Southmpt	1	Liverpool	0	

SEMI-FINAL

Cardiff	3	Blackburn	1	N
Sheff Utd	2	Southmpt	0	N

FINAL

Sheff Utd	1	Cardiff	0	N

1926

FIRST ROUND

Aberdare	4	Bristol R	1	
Accringtn	4	Wrexham	0	
Blyth S	2	Hartlepl	2	
Boston	5	Mansfield	2	
Bournemth	3	Merthyr T	0	
Bradfd PA	2	Lincoln	2	
Brentford	3	Barnet	1	
Brighton	1	Watford	1	
Carlisle	0	Chilton C	2	
Charlton	4	Windsor&E	2	
Chatham	0	Sittingbn	3	
Clapton	3	Norwich	1	
Doncaster	2	Wellingtn	0	
Durham C	4	Ashington	1	
Exeter	1	Swansea	3	
Farnham U	1	Swindon	10	
Gillinghm	6	Southall	0	
Halifax	0	Rotherhm	3	
Horden A	2	Darlingtn	3	
Leyton	1	St Albns C	0	
London C	1	Ilford	2	
Luton	3	Folkestne	0	
New Brig	2	Barrow	0	
N'hamptn	3	Barnsley	1	
Northflt	2	QPR	2	
Oldham	10	Lytham	1	
Rochdale	4	W.Stanley	0	
South Bk	1	Stockton	4	
Southend	5	Dulwich H	1	
Southport	1	Mold	0	
Torquay	1	Reading	1	
Tranmere	0	Crewe	0	
Walsall	0	Grimsby	1	
Wath Ath	0	Chestrfld	5	
Weymouth	0	Newport	1	
Wigan Bor	3	Nelson	0	
Worcester	0	Kettering	0	
Worksop	1	Coventry	0	
Crewe	2	Tranmere	1	re
Hartlepl	1	Blyth S	1	re
Kettering	0	Worcester	0	re
Lincoln	1	Bradfd PA	1	re
QPR	2	Northflt	0	r
Reading	1	Torquay	1	re
Watford	2	Brighton	0	r
Bradfd PA	2	Lincoln	1	r2N
Hartlepl	1	Blyth S	1	r2eN
Kettering	2	Worcester	0	r2N
Reading	2	Torquay	0	r2N
Hartlepl	1	Blyth S	2	r3N

SECOND ROUND

Aberdare	1	Luton	0	
Accringtn	5	Blyth S	0	
Boston	1	Bradfd PA	0	
Brentford	1	Bournemth	2	
Chilton C	1	Rochdale	1	
Clapton	1	Ilford	0	
Crewe	2	Wigan Bor	2	
Doncaster	0	Rotherhm	2	
Durham C	0	Southport	3	
Kettering	1	Grimsby	1	
New Brig	2	Darlingtn	0	
N'hamptn	3	Newport	1	
QPR	1	Charlton	1	
Reading	6	Leyton	0	
Southend	1	Gillinghm	0	
Stockton	4	Oldham	6	
Swansea	3	Watford	2	
Swindon	7	Sittingbn	0	
Worksop	1	Chestrfld	2	
Charlton	1	QPR	0	r
Grimsby	3	Kettering	1	r
Rochdale	1	Chilton C	2	r
Wigan Bor	2	Crewe	1	r

THIRD ROUND

Accringtn	0	Bolton	1	
Birmghm C	2	Grimsby	0	
Blackburn	1	Preston NE	1	
Blackpool	0	Swansea	2	
Bournemth	2	Reading	0	
Cardiff	2	Burnley	2	
Charlton	0	Huddersfd	1	
Chestrfld	0	Clapton O	1	
Clapton	2	Swindon	3	
Corinthns	3	Man City	3	
Derby	0	Portsmth	0	
Everton	1	Fulham	1	
Hull	0	Aston V	3	
Middlesbr	5	Leeds U	1	
Millwall	1	Oldham	1	
New Brig	2	Sheff Wed	1	
Newcastle	4	Aberdare	1	
N'hamptn	3	C.Palace	3	
Nottm For	1	Bradford	0	

Numbers Game

Numbers on shirts were used as an experiment in the 1933 Final, but clubs were generally against the idea because 'Football is a simple game, and numbers are not necessary'.

Notts Co	2	Leicester	0	
Plymouth	1	Chelsea	2	
Port Vale	2	Man Utd	3	
Rotherhm	2	Bury	3	
S.Shields	3	Chilton C	0	
Sheff Utd	2	Stockport	0	
Southmpt	0	Liverpool	0	
Southend	5	Southport	2	
Sunderld	8	Boston	1	
Tottenham	5	West Ham	0	
West Brom	4	Bristol C	1	
Wigan Bor	2	Stoke	5	
Wolves	1	Arsenal	1	
Arsenal	1	Wolves	0	r
Burnley	0	Cardiff	2	r
C.Palace	2	N'hamptn	1	r
Fulham	1	Everton	0	r
Liverpool	1	Southmpt	0	r
Man City	4	Corinthns	0	r
Oldham	0	Millwall	1	r
Portsmth	1	Derby	1	re
Preston NE	1	Blackburn	4	r
Derby	2	Portsmth	0	r2N

FOURTH ROUND

Arsenal	3	Blackburn	1	
Bournemth	2	Bolton	2	
Bury	3	Millwall	3	
Cardiff	0	Newcastle	2	
Clapton O	4	Middlesbr	2	
C.Palace	2	Chelsea	1	
Fulham	3	Liverpool	1	
Man City	4	Huddersfd	0	
Nottm For	2	Swindon	0	
Notts Co	2	New Brig	0	
S.Shields	2	Birmghm C	1	
Sheff Utd	1	Sunderld	2	
Southend	4	Derby	1	
Swansea	6	Stoke	3	
Tottenham	2	Man Utd	2	
West Brom	1	Aston V	2	
Bolton	6	Bournemth	2	r
Man Utd	2	Tottenham	0	r
Millwall	2	Bury	0	r

FIFTH ROUND

Aston V	1	Arsenal	1	
Bolton	3	S.Shields	0	
Clapton O	2	Newcastle	0	
Man City	11	C.Palace	4	
Millwall	0	Swansea	1	
Notts Co	0	Fulham	1	
Southend	0	Nottm For	1	
Sunderld	3	Man Utd	3	
Arsenal	2	Aston V	0	r
Man Utd	2	Sunderld	1	r

SIXTH ROUND

Clapton O	1	Man City	6	
Fulham	1	Man Utd	2	
Nottm For	2	Bolton	2	
Swansea	2	Arsenal	1	
Bolton	0	Nottm For	0	re
Bolton	1	Nottm For	0	r2N

SEMI-FINAL

Bolton	3	Swansea	0	N
Man City	3	Man Utd	0	N

FINAL

Bolton	1	Man City	0	N

WHAT A STAR ✪ ELLIS RIMMER

A tall outside-left from Merseyside, who played in the same school team as the legendary Dixie Dean, Rimmer had a long career with Sheffield Wednesday, and made a big impact on the public because his two greatest games were both at Wembley. He scored twice in a 5-2 defeat of Scotland on his international debut in 1930, and in 1935, with the Cup Final locked at 2-2 and only four minutes to go, he scored two more to give his team a remarkable win over West Brom.

1927

FIRST ROUND				
Accringtn	4	Rochdale	3	
Annfield	2	Chilton C	4	
Barking	0	Gillinghm	0	
Boston	1	N'hamptn	1	
Bournemth	1	Swindon	1	
Brighton	3	Barnet	0	
Bshk Auck	0	Bedlingtn	1	
Carlisle	6	Hartlepl	2	
Chatham	3	St Albns C	1	
Chestrfld	2	Mexboro	1	
Clapton	1	Brentford	1	
Crewe	4	Northn N	1	
C.Palace	0	Norwich	0	
Doncaster	3	Desborgh	0	
Dulwich H	1	Southend	4	
Exeter	3	Aberdare	0	
Grimsby	3	Halifax	2	
Kettering	2	Coventry	3	
Lincoln	2	Rotherhm	0	
Luton	4	London C	2	
Merthyr T	0	Bristol C	2	
Nelson	4	Stockport	1	
Nunhead	9	Kingst'an	0	
Poole	1	Newport	0	
Reading	4	Weymouth	4	
Rhyl Ath	1	Stoke	1	
Sittingbn	1	Northflt	3	
Southport	1	Tranmere	1	
Stockton	1	Ashington	2	
Torquay	1	Bristol R	1	
Walsall	1	Bradfd PA	0	
Watford	10	Lowestoft	1	
Wellingtn	1	Mansfield	2	
Wigan Bor	2	Barrow	2	
Woking	1	Charlton	3	
Workingtn	1	Crook T	2	
Wrexham	1	New Brig	1	
York	4	Worksop	1	
Barrow	0	Wigan Bor	1	r
Brentford	7	Clapton	3	r
Bristol R	1	Torquay	0	r
Gillinghm	2	Barking	0	r
New Brig	2	Wrexham	2	re
N'hamptn	2	Boston	1	r
Norwich	1	C.Palace	0	r
Reading	5	Weymouth	0	r
Stoke	1	Rhyl Ath	1	re
Swindon	3	Bournemth	4	r
Tranmere	1	Southport	2	r
Rhyl Ath	2	Stoke	1	r2N
Wrexham	3	New Brig	1	r2N
SECOND ROUND				
Ashington	2	Nelson	1	
Bristol C	1	Bournemth	1	
Bristol R	4	Charlton	1	
Carlisle	4	Bedlingtn	0	
Chilton C	0	Accringtn	3	
Coventry	1	Lincoln	1	
Crewe	4	Wigan Bor	1	
Doncaster	0	Chestrfld	1	
Exeter	1	N'hamptn	0	
Gillinghm	1	Brentford	1	
Grimsby	2	York	1	
Luton	6	Northflt	2	
Norwich	5	Chatham	0	
Nunhead	1	Poole	2	
Reading	3	Southend	2	
Rhyl Ath	3	Wrexham	1	
Southport	2	Crook T	0	
Walsall	2	Mansfield	0	
Watford	0	Brighton	1	
Bournemth	2	Bristol C	0	r
Brentford	1	Gillinghm	0	r
Lincoln	2	Coventry	1	r
THIRD ROUND				
Ashington	0	Nottm For	2	
Barnsley	6	Crewe	1	
Birmghm C	4	Man City	1	
Blackpool	1	Bolton	3	
Bournemth	1	Liverpool	1	
Bradford	2	Derby	6	
Bristol R	3	Portsmth	3	
Burnley	3	Grimsby	1	
Cardiff	2	Aston V	1	
Carlisle	0	Wolves	2	
Chelsea	4	Luton	0	
Clapton O	1	Port Vale	1	
Darlingtn	2	Rhyl Ath	1	
Everton	3	Poole	1	
Exeter	0	Accringtn	2	
Fulham	4	Chestrfld	3	
Hull	2	West Brom	1	
Leeds U	3	Sunderld	2	
Lincoln	2	Preston NE	4	
Middlesbr	5	Leicester	3	
Millwall	3	Huddersfd	1	
Newcastle	8	Notts Co	1	
Oldham	2	Brentford	4	
Reading	1	Man Utd	1	
S.Shields	3	Plymouth	1	
Sheff Utd	2	Arsenal	3	
Sheff Wed	2	Brighton	0	
Southmpt	3	Norwich	0	
Southport	2	Blackburn	0	
Swansea	4	Bury	1	
Walsall	0	Corinthns	4	
West Ham	3	Tottenham	2	
Liverpool	4	Bournemth	1	r
Man Utd	2	Reading	2	re
Port Vale	5	Clapton O	1	r
Portsmth	4	Bristol R	0	r
Reading	2	Man Utd	1	r2N
FOURTH ROUND				
Barnsley	1	Swansea	3	
Chelsea	7	Accringtn	2	
Corinthns	1	Newcastle	3	
Darlingtn	0	Cardiff	2	
Derby	0	Millwall	2	
Fulham	0	Burnley	4	
Hull	1	Everton	1	
Leeds U	0	Bolton	0	
Liverpool	3	Southport	1	
Port Vale	2	Arsenal	2	
Preston NE	0	Middlesbr	3	
Reading	3	Portsmth	1	
Sheff Wed	1	S.Shields	1	
Southmpt	4	Birmghm C	1	
West Ham	1	Brentford	1	
Wolves	2	Nottm For	0	
Arsenal	1	Port Vale	0	r
Bolton	3	Leeds U	0	r
Brentford	2	West Ham	0	r
Everton	2	Hull	2	re
S.Shields	1	Sheff Wed	0	r
Hull	3	Everton	2	r2eN
FIFTH ROUND				
Arsenal	2	Liverpool	0	
Bolton	0	Cardiff	2	
Chelsea	2	Burnley	1	
Millwall	3	Middlesbr	2	
Reading	1	Brentford	0	
S.Shields	2	Swansea	2	
Southmpt	2	Newcastle	1	
Wolves	1	Hull	0	
Swansea	2	S.Shields	1	r
SIXTH ROUND				
Arsenal	2	Wolves	1	
Chelsea	0	Cardiff	0	
Millwall	0	Southmpt	0	
Swansea	1	Reading	3	
Cardiff	3	Chelsea	2	r

Southmpt	2	Millwall	0	r

SEMI-FINAL

Arsenal	2	Southmpt	1	N
Cardiff	3	Reading	0	N

FINAL

Cardiff	1	Arsenal	0	N

1928

FIRST ROUND

Accringtn	2	Lincoln	5	
Aldershot	2	QPR	1	
Bath C	2	Southall	0	
Botwell M	3	P'boro & F	4	
Bradford	6	Workingtn	0	
Bristol R	4	Walsall	2	
Carlisle	2	Doncaster	1	
Coventry	2	Bournemt	2	
Crewe	2	Ashington	2	
Darlingtn	4	Chestrfld	1	
Dartford	1	C.Palace	3	
Denaby U	2	Southport	3	
Durham C	1	Wrexham	1	
Exeter	9	Aberdare	1	
Gainsbrgh	6	Stockton	0	
Gillinghm	2	Plymouth	1	
Halifax	3	Hartlepl	0	
Ilford	4	Dulwich H	0	
Kettering	2	Chatham	0	
Luton	9	Clapton	0	
Merthyr T	0	Charlton	0	
Nelson	0	Bradfd PA	3	
Newport	0	Swindon	1	
N'hamptn	8	Leyton	0	
Northflt	0	London C	1	
Poole	1	Norwich	1	
Rhyl Ath	4	Wigan Bor	3	
Rochdale	8	Crook T	2	
Shildon	1	New Brig	3	
Shirebrk	1	Tranmere	3	
Southend	1	Wellingtn	0	
Spennym'r	1	Rotherhm	1	
Stockport	5	Oswest T	2	
Watford	1	Brighton	2	
Ashington	0	Crewe	2	r
Bournemt	2	Coventry	0	r
Charlton	2	Merthyr T	1	r
Norwich	5	Poole	0	r
Rotherhm	4	Spennym'r	2	r
Wrexham	4	Durham C	0	r

SECOND ROUND

Bournemt	6	Bristol R	1	
Bradford	2	Rotherhm	3	
Bradfd PA	0	Southport	2	
Charlton	1	Kettering	1	
Crewe	2	Stockport	0	
Darlingtn	2	Rochdale	1	
Exeter	5	Ilford	3	
Gainsbrgh	0	Lincoln	2	
Gillinghm	2	Southend	0	
London C	1	Bath C	0	
Luton	6	Norwich	0	
New Brig	7	Rhyl Ath	2	
N'hamptn	1	Brighton	0	
P'boro & F	2	Aldershot	1	
Swindon	0	C.Palace	0	
Tranmere	3	Halifax	1	
Wrexham	1	Carlisle	0	

Stand By Me

Walsall's 2-0 defeat of Arsenal in 1933 is still recalled as one of the Cup's greatest shocks. The club later named a new stand after one of the scorers that day, Gilbert Alsop....60 years later!

C.Palace	1	Swindon	2	r
Kettering	1	Charlton	2	r

THIRD ROUND

Arsenal	2	West Brom	0	
Birmghm C	4	P'boro & F	3	
Blackburn	4	Newcastle	1	
Blackpool	1	Oldham	4	
Bolton	2	Luton	1	
Bristol C	1	Tottenham	2	
Burnley	0	Aston V	2	
Cardiff	2	Southmpt	1	
Charlton	1	Bury	1	
Huddersfd	4	Lincoln	2	
Hull	0	Leicester	1	
Liverpool	1	Darlingtn	0	
London C	2	Crewe	3	
Man City	1	Leeds U	0	
Man Utd	7	Brentford	1	
Middlesbr	3	S.Shields	0	
Millwall	1	Derby	2	
New Brig	2	Corinthns	1	
Nottm For	1	Tranmere	0	
Notts Co	2	Sheff Utd	3	
Port Vale	3	Barnsley	0	
Portsmth	0	West Ham	2	
Preston NE	0	Everton	3	
Reading	4	Grimsby	0	
Rotherhm	3	Exeter	3	
Sheff Wed	3	Bournemt	0	
Southport	3	Fulham	0	
Stoke	6	Gillinghm	1	
Sunderld	3	N'hamptn	3	
Swindon	2	Clapton O	1	
Wolves	2	Chelsea	1	
Wrexham	2	Swansea	1	
Bury	4	Charlton	3	r
Exeter	3	Rotherhm	1	r
N'hamptn	0	Sunderld	3	r

FOURTH ROUND

Arsenal	4	Everton	3	
Aston V	3	Crewe	0	
Bury	1	Man Utd	1	
Cardiff	2	Liverpool	1	
Derby	0	Nottm For	0	
Exeter	2	Blackburn	2	
Huddersfd	2	West Ham	1	
Port Vale	3	New Brig	0	
Reading	0	Leicester	1	
Sheff Utd	3	Wolves	1	
Southport	0	Middlesbr	3	
Stoke	4	Bolton	2	
Sunderld	1	Man City	2	
Swindon	1	Sheff Wed	2	
Tottenham	3	Oldham	0	
Wrexham	1	Birmghm C	3	
Blackburn	3	Exeter	1	r
Man Utd	1	Bury	0	r
Nottm For	2	Derby	0	r

FIFTH ROUND

Arsenal	4	Aston V	1	
Blackburn	2	Port Vale	1	
Huddersfd	4	Middlesbr	0	
Leicester	0	Tottenham	3	
Man City	0	Stoke	1	
Man Utd	1	Birmghm C	0	
Nottm For	2	Cardiff	1	
Sheff Wed	1	Sheff Utd	1	
Sheff Utd	4	Sheff Wed	1	r

SIXTH ROUND

Arsenal	4	Stoke	1	
Blackburn	2	Man Utd	0	
Huddersfd	6	Tottenham	1	
Sheff Utd	3	Nottm For	0	

SEMI-FINAL

Blackburn	1	Arsenal	0	N
Huddersfd	2	Sheff Utd	2	N
Huddersfd	0	Sheff Utd	0	reN
Huddersfd	1	Sheff Utd	0	r2N

FINAL

Blackburn	3	Huddersfd	1	N

1929

FIRST ROUND

Accringtn	2	S.Shields	1	
Annfield	1	Southport	4	
Bradford	4	Doncaster	1	
Brentford	4	Brighton	1	
Bristol R	2	Wellingbro	1	
Chestrfld	3	Rochdale	2	
Coventry	1	Fulham	4	
C.Palace	2	Kettering	0	
Darlingtn	3	New Brig	0	
Exeter	6	Barking	0	
Gainsbrgh	3	Crewe	1	
Gillinghm	0	Torquay	0	
Grantham	1	Rhyl Ath	0	
Guilford	4	QPR	2	
Horwich R	1	Scarboro	2	
Lancaster	1	Lincoln	3	
Leyton	0	Watford	2	
Luton	5	Southend	1	
Merthyr T	4	Dulwich H	2	
Newport	7	Woking	0	
Northflt	5	Ilford	2	
Norwich	6	Chatham	1	
P'boro & F	0	Charlton	2	
Poole	1	Bournemt	4	
Shirebrk	2	Mansfield	4	
Sittingbn	2	Southall	1	
Spennym'r	5	Hartlepl	2	
Stockport	1	Halifax	0	
Tranmere	2	Rotherhm	1	
Walsall	3	Worcester	1	
Wigan Bor	2	Ashington	0	
Wrexham	0	Carlisle	1	
Yeovil	1	Plymouth	4	
York	0	Barrow	1	

Torquay	5	Gillinghm	1	r
SECOND ROUND				
Accringtn	7	Spennym'r	0	
Barrow	1	Mansfield	2	
Brentford	0	Plymouth	1	
Carlisle	0	Lincoln	1	
C.Palace	3	Bristol R	1	
Fulham	0	Luton	0	
Gainsbrgh	2	Chestrfld	3	
Guilford	1	Bournemt	5	
Northflt	1	Charlton	5	
Norwich	6	Newport	0	
Scarboro	2	Darlingtn	2	
Stockport	3	Southport	0	
Torquay	0	Exeter	1	
Tranmere	0	Bradford	1	
Walsall	2	Sittingbn	1	
Watford	2	Merthyr T	0	
Wigan Bor	2	Grantham	1	
Darlingtn	2	Scarboro	1	r
Luton	4	Fulham	1	r
THIRD ROUND				
Accringtn	1	Bournemt	1	
Arsenal	2	Stoke	1	
Aston V	6	Cardiff	1	
Birmghm C	3	Man City	1	
Blackburn	1	Barnsley	0	
Bolton	2	Oldham	0	
Bradford	2	Stockport	0	
Bristol C	0	Liverpool	2	
Burnley	2	Sheff Utd	1	
Chelsea	2	Everton	0	
Chestrfld	1	Huddersfd	7	
Darlingtn	2	Bury	6	
Derby	4	Notts Co	3	
Exeter	2	Leeds U	2	
Grimsby	1	West Brom	1	
Hull	1	Bradfd PA	1	
Lincoln	0	Leicester	1	
Luton	0	C.Palace	0	
Millwall	1	N'hamptn	1	
Norwich	0	Corinthns	5	
Nottm For	1	Swansea	2	
Plymouth	3	Blackpool	0	
Port Vale	0	Man Utd	3	
Portsmth	2	Charlton	1	

Walker way

Billy Walker, a member of Aston Villa's victorious FA Cup side of 1920, later achieved a unique double success. He remains the only man to have managed two different Cup-winning teams: Sheffield Wednesday in 1935 and Nottingham Forest 24 years later.

Reading	2	Tottenham	0	
Southmpt	0	Clapton O	0	
Swindon	2	Newcastle	0	
Walsall	1	Middlesbr	1	
Watford	1	Preston NE	0	
West Ham	1	Sunderld	0	
Wigan Bor	1	Sheff Wed	3	
Wolves	0	Mansfield	1	
Bournemt	2	Accringtn	0	r
Bradfd PA	3	Hull	1	r
Clapton O	2	Southmpt	1	r
C.Palace	7	Luton	0	r
Leeds U	5	Exeter	1	r
Middlesbr	5	Walsall	1	r
N'hamptn	2	Millwall	2	re
West Brom	2	Grimsby	0	r
Millwall	2	N'hamptn	0	r2N
FOURTH ROUND				
Arsenal	2	Mansfield	0	
Aston V	0	Clapton O	0	
Blackburn	1	Derby	1	
Bournemt	6	Watford	4	
Burnley	3	Swindon	3	
Chelsea	1	Birmghm C	0	
Huddersfd	3	Leeds U	0	
Leicester	1	Swansea	0	
Liverpool	0	Bolton	0	
Man Utd	0	Bury	1	
Millwall	0	C.Palace	0	
Plymouth	0	Bradfd PA	1	
Portsmth	2	Bradford	0	
Reading	1	Sheff Wed	0	
West Brom	1	Middlesbr	0	
West Ham	3	Corinthns	0	
Bolton	5	Liverpool	2	re
Clapton O	0	Aston V	8	r
C.Palace	5	Millwall	3	r
Derby	0	Blackburn	3	r
Swindon	3	Burnley	2	r
FIFTH ROUND				
Blackburn	1	Bury	0	
Bournemt	1	West Ham	1	
Chelsea	1	Portsmth	1	
Huddersfd	5	C.Palace	2	
Leicester	1	Bolton	2	
Reading	1	Aston V	3	
Swindon	0	Arsenal	0	
West Brom	6	Bradfd PA	0	
Arsenal	1	Swindon	0	r
Portsmth	1	Chelsea	0	r
West Ham	3	Bournemt	1	r
SIXTH ROUND				
Aston V	1	Arsenal	0	
Blackburn	1	Bolton	1	
Portsmth	3	West Ham	2	
West Brom	1	Huddersfd	1	
Bolton	2	Blackburn	1	r
Huddersfd	2	West Brom	1	r
SEMI-FINAL				
Bolton	3	Huddersfd	1	N
Portsmth	1	Aston V	0	N
FINAL				
Bolton	2	Portsmth	0	N

1930

FIRST ROUND				
Accringtn	3	Rochdale	1	

Strange but true!

The First Round of the FA Cup in 1929 consisted of 34 ties and only one was drawn - Gillingham v Torquay.

Aldershot	0	N'hamptn	1	
Barrow	1	Newark T	0	
Barry	0	Dagenhm T	0	
Bournemt	2	Torquay	0	
Brighton	4	P'boro & F	0	
Caernvn A	4	Darlingtn	2	
Carlisle	2	Halifax	0	
Clapton O	0	Folkestne	0	
Doncaster	0	Shildon	0	
Dulwich H	0	Plymouth	3	
Fulham	4	Thames	0	
Gainsbrgh	0	Port Vale	0	
Gillinghm	0	Margate	2	
Ilford	0	Watford	3	
Leyton	4	Merthyr T	1	
Lincoln	3	Wigan Bor	1	
Luton	2	QPR	3	
Mansfield	0	Man Cent	2	
Nelson	0	Crewe	3	
New Brig	4	Lancaster	1	
Newport	3	Kettering	2	
Norwich	3	Coventry	3	
Nunhead	0	Bristol R	2	
Rotherhm	3	Ashington	0	
S.Shields	2	Wrexham	4	
Scunthpe	1	Hartlepl	0	
Southend	1	Brentford	0	
Southport	0	Chestrfld	0	
Tunbridge	1	Bath C	3	
Walsall	1	Exeter	0	
Wellingtn	1	Stockport	4	
Wimbledn	1	Northflt	4	
York	2	Tranmere	2	
Chestrfld	3	Southport	2	r
Coventry	2	Norwich	0	r
Dagenhm T	0	Barry	1	rN
Folkestne	2	Clapton O	2	re
Port Vale	5	Gainsbrgh	0	r
Shildon	1	Doncaster	1	re
Tranmere	0	York	1	r
Clapton O	4	Folkestne	1	r2N
Doncaster	3	Shildon	0	r2N
SECOND ROUND				
Brighton	4	Barry	1	
Bristol R	4	Accringtn	1	
Caernvn A	1	Bournemt	1	
Carlisle	4	Crewe	2	
Chestrfld	2	Port Vale	0	
Clapton O	2	Northflt	0	
Coventry	7	Bath C	1	
Doncaster	1	New Brig	0	
Leyton	1	Fulham	4	
Man Cent	0	Wrexham	1	
Newport	2	Walsall	3	
N'hamptn	6	Margate	0	

QPR	2	Lincoln	1	
Scunthpe	3	Rotherhm	3	
Southend	1	York	4	
Stockport	4	Barrow	0	
Watford	1	Plymouth	1	
Bournemt	5	Caernvn A	2	r
Plymouth	3	Watford	0	r
Rotherhm	5	Scunthpe	4	r
THIRD ROUND				
Arsenal	2	Chelsea	0	
Aston V	5	Reading	1	
Barnsley	0	Bradfd PA	1	
Birmghm C	1	Bolton	0	
Blackburn	4	N'hamptn	1	
Blackpool	2	Stockport	1	
Bradford	4	Southmpt	1	
Brighton	1	Grimsby	1	
Bury	0	Huddersfd	0	
Carlisle	2	Everton	4	
Charlton	1	QPR	1	
Chestrfld	1	Middlesbr	1	
Clapton O	1	Bristol R	0	
Corinthns	2	Millwall	2	
Coventry	1	Sunderld	2	
Derby	5	Bristol C	1	
Doncaster	1	Stoke	0	
Fulham	1	Bournemt	1	
Leeds U	8	C.Palace	1	
Liverpool	1	Cardiff	2	
Man Utd	0	Swindon	2	
Newcastle	1	York	1	
Oldham	1	Wolves	0	
Plymouth	3	Hull	4	
Portsmth	2	Preston NE	0	
Rotherhm	0	Nottm For	5	
Sheff Utd	2	Leicester	1	
Sheff Wed	1	Burnley	0	
Tottenham	2	Man City	2	
Walsall	2	Swansea	0	
West Ham	4	Notts Co	0	
Wrexham	1	West Brom	0	
Bournemt	0	Fulham	2	r
Grimsby	0	Brighton	1	r
Huddersfd	3	Bury	1	r
Man City	4	Tottenham	1	r
Middlesbr	4	Chestrfld	3	r
Millwall	1	Corinthns	1	re
QPR	0	Charlton	3	r
York	1	Newcastle	2	r
Millwall	5	Corinthns	1	r2N
FOURTH ROUND				
Arsenal	2	Birmghm C	2	
Aston V	3	Walsall	1	
Blackburn	4	Everton	1	
Derby	1	Bradfd PA	1	
Huddersfd	2	Sheff Utd	1	
Hull	3	Blackpool	1	
Middlesbr	1	Charlton	1	
Millwall	4	Doncaster	0	
Newcastle	3	Clapton O	1	
Nottm For	2	Fulham	1	
Oldham	3	Sheff Wed	4	
Portsmth	0	Brighton	1	
Sunderld	2	Cardiff	1	
Swindon	1	Man City	1	
West Ham	4	Leeds U	1	
Wrexham	0	Bradford	0	
Birmghm C	0	Arsenal	1	r
Bradford	2	Wrexham	1	r
Bradfd PA	2	Derby	1	r
Charlton	1	Middlesbr	1	re
Man City	10	Swindon	1	r
Middlesbr	1	Charlton	0	r2eN
FIFTH ROUND				
Aston V	4	Blackburn	1	
Huddersfd	2	Bradford	1	
Man City	1	Hull	2	
Middlesbr	0	Arsenal	2	
Newcastle	3	Brighton	0	
Sheff Wed	5	Bradfd PA	1	
Sunderld	2	Nottm For	2	
West Ham	4	Millwall	1	
Nottm For	3	Sunderld	1	r
SIXTH ROUND				
Aston V	1	Huddersfd	2	
Newcastle	1	Hull	1	
Nottm For	2	Sheff Wed	2	
West Ham	0	Arsenal	3	
Hull	1	Newcastle	0	r
Sheff Wed	3	Nottm For	1	r
SEMI-FINAL				
Arsenal	2	Hull	2	N
Huddersfd	2	Sheff Wed	1	N
Arsenal	1	Hull	0	rN
FINAL				
Arsenal	2	Huddersfd	0	N
1931				
FIRST ROUND				
Accringtn	3	Lancaster	1	
Aldershot	4	P'boro & F	1	
Bristol R	4	Merthyr T	1	
Carlisle	3	New Brig	1	
Chestrfld	1	Notts Co	2	
Crewe	1	Jarrow	0	
C.Palace	6	Taunton T	0	
Dulwich H	2	Newport	2	
Folkestne	5	Sittingbn	3	
Fulham	1	Wimbledn	1	
Gainsbrgh	1	Scunthpe	0	
Gillinghm	7	Guilford	2	
Halifax	2	Mansfield	2	
Hartlepl	2	Stockport	3	
Ilford	1	Brentford	6	
Lincoln	8	Barrow	3	
Luton	2	Clapton O	2	
Nelson	4	Workingtn	0	
Newark T	2	Rotherhm	1	
N'hamptn	1	Coventry	2	
Northflt	0	Exeter	3	
Norwich	2	Swindon	0	
QPR	5	Thames	0	
Rochdale	1	Doncaster	2	
Scarboro	6	Rhyl Ath	0	
Southend	0	Torquay	1	
Southport	4	Darlingtn	2	
Tranmere	4	Gateshead	4	
Tunbridge	3	Kingst'an	0	
Walsall	1	Bournemt	0	
Walstmw A	1	Watford	5	
Wellingtn	0	Wombwell	0	
Wrexham	2	Wigan Bor	0	
York	3	Gresley R	1	
Clapton O	2	Luton	4	rN
Gateshead	3	Tranmere	2	r
Mansfield	1	Halifax	2	r
Newport	4	Dulwich H	1	r
Wimbledn	0	Fulham	6	r
Wombwell	0	Wellingtn	3	r
SECOND ROUND				
Accringtn	0	Torquay	1	

GIANTKILLERS

1922 Everton 0 Crystal Palace 6

Palace were 14th in the Second Division, Everton 19th in the First, and this First Round result remains the biggest margin of victory in an away Cup-tie won by a team from a lower division. Everton 'keeper Tom Fern injured a hand early on, and Palace were so much on top that their No.1, Jack Alderson, was said to have leant on his goalpost and eaten a couple of oranges thrown from the crowd during the game. In 1931, Palace, then in the Third Division South, were at home to Everton of Division Two in another Cup-tie....and revenge was sweet as the Merseysiders this time won 6-0.

Brentford	1	Norwich	0	
Bristol R	4	Stockport	2	
Carlisle	4	Tunbridge	2	
Crewe	2	QPR	4	
C.Palace	6	Newark T	0	
Doncaster	0	Notts Co	1	
Exeter	1	Coventry	1	
Fulham	4	Halifax	0	
Gainsbrgh	0	Southport	4	
Gateshead	3	Folkestne	2	
Gillinghm	1	Aldershot	3	
Nelson	1	York	1	
Scarboro	6	Lincoln	4	
Walsall	4	Newport	0	
Watford	3	Luton	1	
Wellingtn	2	Wrexham	4	
Coventry	1	Exeter	2	r
York	3	Nelson	2	r
THIRD ROUND				
Aldershot	0	Bradfd PA	1	
Arsenal	2	Aston V	2	
Barnsley	4	Bristol C	1	
Blackburn	1	Walsall	1	
Bolton	1	Carlisle	0	
Brentford	2	Cardiff	2	
Bristol R	3	QPR	1	
Burnley	3	Man City	0	
Bury	1	Torquay	1	
Corinthns	1	Port Vale	3	
C.Palace	1	Reading	1	
Exeter	3	Derby	2	
Fulham	0	Portsmth	2	
Gateshead	2	Sheff Wed	6	
Hull	1	Blackpool	2	
Leeds U	2	Huddersfd	0	
Leicester	1	Brighton	2	
Liverpool	0	Birmghm C	2	
Middlesbr	1	Bradford	1	
Newcastle	4	Nottm For	0	
Notts Co	3	Swansea	1	
Oldham	1	Watford	3	
Plymouth	0	Everton	2	
Scarboro	1	Grimsby	2	
Sheff Utd	1	York	1	
Southport	3	Millwall	1	
Stoke	3	Man Utd	3	
Sunderld	2	Southmpt	0	
Tottenham	3	Preston NE	1	
West Brom	2	Charlton	2	
West Ham	1	Chelsea	3	
Wolves	9	Wrexham	1	
Aston V	1	Arsenal	3	r
Bradford	2	Middlesbr	1	r
Cardiff	1	Brentford	2	r
Charlton	1	West Brom	1	re
Man Utd	0	Stoke	0	re
Reading	1	C.Palace	1	re
Torquay	1	Bury	2	re
Walsall	0	Blackburn	3	r
York	0	Sheff Utd	2	r
C.Palace	2	Reading	0	r2N
Man Utd	4	Stoke	2	r2N
West Brom	3	Charlton	1	r2N
FOURTH ROUND				
Barnsley	2	Sheff Wed	1	
Birmghm C	2	Port Vale	0	
Blackburn	5	Bristol R	1	
Bolton	1	Sunderld	1	
Bradford	0	Wolves	0	
Bradfd PA	2	Burnley	0	
Brentford	0	Portsmth	1	
Bury	1	Exeter	2	
Chelsea	2	Arsenal	1	
C.Palace	0	Everton	6	
Grimsby	1	Man Utd	0	
Leeds U	4	Newcastle	1	
Sheff Utd	4	Notts Co	1	
Southport	2	Blackpool	1	
Watford	2	Brighton	0	
West Brom	1	Tottenham	0	
Sunderld	3	Bolton	1	r
Wolves	4	Bradford	2	r
FIFTH ROUND				
Barnsley	1	Wolves	3	
Birmghm C	3	Watford	0	
Chelsea	3	Blackburn	0	
Everton	5	Grimsby	3	
Exeter	3	Leeds U	1	
Portsmth	0	West Brom	1	
Southport	1	Bradfd PA	0	
Sunderld	2	Sheff Utd	1	
SIXTH ROUND				
Birmghm C	2	Chelsea	2	
Everton	9	Southport	1	
Sunderld	1	Exeter	1	
West Brom	1	Wolves	1	
Chelsea	0	Birmghm C	3	r
Exeter	2	Sunderld	4	r
Wolves	1	West Brom	2	r
SEMI-FINAL				
Birmghm C	2	Sunderld	0	N
West Brom	1	Everton	0	N
FINAL				
West Brom	2	Birmghm C	1	N

1932

FIRST ROUND				
Aldershot	7	Chelmsfd	0	
Barnet	3	QPR	7	
Barrow	3	Doncaster	3	
Bath C	9	Nunhead	0	
Bournemt	1	Northflt	1	
Bristol R	5	Gillinghm	1	
Burton T	w	Wigan Bor	s	
Cardiff	8	Enfield	0	
Chester	4	Hartlepl	1	
Coventry	2	Clapton O	2	
Crewe	2	Gainsbrgh	2	
Crook T	3	Stockport	1	
Darlingtn	1	Walsall	0	
Darwen	4	P'boro & F	1	
Folkestne	2	Brighton	5	
Fulham	2	Guilford	0	
Gateshead	3	Wrexham	2	
Hull	4	Mansfield	1	
Lancaster	0	Blyth S	3	
Man Cent	0	Lincoln	3	
New Brig	3	York	1	
Newark T	1	Halifax	1	
N'hamptn	9	Met Pol	0	
Reading	0	C.Palace	1	
Rotherhm	0	Accringtn	0	
Scunthpe	2	Rochdale	1	
Swindon	0	Luton	5	

Goals galore

Huddersfield and Scotland winger Alex Jackson scored 19 Cup goals in the last three seasons of the 1920s, five of them in Semi-Finals and one in a Final, where he was on the losing side twice.

Thames	2	Watford	2	
Torquay	1	Southend	3	
Tranmere	3	W.Stanley	0	
Tunbridge	1	Brentford	1	
Wimbledn	1	Norwich	3	
Yeovil	3	Hayes	1	
York Ams	1	Carlisle	3	
Accringtn	5	Rotherhm	0	r
Brentford	2	Tunbridge	1	r
Clapton O	2	Coventry	0	r
Doncaster	1	Barrow	1	re
Gainsbrgh	1	Crewe	0	r
Halifax	2	Newark T	1	r
Northflt	0	Bournemt	1	r
Watford	2	Thames	1	re
Barrow	1	Doncaster	1	r2eN
Doncaster	1	Barrow	0r3	eN
SECOND ROUND				
Aldershot	1	Crook T	1	
Bath C	2	C.Palace	1	
Bournemt	1	Blyth S	0	
Brentford	4	Norwich	1	
Brighton	5	Doncaster	0	
Burton T	4	Gateshead	1	
Cardiff	4	Clapton O	0	
Carlisle	0	Darlingtn	2	
Darwen	2	Chester	1	
Fulham	0	Yeovil	0	
Gainsbrgh	2	Watford	5	
Halifax	3	Accringtn	0	
Lincoln	2	Luton	2	
New Brig	0	Hull	4	
N'hamptn	3	Southend	0	
Scunthpe	1	QPR	4	
Tranmere	2	Bristol R	0	
Crook T	1	Aldershot	0	r
Luton	4	Lincoln	1	r
Yeovil	2	Fulham	5	r
THIRD ROUND				
Arsenal	11	Darwen	1	
Barnsley	0	Southport	0	
Birmghm C	1	Bradford	0	
Blackpool	1	Newcastle	1	
Bradfd PA	2	Cardiff	0	
Brentford	2	Bath C	0	
Brighton	1	Port Vale	2	
Burnley	0	Derby	4	
Burton T	0	Blackburn	4	
Bury	2	Swansea	1	
Charlton	1	West Ham	2	

Chestrfld	5	Nottm For	2	
Darlingtn	1	N'hamptn	1	
Everton	1	Liverpool	2	
Grimsby	4	Exeter	1	
Halifax	1	Bournemt	3	
Leicester	7	Crook T	0	
Luton	1	Wolves	2	
Middlesbr	1	Portsmth	1	
Millwall	2	Man City	3	
Notts Co	2	Bristol C	2	
Oldham	1	Huddersfd	1	
Plymouth	4	Man Utd	1	
Preston NE	0	Bolton	0	
QPR	3	Leeds U	1	
Sheff Utd	2	Corinthns	1	
Stoke	3	Hull	0	
Sunderld	0	Southmpt	0	
Tottenham	2	Sheff Wed	2	
Tranmere	2	Chelsea	2	
Watford	1	Fulham	1	
West Brom	1	Aston V	2	
Bolton	2	Preston NE	5	r
Bristol C	3	Notts Co	2	r
Chelsea	5	Tranmere	3	r
Fulham	0	Watford	3	r
Huddersfd	6	Oldham	0	r
Newcastle	1	Blackpool	0	r
N'hamptn	2	Darlingtn	0	r
Portsmth	3	Middlesbr	0	r
Sheff Wed	3	Tottenham	1	r
Southmpt	2	Sunderld	4	r
Southport	4	Barnsley	1	r
FOURTH ROUND				
Arsenal	4	Plymouth	2	
Bradfd PA	4	N'hamptn	2	
Bury	3	Sheff Utd	1	
Chelsea	3	West Ham	1	
Chestrfld	2	Liverpool	4	
Derby	3	Blackburn	2	
Grimsby	2	Birmghm C	1	
Huddersfd	5	QPR	0	
Man City	6	Brentford	1	
Newcastle	1	Southport	1	
Port Vale	1	Leicester	2	
Portsmth	1	Aston V	1	
Preston NE	2	Wolves	0	
Sheff Wed	7	Bournemt	0	
Sunderld	1	Stoke	1	
Watford	2	Bristol C	1	
Aston V	0	Portsmth	1	r
Southport	1	Newcastle	1	re
Stoke	1	Sunderld	1	re
Newcastle	9	Southport	0	r2N
Stoke	2	Sunderld	1	r2eN
FIFTH ROUND				
Bury	3	Stoke	0	
Huddersfd	4	Preston NE	0	
Liverpool	1	Grimsby	0	
Man City	3	Derby	0	
Newcastle	3	Leicester	1	
Portsmth	0	Arsenal	2	
Sheff Wed	1	Chelsea	1	
Watford	1	Bradfd PA	0	
Chelsea	2	Sheff Wed	0	r
SIXTH ROUND				
Bury	3	Man City	4	
Huddersfd	0	Arsenal	1	

It's For Keeps

Dick Pym, a Bolton favourite in the 1920s, was the first of only two goalkeepers with three FA Cup winner's medals. The other is Bruce Grobbelaar of Liverpool.

Liverpool	0	Chelsea	2	
Newcastle	5	Watford	0	
SEMI-FINAL				
Arsenal	1	Man City	0	N
Newcastle	2	Chelsea	1	N
FINAL				
Newcastle	2	Arsenal	1	N

1933

FIRST ROUND				
Accringtn	2	Hereford	1	
Barrow	0	Gateshead	1	
Bristol C	4	Romford	0	
Cardiff	1	Bristol R	1	
Carlisle	1	Denaby U	0	
Chester	4	Rotherhm	0	
Clapton O	0	Aldershot	1	
Crewe	4	Crook T	0	
C.Palace	1	Brighton	2	
Darlingtn	1	Boston	0	
Dartford	0	Yeovil	0	
Doncaster	4	Gainsbrgh	1	
Folkestne	1	Norwich	0	
Gillinghm	1	Wycombe	1	
Guilford	1	Coventry	2	
Halifax	2	Darwen	0	
Luton	2	Kingst'an	2	
Margate	5	Ryde Spts	0	
Marine	2	Hartlepl	5	
Merthyr T	1	QPR	1	
Newport	4	Ilford	2	
N'hamptn	8	Lloyds	1	
Reading	3	Brentford	2	
Rochdale	0	Stockport	2	
Southend	1	Exeter	1	
Southport	3	Nelson	3	
Stalyb C	2	Hull	8	
Swindon	4	Dulwich H	1	
Torquay	0	Bournemt	0	
Tranmere	3	New Brig	0	
Walsall	4	Mansfield	1	
Workingtn	5	Scunthpe	1	
Wrexham	3	Spennym'r	0	
York	1	Scarboro	3	
Bournemt	2	Torquay	2	re
Bristol R	4	Cardiff	1	r
Exeter	0	Southend	1	r
Kingst'an	2	Luton	3	r
Nelson	0	Southport	4	r
QPR	5	Merthyr T	1	r
Wycombe	2	Gillinghm	4	r
Yeovil	4	Dartford	2	r
Torquay	3	Bournemt	2	r2N
SECOND ROUND				
Accringtn	1	Aldershot	2	
Brighton	0	Wrexham	0	
Bristol C	2	Tranmere	2	
Bristol R	1	Gillinghm	1	
Carlisle	1	Hull	1	
Chester	2	Yeovil	1	
Crewe	0	Darlingtn	2	
Folkestne	2	Newport	1	
Gateshead	5	Margate	2	
Halifax	2	Workingtn	1	
N'hamptn	0	Doncaster	1	
Reading	2	Coventry	2	
Southend	4	Scarboro	1	
Southport	1	Swindon	2	
Stockport	2	Luton	3	
Torquay	1	QPR	1	
Walsall	2	Hartlepl	1	
Coventry	3	Reading	3	re
Gillinghm	1	Bristol R	3	r
Hull	2	Carlisle	1	re
QPR	3	Torquay	1	r
Tranmere	3	Bristol C	2	r
Wrexham	2	Brighton	3	re
Reading	1	Coventry	0	r2N
THIRD ROUND				
Aldershot	1	Bristol R	0	
Barnsley	0	Luton	0	
Birmghm C	2	Preston NE	1	
Blackpool	2	Port Vale	1	
Bradford	2	Aston V	2	
Bradfd PA	5	Plymouth	1	
Brighton	2	Chelsea	1	
Bury	2	Nottm For	2	
Charlton	1	Bolton	5	
Chester	5	Fulham	0	
Corinthns	0	West Ham	2	
Darlingtn	2	QPR	0	
Doncaster	0	Halifax	3	
Gateshead	1	Man City	1	
Grimsby	3	Portsmth	2	
Huddersfd	2	Folkestne	0	
Hull	0	Sunderld	2	
Leicester	2	Everton	3	
Lincoln	1	Blackburn	5	
Man Utd	1	Middlesbr	4	
Millwall	1	Reading	1	
Newcastle	0	Leeds U	3	
Oldham	0	Tottenham	6	
Sheff Wed	2	Chestrfld	2	
Stoke	1	Southmpt	0	
Swansea	2	Sheff Utd	3	
Swindon	1	Burnley	2	
Tranmere	2	Notts Co	1	
Walsall	2	Arsenal	0	
Watford	1	Southend	1	
West Brom	2	Liverpool	0	
Wolves	3	Derby	6	
Aston V	2	Bradford	1	r
Chestrfld	4	Sheff Wed	2	r
Luton	2	Barnsley	0	r
Man City	9	Gateshead	0	r
Nottm For	1	Bury	2	r
Reading	0	Millwall	2	r
Southend	2	Watford	0	r

FOURTH ROUND

Home		Away		
Aldershot	1	Millwall	0	
Aston V	0	Sunderld	3	
Birmghm C	3	Blackburn	0	
Blackpool	2	Huddersfd	0	
Bolton	2	Grimsby	1	
Brighton	2	Bradfd PA	1	
Burnley	3	Sheff Utd	1	
Chester	0	Halifax	0	
Darlingtn	0	Chestrfld	2	
Everton	3	Bury	1	
Luton	2	Tottenham	0	
Man City	2	Walsall	0	
Middlesbr	4	Stoke	1	
Southend	2	Derby	3	
Tranmere	0	Leeds U	0	
West Ham	2	West Brom	0	
Halifax	3	Chester	2	r
Leeds U	4	Tranmere	0	r

FIFTH ROUND

Home		Away		
Bolton	2	Man City	4	
Brighton	2	West Ham	2	
Burnley	1	Chestrfld	0	
Derby	2	Aldershot	0	
Everton	2	Leeds U	0	
Halifax	0	Luton	2	
Middlesbr	0	Birmghm C	0	
Sunderld	1	Blackpool	0	
Birmghm C	3	Middlesbr	0	r
West Ham	1	Brighton	0	re

SIXTH ROUND

Home		Away		
Burnley	0	Man City	1	
Derby	4	Sunderld	4	
Everton	6	Luton	0	
West Ham	4	Birmghm C	0	
Sunderld	0	Derby	1	re

SEMI-FINAL

Home		Away		
Everton	2	West Ham	1	N
Man City	3	Derby	2	N

FINAL

Home		Away		
Everton	3	Man City	0	N

1934

FIRST ROUND

Home		Away		
Barrow	4	Doncaster	2	
Bath C	0	Charlton	0	
Bournemt	3	Hayes	0	
Cardiff	0	Aldershot	0	
Carlisle	2	Wrexham	1	
Chelthnm	5	Barnet	1	
Chester	6	Darlingtn	1	
Clapton O	4	Epsom T	2	
Coventry	3	Crewe	0	
C.Palace	3	Norwich	0	
Dulwich H	2	Newport	2	
Folkestne	0	Bristol R	0	
Gainsbrgh	1	Altrinchm	0	
Gateshead	5	Darwen	2	
Halifax	3	Barnsley	2	
Ilford	2	Swindon	4	
Kingst'an	1	Bristol C	7	
Lancaster	0	Stockport	1	
London P	0	Southend	1	
N.Shields	3	Scarboro	0	
New Brig	0	Mansfield	0	
N'hamptn	2	Exeter	0	
Northflt	0	Dartford	2	
Oxford C	1	Gillinghm	5	
QPR	6	Kettering	0	
Rotherhm	3	S.Bank STP	2	
Scunthpe	1	Accringtn	1	
Sutton T	2	Rochdale	1	
Torquay	1	Margate	1	
Tranmere	7	Newark T	0	
Walsall	4	Spennym'r	0	
Watford	0	Reading	3	
Workingtn	1	Southport	0	
York	2	Hartlepl	3	
Accringtn	3	Scunthpe	0	r
Aldershot	3	Cardiff	1	r
Bristol R	3	Folkestne	1	r
Charlton	3	Bath C	1	r
Mansfield	3	New Brig	4	r
Margate	0	Torquay	2	r
Newport	6	Dulwich H	2	r

SECOND ROUND

Home		Away		
Accringtn	1	Bristol R	0	
Bournemt	2	Tranmere	4	
Bristol C	2	Barrow	1	
Carlisle	1	Chelthnm	2	
Charlton	1	Gillinghm	0	
Gainsbrgh	0	Aldershot	2	
Gateshead	1	N.Shields	0	
Halifax	1	Hartlepl	1	
N'hamptn	3	Torquay	0	
QPR	1	New Brig	1	
Rotherhm	2	Coventry	1	
Southend	2	Chester	1	
Stockport	1	C.Palace	2	
Sutton T	1	Reading	2	
Swindon	1	Dartford	0	
Walsall	0	Clapton O	0	
Workingtn	3	Newport	1	
Clapton O	2	Walsall	0	r
Hartlepl	1	Halifax	2	r
New Brig	0	QPR	4	r

THIRD ROUND

Home		Away		
Birmghm C	2	Sheff Utd	1	
Bolton	3	Halifax	1	
Brighton	3	Swindon	1	
Bristol C	1	Derby	1	
Burnley	0	Bury	0	
Charlton	2	Port Vale	0	
Chelsea	1	West Brom	1	
Chelthnm	1	Blackpool	3	
Chestrfld	2	Aston V	2	
C.Palace	1	Aldershot	0	
Grimsby	1	Clapton O	0	
Hull	1	Brentford	0	
Leeds U	0	Preston NE	1	
Leicester	3	Lincoln	0	
Liverpool	1	Fulham	1	
Luton	0	Arsenal	1	
Man City	3	Blackburn	1	
Man Utd	1	Portsmth	1	
Millwall	3	Accringtn	0	
Nottm For	4	QPR	0	
Plymouth	1	Huddersfd	1	
Reading	1	Oldham	2	
Rotherhm	0	Sheff Wed	3	
Southmpt	1	N'hamptn	1	
Stoke	3	Bradfd PA	0	
Sunderld	1	Middlesbr	1	
Swansea	1	Notts Co	0	
Tottenham	3	Everton	0	
Tranmere	3	Southend	0	
West Ham	3	Bradford	2	
Wolves	1	Newcastle	0	

GIANTKILLERS

1924 Corinthians 1 Blackburn 0

Upholders of the noble sporting traditions of honesty and fair play, the Corinthians were held in high regard in English football between the two world wars. They were a very strong amateur side, although they did not play competitive matches until 1922, preferring instead to appear only in friendlies. They did not have their own ground. A goal by A.G. Doggart, who played once for the full England team and later became a vice-president of the Football Association, gave them victory over First Division Blackburn at the old Crystal Palace, and this was followed by further Cup defeats of League clubs in 1927 (Walsall 4-0 away) and 1929 (Norwich 5-0 away).

Strange but true!

Before the newly completed Wembley Stadium could play host to its first Cup Final in 1923 it had to prove it was safe. An infantry battalion and hundreds of local volunteers marched on the terraces for quarter of an hour to ensure the foundations were solid.

Workingtn	4	Gateshead	1	
Aston V	2	Chestrfld	0	r
Bury	3	Burnley	2	r
Derby	1	Bristol C	0	re
Fulham	2	Liverpool	3	re
Huddersfd	6	Plymouth	2	r
Middlesbr	1	Sunderld	2	r
N'hamptn	1	Southmpt	0	r
Portsmth	4	Man Utd	1	r
West Brom	0	Chelsea	1	re

FOURTH ROUND

Arsenal	7	C.Palace	0	
Aston V	7	Sunderld	2	
Birmghm C	1	Charlton	0	
Brighton	1	Bolton	1	
Bury	1	Swansea	1	
Chelsea	1	Nottm For	1	
Derby	3	Wolves	0	
Huddersfd	0	N'hamptn	2	
Hull	2	Man City	2	
Liverpool	3	Tranmere	1	
Millwall	3	Leicester	6	
Oldham	1	Sheff Wed	1	
Portsmth	2	Grimsby	0	
Stoke	3	Blackpool	0	
Tottenham	4	West Ham	1	
Workingtn	1	Preston NE	2	
Bolton	6	Brighton	1	r
Man City	4	Hull	1	r
Nottm For	0	Chelsea	3	r
Sheff Wed	6	Oldham	1	r
Swansea	3	Bury	0	r

FIFTH ROUND

Arsenal	1	Derby	0	
Birmghm C	1	Leicester	2	
Liverpool	0	Bolton	3	
Preston NE	4	N'hamptn	0	
Sheff Wed	2	Man City	2	
Stoke	3	Chelsea	1	
Swansea	0	Portsmth	1	
Tottenham	0	Aston V	1	
Man City	2	Sheff Wed	0	r

SIXTH ROUND

Arsenal	1	Aston V	2	
Bolton	0	Portsmth	3	
Man City	1	Stoke	0	
Preston NE	0	Leicester	1	

SEMI-FINAL

Man City	6	Aston V	1	N
Portsmth	4	Leicester	1	N

FINAL

Man City	2	Portsmth	1	N

1935

FIRST ROUND

Aldershot	4	Bournemt	0	
Ashford	1	Clapton O	4	
Barry	0	N'hamptn	1	
Bedford T	2	Dartford	3	
Blyth S	1	Stockport	1	
Brighton	3	Folkestne	1	
Bristol C	2	Gillinghm	0	
Bristol R	3	Harwich	0	
Burton T	2	York	3	
Cardiff	1	Reading	2	
Carlisle	1	Wigan Ath	6	
Charlton	2	Exeter	2	
Chester	3	Dinningtn	1	
Coventry	7	Scunthpe	0	
Crewe	1	Walsall	2	
Darwen	1	Boston U	2	
Doncaster	0	Barrow	2	
Dulwich H	1	Torquay	2	
Gateshead	1	Darlingtn	4	
Guilford	1	Bath C	2	
Halifax	1	Hartlepl	1	
Mansfield	6	Accringtn	1	
QPR	2	Walstmw A	0	
Rotherhm	2	Spennym'r	0	
Shildon	2	Lincoln	2	
Southend	10	Golders G	1	
Southport	1	New Brig	1	
Swindon	4	Newport	0	
Tranmere	3	Stalyb C	1	
Watford	2	Corinthns	0	
Wimbledn	1	Leyton	1	
Workingtn	2	Birm.C.T	0	
Wrexham	4	Rochdale	1	
Yeovil	3	C.Palace	0	
Exeter	5	Charlton	2	r
Hartlepl	2	Halifax	0	r
Leyton	0	Wimbledn	1	r
Lincoln	4	Shildon	0	r
New Brig	1	Southport	1	re
Stockport	4	Blyth S	1	r
Southport	1	New Brig	2	r2N

SECOND ROUND

Barrow	0	Aldershot	2	
Bath C	2	Boston U	1	
Clapton O	1	Chester	3	
Dartford	0	Bristol R	1	
Hartlepl	0	Coventry	4	
Mansfield	4	Tranmere	2	
N'hamptn	0	Workingtn	0	
QPR	1	Brighton	2	
Reading	3	Wrexham	0	
Rotherhm	1	Bristol C	2	
Stockport	3	Darlingtn	2	
Swindon	4	Lincoln	3	
Watford	1	Walsall	1	
Wigan Ath	3	Torquay	2	
Wimbledn	1	Southend	5	
Yeovil	4	Exeter	1	
York	1	New Brig	0	
Walsall	1	Watford	0	re
Workingtn	0	N'hamptn	1	r

THIRD ROUND

Aldershot	0	Reading	0	
Aston V	1	Bradford	3	
Birmghm C	5	Coventry	1	
Brentford	0	Plymouth	1	
Brighton	0	Arsenal	2	
Bristol C	1	Bury	1	
Bristol R	1	Man Utd	3	
Burnley	4	Mansfield	2	
Chelsea	1	Luton	1	
Chester	0	Nottm For	4	
Everton	6	Grimsby	3	
Hull	1	Newcastle	5	
Leeds U	4	Bradfd PA	1	
Leicester	2	Blackpool	1	
Middlesbr	1	Blackburn	1	
N'hamptn	0	Bolton	2	
Norwich	2	Bath C	0	
Portsmth	1	Huddersfd	1	
Preston NE	0	Barnsley	0	
Sheff Wed	3	Oldham	1	
Southend	0	Sheff Utd	4	
Sunderld	3	Fulham	2	
Swansea	4	Stoke	1	
Swindon	2	Chestrfld	1	
Tottenham	1	Man City	0	
Walsall	1	Southmpt	2	
West Brom	2	Port Vale	1	
West Ham	1	Stockport	1	
Wigan Ath	1	Millwall	4	
Wolves	4	Notts Co	0	
Yeovil	2	Liverpool	6	
York	0	Derby	1	
Barnsley	0	Preston NE	1	r
Blackburn	1	Middlesbr	0	r
Bury	2	Bristol C	2	re
Huddersfd	2	Portsmth	3	r
Luton	2	Chelsea	0	r
Reading	3	Aldershot	1	r
Stockport	1	West Ham	0	r
Bristol C	2	Bury	1	r2N

FOURTH ROUND

Blackburn	1	Liverpool	0	
Bradford	0	Stockport	0	
Burnley	3	Luton	1	
Derby	3	Swansea	0	
Leicester	0	Arsenal	1	
Norwich	3	Leeds U	3	
Nottm For	0	Man Utd	0	
Plymouth	1	Bolton	4	

Fans on song

Community singing was introduced at the 1927 Final, to fill in time before the kick-off. One of the songs that day was called Drink To Me Only.

Terrier's target

In 1920 Huddersfield made a public appeal for cash in order to stay in business. They ended the season by winning promotion and reaching the Cup Final, losing 0-1 to Aston Villa.

Portsmth	0	Bristol C	0	
Reading	1	Millwall	0	
Southmpt	0	Birmghm C	3	
Sunderld	1	Everton	1	
Swindon	0	Preston NE	2	
Tottenham	2	Newcastle	0	
West Brom	7	Sheff Utd	1	
Wolves	1	Sheff Wed	2	
Bristol C	2	Portsmth	0	r
Everton	6	Sunderld	4	r
Leeds U	1	Norwich	2	r
Man Utd	0	Nottm For	3	r
Stockport	3	Bradford	2	re

FIFTH ROUND

Blackburn	1	Birmghm C	2	
Bristol C	0	Preston NE	0	
Everton	3	Derby	1	
Norwich	0	Sheff Wed	1	
Nottm For	0	Burnley	0	
Reading	0	Arsenal	1	
Stockport	0	West Brom	5	
Tottenham	1	Bolton	1	
Bolton	1	Tottenham	1	re
Burnley	3	Nottm For	0	r
Preston NE	5	Bristol C	0	r
Bolton	2	Tottenham	0	r2N

SIXTH ROUND

Burnley	3	Birmghm C	2	
Everton	1	Bolton	2	
Sheff Wed	2	Arsenal	1	
West Brom	1	Preston NE	0	

SEMI-FINAL

Sheff Wed	3	Burnley	0	N
West Brom	1	Bolton	1	N
West Brom	2	Bolton	0	rN

FINAL

Sheff Wed	4	West Brom	2	N

1936

FIRST ROUND

Barrow	4	Wrexham	1	
Brighton	0	Chelthnm	0	
Bristol C	0	C.Palace	1	
Cardiff	0	Dartford	3	
Chester	1	Gateshead	0	
Chestrfld	3	Southport	0	
Clapton O	0	Aldershot	0	
Coventry	1	Scunthpe	1	
Crewe	4	Boston U	2	
Darlingtn	4	Accringtn	2	
Dulwich H	2	Torquay	3	
Exeter	0	Gillinghm	4	
Gainsbrgh	3	Blyth S	1	
Grantham	0	Notts Co	2	
Halifax	4	Rochdale	0	
Kiddermst	4	Bshk Auck	1	
Mansfield	2	Hartlepl	3	
Margate	3	QPR	1	
New Brig	1	Workingtn	3	
Newport	0	Southend	1	
N'hamptn	0	Bristol R	0	
Nunhead	2	Watford	4	
Oldham	6	Ferryhill	1	
Reading	8	Corinthns	3	
Romford	3	Folkestne	3	
Scarboro	2	Darwen	0	
Southall	3	Swindon	1	
Stalyb C	4	Kells U	0	
Tranmere	3	Carlisle	0	
Walsall	2	Lincoln	0	
Walstmw A	1	Bournemt	1	
Wigan Ath	1	Rotherhm	2	
Yeovil	0	Nwpt IOW	1	
York	1	Burton T	5	
Aldershot	0	Clapton O	1	re
Bournemt	8	Walstmw A	1	r
Bristol R	3	N'hamptn	1	r
Chelthnm	0	Brighton	6	r
Folkestne	2	Romford	1	re
Scunthpe	4	Coventry	2	r

SECOND ROUND

Bournemt	5	Barrow	2	
Chester	3	Reading	3	
Chestrfld	0	Walsall	0	
Crewe	2	Gillinghm	1	
Dartford	4	Gainsbrgh	0	
Folkestne	1	Clapton O	2	
Halifax	1	Hartlepl	1	
Margate	3	C.Palace	1	
Notts Co	3	Torquay	0	
Oldham	1	Bristol R	1	
Rotherhm	1	Watford	1	
Scarboro	1	Brighton	1	
Southall	8	Nwpt IOW	0	
Southend	5	Burton T	0	
Stalyb C	0	Darlingtn	1	
Tranmere	6	Scunthpe	2	
Workingtn	5	Kiddermst	1	
Brighton	3	Scarboro	0	r
Bristol R	4	Oldham	1	r
Hartlepl	0	Halifax	0	re
Reading	3	Chester	0	r
Walsall	2	Chestrfld	1	r
Watford	1	Rotherhm	0	r
Halifax	1	Hartlepl	4	r2eN

THIRD ROUND

Aston V	0	Huddersfd	1	
Barnsley	3	Birmghm C	3	
Blackburn	1	Bolton	1	
Blackpool	3	Margate	1	
Bradford	1	Bournemt	0	
Bradfd PA	3	Workingtn	2	
Bristol R	1	Arsenal	5	
Burnley	0	Sheff Utd	0	
Clapton O	3	Charlton	0	
Crewe	1	Sheff Wed	1	
Darlingtn	2	Bury	3	
Derby	3	Dartford	2	
Doncaster	1	Nottm For	2	
Everton	1	Preston NE	3	
Fulham	2	Brighton	1	
Hartlepl	0	Grimsby	0	
Leicester	1	Brentford	0	
Liverpool	1	Swansea	0	
Man City	3	Portsmth	1	
Middlesbr	1	Southmpt	0	
Millwall	0	Stoke	0	
Norwich	1	Chelsea	1	
Notts Co	0	Tranmere	0	
Reading	1	Man Utd	3	
Southall	1	Watford	4	
Stockport	2	Plymouth	3	
Sunderld	2	Port Vale	2	
Tottenham	4	Southend	4	
Walsall	0	Newcastle	2	
West Brom	2	Hull	0	
West Ham	2	Luton	2	
Wolves	1	Leeds U	1	
Birmghm C	0	Barnsley	2	r
Bolton	0	Blackburn	1	re
Chelsea	3	Norwich	1	r
Grimsby	4	Hartlepl	1	r
Leeds U	3	Wolves	1	r
Luton	4	West Ham	0	r
Port Vale	2	Sunderld	0	r
Sheff Utd	2	Burnley	1	r
Sheff Wed	3	Crewe	1	re
Southend	1	Tottenham	2	r
Stoke	4	Millwall	0	r
Tranmere	4	Notts Co	3	r

FOURTH ROUND

Bradford	3	Blackburn	1	
Bradfd PA	1	West Brom	1	
Chelsea	4	Plymouth	1	
Derby	2	Nottm For	0	
Fulham	5	Blackpool	2	
Leeds U	3	Bury	2	
Leicester	6	Watford	3	
Liverpool	0	Arsenal	2	
Man City	2	Luton	1	
Middlesbr	3	Clapton O	0	
Port Vale	0	Grimsby	4	
Preston NE	0	Sheff Utd	0	
Sheff Wed	1	Newcastle	1	
Stoke	0	Man Utd	0	
Tottenham	1	Huddersfd	0	
Tranmere	2	Barnsley	4	
Man Utd	0	Stoke	2	r
Newcastle	3	Sheff Wed	1	r
Sheff Utd	2	Preston NE	0	r
West Brom	1	Bradfd PA	1	re
Bradfd PA	2	West Brom	0	r2N

FIFTH ROUND

Barnsley	2	Stoke	1	
Bradford	0	Derby	1	
Bradfd PA	0	Tottenham	0	
Chelsea	0	Fulham	0	
Grimsby	3	Man City	2	
Middlesbr	2	Leicester	1	
Newcastle	3	Arsenal	3	
Sheff Utd	3	Leeds U	1	
Arsenal	3	Newcastle	0	r
Fulham	3	Chelsea	2	r
Tottenham	2	Bradfd PA	1	r

SIXTH ROUND

Arsenal	4	Barnsley	1	

Fulham	3	Derby	0	
Grimsby	3	Middlesbr	1	
Sheff Utd	3	Tottenham	1	
SEMI-FINAL				
Arsenal	1	Grimsby	0	N
Sheff Utd	2	Fulham	1	N
FINAL				
Arsenal	1	Sheff Utd	0	N

1937

FIRST ROUND				
Accringtn	3	Wellingtn	1	
Aldershot	1	Millwall	6	
Barrow	0	Mansfield	4	
Bath C	1	Tunbridge	2	
Blyth S	0	Wrexham	2	
Boston U	1	Spennym'r	1	
Bournemt	5	Harwich	1	
Burton T	5	Wigan Ath	1	
Cardiff	3	Southall	1	
Carlisle	2	Stockport	1	
Clapton O	2	Torquay	1	
Corinthns	0	Bristol R	2	
Crewe	5	Rochdale	1	
C.Palace	1	Southend	1	
Dartford	3	Peterboro	0	
Exeter	3	Folkestne	0	
Frickley	0	Southport	2	
Gateshead	2	Notts Co	0	
Halifax	1	Darlingtn	2	
Ilford	2	Reading	4	
Ipswich	2	Watford	1	
Lincoln	1	New Brig	1	
Newport	3	Bristol C	0	
Oldham	1	Tranmere	0	
QPR	5	Brighton	1	
Rotherhm	4	Hartlepl	4	
Ryde Spts	1	Gillinghm	5	
S.L'pool	1	Morecambe	0	
Shildon	4	Stalyb C	2	
Swindon	6	Dulwich H	0	
Walsall	3	Scunthpe	0	
Walstmw A	6	N'hamptn	1	
Yeovil	4	Worthing	3	
York	5	Hull	2	
Hartlepl	2	Rotherhm	0	r
New Brig	2	Lincoln	3	re
Southend	2	C.Palace	0	r
Spennym'r	2	Boston U	0	r
SECOND ROUND				
Accringtn	1	Tunbridge	0	
Bristol R	2	Southport	1	
Burton T	1	Darlingtn	2	
Cardiff	2	Swindon	1	
Carlisle	4	Clapton O	1	
Crewe	1	Hartlepl	1	
Ipswich	1	Spennym'r	2	
Lincoln	2	Oldham	3	
Mansfield	0	Bournemt	3	
Millwall	7	Gateshead	0	
Reading	7	Newport	2	
S.L'pool	0	QPR	1	
Shildon	0	Dartford	3	
Southend	3	York	3	
Walsall	1	Yeovil	1	
Walstmw A	2	Exeter	3	
Wrexham	2	Gillinghm	0	
Hartlepl	1	Crewe	2	r
Yeovil	0	Walsall	1	r
York	2	Southend	1	r
THIRD ROUND				
Aston V	2	Burnley	3	
Blackburn	2	Accringtn	2	
Bradford	2	York	2	
Bradfd PA	0	Derby	4	
Brentford	5	Huddersfd	0	
Bristol R	2	Leicester	5	
Bury	1	QPR	0	
Cardiff	1	Grimsby	3	
Chelsea	4	Leeds U	0	
Chester	4	Doncaster	0	
Chestrfld	1	Arsenal	5	
Coventry	2	Charlton	0	
Crewe	0	Plymouth	2	
Dartford	0	Darlingtn	1	
Everton	5	Bournemt	0	
Exeter	3	Oldham	0	
Luton	3	Blackpool	3	
Man Utd	1	Reading	0	
Millwall	2	Fulham	0	
Norwich	3	Liverpool	0	
Nottm For	2	Sheff Utd	4	
Portsmth	0	Tottenham	5	
Preston NE	2	Newcastle	0	
Sheff Wed	2	Port Vale	0	
Southmpt	2	Sunderld	3	
Stoke	4	Birmghm C	1	
Swansea	1	Carlisle	0	
Walsall	3	Barnsley	1	
West Brom	7	Spennym'r	1	
West Ham	0	Bolton	0	
Wolves	6	Middlesbr	1	
Wrexham	1	Man City	3	
Accringtn	3	Blackburn	1	re
Blackpool	1	Luton	2	r
Bolton	1	West Ham	0	r
York	1'	Bradford	0	r
FOURTH ROUND				
Arsenal	5	Man Utd	0	
Bolton	1	Norwich	1	
Burnley	4	Bury	1	
Coventry	2	Chester	0	
Derby	3	Brentford	0	
Everton	3	Sheff Wed	0	
Exeter	3	Leicester	1	
Grimsby	5	Walsall	1	
Luton	2	Sunderld	2	
Man City	2	Accringtn	0	
Millwall	3	Chelsea	0	
Preston NE	5	Stoke	1	
Swansea	0	York	0	
Tottenham	1	Plymouth	0	
West Brom	3	Darlingtn	2	
Wolves	2	Sheff Utd	2	
Norwich	1	Bolton	2	re
Sheff Utd	1	Wolves	2	r
Sunderld	3	Luton	1	r
York	1	Swansea	3	r
FIFTH ROUND				
Bolton	0	Man City	5	
Burnley	1	Arsenal	7	
Coventry	2	West Brom	3	
Everton	1	Tottenham	1	
Grimsby	1	Wolves	1	
Millwall	2	Derby	1	
Preston NE	5	Exeter	3	
Sunderld	3	Swansea	0	
Tottenham	4	Everton	3	r
Wolves	6	Grimsby	2	r
SIXTH ROUND				
Millwall	2	Man City	0	
Tottenham	1	Preston NE	3	
West Brom	3	Arsenal	1	
Wolves	1	Sunderld	1	
Sunderld	2	Wolves	2	re
Sunderld	4	Wolves	0	r2N
SEMI-FINAL				
Preston NE	4	West Brom	1	N
Sunderld	2	Millwall	1	N
FINAL				
Sunderld	3	Preston NE	1	N

Strange but true!

Dixie Dean captained Everton when they won the Cup in 1933. His brother-in-law was sacked for taking time off from work to travel to the match.

Trotters by foot

Such was the chaos caused at Wembley when hundreds of thousands of fans turned up to watch the Cup Final in 1923 - the first at the new stadium - that the Bolton team had to abandon their coach a mile from the ground and complete their journey by foot.

1938

FIRST ROUND			
Accringtn	1	Lancaster	1
Barrow	0	Crewe	1
Bournemt	0	Dartford	0
Brighton	5	Tunbridge	1
Bristol C	3	Enfield	0
Bristol R	1	QPR	8
Burton T	1	Rotherhm	1
Corinthns	0	Southend	2
C.Palace	2	Kettering	2
Darlingtn	0	Scarboro	2
Doncaster	7	Blyth S	0

Dulwich H	1	Aldershot	2	
Exeter	1	Folkestne	0	
Gillinghm	3	Swindon	4	
Guilford	1	Reading	0	
Hartlepl	3	Southport	1	
Hull	4	Scunthpe	0	
Kiddermst	2	Newport	2	
King's Ln	0	Bromley	4	
New Brig	5	Workingtn	0	
N'hamptn	1	Cardiff	2	
Port Vale	1	Gainsbrgh	1	
Rochdale	1	Lincoln	1	
Torquay	1	Clapton O	2	
Tranmere	2	Carlisle	1	
Walker C	1	Bradford	1	
Walsall	4	Gateshead	0	
Watford	3	Chelthnm	0	
Wellingtn	1	Mansfield	2	
Westbury U	1	Walstmw A	3	
Wigan Ath	1	S.L'pool	4	
Wrexham	2	Oldham	1	
Yeovil	2	Ipswich	1	
York	1	Halifax	1	
Bradford	11	Walker C	3	r
Dartford	0	Bournemt	6	r
Gainsbrgh	2	Port Vale	1	re
Halifax	0	York	1	r
Kettering	0	C.Palace	4	r
Lancaster	1	Accringtn	1	re
Lincoln	2	Rochdale	0	r
Newport	4	Kiddermst	1	r
Rotherhm	3	Burton T	0	r
Accringtn	4	Lancaster	0	r2N
SECOND ROUND				
Accringtn	0	C.Palace	1	
Cardiff	1	Bristol C	1	
Clapton O	2	York	2	
Crewe	2	New Brig	2	
Doncaster	4	Guilford	0	
Exeter	1	Hull	2	
Mansfield	2	Lincoln	1	
Newport	2	Bournemt	1	
Rotherhm	1	Aldershot	3	
S.L'pool	1	Brighton	1	
Scarboro	4	Bromley	1	
Swindon	2	QPR	1	
Tranmere	3	Hartlepl	1	
Walstmw A	0	Southend	1	
Watford	3	Walsall	0	
Wrexham	1	Bradford	2	
Yeovil	2	Gainsbrgh	1	
Brighton	6	S.L'pool	0	r
Bristol C	0	Cardiff	2	r
New Brig	4	Crewe	1	r
York	1	Clapton O	0	r
THIRD ROUND				
Aldershot	1	Notts Co	3	
Arsenal	3	Bolton	1	
Birmghm C	0	Blackpool	1	
Bradford	1	Chestrfld	1	
Bradfd PA	7	Newport	4	
Brentford	3	Fulham	1	
Bury	2	Brighton	0	
Charlton	5	Cardiff	0	
Chelsea	0	Everton	1	
C.Palace	0	Liverpool	0	
Derby	1	Stoke	2	

Doncaster	0	Sheff Utd	2	
Grimsby	1	Swindon	1	
Huddersfd	3	Hull	1	
Leeds U	3	Chester	1	
Man Utd	3	Yeovil	0	
Mansfield	1	Leicester	2	
Middlesbr	2	Stockport	0	
Millwall	2	Man City	2	
New Brig	1	Plymouth	0	
Norwich	2	Aston V	3	
Nottm For	3	Southmpt	1	
Preston NE	3	West Ham	0	
Scarboro	1	Luton	1	
Sheff Wed	1	Burnley	1	
Southend	2	Barnsley	2	
Sunderld	1	Watford	0	
Swansea	0	Wolves	4	
Tottenham	3	Blackburn	2	
Tranmere	1	Portsmth	2	
West Brom	1	Newcastle	0	
York	3	Coventry	2	
Barnsley	2	Southend	1	r
Burnley	3	Sheff Wed	1	r
Chestrfld	1	Bradford	1	re
Liverpool	3	C.Palace	1	re
Luton	5	Scarboro	1	r
Man City	3	Millwall	1	r
Swindon	2	Grimsby	1	re
Bradford	0	Chestrfld	2	r2N
FOURTH ROUND				
Aston V	4	Blackpool	0	
Barnsley	2	Man Utd	2	
Bradfd PA	1	Stoke	1	
Brentford	2	Portsmth	1	
Charlton	2	Leeds U	1	
Chestrfld	3	Burnley	2	
Everton	0	Sunderld	1	
Huddersfd	1	Notts Co	0	
Luton	2	Swindon	1	
Man City	3	Bury	1	
New Brig	0	Tottenham	0	
Nottm For	1	Middlesbr	3	
Preston NE	2	Leicester	0	
Sheff Utd	1	Liverpool	1	
Wolves	1	Arsenal	2	
York	3	West Brom	2	
Liverpool	1	Sheff Utd	0	r
Man Utd	1	Barnsley	0	r
Stoke	1	Bradfd PA	2	r
Tottenham	5	New Brig	2	r
FIFTH ROUND				
Arsenal	0	Preston NE	1	
Brentford	2	Man Utd	0	
Charlton	1	Aston V	1	
Chestrfld	2	Tottenham	2	
Liverpool	0	Huddersfd	1	
Luton	1	Man City	3	
Sunderld	1	Bradfd PA	0	
York	1	Middlesbr	0	
Aston V	2	Charlton	2	re
Tottenham	2	Chestrfld	1	r
Aston V	4	Charlton	1	r2N
SIXTH ROUND				
Aston V	3	Man City	2	
Brentford	0	Preston NE	3	
Tottenham	0	Sunderld	1	
York	0	Huddersfd	0	

Huddersfd	2	York	1	r
SEMI-FINAL				
Huddersfd	3	Sunderld	1	N
Preston NE	2	Aston V	1	N
FINAL				
Preston NE	1	Huddersfd	0	eN

1939

FIRST ROUND				
Aldershot	1	Guilford	1	
Bournemt	2	Bristol C	1	
Bristol R	4	Peterboro	1	
Bromley	2	Apsley	1	
Chelmsfd	4	Kiddermst	0	
Chelthnm	1	Cardiff	1	
Chester	3	Bradford	1	
Clapton O	3	Hayes	1	
C.Palace	1	QPR	1	
Darlingtn	4	Stalyb C	0	
Doncaster	4	New Brig	2	
Folkestne	2	Colchester	1	
Gainsbrgh	2	Gateshead	1	
Halifax	7	Rochdale	3	
Hartlepl	2	Accringtn	1	
Horden CW	1	Chorley	1	
Hull	4	Rotherhm	1	
Ipswich	7	Street	0	
Lincoln	4	Barrow	1	
N.Shields	1	Stockport	4	
Oldham	2	Crewe	2	
Reading	3	Newport	3	
Runcorn	3	Wellingtn	0	
Scarboro	0	Southport	0	
Scunthpe	4	Lancaster	2	
Southend	3	Corinthns	0	
Swindon	6	Lowestoft	0	
Torquay	3	Exeter	1	
Walsall	4	Carlisle	1	
Walstmw A	4	Tunbridge	1	
Watford	4	N'hamptn	1	
Workingtn	1	Mansfield	1	
Wrexham	1	Port Vale	2	
Yeovil	2	Brighton	1	
Cardiff	1	Chelthnm	0	r
Chorley	1	Horden CW	2	r
Crewe	1	Oldham	0	r
Guilford	3	Aldershot	4	r
Mansfield	2	Workingtn	1	r
Newport	3	Reading	1	r
QPR	3	C.Palace	0	r
Southport	5	Scarboro	3	r
SECOND ROUND				

Ancient Warrior

Billy Hampson was aged 41 years and eight months when he played for Newcastle in the 1924 Final. He seems certain to hold the 'oldest player' record for all time.

Bristol R	0	Bournemt	3	
Cardiff	1	Crewe	0	
Chelmsfd	3	Darlingtn	1	
Chester	2	Hull	2	
Folkestne	1	Yeovil	1	
Gainsbrgh	0	Doncaster	1	
Halifax	1	Mansfield	1	
Hartlepl	0	QPR	2	
Horden CW	2	Newport	3	
Ipswich	4	Torquay	1	
Lincoln	8	Bromley	1	
Port Vale	0	Southend	1	
Runcorn	3	Aldershot	1	
Scunthpe	1	Watford	2	
Southport	2	Swindon	0	
Stockport	0	Walstmw A	0	
Walsall	4	Clapton O	2	
Hull	0	Chester	1	r
Mansfield	3	Halifax	3	re
Walstmw A	1	Stockport	3	r
Yeovil	1	Folkestne	0	r
Mansfield	0	Halifax	0	r2eN
Mansfield	1	Halifax	2	r3N
THIRD ROUND				
Aston V	1	Ipswich	1	
Barnsley	1	Stockport	2	
Birmghm C	2	Halifax	0	
Blackburn	2	Swansea	0	
Blackpool	1	Sheff Utd	2	
Brentford	0	Newcastle	2	
Cardiff	1	Charlton	0	
Chelmsfd	4	Southmpt	1	
Chelsea	2	Arsenal	1	
Chester	1	Coventry	0	
Chestrfld	1	Southend	1	
Derby	0	Everton	1	
Fulham	6	Bury	0	
Grimsby	6	Tranmere	0	
Huddersfd	0	Nottm For	0	
Leeds U	3	Bournemt	1	
Liverpool	3	Luton	0	
Middlesbr	0	Bolton	0	
Newport	0	Walsall	2	
Norwich	0	Man City	5	
Notts Co	3	Burnley	1	
Portsmth	4	Lincoln	0	
QPR	1	West Ham	2	
Runcorn	2	Preston NE	4	
Sheff Wed	1	Yeovil	1	
Southport	1	Doncaster	1	
Stoke	1	Leicester	1	
Sunderld	3	Plymouth	0	
Tottenham	7	Watford	1	
West Brom	0	Man Utd	0	
Wolves	3	Bradfd PA	1	
York	0	Millwall	5	
Bolton	0	Middlesbr	0	re
Doncaster	2	Southport	1	r
Ipswich	1	Aston V	2	r
Leicester	2	Stoke	1	r
Man Utd	1	West Brom	5	r
Nottm For	0	Huddersfd	3	r
Southend	4	Chestrfld	3	re
Yeovil	1	Sheff Wed	2	r
Bolton	0	Middlesbr	1	r2N
FOURTH ROUND				
Birmghm C	6	Chelmsfd	0	
Blackburn	4	Southend	2	
Cardiff	0	Newcastle	0	
Chelsea	3	Fulham	0	
Everton	8	Doncaster	0	
Leeds U	2	Huddersfd	4	
Liverpool	5	Stockport	1	
Middlesbr	0	Sunderld	2	
Millwall	2	Grimsby	2	
Notts Co	0	Walsall	0	
Portsmth	2	West Brom	0	
Preston NE	2	Aston V	0	
Sheff Utd	2	Man City	0	
Sheff Wed	1	Chester	1	
West Ham	3	Tottenham	3	
Wolves	5	Leicester	1	
Chester	1	Sheff Wed	1	re
Grimsby	3	Millwall	2	r
Newcastle	4	Cardiff	1	r
Tottenham	1	West Ham	1	re
Walsall	4	Notts Co	0	r
Sheff Wed	2	Chester	0	r2N
West Ham	2	Tottenham	1	r2N
FIFTH ROUND				
Birmghm C	2	Everton	2	
Chelsea	1	Sheff Wed	1	
Huddersfd	3	Walsall	0	
Newcastle	1	Preston NE	2	
Portsmth	2	West Ham	0	
Sheff Utd	0	Grimsby	0	
Sunderld	1	Blackburn	1	
Wolves	4	Liverpool	1	
Blackburn	0	Sunderld	0	re
Everton	2	Birmghm C	1	r
Grimsby	1	Sheff Utd	0	r
Sheff Wed	0	Chelsea	0	re
Blackburn	1	Sunderld	0	r2N
Chelsea	3	Sheff Wed	1	r2N
SIXTH ROUND				
Chelsea	0	Grimsby	1	
Huddersfd	1	Blackburn	1	
Portsmth	1	Preston NE	0	
Wolves	2	Everton	0	
Blackburn	1	Huddersfd	2	r
SEMI-FINAL				
Portsmth	2	Huddersfd	1	N
Wolves	5	Grimsby	0	N
FINAL				
Portsmth	4	Wolves	1	N

Strange but true!

It's an Arsenal tradition that no 'keeper takes to the field in a brand new jersey. This is because Highbury coach Tom Whittaker blamed Dan Lewis's shiny shirt for the goal which won the Cup for Cardiff City in 1927 - when the ball slipped off Lewis's chest in the Final.

GIANTKILLERS

1933 Walsall 2 Arsenal 0

Perhaps the biggest Cup upset of all time, with Walsall - then in the Third Division North - beating the mighty Gunners in the Third Round, and beating them well. Arsenal, who won the Championship that season and for the next two, blundered by under-estimating their opponents and giving first-team debuts to three players - one of whom conceded a penalty for the second goal with an horrendous foul, and was transferred within a week. On a high, Walsall beat Mansfield Town 8-1 in their next League game, but the party was soon over. They lost 4-0 to Manchester City in the Fourth Round and finished 16th in the League table.

1946-1959

TRAGEDY STRIKES AT BOLTON

Strange but true!
Players named Harrison appeared in the Finals of 1946 (Derby), 1947 (Burnley) and 1949 (Leicester, two of them). But no Harrison has been in a Final since.

The first competition after World War II broke with tradition, when for the first and only time, matches between the First Round proper and the Sixth Round were played on a home and away basis.

This was partly due to a severe shortage of funds following the war, and this change brought about some marathon ties - and some mammoth cup crowds - with matches being played to a conclusion in the second-legs, even after extra-time.

But, tragically, one of those large crowds witnessed - and contributed to - the first ground disaster in England. Sixty five thousand people crammed into Bolton's Burnden Park to see the second leg of their Sixth Round tie against Stanley Matthews' Stoke City.

But as the crowds surged, fences were trampled, a brick wall toppled and crowd barriers collapsed.

Geordie Gems
Newcastle were the first club to win successive Wembley Finals, in 1951 and 1952.

In the resulting crush, 33 people died and 500 were injured. It was a terrible tragedy but one that could have happened at any of a number of grounds that were unsafe after six years of neglect during hostilities.

On a happier note, Derby County won the first Final after the war with a 4-1 win over Charlton, but the Londoners returned to Wembley a year later to claim the trophy for the first, and to date only, time with a 1-0 victory over Bolton.

And what makes those two Finals even more fascinating is the fact that on both occasions the ball burst - the only incidents of this type in FA Cup Finals.

Ground Hell
Manchester United's home tie with Liverpool in 1948 was played at Everton - because Old Trafford was still unusable after bomb damage from the war.

As football moved into the 50s, Newcastle dominated the FA Cup, winning the trophy in 1951, 1952 and 1955.

Special mention in this decade should also go to Nottingham Forest, who won the Cup against Luton in 1959 with only ten men, after Roy Dwight - the uncle of pop star Elton John - was carried off with a broken leg.

WHAT A STAR ✪ STANLEY MORTENSEN

'They named a Cup Final after him - the Matthews Final' is a well-worn soccer joke. Mortensen, the 'other Stanley', survived a war-time plane crash to become a prolific scorer with lightning pace and enormous bravery. After accompanying Matthews to defeat in the 1948 and 1951 Finals, he too had his greatest day in 1953, scoring with an in-off, a toe-poke from a yard out, and then a blistering 20-yard free-kick shortly before the final whistle, leaving the inspirational Matthews just enough time to make the winner for Bill Perry.

1946

FIRST ROUND

Barnet	2	QPR	6	
Barrow	1	Netherfld	0	
Bath C	3	Chelthnm	2	
Brighton	3	Romford	1	
Bromley	6	Slough U	1	
Carlisle	5	N.Shields	1	
Chorley	2	Accringtn	1	
Crewe	4	Wrexham	2	
Darlingtn	2	Stockton	0	
Doncaster	0	Rotherhm	1	
Gateshead	6	Hartlepl	2	
Halifax	1	York	0	
Kettering	1	Grantham	5	
Leyton O	2	Nwpt IOW	1	
Lovells A	4	Bournemt	1	
Mansfield	3	Gainsbrgh	0	
Marine	4	Stalyb C	0	
N'hamptn	5	Chelmsfd	1	
Notts Co	2	Bradford	2	
Port Vale	4	Wellingtn	0	
Reading	3	Aldershot	0	
S.L'pool	1	Tranmere	1	
Shrewsby	5	Walsall	0	
Southport	1	Oldham	2	
Stockport	1	Rochdale	2	
Sutton U	1	Walstmw A	4	
Swindon	1	Bristol R	0	
Torquay	0	Newport	1	
Trowbdge	1	Exeter	3	
Watford	1	Southend	1	
Willingtn	0	Bshk Auck	5	
Wisbech	0	Ipswich	3	
Yeovil	2	Bristol C	2	
York Ams	1	Lincoln	0	
Accringtn	2	Chorley	0	s
Aldershot	7	Reading	3	s
Bournemt	3	Lovells A	2	s
Bradford	1	Notts Co	2	s
Bristol C	3	Yeovil	0	s
Bristol R	4	Swindon	1	s
Bshk Auck	0	Willingtn	2	s
Chelmsfd	0	N'hamptn	5	s
Chelthnm	0	Bath C	2	s
Exeter	7	Trowbdge	2	s
Gainsbrgh	4	Mansfield	2	se
Grantham	2	Kettering	2	s
Hartlepl	1	Gateshead	2	s
Ipswich	5	Wisbech	0	s
Lincoln	5	York Ams	1	s
N.Shields	2	Carlisle	3	s
Netherfld	2	Barrow	2	s
Newport	1	Torquay	1	s
Nwpt IOW	2	Leyton O	0	s
Oldham	3	Southport	1	s
QPR	2	Barnet	1	s
Rochdale	1	Stockport	1	s
Romford	1	Brighton	1	s
Rotherhm	2	Doncaster	1	s
Slough U	1	Bromley	0	s
Southend	0	Watford	3	s
Stalyb C	3	Marine	3	s
Stockton	1	Darlingtn	4	s
Tranmere	6	S.L'pool	1	s
Walsall	4	Shrewsby	1	s
Walstmw A	7	Sutton U	2	s
Wellingtn	0	Port Vale	2	s
Wrexham	3	Crewe	0	s
York	4	Halifax	2	s

SECOND ROUND

Aldershot	7	Nwpt IOW	0	
Barrow	4	Carlisle	2	
Bristol C	4	Bristol R	2	
Bromley	1	Watford	3	
Bshk Auck	1	York	2	
Gateshead	1	Darlingtn	2	
Grantham	1	Mansfield	2	
Lovells A	2	Bath C	1	
Newport	5	Exeter	1	
N'hamptn	3	Notts Co	1	
Oldham	2	Accringtn	1	
Port Vale	3	Marine	1	
QPR	4	Ipswich	0	
Rotherhm	2	Lincoln	1	
Shrewsby	0	Wrexham	1	
Tranmere	3	Rochdale	1	
Walstmw A	1	Brighton	1	
Accringtn	3	Oldham	1	s
Bath C	2	Lovells A	5	s
Brighton	4	Walstmw A	2	s
Bristol R	0	Bristol C	2	s
Carlisle	3	Barrow	4	s
Darlingtn	2	Gateshead	4	s
Exeter	1	Newport	3	s
Ipswich	0	QPR	2	s
Lincoln	1	Rotherhm	1	s
Mansfield	2	Grantham	1	s
Marine	1	Port Vale	1	s
Nwpt IOW	0	Aldershot	5	s
Notts Co	1	N'hamptn	0	s
Rochdale	3	Tranmere	0	s
Watford	1	Bromley	1	s
Wrexham	1	Shrewsby	1	s
York	3	Bshk Auck	0	s

THIRD ROUND

Accringtn	2	Man Utd	2	
Aldershot	2	Plymouth	0	
Birmghm C	1	Portsmth	0	
Bolton	1	Blackburn	0	
Bradfd PA	2	Port Vale	1	
Bristol C	5	Swansea	1	
Bury	3	Rochdale	3	
Cardiff	1	West Brom	1	
Charlton	3	Fulham	1	
Chelsea	1	Leicester	1	
Chester	0	Liverpool	2	
Chestrfld	1	York	1	
Coventry	2	Aston V	1	
Grimsby	1	Sunderld	3	
Huddersfld	1	Sheff Utd	1	
Leeds U	4	Middlesbr	4	
Lovells A	2	Wolves	4	
Luton	0	Derby	6	
Man City	6	Barrow	2	
Mansfield	0	Sheff Wed	0	
Newcastle	4	Barnsley	2	
N'hamptn	2	Millwall	2	
Norwich	1	Brighton	2	
Nottm For	1	Watford	1	
Preston NE	2	Everton	1	
QPR	0	C.Palace	0	
Rotherhm	2	Gateshead	2	
Southmptn	4	Newport	3	
Stoke	3	Burnley	1	
Tottenham	2	Brentford	2	
West Ham	6	Arsenal	0	
Wrexham	1	Blackpool	4	
Arsenal	1	West Ham	0	s
Aston V	2	Coventry	0	s
Barnsley	3	Newcastle	0	s
Barrow	2	Man City	2	s
Blackburn	1	Bolton	3	s
Blackpool	4	Wrexham	1	s
Brentford	2	Tottenham	0	s
Brighton	4	Norwich	1	s
Burnley	2	Stoke	1	s
C.Palace	0	QPR	0	sa
Derby	3	Luton	0	s
Everton	2	Preston NE	2	se

Fulham	2	Charlton	1	s
Gateshead	0	Rotherhm	2	s
Leicester	0	Chelsea	2	s
Liverpool	2	Chester	1	s
Man Utd	5	Accringtn	1	s
Middlesbr	7	Leeds U	2	s
Millwall	3	N'hamptn	0	s
Newport	1	Southmptn	2	s
Plymouth	0	Aldershot	1	s
Port Vale	1	Bradfd PA	1	s
Portsmth	0	Birmghm C	0	s
Rochdale	2	Bury	4	s
Sheff Utd	2	Huddersfld	0	s
Sheff Wed	5	Mansfield	0	s
Sunderld	2	Grimsby	1	s
Swansea	2	Bristol C	2	s
Watford	1	Nottm For	1	se
West Brom	4	Cardiff	0	s
Wolves	8	Lovells A	1	s
York	3	Chestrfld	2	se
Nottm For	0	Watford	1	reN
QPR	1	C.Palace	0	rN

FOURTH ROUND

Barnsley	3	Rotherhm	0	
Birmghm C	5	Watford	0	
Blackpool	3	Middlesbr	2	
Bolton	5	Liverpool	0	
Bradfd PA	1	Man City	3	
Brighton	3	Aldershot	0	
Bristol C	2	Brentford	1	
Charlton	5	Wolves	2	
Chelsea	2	West Ham	0	
Derby	1	West Brom	0	
Man Utd	1	Preston NE	0	
Millwall	2	Aston V	4	
Sheff Wed	5	York	1	
Southmptn	0	QPR	1	
Stoke	2	Sheff Utd	0	
Sunderld	3	Bury	1	
Aldershot	1	Brighton	4	s
Aston V	9	Millwall	1	s
Brentford	5	Bristol C	0	s
Bury	5	Sunderld	4	se
Liverpool	2	Bolton	0	s
Man City	2	Bradfd PA	8	s
Middlesbr	3	Blackpool	2	se
Preston NE	3	Man Utd	1	s
QPR	4	Southmptn	3	s
Rotherhm	2	Barnsley	1	s
Sheff Utd	3	Stoke	2	s
Watford	1	Birmghm C	1	s
West Brom	1	Derby	3	s
West Ham	1	Chelsea	0	s
Wolves	1	Charlton	1	s
York	1	Sheff Wed	6	s
Blackpool	0	Middlesbr	1	reN

FIFTH ROUND

Barnsley	0	Bradfd PA	1	
Bolton	1	Middlesbr	0	
Brighton	1	Derby	4	
Chelsea	0	Aston V	1	
Preston NE	1	Charlton	1	
QPR	1	Brentford	3	
Stoke	2	Sheff Wed	0	
Sunderld	1	Birmghm C	0	
Aston V	1	Chelsea	0	s
Birmghm C	3	Sunderld	1	s
Bradfd PA	1	Barnsley	1	s
Brentford	0	QPR	0	s
Charlton	6	Preston NE	0	s
Derby	6	Brighton	0	s
Middlesbr	1	Bolton	1	s
Sheff Wed	0	Stoke	0	s

SIXTH ROUND

Aston V	3	Derby	4	
Bradfd PA	2	Birmghm C	2	
Charlton	6	Brentford	3	
Stoke	0	Bolton	2	
Birmghm C	6	Bradfd PA	0	s
Bolton	0	Stoke	0	s
Brentford	1	Charlton	3	s
Derby	1	Aston V	1	s

SEMI-FINAL

Charlton	2	Bolton	0	N
Derby	1	Birmghm C	1	N
Derby	4	Birmghm C	0	reN

FINAL

Derby	4	Charlton	1	eN

1947

FIRST ROUND

Aldershot	4	Chelthnm	2	
Barnet	3	Sutton U	0	
Barrow	0	Halifax	0	
Bournemt	4	Exeter	2	
Bristol C	9	Hayes	3	
Brush Sp	1	Southend	6	
Carlisle	4	Runcorn	0	
Doncaster	2	Accringtn	2	
Gainsbrgh	1	Darlingtn	2	
Gateshead	3	Bradford	1	
Gillinghm	4	Gravesend	1	
Hartlepl	6	N.Shields	0	
Hull	0	New Brig	0	
Ipswich	2	Torquay	0	
Lancaster	1	Spennym'r	0	
Leyton O	1	Notts Co	2	
Leytonstn	1	Walsall	6	
Mert Tyd	3	Bristol R	1	
N'hamptn	2	Mansfield	0	
Norwich	7	Brighton	2	
Oldham	1	Tranmere	0	
Port Vale	5	Finchley	0	
QPR	2	Poole T	2	
Reading	5	Colchester	0	
Rochdale	6	Bshk Auck	1	
Rotherhm	2	Crewe	0	
S.L'pool	2	Workingtn	1	
Stockport	2	Southport	0	
Stockton	2	Lincoln	4	
Swindon	4	Cambs T	1	
Wellingtn	1	Watford	1	
Wrexham	5	Marine	0	
Yeovil T	2	Peterboro	2	
York	0	Scunthpe	1	
Accringtn	0	Doncaster	5	r
Halifax	1	Barrow	0	re
New Brig	1	Hull	2	re
Peterboro	1	Yeovil T	0	r
Poole T	0	QPR	6	r
Watford	1	Wellingtn	0	r

No Mercer

Joe Mercer, Arsenal captain in the 1950 Final, lived on Merseyside and did a lot of his training with Liverpool - the club The Gunners beat at Wembley that year.

SECOND ROUND

Barnet	2	Southend	9	
Bournemt	4	Aldershot	2	
Bristol C	1	Gillinghm	2	
Darlingtn	1	Hull	2	
Gateshead	4	Lancaster	0	
Halifax	1	Stockport	1	
Lincoln	1	Wrexham	1	
Mert Tyd	1	Reading	3	
Norwich	4	QPR	4	
Notts Co	2	Swindon	1	
Oldham	1	Doncaster	2	
Peterboro	1	N'hamptn	1	
Rochdale	6	Hartlepl	1	
Rotherhm	4	Scunthpe	1	
S.L'pool	2	Carlisle	3	
Walsall	0	Ipswich	0	
Watford	1	Port Vale	1	
Ipswich	0	Walsall	1	r
N'hamptn	1	Peterboro	1	re
Port Vale	2	Watford	1	r
QPR	2	Norwich	0	r
Stockport	2	Halifax	1	r
Wrexham	3	Lincoln	3	re
Lincoln	2	Wrexham	1	r2N
N'hamptn	8	Peterboro	1	r2N

THIRD ROUND

Blackburn	1	Hull	1	
Bolton	5	Stockport	1	
Bournemt	0	Derby	2	
Bradfd PA	0	Man Utd	3	
Brentford	1	Cardiff	0	
Burnley	5	Aston V	1	
Charlton	3	Rochdale	1	
Chelsea	1	Arsenal	1	
Chester	2	Plymouth	0	
Chestrfld	2	Sunderld	1	
Coventry	5	Newport	2	
Doncaster	2	Portsmth	3	
Everton	4	Southend	2	
Fulham	1	Birmghm C	2	
Huddersfld	3	Barnsley	4	
Lincoln	0	Nottm For	1	
Luton	6	Notts Co	0	
Man City	3	Gateshead	0	
Millwall	0	Port Vale	3	
Newcastle	6	C.Palace	2	
N'hamptn	1	Preston NE	2	
QPR	1	Middlesbr	1	
Reading	2	Grimsby	2	
Sheff Utd	3	Carlisle	0	
Sheff Wed	4	Blackpool	1	
Southmptn	5	Bury	1	
Swansea	4	Gillinghm	1	
Tottenham	2	Stoke	2	

Walsall	2	Liverpool	5	
West Brom	2	Leeds U	1	
West Ham	1	Leicester	2	
Wolves	3	Rotherhm	0	
Arsenal	1	Chelsea	1	re
Grimsby	3	Reading	1	r
Hull	0	Blackburn	3	r
Middlesbr	3	QPR	1	r
Stoke	1	Tottenham	0	r
Arsenal	0	Chelsea	2	r2N
FOURTH ROUND				
Birmghm C	1	Portsmth	0	
Blackburn	2	Port Vale	0	
Bolton	3	Man City	3	
Brentford	0	Leicester	0	
Burnley	2	Coventry	0	
Chelsea	2	Derby	2	
Chester	0	Stoke	0	
Liverpool	2	Grimsby	0	
Luton	2	Swansea	0	
Man Utd	0	Nottm For	2	
Middlesbr	2	Chestrfld	1	
Newcastle	3	Southmptn	1	
Preston NE	6	Barnsley	0	
Sheff Wed	2	Everton	1	
West Brom	1	Charlton	2	
Wolves	0	Sheff Utd	0	
Derby	1	Chelsea	0	re
Leicester	0	Brentford	0	re
Man City	1	Bolton	0	r
Sheff Utd	2	Wolves	0	r
Stoke	3	Chester	2	r
Leicester	4	Brentford	1	r2N
FIFTH ROUND				
Birmghm C	5	Man City	0	
Charlton	1	Blackburn	0	
Liverpool	1	Derby	0	
Luton	0	Burnley	0	
Newcastle	1	Leicester	1	
Nottm For	2	Middlesbr	2	
Sheff Wed	0	Preston NE	2	
Stoke	0	Sheff Utd	1	
Burnley	3	Luton	0	r
Leicester	1	Newcastle	2	r
Middlesbr	6	Nottm For	2	r
SIXTH ROUND				
Charlton	2	Preston NE	1	
Liverpool	4	Birmghm C	1	
Middlesbr	1	Burnley	1	
Sheff Utd	0	Newcastle	2	

Old Pals Act

Forest full-back Joe McDonald and Luton winger Billy Bingham were in direct opposition in the 1959 Final, after playing in the same losing Sunderland side in two earlier Semi-Finals.

Burnley	1	Middlesbr	0	re
SEMI-FINAL				
Burnley	0	Liverpool	0	eN
Charlton	4	Newcastle	0	N
Burnley	1	Liverpool	0	rN
FINAL				
Charlton	1	Burnley	0	eN

1948

FIRST ROUND				
Aldershot	2	Bromsgrv	1	
Barrow	3	Carlisle	2	
Bournemt	2	Guilford	0	
Bristol R	3	Leytonstn	2	
Bromley	3	Reading	3	e
Chelthnm	5	Street	0	
Chester	3	Bshk Auck	1	
Colchester	2	Banbury S	1	
Crewe	4	S.Shields	1	
C.Palace	2	Port Vale	1	
Dartford	0	Bristol C	0	e
Exeter	1	N'hamptn	1	e
Gateshead	1	Bradford	3	
Gillinghm	1	Leyton O	0	
G.Yarmth	1	Shrewsby	4	
Hartlepl	1	Darlingtn	0	
Hull	1	Southport	1	e
Lincoln	0	Workingtn	2	
New Brig	4	Marine	0	
Newport	3	Southend	2	
Norwich	3	Mert Tyd	0	
Notts Co	9	Horsham	1	
Oldham	6	Lancaster	0	
Runcorn	4	Scunthpe	2	
Stockport	3	Accringtn	1	
Stockton	2	Grantham	1	
Swindon	4	Ipswich	2	
Tranmere	2	Stalyb C	0	
Trowbdge	1	Brighton	1	e
Vauxhall	1	Walsall	2	N
Watford	1	Torquay	1	e
Wimbledn	0	Mansfield	1	
Wrexham	5	Halifax	0	
York	0	Rochdale	1	
Brighton	5	Trowbdge	0	r
Bristol C	9	Dartford	2	r
N'hamptn	2	Exeter	0	r
Reading	3	Bromley	0	r
Southport	2	Hull	3	r
Torquay	3	Watford	0	r
SECOND ROUND				
Aldershot	0	Swindon	0	e
Bournemt	1	Bradford	0	
Bristol C	0	C.Palace	1	e
Bristol R	4	New Brig	0	
Colchester	1	Wrexham	0	
Hartlepl	1	Brighton	1	e
Hull	4	Chelthnm	2	
N'hamptn	1	Torquay	1	e
Norwich	2	Walsall	2	e
Notts Co	1	Stockton	1	e
Oldham	0	Mansfield	1	
Reading	2	Newport	0	
Rochdale	1	Gillinghm	1	e
Runcorn	0	Barrow	1	
Stockport	1	Shrewsby	1	
Tranmere	0	Chester	1	

Workingtn	1	Crewe	2	
Brighton	2	Hartlepl	1	r
Gillinghm	3	Rochdale	0	r
Shrewsby	2	Stockport	2	re
Stockton	1	Notts Co	4	rN
Swindon	2	Aldershot	0	r
Torquay	2	N'hamptn	0	r
Walsall	3	Norwich	2	r
Stockport	3	Shrewsby	2	r2eN
THIRD ROUND				
Arsenal	0	Bradfd PA	1	
Aston V	4	Man Utd	6	
Birmghm C	0	Notts Co	2	
Blackburn	0	West Ham	0	e
Blackpool	4	Leeds U	0	
Bolton	0	Tottenham	2	e
Bournemt	1	Wolves	2	
Bristol R	3	Swansea	0	
Burnley	0	Swindon	2	
Cardiff	1	Sheff Wed	2	e
Charlton	2	Newcastle	1	
Chelsea	5	Barrow	0	
Colchester	1	Huddersfld	0	
Coventry	2	Walsall	1	
Crewe	3	Sheff Utd	1	
C.Palace	0	Chester	1	
Derby	2	Chestrfld	0	
Fulham	2	Doncaster	0	
Gillinghm	1	QPR	1	e
Grimsby	1	Everton	4	
Hull	1	Middlesbr	3	
Leicester	1	Bury	0	
Liverpool	4	Nottm For	1	
Man City	2	Barnsley	1	
Mansfield	2	Stoke	4	
Millwall	1	Preston NE	2	
Plymouth	2	Luton	4	
Portsmth	4	Brighton	1	
Rotherhm	0	Brentford	3	
Southmptn	1	Sunderld	0	
Stockport	3	Torquay	0	
West Brom	2	Reading	0	
QPR	3	Gillinghm	1	r
West Ham	2	Blackburn	4	re
FOURTH ROUND				
Blackpool	4	Chester	0	
Brentford	1	Middlesbr	2	
Charlton	3	Stockport	0	
Colchester	3	Bradfd PA	2	
Crewe	0	Derby	3	
Fulham	5	Bristol R	2	
Leicester	2	Sheff Wed	1	
Luton	3	Coventry	2	
Man City	2	Chelsea	0	e
Man Utd	3	Liverpool	0	N
Portsmth	1	Preston NE	3	
QPR	3	Stoke	0	
Southmptn	3	Blackburn	2	
Swindon	1	Notts Co	0	
Tottenham	3	West Brom	1	
Wolves	1	Everton	1	e
Everton	3	Wolves	2	re
FIFTH ROUND				
Blackpool	5	Colchester	0	
Fulham	1	Everton	1	e
Man City	0	Preston NE	1	
Man Utd	2	Charlton	0	N

WHAT A STAR ✪ STANLEY MATTHEWS

He played until he was 50, and was probably the most popular footballer in England for 25 years or more. A magical winger of no great size, Matthews hated heading the ball and was hardly ever known to tackle. But nobody of his time - and few since - could match him at beating his man. He started and finished with Stoke, but his greatest days were with Blackpool in the early post-war years, when he lost two Cup Finals but won at the third attempt in the most dramatic of them all in 1953, 4-3 against Bolton after being 3-1 down with just 20 minutes to go. He was knighted in 1965.

Middlesbr	1	Derby	2	
QPR	3	Luton	1	
Southmptn	3	Swindon	0	
Tottenham	5	Leicester	2	
Everton	0	Fulham	1	r
SIXTH ROUND				
Fulham	0	Blackpool	2	
Man Utd	4	Preston NE	1	
QPR	1	Derby	1	e
Southmptn	0	Tottenham	1	
Derby	5	QPR	0	r
SEMI-FINAL				
Blackpool	3	Tottenham	1	eN
Man Utd	3	Derby	1	N
FINAL				
Man Utd	4	Blackpool	2	N

1949

FIRST ROUND				
Barnet	2	Exeter	6	
Bradford	4	Doncaster	3	
Colchester	2	Reading	4	
Crewe	5	Billngh S	0	
C.Palace	0	Bristol C	1	e
Dartford	2	Leyton O	3	
Gainsbrgh	1	Witton Ab	0	
Gateshead	3	Netherfld	0	
Halifax	0	Scunthpe	0	e
Hartlepl	1	Chester	3	
Hull	3	Accringtn	1	
Ipswich	0	Aldershot	3	
Kiddermst	0	Hereford	3	
Leytonstn	2	Watford	1	
Mansfield	4	Gloc City	0	
Millwall	1	Tooting	0	
New Brig	1	Carlisle	0	
Newport	3	Brighton	1	
N'hamptn	2	Dulwich H	1	
Norwich	1	Wellingtn	0	
Notts Co	2	Port Vale	1	
Peterboro	0	Torquay	1	
Rhyl	0	Scarboro	2	
Rochdale	1	Barrow	1	eN
Southend	1	Swansea	2	
Southport	2	Horden CW	1	
Tranmere	1	Darlingtn	2	
Walsall	2	Bristol R	1	
Walstmw A	3	Cambs T	2	
Weymouth	2	Chelmsfd	1	
Workingtn	0	Stockport	3	
Wrexham	0	Oldham	3	
Yeovil T	4	Romford	0	
York	2	Runcorn	1	
Barrow	2	Rochdale	0	r
Scunthpe	1	Halifax	0	r
SECOND ROUND				
Aldershot	1	Chester	0	
Bradford	0	New Brig	0	
Bristol C	3	Swansea	1	
Crewe	3	Millwall	2	
Darlingtn	1	Leyton O	0	
Exeter	2	Hereford	1	
Gateshead	3	Scarboro	0	
Hull	0	Reading	0	e
Leytonstn	3	Newport	4	e
Mansfield	2	N'hamptn	1	e
Notts Co	3	Barrow	2	
Scunthpe	0	Stockport	1	
Southport	2	York	2	e
Torquay	3	Norwich	1	
Walsall	4	Gainsbrgh	3	
Walstmw A	2	Oldham	2	e
Weymouth	0	Yeovil T	4	
New Brig	1	Bradford	0	r
Oldham	3	Walstmw A	1	r
Reading	1	Hull	2	r
York	0	Southport	2	r
THIRD ROUND				
Arsenal	3	Tottenham	0	
Aston V	1	Bolton	1	e
Barnsley	0	Blackpool	1	
Birmghm C	1	Leicester	1	e
Blackburn	1	Hull	2	e
Brentford	3	Middlesbr	2	e
Bristol C	1	Chelsea	3	
Burnley	2	Charlton	1	e
Crewe	0	Sunderld	2	
Derby	4	Southport	1	
Everton	1	Man City	0	
Fulham	0	Walsall	1	e
Gateshead	3	Aldershot	1	
Grimsby	2	Exeter	1	
Leeds U	1	Newport	3	
Lincoln	0	West Brom	1	
Luton	3	West Ham	1	
Man Utd	6	Bournemt	0	
Newcastle	0	Bradfd PA	2	
Nottm For	2	Liverpool	2	e
Oldham	2	Cardiff	3	
Plymouth	0	Notts Co	1	e
Portsmth	7	Stockport	0	
Preston NE	2	Mansfield	1	
QPR	0	Huddersfld	0	e
Rotherhm	4	Darlingtn	2	
Sheff Utd	5	New Brig	2	
Sheff Wed	2	Southmptn	1	
Swindon	1	Stoke	3	
Torquay	1	Coventry	0	
Wolves	6	Chestrfld	0	
Yeovil T	3	Bury	1	
Bolton	0	Aston V	0	re
Huddersfld	5	QPR	0	r
Leicester	1	Birmghm C	1	re
Liverpool	4	Nottm For	0	r
Aston V	2	Bolton	1	r2e
Birmghm C	1	Leicester	2	r2
FOURTH ROUND				
Aston V	1	Cardiff	2	
Brentford	1	Torquay	0	
Chelsea	2	Everton	0	
Derby	1	Arsenal	0	
Gateshead	1	West Brom	3	e
Grimsby	2	Hull	3	
Leicester	2	Preston NE	0	
Liverpool	1	Notts Co	0	
Luton	4	Walsall	0	
Man Utd	1	Bradfd PA	1	e
Newport	3	Huddersfld	3	e
Portsmth	2	Sheff Wed	1	
Rotherhm	0	Burnley	1	
Sheff Utd	0	Wolves	3	
Stoke	1	Blackpool	1	e
Yeovil T	2	Sunderld	1	e
Blackpool	0	Stoke	1	r
Bradfd PA	1	Man Utd	1	re
Huddersfld	1	Newport	3	r
Man Utd	5	Bradfd PA	0	r2e
FIFTH ROUND				
Brentford	4	Burnley	2	
Derby	2	Cardiff	1	
Luton	5	Leicester	5	e
Man Utd	8	Yeovil T	0	
Portsmth	3	Newport	2	e
Stoke	0	Hull	2	
West Brom	3	Chelsea	0	
Wolves	3	Liverpool	1	
Leicester	5	Luton	3	r

GIANTKILLERS

1948 Colchester 1 Huddersfield 0

Colchester had not gone beyond the First Round in the Cup before, but they set a record for a non-League club by beating three opponents of League status - Wrexham (Third Division North), Huddersfield (First) and Bradford Park Avenue (Second) before losing 5-0 at Blackpool. Under clever manager Ted Fenton and 'dieting' on the area's celebrated oysters, they generated enormous publicity by the standards of the time, enjoyed every minute of it, and gained their reward two years later by winning a place in the Football League.

SIXTH ROUND				
Brentford	0	Leicester	2	
Hull	0	Man Utd	1	
Portsmth	2	Derby	1	
Wolves	1	West Brom	0	
SEMI-FINAL				
Leicester	3	Portsmth	1	N
Man Utd	1	Wolves	1	eN
Man Utd	0	Wolves	1	rN
FINAL				
Wolves	3	Leicester	1	N

1950

FIRST ROUND				
Accringtn	0	Hartlepl	1	
Bradford	9	Fleetwood	0	
Bromley	1	Watford	2	
Carlisle	1	Lincoln	0	
Chester	4	Goole T	1	
C.Palace	0	Newport	3	
Darlingtn	2	Crewe	2	
Doncaster	5	New Brig	1	
Gateshead	3	York	1	
Gloc City	2	Norwich	3	
Gravesend	1	Torquay	3	
Hasting U	1	Gillinghm	3	
Hereford	3	Bromsgrv	0	
Ipswich	2	Brighton	1	
Leyton O	0	Southend	2	
Leytonstn	1	Chelmsfd	2	
Mansfield	4	Walsall	1	
Millwall	3	Exeter	5	
Netherfld	4	N.Shields	3	
N'hamptn	4	Walstmw A	1	
Nottm For	1	Bristol C	0	
Notts Co	4	Tilbury	0	
Nuneaton	2	King's Ln	1	
Oldham	4	Stockton	0	
Port Vale	1	Wealdstne	0	
Rhyl	0	Rochdale	3	
Southport	1	Barrow	1	
Stockport	3	Billngh S	0	
Swindon	1	Bristol R	0	
Tranmere	2	Halifax	1	
Weymouth	2	Aldershot	2	
Witton Ab	0	Mossley	1	
Wrexham	4	Grantham	1	
Yeovil T	4	Romford	1	
Aldershot	2	Weymouth	3	r
Barrow	0	Southport	1	r
Crewe	1	Darlingtn	0	r
SECOND ROUND				
Carlisle	2	Swindon	0	
Chelmsfd	1	Ipswich	1	
Crewe	1	Oldham	1	
Doncaster	1	Mansfield	0	
Exeter	2	Chester	0	
Hartlepl	1	Norwich	1	
Newport	1	Gateshead	1	
N'hamptn	4	Torquay	2	
Nottm For	0	Stockport	2	
Nuneaton	0	Mossley	0	
Port Vale	1	Tranmere	0	
Rochdale	1	Notts Co	2	
Southport	2	Bradford	1	
Watford	6	Netherfld	0	
Weymouth	2	Hereford	1	
Wrexham	2	Southend	2	
Yeovil T	3	Gillinghm	1	
Gateshead	1	Newport	2	re
Ipswich	1	Chelmsfd	0	re
Mossley	0	Nuneaton	3	r
Norwich	5	Hartlepl	1	r
Oldham	0	Crewe	0	re
Southend	2	Wrexham	0	r
Crewe	0	Oldham	3	r2N
THIRD ROUND				
Arsenal	1	Sheff Wed	0	
Aston V	2	Middlesbr	2	
Blackburn	0	Liverpool	0	
Blackpool	4	Southend	0	
Bradfd PA	0	Bournemt	1	
Brentford	0	Chelsea	1	
Bury	5	Rotherhm	4	
Cardiff	2	West Brom	2	
Carlisle	2	Leeds U	5	
Charlton	2	Fulham	2	
Chestrfld	3	Yeovil T	1	
Coventry	1	Bolton	2	
Exeter	3	Nuneaton	0	
Luton	3	Grimsby	4	
Man City	3	Derby	5	
Man Utd	4	Weymouth	0	
Newport	1	Port Vale	2	
N'hamptn	1	Southmptn	1	
Notts Co	1	Burnley	4	
Oldham	2	Newcastle	7	
Plymouth	1	Wolves	1	
Portsmth	1	Norwich	1	
QPR	0	Everton	2	
Reading	2	Doncaster	3	
Sheff Utd	3	Leicester	1	
Southport	0	Hull	0	
Stockport	4	Barnsley	2	
Stoke	0	Tottenham	1	
Sunderld	6	Huddersfld	0	
Swansea	3	Birmghm C	0	
Watford	2	Preston NE	2	
West Ham	5	Ipswich	1	
Fulham	1	Charlton	2	r
Hull	5	Southport	0	r
Liverpool	2	Blackburn	1	r
Middlesbr	0	Aston V	0	re
Norwich	0	Portsmth	2	r
Preston NE	0	Watford	1	r
Southmptn	2	N'hamptn	3	r
West Brom	0	Cardiff	1	r
Wolves	3	Plymouth	0	r
Aston V	0	Middlesbr	3	r2N
FOURTH ROUND				
Arsenal	2	Swansea	1	
Blackpool	2	Doncaster	1	
Bournemt	1	N'hamptn	1	
Burnley	2	Port Vale	1	
Bury	2	Derby	2	
Charlton	1	Cardiff	1	
Chelsea	3	Newcastle	0	
Chestrfld	3	Middlesbr	2	
Leeds U	1	Bolton	1	
Liverpool	3	Exeter	1	
Portsmth	5	Grimsby	0	
Stockport	0	Hull	0	
Tottenham	5	Sunderld	1	
Watford	0	Man Utd	1	
West Ham	1	Everton	2	
Wolves	0	Sheff Utd	0	
Bolton	2	Leeds U	3	re
Cardiff	2	Charlton	0	r
Derby	5	Bury	2	r
Hull	0	Stockport	2	r
N'hamptn	2	Bournemt	1	r
Sheff Utd	3	Wolves	4	r
FIFTH ROUND				
Arsenal	2	Burnley	0	
Chestrfld	1	Chelsea	1	
Derby	4	N'hamptn	2	
Everton	1	Tottenham	0	

Leeds U	3	Cardiff	1	
Man Utd	3	Portsmth	3	
Stockport	1	Liverpool	2	
Wolves	0	Blackpool	0	
Blackpool	1	Wolves	0	r
Chelsea	3	Chestrfld	0	r
Portsmth	1	Man Utd	3	r

SIXTH ROUND

Arsenal	1	Leeds U	0	
Chelsea	2	Man Utd	0	
Derby	1	Everton	2	
Liverpool	2	Blackpool	1	

SEMI-FINAL

Arsenal	2	Chelsea	2	N
Liverpool	2	Everton	0	N
Chelsea	0	Arsenal	1	reN

FINAL

Arsenal	2	Liverpool	0	N

1951

FIRST ROUND

Aldershot	2	Bromley	2	
Bournemt	1	Colchester	0	
Bradford	2	Oldham	2	
Bristol C	4	Gloc City	0	
Bristol R	1	Llanelli	1	
Bromsgrv	1	Hereford	3	
Bshk Auck	2	York	2	
Carlisle	2	Barrow	1	
Chelmsfd	2	Tonbridge	2	
Chester	1	Bradfd PA	2	
Cleator M	0	Tranmere	5	N
Crewe	4	N.Shields	0	
C.Palace	1	Millwall	4	
Darlingtn	2	Rotherhm	7	
Gainsbrgh	0	Plymouth	3	
Glastonby	1	Exeter	2	
Guilford	1	Dartford	5	
Halifax	2	Ashington	3	
Leyton O	1	Ipswich	2	
Linby Col	1	Gillinghm	4	
Lincoln	1	Southport	1	
Mansfield	1	Walstmw A	0	
Newport	4	Walsall	2	
Norwich	2	Watford	0	
Nottm For	6	Torquay	1	
Port Vale	3	New Brig	2	
Reading	3	Chelthnm	1	
Rochdale	3	Willingtn	1	
Scarboro	1	Rhyl	2	
Southend	0	Swindon	3	
Tooting	2	Brighton	3	
Witton Ab	1	Nelson	2	
Worcester	1	Hartlepl	4	
Wrexham	1	Accringtn	0	
Bromley	0	Aldershot	1	r
Llanelli	1	Bristol R	1	re
Oldham	2	Bradford	1	r
Southport	3	Lincoln	2	r
Tonbridge	0	Chelmsfd	1	re
York	2	Bshk Auck	1	r
Bristol R	3	Llanelli	1	r2eN

SECOND ROUND

Aldershot	3	Bournemt	0	
Ashington	1	Rochdale	2	
Brighton	2	Ipswich	0	
Bristol C	2	Wrexham	1	
Bristol R	2	Gillinghm	2	
Chelmsfd	1	Mansfield	4	
Crewe	2	Plymouth	2	
Exeter	3	Swindon	0	
Hartlepl	1	Oldham	2	
Hereford	0	Newport	3	
Millwall	1	Bradfd PA	1	
Port Vale	3	Nelson	2	
Reading	4	Dartford	0	
Rhyl	0	Norwich	1	
Rotherhm	3	Nottm For	1	
Southport	1	Carlisle	3	
York	2	Tranmere	1	
Bradfd PA	0	Millwall	1	r
Gillinghm	1	Bristol R	1	re
Plymouth	3	Crewe	0	r
Bristol R	2	Gillinghm	1	r2N

THIRD ROUND

Arsenal	0	Carlisle	0	
Aston V	2	Burnley	0	
Birmghm C	2	Man City	0	
Bolton	3	York	0	
Brighton	2	Chestrfld	1	
Bristol C	2	Blackburn	1	
Bristol R	5	Aldershot	1	
Charlton	2	Blackpool	2	
Derby	2	West Brom	2	
Fulham	1	Sheff Wed	0	
Grimsby	3	Exeter	3	
Huddersfld	2	Tottenham	0	
Hull	2	Everton	0	
Leeds U	1	Middlesbr	0	
Leicester	0	Preston NE	3	
Luton	2	Portsmth	0	
Man Utd	4	Oldham	1	
Mansfield	2	Swansea	0	
Newcastle	4	Bury	1	
Newport	3	Reading	2	
N'hamptn	3	Barnsley	1	
Norwich	3	Liverpool	1	
Notts Co	3	Southmptn	4	
Plymouth	1	Wolves	2	
QPR	3	Millwall	4	
Rochdale	2	Chelsea	3	
Rotherhm	2	Doncaster	1	
Sheff Utd	1	Gateshead	0	
Stockport	2	Brentford	1	
Stoke	2	Port Vale	2	
Sunderld	2	Coventry	0	
West Ham	2	Cardiff	1	
Blackpool	3	Charlton	0	r
Carlisle	1	Arsenal	4	r
Exeter	4	Grimsby	2	r
Port Vale	0	Stoke	1	r
West Brom	0	Derby	1	r

FOURTH ROUND

Arsenal	3	N'hamptn	2	
Blackpool	2	Stockport	1	
Bristol C	1	Brighton	0	
Derby	1	Birmghm C	3	
Exeter	1	Chelsea	1	
Hull	2	Rotherhm	0	
Luton	1	Bristol R	2	
Man Utd	4	Leeds U	0	
Millwall	0	Fulham	1	
Newcastle	3	Bolton	2	
Newport	0	Norwich	2	
Preston NE	0	Huddersfld	2	
Sheff Utd	0	Mansfield	0	
Stoke	1	West Ham	0	
Sunderld	2	Southmptn	0	
Wolves	3	Aston V	1	
Chelsea	2	Exeter	0	r
Mansfield	2	Sheff Utd	1	r

FIFTH ROUND

Birmghm C	2	Bristol C	0	
Blackpool	2	Mansfield	0	
Bristol R	3	Hull	0	
Chelsea	1	Fulham	1	
Man Utd	1	Arsenal	0	

WHAT A STAR ✪ JACKIE MILBURN

Milburn has a statue in Newcastle city centre and a place in all Geordie hearts, as a winger-cum-striker who was a dominant personality for nearly 20 years. His goals for club and country were often of the spectacular variety, as in two of his three Cup Finals. In 1951 he ran from the halfway line for the first and crashed in a left-footer from 25 yards for the second. In 1955 he headed one - something rare for him - in the first minute. He picked up another medal in 1952, without doing much, but that was one of his rare off days. Usually 'wor Jackie' was a complete menace.

Stoke	2	Newcastle	4	
Sunderld	3	Norwich	1	
Wolves	2	Huddersfld	0	
Fulham	3	Chelsea	0	r

SIXTH ROUND

Birmghm C	1	Man Utd	0	
Blackpool	1	Fulham	0	
Newcastle	0	Bristol R	0	
Sunderld	1	Wolves	1	
Bristol R	1	Newcastle	3	r
Wolves	3	Sunderld	1	r

SEMI-FINAL

Blackpool	0	Birmghm C	0	N
Newcastle	0	Wolves	0	N
Birmghm C	1	Blackpool	2	rN
Wolves	1	Newcastle	2	rN

FINAL

Newcastle	2	Blackpool	0	N

1952

FIRST ROUND

Accringtn	1	Chester	2	
Aylesbury	0	Watford	5	
Bangor C	2	Southport	2	
Barnstple	2	Folkestne	2	
Barrow	0	Chestrfld	2	
Blkhall C	2	Workingtn	5	
Blyth S	2	Bshk Auck	1	
Bradford	6	Carlisle	1	
Brighton	1	Bristol C	2	
Bristol R	3	Kettering	0	
Brush Sp	2	Weymouth	3	
Colchester	3	Port Vale	1	
Crewe	2	Lincoln	4	
C.Palace	0	Gillinghm	1	
Grimsby	4	Darlingtn	0	
Guilford	4	Hereford	1	
Hartlepl	2	Rhyl	0	
Ilkeston	0	Rochdale	2	
King's Ln	1	Exeter	3	
Leyton	3	Chippenhm	0	
Leyton O	2	Gorleston	2	
Leytonstn	2	Shrewsby	0	
Mert Tyd	2	Ipswich	2	e
Millwall	1	Plymouth	0	
Nelson	0	Oldham	4	
Newport	4	Barry T	0	
Norwich	3	N'hamptn	2	
Rawmarsh	1	Buxton	4	
Reading	1	Walsall	0	
Scunthpe	5	Billngh S	0	
Southend	6	Bournemt	1	
Stockport	2	Gateshead	2	
Stockton	1	Mansfield	1	
Swindon	2	Bedford T	0	
Tonbridge	0	Aldershot	0	
Torquay	3	Bromley	2	
Tranmere	4	Goole T	2	
Witton Ab	2	Gainsbrgh	1	
Wrexham	3	Halifax	0	
York	1	Bradfd PA	1	
Aldershot	3	Tonbridge	2	re
Bradfd PA	1	York	1	re
Folkestne	5	Barnstple	2	r
Gateshead	1	Stockport	1	re
Gorleston	0	Leyton O	0	re
Ipswich	1	Mert Tyd	0	r

Brown and out

Allan Brown, a Scottish international forward, missed two Finals through injury while with Blackpool, before playing, and losing, with Luton Town in 1959.

Mansfield	0	Stockton	2	r
Southport	3	Bangor C	0	r
Leyton O	5	Gorleston	4	r2N
Stockport	1	Gateshead	2	r2N
York	0	Bradfd PA	4	r2N

SECOND ROUND

Bradfd PA	3	Bradford	2	
Bristol R	2	Weymouth	0	
Buxton	4	Aldershot	3	
Chester	5	Leyton	2	
Colchester	2	Bristol C	1	
Gateshead	2	Guilford	0	
Gillinghm	0	Rochdale	3	
Ipswich	4	Exeter	0	
Leytonstn	2	Newport	2	
Lincoln	3	Grimsby	1	
Millwall	0	Scunthpe	0	
Norwich	3	Chestrfld	1	
Reading	1	Southport	1	
Southend	5	Oldham	0	
Stockton	2	Folkestne	1	
Swindon	3	Torquay	3	
Tranmere	1	Blyth S	1	
Watford	1	Hartlepl	2	
Witton Ab	3	Workingtn	3	
Wrexham	1	Leyton O	1	
Blyth S	1	Tranmere	1	ra
Leyton O	3	Wrexham	2	re
Newport	3	Leytonstn	0	r
Scunthpe	3	Millwall	0	r
Southport	1	Reading	1	re
Torquay	1	Swindon	1	re
Workingtn	1	Witton Ab	0	r
Reading	2	Southport	0	r2N
Swindon	3	Torquay	1	r2N
Tranmere	2	Blyth S	2	r2eN
Tranmere	5	Blyth S	1	r3N

THIRD ROUND

Barnsley	3	Colchester	0	
Bradfd PA	2	Sheff Wed	1	
Brentford	3	QPR	1	
Bristol R	2	Preston NE	0	
Burnley	1	Hartlepl	0	
Cardiff	1	Swindon	1	
Chelsea	2	Chester	2	
Doncaster	2	Buxton	0	
Fulham	0	Birmghm C	1	
Huddersfld	1	Tranmere	2	
Ipswich	2	Gateshead	2	
Leicester	1	Coventry	1	
Leyton O	0	Everton	0	
Liverpool	1	Workingtn	0	
Luton	1	Charlton	0	
Man City	2	Wolves	2	
Man Utd	0	Hull	2	
Middlesbr	2	Derby	2	
Newcastle	4	Aston V	2	
Norwich	0	Arsenal	5	
Nottm For	2	Blackburn	2	
Notts Co	4	Stockton	0	
Portsmth	4	Lincoln	0	
Reading	0	Swansea	3	
Rochdale	0	Leeds U	2	
Rotherhm	2	Bury	1	
Scunthpe	0	Tottenham	3	
Sheff Utd	2	Newport	0	
Southend	3	Southmptn	0	
Sunderld	0	Stoke	0	
West Brom	4	Bolton	0	
West Ham	2	Blackpool	1	
Blackburn	2	Nottm For	0	r
Chester	2	Chelsea	3	re
Coventry	4	Leicester	1	r
Derby	0	Middlesbr	2	r
Everton	1	Leyton O	3	r
Gateshead	3	Ipswich	3	re
Stoke	3	Sunderld	1	r
Swindon	1	Cardiff	0	re
Wolves	4	Man City	1	r
Ipswich	1	Gateshead	2	r2eN

FOURTH ROUND

Arsenal	4	Barnsley	0	
Birmghm C	0	Leyton O	1	
Blackburn	2	Hull	0	
Burnley	2	Coventry	0	
Chelsea	4	Tranmere	0	
Gateshead	0	West Brom	2	N
Leeds U	2	Bradfd PA	0	
Liverpool	2	Wolves	1	
Luton	2	Brentford	2	
Middlesbr	1	Doncaster	4	
Notts Co	1	Portsmth	3	
Southend	2	Bristol R	1	
Swansea	3	Rotherhm	0	
Swindon	1	Stoke	1	
Tottenham	0	Newcastle	3	
West Ham	0	Sheff Utd	0	
Brentford	0	Luton	0	re
Sheff Utd	4	West Ham	2	r
Stoke	0	Swindon	1	r
Luton	3	Brentford	2	r2eN

FIFTH ROUND

Blackburn	1	West Brom	0	
Burnley	2	Liverpool	0	
Leeds U	1	Chelsea	1	
Leyton O	0	Arsenal	3	
Luton	3	Swindon	1	
Portsmth	4	Doncaster	0	
Southend	1	Sheff Utd	2	
Swansea	0	Newcastle	1	
Chelsea	1	Leeds U	1	re
Leeds U	1	Chelsea	5	r2N

SIXTH ROUND

Blackburn	3	Burnley	1	
Luton	2	Arsenal	3	
Portsmth	0	Newcastle	4	
Sheff Utd	0	Chelsea	1	

SEMI-FINAL

Chelsea	1	Arsenal	1	N

Newcastle	0	Blackburn	0	N
Arsenal	3	Chelsea	0	rN
Blackburn	1	Newcastle	2	rN
FINAL				
Newcastle	1	Arsenal	0	N

1953

FIRST ROUND				
Aldershot	0	Millwall	0	
Bath C	3	Southend	1	
Beighton	0	Wrexham	3	N
Boston U	1	Oldham	2	
Bradford	4	Rhyl	0	
Bradfd PA	2	Rochdale	1	
Chester	0	Hartlepl	1	
Chestrfld	1	Workingtn	0	
Coventry	2	Bristol C	0	
C.Palace	1	Reading	1	
Darlingtn	2	Grimsby	3	
Gainsbrgh	1	Netherfld	1	
Gateshead	2	Crewe	0	
Grays Ath	0	Llanelli	5	
Guilford	2	G.Yarmth	2	
Halifax	1	Ashton U	1	
Hendon	0	N'hamptn	0	
Horden CW	1	Accringtn	2	
Ipswich	2	Bournemt	2	
Kiddermst	0	Finchley	1	
Leyton	0	Hereford	0	
Leyton O	1	Bristol R	1	
Leytonstn	0	Watford	2	
N.Shields	3	Stockport	6	
Newport	2	Walsall	1	
Peterboro	2	Torquay	1	
Port Vale	2	Exeter	1	
QPR	2	Shrewsby	2	
Scarboro	0	Mansfield	8	
Scunthpe	1	Carlisle	0	
Selby T	1	Bshk Auck	5	
Southport	3	Bangor C	1	
Swindon	5	Nwpt IOW	0	
Tonbridge	2	Norwich	2	
Tranmere	8	Ashington	1	
Walstmw A	2	Wimbledn	2	
Wellingtn	1	Gillinghm	1	
Weymouth	1	Colchester	1	
Yeovil T	1	Brighton	4	
York	1	Barrow	2	
Ashton U	1	Halifax	2	r
Bournemt	2	Ipswich	2	re
Bristol R	1	Leyton O	0	r
Colchester	4	Weymouth	0	r
Gillinghm	3	Wellingtn	0	r
G.Yarmth	1	Guilford	0	r
Hereford	3	Leyton	2	r
Millwall	7	Aldershot	1	r
Netherfld	0	Gainsbrgh	3	r
N'hamptn	2	Hendon	0	r
Norwich	1	Tonbridge	0	r
Reading	1	C.Palace	3	r
Shrewsby	2	QPR	2	re
Wimbledn	0	Walstmw A	3	r
Ipswich	3	Bournemt	2	r2N
QPR	1	Shrewsby	4	r2N
SECOND ROUND				
Accringtn	0	Mansfield	2	
Barrow	2	Millwall	2	
Bradford	1	Ipswich	1	
Bradfd PA	1	Gateshead	2	
Brighton	2	Norwich	0	
Bshk Auck	1	Coventry	4	
Colchester	3	Llanelli	2	
Finchley	3	C.Palace	1	
Grimsby	1	Bath C	0	
G.Yarmth	1	Wrexham	2	
Halifax	4	Southport	2	
Hereford	0	Scunthpe	0	
Newport	2	Gainsbrgh	1	
Peterboro	0	Bristol R	1	
Port Vale	0	Oldham	3	
Shrewsby	0	Chestrfld	0	
Stockport	3	Gillinghm	1	
Swindon	2	N'hamptn	0	
Tranmere	2	Hartlepl	1	
Walstmw A	1	Watford	1	
Chestrfld	2	Shrewsby	4	r
Ipswich	5	Bradford	1	r
Millwall	4	Barrow	1	r
Scunthpe	2	Hereford	1	r
Watford	1	Walstmw A	2	re
THIRD ROUND				
Arsenal	4	Doncaster	0	
Aston V	3	Middlesbr	1	
Barnsley	4	Brighton	3	
Bolton	3	Fulham	1	
Brentford	2	Leeds U	1	
Derby	4	Chelsea	4	
Everton	3	Ipswich	2	
Gateshead	1	Liverpool	0	
Grimsby	1	Bury	3	
Halifax	3	Cardiff	1	
Huddersfld	2	Bristol R	0	
Hull	3	Charlton	1	
Leicester	2	Notts Co	4	
Lincoln	1	Southmptn	1	
Luton	6	Blackburn	1	
Man City	7	Swindon	0	
Mansfield	0	Nottm For	1	
Millwall	0	Man Utd	1	
Newcastle	3	Swansea	0	
Newport	1	Sheff Utd	4	
Oldham	1	Birmghm C	3	
Plymouth	4	Coventry	1	
Portsmth	1	Burnley	1	
Preston NE	5	Wolves	2	
Rotherhm	2	Colchester	2	
Sheff Wed	1	Blackpool	2	
Shrewsby	2	Finchley	0	
Stoke	2	Wrexham	1	
Sunderld	1	Scunthpe	1	
Tranmere	1	Tottenham	1	
Walstmw A	2	Stockport	1	
West Ham	1	West Brom	4	
Burnley	3	Portsmth	1	r
Chelsea	1	Derby	0	re
Colchester	0	Rotherhm	2	r
Scunthpe	1	Sunderld	2	r
Southmptn	2	Lincoln	1	r
Tottenham	9	Tranmere	1	r
FOURTH ROUND				
Arsenal	6	Bury	2	
Aston V	0	Brentford	0	
Blackpool	1	Huddersfld	0	
Bolton	1	Notts Co	1	
Burnley	2	Sunderld	0	
Chelsea	1	West Brom	1	
Everton	4	Nottm For	1	
Halifax	1	Stoke	0	
Hull	1	Gateshead	2	
Man City	1	Luton	1	
Man Utd	1	Walstmw A	1	
Newcastle	1	Rotherhm	3	
Plymouth	1	Barnsley	0	
Preston NE	2	Tottenham	2	

GIANTKILLERS

1949 Yeovil 2 Sunderland 1

Yeovil have the best Cup-fighting record of any non-League team, and this win over the 'Bank of England' club remains their greatest ever. It happened in the Fourth Round after an earlier victory over Second Division Bury, and gave the little Somerset club from the Southern League an indelible place in soccer history. Player-manager Alec Stock, who got to an FA Cup Final with Fulham 26 years later, scored the first goal and made the second, but they were all heroes. Even an 8-0 defeat by Manchester United in the next round failed to take the shine off Yeovil's glory.

Sheff Utd	1	Birmghm C	1	
Shrewsby	1	Southmptn	4	
Birmghm C	3	Sheff Utd	1	r
Brentford	1	Aston V	2	r
Luton	5	Man City	1	r
Notts Co	2	Bolton	2	re
Tottenham	1	Preston NE	0	r
Walstmw A	2	Man Utd	5	rN
West Brom	0	Chelsea	0	re
Bolton	1	Notts Co	0	r2N
Chelsea	1	West Brom	1	r2eN
West Brom	0	Chelsea	4	r3N
FIFTH ROUND				
Blackpool	1	Southmptn	1	
Burnley	0	Arsenal	2	
Chelsea	0	Birmghm C	4	
Everton	2	Man Utd	1	
Halifax	0	Tottenham	3	
Luton	0	Bolton	1	
Plymouth	0	Gateshead	1	
Rotherhm	1	Aston V	3	
Southmptn	1	Blackpool	2	r
SIXTH ROUND				
Arsenal	1	Blackpool	2	
Aston V	0	Everton	1	
Birmghm C	1	Tottenham	1	
Gateshead	0	Bolton	1	
Tottenham	2	Birmghm C	2	re
Birmghm C	0	Tottenham	1	r2N
SEMI-FINAL				
Blackpool	2	Tottenham	1	N
Bolton	4	Everton	3	N
FINAL				
Blackpool	4	Bolton	3	N

1954

FIRST ROUND				
Aldershot	5	Wellingtn	3	
Barnsley	5	York	2	
Bath C	0	Walsall	3	
Blyth S	0	Accringtn	1	
Brighton	5	Coventry	1	
Cambridge	2	Newport	2	
Colchester	1	Millwall	1	
Crewe	0	Bradford	0	
Darlingtn	1	Port Vale	3	
Exeter	1	Hereford	1	
Finchley	1	Southend	3	
Gainsbrgh	1	Chestrfld	4	
Gateshead	1	Tranmere	2	
Grimsby	2	Rochdale	0	
G.Yarmth	1	C.Palace	0	
Halifax	0	Rhyl	0	
Hartlepl	1	Mansfield	1	
Harwich	2	Headingtn	3	
Hasting U	1	Guilford	0	
Hitchin	1	Peterboro	3	
Horden CW	0	Wrexham	1	
Ipswich	4	Reading	1	
Leyton O	3	Kettering	0	
N'hamptn	3	Llanelli	0	
Nuneaton	3	Watford	0	
QPR	2	Shrewsby	0	
Scunthpe	9	Boston U	0	
Selby T	0	Bradfd PA	2	
Southmptn	1	Bournemt	1	
Southport	1	Carlisle	0	
Spennym'r	0	Barrow	3	
Stockport	4	Chester	2	
Swindon	2	Nwpt IOW	1	
Torquay	1	Bristol C	3	
Walstmw A	1	Gillinghm	0	
Weymouth	2	Bedford T	0	
Wigan Ath	4	Scarboro	0	
Witton Ab	4	Nelson	1	
Workingtn	3	Ferryhill	0	
Yeovil T	0	Norwich	2	
Bournemt	3	Southmptn	1	r
Bradford	0	Crewe	1	r
Hereford	2	Exeter	0	r
Mansfield	0	Hartlepl	3	r
Millwall	4	Colchester	0	r
Newport	1	Cambridge	2	r
Rhyl	4	Halifax	3	re
SECOND ROUND				
Accringtn	2	Tranmere	2	
Barrow	5	G.Yarmth	2	
Cambridge	1	Bradfd PA	2	
Hasting U	4	Swindon	1	
Ipswich	2	Walstmw A	2	
Leyton O	4	Weymouth	0	
Millwall	3	Headingtn	3	
N'hamptn	1	Hartlepl	1	
Norwich	2	Barnsley	1	
Peterboro	2	Aldershot	1	
QPR	1	Nuneaton	1	
Rhyl	0	Bristol C	3	
Scunthpe	1	Bournemt	0	
Southend	1	Chestrfld	2	
Southport	1	Port Vale	1	
Stockport	2	Workingtn	1	
Walsall	3	Crewe	0	
Wigan Ath	4	Hereford	1	
Witton Ab	1	Grimsby	1	
Wrexham	1	Brighton	1	
Brighton	1	Wrexham	1	re
Grimsby	6	Witton Ab	1	r
Hartlepl	1	N'hamptn	0	re
Headingtn	1	Millwall	0	r
Nuneaton	1	QPR	2	r
Port Vale	2	Southport	0	r
Tranmere	5	Accringtn	1	r
Walstmw A	0	Ipswich	1	r
Wrexham	3	Brighton	1	r2N
THIRD ROUND				
Arsenal	5	Aston V	1	
Barrow	2	Swansea	2	
Blackpool	1	Luton	1	
Bolton	1	Liverpool	0	
Bradfd PA	2	Man City	5	
Brentford	0	Hull	0	
Bristol C	1	Rotherhm	3	
Bristol R	0	Blackburn	1	
Burnley	5	Man Utd	3	
Cardiff	3	Peterboro	1	
Chestrfld	2	Bury	0	
Derby	0	Preston NE	2	
Everton	2	Notts Co	1	
Grimsby	5	Fulham	5	
Hasting U	3	Norwich	3	
Ipswich	3	Oldham	3	
Leeds U	3	Tottenham	3	
Lincoln	1	Walsall	1	
Middlesbr	0	Leicester	0	
Newcastle	2	Wigan Ath	2	
Plymouth	2	Nottm For	0	
Portsmth	3	Charlton	3	
QPR	0	Port Vale	1	
Sheff Wed	1	Sheff Utd	1	
Stockport	0	Headingtn	0	
Stoke	6	Hartlepl	2	
Sunderld	0	Doncaster	2	
Tranmere	2	Leyton O	2	
West Brom	1	Chelsea	0	
West Ham	4	Huddersfld	0	
Wolves	1	Birmghm C	2	
Wrexham	3	Scunthpe	3	
Charlton	2	Portsmth	3	re
Fulham	3	Grimsby	1	r
Headingtn	1	Stockport	0	r

GIANTKILLERS

1953 Port Vale 2 Blackpool 0

Port Vale had one of the most successful seasons of any club. They won the Third Division North title with 11 points to spare and lost only four matches of a 54-game season. They conceded just 25 goals, and Albert Leake scored in six of their seven Cup rounds, including the pair that knocked out holders Blackpool in the Fifth Round. Leake also scored the first in the Semi-Final before West Brom came back to win 2-1, with a freak goal and a disputed penalty.

Hull	2	Brentford	2	re
Leicester	3	Middlesbr	2	r
Leyton O	4	Tranmere	1	r
Luton	0	Blackpool	0	re
Norwich	3	Hasting U	0	r
Oldham	0	Ipswich	1	r
Scunthpe	3	Wrexham	1	r
Sheff Utd	1	Sheff Wed	3	r
Swansea	4	Barrow	2	r
Tottenham	1	Leeds U	0	r
Walsall	1	Lincoln	1	re
Wigan Ath	2	Newcastle	3	r
Blackpool	1	Luton	1	r2eN
Brentford	2	Hull	5	r2N
Lincoln	2	Walsall	1	r2N
Luton	0	Blackpool	2	r3N

FOURTH ROUND

Arsenal	1	Norwich	2	
Blackburn	2	Hull	2	
Burnley	1	Newcastle	1	
Cardiff	0	Port Vale	2	
Everton	3	Swansea	0	
Headingtn	2	Bolton	4	
Ipswich	1	Birmghm C	0	
Leyton O	2	Fulham	1	
Lincoln	0	Preston NE	2	
Man City	0	Tottenham	1	
Plymouth	0	Doncaster	2	
Scunthpe	1	Portsmth	1	
Sheff Wed	0	Chestrfld	0	
Stoke	0	Leicester	0	
West Brom	4	Rotherhm	0	
West Ham	1	Blackpool	1	
Blackpool	3	West Ham	1	r
Chestrfld	2	Sheff Wed	4	r
Hull	2	Blackburn	1	r
Leicester	3	Stoke	1	r
Newcastle	1	Burnley	0	r
Portsmth	2	Scunthpe	2	re
Scunthpe	0	Portsmth	4	r2N

FIFTH ROUND

Bolton	0	Portsmth	0	
Hull	1	Tottenham	1	
Leyton O	3	Doncaster	1	
Norwich	1	Leicester	2	
Port Vale	2	Blackpool	0	
Preston NE	6	Ipswich	1	
Sheff Wed	3	Everton	1	
West Brom	3	Newcastle	2	
Portsmth	1	Bolton	2	r
Tottenham	2	Hull	0	r

SIXTH ROUND

Leicester	1	Preston NE	1	
Leyton O	0	Port Vale	1	
Sheff Wed	1	Bolton	1	
West Brom	3	Tottenham	0	
Bolton	0	Sheff Wed	2	r
Preston NE	2	Leicester	2	re
Leicester	1	Preston NE	3	r2N

SEMI-FINAL

Preston NE	2	Sheff Wed	0	N
West Brom	2	Port Vale	1	N

FINAL

West Brom	3	Preston NE	2	N

1955

FIRST ROUND

Accringtn	7	Cresswl C	1	
Aldershot	3	Chelmsfd	1	
Barnet	1	Southmptn	4	
Barnsley	3	Wigan Ath	2	
Barnstple	1	Bournemt	4	
Barrow	1	Darlingtn	1	
Boston U	1	Blyth S	1	
Bradford	3	Mansfield	1	
Bradfd PA	2	Southport	0	
Brentford	2	Nuneaton	1	
Brighton	5	Tunbge W	0	
Bristol C	1	Southend	2	
Bshk Auck	5	Kettering	1	
Corby T	0	Watford	2	
Crook T	5	Stanley	3	
Dorchstr	2	Bedford T	0	
Frome T	0	Leyton O	3	
Gateshead	6	Chester	0	
Gillinghm	2	Newport	0	
Grimsby	2	Halifax	1	
Hartlepl	1	Chestrfld	0	
Hinckley A	4	Nwpt IOW	3	
Horden CW	0	Scunthpe	1	
Hounslow	2	Hasting U	4	
Mert Tyd	1	Wellingtn	1	
Millwall	3	Exeter	2	
Netherfld	3	Wrexham	3	
N'hamptn	0	Coventry	1	
Norwich	4	Headingtn	2	
Oldham	1	Crewe	0	
QPR	2	Walstmw A	2	
Reading	3	Colchester	3	
Selby T	2	Rhyl	1	
Stockport	0	Carlisle	1	
Swindon	0	C.Palace	2	
Torquay	4	Cambridge	0	
Tranmere	3	Rochdale	3	
Walsall	5	Shrewsby	2	
Workingtn	5	Hyde Utd	1	
York	3	Scarboro	2	
Blyth S	5	Boston U	4	r
Colchester	1	Reading	2	r
Darlingtn	2	Barrow	1	r
Rochdale	1	Tranmere	0	r
Walstmw A	2	QPR	2	re
Wellingtn	1	Mert Tyd	6	r
Wrexham	4	Netherfld	0	r
QPR	0	Walstmw A	4	r2N

SECOND ROUND

Blyth S	1	Torquay	3	
Bournemt	1	Oldham	0	
Bradford	7	Mert Tyd	1	
Bradfd PA	2	Southend	3	
Brentford	4	Crook T	1	
Carlisle	2	Watford	2	
Coventry	4	Scunthpe	0	
C.Palace	2	Bshk Auck	4	
Dorchstr	2	York	5	
Gateshead	3	Barnsley	3	
Gillinghm	1	Reading	1	
Grimsby	4	Southmptn	1	
Hartlepl	4	Aldershot	0	
Leyton O	0	Workingtn	1	
Millwall	3	Accringtn	2	
Norwich	0	Brighton	0	
Rochdale	2	Hinckley A	1	
Selby T	0	Hasting U	2	

Just two

Bobby Charlton and Bill Foulkes were the only two of Man Utd's 1957 Final team who also played in the Final a year later... after the Munich air crash killed eight of their former team-mates.

Walstmw A	0	Darlingtn	3	
Wrexham	1	Walsall	2	
Barnsley	0	Gateshead	1	r
Brighton	5	Norwich	1	r
Reading	5	Gillinghm	3	r
Watford	4	Carlisle	1	r

THIRD ROUND

Arsenal	1	Cardiff	0	
Blackburn	0	Swansea	2	
Blackpool	0	York	2	
Bolton	3	Millwall	1	
Bournemt	0	West Brom	1	
Brentford	1	Bradford	1	
Brighton	2	Aston V	2	
Bristol R	2	Portsmth	1	
Bury	1	Stoke	1	
Chelsea	2	Walsall	0	
Derby	1	Man City	3	
Everton	3	Southend	1	
Fulham	2	Preston NE	3	
Gateshead	0	Tottenham	2	
Grimsby	2	Wolves	5	
Hartlepl	1	Darlingtn	1	
Huddersfld	3	Coventry	3	
Hull	0	Birmghm C	2	
Ipswich	2	Bshk Auck	2	
Leeds U	2	Torquay	2	
Lincoln	1	Liverpool	1	
Luton	5	Workingtn	0	
Middlesbr	1	Notts Co	4	
Plymouth	0	Newcastle	1	
Reading	1	Man Utd	1	
Rochdale	1	Charlton	3	
Rotherhm	1	Leicester	0	
Sheff Utd	1	Nottm For	3	
Sheff Wed	2	Hasting U	1	
Sunderld	1	Burnley	0	
Watford	1	Doncaster	2	
West Ham	2	Port Vale	2	
Aston V	4	Brighton	2	r
Bradford	2	Brentford	2	re
Bshk Auck	3	Ipswich	0	r
Coventry	1	Huddersfld	2	re
Darlingtn	2	Hartlepl	2	re
Liverpool	1	Lincoln	0	re
Man Utd	4	Reading	1	r
Port Vale	3	West Ham	1	r
Stoke	1	Bury	1	r
Torquay	4	Leeds U	0	r
Brentford	1	Bradford	0	r2N
Bury	3	Stoke	3	r2eN
Hartlepl	2	Darlingtn	0	r2N

Stoke	2	Bury	2	r3eN
Bury	2	Stoke	3	r4eN

FOURTH ROUND

Birmghm C	2	Bolton	1	
Bristol R	1	Chelsea	3	
Bshk Auck	1	York	3	
Doncaster	0	Aston V	0	
Everton	0	Liverpool	4	
Hartlepl	1	Nottm For	1	
Man City	2	Man Utd	0	
Newcastle	3	Brentford	2	
Preston NE	3	Sunderld	3	
Rotherhm	1	Luton	5	
Sheff Wed	1	Notts Co	1	
Swansea	3	Stoke	1	
Torquay	0	Huddersfld	1	
Tottenham	4	Port Vale	2	
West Brom	2	Charlton	4	
Wolves	1	Arsenal	0	
Aston V	2	Doncaster	2	re
Nottm For	2	Hartlepl	1	re
Notts Co	1	Sheff Wed	0	re
Sunderld	2	Preston NE	0	r
Doncaster	1	Aston V	1	r2eN
Aston V	0	Doncaster	0	r3N
Doncaster	3	Aston V	1	r4N

FIFTH ROUND

Birmghm C	2	Doncaster	1	
Liverpool	0	Huddersfld	2	
Luton	0	Man City	2	
Nottm For	1	Newcastle	1	
Notts Co	1	Chelsea	0	
Swansea	2	Sunderld	2	
Wolves	4	Charlton	1	
York	3	Tottenham	1	
Newcastle	2	Nottm For	2	re
Sunderld	1	Swansea	0	r
Newcastle	2	Nottm For	1	r2e

SIXTH ROUND

Birmghm C	0	Man City	1	
Huddersfld	1	Newcastle	1	
Notts Co	0	York	1	
Sunderld	2	Wolves	0	
Newcastle	2	Huddersfld	0	re

SEMI-FINAL

Man City	1	Sunderld	0	N
Newcastle	1	York	1	N
York	0	Newcastle	2	rN

FINAL

Newcastle	3	Man City	1	N

1956

FIRST ROUND

Accringtn	3	Wrexham	1	
Barrow	0	Crewe	0	
Bedford T	3	Leyton	0	
Boston U	3	Northwich	2	
Bradford	3	Oldham	1	
Brentford	4	March	0	
Brighton	8	Newport	1	
Bshk Auck	3	Durham C	1	
Chestrfld	1	Chester	0	
Coventry	0	Exeter	1	
Crook T	2	Derby	2	
C.Palace	0	Southmptn	0	
Darlingtn	0	Carlisle	0	
Easington	0	Tranmere	2	
Gillinghm	1	Shrewsby	1	
Goole T	1	Halifax	2	
Halesowen	2	Hendon	4	
Hartlepl	3	Gateshead	0	
Hasting U	6	Southall	1	
Leyton O	7	Lovells A	1	
Mansfield	2	Stockport	0	
Margate	2	Walsall	2	
Netherfld	1	Grimsby	5	
N'hamptn	4	Millwall	1	
Norwich	4	Dorchstr	0	
Peterboro	3	Ipswich	1	
Reading	1	Bournemt	0	
Rhyl	0	Bradfd PA	3	
Rochdale	0	York	1	
Scunthpe	3	Shildon	0	
Skegness	0	Worksop	4	
Southend	2	QPR	0	
Southport	6	Ashton U	1	
Swindon	4	Hereford	0	
Torquay	2	Colchester	0	
Watford	5	Ramsgate A	3	
Weymouth	3	Salisbury	2	
Workingtn	4	Scarboro	2	
Wycombe	1	Burton Al	3	
Yeovil T	1	Aldershot	1	
Aldershot	1	Yeovil T	1	re
Carlisle	0	Darlingtn	0	re
Crewe	2	Barrow	3	re
Derby	5	Crook T	1	r
Shrewsby	4	Gillinghm	1	re
Southmptn	2	C.Palace	0	r
Walsall	6	Margate	1	r
Darlingtn	3	Carlisle	1	r2N
Yeovil T	0	Aldershot	3	r2N

Strange but true!

Leicester, beaten by Wolves in the 1949 Final, finished that season 19th in Division Two.

SECOND ROUND

Bedford T	3	Watford	2	
Bradford	2	Worksop	2	
Bradfd PA	4	Workingtn	3	
Brighton	1	Norwich	2	
Bshk Auck	0	Scunthpe	0	
Chestrfld	1	Hartlepl	2	
Darlingtn	0	Accringtn	1	
Derby	1	Boston U	6	
Exeter	6	Hendon	2	
Halifax	0	Burton Al	0	
Leyton O	4	Brentford	1	
N'hamptn	4	Hasting U	1	
Reading	2	Aldershot	2	
Shrewsby	0	Torquay	0	
Southport	0	Grimsby	0	
Swindon	1	Peterboro	1	
Tranmere	0	Barrow	3	
Walsall	2	Southmptn	1	
Weymouth	0	Southend	1	
York	2	Mansfield	1	
Aldershot	3	Reading	0	re
Burton Al	1	Halifax	0	r
Grimsby	3	Southport	2	r
Peterboro	1	Swindon	2	re
Scunthpe	2	Bshk Auck	0	r
Torquay	5	Shrewsby	1	r
Worksop	1	Bradford	0	r

THIRD ROUND

Aldershot	1	Barnsley	2	
Arsenal	2	Bedford T	2	
Aston V	1	Hull	1	
Bolton	3	Huddersfld	0	
Bradfd PA	0	Middlesbr	4	
Bristol R	4	Man Utd	0	
Bury	0	Burnley	1	
Charlton	7	Burton Al	0	
Doncaster	3	Nottm For	0	
Everton	3	Bristol C	1	
Exeter	0	Stoke	0	
Hartlepl	0	Chelsea	1	
Leeds U	1	Cardiff	2	
Leyton O	1	Plymouth	0	
Lincoln	2	Southend	3	
Liverpool	2	Accringtn	0	
Luton	0	Leicester	4	
Man City	2	Blackpool	1	
N'hamptn	1	Blackburn	2	
Notts Co	0	Fulham	1	
Portsmth	3	Grimsby	1	
Rotherhm	1	Scunthpe	1	
Sheff Utd	5	Barrow	0	
Sheff Wed	1	Newcastle	3	
Sunderld	4	Norwich	2	
Swansea	1	York	2	
Swindon	1	Worksop	0	
Torquay	1	Birmghm C	7	
Tottenham	4	Boston U	0	
Walsall	0	Port Vale	1	
West Ham	5	Preston NE	2	
Wolves	1	West Brom	2	
Bedford T	1	Arsenal	2	re
Hull	1	Aston V	2	r
Scunthpe	4	Rotherhm	2	r
Stoke	3	Exeter	0	r

FOURTH ROUND

Arsenal	4	Aston V	1	
Barnsley	0	Blackburn	1	
Bolton	1	Sheff Utd	2	
Bristol R	1	Doncaster	1	
Burnley	1	Chelsea	1	
Charlton	2	Swindon	1	
Fulham	4	Newcastle	5	
Leicester	3	Stoke	3	
Leyton O	0	Birmghm C	4	
Liverpool	3	Scunthpe	3	
Port Vale	2	Everton	3	
Southend	0	Man City	1	
Tottenham	3	Middlesbr	1	
West Brom	2	Portsmth	0	
West Ham	2	Cardiff	1	
York	0	Sunderld	0	
Chelsea	1	Burnley	1	re
Doncaster	1	Bristol R	0	r
Scunthpe	1	Liverpool	2	re
Stoke	2	Leicester	1	r
Sunderld	2	York	1	r
Burnley	2	Chelsea	2	r2eN

Chelsea 0 Burnley 0 r3eN
Burnley 0 Chelsea 2 r4N

FIFTH ROUND
Charlton 0 Arsenal 2
Doncaster 0 Tottenham 2
Everton 1 Chelsea 0
Man City 0 Liverpool 0
Newcastle 2 Stoke 1
Sheff Utd 0 Sunderld 0
West Brom 0 Birmghm C 1
West Ham 0 Blackburn 0
Blackburn 2 West Ham 3 r
Liverpool 1 Man City 2 r
Sunderld 1 Sheff Utd 0 r

SIXTH ROUND
Arsenal 1 Birmghm C 3
Man City 2 Everton 1
Newcastle 0 Sunderld 2
Tottenham 3 West Ham 3
West Ham 1 Tottenham 2 r

SEMI-FINAL
Birmghm C 3 Sunderld 0 N
Man City 1 Tottenham 0 N

FINAL
Man City 3 Birmghm C 1 N

1957

FIRST ROUND
Accringtn 4 Morecambe 1
Boston U 0 Bradfd PA 2
Bournemt 8 Burton Al 0
Brentford 3 Guilford 0
Brighton 1 Millwall 1
Bshk Auck 2 Tranmere 1
Carlisle 6 Billngh S 1
Chelthnm 1 Reading 2
Chester 0 Barrow 0
Colchester 1 Southend 4
Crewe 2 Wrexham 2
C.Palace 2 Walstmw A 0
Darlingtn 7 Evenwood 2
Derby 2 Bradford 1
Ely City 2 Torquay 6
Exeter 0 Plymouth 2
Halifax 2 Oldham 3
Hartlepl 3 Selby T 1
Hereford 3 Aldershot 2
Hull 4 Gateshead 0
Ilkeston 1 Blyth S 5
Ipswich 4 Hasting U 0
Mansfield 1 Workingtn 1
Margate 3 Dunstable 1
New Brig 3 Stockport 3
Nwpt IOW 0 Watford 6
Norwich 2 Bedford T 4
QPR 4 Dorchstr 0
Rhyl 3 Scarboro 2
S.Shields 2 Chestrfld 2
Scunthpe 1 Rochdale 0
Southmptn 2 N'hamptn 0
Southport 0 York 0
Swindon 2 Coventry 1
Tooting 2 Bromsgrv 1
Walsall 0 Newport 1
Weymouth 1 Shrewsby 0
Wigan Ath 1 Goole T 2
Yeovil T 1 Peterboro 3
Yiewsley 2 Gillinghm 2
Barrow 3 Chester 1 r
Chestrfld 4 S.Shields 0 r
Gillinghm 2 Yiewsley 0 r
Millwall 3 Brighton 1 r
Stockport 2 New Brig 3 r
Workingtn 2 Mansfield 1 r
Wrexham 2 Crewe 1 r
York 2 Southport 1 r

SECOND ROUND
Accringtn 2 Oldham 1
Blyth S 0 Hartlepl 1
Brentford 1 C.Palace 1
Carlisle 2 Darlingtn 1
Chestrfld 4 Barrow 1
Derby 1 New Brig 3
Gillinghm 1 Newport 2
Goole T 2 Workingtn 2
Hereford 2 Southend 3
Hull 2 York 1
Millwall 4 Margate 0
Peterboro 3 Bradfd PA 0
Reading 1 Bedford T 0
Rhyl 3 Bshk Auck 1
Scunthpe 0 Wrexham 0
Southmptn 3 Weymouth 2
Swindon 0 Bournemt 1
Tooting 0 QPR 2
Torquay 1 Plymouth 0
Watford 1 Ipswich 3
C.Palace 3 Brentford 2 re
Workingtn 0 Goole T 1 r
Wrexham 6 Scunthpe 2 re

THIRD ROUND
Arsenal 4 Stoke 2
Barnsley 3 Port Vale 3
Bolton 2 Blackpool 3
Bournemt 2 Accringtn 0
Bristol C 4 Rotherhm 1
Burnley 7 Chestrfld 0
Bury 1 Portsmth 3
Carlisle 3 Birmghm C 3
Doncaster 1 West Brom 1
Everton 1 Blackburn 0
Hartlepl 3 Man Utd 4
Huddersfld 0 Sheff Utd 0
Hull 3 Bristol R 4
Ipswich 2 Fulham 3
Leeds U 1 Cardiff 2
Leyton O 0 Chelsea 2
Luton 2 Aston V 2
Middlesbr 1 Charlton 1
Millwall 2 C.Palace 0
New Brig 2 Torquay 1
Newcastle 1 Man City 1
Newport 3 Southmptn 3
Nottm For 6 Goole T 0
Notts Co 1 Rhyl 3
Peterboro 2 Lincoln 2
Preston NE 0 Sheff Wed 0
Southend 2 Liverpool 1
Sunderld 4 QPR 0
Tottenham 2 Leicester 0
West Ham 5 Grimsby 3
Wolves 5 Swansea 3
Wrexham 1 Reading 1
Aston V 2 Luton 0 r
Birmghm C 4 Carlisle 0 r
Charlton 2 Middlesbr 3 r
Lincoln 4 Peterboro 5 re
Man City 4 Newcastle 5 re
Port Vale 0 Barnsley 1 r
Reading 1 Wrexham 2 r
Sheff Utd 1 Huddersfld 1 re
Sheff Wed 2 Preston NE 2 re
Southmptn 0 Newport 1 r
West Brom 2 Doncaster 0 r
Huddersfld 2 Sheff Utd 1 r2N
Preston NE 5 Sheff Wed 1 r2N

FOURTH ROUND
Blackpool 6 Fulham 2
Bristol C 3 Rhyl 0
Bristol R 1 Preston NE 4
Burnley 9 New Brig 0
Cardiff 0 Barnsley 1
Everton 2 West Ham 1
Huddersfld 3 Peterboro 1
Middlesbr 2 Aston V 3
Millwall 2 Newcastle 1
Newport 0 Arsenal 2
Portsmth 1 Nottm For 3
Southend 1 Birmghm C 6
Tottenham 4 Chelsea 0
West Brom 4 Sunderld 2
Wolves 0 Bournemt 1
Wrexham 0 Man Utd 5

FIFTH ROUND
Aston V 2 Bristol C 1
Barnsley 1 Nottm For 2
Blackpool 0 West Brom 0
Bournemt 3 Tottenham 1
Huddersfld 1 Burnley 2
Man Utd 1 Everton 0
Millwall 1 Birmghm C 4
Preston NE 3 Arsenal 3
Arsenal 2 Preston NE 1 r
West Brom 2 Blackpool 1 r

SIXTH ROUND
Birmghm C 0 Nottm For 0
Bournemt 1 Man Utd 2
Burnley 1 Aston V 1
West Brom 2 Arsenal 2
Arsenal 1 West Brom 2 r
Aston V 2 Burnley 0 r
Nottm For 0 Birmghm C 1 r

SEMI-FINAL
Aston V 2 West Brom 2 N
Man Utd 2 Birmghm C 0 N
West Brom 0 Aston V 1 rN

FINAL
Aston V 2 Man Utd 1 N

Beer we go...

Derby's winning team in 1946 had a part-time manager, Stuart McMillan. His other job was running a pub, the Nag's Head.

1958

FIRST ROUND

Aldershot	0	Worcester	0	
Bath C	2	Exeter	1	
Boston U	5	Billngh S	2	
Bradford	6	Scarboro	0	
Brighton	2	Walsall	1	
Bshk Auck	0	Bury	0	
Carlisle	5	Rhyl	1	
Chester	4	Gateshead	3	
Clapton	1	QPR	1	
Coventry	1	Walstmw A	0	
Dorchstr	3	Wycombe	2	
Durham C	3	Spalding	1	
Gillinghm	10	Gorleston	1	
Guilford	2	Yeovil T	2	
Hartlepl	5	Prescot C	0	
Hull	2	Crewe	1	
Mansfield	2	Halifax	0	
Margate	2	C.Palace	3	
Millwall	1	Brentford	0	
Nwpt IOW	0	Hereford	3	
N'hamptn	3	Newport	0	
Norwich	6	Redhill	1	
Oldham	2	Bradfd PA	0	
Oswest T	1	Bournemt	5	
Peterboro	3	Torquay	3	
Plymouth	6	Watford	2	
Port Vale	2	Shrewsby	1	
Reading	1	Swindon	0	
Rochdale	0	Darlingtn	2	
S.Shields	3	Frickley	2	
Scunthpe	2	Goole T	1	
Southport	1	Wigan Ath	2	
Stockport	2	Barrow	1	
Tranmere	2	Witton Ab	1	
Trowbdge	0	Southend	2	
Walton&H	1	Southmptn	6	
Wisbech	1	Colchester	0	
Workingtn	8	Crook T	1	
Wrexham	0	Accringtn	1	
York	1	Chestrfld	0	
Bury	4	Bshk Auck	1	r
QPR	3	Clapton	1	r
Torquay	1	Peterboro	0	r
Worcester	2	Aldershot	2	re
Yeovil T	1	Guilford	0	r
Aldershot	3	Worcester	2	r2eN

SECOND ROUND

Aldershot	4	Coventry	1	
Carlisle	1	Accringtn	1	
Chester	3	Bradford	3	
C.Palace	1	Southmptn	0	
Darlingtn	5	Boston U	3	
Durham C	0	Tranmere	3	
Hereford	6	QPR	1	
Millwall	1	Gillinghm	1	
N'hamptn	4	Bournemt	1	
Norwich	1	Brighton	1	
Oldham	1	Workingtn	5	
Plymouth	5	Dorchstr	2	
Port Vale	2	Hull	2	
Reading	2	Wisbech	1	
S.Shields	1	York	3	
Scunthpe	2	Bury	0	
Stockport	2	Hartlepl	1	
Torquay	1	Southend	1	
Wigan Ath	1	Mansfield	1	
Yeovil T	2	Bath C	0	
Accringtn	3	Carlisle	2	r
Bradford	3	Chester	1	r
Brighton	1	Norwich	2	r
Gillinghm	6	Millwall	1	r
Hull	4	Port Vale	3	re
Mansfield	3	Wigan Ath	1	r
Southend	2	Torquay	1	r

THIRD ROUND

Accringtn	2	Bristol C	2	
Bristol R	5	Mansfield	0	
Burnley	4	Swansea	2	
C.Palace	0	Ipswich	1	
Doncaster	0	Chelsea	2	
Fulham	4	Yeovil T	0	
Hereford	0	Sheff Wed	3	
Huddersfld	2	Charlton	2	
Hull	1	Barnsley	1	
Leeds U	1	Cardiff	2	
Leyton O	1	Reading	0	
Lincoln	0	Wolves	1	
Liverpool	1	Southend	1	
Middlesbr	5	Derby	0	
N'hamptn	3	Arsenal	1	
Norwich	1	Darlingtn	2	
Nottm For	2	Gillinghm	0	
Notts Co	2	Tranmere	0	
Plymouth	1	Newcastle	6	
Portsmth	5	Aldershot	1	
Preston NE	0	Bolton	3	
Rotherhm	1	Blackburn	4	
Scunthpe	1	Bradford	0	
Sheff Utd	5	Grimsby	1	
Stockport	3	Luton	0	
Stoke	1	Aston V	1	
Sunderld	2	Everton	2	
Tottenham	4	Leicester	0	
West Brom	5	Man City	1	
West Ham	5	Blackpool	1	
Workingtn	1	Man Utd	3	
York	3	Birmghm C	0	
Aston V	3	Stoke	3	re
Barnsley	0	Hull	2	r
Bristol C	3	Accringtn	1	r
Charlton	1	Huddersfld	0	r
Everton	3	Sunderld	1	r
Southend	2	Liverpool	3	r
Stoke	2	Aston V	0	r2N

FOURTH ROUND

Bristol R	2	Burnley	2	
Cardiff	4	Leyton O	1	
Chelsea	3	Darlingtn	3	
Everton	1	Blackburn	2	
Fulham	1	Charlton	1	
Liverpool	3	N'hamptn	1	
Man Utd	2	Ipswich	0	
Newcastle	1	Scunthpe	3	
Notts Co	1	Bristol C	2	
Sheff Wed	4	Hull	3	
Stoke	3	Middlesbr	1	
Tottenham	0	Sheff Utd	3	
West Brom	3	Nottm For	3	
West Ham	3	Stockport	2	
Wolves	5	Portsmth	1	
York	0	Bolton	0	
Bolton	3	York	0	r
Burnley	2	Bristol R	3	r
Charlton	0	Fulham	2	r
Darlingtn	4	Chelsea	1	r
Nottm For	1	West Brom	5	r

Strange but true!

Man City full-back Jimmy Meadows was so badly injured during the 1955 Final defeat by Newcastle that he never played again. He was 23.

FIFTH ROUND

Bolton	3	Stoke	1	
Bristol C	3	Bristol R	4	
Cardiff	0	Blackburn	0	
Man Utd	3	Sheff Wed	0	
Scunthpe	0	Liverpool	1	
Sheff Utd	1	West Brom	1	
West Ham	2	Fulham	3	
Wolves	6	Darlingtn	1	
Blackburn	2	Cardiff	1	r
West Brom	4	Sheff Utd	1	r

SIXTH ROUND

Blackburn	2	Liverpool	1	
Bolton	2	Wolves	1	
Fulham	3	Bristol R	1	
West Brom	2	Man Utd	2	
Man Utd	1	West Brom	0	r

SEMI-FINAL

Bolton	2	Blackburn	1	N
Man Utd	2	Fulham	2	N
Fulham	3	Man Utd	5	rN

FINAL

Bolton	2	Man Utd	0	N

1959

FIRST ROUND

Accringtn	5	Workingtn	1
Ashford	0	C.Palace	1
Brentford	3	Exeter	2
Bury	1	York	0
Buxton	4	Crook T	1
Chelmsfd	0	Worcester	0
Chester	3	Boston U	2
Chestrfld	3	Rhyl	0
Colchester	2	Bath C	0
Crewe	2	S.Shields	2
Denaby U	0	Oldham	2
Doncaster	5	Consett	0
Gateshead	1	Bradfd PA	4
Guilford	1	Hereford	2
Hartlepl	1	Rochdale	1
Headingtn	3	Margate	2
Heanor	1	Carlisle	5
Hitchin	1	Millwall	1
Hull	0	Stockport	1
King's Ln	2	Mert Tyd	1
Mansfield	3	Bradford	4
Morecambe	1	Blyth S	2
Nwpt IOW	0	Shrewsby	0

N'hamptn	2	Wycombe	0	
Norwich	3	Ilford	1	
Notts Co	1	Barrow	2	
Peterboro	2	Kettering	2	
Plymouth	2	Gillinghm	2	
Southmptn	4	Woking	1	
Southend	0	Yeovil T	0	
Southport	0	Halifax	2	
Swindon	5	Aldershot	0	
Tooting	3	Bournemt	1	
Torquay	1	Port Vale	0	
Tranmere	8	Bshk Auck	1	
Walsall	0	QPR	1	
Watford	1	Reading	1	
Weymouth	2	Coventry	5	
Wisbech	2	Newport	2	
Wrexham	1	Darlingtn	2	
Gillinghm	1	Plymouth	4	r
Kettering	2	Peterboro	3	re
Millwall	2	Hitchin	1	r
Newport	4	Wisbech	1	re
Reading	0	Watford	2	r
Rochdale	3	Hartlepl	3	re
S.Shields	5	Crewe	0	r
Shrewsby	5	Nwpt IOW	0	r
Worcester	3	Chelmsfd	1	r
Yeovil T	1	Southend	0	r
Hartlepl	2	Rochdale	1	r2N

SECOND ROUND

Accringtn	6	Buxton	1	
Barrow	2	Hartlepl	0	
Blyth S	3	Stockport	4	
Bradfd PA	0	Bradford	2	
Brentford	3	King's Ln	1	
Carlisle	0	Chestrfld	0	
Chester	1	Bury	1	
Colchester	1	Yeovil T	1	
Coventry	1	Plymouth	3	
C.Palace	2	Shrewsby	2	
Halifax	1	Darlingtn	1	
Hereford	0	Newport	2	
Oldham	2	S.Shields	0	
Peterboro	4	Headingtn	2	
QPR	0	Southmptn	1	
Swindon	1	Norwich	1	
Tooting	2	N'hamptn	1	
Torquay	2	Watford	0	
Tranmere	1	Doncaster	2	
Worcester	5	Millwall	2	
Bury	2	Chester	1	r
Chestrfld	1	Carlisle	0	r
Darlingtn	3	Halifax	0	r
Norwich	1	Swindon	0	r
Shrewsby	2	C.Palace	2	re
Yeovil T	1	Colchester	7	r
C.Palace	4	Shrewsby	1	r2N

THIRD ROUND

Accringtn	3	Darlingtn	0	
Aston V	2	Rotherhm	1	
Barrow	2	Wolves	4	
Blackburn	4	Leyton O	2	
Brentford	2	Barnsley	0	
Brighton	0	Bradford	2	
Bristol R	0	Charlton	4	
Bury	0	Arsenal	1	
Colchester	2	Chestrfld	0	
Derby	2	Preston NE	2	
Doncaster	0	Bristol C	2	
Everton	4	Sunderld	0	
Fulham	0	Peterboro	0	
Grimsby	2	Man City	2	
Ipswich	1	Huddersfld	0	
Leicester	1	Lincoln	1	
Luton	5	Leeds U	1	
Middlesbr	0	Birmghm C	1	
Newcastle	1	Chelsea	4	
Newport	0	Torquay	0	
Norwich	3	Man Utd	0	
Plymouth	0	Cardiff	3	
Portsmth	3	Swansea	1	
Scunthpe	0	Bolton	2	
Sheff Utd	2	C.Palace	0	
Sheff Wed	0	West Brom	2	
Southmptn	1	Blackpool	2	
Stockport	1	Burnley	3	
Stoke	5	Oldham	1	
Tooting	2	Nottm For	2	
Tottenham	2	West Ham	0	
Worcester	2	Liverpool	1	
Lincoln	0	Leicester	2	r
Man City	1	Grimsby	2	r
Nottm For	3	Tooting	0	r
Peterboro	0	Fulham	1	r
Preston NE	4	Derby	2	re
Torquay	0	Newport	1	r

FOURTH ROUND

Accringtn	0	Portsmth	0	
Birmghm C	1	Fulham	1	
Blackburn	1	Burnley	2	
Bristol C	1	Blackpool	1	
Charlton	2	Everton	2	
Chelsea	1	Aston V	2	
Colchester	2	Arsenal	2	
Leicester	1	Luton	1	
Norwich	3	Cardiff	2	
Nottm For	4	Grimsby	1	
Preston NE	3	Bradford	2	
Stoke	0	Ipswich	1	
Tottenham	4	Newport	1	
West Brom	2	Brentford	0	
Wolves	1	Bolton	2	
Worcester	0	Sheff Utd	2	
Arsenal	4	Colchester	0	r
Blackpool	1	Bristol C	0	r
Everton	4	Charlton	1	re
Fulham	2	Birmghm C	3	r
Luton	4	Leicester	1	r
Portsmth	4	Accringtn	1	r

FIFTH ROUND

Arsenal	2	Sheff Utd	2	
Birmghm C	1	Nottm For	1	
Blackpool	3	West Brom	1	
Bolton	2	Preston NE	2	
Burnley	1	Portsmth	0	
Everton	1	Aston V	4	
Ipswich	2	Luton	5	
Tottenham	1	Norwich	1	
Norwich	1	Tottenham	0	r
Nottm For	1	Birmghm C	1	re
Preston NE	1	Bolton	1	re
Sheff Utd	3	Arsenal	0	r
Birmghm C	0	Nottm For	5	r2N
Bolton	1	Preston NE	0	r2N

SIXTH ROUND

Aston V	0	Burnley	0	
Blackpool	1	Luton	1	
Nottm For	2	Bolton	1	
Sheff Utd	1	Norwich	1	
Burnley	0	Aston V	2	r
Luton	1	Blackpool	0	r
Norwich	3	Sheff Utd	2	r

SEMI-FINAL

Luton	1	Norwich	1	N
Nottm For	1	Aston V	0	N
Norwich	0	Luton	1	rN

FINAL

Nottm For	2	Luton	1	N

WHAT A STAR ✪ ROY DWIGHT

He played for Nottingham Forest in the 1959 Final against Luton, but sadly he is remembered not so much for the part he played in the match, but for the part he didn't. He scored a fine first goal after just ten minutes and was around long enough to see Tommy Wilson make it 2-0, but in the 30th minute Dwight broke a leg and was stretchered off to watch the rest of the match on television. Fortunately, ten-man Forest - there were no subs in those days - held on to win and Dwight got his medal. Nowadays he's almost as well-known for being the uncle of pop star Elton John (real name Reg Dwight).

1960-1969

SUPER SPURS

Once again at the start of a new decade it was Tottenham Hotspur making the FA Cup headlines. What is it about them and years ending in '1'?

They had won the Cup in 1901 and 1921 and so, justifiably perhaps considering their fine team of the age, felt confident of triumphing at Wembley in 1961.

Triple triumph

Bill Nicholson managed Spurs in all their three winning Finals during the 60s, while Dave Mackay was the only player to appear in all three.

But whether they expected the spectacular success they achieved is doubtful. Not only did the men from White Hart Lane win the FA Cup - courtesy of a 2-0 win over Leicester - they also became the first club in the 20th century to complete the League and Cup double.

Preston and Aston Villa had both achieved the feat in the 1800s but by now the game was vastly different and success on two levels a rare, and rightly applauded, achievement.

Spurs managed it under the guidance of manager Bill Nicholson, who moulded a fabulous side containing such footballing greats as Danny Blanchflower and Dave Mackay.

Indeed, captain Blanchflower always believed their success was possible. "Our conviction was the key to everything," he said, and as if to emphasise the point Spurs duly defended the FA Cup in 1962.

They also won the trophy in 1967 to complete a golden decade for them, but there were other notable FA Cup triumphs during the swinging sixties.

Not least of all was Liverpool's 1965 win over Leeds, a victory which laid the foundations for the Anfield club to go on and dominate the English game throughout the 1970s and 80s.

The Reds had never previously won the FA Cup but goals from Roger Hunt and Ian St John changed all that, and perhaps the words of manager Bill Shankly that day best sum up what the FA Cup means.

"We had won the Cup for the first time, grown men were crying and it was the greatest feeling any human being could have to see what we had done," explained Shanks.

"There have been many proud moments. Wonderful, fantastic moments. But that was the greatest day."

Three 'n' Easy

West Ham scored three goals in all of their six winning FA Cup ties in 1964, finishing with a 3-2 defeat of Preston at Wembley.

1960

FIRST ROUND				
Accringtn	1	Mansfield	2	
Barnsley	3	Bradford	3	
Bath C	3	Millwall	1	
Bedford T	0	Gillinghm	4	
Bradfd PA	6	Scarboro	1	
Brentford	5	Ashford	0	
Burscough	1	Crewe	3	
Bury	5	Hartlepl	0	
Chelthnm	0	Watford	0	
Colchester	2	QPR	3	
Coventry	1	Southmptn	1	
Crook T	2	Matlock T	2	
C.Palace	5	Chelmsfd	1	
Darlingtn	4	Prescot C	0	
Doncaster	3	Gainsbrgh	3	
Dorchstr	1	Port Vale	2	
Enfield	4	Headingtn	3	
Exeter	4	Barnstple	0	
Gateshead	3	Halifax	4	
Hasting U	1	Notts Co	2	
Kettering	1	Margate	1	
King's Ln	3	Aldershot	1	
Newport	4	Hereford	2	
Norwich	1	Reading	1	
Peterboro	4	Shrewsby	3	
Rhyl	1	Grimsby	2	
Rochdale	2	Carlisle	2	
S.Shields	2	Chestrfld	1	
Salisbury	1	Barnet	0	
Shildon	1	Oldham	1	
Southend	6	Oswest T	0	
Southport	2	Workingtn	2	
Swindon	2	Walsall	3	
Torquay	7	N'hamptn	1	
Tranmere	0	Chester	1	
W.Auchld	2	Stockport	6	
Walstmw A	2	Bournemth	3	
Wrexham	2	Blyth S	1	
Wycombe	4	Wisbech	2	
York	3	Barrow	1	
Bradford	2	Barnsley	1	r
Carlisle	1	Rochdale	3	re
Gainsbrgh	0	Doncaster	1	r
Margate	3	Kettering	2	r
Matlock T	0	Crook T	1	r
Oldham	3	Shildon	0	r
Reading	2	Norwich	1	r
Southmptn	5	Coventry	1	r
Watford	3	Chelthnm	0	r
Workingtn	3	Southport	0	r
SECOND ROUND				
Bury	2	Oldham	1	
Crook T	0	York	1	
Doncaster	3	Darlingtn	2	
Enfield	1	Bournemth	5	
Exeter	3	Brentford	1	
Gillinghm	2	Torquay	2	
Grimsby	2	Wrexham	3	
Mansfield	2	Chester	0	
Margate	0	C.Palace	0	
Notts Co	0	Bath C	1	
QPR	3	Port Vale	3	
Reading	4	King's Ln	2	
Rochdale	1	Bradford	1	
S.Shields	1	Bradfd PA	5	
Salisbury	0	Newport	1	
Southmptn	3	Southend	0	
Stockport	0	Crewe	0	
Walsall	2	Peterboro	3	
Watford	5	Wycombe	1	
Workingtn	1	Halifax	0	
Bradford	2	Rochdale	1	r
Crewe	2	Stockport	0	r
C.Palace	3	Margate	0	r
Port Vale	2	QPR	1	r
Torquay	1	Gillinghm	2	r
THIRD ROUND				
Aston V	2	Leeds U	1	
Bath C	0	Brighton	1	
Blackpool	3	Mansfield	0	
Bournemth	1	York	0	
Bradford	3	Everton	0	
Bristol C	2	Charlton	3	
Bristol R	0	Doncaster	0	
Bury	1	Bolton	1	
Cardiff	0	Port Vale	2	
Chelsea	5	Bradfd PA	1	
Crewe	2	Workingtn	0	
Derby	2	Man Utd	4	
Exeter	1	Luton	2	
Fulham	5	Hull	0	
Gillinghm	1	Swansea	4	
Huddersfld	1	West Ham	1	
Ipswich	2	Peterboro	3	
Lincoln	1	Burnley	1	
Liverpool	2	Leyton O	1	
Man City	1	Southmptn	5	
Newcastle	2	Wolves	2	
Newport	0	Tottenham	4	
Nottm For	1	Reading	0	
Rotherhm	2	Arsenal	2	
Scunthpe	1	C.Palace	0	
Sheff Utd	3	Portsmth	0	
Sheff Wed	2	Middlesbro	1	
Stoke	1	Preston NE	1	
Sunderld	1	Blackburn	1	
Watford	2	Birmghm C	1	
West Brom	3	Plymouth	2	
Wrexham	1	Leicester	2	
Arsenal	1	Rotherhm	1	re
Blackburn	4	Sunderld	1	r
Bolton	4	Bury	2	r
Burnley	2	Lincoln	0	r
Doncaster	1	Bristol R	2	r
Preston NE	3	Stoke	1	r
West Ham	1	Huddersfld	5	r
Wolves	4	Newcastle	2	r
Rotherhm	2	Arsenal	0	r2N
FOURTH ROUND				
Blackburn	1	Blackpool	1	
Bradford	3	Bournemth	1	
Bristol R	3	Preston NE	3	
Chelsea	1	Aston V	2	
Crewe	2	Tottenham	2	
Huddersfld	0	Luton	1	
Leicester	2	Fulham	1	
Liverpool	1	Man Utd	3	
Rotherhm	1	Brighton	1	
Scunthpe	0	Port Vale	1	
Sheff Utd	3	Nottm For	0	
Sheff Wed	2	Peterboro	0	
Southmptn	2	Watford	2	
Swansea	0	Burnley	0	
West Brom	2	Bolton	0	
Wolves	2	Charlton	1	
Blackpool	0	Blackburn	3	r
Brighton	1	Rotherhm	1	re
Burnley	2	Swansea	1	r
Preston NE	5	Bristol R	1	r
Tottenham	13	Crewe	2	r
Watford	1	Southmptn	0	r
Rotherhm	0	Brighton	6	r2N
FIFTH ROUND				
Bradford	2	Burnley	2	
Leicester	2	West Brom	1	
Luton	1	Wolves	4	
Man Utd	0	Sheff Wed	1	
Port Vale	1	Aston V	2	
Preston NE	2	Brighton	1	
Sheff Utd	3	Watford	2	
Tottenham	1	Blackburn	3	
Burnley	5	Bradford	0	r
SIXTH ROUND				
Aston V	2	Preston NE	0	
Burnley	3	Blackburn	3	
Leicester	1	Wolves	2	
Sheff Utd	0	Sheff Wed	2	
Blackburn	2	Burnley	0	r
SEMI-FINAL				
Blackburn	2	Sheff Wed	1	N
Wolves	1	Aston V	0	N
FINAL				
Wolves	3	Blackburn	0	N

Strange but true!

Burnley's skipper in the 1962 Final, Jimmy Adamson, acted as England's assistant-manager in the World Cup later that year. He was offered the top job when Walter Winterbottom later resigned, but he turned it down.

1961

FIRST ROUND				
Accringtn	2	Barrow	1	
Aldershot	2	Notts Co	0	
Ashford	1	Gillinghm	2	
Bangor C	1	Wrexham	0	
Bradford	0	Scarboro	0	
Bridgwtr	3	Hereford	0	
Bristol C	11	Chichstr	0	
Bshk Auck	3	Bridlingtn	2	
Chelmsfd	2	Port Vale	3	
Chester	0	Carlisle	1	
Chestrfld	3	Doncaster	3	
Clacton T	1	Southend	3	
Colchester	5	Maidenh U	0	
Crewe	1	Rochdale	1	

GIANTKILLERS

1960 Manchester City 1 Southampton 5

Saints were on their way to the Third Division Championship and City were struggling against relegation to the Second - which they narrowly avoided - but few people could have expected such a rout. During the season, Southampton scored 106 goals in 46 League matches and another 16 in six Cup games, with Derek Reeves claiming 39 - the Third Division record - plus four at Maine Road. City had not won a Cup-tie since Wembley in 1956 and their goal in this disaster was scored by Colin Barlow, now their managing director.

C.Palace	6	Hitchin	2	
Darlingtn	2	Grimsby	0	
Dover	1	Peterboro	4	
Exeter	1	Bournemth	1	
Gateshead	0	Barnsley	0	
Halifax	5	Hartlepl	1	
Hendon	2	Oxford	2	
Hull	3	Sutton T	0	
Loughbr U	0	King's Ln	0	
Mansfield	3	Blyth S	1	
N'hamptn	2	Hasting U	1	
QPR	3	Walstmw A	2	
Reading	6	Millwall	2	
Rhyl	0	Oldham	1	
Shrewsby	4	Newport	1	
Southport	7	Macclesfd	2	
Stockport	1	Workingtn	0	
Sutton U	2	Romford	2	
Swindon	2	Bath C	2	
Tranmere	1	Bury	0	
Walsall	0	Yeovil T	1	
Watford	2	Brentford	2	
Weymouth	1	Torquay	3	
Worcester	1	Coventry	4	
Wycombe	1	Kettering	2	
York	0	Bradfd PA	0	
Barnsley	2	Gateshead	0	r
Bath C	4	Swindon	6	r
Bournemth	3	Exeter	1	r
Bradfd PA	0	York	2	r
Brentford	0	Watford	2	r
Doncaster	0	Chestrfld	1	r
King's Ln	3	Loughbr U	0	r
Oxford	3	Hendon	2	r
Rochdale	1	Crewe	2	r
Romford	5	Sutton U	0	r
Scarboro	1	Bradford	2	re
SECOND ROUND				
Accringtn	3	Mansfield	0	
Aldershot	3	Colchester	1	
Bangor C	1	Southport	1	
Bournemth	3	Yeovil T	1	
Bradford	1	Barnsley	2	
Chestrfld	4	Oldham	4	
C.Palace	0	Watford	0	
Darlingtn	1	Hull	1	
Gillinghm	3	Southend	2	
Halifax	2	Crewe	2	
King's Ln	2	Bristol C	2	
Oxford	2	Bridgwtr	1	
Port Vale	2	Carlisle	1	
QPR	1	Coventry	2	
Reading	4	Kettering	2	
Romford	1	N'hamptn	5	
Stockport	2	Bshk Auck	0	
Swindon	0	Shrewsby	1	
Torquay	1	Peterboro	3	
Tranmere	1	York	1	
Bristol C	3	King's Ln	0	r
Crewe	3	Halifax	0	r
Hull	1	Darlingtn	1	re
Oldham	0	Chestrfld	3	r
Southport	3	Bangor C	1	r
Watford	1	C.Palace	0	r
York	2	Tranmere	1	r
Darlingtn	1	Hull	1	r2aN
Hull	0	Darlingtn	0	r3eN
Darlingtn	0	Hull	3	r4N
THIRD ROUND				
Aldershot	1	Shrewsby	1	
Brighton	3	Derby	1	
Bristol R	1	Aston V	1	
Burnley	1	Bournemth	0	
Cardiff	1	Man City	1	
Chelsea	1	Crewe	2	
Chestrfld	0	Blackburn	0	
Everton	0	Sheff Utd	1	
Gillinghm	2	Leyton O	6	
Hull	0	Bolton	1	
Leicester	3	Oxford	1	
Lincoln	3	West Brom	1	
Liverpool	3	Coventry	2	
Luton	4	N'hamptn	0	
Man Utd	3	Middlesbro	0	
Newcastle	5	Fulham	0	
Nottm For	0	Birmghm C	2	
Plymouth	0	Bristol C	1	
Portsmth	1	Peterboro	2	
Preston NE	1	Accringtn	1	
Reading	1	Barnsley	1	
Rotherhm	1	Watford	0	
Scunthpe	6	Blackpool	2	
Sheff Wed	2	Leeds U	0	
Southmptn	7	Ipswich	1	
Stockport	3	Southport	1	
Sunderld	2	Arsenal	1	
Swansea	3	Port Vale	0	
Tottenham	3	Charlton	2	
West Ham	2	Stoke	2	
Wolves	1	Huddersfld	1	
York	1	Norwich	1	
Accringtn	0	Preston NE	4	r
Aston V	4	Bristol R	0	r
Barnsley	3	Reading	1	r
Blackburn	3	Chestrfld	0	r
Huddersfld	2	Wolves	1	r
Man City	0	Cardiff	0	re
Norwich	1	York	0	r
Shrewsby	2	Aldershot	2	re
Stoke	1	West Ham	0	r
Aldershot	2	Shrewsby	0	r2N
Cardiff	0	Man City	2	r2eN
FOURTH ROUND				
Birmghm C	4	Rotherhm	0	
Bolton	3	Blackburn	3	
Brighton	3	Burnley	3	
Huddersfld	1	Barnsley	1	
Leicester	5	Bristol C	1	
Liverpool	0	Sunderld	2	
Luton	3	Man City	1	
Newcastle	4	Stockport	0	
Peterboro	1	Aston V	1	
Scunthpe	1	Norwich	4	
Sheff Utd	3	Lincoln	1	
Sheff Wed	1	Man Utd	1	
Southmptn	0	Leyton O	1	
Stoke	0	Aldershot	0	
Swansea	2	Preston NE	1	
Tottenham	5	Crewe	1	
Aldershot	0	Stoke	0	re
Aston V	2	Peterboro	1	r
Barnsley	1	Huddersfld	0	r
Blackburn	4	Bolton	0	r
Burnley	2	Brighton	0	r
Man Utd	2	Sheff Wed	7	r
Stoke	3	Aldershot	0	r2N
FIFTH ROUND				
Aston V	0	Tottenham	2	
Barnsley	1	Luton	0	
Birmghm C	1	Leicester	1	
Burnley	4	Swansea	0	
Leyton O	0	Sheff Wed	2	
Newcastle	3	Stoke	1	
Norwich	0	Sunderld	1	
Sheff Utd	2	Blackburn	1	
Leicester	2	Birmghm C	1	r
SIXTH ROUND				

Leicester	0	Barnsley	0	
Newcastle	1	Sheff Utd	3	
Sheff Wed	0	Burnley	0	
Sunderld	1	Tottenham	1	
Barnsley	1	Leicester	2	r
Burnley	2	Sheff Wed	0	r
Tottenham	5	Sunderld	0	r
SEMI-FINAL				
Leicester	0	Sheff Utd	0	N
Tottenham	3	Burnley	0	N
Sheff Utd	0	Leicester	0	reN
Leicester	2	Sheff Utd	0	r2eN
FINAL				
Tottenham	2	Leicester	0	N

1962

FIRST ROUND				
Aldershot	3	Tunbge WU	1	
Barry T	1	QPR	1	
Bournemth	0	Margate	3	
Bradford	1	York	0	
Bradfd PA	0	Port Vale	1	
Brentford	3	Oxford	0	
Bridgwtr	0	Weston SM	0	
Brierley	3	Grantham	0	
Bristol C	1	Hereford	1	
Chelmsfd	1	King's Ln	2	
Chester	4	Ashington	1	
Coventry	2	Gillinghm	0	
Crewe	2	Lincoln	0	
C.Palace	3	Portsmth	0	
Darlingtn	0	Carlisle	4	
Doncaster	0	Chestrfld	4	
Exeter	3	Dartford	3	
Hartlepl	5	Blyth S	1	
Hull	5	Rhyl	0	
Mansfield	3	Grimsby	2	
Morecambe	2	S.Shields	1	
N'hamptn	2	Millwall	0	
Notts Co	4	Yeovil T	2	
Oldham	5	Shildon	2	
Peterboro	3	Colchester	3	
Reading	1	Newport	1	
Rochdale	2	Halifax	0	
Shrewsby	7	Banbury S	1	
Southend	0	Watford	2	
Southport	1	Northwich	0	
Stockport	0	Accringtn	1	
Swindon	2	Kettering	2	
Torquay	5	Harwich	1	
Tranmere	2	Gateshead	3	
W.Auchld	3	Barnsley	3	
Walstmw A	2	Romford	3	
Weymouth	1	Barnet	0	
Workingtn	2	Worksop	0	
Wrexham	3	Barrow	2	
Wycombe	0	Ashford	0	
Ashford	3	Wycombe	0	r
Barnsley	2	W.Auchld	0	r
Colchester	2	Peterboro	2	re
Dartford	2	Exeter	1	r
Hereford	2	Bristol C	5	r
Kettering	3	Swindon	0	r
Newport	1	Reading	0	r
QPR	7	Barry T	0	r
Weston SM	0	Bridgwtr	1	r
Peterboro	3	Colchester	0	r2N
SECOND ROUND				
Aldershot	2	Brentford	2	
Ashford	0	QPR	3	
Barnsley	1	Carlisle	2	
Bridgwtr	0	C.Palace	3	
Bristol C	8	Dartford	2	
Chester	0	Morecambe	1	
Chestrfld	2	Oldham	2	
Coventry	1	King's Ln	2	
Crewe	1	Port Vale	1	
Gateshead	0	Workingtn	2	
Hartlepl	2	Accringtn	1	
Hull	0	Bradford	2	
Margate	1	Notts Co	1	
N'hamptn	3	Kettering	0	
Rochdale	1	Wrexham	2	
Romford	1	Watford	3	
Shrewsby	3	Brierley	0	
Southport	4	Mansfield	2	
Torquay	1	Peterboro	4	
Weymouth	1	Newport	0	
Brentford	2	Aldershot	0	r
Notts Co	3	Margate	1	r
Oldham	4	Chestrfld	2	re
Port Vale	3	Crewe	0	r
THIRD ROUND				
Arsenal	3	Bradford	0	
Aston V	4	C.Palace	3	
Birmghm C	3	Tottenham	3	
Blackpool	0	West Brom	0	
Brentford	1	Leyton O	1	
Brighton	0	Blackburn	3	
Bristol C	0	Walsall	0	
Bristol R	1	Oldham	1	
Burnley	6	QPR	1	
Bury	0	Sheff Utd	0	
Charlton	1	Scunthpe	0	
Everton	4	King's Ln	0	
Fulham	3	Hartlepl	1	

Danny Blanchflower lifts the FA Cup for Tottenham

WHAT A STAR ✪ BOBBY SMITH

Big Bobby Smith was often criticised, but any Spurs fan will tell of the debt the club owe to him. In both the 1961 and 1962 Finals Spurs were looking for a goal when Smith did the job, in similar style both times, turning and dragging the ball away from his marker, then thumping a right-footer past an international keeper, first Banks and then Blacklaw. He earned his medals, plus one for the Championship and another for the Cup-Winners' Cup, but has paid a heavy price for the leg injuries he withstood so bravely during his playing career.

Home		Away		
Huddersfld	4	Rotherhm	3	
Ipswich	1	Luton	1	
Leeds U	2	Derby	2	
Leicester	1	Stoke	1	
Liverpool	4	Chelsea	3	
Man Utd	2	Bolton	1	
Middlesbro	1	Cardiff	0	
Morecambe	0	Weymouth	1	
Newcastle	0	Peterboro	1	
Norwich	3	Wrexham	1	
Notts Co	0	Man City	1	
Plymouth	3	West Ham	0	
Port Vale	3	N'hamptn	1	
Preston NE	3	Watford	2	
Sheff Wed	1	Swansea	0	
Southmptn	2	Sunderld	2	
Southport	1	Shrewsby	3	
Wolves	3	Carlisle	1	
Workingtn	1	Nottm For	2	
Derby	3	Leeds U	1	r
Leyton O	2	Brentford	1	r
Luton	1	Ipswich	1	re
Oldham	2	Bristol R	0	r
Sheff Utd	2	Bury	2	re
Stoke	5	Leicester	2	r
Sunderld	3	Southmptn	0	r
Tottenham	4	Birmghm C	2	r
Walsall	4	Bristol C	1	r
West Brom	2	Blackpool	1	r
Bury	0	Sheff Utd	2	r2N
Ipswich	5	Luton	1	r2N
FOURTH ROUND				
Aston V	2	Huddersfld	1	
Burnley	1	Leyton O	1	
Charlton	2	Derby	1	
Everton	2	Man City	0	
Fulham	2	Walsall	2	
Man Utd	1	Arsenal	0	
Norwich	1	Ipswich	1	
Nottm For	0	Sheff Wed	2	
Oldham	1	Liverpool	2	
Peterboro	1	Sheff Utd	3	
Plymouth	1	Tottenham	5	
Preston NE	2	Weymouth	0	
Shrewsby	2	Middlesbro	2	
Stoke	0	Blackburn	1	
Sunderld	0	Port Vale	0	
Wolves	1	West Brom	2	
Ipswich	1	Norwich	2	r
Leyton O	0	Burnley	1	r
Middlesbro	5	Shrewsby	1	r
Port Vale	3	Sunderld	1	r
Walsall	0	Fulham	2	r
FIFTH ROUND				
Aston V	2	Charlton	1	
Blackburn	2	Middlesbro	1	
Burnley	3	Everton	1	
Fulham	1	Port Vale	0	
Liverpool	0	Preston NE	0	
Man Utd	0	Sheff Wed	0	
Sheff Utd	3	Norwich	1	
West Brom	2	Tottenham	4	
Preston NE	0	Liverpool	0	re
Sheff Wed	0	Man Utd	2	r
Liverpool	0	Preston NE	1	r2N
SIXTH ROUND				
Fulham	2	Blackburn	2	
Preston NE	0	Man Utd	0	
Sheff Utd	0	Burnley	1	
Tottenham	2	Aston V	0	
Blackburn	0	Fulham	1	r
Man Utd	2	Preston NE	1	r
SEMI-FINAL				
Burnley	1	Fulham	1	N
Tottenham	3	Man Utd	1	N
Fulham	1	Burnley	2	rN
FINAL				
Tottenham	3	Burnley	1	N

1963

Home		Away		
FIRST ROUND				
Aldershot	1	Brentford	0	
Andover	0	Gillinghm	1	
Barnsley	4	Rhyl	0	
Bedford T	2	Cambridge	1	
Blyth S	2	Morecambe	1	
Boston U	1	King's Ln	2	
Bristol C	4	Wellingtn	2	
Bristol R	0	Port Vale	2	
Buxton	2	Barrow	2	
Carlisle	2	Hartlepl	1	
Chelmsfd	2	Shrewsby	6	
Chelthnm	3	Enfield	6	
Chester	0	Tranmere	2	
Chestrfld	4	Stockport	1	
Coventry	1	Bournemth	0	
Crewe	1	Scarboro	1	
C.Palace	2	Hereford	0	
Falmouth	1	Oxford	2	
Gateshead	2	Wigan Ath	1	
Gravesend	3	Exeter	2	
Halifax	1	Bradfd PA	0	
Hinckley A	3	Sittingbn	0	
Hounslow	3	Mansfield	3	
Hull	5	Crook T	4	
Lincoln	1	Darlingtn	1	
Maidenh U	0	Wycombe	3	
Millwall	3	Margate	1	
N.Shields	2	Workingtn	2	
N'hamptn	1	Torquay	2	
Notts Co	0	Peterboro	3	
Oldham	2	Bradford	5	
QPR	3	Newport	2	
S.Shields	0	Doncaster	0	
Southend	2	Brighton	1	
Southport	1	Wrexham	1	
Swindon	4	Reading	2	
Watford	2	Poole T	2	
Wimbledn	2	Colchester	1	
Yeovil T	3	Dartford	2	
York	0	Rochdale	0	
Barrow	3	Buxton	1	r
Darlingtn	1	Lincoln	2	r
Doncaster	2	S.Shields	1	r
Mansfield	9	Hounslow	2	r
Poole T	1	Watford	2	r
Rochdale	1	York	2	r
Scarboro	2	Crewe	3	re
Workingtn	7	N.Shields	2	r
Wrexham	3	Southport	2	r
SECOND ROUND				
Barnsley	2	Chestrfld	1	
Blyth S	0	Carlisle	2	
Bradford	3	Gateshead	2	
Bristol C	2	Wimbledn	1	
C.Palace	2	Mansfield	2	
Doncaster	1	Tranmere	4	
Gillinghm	3	Bedford T	0	
Gravesend	3	Wycombe	1	
Hull	2	Workingtn	0	
King's Ln	1	Oxford	2	
Lincoln	1	Halifax	0	
Millwall	0	Coventry	0	
Peterboro	1	Enfield	0	
Port Vale	2	Aldershot	0	
QPR	7	Hinckley A	2	
Shrewsby	2	Torquay	1	
Southend	0	Watford	2	
Wrexham	5	Barrow	2	
Yeovil T	0	Swindon	2	
York	2	Crewe	1	
Coventry	2	Millwall	1	r
Mansfield	7	C.Palace	2	r
THIRD ROUND				
Arsenal	5	Oxford	1	
Barnsley	0	Everton	3	
Birmghm C	3	Bury	3	
Blackburn	1	Middlesbro	1	
Bradford	1	Newcastle	6	
Bristol C	1	Aston V	1	
Carlisle	0	Gravesend	1	
Charlton	1	Cardiff	0	
Derby	2	Peterboro	0	
Gillinghm	2	Port Vale	4	
Grimsby	1	Leicester	3	
Leeds U	3	Stoke	1	
Leyton O	1	Hull	1	
Lincoln	1	Coventry	5	
Luton	0	Swindon	2	
Man Utd	5	Huddersfld	0	
Mansfield	2	Ipswich	3	
Norwich	1	Blackpool	1	
Nottm For	4	Wolves	3	
Plymouth	1	West Brom	5	
Portsmth	1	Scunthpe	1	
Preston NE	1	Sunderld	4	
Sheff Utd	3	Bolton	1	
Shrewsby	1	Sheff Wed	1	
Southmptn	5	York	0	
Swansea	2	QPR	0	
Tottenham	0	Burnley	3	
Tranmere	2	Chelsea	2	
Walsall	0	Man City	1	
Watford	2	Rotherhm	0	

Preston Woe

Preston, losing to West Ham by Ron Boyce's last minute goal in 1964, thus became the first club to be beaten in three Finals after leading in all of them. They did so in 1937 and 1954 as well.

GIANTKILLERS

1965 Peterborough 2 Arsenal 1

Any club knocking out Salisbury, QPR, Chesterfield, Arsenal and Swansea in the course of one Cup run deserves a medal, even if they do fall 5-1 to Chelsea at the end of it. When that club's experience of the Football League goes back only five seasons, the medal should be an exceptionally big one. Welsh international Vic Crowe was an inspirational player-coach for the Posh around that time, and Derek Dougan, one-time chairman of the PFA, got one of their goals in the win over Arsenal. Former England favourite Billy Wright was then manager of a below-average Arsenal side.

West Ham	0	Fulham	0	
Wrexham	0	Liverpool	3	
Aston V	3	Bristol C	2	r
Blackpool	1	Norwich	3	re
Bury	2	Birmghm C	0	r
Chelsea	3	Tranmere	1	r
Fulham	1	West Ham	2	r
Hull	0	Leyton O	2	re
Middlesbro	3	Blackburn	1	r
Scunthpe	1	Portsmth	2	r
Sheff Wed	2	Shrewsby	1	r
FOURTH ROUND				
Arsenal	2	Sheff Wed	0	
Burnley	1	Liverpool	1	
Charlton	0	Chelsea	3	
Gravesend	1	Sunderld	1	
Leicester	3	Ipswich	1	
Leyton O	3	Derby	0	
Man City	1	Bury	0	
Man Utd	1	Aston V	0	
Middlesbro	0	Leeds U	2	
Norwich	5	Newcastle	0	
Port Vale	1	Sheff Utd	2	
Portsmth	1	Coventry	1	
Southmptn	3	Watford	1	
Swindon	1	Everton	5	
West Brom	0	Nottm For	0	
West Ham	1	Swansea	0	
Coventry	2	Portsmth	2	re
Liverpool	2	Burnley	1	re
Nottm For	2	West Brom	1	re
Sunderld	5	Gravesend	2	r
Portsmth	1	Coventry	2	r2N
FIFTH ROUND				
Arsenal	1	Liverpool	2	
Coventry	2	Sunderld	1	
Leyton O	0	Leicester	1	
Man City	1	Norwich	2	
Man Utd	2	Chelsea	1	
Nottm For	3	Leeds U	0	
Southmptn	1	Sheff Utd	0	
West Ham	1	Everton	0	
SIXTH ROUND				
Coventry	1	Man Utd	3	
Liverpool	1	West Ham	0	
Norwich	0	Leicester	2	
Nottm For	1	Southmptn	1	
Southmptn	3	Nottm For	3	re
Nottm For	0	Southmptn	5	r2N
SEMI-FINAL				
Leicester	1	Liverpool	0	N
Man Utd	1	Southmptn	0	N
FINAL				
Man Utd	3	Leicester	1	N

1964

FIRST ROUND				
Altrinchm	0	Wrexham	0	
Barnsley	1	Stockport	0	
Barrow	3	Bangor C	2	
Bexley U	1	Wimbledn	5	
Bournemth	1	Bristol R	3	
Bradford	1	Port Vale	2	
Bradfd PA	3	Heanor	1	
Brentford	2	Margate	2	
Bridgwtr	0	Luton	3	
Brighton	0	Colchester	1	
Cambridge	0	Chelmsfd	1	
Chester	3	Blyth S	2	
Corby T	1	Bristol C	3	
Crook T	1	Chestrfld	2	
C.Palace	8	Harwich	2	
Darlingtn	1	Gateshead	4	
Doncaster	3	Tranmere	0	
Exeter	2	Shrewsby	1	
Hartlepl	0	Lincoln	1	
Hereford	1	Newport	1	
Hull	2	Crewe	2	
Kettering	1	Millwall	1	
Maidenh U	0	Bath C	2	
Netherfld	6	Loughbr U	1	
Notts Co	2	Frickley	1	
Oldham	3	Mansfield	2	
Oxford	2	Folkestne	0	
Peterboro	1	Watford	1	
QPR	4	Gillinghm	1	
Reading	2	Enfield	2	
Rochdale	2	Chorley	1	
Southport	2	Walsall	1	
Sutton U	0	Aldershot	4	
Tooting	1	Gravesend	2	
Torquay	6	Barnet	2	
Trowbdge	1	Coventry	6	
Weymouth	1	Bedford T	1	
Workingtn	4	Halifax	1	
Yeovil T	1	Southend	0	
York	2	Carlisle	5	
Bedford T	1	Weymouth	0	r
Crewe	0	Hull	3	r
Enfield	2	Reading	4	re
Margate	0	Brentford	2	r
Millwall	2	Kettering	3	r
Newport	4	Hereford	0	r
Watford	2	Peterboro	1	re
Wrexham	3	Altrinchm	0	r
SECOND ROUND				
Barnsley	3	Rochdale	1	
Brentford	1	Gravesend	0	
Carlisle	4	Gateshead	3	
Chelmsfd	0	Bedford T	1	
Chester	0	Barrow	2	
Colchester	0	QPR	1	
Coventry	1	Bristol R	2	
Doncaster	1	Notts Co	1	
Exeter	0	Bristol C	2	
Lincoln	2	Southport	0	
Luton	2	Reading	1	
Netherfld	1	Chestrfld	1	
Newport	2	Watford	0	
Oldham	2	Bradfd PA	0	
Oxford	2	Kettering	1	
Port Vale	2	Workingtn	1	
Torquay	2	Aldershot	3	
Wimbledn	2	Bath C	2	
Wrexham	0	Hull	2	
Yeovil T	3	C.Palace	1	
Bath C	4	Wimbledn	0	r
Chestrfld	4	Netherfld	1	r
Notts Co	1	Doncaster	2	r
THIRD ROUND				
Arsenal	2	Wolves	1	
Aston V	0	Aldershot	0	
Bath C	1	Bolton	1	
Birmghm C	1	Port Vale	2	
Blackburn	4	Grimsby	0	
Brentford	2	Middlesbro	1	
Bristol R	2	Norwich	1	
Burnley	1	Rotherhm	1	
Cardiff	0	Leeds U	1	
Carlisle	2	QPR	0	
Doncaster	2	Bristol C	2	

Fulham	4	Luton	1	
Hull	1	Everton	1	
Ipswich	6	Oldham	3	
Leicester	2	Leyton O	3	
Lincoln	0	Sheff Utd	4	
Liverpool	5	Derby	0	
Newcastle	1	Bedford T	2	
Newport	3	Sheff Wed	2	
Nottm For	0	Preston NE	0	
Oxford	1	Chestrfld	0	
Plymouth	0	Huddersfld	1	
Scunthpe	2	Barnsley	2	
Southmptn	2	Man Utd	3	
Stoke	4	Portsmth	1	
Sunderld	2	N'hamptn	0	
Swansea	4	Barrow	1	
Swindon	2	Man City	1	
Tottenham	1	Chelsea	1	
West Brom	2	Blackpool	2	
West Ham	3	Charlton	0	
Yeovil T	0	Bury	2	
Aldershot	2	Aston V	1	r
Barnsley	3	Scunthpe	2	re
Blackpool	0	West Brom	1	r
Bolton	3	Bath C	0	r
Bristol C	2	Doncaster	0	r
Chelsea	2	Tottenham	0	r
Everton	2	Hull	1	r
Preston NE	1	Nottm For	0	r
Rotherhm	2	Burnley	3	r
FOURTH ROUND				
Aldershot	1	Swindon	2	
Barnsley	2	Bury	1	
Bedford T	0	Carlisle	3	
Blackburn	2	Fulham	0	
Bolton	2	Preston NE	2	
Burnley	2	Newport	1	
Chelsea	1	Huddersfld	2	
Ipswich	1	Stoke	1	
Leeds U	1	Everton	1	
Leyton O	1	West Ham	1	
Liverpool	0	Port Vale	0	
Man Utd	4	Bristol R	1	
Oxford	2	Brentford	2	
Sheff Utd	1	Swansea	1	
Sunderld	6	Bristol C	1	
West Brom	3	Arsenal	3	
Arsenal	2	West Brom	0	r
Brentford	1	Oxford	2	r
Everton	2	Leeds U	0	r
Port Vale	1	Liverpool	2	re
Preston NE	2	Bolton	1	r
Stoke	1	Ipswich	0	r
Swansea	4	Sheff Utd	0	r
West Ham	3	Leyton O	0	r
FIFTH ROUND				
Arsenal	0	Liverpool	1	
Barnsley	0	Man Utd	4	
Burnley	3	Huddersfld	0	
Oxford	3	Blackburn	1	
Preston NE	1	Carlisle	0	
Stoke	2	Swansea	2	
Sunderld	3	Everton	1	
Swindon	1	West Ham	3	
Swansea	2	Stoke	0	r
SIXTH ROUND				
Liverpool	1	Swansea	2	
Man Utd	3	Sunderld	3	
Oxford	1	Preston NE	2	
West Ham	3	Burnley	2	
Sunderld	2	Man Utd	2	re
Sunderld	1	Man Utd	5	r2N
SEMI-FINAL				
Preston NE	2	Swansea	1	N
West Ham	3	Man Utd	1	N
FINAL				
West Ham	3	Preston NE	2	N

1965

FIRST ROUND				
Barnet	2	Cambridge	1	
Barrow	1	Grimsby	1	
Bournemth	7	Gravesend	0	
Bradfd PA	2	Doncaster	3	
Bristol C	1	Brighton	0	
Canterby	0	Torquay	6	
Chester	5	Crewe	0	
Chestrfld	2	S.Shields	0	
Colchester	3	Bideford	3	
Corby T	1	Hartlepl	3	
Crook T	1	Carlisle	0	
Dartford	1	Aldershot	1	
Exeter	1	Hayes	0	
Guilford	2	Gillinghm	2	
Halifax	2	S.L'pool	2	
Kiddermst	1	Hull	4	
King's Ln	0	Shrewsby	1	
Luton	1	Southend	0	
Macclesfd	1	Wrexham	2	
Millwall	2	Kettering	0	
Netherfld	1	Barnsley	3	
Newport	5	Spalding	3	
Notts Co	2	Chelmsfd	0	
Oldham	4	Hereford	0	
Oxford	0	Mansfield	1	
Peterboro	5	Salisbury	1	
Port Vale	2	Hendon	1	
QPR	2	Bath C	0	
Reading	3	Watford	1	
Romford	0	Enfield	0	
Scarboro	1	Bradford	0	
Scunthpe	1	Darlingtn	2	
Southport	6	Annfield	1	
Stockport	2	Wigan Ath	1	
Tranmere	0	Lincoln	0	
Walsall	0	Bristol R	2	
Welton R	1	Weymouth	1	
Wisbech	0	Brentford	2	
Workingtn	2	Rochdale	0	
York	5	Bangor C	1	
Aldershot	1	Dartford	0	r
Bideford	1	Colchester	2	r
Enfield	0	Romford	0	re
Gillinghm	1	Guilford	0	r
Grimsby	2	Barrow	2	re
Lincoln	1	Tranmere	0	r
S.L'pool	4	Halifax	2	r
Weymouth	4	Welton R	3	r
Barrow	0	Grimsby	2	r2N
Romford	2	Enfield	4	r2N
SECOND ROUND				
Aldershot	1	Reading	3	
Barnsley	2	Chester	5	
Bournemth	0	Bristol C	3	
Brentford	4	Notts Co	0	
Bristol R	4	Weymouth	1	
Chestrfld	2	York	1	
Crook T	0	Oldham	1	
Doncaster	0	Scarboro	0	
Enfield	4	Barnet	4	
Exeter	1	Shrewsby	2	
Hartlepl	0	Darlingtn	0	
Hull	1	Lincoln	1	
Luton	1	Gillinghm	0	
Millwall	4	Port Vale	0	
Newport	3	Mansfield	0	
QPR	3	Peterboro	3	
S.L'pool	0	Workingtn	2	
Stockport	1	Grimsby	0	
Torquay	2	Colchester	0	
Wrexham	2	Southport	3	
Barnet	3	Enfield	0	r
Darlingtn	4	Hartlepl	1	r
Lincoln	3	Hull	1	r
Peterboro	2	QPR	1	r
Scarboro	1	Doncaster	2	r
THIRD ROUND				
Aston V	3	Coventry	0	
Barnet	2	Preston NE	3	
Bolton	4	Workingtn	1	
Bristol C	1	Sheff Utd	1	
Bristol R	0	Stockport	0	
Burnley	1	Brentford	1	
Cardiff	1	Charlton	2	
Chelsea	4	N'hamptn	1	

Strange but true!

Gordon Milne missed Liverpool's 1965 victory, their first-ever Cup win, because of injury. In 1938 his father had missed Preston's success for the same reason. Gordon's manager, Bill Shankly, had been in the Preston side with Milne senior.

Mobley Sick

Vic Mobley of Sheffield Wednesday missed the 1966 Final through injury, and had to pull out of an England squad as well. Unlucky Vic never got to play in a Final...and never won a cap either.

Home		Away		
Chestrfld	0	Peterboro	3	
C.Palace	5	Bury	1	
Darlingtn	0	Arsenal	2	
Doncaster	0	Huddersfld	1	
Everton	2	Sheff Wed	2	
Fulham	3	Millwall	3	
Leeds U	3	Southport	0	
Leicester	2	Blackburn	2	
Luton	0	Sunderld	3	
Man City	1	Shrewsby	1	
Man Utd	2	Chester	1	
Middlesbro	6	Oldham	2	
Nottm For	1	Norwich	0	
Plymouth	4	Derby	2	
Portsmth	0	Wolves	0	
Reading	2	Newport	2	
Rotherhm	5	Lincoln	1	
Southmptn	3	Leyton O	1	
Stoke	4	Blackpool	1	
Swansea	1	Newcastle	0	
Swindon	1	Ipswich	2	
Torquay	3	Tottenham	3	
West Brom	1	Liverpool	2	
West Ham	4	Birmghm C	2	
Blackburn	1	Leicester	2	r
Brentford	0	Burnley	2	r
Millwall	2	Fulham	0	r
Newport	0	Reading	1	r
Sheff Utd	3	Bristol C	0	r
Sheff Wed	0	Everton	3	r
Shrewsby	3	Man City	1	r
Stockport	3	Bristol R	2	r
Tottenham	5	Torquay	1	r
Wolves	3	Portsmth	2	r
FOURTH ROUND				
Charlton	1	Middlesbro	1	
Leeds U	1	Everton	1	
Leicester	5	Plymouth	0	
Liverpool	1	Stockport	1	
Millwall	1	Shrewsby	2	
Peterboro	2	Arsenal	1	
Preston NE	1	Bolton	2	
Reading	1	Burnley	1	
Sheff Utd	0	Aston V	2	
Southmptn	1	C.Palace	2	
Stoke	0	Man Utd	0	
Sunderld	1	Nottm For	3	
Swansea	1	Huddersfld	0	
Tottenham	5	Ipswich	0	
West Ham	0	Chelsea	1	
Wolves	2	Rotherhm	2	
Burnley	1	Reading	0	r
Everton	1	Leeds U	2	r
Man Utd	1	Stoke	0	r
Middlesbro	2	Charlton	1	r
Rotherhm	0	Wolves	3	r
Stockport	0	Liverpool	2	r
FIFTH ROUND				
Aston V	1	Wolves	1	
Bolton	0	Liverpool	1	
Chelsea	1	Tottenham	0	
C.Palace	3	Nottm For	1	
Leeds U	2	Shrewsby	0	
Man Utd	2	Burnley	1	
Middlesbro	0	Leicester	3	
Peterboro	0	Swansea	0	
Swansea	0	Peterboro	2	r
Wolves	0	Aston V	0	re
Aston V	1	Wolves	3	r2N
SIXTH ROUND				
Chelsea	5	Peterboro	1	
C.Palace	0	Leeds U	3	
Leicester	0	Liverpool	0	
Wolves	3	Man Utd	5	
Liverpool	1	Leicester	0	r
SEMI-FINAL				
Leeds U	0	Man Utd	0	N
Liverpool	2	Chelsea	0	N
Man Utd	0	Leeds U	1	rN
FINAL				
Liverpool	2	Leeds U	1	eN

1966

Home		Away		
FIRST ROUND				
Aldershot	2	Wellingbro	1	
Altrinchm	6	Scarboro	0	
Barnet	0	Dartford	2	
Barrow	1	Grimsby	2	
Bath C	2	Newport	0	
Bournemth	0	Weymouth	0	
Bradfd PA	2	Hull	3	
Brentford	2	Yeovil T	1	
Brighton	10	Wisbech	1	
Chestrfld	0	Chester	2	
Colchester	3	QPR	3	
Cor Casls	1	Watford	5	
Corby T	6	Burton Al	3	
Crewe	3	Scunthpe	0	
Darlingtn	3	Bradford	2	
Doncaster	2	Wigan Ath	2	
Exeter	1	Bedford T	2	
Fleetwood	2	Rochdale	2	
Gateshead	4	Crook T	2	
Gillinghm	1	Folkestne	2	
Grantham	4	Hendon	1	
Guilford	2	Wycombe	2	
Hartlepl	3	Workingtn	1	
Leytonstn	0	Hereford	1	
Lincoln	1	Barnsley	3	
Mansfield	1	Oldham	3	
Millwall	3	Wealdstne	1	
Oxford	2	Port Vale	2	
Peterboro	2	Kiddermst	1	
Reading	3	Bristol R	2	
Romford	1	Luton	1	
S.Shields	3	York	1	
Shrewsby	2	Torquay	1	
Southend	3	Notts Co	1	
Southport	2	Halifax	0	
Swindon	5	Mert Tyd	1	
Tranmere	0	Stockport	1	
Walsall	6	Swansea	3	
Wimbledn	4	Gravesend	1	
Wrexham	4	S.L'pool	1	
Luton	1	Romford	0	r
Port Vale	3	Oxford	2	r
QPR	4	Colchester	0	r
Rochdale	5	Fleetwood	0	r
Weymouth	1	Bournemth	4	r
Wigan Ath	3	Doncaster	1	r
Wycombe	0	Guilford	1	r
SECOND ROUND				
Aldershot	0	Walsall	2	
Barnsley	1	Grimsby	1	
Bournemth	5	Bath C	3	
Brighton	1	Bedford T	1	
Chester	2	Wigan Ath	1	
Corby T	2	Luton	2	
Crewe	3	S.Shields	1	
Darlingtn	0	Oldham	1	
Gateshead	0	Hull	4	
Grantham	1	Swindon	6	
Hartlepl	2	Wrexham	0	
Hereford	1	Millwall	0	
Port Vale	1	Dartford	0	
QPR	3	Guilford	0	
Reading	5	Brentford	0	
Rochdale	1	Altrinchm	3	
Shrewsby	3	Peterboro	2	
Southend	2	Watford	1	
Southport	3	Stockport	3	
Wimbledn	0	Folkestne	1	
Bedford T	2	Brighton	1	r
Grimsby	2	Barnsley	0	re
Luton	0	Corby T	1	r
Stockport	0	Southport	2	r
THIRD ROUND				
Aston V	1	Leicester	2	
Bedford T	2	Hereford	1	
Birmghm C	3	Bristol C	2	
Blackburn	3	Arsenal	0	
Blackpool	1	Man City	1	
Bolton	3	West Brom	0	
Bournemth	1	Burnley	1	
Cardiff	2	Port Vale	1	
Carlisle	3	C.Palace	0	
Charlton	2	Preston NE	3	
Chester	1	Newcastle	3	
Derby	2	Man Utd	5	
Everton	3	Sunderld	0	
Folkestne	1	Crewe	5	
Grimsby	0	Portsmth	0	
Huddersfld	3	Hartlepl	1	
Hull	1	Southmptn	0	
Leeds U	6	Bury	0	
Leyton O	1	Norwich	3	
Liverpool	1	Chelsea	2	
N'hamptn	1	Nottm For	2	
Oldham	2	West Ham	2	
Plymouth	6	Corby T	0	

Peter Pain

Peter Shilton is the youngest-ever Final goalkeeper. He was only 19 years 221 days when he played for a Leicester side beaten 1-0 by Manchester City, in 1969. It was the fourth successive season that the two clubs had met in the competition.

Pro-File: JIMMY GREAVES

If you were to ask anyone in England to name their top five strikers, the chances are that Jimmy Greaves' name would pop up more often than not - just like the player himself.

It's almost impossible to compare players from different eras, but the former England and Tottenham striker's goalscoring record speaks for itself.

He notched up more than 350 League goals in just over 500 appearances, and that is an astonishing total by anybody's standards.

But the thing that marked Greaves out from his fellow strikers of the 1960s - and so many of the game's stars today - was the way in which he scored so many of his goals.

He appeared to almost pass the ball into the net, but such was his accuracy that extra power was never necessary to leave the goalkeeper absolutely helpless.

The greatest English striker ever? Again, it's impossible to say with any degree of certainty but one's thing's for sure...if Jimmy Greaves were playing today he'd be worth a fortune.

Career details

●**Represented:** England, Chelsea, AC Milan (Italy), Tottenham, West Ham ●**Position:** Striker ●**Born:** East Ham, 20.02.40 ●**Height:** 5ft 7in ●**Weight:** 10st 7lbs ●**Club honours:** FA Cup 1962, 1967; European Cup-Winners' Cup 1963 ●**International honours:** England 12 U23, 57 full caps; Football League representative

Club League Record

Era	Club	Games	Goals
57/60	Chelsea	157	124
60/61	AC Milan	14	9
61/69	Tottenham	321	220
69/70	West Ham	38	13

Cup Highlights

May 5 1962: Greaves scores the first goal, after only three minutes, as Spurs beat Burnley 3-1 in the FA Cup Final. It is his first major club honour.

May 15 1963: Having helped guide his new club to FA Cup glory the previous season, Jimmy Greaves scores twice as Spurs trounce Spanish giants Atletico Madrid 5-1 in the European Cup-Winners' Cup Final in Rotterdam.

May 20 1967: Greaves appears in his second FA Cup Final, against his former club Chelsea - and he collects his second winners' medal as Spurs run out 2-1 winners.

Greaves On:

●Eric is no longer a footballer, he is an issue. He is either loved or hated like a chart-topping teeny band. **His thoughts on Eric Cantona**

●Just when you thought there were truly no surprises left in football, Vinnie Jones turns out to be an international player. **Greaves on Vinny Jones**

DID YOU KNOW THAT...

●Jimmy Greaves scored on his debut for every team he played for, including England.

●Always the showman, he scored a hat-trick on his League debut for Spurs against Blackpool.

●He missed the 1966 World Cup Final while still suffering with the after-effects of a bout of hepatitis. His replacement was one Geoff Hurst and the rest, as they say, is history.

●Jimmy is a reformed alcoholic. He wrote all about his on-going battle against the bottle in his autobiography, 'This One's On Me'.

●He scored 44 goals for England, placing him third in the all-time scorers list behind Bobby Charlton and Gary Lineker.

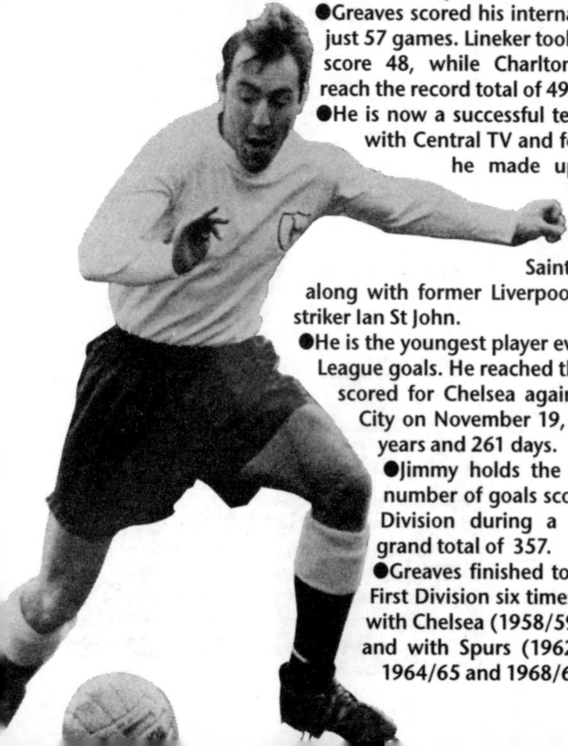

●Greaves scored his international goals in just 57 games. Lineker took 80 matches to score 48, while Charlton took 106 to reach the record total of 49.

●He is now a successful television pundit with Central TV and for several years he made up one half of the hugely successful TV partnership Saint & Greavsie, along with former Liverpool and Scotland striker Ian St John.

●He is the youngest player ever to score 100 League goals. He reached the ton when he scored for Chelsea against Manchester City on November 19, 1960, aged 20 years and 261 days.

●Jimmy holds the record for the number of goals scored in the First Division during a career with a grand total of 357.

●Greaves finished top scorer in the First Division six times in 11 seasons, with Chelsea (1958/59 and 1960/61) and with Spurs (1962/63, 1963/64, 1964/65 and 1968/69).

WHAT A STAR ✪ MIKE TREBILCOCK

This unknown Cornishman with the difficult to pronounce name took all the headlines in the 1966 Final, when Everton came from behind to beat Sheffield Wednesday 3-2. Trebilcock, surprisingly preferred to England international Fred Pickering, scored twice in five minutes, both with fierce right-foot volleys, to level the scores, and Everton battled on to win. Trebilcock had done little before that game and did little afterwards, ending his career early and emigrating to the USA. But he'll never be forgotten on Merseyside.

QPR	0	Shrewsby	0	
Reading	2	Sheff Wed	3	
Rotherhm	3	Southend	2	
Sheff Utd	3	Fulham	1	
Southport	0	Ipswich	0	
Stoke	0	Walsall	2	
Swindon	1	Coventry	2	
Tottenham	4	Middlesbro	0	
Wolves	5	Altrinchm	0	
Burnley	7	Bournemth	0	r
Ipswich	2	Southport	3	r
Man City	3	Blackpool	1	r
Portsmth	1	Grimsby	3	r
Shrewsby	1	QPR	0	r
West Ham	2	Oldham	1	r
FOURTH ROUND				
Bedford T	0	Everton	3	
Birmghm C	1	Leicester	2	
Bolton	1	Preston NE	1	
Chelsea	1	Leeds U	0	
Crewe	1	Coventry	1	
Hull	2	Nottm For	0	
Man City	2	Grimsby	0	
Man Utd	0	Rotherhm	0	
Newcastle	1	Sheff Wed	2	
Norwich	3	Walsall	2	
Plymouth	0	Huddersfld	2	
Shrewsby	0	Carlisle	0	
Southport	2	Cardiff	0	
Tottenham	4	Burnley	3	
West Ham	3	Blackburn	3	
Wolves	3	Sheff Utd	0	
Blackburn	4	West Ham	1	r
Carlisle	1	Shrewsby	1	re
Coventry	4	Crewe	1	r
Preston NE	3	Bolton	2	r
Rotherhm	0	Man Utd	1	re
Shrewsby	4	Carlisle	3	r2eN
FIFTH ROUND				
Chelsea	3	Shrewsby	2	
Everton	3	Coventry	0	
Huddersfld	1	Sheff Wed	2	
Hull	2	Southport	0	
Man City	2	Leicester	2	
Norwich	2	Blackburn	2	
Preston NE	2	Tottenham	1	
Wolves	2	Man Utd	4	
Blackburn	3	Norwich	2	r
Leicester	0	Man City	1	r
SIXTH ROUND				

Blackburn	1	Sheff Wed	2	
Chelsea	2	Hull	2	
Man City	0	Everton	0	
Preston NE	1	Man Utd	1	
Everton	0	Man City	0	re
Hull	1	Chelsea	3	r
Man Utd	3	Preston NE	1	r
Everton	2	Man City	0	r2N
SEMI-FINAL				
Everton	1	Man Utd	0	N
Sheff Wed	2	Chelsea	0	N
FINAL				
Everton	3	Sheff Wed	2	N

1967

FIRST ROUND				
Aldershot	2	Torquay	1	
Ashford	4	Cambs C	1	
Barnsley	3	Southport	1	
Bath C	1	Sutton U	0	
Bournemth	3	Welton R	0	
Bradford	1	Port Vale	2	
Bradfd PA	3	Witton Ab	2	
Brentford	1	Chelmsfd	0	
Bshk Auck	1	Blyth S	1	
Chester	2	Middlesbro	5	
Crewe	1	Grimsby	1	
Darlingtn	0	Stockport	0	
Enfield	6	Chesham U	0	
Exeter	1	Luton	1	
Folkestne	2	Swansea	2	
Gainsbrgh	0	Colchester	1	
Gillinghm	4	Tamworth	1	
Grantham	2	Wimbledn	1	
Halifax	2	Doncaster	2	

Great Scots

Both captains in the 1965 Final were Scots - the first time this had happened. Liverpool skipper Ron Yeats stood almost a foot taller than Bobby Collins of Leeds.

Hendon	1	Reading	3	
Horsham	0	Swindon	3	
Leyton O	2	Lowestoft	1	
Lincoln	3	Scunthpe	4	
Mansfield	4	Bangor C	1	
Newport	1	Brighton	2	
Oldham	3	Notts Co	1	
Oxford C	2	Bristol R	2	
Peterboro	4	Hereford	1	
QPR	3	Poole T	2	
Rochdale	1	Barrow	3	
S.Shields	1	Workingtn	4	
Shrewsby	5	Hartlepl	2	
Tranmere	1	Wigan Ath	1	
Walsall	2	St Neots	0	
Watford	1	Southend	0	
Wealdstne	0	Nuneaton	2	
Wrexham	3	Chestrfld	2	
Wycombe	1	Bedford T	1	
Yeovil T	1	Oxford	3	
York	0	Morecambe	0	
Bedford T	3	Wycombe	3	re
Blyth S	0	Bshk Auck	0	re
Bristol R	4	Oxford C	0	r
Doncaster	1	Halifax	3	re
Grimsby	0	Crewe	1	r
Luton	2	Exeter	0	r
Morecambe	1	York	1	re
Stockport	1	Darlingtn	1	re
Swansea	7	Folkestne	2	r
Wigan Ath	0	Tranmere	1	r
Bshk Auck	3	Blyth S	3	r2eN
Darlingtn	4	Stockport	2	r2N
Wycombe	1	Bedford T	1	r2
York	1	Morecambe	0	r2N
Bedford T	3	Wycombe	2	r3
Blyth S	1	Bshk Auck	4	r3N
SECOND ROUND				
Aldershot	1	Reading	0	
Barnsley	1	Port Vale	1	
Barrow	2	Tranmere	1	
Bath C	0	Brighton	5	
Bradfd PA	3	Workingtn	1	
Bristol R	3	Luton	2	
Bshk Auck	0	Halifax	0	
Colchester	0	Peterboro	3	
Crewe	2	Darlingtn	1	
Enfield	2	Watford	4	
Grantham	0	Oldham	4	
Leyton O	0	Brentford	0	

Mansfield	2	Scunthpe	1	
Middlesbro	1	York	1	
Nuneaton	2	Swansea	0	
Oxford	1	Bedford T	1	
QPR	2	Bournemth	0	
Shrewsby	5	Wrexham	1	
Swindon	5	Ashford	0	
Walsall	3	Gillinghm	1	
Bedford T	1	Oxford	0	r
Brentford	3	Leyton O	1	r
Halifax	7	Bshk Auck	0	r
Port Vale	1	Barnsley	3	r
York	0	Middlesbro	0	re
Middlesbro	4	York	1	r2N

THIRD ROUND

Aldershot	0	Brighton	0	
Barnsley	1	Cardiff	1	
Barrow	2	Southmptn	2	
Bedford T	2	Peterboro	6	
Birmghm C	2	Blackpool	1	
Blackburn	1	Carlisle	2	
Bolton	1	Crewe	0	
Bradfd PA	1	Fulham	3	
Bristol R	0	Arsenal	3	
Burnley	0	Everton	0	
Bury	2	Walsall	0	
Charlton	0	Sheff Utd	1	
Coventry	3	Newcastle	4	
Halifax	1	Bristol C	1	
Huddersfld	1	Chelsea	2	
Hull	1	Portsmth	1	
Ipswich	4	Shrewsby	1	
Leeds U	3	C.Palace	0	
Man City	2	Leicester	1	
Man Utd	2	Stoke	0	
Mansfield	2	Middlesbro	0	
Millwall	0	Tottenham	0	
N'hamptn	1	West Brom	3	
Norwich	3	Derby	0	
Nottm For	2	Plymouth	1	
Nuneaton	1	Rotherhm	1	
Oldham	2	Wolves	2	
Preston NE	0	Aston V	1	
Sheff Wed	3	QPR	0	
Sunderld	5	Brentford	2	
Watford	0	Liverpool	0	
West Ham	3	Swindon	3	
Brighton	3	Aldershot	1	r
Bristol C	4	Halifax	1	r
Cardiff	2	Barnsley	1	r
Everton	2	Burnley	1	r
Liverpool	3	Watford	1	r
Portsmth	2	Hull	2	re
Rotherhm	1	Nuneaton	0	r
Southmptn	3	Barrow	0	r
Swindon	3	West Ham	1	r
Tottenham	1	Millwall	0	r
Wolves	4	Oldham	1	r
Hull	1	Portsmth	3	r2N

FOURTH ROUND

Bolton	0	Arsenal	0	
Brighton	1	Chelsea	1	
Bristol C	1	Southmptn	0	
Cardiff	1	Man City	1	
Fulham	1	Sheff Utd	1	
Ipswich	2	Carlisle	0	
Leeds U	5	West Brom	0	
Liverpool	1	Aston V	0	
Man Utd	1	Norwich	2	
Nottm For	3	Newcastle	0	
Rotherhm	0	Birmghm C	0	
Sheff Wed	4	Mansfield	0	
Sunderld	7	Peterboro	1	
Swindon	2	Bury	1	
Tottenham	3	Portsmth	1	
Wolves	1	Everton	1	
Arsenal	3	Bolton	0	r
Birmghm C	2	Rotherhm	1	r
Chelsea	4	Brighton	0	r
Everton	3	Wolves	1	r
Man City	3	Cardiff	1	r
Sheff Utd	3	Fulham	1	r

FIFTH ROUND

Birmghm C	1	Arsenal	0	
Chelsea	2	Sheff Utd	0	
Everton	1	Liverpool	0	
Man City	1	Ipswich	1	
Norwich	1	Sheff Wed	3	
Nottm For	0	Swindon	0	
Sunderld	1	Leeds U	1	
Tottenham	2	Bristol C	0	
Ipswich	0	Man City	3	r
Leeds U	1	Sunderld	1	re
Swindon	1	Nottm For	1	re
Nottm For	3	Swindon	0	r2N
Sunderld	1	Leeds U	2	r2N

SIXTH ROUND

Birmghm C	0	Tottenham	0	
Chelsea	1	Sheff Wed	0	
Leeds U	1	Man City	0	
Nottm For	3	Everton	2	
Tottenham	6	Birmghm C	0	r

SEMI-FINAL

Chelsea	1	Leeds U	0	N
Tottenham	2	Nottm For	1	N

FINAL

Tottenham	2	Chelsea	1	N

1968

FIRST ROUND

Arnold	0	Bristol R	3
Barrow	2	Oldham	0
Bournemth	2	N'hamptn	0
Bradford	7	Wrexham	1
Brentford	2	Guilford	2
Brighton	1	Southend	0
Chelmsfd	3	Oxford	3
Chestrfld	2	Barnsley	0
Corby T	0	Boston U	3
Dagenham	1	Tonbridge	0
Goole T	0	Spennym'r	0
Grantham	0	Altrinchm	3
Grimsby	1	Bradfd PA	1
Halifax	3	Crewe	2
Hartlepl	2	Bury	3
Hereford	3	Barnet	2
Leytonstn	0	Walsall	1
Lowestoft	0	Watford	1
Luton	2	Oxford C	1
Newport	3	Gillinghm	0
Nuneaton	0	Exeter	0
Peterboro	5	Falmouth	2
Port Vale	1	Chester	2
Reading	6	Aldershot	2
Runcorn	1	Notts Co	0
Ryhope CW	0	Workingtn	1
Scunthpe	2	Skelmersd	0
Shrewsby	3	Darlingtn	0
Southport	3	Lincoln	1
Stockport	1	Macclesfd	1
Swansea	2	Enfield	0
Swindon	4	Salisbury	0
Torquay	1	Colchester	1
Tow Law	5	Mansfield	1
Tranmere	5	Rochdale	1
Walstmw A	2	Kiddermst	1
Weymouth	0	Leyton O	2

GIANTKILLERS

1967 Manchester United 1 Norwich 2

United had won the Cup once and lost in four Semi-Finals in the five years before this one, and they won the League title that season without losing at home, but on the day they came badly unstuck against Norwich, mid-table in the Second Division. Not even a goal by Denis Law, en route to a record of 41 in the FA Cup, could save United. They were managed by Matt Busby, of course, but give yourself a bonus point for spotting the opposing boss. He was the largely forgotten - even in Norwich - Lol Morgan.

Wimbledn	3	Romford	0	
Yeovil T	1	Margate	3	
York	0	Doncaster	1	
Bradfd PA	4	Grimsby	1	r
Colchester	2	Torquay	1	r
Exeter	0	Nuneaton	0	re
Guilford	2	Brentford	1	r
Macclesfd	2	Stockport	1	r
Oxford	3	Chelmsfd	3	re
Spennym'r	3	Goole T	1	r
Chelmsfd	1	Oxford	0	r2N
Nuneaton	0	Exeter	1	r2N

SECOND ROUND

Altrinchm	1	Barrow	2	
Boston U	1	Leyton O	1	
Bradford	2	Bury	3	
Bradfd PA	2	Tranmere	3	
Chelmsfd	0	Colchester	2	
Chester	0	Chestrfld	1	
Doncaster	1	Workingtn	1	
Exeter	1	Walsall	3	
Guilford	0	Newport	1	
Halifax	1	Scunthpe	0	
Macclesfd	2	Spennym'r	0	
Margate	0	Peterboro	4	
Reading	1	Dagenham	1	
Southport	4	Runcorn	2	
Swansea	2	Brighton	1	
Swindon	3	Luton	2	
Tow Law	1	Shrewsby	1	
Walstmw A	1	Bournemth	3	
Watford	3	Hereford	0	
Wimbledn	0	Bristol R	4	
Dagenham	0	Reading	1	r
Leyton O	2	Boston U	1	r
Shrewsby	6	Tow Law	2	r
Workingtn	1	Doncaster	2	re

THIRD ROUND

Aston V	3	Millwall	0	
Barrow	1	Leicester	2	
Blackpool	2	Chestrfld	1	
Bournemth	0	Liverpool	0	
Bristol C	0	Bristol R	0	
Burnley	1	West Ham	3	
Chelsea	3	Ipswich	0	
Colchester	1	West Brom	1	
Coventry	3	Charlton	0	
Doncaster	0	Swansea	2	
Fulham	4	Macclesfd	2	
Halifax	2	Birmghm C	4	
Leeds U	2	Derby	0	
Leyton O	1	Bury	0	
Man City	0	Reading	0	
Man Utd	2	Tottenham	2	
Middlesbro	1	Hull	1	
Newcastle	0	Carlisle	1	
Norwich	1	Sunderld	1	
Nottm For	4	Bolton	2	
Peterboro	0	Portsmth	1	
QPR	1	Preston NE	3	
Rotherhm	1	Wolves	0	
Sheff Wed	3	Plymouth	0	
Shrewsby	1	Arsenal	1	
Southmptn	1	Newport	1	
Southport	0	Everton	1	
Stoke	4	Cardiff	1	
Swindon	1	Blackburn	0	
Tranmere	2	Huddersfld	1	
Walsall	1	C.Palace	1	
Watford	0	Sheff Utd	1	
Arsenal	2	Shrewsby	0	r
Bristol R	1	Bristol C	2	r
C.Palace	1	Walsall	2	r
Hull	2	Middlesbro	2	re
Liverpool	4	Bournemth	1	r
Newport	2	Southmptn	3	r
Reading	0	Man City	7	r
Sunderld	0	Norwich	1	r
Tottenham	1	Man Utd	0	re
West Brom	4	Colchester	0	r
Middlesbro	1	Hull	0	r2N

Strange but true!

Goalkeeper Jim Standen achieved an odd double in 1964. He helped West Ham to win the FA Cup Final, and then won a County Championship cricket medal with Worcestershire that summer.

FOURTH ROUND

Aston V	0	Rotherhm	1	
Birmghm C	3	Leyton O	0	
Carlisle	0	Everton	2	
Chelsea	1	Norwich	0	
Coventry	1	Tranmere	1	
Fulham	0	Portsmth	0	
Leeds U	2	Nottm For	1	
Man City	0	Leicester	0	
Middlesbro	1	Bristol C	1	
Sheff Utd	2	Blackpool	1	
Sheff Wed	2	Swindon	1	
Stoke	0	West Ham	3	
Swansea	0	Arsenal	1	
Tottenham	3	Preston NE	1	
Walsall	0	Liverpool	0	
West Brom	1	Southmptn	1	
Bristol C	2	Middlesbro	1	r
Leicester	4	Man City	3	r
Liverpool	5	Walsall	2	r
Portsmth	1	Fulham	0	r
Southmptn	2	West Brom	3	r
Tranmere	2	Coventry	0	r

FIFTH ROUND

Arsenal	1	Birmghm C	1	
Everton	2	Tranmere	0	
Leeds U	2	Bristol C	0	
Portsmth	1	West Brom	2	
Rotherhm	1	Leicester	1	
Sheff Wed	2	Chelsea	2	
Tottenham	1	Liverpool	1	
West Ham	1	Sheff Utd	2	
Birmghm C	2	Arsenal	1	r
Chelsea	2	Sheff Wed	0	r
Leicester	2	Rotherhm	0	re

Early Starters

Barry Stobart won the Cup with Wolves in 1960 after making only five previous first-team appearances. A year later Hugh McIlmoyle was a loser with Leicester in only his eighth senior game.

Liverpool	2	Tottenham	1	r

SIXTH ROUND

Birmghm C	1	Chelsea	0	
Leeds U	1	Sheff Utd	0	
Leicester	1	Everton	3	
West Brom	0	Liverpool	0	
Liverpool	1	West Brom	1	re
West Brom	2	Liverpool	1	r2N

SEMI-FINAL

Everton	1	Leeds U	0	N
West Brom	2	Birmghm C	0	N

FINAL

West Brom	1	Everton	0	eN

1969

FIRST ROUND

Altrinchm	0	Crewe	1	
Bangor C	2	Morecambe	3	
Barnet	1	Brentwd T	1	
Barnsley	0	Rochdale	0	
Bilston	1	Halifax	3	
Bradford	1	Chester	2	
Brentford	2	Woking	0	
Brighton	2	Kiddermst	2	
Bristol R	3	Peterboro	1	
Bury Town	0	Bournemth	0	
Chelthnm	0	Watford	4	
Chestrfld	2	Skelmersd	0	
Colchester	5	Chesham U	0	
Darlingtn	2	Grimsby	0	
Dartford	3	Aldershot	1	
Doncaster	1	Notts Co	0	
Exeter	0	Newport	0	
Goole T	1	Barrow	3	
Grantham	2	Chelmsfd	1	
Hartlepl	1	Rotherhm	1	
Hereford	0	Torquay	0	
Leyton O	1	Gillinghm	1	
Leytonstn	0	Walsall	1	
Luton	6	Ware	1	
Macclesfd	1	Lincoln	3	
Mansfield	4	Tow Law	1	
N'hamptn	3	Margate	1	
Oxford C	2	Swansea	3	
Reading	1	Plymouth	0	
S.Shields	0	York	6	
Shrewsby	1	Port Vale	1	
Southend	9	King's Ln	0	
Stockport	3	Bradfd PA	0	

Swindon	1	Canterby	0	
Tranmere	0	Southport	1	
Waterlve	1	Kettering	2	
Wealdstne	1	St Albns C	1	
Weymouth	2	Yeovil T	1	
Workingtn	2	Scunthpe	0	
Wrexham	4	Oldham	2	
Bournemth	3	Bury Town	0	r
Brentwd T	1	Barnet	0	r
Gillinghm	2	Leyton O	1	r
Kiddermst	0	Brighton	1	r
Newport	1	Exeter	3	r
Port Vale	3	Shrewsby	1	r
Rochdale	0	Barnsley	1	r
Rotherhm	3	Hartlepl	0	r
St Albns C	1	Wealdstne	0	r
Torquay	4	Hereford	2	r
SECOND ROUND				
Bournemth	0	Bristol R	0	
Brighton	1	N'hamptn	2	
Chester	1	Lincoln	1	
Chestrfld	2	Wrexham	1	
Colchester	0	Exeter	1	
Darlingtn	0	Barnsley	0	
Doncaster	2	Southport	1	
Grantham	0	Swindon	2	
Halifax	1	Crewe	1	
Kettering	5	Dartford	0	
Luton	3	Gillinghm	1	
Port Vale	1	Workingtn	1	
Reading	0	Torquay	0	
Rotherhm	2	Mansfield	2	
Southend	10	Brentwd T	1	
St Albns C	1	Walsall	1	
Stockport	2	Barrow	0	
Watford	1	Brentford	0	
Weymouth	1	Swansea	1	
York	2	Morecambe	0	
Barnsley	1	Darlingtn	0	re
Bristol R	1	Bournemth	0	r
Crewe	1	Halifax	3	r
Lincoln	2	Chester	1	r
Mansfield	1	Rotherhm	0	r
Swansea	2	Weymouth	0	r
Torquay	1	Reading	2	r
Walsall	3	St Albns C	1	r
Workingtn	1	Port Vale	2	r
THIRD ROUND				
Aston V	2	QPR	1	
Barnsley	1	Leicester	1	
Birmghm C	2	Lincoln	1	
Blackburn	2	Stockport	0	
Bolton	2	N'hamptn	1	
Bristol R	1	Kettering	1	
Burnley	3	Derby	1	
Bury	1	Huddersfld	2	
Cardiff	0	Arsenal	0	
Charlton	0	C.Palace	0	
Chelsea	2	Carlisle	0	
Coventry	3	Blackpool	1	
Everton	2	Ipswich	1	
Exeter	1	Man Utd	3	
Hull	1	Wolves	3	
Liverpool	2	Doncaster	0	
Man City	1	Luton	0	
Mansfield	2	Sheff Utd	1	
Middlesbro	1	Millwall	1	
Newcastle	4	Reading	0	
Oxford	1	Southmptn	1	
Portsmth	3	Chestrfld	0	
Preston NE	3	Nottm For	0	
Sheff Wed	1	Leeds U	1	
Sunderld	1	Fulham	4	
Swansea	0	Halifax	1	
Swindon	0	Southend	2	
Walsall	0	Tottenham	1	
Watford	2	Port Vale	0	
West Brom	3	Norwich	0	
West Ham	3	Bristol C	2	
York	0	Stoke	2	
Arsenal	2	Cardiff	0	r
C.Palace	0	Charlton	2	r
Kettering	1	Bristol R	2	r
Leeds U	1	Sheff Wed	3	r
Leicester	2	Barnsley	1	r
Millwall	1	Middlesbro	0	r
Southmptn	2	Oxford	0	r
FOURTH ROUND				
Arsenal	2	Charlton	0	
Blackburn	4	Portsmth	0	
Bolton	1	Bristol R	2	
Everton	2	Coventry	0	
Fulham	1	West Brom	2	
Huddersfld	0	West Ham	2	
Liverpool	2	Burnley	1	
Man City	0	Newcastle	0	
Man Utd	1	Watford	1	
Mansfield	2	Southend	1	
Millwall	0	Leicester	1	
Preston NE	0	Chelsea	0	

Top Finnish

Graham Williams, captain of WBA's 1968 winners, was a Welsh international who later coached Rovaniemi, a Finnish club inside the Arctic circle. The local authority there run trips by reindeer sleigh to see Santa Claus.

Sheff Wed	2	Birmghm C	2	
Southmptn	2	Aston V	2	
Stoke	1	Halifax	1	
Tottenham	2	Wolves	1	
Aston V	2	Southmptn	1	r
Birmghm C	2	Sheff Wed	1	r
Chelsea	2	Preston NE	1	r
Halifax	0	Stoke	3	r
Newcastle	0	Man City	2	r
Watford	0	Man Utd	2	r
FIFTH ROUND				
Birmghm C	2	Man Utd	2	
Chelsea	3	Stoke	2	
Everton	1	Bristol R	0	
Leicester	0	Liverpool	0	
Man City	4	Blackburn	1	
Mansfield	3	West Ham	0	
Tottenham	3	Aston V	2	
West Brom	1	Arsenal	0	
Liverpool	0	Leicester	1	r
Man Utd	6	Birmghm C	2	r
SIXTH ROUND				
Chelsea	1	West Brom	2	
Man City	1	Tottenham	0	
Man Utd	0	Everton	1	
Mansfield	0	Leicester	1	
SEMI-FINAL				
Leicester	1	West Brom	0	N
Man City	1	Everton	0	N
FINAL				
Man City	1	Leicester	0	N

WHAT A STAR ✪ GERRY BYRNE

Gerry Byrne unfortunately put through his own goal on his League debut for Liverpool, disappeared back into the reserves, then emerged to become a hero in the 1965 Cup Final. After only two minutes he broke a collarbone in a collision, but not only did he play on until the end of extra-time, and help make the first goal, but he disguised the injury so well that Leeds never caught on, and Liverpool won the trophy for the first time. The hard-working Byrne was later named in the England squad for the World Cup the following year.

1970-1979

UNDERDOGS MAKE THEIR MARK

Arsenal emulated their North London rivals Tottenham's achievement of ten years earlier by completing the 'double' with a Cup Final victory over Liverpool in 1971.

Eddie Kelly and Charlie George - with a memorable goal and even more memorable flat-on-the-back celebration - were the heroes of The Gunners' 2-1 win, but the 70s will be remembered as the decade of the underdog.

Strange but true!

Phil Boersma, left out of the Liverpool Wembley team in 1974, walked out of the ground and travelled home rather than stay to watch.

Sunderland, Southampton and Ipswich Town all carried off the great trophy after beating sides they were supposedly inferior to. Perhaps the most romantic FA Cup win of all-time was in 1973, when Bob Stokoe took his Second Division Sunderland side to Wembley to face Leeds United, the best team of that era.

But, as The Wanderers proved against Royal Engineers way back in 1872, reputations count for nothing in the FA Cup. So the form book was ripped up, tossed away and The Rokerites strolled off into the sunset clutching the silverware.

Ian Porterfield grabbed the decisive goal, but it was goalkeeper Jim Montgomery who stole the headlines, mainly for a stunning save from Peter Lorimer which broke the Yorkshiremen's hearts.

But those expecting that to signal an end to the fairytales and for the big clubs to reclaim their 'right' to the Cup were sadly mistaken.

Three years later, Southampton, also from the Second Division, sprung another almighty surprise by beating mighty Man Utd.

United boss Tommy Docherty had been scathing of his side's opponents in the build-up to the Final but was made to eat his words when little Bobby Stokes drilled home the winning goal just seven minutes from time.

And there was still time for one more shock, although it wasn't such a heart-stopper as the first two.

Ipswich, although a good side, were in their first ever Final and not expected to be a match for Arsenal in the '78 showpiece, but yet again no-one told the underdogs.

And when Suffolk-born midfielder Roger Osborne drilled home the winning goal 14 minutes from time - before collapsing with a mixture of exhaustion and emotion - it signalled that the 1970s really was the decade of the upset.

1970

FIRST ROUND				
Alfreton	1	Barrow	1	
Bangor C	6	Kirkby T	0	
Bournemth	1	Luton	1	
Bradford	2	Grimsby	1	
Brentford	0	Plymouth	0	
Brentwd T	1	Reading	0	
Brighton	2	Enfield	1	
Bury	2	Manfield	2	
Chelmsfd	1	Hereford	2	
Chelthnm	0	Oxford C	2	
Dagenham	0	Sutton U	1	
Darlingtn	0	Barnsley	0	
Doncaster	1	Crewe	1	
Exeter	2	Fulham	0	
Falmouth	1	Peterboro	4	
Halifax	3	Chester	3	
Hartlepl	3	N.Shields	0	
Hendon	5	Carshlton	3	
Hillingdn	2	Wimbledn	0	
Kettering	0	Swansea	2	
Lincoln	2	Southport	0	
Macclesfd	1	Scunthpe	1	
Margate	2	Aldershot	7	
Newport	2	Colchester	1	
N'hamptn	0	Weymouth	0	
Notts Co	0	Rotherhm	3	
Oldham	3	Grantham	1	
S.Shields	2	Bradfd PA	1	
Southend	0	Gillinghm	0	
Spennym'r	1	Wrexham	4	
Stockport	1	Mossley	1	
Tamworth	2	Torquay	1	
Telford U	0	Bristol R	3	
Tranmere	3	Chestrfld	0	
Walsall	0	Leyton O	0	
Walton&H	0	Barnet	1	
Wigan Ath	1	Port Vale	1	
Workingtn	2	Rochdale	1	
Yeovil T	2	Shrewsby	3	
York	2	Whitby T	0	
Barnsley	2	Darlingtn	0	r
Barrow	0	Alfreton	0	re
Chester	1	Halifax	0	r
Crewe	0	Doncaster	1	r
Gillinghm	2	Southend	1	r
Leyton O	0	Walsall	2	r
Luton	3	Bournemth	1	r
Manfield	2	Bury	0	r
Mossley	0	Stockport	1	r
Plymouth	2	Brentford	0	r
Port Vale	2	Wigan Ath	2	re
Scunthpe	4	Macclesfd	2	r
Weymouth	1	N'hamptn	3	r
Alfreton	2	Barrow	2	r2eN
Port Vale	1	Wigan Ath	0	r2eN
Barrow	2	Alfreton	0	r3N
SECOND ROUND				
Aldershot	3	Bristol R	1	
Bangor C	0	York	0	
Barnet	0	Sutton U	2	
Barnsley	3	Barrow	0	
Bradford	3	Lincoln	0	
Brighton	1	Walsall	1	
Chester	1	Doncaster	1	
Gillinghm	6	Tamworth	0	
Hartlepl	0	Wrexham	1	
Hendon	0	Brentwd T	2	
Hillingdn	2	Luton	1	
Newport	2	Hereford	1	
N'hamptn	1	Exeter	1	
Oxford C	1	Swansea	5	
Peterboro	2	Plymouth	0	
Port Vale	2	Tranmere	2	
Rotherhm	3	Workingtn	0	
S.Shields	0	Oldham	0	
Shrewsby	1	Manfield	2	
Stockport	0	Scunthpe	0	
Doncaster	0	Chester	2	r
Exeter	0	N'hamptn	0	re
Oldham	1	S.Shields	2	r
Scunthpe	4	Stockport	0	r
Tranmere	3	Port Vale	1	r
Walsall	1	Brighton	1	re
York	2	Bangor C	0	r
Brighton	0	Walsall	0	r2eN
N'hamptn	2	Exeter	1	r2N
Brighton	1	Walsall	2	r3N
THIRD ROUND				
Arsenal	1	Blackpool	1	
Aston V	1	Charlton	1	
Blackburn	0	Swindon	4	
Bolton	1	Watford	2	
Bradford	2	Tottenham	2	
Brentwd T	0	N'hamptn	1	
Burnley	3	Wolves	0	
Chelsea	3	Birmghm C	0	
Chester	2	Bristol C	1	
Coventry	1	Liverpool	1	
C.Palace	2	Walsall	0	
Gillinghm	1	Newport	0	
Hillingdn	0	Sutton U	0	
Huddersfld	1	Aldershot	1	
Hull	0	Man City	1	
Ipswich	0	Man Utd	1	
Leeds U	2	Swansea	1	
Leicester	1	Sunderld	0	
Manfield	3	Barnsley	2	
Middlesbro	2	West Ham	1	
Norwich	1	Wrexham	2	
Nottm For	0	Carlisle	0	
Oxford	0	Stoke	0	
Portsmth	1	Tranmere	2	
Preston NE	1	Derby	1	
QPR	4	S.Shields	1	
Rotherhm	0	Peterboro	1	
Scunthpe	2	Millwall	1	
Sheff Utd	2	Everton	1	
Sheff Wed	2	West Brom	1	
Southmptn	3	Newcastle	0	
York	1	Cardiff	1	
Aldershot	3	Huddersfld	1	r
Blackpool	3	Arsenal	2	r
Cardiff	1	York	1	re
Carlisle	2	Nottm For	1	r
Charlton	1	Aston V	0	r
Derby	4	Preston NE	1	r
Liverpool	3	Coventry	0	r
Stoke	3	Oxford	2	r
Sutton U	4	Hillingdn	1	r
Tottenham	5	Bradford	0	r
Cardiff	1	York	3	r2eN
FOURTH ROUND				
Blackpool	0	Manfield	2	
Carlisle	2	Aldershot	2	
Charlton	2	QPR	3	
Chelsea	2	Burnley	2	
Derby	3	Sheff Utd	0	
Gillinghm	5	Peterboro	1	

GIANTKILLERS

1971 Colchester 3 Leeds 2

This was one of the really big shocks of Cup history, when a mid-table Fourth Division team containing six men obtained on free transfers beat one of the world's strongest clubs, even though they were almost overhauled after leading 3-0 with half-an-hour to go. A 5-0 defeat at Everton at the next stage was something of an anti-climax for Colchester, but that does not mar the memory of Ray Crawford (ex-Ipswich and England), Mick Mahon, Dave Simmons and the rest, plus manager Dick Graham, a sergeant-major type who outfoxed even the wily Don Revie for 90 glorious minutes.

Liverpool	3	Wrexham	1	
Man Utd	3	Man City	0	
Middlesbro	4	York	1	
Sheff Wed	1	Scunthpe	2	
Southmptn	1	Leicester	1	
Sutton U	0	Leeds U	6	
Swindon	4	Chester	2	
Tottenham	0	C.Palace	0	
Tranmere	0	N'hamptn	0	
Watford	1	Stoke	0	
Aldershot	1	Carlisle	4	r
Burnley	1	Chelsea	3	re
C.Palace	1	Tottenham	0	r
Leicester	4	Southmptn	2	re
N'hamptn	2	Tranmere	1	r
FIFTH ROUND				
Carlisle	1	Middlesbro	2	
C.Palace	1	Chelsea	4	
Leeds U	2	Manfield	0	
Liverpool	0	Leicester	0	
N'hamptn	2	Man Utd	8	
QPR	1	Derby	0	
Swindon	3	Scunthpe	1	
Watford	2	Gillinghm	1	
Leicester	0	Liverpool	2	r
SIXTH ROUND				
Middlesbro	1	Man Utd	1	
QPR	2	Chelsea	4	
Swindon	0	Leeds U	2	
Watford	1	Liverpool	0	
Man Utd	2	Middlesbro	1	r
SEMI-FINAL				
Chelsea	5	Watford	1	N
Man Utd	0	Leeds U	0	N
Man Utd	0	Leeds U	0	reN
Man Utd	0	Leeds U	1	r2N
FINAL				
Chelsea	2	Leeds U	2	eN
Chelsea	2	Leeds U	1	reN

1971

FIRST ROUND				
Barnet	6	Newport	1	
Barnsley	1	Bradfd PA	0	
Bradford	3	Macclesfd	2	
Brentford	2	Gillinghm	1	
Brighton	4	Chelthnm	0	
Chestrfld	2	Halifax	0	
Colchester	3	Ringmer	0	
Crawley T	1	Chelmsfd	1	
Crewe	0	Doncaster	0	
Dagenham	2	Margate	0	
Darlingtn	5	Bangor C	1	
Enfield	0	Cambridge	1	
Fulham	1	Bristol R	2	
Grantham	2	Stockport	1	
Grimsby	0	Bury	1	
G.Harwood	2	Rotherhm	6	
Hendon	0	Aldershot	2	
Hereford	2	N'hamptn	2	
Lincoln	2	Barrow	1	
Manfield	2	Wrexham	0	
Minehead	1	Shrewsby	2	
Notts Co	1	Port Vale	0	
Oxford C	1	Bournemth	1	
Peterboro	3	Wimbledn	1	
Preston NE	1	Chester	1	
Reading	6	Bshp Stor	1	
Rhyl	1	Hartlepl	0	
Rochdale	2	Oldham	0	
S.Shields	1	Wigan Ath	1	
Scarboro	2	Workingtn	3	
Southend	7	Weymouth	0	
Southport	0	Boston U	2	
Swansea	4	Exeter	1	
Tamworth	0	York	0	
Torquay	3	Aston V	1	
Tranmere	1	Scunthpe	1	
Walsall	3	Plymouth	0	
Walton&H	2	Telford U	5	
Wycombe	1	Slough T	1	
Yeovil T	1	Averley	0	
Bournemth	8	Oxford C	1	r
Chelmsfd	6	Crawley T	1	r
Chester	1	Preston NE	0	r
Doncaster	1	Crewe	3	r
N'hamptn	1	Hereford	2	r
Scunthpe	0	Tranmere	0	re
Slough T	1	Wycombe	0	r
Wigan Ath	2	S.Shields	0	r
York	5	Tamworth	0	r
Tranmere	0	Scunthpe	1	r2eN
SECOND ROUND				
Aldershot	1	Bristol R	1	
Boston U	1	York	2	
Bournemth	0	Yeovil T	1	
Brentford	1	Walsall	0	
Bury	1	Notts Co	1	
Chelmsfd	0	Torquay	1	
Chester	1	Crewe	0	
Chestrfld	0	Workingtn	0	
Colchester	3	Cambridge	0	
Darlingtn	0	Rochdale	2	
Grantham	1	Rotherhm	4	
Hereford	1	Brighton	2	
Lincoln	2	Bradford	2	
Rhyl	0	Barnsley	0	
Scunthpe	3	Manfield	0	
Shrewsby	2	Reading	2	
Slough T	0	Barnet	1	
Southend	1	Dagenham	0	
Swansea	6	Telford U	2	
Wigan Ath	2	Peterboro	1	
Barnsley	1	Rhyl	1	re
Bradford	2	Lincoln	2	re
Bristol R	1	Aldershot	3	r
Notts Co	3	Bury	0	r
Reading	1	Shrewsby	0	r
Workingtn	3	Chestrfld	2	r
Lincoln	4	Bradford	1	r2N
Rhyl	2	Barnsley	0	r2N
THIRD ROUND				
Barnet	0	Colchester	1	
Blackpool	4	West Ham	0	
Cardiff	1	Brighton	0	
Chester	1	Derby	2	
C.Palace	2	Chelsea	2	
Everton	2	Blackburn	0	
Huddersfld	1	Birmghm C	1	
Hull	3	Charlton	0	
Leicester	2	Notts Co	0	
Liverpool	1	Aldershot	0	
Man City	1	Wigan Ath	0	
Man Utd	0	Middlesbro	0	
Newcastle	1	Ipswich	1	
Nottm For	1	Luton	1	
Oxford	3	Burnley	0	
Portsmth	2	Sheff Utd	0	

Crowded Houses

Leeds were watched by a then-capacity 100,000 crowd in the 1970 FA Cup Final, but four days later they were seen by an even larger number - 136,505 for the European Cup Semi-Final against Celtic at Hampden Park.

WHAT A STAR ✪ DICKIE GUY

An unknown goalkeeper became national news when he helped Wimbledon, then a non-League club, hold Leeds to a Fourth Round draw by saving a Peter Lorimer penalty near the end. In their 1975 replay, watched by nearly 46,000 at Selhurst Park, Guy again made a string of saves before finally being beaten by a shot which deflected off team-mate Dave Bassett. In the previous round, Dons had beaten First Division Burnley on their own ground, largely thanks to Guy.

GIANTKILLERS

1972 Hereford 2 Newcastle 1

The goal of the season, Ronnie Radford's 30-yard thump out of a mud patch, did more than equalise for non-League Hereford after Malcolm Macdonald had put First Division Newcastle in front. That goal, plus Ricky George's winner, and the team's overall performances both at Edgar Street and in the earlier 2-2 draw on Tyneside, persuaded the Football League to vote Hereford into the Fourth Division for the following season. On a less important scale, John Motson's TV commentary established him in the public eye...or ear.

QPR	1	Swindon	2	
Rochdale	2	Coventry	1	
Rotherhm	0	Leeds U	0	
Southmptn	3	Bristol C	0	
Southend	0	Carlisle	3	
Stoke	2	Millwall	1	
Sunderld	0	Leyton O	3	
Swansea	6	Rhyl	1	
Torquay	4	Lincoln	3	
Tottenham	4	Sheff Wed	1	
Watford	5	Reading	0	
West Brom	0	Scunthpe	0	
Wolves	5	Norwich	1	
Workingtn	0	Brentford	1	
Yeovil T	0	Arsenal	3	
York	2	Bolton	0	
Birmghm C	0	Huddersfld	2	r
Chelsea	2	C.Palace	0	r
Ipswich	2	Newcastle	1	r
Leeds U	3	Rotherhm	2	r
Luton	3	Nottm For	4	r
Middlesbro	2	Man Utd	1	r
Scunthpe	1	West Brom	3	r

FOURTH ROUND

Cardiff	0	Brentford	2	
Carlisle	2	Tottenham	3	
Chelsea	0	Man City	3	
Derby	2	Wolves	1	
Everton	3	Middlesbro	0	
Hull	2	Blackpool	0	
Leeds U	4	Swindon	0	
Leicester	3	Torquay	0	
Liverpool	3	Swansea	0	
Nottm For	1	Leyton O	1	
Oxford	1	Watford	1	
Portsmth	1	Arsenal	1	
Rochdale	3	Colchester	3	
Stoke	3	Huddersfld	3	
West Brom	1	Ipswich	1	
York	3	Southmptn	3	
Arsenal	3	Portsmth	2	r
Colchester	5	Rochdale	0	r
Huddersfld	0	Stoke	0	re
Ipswich	3	West Brom	0	r
Leyton O	0	Nottm For	1	r
Southmptn	3	York	2	r
Watford	1	Oxford	2	r
Stoke	1	Huddersfld	0	r2N

FIFTH ROUND

Colchester	3	Leeds U	2	
Everton	1	Derby	0	
Hull	2	Brentford	1	
Leicester	1	Oxford	1	
Liverpool	1	Southmptn	0	
Man City	1	Arsenal	2	
Stoke	0	Ipswich	0	
Tottenham	2	Nottm For	1	
Ipswich	0	Stoke	1	r
Oxford	1	Leicester	3	re

SIXTH ROUND

Everton	5	Colchester	0	
Hull	2	Stoke	3	
Leicester	0	Arsenal	0	
Liverpool	0	Tottenham	0	
Arsenal	1	Leicester	0	r
Tottenham	0	Liverpool	1	r

SEMI-FINAL

Arsenal	2	Stoke	2	N
Liverpool	2	Everton	1	N
Stoke	0	Arsenal	2	rN

FINAL

Arsenal	2	Liverpool	1	eN

1972

FIRST ROUND

Aldershot	4	Alvechurch	2	
Barrow	0	Darlingtn	2	
BasingstokeT	1	N'hamptn	5	
Blackburn	1	Port Vale	1	
Bolton	3	Bangor C	0	
Bournemth	11	Margate	0	
Bridgwtr	0	Reading	3	
Brighton	7	Hillingdn	1	
Bristol R	3	Telford U	0	
Cambridge	2	Weymouth	1	
Chester	1	Manfield	1	
Chestrfld	3	Oldham	0	
Colchester	1	Shrewsby	4	
Crawley T	0	Exeter	0	
Crewe	0	Blyth S	1	
Doncaster	1	Stockport	2	
Ellesmere	0	Boston U	3	
Enfield	2	Maidenh U	0	
Frickley	2	Rotherhm	2	
Gillinghm	3	Plymouth	2	
Guilford	0	Dover	0	
Hartlepl	6	Scarboro	1	
Kettering	2	Barnet	4	
King's Ln	0	Hereford	0	
Lincoln	1	Bury	2	
Notts Co	6	Newport	0	
Redditch	1	Peterboro	1	
Rochdale	1	Barnsley	3	
Rossendl U	1	Altrinchm	0	
S.Shields	3	Scunthpe	3	
Skelmersd	0	Tranmere	4	
Southend	1	Aston V	0	
Southport	1	Workingtn	3	
Swansea	1	Brentford	1	
Torquay	1	Nuneaton	0	
Walsall	4	Dagenham	1	
Wigan Ath	2	Halifax	1	
Witney T	0	Romford	3	
Wrexham	5	Bradford	1	
York	4	Grimsby	2	
Brentford	2	Swansea	3	r
Dover	0	Guilford	2	r
Exeter	2	Crawley T	0	r
Hereford	1	King's Ln	0	r
Manfield	4	Chester	3	r
Peterboro	6	Redditch	0	r
Port Vale	3	Blackburn	1	r
Rotherhm	4	Frickley	0	r
Scunthpe	2	S.Shields	3	r

SECOND ROUND

Barnet	1	Torquay	4	
Barnsley	0	Chestrfld	0	
Blyth S	1	Stockport	0	
Boston U	2	Hartlepl	1	
Bournemth	2	Southend	0	
Brighton	1	Walsall	1	
Bristol R	3	Cambridge	0	
Hereford	0	N'hamptn	0	
Manfield	2	Tranmere	2	
Peterboro	4	Enfield	0	
Port Vale	1	Darlingtn	0	
Reading	1	Aldershot	0	
Romford	0	Gillinghm	1	
Rossendl U	1	Bolton	4	N
Rotherhm	1	York	1	
S.Shields	1	Notts Co	3	
Shrewsby	2	Guilford	1	
Swansea	0	Exeter	0	
Workingtn	1	Bury	3	
Wrexham	4	Wigan Ath	0	
Chestrfld	1	Barnsley	0	r
Exeter	0	Swansea	1	r

N'hamptn	2	Hereford	2	re
Tranmere	4	Manfield	2	r
Walsall	2	Brighton	1	r
York	2	Rotherhm	3	re
Hereford	2	N'hamptn	1	r2eN
THIRD ROUND				
Birmghm C	3	Port Vale	0	
Blackpool	0	Chelsea	1	
Blyth S	2	Reading	2	
Bolton	2	Torquay	1	
Boston U	0	Portsmth	1	
Burnley	0	Huddersfld	1	
Bury	1	Rotherhm	1	
Charlton	0	Tranmere	0	
C.Palace	2	Everton	2	
Derby	2	Shrewsby	0	
Leeds U	4	Bristol R	1	
Leyton O	3	Wrexham	0	
Man City	1	Middlesbro	1	
Millwall	3	Nottm For	1	
Newcastle	2	Hereford	2	
Norwich	0	Hull	3	
Oxford	0	Liverpool	3	
Peterboro	0	Ipswich	2	
Preston NE	4	Bristol C	2	
QPR	1	Fulham	1	
Sheff Utd	1	Cardiff	3	
Southmptn	1	Man Utd	1	
Stoke	2	Chestrfld	1	
Sunderld	3	Sheff Wed	0	
Swansea	1	Gillinghm	0	
Swindon	0	Arsenal	2	
Tottenham	1	Carlisle	1	
Walsall	1	Bournemth	0	
Watford	1	Notts Co	4	
West Brom	1	Coventry	2	
West Ham	2	Luton	1	
Wolves	1	Leicester	1	
Carlisle	1	Tottenham	3	r
Everton	3	C.Palace	2	r
Fulham	2	QPR	1	r
Hereford	2	Newcastle	1	r
Leicester	2	Wolves	0	r
Man Utd	4	Southmptn	1	re
Middlesbro	1	Man City	0	r
Reading	6	Blyth S	1	r

Peter Perfect

Chelsea's Peter Osgood is the 12th and last player to score in every round of the Cup in one season. He did so in 1970, grabbing eight goals in eight games. When Osgood helped Southampton to win the trophy in 1976, he did not get a single goal in the entire competition.

Ian Porterfield strikes for Sunderland against Leeds in 1973

Rotherhm	2	Bury	1	r
Tranmere	4	Charlton	2	r
FOURTH ROUND				
Birmghm C	1	Ipswich	0	
Cardiff	1	Sunderld	1	
Chelsea	3	Bolton	0	
Coventry	0	Hull	1	
Derby	6	Notts Co	0	
Everton	2	Walsall	1	
Hereford	0	West Ham	0	
Huddersfld	3	Fulham	0	
Leicester	0	Leyton O	2	
Liverpool	0	Leeds U	0	
Millwall	2	Middlesbro	2	
Portsmth	2	Swansea	0	
Preston NE	0	Man Utd	2	
Reading	1	Arsenal	2	
Tottenham	2	Rotherhm	0	
Tranmere	2	Stoke	2	
Leeds U	2	Liverpool	0	r
Middlesbro	2	Millwall	1	r
Stoke	2	Tranmere	0	r
Sunderld	1	Cardiff	1	re
West Ham	3	Hereford	1	r
Cardiff	3	Sunderld	1	r2N
FIFTH ROUND				
Birmghm C	3	Portsmth	1	
Cardiff	0	Leeds U	2	
Derby	2	Arsenal	2	
Everton	0	Tottenham	2	
Huddersfld	4	West Ham	2	
Leyton O	3	Chelsea	2	
Man Utd	0	Middlesbro	0	
Stoke	4	Hull	1	
Arsenal	0	Derby	0	re
Middlesbro	0	Man Utd	3	r
Derby	0	Arsenal	1	r2N
SIXTH ROUND				
Birmghm C	3	Huddersfld	1	
Leeds U	2	Tottenham	1	
Leyton O	0	Arsenal	1	
Man Utd	1	Stoke	1	
Stoke	2	Man Utd	1	re
SEMI-FINAL				
Arsenal	1	Stoke	1	N
Leeds U	3	Birmghm C	0	N
Stoke	1	Arsenal	2	rN

FINAL				
Leeds U	1	Arsenal	0	N

1973

FIRST ROUND				
Altrinchm	0	Notts Co	1	
Banbury U	0	Barnet	2	
Barnsley	1	Halifax	1	
Barnstple	0	Bilston	2	
Bolton	1	Chester	1	
Boston U	1	Lancaster	2	
Bournemth	5	Cambridge	1	
Bradford	3	Grantham	0	
Chelmsfd	2	Hillingdn	0	
Chestrfld	4	Rhyl	2	
Colchester	6	Bognor R	0	
Crewe	1	Staffd Rg	0	
Darlingtn	1	Wrexham	1	
Doncaster	3	Bury	1	
Enfield	1	Bshp Stor	1	
Gillinghm	1	Reading	2	
Grimsby	2	Wigan Ath	1	
Hartlepl	0	Scunthpe	0	
Hayes	1	Bristol R	0	
Lincoln	2	Blackburn	2	
Margate	1	Swansea	0	
Newport	5	Alton T	1	
Oldham	1	Scarboro	1	
Peterboro	1	N'hamptn	0	
Plymouth	1	Hendon	0	
Port Vale	2	Southport	1	
Rochdale	1	Bangor C	2	
Rotherhm	4	S.Shields	0	
S.L'pool	0	Tranmere	2	
Southend	0	Aldershot	2	
Spennym'r	1	Shrewsby	1	
Stockport	1	Workingtn	0	
Telford U	3	Nuneaton	2	
Tonbridge	0	Charlton	5	
Torquay	3	Hereford	0	
Walsall	3	Kettering	3	
Walton&H	2	Exeter	1	
Watford	4	Guilford	2	
Yeovil T	2	Brentford	1	
York	2	Manfield	1	
Blackburn	4	Lincoln	1	r
Bshp Stor	1	Enfield	0	r

Chester	0	Bolton	1	r
Halifax	2	Barnsley	1	r
Kettering	1	Walsall	2	r
Scarboro	2	Oldham	1	r
Scunthpe	0	Hartlepl	0	re
Shrewsby	3	Spennym'r	1	r
Wrexham	5	Darlingtn	0	r
Hartlepl	1	Scunthpe	2	r2eN
SECOND ROUND				
Bangor C	2	York	3	
Barnet	1	Bilston	1	
Blackburn	0	Crewe	1	
Bolton	3	Shrewsby	0	
Bournemth	0	Colchester	0	
Bradford	2	Tranmere	1	
Bshp Stor	2	Peterboro	2	
Chelmsfd	5	Telford U	0	
Grimsby	2	Chestrfld	2	
Notts Co	2	Lancaster	1	
Port Vale	1	Wrexham	0	
Reading	0	Hayes	0	
Rotherhm	0	Stockport	1	
Scarboro	1	Doncaster	2	
Scunthpe	3	Halifax	2	
Torquay	0	Newport	1	
Walsall	1	Charlton	2	
Walton&H	0	Margate	1	
Watford	2	Aldershot	0	
Yeovil T	0	Plymouth	2	
Bilston	0	Barnet	1	r
Chestrfld	0	Grimsby	1	r
Colchester	0	Bournemth	2	r
Hayes	0	Reading	1	r
Peterboro	3	Bshp Stor	1	r
THIRD ROUND				
Arsenal	2	Leicester	2	
Bradford	2	Blackpool	1	
Brighton	0	Chelsea	2	
Burnley	0	Liverpool	0	
Carlisle	2	Huddersfld	2	
Charlton	1	Bolton	1	
Chelmsfd	1	Ipswich	3	
C.Palace	2	Southmptn	0	
Everton	3	Aston V	2	
Grimsby	0	Preston NE	0	
Leyton O	1	Coventry	4	
Luton	2	Crewe	0	
Man City	3	Stoke	2	
Margate	0	Tottenham	6	
Millwall	3	Newport	0	
Newcastle	2	Bournemth	0	

Norwich	1	Leeds U	1	
Notts Co	1	Sunderld	1	
Peterboro	0	Derby	1	
Plymouth	1	Middlesbro	0	
Port Vale	0	West Ham	1	
Portsmth	1	Bristol C	1	
QPR	0	Barnet	0	
Reading	2	Doncaster	0	
Scunthpe	2	Cardiff	3	
Sheff Wed	2	Fulham	0	
Stockport	0	Hull	0	
Swindon	2	Birmghm C	0	
Watford	0	Sheff Utd	1	
West Brom	1	Nottm For	1	
Wolves	1	Man Utd	0	
York	0	Oxford	1	
Barnet	0	QPR	3	r
Bolton	4	Charlton	0	r
Bristol C	4	Portsmth	1	r
Huddersfld	0	Carlisle	1	r
Hull	2	Stockport	0	re
Leeds U	1	Norwich	1	re
Leicester	1	Arsenal	2	r
Liverpool	3	Burnley	0	r
Nottm For	0	West Brom	0	re
Preston NE	0	Grimsby	1	r
Sunderld	2	Notts Co	0	r
Norwich	0	Leeds U	5	r2N
West Brom	3	Nottm For	1	r2N
FOURTH ROUND				
Arsenal	2	Bradford	0	
Bolton	2	Cardiff	2	
Carlisle	2	Sheff Utd	1	
Chelsea	2	Ipswich	0	
Coventry	1	Grimsby	0	
Derby	1	Tottenham	1	
Everton	0	Millwall	2	
Hull	1	West Ham	0	
Leeds U	2	Plymouth	1	
Liverpool	0	Man City	0	
Newcastle	0	Luton	2	
Oxford	0	QPR	2	
Sheff Wed	1	C.Palace	1	
Sunderld	1	Reading	1	
West Brom	2	Swindon	0	
Wolves	1	Bristol C	0	
Cardiff	1	Bolton	1	re
C.Palace	1	Sheff Wed	1	re
Man City	2	Liverpool	0	r
Reading	1	Sunderld	3	r
Tottenham	3	Derby	5	re

Bolton	1	Cardiff	0	r2N
Sheff Wed	3	C.Palace	2	r2N
FIFTH ROUND				
Bolton	0	Luton	1	
Carlisle	1	Arsenal	2	
Coventry	3	Hull	0	
Derby	4	QPR	2	
Leeds U	2	West Brom	0	
Man City	2	Sunderld	2	
Sheff Wed	1	Chelsea	2	
Wolves	1	Millwall	0	
Sunderld	3	Man City	1	r
SIXTH ROUND				
Chelsea	2	Arsenal	2	
Derby	0	Leeds U	1	
Sunderld	2	Luton	0	
Wolves	2	Coventry	0	
Arsenal	2	Chelsea	1	r
SEMI-FINAL				
Leeds U	1	Wolves	0	N
Sunderld	2	Arsenal	1	N
FINAL				
Sunderld	1	Leeds U	0	N

1974

FIRST ROUND				
Alfreton	0	Blyth S	0	
Altrinchm	2	Hartlepl	0	
Banbury U	0	N'hamptn	0	
Bideford	0	Bristol R	2	
Boston U	0	Hayes	0	
Bournemth	1	Charlton	0	
Bradford	2	Workingtn	0	
Cambridge	3	Gillinghm	2	
Chester	1	Telford U	0	
Chestrfld	0	Barnsley	0	
Colchester	2	Peterboro	3	
Crewe	0	Scarboro	0	
Dagenham	0	Aldershot	4	
Doncaster	1	Lincoln	0	
Exeter	0	Alvechurch	1	
Formby	0	Oldham	2	
Halifax	6	Frickley	1	
Hendon	3	Leytonstn	0	
Hereford	3	Torquay	1	
Hillingdn	0	Grantham	4	
Hitchin	1	Guilford	1	
Huddersfld	2	Wigan Ath	0	
King's Ln	1	Wimbledn	0	
Plymouth	2	Brentford	1	
Reading	3	Slough T	0	

WHAT A STAR ✪ JIM MONTGOMERY

From St. Hilda's School in Sunderland to Roker Park and a total of 623 appearances for the club - but everybody knows Jim Montgomery for a few seconds in the 1973 Final. He made a fine save from Trevor Cherry of Leeds, then somehow turned Peter Lorimer's follow-up shot on to the bar. It was on a par with Gordon Banks's save from Pele in the 1970 World Cup, probably the best in Wembley history. And it helped Second Division Sunderland, then without a single international in the team, to beat mighty Leeds - and deservedly so.

Rochdale	2	S.Shields	0	
Rotherhm	2	Southport	1	
Runcorn	0	Grimsby	1	
Scunthpe	1	Darlingtn	0	
Southend	3	Boreham W	0	
Stockport	0	Port Vale	1	
Tranmere	2	Bury	1	
Walsall	1	Swansea	0	
Walton&H	0	Brighton	0	
Watford	1	Chelmsfd	0	
Weymouth	0	Mert Tyd	1	
Willingtn	0	Blackburn	0	
Wrexham	1	Shrewsby	1	
Wycombe	3	Newport	1	
York	0	Manfield	0	
Barnsley	2	Chestrfld	1	r
Blackburn	6	Willingtn	1	r
Blyth S	2	Alfreton	1	r
Brighton	0	Walton&H	4	r
Guilford	1	Hitchin	4	r
Hayes	1	Boston U	2	re
Manfield	5	York	3	r
N'hamptn	3	Banbury U	2	r
Scarboro	2	Crewe	1	r
Shrewsby	0	Wrexham	1	r

SECOND ROUND

Aldershot	1	Cambridge	2	
Alvechurch	6	King's Ln	1	
Barnsley	1	Bradford	1	
Blackburn	0	Altrinchm	0	
Boston U	1	Hitchin	0	
Chester	3	Huddersfld	2	
Doncaster	3	Tranmere	0	
Grantham	1	Rochdale	1	
Grimsby	1	Blyth S	1	
Halifax	0	Oldham	1	
Hereford	3	Walton&H	0	
Manfield	1	Scunthpe	1	
Mert Tyd	0	Hendon	3	
N'hamptn	1	Bristol R	2	
Plymouth	1	Walsall	0	
Port Vale	2	Scarboro	1	
Southend	2	Reading	0	
Watford	0	Bournemth	1	
Wrexham	3	Rotherhm	0	
Wycombe	1	Peterboro	3	
Altrinchm	0	Blackburn	2	r
Blyth S	0	Grimsby	2	r
Bradford	2	Barnsley	1	r
Rochdale	3	Grantham	5	re
Scunthpe	1	Manfield	0	r

THIRD ROUND

Aston V	3	Chester	1	
Birmghm C	5	Cardiff	2	
Bolton	3	Stoke	2	
Bradford	4	Alvechurch	2	
Bristol C	1	Hull	1	
Cambridge	2	Oldham	2	
Carlisle	0	Sunderld	0	
Chelsea	0	QPR	0	
C.Palace	0	Wrexham	2	
Derby	0	Boston U	0	
Everton	3	Blackburn	0	
Fulham	1	Preston NE	0	
Grantham	0	Middlesbro	2	
Grimsby	0	Burnley	2	
Ipswich	3	Sheff Utd	2	
Leicester	1	Tottenham	0	
Leyton O	2	Bournemth	1	
Liverpool	2	Doncaster	2	
Man Utd	1	Plymouth	0	
Millwall	1	Scunthpe	1	
Newcastle	1	Hendon	1	
Norwich	0	Arsenal	1	
Nottm For	4	Bristol R	3	
Oxford	2	Man City	5	
Peterboro	3	Southend	1	
Port Vale	1	Luton	1	
Portsmth	3	Swindon	3	
Sheff Wed	0	Coventry	0	
Southmptn	2	Blackpool	1	
West Brom	4	Notts Co	0	
West Ham	1	Hereford	1	
Wolves	1	Leeds U	1	
Boston U	1	Derby	6	r
Coventry	3	Sheff Wed	1	r
Doncaster	0	Liverpool	2	r
Hendon	0	Newcastle	4	rN
Hereford	2	West Ham	1	r
Hull	0	Bristol C	1	r
Leeds U	1	Wolves	0	r
Luton	4	Port Vale	2	r
Oldham	3	Cambridge	3	re
QPR	1	Chelsea	0	r
Scunthpe	1	Millwall	0	r
Sunderld	0	Carlisle	1	r
Swindon	0	Portsmth	1	r
Cambridge	1	Oldham	2	r2N

FOURTH ROUND

Arsenal	1	Aston V	1	
Coventry	0	Derby	0	
Everton	0	West Brom	0	
Fulham	1	Leicester	1	
Hereford	0	Bristol C	1	
Liverpool	0	Carlisle	0	
Luton	3	Bradford	0	
Man Utd	0	Ipswich	1	
Newcastle	1	Scunthpe	1	
Nottm For	4	Man City	1	
Oldham	1	Burnley	4	
Peterboro	1	Leeds U	4	
Portsmth	0	Leyton O	0	
QPR	2	Birmghm C	0	
Southmptn	3	Bolton	3	
Wrexham	1	Middlesbro	0	
Aston V	2	Arsenal	0	r
Bolton	0	Southmptn	2	re
Carlisle	0	Liverpool	2	r
Derby	0	Coventry	1	re
Leicester	2	Fulham	1	re
Leyton O	1	Portsmth	1	re
Scunthpe	0	Newcastle	3	r
West Brom	1	Everton	0	r
Portsmth	2	Leyton O	0	r2N

Strange but true!

There were only eight Englishmen among the 23 players who appeared in the 1979 Final between Arsenal and Manchester United, plus eight Irish, six Scots and a Welshman.

Kelly's Aye

Substitute Eddie Kelly is the 'official' scorer of Arsenal's first goal in the 1971 win over Liverpool, but George Graham still insists that he had the final touch in the scramble before the ball crossed the line. Even video evidence is inconclusive.

FIFTH ROUND

Bristol C	1	Leeds U	1	
Burnley	1	Aston V	0	
Coventry	0	QPR	0	
Liverpool	2	Ipswich	0	
Luton	0	Leicester	4	
Nottm For	1	Portsmth	0	
Southmptn	0	Wrexham	1	
West Brom	0	Newcastle	3	
Leeds U	0	Bristol C	1	r
QPR	3	Coventry	2	r

SIXTH ROUND

Bristol C	0	Liverpool	1	
Burnley	1	Wrexham	0	
Newcastle	4	Nottm For	3	v
QPR	0	Leicester	2	
Newcastle	0	Nottm For	0	rN
Newcastle	1	Nottm For	0	r2N

SEMI-FINAL

Liverpool	0	Leicester	0	N
Newcastle	2	Burnley	0	N
Leicester	1	Liverpool	3	rN

FINAL

Liverpool	3	Newcastle	0	N

1975

FIRST ROUND

AP Leamgtn	1	Southend	2	
Ashford	1	Walsall	3	
Barnsley	1	Halifax	2	
Blyth S	1	Preston NE	1	
Bournemth	5	Southwk	0	
Brighton	3	Aldershot	1	
Bshk Auck	5	Morecambe	0	
Bshp Stor	0	Leatherhd	0	
Bury	4	Southport	2	
Chelmsfd	0	Charlton	1	
Chestrfld	3	Boston U	1	
Crewe	2	Gateshd U	2	
Darlingtn	1	Workingtn	0	
Dartford	2	Plymouth	3	
Exeter	1	Newport	2	

Farsley C	0	Tranmere	2	
Grimsby	1	Huddersfld	0	
Hartlepl	1	Bradford	0	
Hereford	1	Gillinghm	0	
Hitchin	0	Cambridge	0	
Manfield	3	Wrexham	1	
Matlock T	1	Blackburn	4	
Nuneaton	2	Maidstone	2	
Oswest T	1	Doncaster	3	
Peterboro	0	Weymouth	0	
Port Vale	2	Lincoln	2	
Rochdale	0	Marine	0	
Romford	0	Ilford	2	
Rotherhm	1	Chester	0	
Scunthpe	1	Altrinchm	1	
Shrewsby	1	Wigan Ath	1	
Slough T	1	Brentford	4	
Stockport	0	Staffd Rg	0	
Swansea	1	Kettering	1	
Swindon	4	Reading	0	
Tooting	1	C.Palace	2	
Torquay	0	N'hamptn	1	
Watford	0	Colchester	1	
Wimbledn	1	Bath C	0	
Wycombe	3	Chelthnm	1	
Altrinchm	3	Scunthpe	1	r
Cambridge	3	Hitchin	0	r
Gateshd U	1	Crewe	0	re
Kettering	3	Swansea	1	r
Leatherhd	2	Bshp Stor	0	r
Lincoln	2	Port Vale	0	r
Maidstone	2	Nuneaton	0	r
Marine	1	Rochdale	2	re
Preston NE	5	Blyth S	1	r
Staffd Rg	1	Stockport	0	r
Weymouth	3	Peterboro	3	re
Wigan Ath	2	Shrewsby	1	r
Peterboro	3	Weymouth	0	r2

SECOND ROUND

Altrinchm	3	Gateshd U	0	
Blackburn	1	Darlingtn	0	
Brighton	1	Brentford	0	
Bshk Auck	0	Preston NE	2	
Cambridge	2	Hereford	0	
Chestrfld	1	Doncaster	0	
Grimsby	1	Bury	1	
Hartlepl	0	Lincoln	0	
Ilford	0	Southend	2	
Leatherhd	1	Colchester	0	
Newport	1	Walsall	3	
Peterboro	3	Charlton	0	
Plymouth	2	C.Palace	1	
Rochdale	1	Tranmere	1	
Rotherhm	2	N'hamptn	1	
Staffd Rg	2	Halifax	1	
Swindon	3	Maidstone	1	
Wigan Ath	1	Manfield	1	
Wimbledn	2	Kettering	0	
Wycombe	0	Bournemth	0	
Bournemth	1	Wycombe	2	r
Bury	2	Grimsby	1	r
Lincoln	1	Hartlepl	0	r
Manfield	3	Wigan Ath	1	r
Tranmere	1	Rochdale	0	r

Double Trouble

Alan Taylor, signed for £40,000 from Rochdale in November 1974, helped West Ham to win the Cup the following year by scoring twice in the Sixth Round, twice in the Semi-Final and twice in the Final.

THIRD ROUND

Arsenal	1	York	1	
Blackburn	1	Bristol R	2	
Bolton	0	West Brom	0	
Brighton	0	Leatherhd	1	
Burnley	0	Wimbledn	1	
Bury	2	Millwall	2	
Chelsea	3	Sheff Wed	2	
Coventry	2	Norwich	0	
Everton	1	Altrinchm	1	
Fulham	1	Hull	1	
Leeds U	4	Cardiff	1	
Leicester	3	Oxford	1	
Leyton O	2	Derby	2	
Liverpool	2	Stoke	0	
Luton	0	Birmghm C	1	
Man City	0	Newcastle	2	
Man Utd	0	Walsall	0	
Manfield	1	Cambridge	0	
Nottm For	1	Tottenham	1	
Notts Co	3	Portsmth	1	
Oldham	0	Aston V	3	
Peterboro	1	Tranmere	0	
Plymouth	2	Blackpool	0	
Preston NE	0	Carlisle	1	
Sheff Utd	2	Bristol C	0	
Southmptn	1	West Ham	2	
Southend	2	QPR	2	
Staffd Rg	0	Rotherhm	0	
Sunderld	2	Chestrfld	0	
Swindon	2	Lincoln	0	
Wolves	1	Ipswich	2	
Wycombe	0	Middlesbro	0	
Altrinchm	0	Everton	2	rN
Derby	2	Leyton O	1	r
Hull	2	Fulham	2	re
Middlesbro	1	Wycombe	0	r
Millwall	1	Bury	1	re
QPR	2	Southend	0	r
Rotherhm	0	Staffd Rg	2	r
Tottenham	0	Nottm For	1	r
Walsall	3	Man Utd	2	re
West Brom	4	Bolton	0	r
York	1	Arsenal	3	re
Bury	2	Millwall	0	r2N
Fulham	1	Hull	0	r2N

FOURTH ROUND

Aston V	4	Sheff Utd	1	
Bury	1	Manfield	2	
Carlisle	3	West Brom	2	
Chelsea	0	Birmghm C	1	
Coventry	1	Arsenal	1	
Derby	2	Bristol R	0	
Fulham	0	Nottm For	0	
Ipswich	1	Liverpool	0	
Leeds U	0	Wimbledn	0	
Leicester	3	Leatherhd	2	
Middlesbro	3	Sunderld	1	
Plymouth	1	Everton	3	
QPR	3	Notts Co	0	
Staffd Rg	1	Peterboro	2	N
Walsall	1	Newcastle	0	
West Ham	1	Swindon	1	
Arsenal	3	Coventry	0	r
Nottm For	1	Fulham	1	re
Swindon	1	West Ham	2	r
Wimbledn	0	Leeds U	1	rN
Fulham	1	Nottm For	1	r2e
Nottm For	1	Fulham	2	r3

FIFTH ROUND

Arsenal	0	Leicester	0	
Birmghm C	2	Walsall	1	
Derby	0	Leeds U	1	
Everton	1	Fulham	2	
Ipswich	3	Aston V	2	
Manfield	0	Carlisle	1	
Peterboro	1	Middlesbro	1	
West Ham	2	QPR	1	
Leicester	1	Arsenal	1	re
Middlesbro	2	Peterboro	0	r
Leicester	0	Arsenal	1	r2e

SIXTH ROUND

Arsenal	0	West Ham	2	
Birmghm C	1	Middlesbro	0	
Carlisle	0	Fulham	1	
Ipswich	0	Leeds U	0	
Leeds U	1	Ipswich	1	re
Ipswich	0	Leeds U	0	r2eN
Leeds U	2	Ipswich	3	r3N

SEMI-FINAL

Fulham	1	Birmghm C	1	N
West Ham	0	Ipswich	0	N
Birmghm C	0	Fulham	1	reN
Ipswich	1	West Ham	2	rN

FINAL

West Ham	2	Fulham	0	N

1976

FIRST ROUND

AP Leamgtn	2	Staffd Rg	3	
Aldershot	4	Wealdstne	3	
Boston U	0	Lincoln	1	
Bradford	1	Chestrfld	0	
Brentford	2	N'hamptn	0	
Bury	4	Doncaster	2	
Cardiff	6	Exeter	2	
Colchester	3	Dover	3	
Coventy S	2	Tranmere	0	N
C.Palace	1	Walton&H	0	
Darlingtn	0	Chester	0	
Dartford	1	Bshp Stor	4	
Grantham	2	Port Vale	2	
Grimsby	1	Gateshd U	3	
Halifax	3	Altrinchm	1	
Hartlepl	3	Stockport	0	
Hendon	1	Reading	0	
Hereford	2	Torquay	0	
Leatherhd	2	Cambridge	0	
Manfield	1	Wrexham	1	

Pro-File: KEVIN KEEGAN

Kevin Keegan may not have been the most naturally gifted footballer of all time, but he was certainly one of the best.

The pocket-sized striker combined talent with a great deal of hard work to become one of the most feared front-runners in Europe and beyond.

Both in domestic and international football, Keegan proved that if you are dedicated enough you can get right to the very top.

He helped Liverpool conquer the English game - and win the European Cup for the first time in 1977 - before enjoying hugely successful spells with German club Hamburg, then with Southampton and Newcastle back in Britain.

Keegan also captained England and played in the 1982 World Cup finals in Spain, although injury restricted his participation.

On his retirement in 1983, he moved to Spain and was out of the game for eight years before making a surprise return as manager of Newcastle.

His impact there can never be underestimated and if anyone deserved success it was Keegan. Sadly, it wasn't to be and his decision to quit, in January 1997, was as big a shock as his move to St James' Park in the first place.

Career details

●**Represented:** England, Scunthorpe, Liverpool, SV Hamburg (Germany), Southampton, Newcastle ●**Position:** Striker ●**Born:** Doncaster, 14.02.51 ●**Height:** 5ft 8in ●**Weight:** 11st 7lbs ●**Club honours:** League Championship 1972/73, 1975/76, 1976/77; FA Cup 1974; European Cup 1977, UEFA Cup 1973, 1976; FWA Footballer of the Year 1976; PFA Player of the Year 1982; European Footballer of the Year 1978, 1979 ●**International honours:** England 5 U23, 63 full caps

Club League Record

Era	Club	Games	Goals
68/70	Scunthorpe	124	18
71/77	Liverpool	230	68
77/80	SV Hamburg	92	30
80/82	Southampton	68	37
82/84	Newcastle	78	48

Cup Highlights

April 3 1974: Keegan scores Liverpool's second goal as they reach their first FA Cup Final by beating Leicester 3-1 at Villa Park.

May 4, 1974: Liverpool turn on the style to win the Final 3-0 against Newcastle. Keegan scores twice.

On Keegan:

●If Kevin Keegan fell into the Tyne, he'd come up with a salmon in his mouth. **Jack Charlton on Keegan's habit of falling on his feet**

Keegan On:

●As a manager, you always have a gun to your head. It's a question of whether there is a bullet in the barrel. **On the pressures of management**

DID YOU KNOW THAT...

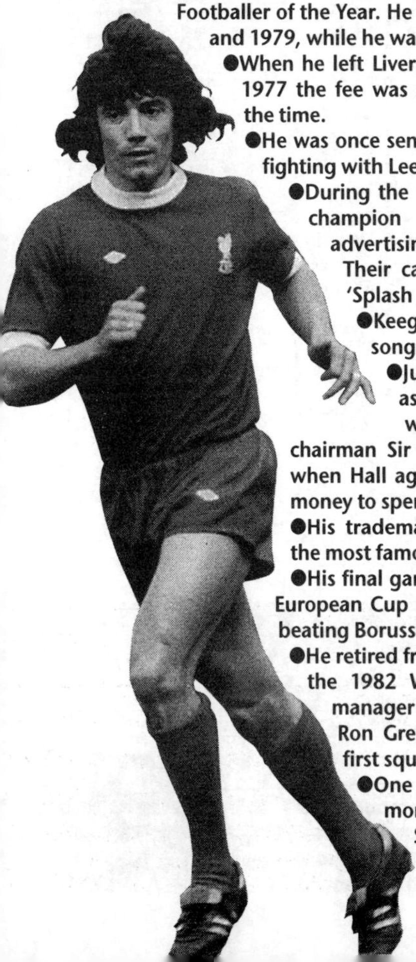

●Keegan is the last English player to be named European Footballer of the Year. He won the award twice, in 1978 and 1979, while he was playing for SV Hamburg.

●When he left Liverpool for SV Hamburg in June 1977 the fee was £500,000, a British record at the time.

●He was once sent-off in the Charity Shield, for fighting with Leeds United's Billy Bremner.

●During the 1970s, he and former boxing champion Henry Cooper were the advertising faces of Brut aftershave. Their catchphrase for the scent was 'Splash it all over'.

●Keegan had a top 40 hit with a song called 'Head Over Heels'.

●Just a few weeks into his reign as Newcastle manager, Keegan walked out after a row with chairman Sir John Hall. He later returned when Hall agreed to his demand for more money to spend on players.

●His trademark curly perm was probably the most famous haircut of the 1970s.

●His final game for Liverpool was the 1977 European Cup Final, which the Reds won by beating Borussia Moenchengladbach 3-1.

●He retired from international football after the 1982 World Cup finals when new manager Bobby Robson - successor to Ron Greenwood - left him out of his first squad.

●One of Keegan's most famous moments came on the TV show Superstars. During the cycling race he came off his bike and skidded wildly along the floor.

England Expects

The West Ham Cup-winning side in 1975 was made up of 11 Englishmen, and their Fulham opponents had ten English and one Irishman - Jimmy Conway, who was one of 17 children.

Marine	3	Barnsley	1	
Newport	2	Swindon	2	
Nuneaton	0	Wimbledn	1	
Peterboro	4	Winsford	1	
Preston NE	2	Scunthpe	1	
Romford	0	Tooting	1	
Rossendl U	0	Shrewsby	1	
Rotherhm	2	Crewe	1	
Scarboro	2	Morecambe	0	
Sheff Wed	3	Macclesfd	1	
Southend	2	Swansea	0	
Spennym'r	4	Southport	1	
Sutton U	1	Bournemth	1	
Walsall	0	Huddersfld	1	
Watford	0	Brighton	3	
Weymouth	0	Gillinghm	2	
Wigan Ath	4	Matlock T	1	
Workingtn	1	Rochdale	1	
Wycombe	0	Bedford T	0	
Yeovil T	1	Millwall	1	
Bedford T	2	Wycombe	2	re
Bournemth	1	Sutton U	0	r
Chester	2	Darlingtn	0	r
Dover	4	Colchester	1	re
Millwall	2	Yeovil T	2	re
Port Vale	4	Grantham	1	r
Rochdale	2	Workingtn	1	re
Swindon	3	Newport	0	r
Wrexham	1	Manfield	1	re
Manfield	2	Wrexham	1	r2N
Wycombe	2	Bedford T	1	r2
Yeovil T	0	Millwall	1	r2N

SECOND ROUND

Aldershot	2	Bshp Stor	0	
Bournemth	2	Hereford	2	
Bury	3	Spennym'r	0	
Cardiff	1	Wycombe	0	
Coventy S	0	Peterboro	4	N
Gateshd U	1	Rochdale	1	
Gillinghm	0	Brighton	1	
Hendon	0	Swindon	1	
Huddersfld	2	Port Vale	1	
Leatherhd	0	Tooting	0	
Manfield	1	Lincoln	2	
Marine	1	Hartlepl	1	
Millwall	1	C.Palace	1	
Rotherhm	0	Bradford	3	
Scarboro	3	Preston NE	2	
Sheff Wed	2	Wigan Ath	0	
Shrewsby	3	Chester	1	
Southend	4	Dover	1	
Staffd Rg	1	Halifax	3	
Wimbledn	0	Brentford	2	
C.Palace	2	Millwall	1	r
Hartlepl	6	Marine	3	r
Hereford	2	Bournemth	0	r
Rochdale	3	Gateshd U	1	r
Tooting	2	Leatherhd	1	re

THIRD ROUND

Aldershot	1	Lincoln	2	
Blackpool	1	Burnley	0	
Brentford	0	Bolton	0	
Charlton	2	Sheff Wed	1	
Chelsea	1	Bristol R	1	
Coventry	2	Bristol C	1	
Derby	2	Everton	1	
Fulham	2	Huddersfld	3	
Hull	1	Plymouth	1	
Ipswich	3	Halifax	1	
Leicester	3	Sheff Utd	0	
Leyton O	0	Cardiff	1	
Luton	2	Blackburn	0	
Man City	6	Hartlepl	0	
Man Utd	2	Oxford	1	
Middlesbro	0	Bury	0	
Norwich	1	Rochdale	1	
Nottm For	0	Peterboro	0	
Notts Co	0	Leeds U	1	
Portsmth	1	Birmghm C	1	
QPR	0	Newcastle	0	
Scarboro	1	C.Palace	2	
Shrewsby	1	Bradford	2	
Southmptn	1	Aston V	1	
Southend	2	Brighton	1	
Sunderld	2	Oldham	0	
Swindon	2	Tooting	2	
Tottenham	1	Stoke	1	
West Brom	3	Carlisle	1	
West Ham	0	Liverpool	2	
Wolves	3	Arsenal	0	
York	2	Hereford	1	
Aston V	1	Southmptn	2	re
Birmghm C	0	Portsmth	1	r
Bolton	2	Brentford	0	r
Bristol R	0	Chelsea	1	r
Bury	3	Middlesbro	2	r
Newcastle	2	QPR	1	r
Peterboro	1	Nottm For	0	r
Plymouth	1	Hull	4	r
Rochdale	0	Norwich	0	re
Stoke	2	Tottenham	1	r
Tooting	2	Swindon	1	r
Norwich	2	Rochdale	1	r2

FOURTH ROUND

Bradford	3	Tooting	1	
Charlton	1	Portsmth	1	
Coventry	1	Newcastle	1	
Derby	1	Liverpool	0	
Huddersfld	0	Bolton	1	
Ipswich	0	Wolves	0	
Leeds U	0	C.Palace	1	
Leicester	1	Bury	0	
Man Utd	3	Peterboro	1	
Norwich	2	Luton	0	
Southmptn	3	Blackpool	1	
Southend	2	Cardiff	1	
Stoke	1	Man City	0	
Sunderld	1	Hull	0	
West Brom	3	Lincoln	2	
York	0	Chelsea	2	
Newcastle	5	Coventry	0	r
Portsmth	0	Charlton	3	r
Wolves	1	Ipswich	0	r

FIFTH ROUND

Bolton	3	Newcastle	3	
Chelsea	2	C.Palace	3	
Derby	1	Southend	0	
Leicester	1	Man Utd	2	
Norwich	1	Bradford	2	
Stoke	0	Sunderld	0	

GIANTKILLERS

1975 Brighton 0 Leatherhead 1

Chris Kelly, known as the Leatherhead Lip, shot his Isthmian League club to a memorable Third Round win over Brighton at the Goldstone Ground, helped to a large extent by amateur international John Swannell's fine goalkeeping. Kelly, who also occupied a fair few column inches with his outspoken views, was one of amateur football's top strikers. He scored in the next round, too, but the Surrey club - having given up home advantage in order to get a bigger share of the gate - lost 3-2 at Leicester, after leading 2-0.

GIANTKILLERS

1976 Manchester United 0 Southampton 1

Tommy Docherty's words came back to haunt him as Second Division Southampton humbled his mighty side at Wembley. United had been drawn against fellow top flight club Derby in the Semi-Finals, with Southampton and Crystal Palace, of Division Three, contesting the other. "This is the first time a Cup Final will be played at Hillsborough," said The Doc. "The other Semi-Final is a bit of a joke really." But he wasn't laughing at Wembley as Bobby Stokes's 83rd minute winner gave The Saints the trophy. Sadly, Stokes died in May 1995 aged just 44.

West Brom	1	Southmptn	1	
Wolves	3	Charlton	0	
Newcastle	0	Bolton	0	re
Southmptn	4	West Brom	0	r
Sunderld	2	Stoke	1	r
Bolton	1	Newcastle	2	r2N
SIXTH ROUND				
Bradford	0	Southmptn	1	
Derby	4	Newcastle	2	
Man Utd	1	Wolves	1	
Sunderld	0	C.Palace	1	
Wolves	2	Man Utd	3	re
SEMI-FINAL				
Man Utd	2	Derby	0	N
Southmptn	2	C.Palace	0	N
FINAL				
Southmptn	1	Man Utd	0	N

1977

FIRST ROUND				
Aldershot	1	Portsmth	1	
Barnsley	3	Boston	1	
Barrow	0	Goole T	2	
Bournemth	0	Newport	0	
Brentford	2	Chesham U	0	
Brighton	2	C.Palace	2	
Bury	6	Workingtn	0	
Cambridge	1	Colchester	1	
Chester	1	Hartlepl	0	
Crewe	1	Preston NE	1	
Crook T	1	Nuneaton	4	
Doncaster	2	Shrewsby	2	
Droylsden	0	Grimsby	0	
Dudley T	1	York	1	
Enfield	0	Harwich	0	
Exeter	1	Southend	1	
Gillinghm	0	Watford	1	
Huddersfld	0	Manfield	0	
Kettering	1	Oxford	1	
Leatherhd	2	N'hamptn	0	
Lincoln	1	Morecambe	0	
Matlock T	2	Wigan Ath	0	
Reading	1	Wealdstne	0	
Rochdale	1	Northwich	1	
Rotherhm	5	Altrinchm	0	
Scarboro	0	Darlingtn	0	
Scunthpe	1	Chestrfld	2	
Sheff Wed	2	Stockport	0	
Southport	1	Port Vale	2	
Staffd Rg	0	Halifax	0	
Swansea	0	Minehead	1	
Swindon	7	Bromley	0	
Tooting	4	Dartford	2	
Torquay	1	Hillingdn	2	
Tranmere	0	Peterboro	4	
Walsall	0	Bradford	0	
Waterlve	1	Wycombe	2	
Weymouth	1	Hitchin	1	
Wimbledn	1	Woking	0	
Wrexham	6	Gateshd U	0	
Bradford	0	Walsall	2	r
Colchester	2	Cambridge	0	r
C.Palace	1	Brighton	1	re
Darlingtn	4	Scarboro	1	r
Grimsby	5	Droylsden	3	r
Halifax	1	Staffd Rg	0	r
Harwich	0	Enfield	3	r
Hitchin	2	Weymouth	2	re
Manfield	2	Huddersfld	1	r
Newport	3	Bournemth	0	r
Northwich	0	Rochdale	0	re
Oxford	0	Kettering	1	r
Portsmth	2	Aldershot	1	r
Preston NE	2	Crewe	2	re
Shrewsby	4	Doncaster	3	r
Southend	2	Exeter	1	re
York	4	Dudley T	1	r
Brighton	0	C.Palace	1	r2N
Crewe	0	Preston NE	3	r2N
Rochdale	1	Northwich	2	r2N
Weymouth	3	Hitchin	3	r2eN
Hitchin	3	Weymouth	1	r3N
SECOND ROUND				
Bury	0	Shrewsby	0	
Chestrfld	1	Walsall	1	
Colchester	3	Brentford	2	
C.Palace	4	Enfield	0	
Darlingtn	1	Sheff Wed	0	
Grimsby	0	Chester	1	
Halifax	1	Preston NE	0	
Hillingdn	2	Watford	3	
Hitchin	1	Swindon	1	
Kettering	1	Tooting	0	
Leatherhd	1	Wimbledn	3	
Lincoln	6	Nuneaton	0	
Manfield	2	Matlock T	5	
Northwich	4	Peterboro	0	
Port Vale	3	Barnsley	0	
Portsmth	2	Minehead	1	
Rotherhm	0	York	0	
Southend	3	Newport	0	
Wrexham	1	Goole T	1	
Wycombe	1	Reading	2	
Goole T	0	Wrexham	1	r
Shrewsby	2	Bury	1	r
Swindon	3	Hitchin	1	re
Walsall	0	Chestrfld	0	re
York	1	Rotherhm	1	re
Chestrfld	0	Walsall	1	r2N
Rotherhm	2	York	1	r2e
THIRD ROUND				
Birmghm C	1	Portsmth	0	
Blackpool	0	Derby	0	
Burnley	2	Lincoln	2	
Cardiff	1	Tottenham	0	
Carlisle	5	Matlock T	1	
Charlton	1	Blackburn	1	
Coventry	1	Millwall	0	
Darlingtn	2	Leyton O	2	
Everton	2	Stoke	0	
Fulham	3	Swindon	3	
Halifax	0	Luton	1	
Hereford	1	Reading	0	
Hull	1	Port Vale	1	
Ipswich	4	Bristol C	1	
Kettering	2	Colchester	3	
Leeds U	5	Norwich	2	
Leicester	0	Aston V	1	
Liverpool	0	C.Palace	0	
Man City	1	West Brom	1	
Man Utd	1	Walsall	0	
Northwich	3	Watford	2	
Nottm For	1	Bristol R	1	
Notts Co	0	Arsenal	1	
Oldham	3	Plymouth	0	
QPR	2	Shrewsby	1	
Sheff Utd	0	Newcastle	0	
Southmptn	1	Chelsea	1	
Southend	0	Chester	4	
Sunderld	2	Wrexham	2	
West Ham	2	Bolton	1	

WHAT A STAR ✪ ROGER OSBORNE

He had 14 years as a pro, with Ipswich and Colchester, but scored only one FA Cup goal - the winner in the 1978 Final. Local boy Roger Osborne and the Ipswich outsiders outplayed favourites Arsenal, hitting the woodwork three times before Osborne's decider. He was so overcome by the tension of it all that he had to be replaced by the substitute, but his place in the history books was secure.

Wimbledn	0	Middlesbro	0	
Wolves	3	Rotherhm	2	
Blackburn	2	Charlton	0	r
Bristol R	1	Nottm For	1	re
Chelsea	0	Southmptn	3	re
C.Palace	2	Liverpool	3	r
Derby	3	Blackpool	2	r
Leyton O	0	Darlingtn	0	re
Lincoln	0	Burnley	1	r
Middlesbro	1	Wimbledn	0	r
Newcastle	3	Sheff Utd	1	r
Port Vale	3	Hull	1	re
Swindon	5	Fulham	0	r
West Brom	0	Man City	1	r
Wrexham	1	Sunderld	0	r
Darlingtn	0	Leyton O	3	r2N
Nottm For	6	Bristol R	0	r2N

FOURTH ROUND

Arsenal	3	Coventry	1	
Aston V	3	West Ham	0	
Birmghm C	1	Leeds U	2	
Blackburn	3	Leyton O	0	
Cardiff	3	Wrexham	2	
Chester	1	Luton	0	
Colchester	1	Derby	1	
Ipswich	2	Wolves	2	
Liverpool	3	Carlisle	0	
Man Utd	1	QPR	0	
Middlesbro	4	Hereford	0	
Newcastle	1	Man City	3	
Northwich	1	Oldham	3	N
Nottm For	3	Southmptn	3	
Port Vale	2	Burnley	1	
Swindon	2	Everton	2	
Derby	1	Colchester	0	r
Everton	2	Swindon	1	r
Southmptn	2	Nottm For	1	r
Wolves	1	Ipswich	0	r

FIFTH ROUND

Aston V	3	Port Vale	0	
Cardiff	1	Everton	2	
Derby	3	Blackburn	1	
Leeds U	1	Man City	0	
Liverpool	3	Oldham	1	
Middlesbro	4	Arsenal	1	
Southmptn	2	Man Utd	2	
Wolves	1	Chester	0	
Man Utd	2	Southmptn	1	r

SIXTH ROUND

Everton	2	Derby	0	
Liverpool	2	Middlesbro	0	
Man Utd	2	Aston V	1	
Wolves	0	Leeds U	1	

SEMI-FINAL

Liverpool	2	Everton	2	N
Man Utd	2	Leeds U	1	N
Everton	0	Liverpool	3	rN

FINAL

Man Utd	2	Liverpool	1	N

1978

FIRST ROUND

AP Leamgtn	6	Enderby T	1	
Arnold	0	Port Vale	0	
Barnet	1	Peterboro	2	
Barnsley	1	Huddersfld	0	
Bath C	0	Plymouth	0	
Blyth S	1	Burscough	0	
Boreham W	0	Swindon	0	
Bradford	0	Crewe	1	
Brentford	2	Folk & Sh	0	
Carlisle	2	Staffd Rg	0	
Chester	4	Darlingtn	1	
Chestrfld	1	Halifax	0	
Colchester	1	Bournemth	1	
Doncaster	0	Shrewsby	1	
Enfield	3	Wimbledn	0	
Gillinghm	1	Weymouth	1	
Leatherhd	0	Swansea	0	
Lowestoft	0	Cambridge	2	
Minehead	2	Wycombe	0	
Newport	1	Exeter	1	
Nuneaton	2	Oxford	0	
Portsmth	3	Bideford	1	
Preston NE	3	Lincoln	2	
Reading	3	Aldershot	1	
Rotherhm	3	Mossley	0	
Scarboro	4	Rochdale	2	
Sheff Wed	1	Bury	0	
Southport	2	Runcorn	2	
Spennym'r	3	Goole T	1	
Stockport	3	Scunthpe	0	
Tilbury	0	Kettering	1	v
Tooting	1	N'hamptn	2	
Torquay	1	Southend	2	
Tranmere	1	Hartlepl	1	
Walsall	1	Dagenham	0	
Watford	2	Hendon	0	
Wealdstne	0	Hereford	0	
Wigan Ath	1	York	0	
Workingtn	0	Grimsby	2	
Wrexham	2	Burton Al	0	
Bournemth	0	Colchester	0	re
Exeter	4	Newport	2	r
Hartlepl	3	Tranmere	1	r
Hereford	2	Wealdstne	3	r
Plymouth	2	Bath C	0	r
Port Vale	5	Arnold	2	r
Runcorn	1	Southport	0	r
Swansea	2	Leatherhd	1	r
Swindon	2	Boreham W	0	r

Brian Talbot celebrates his opening goal v Man Utd in 1979

Tilbury	2	Kettering	2	r
Weymouth	0	Gillinghm	1	r
Bournemth	1	Colchester	4	r2N
Kettering	2	Tilbury	3	r2
SECOND ROUND				
AP Leamgtn	0	Southend	0	
Blyth S	1	Chestrfld	0	
Carlisle	3	Chester	1	
Crewe	0	Scarboro	0	
Gillinghm	1	Peterboro	1	
Grimsby	2	Barnsley	0	
Hartlepl	4	Runcorn	2	
Minehead	0	Exeter	3	
N'hamptn	0	Enfield	2	
Nuneaton	1	Tilbury	2	
Plymouth	1	Cambridge	0	
Portsmth	2	Swansea	2	
Preston NE	0	Wrexham	2	
Rotherhm	6	Spennym'r	0	
Shrewsby	1	Stockport	1	
Swindon	2	Brentford	1	
Walsall	1	Port Vale	1	
Watford	2	Colchester	0	
Wealdstne	2	Reading	1	
Wigan Ath	1	Sheff Wed	0	
Peterboro	2	Gillinghm	0	r
Port Vale	1	Walsall	3	r
Scarboro	2	Crewe	0	r
Southend	4	AP Leamgtn	0	r
Stockport	1	Shrewsby	2	r
Swansea	2	Portsmth	1	r
THIRD ROUND				
Birmghm C	4	Wigan Ath	0	
Blackburn	2	Shrewsby	1	
Blyth S	1	Enfield	0	
Brighton	3	Scarboro	0	
Bristol C	4	Wrexham	4	
Burnley	1	Fulham	0	
Cardiff	0	Ipswich	2	
Carlisle	1	Man Utd	1	
Charlton	0	Notts Co	2	
Chelsea	4	Liverpool	2	
Derby	3	Southend	2	
Everton	4	Aston V	1	
Exeter	2	Wolves	2	
Grimsby	0	Southmptn	0	
Hartlepl	2	C.Palace	1	
Hull	0	Leicester	1	
Leeds U	1	Man City	2	

Honest Bob

Bobby Stokes, scorer of Second Division Southampton's winner against Manchester United in 1976, admitted later that he thought he was off-side at the time. Stokes died suddenly in 1995, aged 44.

Leyton O	1	Norwich	1	
Luton	1	Oldham	1	
Manfield	1	Plymouth	0	
Middlesbro	3	Coventry	0	
Nottm For	4	Swindon	1	
Peterboro	1	Newcastle	1	
QPR	4	Wealdstne	0	
Rotherhm	1	Millwall	1	
Sheff Utd	0	Arsenal	5	
Stoke	4	Tilbury	0	
Sunderld	0	Bristol R	1	
Tottenham	2	Bolton	2	
Walsall	4	Swansea	1	
West Brom	4	Blackpool	1	
West Ham	1	Watford	0	
Bolton	2	Tottenham	1	re
Man Utd	4	Carlisle	2	r
Millwall	2	Rotherhm	0	r
Newcastle	2	Peterboro	0	r
Norwich	0	Leyton O	1	r
Oldham	1	Luton	2	r
Southmptn	0	Grimsby	0	re
Wolves	3	Exeter	1	r
Wrexham	3	Bristol C	0	r
Grimsby	1	Southmptn	4	r2N
FOURTH ROUND				
Arsenal	2	Wolves	1	
Bolton	1	Manfield	0	
Brighton	1	Notts Co	2	
Bristol R	2	Southmptn	0	
Chelsea	6	Burnley	2	
Derby	2	Birmghm C	1	
Ipswich	4	Hartlepl	1	
Leyton O	3	Blackburn	1	
Man Utd	1	West Brom	1	
Middlesbro	3	Everton	2	
Millwall	4	Luton	0	
Newcastle	2	Wrexham	2	
Nottm For	2	Man City	1	
Stoke	2	Blyth S	3	
Walsall	1	Leicester	0	
West Ham	1	QPR	1	
QPR	6	West Ham	1	r
West Brom	3	Man Utd	2	re
Wrexham	4	Newcastle	1	r
FIFTH ROUND				
Arsenal	4	Walsall	1	
Bristol R	2	Ipswich	2	
Derby	2	West Brom	3	
Leyton O	0	Chelsea	0	
Middlesbro	2	Bolton	0	
Millwall	2	Notts Co	1	
QPR	1	Nottm For	1	
Wrexham	1	Blyth S	1	
Blyth S	1	Wrexham	2	rN
Chelsea	1	Leyton O	2	r
Ipswich	3	Bristol R	0	r
Nottm For	1	QPR	1	re
Nottm For	3	QPR	1	r2
SIXTH ROUND				
Middlesbro	0	Leyton O	0	
Millwall	1	Ipswich	6	
West Brom	2	Nottm For	0	
Wrexham	2	Arsenal	3	
Leyton O	2	Middlesbro	1	r
SEMI-FINAL				
Arsenal	3	Leyton O	0	N

Hero Halom

Vic Halom, who played in Sunderland's 1973 Cup-winning side against Leeds, also finished that season as top scorer for his previous club, Luton. He had scored ten goals before his transfer to Roker Park.

Ipswich	3	West Brom	1	N
FINAL				
Ipswich	1	Arsenal	0	N

1979

FIRST ROUND				
Aldershot	1	Weymouth	1	
Altrinchm	4	Southport	3	
Barnet	3	Woking	3	
Barnsley	5	Worksop	1	
Blackpool	2	Lincoln	1	
Bournemth	2	Hitchin	1	
Bradford	1	Port Vale	0	
Carlisle	1	Halifax	0	
Chester	1	Runcorn	1	
Chorley	0	Scarboro	1	
Colchester	4	Oxford	2	
Darlingtn	1	Chestrfld	1	
Dartford	1	AP Leamgtn	2	
Doncaster	2	Huddersfld	1	
Exeter	1	Brentford	0	
Gravesend	0	Wimbledn	0	
Hartlepl	1	Grimsby	0	
Hereford	0	Newport	1	
Hull	2	Staffd Rg	1	
Leatherhd	2	Mert Tyd	1	
Maidstone	1	Wycombe	0	
Manfield	0	Shrewsby	2	
Nuneaton	0	Crewe	2	
Portsmth	2	N'hamptn	0	
Reading	0	Gillinghm	0	
Rochdale	0	Droylsden	1	
Rotherhm	3	Workingtn	0	
Scunthpe	1	Sheff Wed	1	
Southend	3	Peterboro	2	
Stockport	5	Morecambe	1	
Swansea	4	Hillingdn	1	
Swindon	2	March	0	
Tranmere	2	Boston U	1	
Walsall	0	Torquay	2	
Watford	3	Dagenham	0	
Wealdstne	0	Enfield	5	
Wigan Ath	2	Bury	2	
Worcester	2	Plymouth	0	
Yeovil T	0	Barking	1	
York	1	Blyth S	1	
Blyth S	3	York	5	re
Bury	4	Wigan Ath	1	r
Chestrfld	0	Darlingtn	1	r

GIANTKILLERS

1978 Stoke 2 Blyth Spartans 3

Blyth Spartans had long been renowned as one of the leading non-League outfits in the north, and Second Division Stoke duly became their seventh League victims when they lost 3-2 in a Fourth Round thriller on their own pitch. Stoke had three players with Cup Final experience - Howard Kendall, Alec Lindsay and Viv Busby - and another, Garth Crooks, who went on to help Spurs to two Wembley wins. Spartans, beaten by Wrexham in a replay in Round Five, finished second in the Northern League that season.

Gillinghm	1	Reading	2	re
Runcorn	0	Chester	5	r
Sheff Wed	1	Scunthpe	0	r
Weymouth	0	Aldershot	2	r
Wimbledn	1	Gravesend	0	r
Woking	3	Barnet	3	re
Woking	3	Barnet	0	r2N

SECOND ROUND

AP Leamgtn	0	Torquay	1	
Barking	1	Aldershot	2	
Barnsley	1	Rotherhm	1	
Bury	3	Blackpool	1	
Carlisle	3	Hull	0	
Crewe	0	Hartlepl	1	
Darlingtn	2	Chester	1	
Doncaster	0	Shrewsby	3	
Droylsden	0	Altrinchm	2	
Leatherhd	1	Colchester	1	
Maidstone	1	Exeter	0	
Newport	0	Worcester	0	
Portsmth	0	Reading	1	
Stockport	4	Bradford	2	
Swansea	2	Woking	2	
Swindon	3	Enfield	0	
Tranmere	1	Sheff Wed	1	
Watford	1	Southend	1	
Wimbledn	1	Bournemth	1	
York	3	Scarboro	0	
Bournemth	1	Wimbledn	2	re
Colchester	4	Leatherhd	0	r
Rotherhm	2	Barnsley	1	r
Sheff Wed	4	Tranmere	0	r
Southend	1	Watford	0	r
Woking	3	Swansea	5	re
Worcester	1	Newport	2	r

THIRD ROUND

Birmghm C	0	Burnley	2	
Blackburn	2	Millwall	1	
Brighton	2	Wolves	3	
Bristol C	3	Bolton	1	
Charlton	1	Maidstone	1	
Coventry	2	West Brom	2	
Darlingtn	0	Colchester	1	
Fulham	2	QPR	0	
Hartlepl	2	Leeds U	6	
Ipswich	3	Carlisle	2	
Leicester	3	Norwich	0	
Leyton O	3	Bury	2	
Man City	0	Rotherhm	0	
Man Utd	3	Chelsea	0	
Middlesbro	1	C.Palace	1	
Newcastle	3	Torquay	1	
Newport	2	West Ham	1	
Nottm For	2	Aston V	0	
Notts Co	4	Reading	2	
Preston NE	3	Derby	0	
Sheff Utd	0	Aldershot	0	
Sheff Wed	1	Arsenal	1	
Shrewsby	3	Cambridge	1	
Southend	0	Liverpool	0	
Stoke	0	Oldham	1	
Sunderld	2	Everton	1	
Swansea	0	Bristol R	1	
Swindon	3	Cardiff	0	
Tottenham	1	Altrinchm	1	
Wimbledn	0	Southmptn	2	
Wrexham	6	Stockport	2	
York	2	Luton	0	
Aldershot	1	Sheff Utd	0	r
Altrinchm	0	Tottenham	3	rN
Arsenal	1	Sheff Wed	1	re
C.Palace	1	Middlesbro	0	r
Liverpool	3	Southend	0	r
Maidstone	1	Charlton	2	r
Rotherhm	2	Man City	4	r
West Brom	4	Coventry	0	r
Sheff Wed	2	Arsenal	2	r2eN
Arsenal	3	Sheff Wed	3	r3eN
Sheff Wed	0	Arsenal	2	r4N

FOURTH ROUND

Aldershot	2	Swindon	1	
Arsenal	2	Notts Co	0	
Bristol R	1	Charlton	0	
Burnley	1	Sunderld	1	
C.Palace	3	Bristol C	0	
Fulham	1	Man Utd	1	
Ipswich	0	Leyton O	0	
Liverpool	1	Blackburn	0	
Newcastle	1	Wolves	1	
Newport	0	Colchester	0	
Nottm For	3	York	1	
Oldham	3	Leicester	1	
Preston NE	0	Southmptn	1	
Shrewsby	2	Man City	0	
Tottenham	3	Wrexham	3	
West Brom	3	Leeds U	3	
Colchester	1	Newport	0	r
Leyton O	0	Ipswich	2	r
Man Utd	1	Fulham	0	r
Sunderld	0	Burnley	3	r
West Brom	2	Leeds U	0	re
Wolves	1	Newcastle	0	r
Wrexham	2	Tottenham	3	re

FIFTH ROUND

Aldershot	2	Shrewsby	2	
Colchester	0	Man Utd	1	
C.Palace	0	Wolves	1	
Ipswich	6	Bristol R	1	
Liverpool	3	Burnley	0	
Nottm For	0	Arsenal	1	
Oldham	0	Tottenham	1	
West Brom	1	Southmptn	1	
Shrewsby	3	Aldershot	1	re
Southmptn	2	West Brom	1	re

SIXTH ROUND

Ipswich	0	Liverpool	1	
Southmptn	1	Arsenal	1	
Tottenham	1	Man Utd	1	
Wolves	1	Shrewsby	1	
Arsenal	2	Southmptn	0	r
Man Utd	2	Tottenham	0	r
Shrewsby	1	Wolves	3	r

SEMI-FINAL

Arsenal	2	Wolves	0	N
Man Utd	2	Liverpool	2	N
Liverpool	0	Man Utd	1	rN

FINAL

Arsenal	3	Man Utd	2	N

Heighway Patrol

Steve Heighway, of Liverpool, became the first Irishman to score in more than one Final when he added a goal in the winning 1974 team, against Newcastle, to the one he got for the losers in 1971, against Arsenal.

1980-1989

CRAZY GANG RULE

The 1980s were a bleak time for English football with the Bradford fire, the Heysel disaster and, of course, Hillsborough.

Ninety-five Liverpool fans lost their lives when overcrowding at Sheffield Wednesday's ground resulted in crushing at the 1989 Semi-Final between Liverpool and Nottingham Forest.

Perhaps it was fitting that the Final that year should be an all-Merseyside affair between Liverpool and Everton. The fences came down, the sun shone and Liverpool won, as they had also done against Everton in 1986.

But away from this tragic backdrop the FA Cup continued to throw up some wonderful stories along the road to the Twin Towers.

There was Trevor Brooking winning the Cup for West Ham in 1980 with a collectors' item headed goal; there was Argentinian Ricky Villa scoring arguably Wembley's best ever goal for Spurs in the '81 Final replay; there was Elton John in tears as his Watford side reached Wembley in 1984, before losing 2-0 to Everton; and there was Keith Houchen's diving header to help clinch the Cup for Coventry in 1987.

But perhaps the greatest story of all, and one to rival Sunderland's magnificent 1973 achievement, was the fairytale which was Wimbledon Football Club.

The Dons were only elected into the Football League in 1977, and as recently as 1983 they were a Fourth Division club.

But, on a glorious afternoon on May 14th, 1988, the team dubbed the Crazy Gang made a mockery of all that to beat Liverpool and win the FA Cup.

There were many heroes in blue that day, but it was goalkeeper Dave Beasant who stole the glory, even away from Lawrie Sanchez, scorer of the game's only goal.

For it was Beasant who became the first goalkeeper to captain an FA Cup-winning side, and also the first keeper to save a penalty in an FA Cup Final at Wembley, with John Aldridge the unlucky taker.

Strange but true!

David Cross (West Ham) and Pat Jennings (Arsenal) were on opposing sides in the 1980 Final - seven years after they had been opponents in a League Cup Final with different clubs. Cross was then with Norwich and Jennings with Spurs.

Keeping on going

Ray Clemence set a long-distance record as a 38-year-old by appearing in a sixth Final, for Spurs in 1987, 16 years after his first, for Liverpool in 1971.

1980

FIRST ROUND

Aldershot	4	Exeter	1	
Altrinchm	3	Crewe	0	
Barking	1	Oxford	0	
Barnsley	5	Hartlepl	2	
Blackpool	1	Wigan Ath	1	
Blyth S	0	Manfield	2	
Brandon U	0	Bradford	3	N
Burton Al	0	Bury	2	
Carlisle	3	Hull	3	
Chester	5	Workingtn	1	
Colchester	1	Plymouth	1	
Darlingtn	1	Huddersfld	1	
Enfield	0	Yeovil T	1	
Fareham T	2	Mert Tyd	3	
Gillinghm	0	Wimbledn	0	
Gravesend	0	Torquay	1	
Grimsby	1	Chestrfld	1	
Halifax	2	Scarboro	0	
Harlow T	2	Ley/Ilf	1	
Hereford	1	N'hamptn	0	
Kiddermst	0	Blackburn	2	
Minehead	1	Chesham U	2	
Morecambe	1	Rotherhm	1	
Nuneaton	3	Northwich	3	
Peterboro	1	Bournemth	2	
Port Vale	1	Doncaster	3	
Portsmth	1	Newport	0	
Reading	4	Kettering	2	
Rochdale	2	Scunthpe	1	
Salisbury	1	Millwall	2	N
Sheff Utd	3	Burscough	0	
Sheff Wed	3	Lincoln	0	
Slough T	3	Hungerfd	1	
Staffd Rg	3	Moor Grn	2	
Swindon	4	Brentford	1	
Tranmere	9	AP Leamgtn	0	
Walsall	2	Stockport	0	
Wealdstne	0	Southend	1	
Wycombe	0	Croydon	3	
York	5	Mossley	2	
Chestrfld	2	Grimsby	3	r
Huddersfld	0	Darlingtn	1	r
Hull	0	Carlisle	2	r
Northwich	3	Nuneaton	0	r
Plymouth	0	Colchester	1	re
Rotherhm	2	Morecambe	0	r
Wigan Ath	2	Blackpool	0	r
Wimbledn	4	Gillinghm	2	r

SECOND ROUND

Blackburn	2	Staffd Rg	0	
Bury	0	York	0	
Carlisle	3	Sheff Wed	0	
Chesham U	1	Mert Tyd	1	
Chester	1	Barnsley	0	
Colchester	1	Bournemth	0	
Croydon	1	Millwall	1	N
Darlingtn	0	Bradford	1	
Doncaster	1	Manfield	2	
Grimsby	2	Sheff Utd	0	
Hereford	1	Aldershot	2	
Northwich	2	Wigan Ath	2	
Reading	3	Barking	1	
Rotherhm	0	Altrinchm	2	
Southend	1	Harlow T	1	
Torquay	3	Swindon	3	
Tranmere	2	Rochdale	2	
Walsall	1	Halifax	1	
Wimbledn	0	Portsmth	0	
Yeovil T	1	Slough T	0	
Halifax	1	Walsall	1	re
Harlow T	1	Southend	0	r
Mert Tyd	1	Chesham U	3	r
Millwall	3	Croydon	2	re
Portsmth	3	Wimbledn	3	re
Rochdale	2	Tranmere	1	r
Swindon	3	Torquay	2	r
Wigan Ath	1	Northwich	0	r
York	0	Bury	2	r
Halifax	2	Walsall	0	r2e
Wimbledn	0	Portsmth	1	r2

THIRD ROUND

Altrinchm	1	Leyton O	1	
Birmghm C	2	Southmptn	1	
Blackburn	1	Fulham	1	
Bristol C	6	Derby	2	
Bristol R	1	Aston V	2	
Burnley	1	Stoke	0	
Cardiff	0	Arsenal	0	
Carlisle	3	Bradford	2	
Chelsea	0	Wigan Ath	1	
Chesham U	0	Cambridge	2	
Everton	4	Aldershot	1	
Halifax	1	Man City	0	
Leeds U	1	Nottm For	4	
Leicester	1	Harlow T	1	
Liverpool	5	Grimsby	0	
Luton	0	Swindon	2	
Manfield	0	Brighton	2	
Millwall	5	Shrewsby	1	
Newcastle	0	Chester	2	
Notts Co	1	Wolves	3	
Oldham	0	Coventry	1	
Portsmth	1	Middlesbro	1	
Preston NE	0	Ipswich	3	
QPR	1	Watford	2	
Reading	2	Colchester	0	
Rochdale	1	Bury	1	
Sunderld	0	Bolton	1	
Swansea	2	C.Palace	2	
Tottenham	1	Man Utd	1	
West Brom	1	West Ham	1	
Wrexham	6	Charlton	0	
Yeovil T	0	Norwich	3	
Arsenal	2	Cardiff	1	r
Bury	3	Rochdale	2	r
C.Palace	3	Swansea	3	re
Fulham	0	Blackburn	1	r
Harlow T	1	Leicester	0	r
Leyton O	2	Altrinchm	1	r
Man Utd	0	Tottenham	1	re
Middlesbro	3	Portsmth	0	r
West Ham	2	West Brom	1	r
Swansea	2	C.Palace	1	r2N

FOURTH ROUND

Arsenal	2	Brighton	0	
Birmghm C	2	Middlesbro	1	
Blackburn	1	Coventry	0	
Bolton	2	Halifax	0	
Bristol C	1	Ipswich	2	
Bury	1	Burnley	0	
Cambridge	1	Aston V	1	
Carlisle	0	Wrexham	0	
Chester	2	Millwall	0	
Everton	3	Wigan Ath	0	
Leyton O	2	West Ham	3	

A lot of bottle

Goalkeeper Peter Hucker, who played for QPR in the 1982 Final under manager Terry Venables, later became a milkman.

GIANTKILLERS

1980 Chelsea 0 Wigan 1

This was hardly vintage Chelsea, then in the Second Division and with only one international on the books - manager Geoff Hurst. Even so, visiting Wigan did well to lift their game above the Fourth Division norm - they had had to survive a replay against Northwich Victoria of the Northern Premier a week earlier - to win with a goal from midfielder Tommy Gore, one of five Liverpudlians in their team. Ironically, Wigan's giant-killing came to an end on Merseyside, when they lost to Everton in the Fourth Round.

WHAT A STAR ✪ RICKY VILLA

He was perhaps lucky to play in the 1981 Final replay, having done so poorly in the first game that he was substituted. But Tottenham manager Keith Burkinshaw kept faith with Villa, one of the Argentinian duo he had signed nearly three years earlier - and Villa repaid that faith with two goals. The second, which gave Spurs a 3-2 win over Manchester City, is widely regarded as the greatest Wembley solo effort, a run past five defenders before sliding the ball home.

Nottm For	0	Liverpool	2	
Swansea	4	Reading	1	
Swindon	0	Tottenham	0	
Watford	4	Harlow T	3	
Wolves	1	Norwich	1	
Aston V	4	Cambridge	1	r
Norwich	2	Wolves	3	r
Tottenham	2	Swindon	1	r
Wrexham	3	Carlisle	1	r
FIFTH ROUND				
Blackburn	1	Aston V	1	
Bolton	1	Arsenal	1	
Everton	5	Wrexham	2	
Ipswich	2	Chester	1	
Liverpool	2	Bury	0	
Tottenham	3	Birmghm C	1	
West Ham	2	Swansea	0	
Wolves	0	Watford	3	
Arsenal	3	Bolton	0	r
Aston V	1	Blackburn	0	r
SIXTH ROUND				
Everton	2	Ipswich	1	
Tottenham	0	Liverpool	1	
Watford	1	Arsenal	2	
West Ham	1	Aston V	0	
SEMI-FINAL				
Arsenal	0	Liverpool	0	N
West Ham	1	Everton	1	N
Everton	1	West Ham	2	rN
Liverpool	1	Arsenal	1	reN
Arsenal	1	Liverpool	1	r2eN
Liverpool	0	Arsenal	1	r3N
FINAL				
West Ham	1	Arsenal	0	N

1981

FIRST ROUND				
Barnet	2	Minehead	2	
Blackpool	4	Fleetwd T	0	
Blyth S	2	Burton Al	1	
Boston U	0	Rotherhm	4	
Brentford	2	Addlstn&W	2	
Burnley	1	Scarboro	0	
Burscough	1	Altrinchm	2	
Chester	1	Barnsley	2	
Colchester	3	Portsmth	0	
Darlingtn	0	Bury	2	
Enfield	3	Wembley	0	
Exeter	5	Leatherhd	0	
Gillinghm	2	Dagenham	1	
Gravesend	1	St Albns C	2	
Harlow T	0	Charlton	2	
Hull	2	Halifax	1	
Kettering	1	Maidstone	1	
Kiddermst	1	Millwall	1	
Lincoln	1	Gateshead	0	
Manfield	3	Rochdale	1	
Mossley	1	Crewe	0	
N'hamptn	1	Peterboro	4	
Northwich	1	Huddersfld	1	
Oxford	1	Aldershot	0	
Plymouth	2	Newport	0	
Port Vale	4	Bradford	2	
Reading	1	Fulham	2	
Scunthpe	3	Hartlepl	1	
Southend	0	Hereford	1	
Stockport	0	Sheff Utd	0	
Sutton Cd	0	Doncaster	2	
Swindon	3	Weymouth	2	
Torquay	2	Barton R	0	
Tranmere	0	York	0	
Walsall	3	Staffd Rg	0	
Wigan Ath	2	Chestrfld	2	
Wimbledn	7	Windsor&E	2	
Workingtn	0	Carlisle	0	
Wycombe	0	Bournemth	3	
Yeovil T	2	Farnborgh	1	
Brentford	2	Addlstn&W	0	r
Carlisle	4	Workingtn	1	r
Chestrfld	2	Wigan Ath	0	r
Huddersfld	6	Northwich	0	r
Maidstone	0	Kettering	0	re
Millwall	1	Kiddermst	0	r
Minehead	1	Barnet	2	r
Sheff Utd	3	Stockport	2	re
York	1	Tranmere	2	re
Maidstone	3	Kettering	1	r2
SECOND ROUND				
Barnet	0	Peterboro	1	
Burnley	1	Port Vale	1	
Bury	2	Lincoln	0	
Carlisle	3	Walsall	0	
Charlton	2	Bournemth	1	
Colchester	1	Yeovil T	1	
Doncaster	2	Blackpool	1	
Enfield	2	Hereford	0	
Fulham	1	Brentford	0	
Gillinghm	0	Maidstone	0	
Hull	1	Blyth S	1	
Millwall	0	Exeter	1	
Mossley	1	Manfield	3	
Plymouth	3	Oxford	0	
Rotherhm	0	Barnsley	1	
Scunthpe	0	Altrinchm	0	
Sheff Utd	1	Chestrfld	1	
St Albns C	1	Torquay	1	
Tranmere	0	Huddersfld	3	
Wimbledn	2	Swindon	0	
Altrinchm	1	Scunthpe	0	r
Blyth S	2	Hull	2	re
Chestrfld	1	Sheff Utd	0	r
Maidstone	0	Gillinghm	0	re
Port Vale	2	Burnley	0	r
Torquay	4	St Albns C	1	r
Yeovil T	0	Colchester	2	r
Gillinghm	0	Maidstone	2	r2
Hull	2	Blyth S	1	r2eN
THIRD ROUND				
Barnsley	2	Torquay	1	
Birmghm C	1	Sunderld	1	
Bury	1	Fulham	1	
Colchester	0	Watford	1	
Derby	0	Bristol C	0	
Everton	2	Arsenal	0	
Huddersfld	0	Shrewsby	3	
Hull	1	Doncaster	0	
Ipswich	1	Aston V	0	
Leeds U	1	Coventry	1	
Leicester	3	Cardiff	0	
Leyton O	1	Luton	3	
Liverpool	4	Altrinchm	1	
Maidstone	2	Exeter	4	
Man City	4	C.Palace	0	
Man Utd	2	Brighton	2	
Manfield	2	Carlisle	2	
Newcastle	2	Sheff Wed	1	
Norwich	1	Cambridge	0	
Nottm For	3	Bolton	3	
Notts Co	2	Blackburn	1	
Peterboro	1	Chestrfld	1	

Strange but true!

Lawrie Sanchez, not renowned as a regular marksman, headed the only goal when Wimbledon beat Liverpool in 1988...after his brother had drawn him in a first-scorer sweepstake!

Pro-File: BRYAN ROBSON

Bryan Robson was one of the most inspirational players ever to grace a football pitch.

His determination and will-to-win were second to none and he was a fantastic leader of both his club, Manchester United, and his country.

He was nicknamed Captain Marvel and was respected all over the world for his performances, both at home and in Europe.

As captain of United he led the Red Devils to every domestic honour and to the European Cup-Winners' Cup in 1991, during a glorious 13-year career at Old Trafford.

And were it not for a succession of injuries he would surely have challenged Peter Shilton's record of 125 caps for England. Certainly he would have eclipsed Bobby Moore's total of 108 caps, the highest number for an outfield player.

As it was, he played 90 times for his country, many of them as captain, including the World Cup finals in 1982, 1986 and 1990.

His Old Trafford career came to an end in 1994 when he agreed to join Middlesbrough as player-manager.

Fittingly, and not surprisingly, he led them to promotion to the Premiership during his first season in charge and although that was followed by relegation in 1996/97, he still managed to take the Riverside club to two Wembley Cup Finals - both lost - the same year.

Career details

●**Represented:** England, West Bromwich Albion, Manchester United, Middlesbrough ●**Position:** Midfield ●**Born:** Chester-le-Street, 11.01.57 ●**Height:** 5ft 10in ●**Weight:** 12st 5lbs ●**Club honours:** League Championship 1993, 1994; First Division Championship 1995; FA Cup 1983, 1985, 1990; League Cup runners-up 1991; European Cup-Winners' Cup 1991 ●**International honours:** England 7 Youth, 7 U21, 6 'B', 90 full caps

Club League Record

Era	Club	Games	Goals
74/81	West Brom	198	39
81/94	Manchester United	345	74
94/97	Middlesbrough	25	1

Cup Highlights

May 21 1983: Robson appears in his first FA Cup Final. The match against Brighton ends in a 2-2 draw.

May 26 1983: Scores twice as United thrash Brighton 4-0 in the replay to take the FA Cup - the first time he lifts the trophy.

May 18 1985: He gets his hands on the FA Cup for the second time in three years as United beat Everton 1-0 after extra-time, despite having Kevin Moran sent-off.

May 12 1990: Robbo is on target in the FA Cup Final again - this time in a 3-3 draw with Crystal Palace.

May 17 1990: History is made as Robbo lifts the FA Cup for the third time after a 1-0 replay win over Palace.

On Robson:

●His strengths as a manager are the same as they were as a player. He is single-minded, stubborn even, very determined. **Alex Ferguson**

Robson On:

●Maybe we should give him a snowplough instead of a club car. **Robbo on reports that Juninho wouldn't be able to cope with the cold in the North-East**

DID YOU KNOW THAT...

●Bryan Robson made his League debut in April 1975, for West Brom against York. Albion won 3-1 at Bootham Crescent.

●His home debut came a week later against Cardiff and he scored the first goal in a 2-0 win. He scored again the following week, the last day of the season, in a 2-1 defeat at Nottingham Forest.

●When he joined United in October 1981 it was for a British record fee of £1.5 million.

●Robbo played in three World Cup finals for England - Spain in 1982, Mexico in 1986 and Italy in 1990.

●His goal against France in England's first World Cup match at Spain 1982 was scored after only 27 SECONDS - the second quickest strike in World Cup finals history.

●That goal against France is also the quickest ever scored by an England player.

●Robson is the only man in the history of football to lift the FA Cup three times for the same club.

●Away from football, Robson has a business interest in a thriving greetings card company.

●When Robson signed Fabrizio Ravanelli in the summer of 1996 for £7 million it took his spending to £24 million for Boro - nearly twice the amount it cost the club to build the Riverside Stadium.

●Robson's 26 goals make him England's second top scorer from midfield. Only David Platt, with 28, has scored more.

Plymouth	1	Charlton	2	
Port Vale	1	Enfield	1	
Preston NE	3	Bristol R	4	
QPR	0	Tottenham	0	
Southmptn	3	Chelsea	1	
Stoke	2	Wolves	2	
Swansea	0	Middlesbro	5	
West Brom	3	Grimsby	0	
West Ham	1	Wrexham	1	
Wimbledn	0	Oldham	0	
Bolton	0	Nottm For	1	re
Brighton	0	Man Utd	2	r
Bristol C	2	Derby	0	r
Carlisle	2	Manfield	1	r
Chestrfld	1	Peterboro	2	r
Coventry	1	Leeds U	0	r
Enfield	3	Port Vale	0	r
Fulham	0	Bury	0	re
Oldham	0	Wimbledn	1	r
Sunderld	1	Birmghm C	2	re
Tottenham	3	QPR	1	r
Wolves	2	Stoke	1	r
Wrexham	0	West Ham	0	re
Bury	0	Fulham	1	r2N
Wrexham	1	West Ham	0	r2e
FOURTH ROUND				
Barnsley	1	Enfield	1	
Carlisle	1	Bristol C	1	
Coventry	3	Birmghm C	2	
Everton	2	Liverpool	1	
Fulham	1	Charlton	2	
Leicester	1	Exeter	1	
Man City	6	Norwich	0	
Middlesbro	1	West Brom	0	
Newcastle	2	Luton	1	
Nottm For	1	Man Utd	0	
Notts Co	0	Peterboro	1	
Shrewsby	0	Ipswich	0	
Southmptn	3	Bristol R	1	
Tottenham	2	Hull	0	
Watford	1	Wolves	1	
Wrexham	2	Wimbledn	1	
Bristol C	5	Carlisle	0	r
Enfield	0	Barnsley	3	rN
Exeter	3	Leicester	1	r
Ipswich	3	Shrewsby	0	r
Wolves	2	Watford	1	r
FIFTH ROUND				
Ipswich	2	Charlton	0	
Middlesbro	2	Barnsley	1	
Newcastle	1	Exeter	1	
Nottm For	2	Bristol C	1	
Peterboro	0	Man City	1	
Southmptn	0	Everton	0	
Tottenham	3	Coventry	1	
Wolves	3	Wrexham	1	
Everton	1	Southmptn	0	re
Exeter	4	Newcastle	0	r
SIXTH ROUND				
Everton	2	Man City	2	
Middlesbro	1	Wolves	1	
Nottm For	3	Ipswich	3	
Tottenham	2	Exeter	0	
Ipswich	1	Nottm For	0	r
Man City	3	Everton	1	r
Wolves	3	Middlesbro	1	re
SEMI-FINAL				
Man City	1	Ipswich	0	eN
Tottenham	2	Wolves	2	eN
Wolves	0	Tottenham	3	rN
FINAL				
Tottenham	1	Man City	1	eN
Tottenham	3	Man City	2	rN

1982

FIRST ROUND				
Aldershot	2	Ley/Ilf	0	
Bedford T	0	Wimbledn	2	
Bideford	1	Barking	2	
Blyth S	1	Walsall	2	
Boston U	0	Kettering	1	
Bournemth	1	Reading	0	
Brentford	2	Exeter	0	
Bristol C	0	Torquay	0	
Bristol R	1	Fulham	2	
Bshk Auck	4	Nuneaton	1	
Bshp Stor	2	Sutton U	2	
Burnley	0	Runcorn	0	
Chestrfld	4	Preston NE	1	
Colchester	2	Newport	0	
Dagenham	2	Yeovil T	2	
Darlingtn	2	Carlisle	2	
Dorchstr	3	Minehead	3	
Dover	0	Oxford	2	
Enfield	2	Hasting U	0	
Halifax	0	Peterboro	3	
Harlow T	0	Barnet	0	
Hendon	1	Wycombe	1	
Hereford	3	Southend	1	
Horden CW	0	Blackpool	1	N
Lincoln	2	Port Vale	2	
Manfield	0	Doncaster	1	
Penrith	1	Chester	0	
Plymouth	0	Gillinghm	0	
Portsmth	1	Millwall	1	
Rochdale	2	Hull	2	
Scunthpe	1	Bradford	0	
Sheff Utd	2	Altrinchm	2	
Staffd Rg	1	York	2	
Stockport	3	Mossley	1	
Swindon	2	Taunton T	1	
Tranmere	1	Bury	1	
Weymouth	0	N'hamptn	0	
Wigan Ath	2	Hartlepl	2	
Willenh'l	0	Crewe	1	
Workingtn	1	Huddersfld	1	
Altrinchm	3	Sheff Utd	0	r
Barnet	1	Harlow T	0	r
Bury	3	Tranmere	1	r
Carlisle	3	Darlingtn	1	r
Gillinghm	1	Plymouth	0	r
Hartlepl	1	Wigan Ath	0	r
Huddersfld	5	Workingtn	0	r
Hull	2	Rochdale	2	re
Millwall	3	Portsmth	2	re
Minehead	0	Dorchstr	4	r

Tears of joy

In the exciting Final in 1980 between West Ham and Arsenal, Paul Allen - aged 17 years, 256 days - became the youngest player to have appeared in a Wembley Final, and the youngest Cup Finalist for 121 years. He cried after Trevor Brooking's header won the Cup for his club.

GIANTKILLERS

1981 Exeter 3 Leicester 1

Tony Kellow, who scored 33 goals during the season, got three of them in this Fourth Round replay as Third Division Exeter, unlucky not to win the first meeting, outplayed a Leicester side on their way to relegation from the First. Leicester might have done better if they had picked the young Gary Lineker instead of leaving him out. Exeter then beat Second Division Newcastle 4-0 in another replay, before their best-ever Cup run - achieved despite being drawn away five times in a row - was ended by Tottenham, the eventual winners.

WHAT A STAR ★ JIMMY MELIA

White shoes, disco music and a helicopter to Wembley - that was manager Jimmy Melia when Brighton got there in 1983. After a long playing career, spent mainly with Liverpool, balding Jimmy turned to management and surprised everybody by not only reaching the Cup Final against Manchester United, but going very close to winning it. Even though Brighton collapsed in the replay - beaten 4-0 - and were relegated as well, Melia was a big name in the game at last.

N'hamptn	6	Weymouth	2	r
Port Vale	0	Lincoln	0	re
Runcorn	1	Burnley	2	r
Sutton U	2	Bshp Stor	1	r
Torquay	1	Bristol C	2	r
Wycombe	2	Hendon	0	r
Yeovil T	0	Dagenham	1	re
Hull	1	Rochdale	0	r2eN
Port Vale	2	Lincoln	0	r2
SECOND ROUND				
Aldershot	2	Oxford	2	
Barnet	2	Wycombe	0	
Brentford	1	Colchester	1	
Bristol C	3	N'hamptn	0	
Bury	1	Burnley	1	
Carlisle	1	Bshk Auck	0	N
Chestrfld	0	Huddersfld	1	
Crewe	1	Scunthpe	3	
Dagenham	1	Millwall	2	
Doncaster	3	Penrith	0	
Dorchstr	1	Bournemth	1	
Enfield	4	Wimbledn	1	
Gillinghm	1	Barking	1	
Hereford	1	Fulham	0	
Hull	2	Hartlepl	0	
Kettering	0	Blackpool	3	
Peterboro	2	Walsall	1	
Port Vale	4	Stockport	1	
Swindon	2	Sutton U	1	
York	0	Altrinchm	0	
Altrinchm	4	York	3	r
Bournemth	2	Dorchstr	1	re
Burnley	2	Bury	1	re
Colchester	1	Brentford	0	r
Gillinghm	3	Barking	1	re
Oxford	4	Aldershot	2	r
THIRD ROUND				
Barnet	0	Brighton	0	
Barnsley	0	Blackpool	2	
Birmghm C	2	Ipswich	3	
Bolton	3	Derby	1	
Bournemth	0	Oxford	2	
Burnley	6	Altrinchm	1	
Carlisle	2	Huddersfld	3	
Chelsea	0	Hull	0	
Coventry	3	Sheff Wed	1	
Doncaster	2	Cambridge	1	
Enfield	2	C.Palace	3	
Gillinghm	2	Oldham	1	
Leicester	3	Southmptn	1	
Leyton O	1	Charlton	0	
Luton	2	Swindon	1	
Man City	3	Cardiff	1	
Millwall	1	Grimsby	6	
Newcastle	1	Colchester	1	
Nottm For	1	Wrexham	3	
Notts Co	0	Aston V	6	
Peterboro	0	Bristol C	1	
QPR	1	Middlesbro	1	
Rotherhm	1	Sunderld	1	
Scunthpe	1	Hereford	1	
Shrewsby	1	Port Vale	0	
Stoke	0	Norwich	1	
Swansea	0	Liverpool	4	
Tottenham	1	Arsenal	0	
Watford	1	Man Utd	0	
West Brom	3	Blackburn	2	
West Ham	2	Everton	1	
Wolves	1	Leeds U	3	
Brighton	3	Barnet	1	r
Colchester	3	Newcastle	4	re
Hereford	4	Scunthpe	1	r
Hull	0	Chelsea	2	r
Middlesbro	2	QPR	3	re
Sunderld	1	Rotherhm	0	r
FOURTH ROUND				
Blackpool	0	QPR	0	
Brighton	0	Oxford	3	
Bristol C	0	Aston V	1	
Chelsea	0	Wrexham	0	
C.Palace	1	Bolton	0	
Gillinghm	0	West Brom	1	
Hereford	0	Leicester	1	
Huddersfld	1	Leyton O	1	
Luton	0	Ipswich	3	
Man City	1	Coventry	3	
Newcastle	1	Grimsby	2	
Norwich	2	Doncaster	1	
Shrewsby	1	Burnley	0	
Sunderld	0	Liverpool	3	
Tottenham	1	Leeds U	0	
Watford	2	West Ham	0	
Leyton O	2	Huddersfld	0	r
QPR	5	Blackpool	1	r
Wrexham	1	Chelsea	1	re
Wrexham	1	Chelsea	2	r2
FIFTH ROUND				
Chelsea	2	Liverpool	0	
Coventry	4	Oxford	0	
C.Palace	0	Leyton O	0	
Leicester	2	Watford	0	
QPR	3	Grimsby	1	
Shrewsby	2	Ipswich	1	
Tottenham	1	Aston V	0	
West Brom	1	Norwich	0	
Leyton O	0	C.Palace	1	r
SIXTH ROUND				
Chelsea	2	Tottenham	3	
Leicester	5	Shrewsby	2	
QPR	1	C.Palace	0	
West Brom	2	Coventry	0	
SEMI-FINAL				
QPR	1	West Brom	0	N
Tottenham	2	Leicester	0	N
FINAL				
Tottenham	1	QPR	1	eN
Tottenham	1	QPR	0	rN

Price is Right

He broke a leg twice before he had made a Football League appearance, but Paul Price went on to help Spurs to win the Cup in 1982, and also captained Wales on several occasions.

1983

FIRST ROUND				
Aldershot	4	Wimborne	0	
Altrinchm	2	Rochdale	1	
Blackpool	3	Horwich R	0	
Boston U	3	Crewe	1	
Bournemth	0	Southend	2	
Brentford	7	Windsor&E	0	
Bristol R	1	Wycombe	0	
Carshlton	4	Barnet	0	
Chesham U	0	Yeovil T	1	
Chester	1	Northwich	1	
Chestrfld	2	Peterboro	2	
Colchester	0	Torquay	2	
Darlingtn	0	Scunthpe	1	
Enfield	0	Newport	0	
Gillinghm	1	Dagenham	0	
Halifax	0	N.Shields	1	
Hartlepl	3	Lincoln	0	
Holbeach	0	Wrexham	4	N

GIANTKILLERS

1984 Bournemouth 2 Manchester United 0

The scoreline masks a remarkable statistic. Defeat at Dean Court for the Cup holders was United's first loss in the opening round of the competition for nine years, and it has not happened since. When they had to go to Bournemouth again a year later they won easily, but this time - even with ten internationals among the 12 men on duty - they were second best. Goals by Milton Graham and Ian Thompson saw off United, who had lost in the League Cup to another Third Division outfit, Oxford, three weeks earlier. Unfortunately, Bournemouth manager Harry Redknapp could not bring about a repeat in the next round, against Middlesbrough.

Huddersfld	1	Mossley	0	
Hull	1	Sheff Utd	1	
Leyton O	4	Bristol C	1	
Macclesfd	1	Worcester	5	
Manfield	3	Stockport	2	
N'hamptn	2	Wimbledn	2	
Oxford	5	Folkestne	2	
Plymouth	2	Exeter	0	
Port Vale	0	Bradford	1	
Portsmth	4	Hereford	1	
Preston NE	5	Shepshed C	1	
Reading	1	Bshp Stor	2	
Slough T	1	Millwall	0	
Swindon	2	Wealdstne	0	
Tranmere	4	Scarboro	2	
Walsall	3	Kettering	0	
Weymouth	4	Maidstone	3	
Wigan Ath	0	Telford U	0	
Wokingtm	1	Cardiff	1	
Workingtn	1	Doncaster	2	
Worthing	2	Dartford	1	
York	3	Bury	1	
Cardiff	3	Wokingtm	0	r
Newport	4	Enfield	2	r
Northwich	3	Chester	1	re
Peterboro	2	Chestrfld	1	r
Sheff Utd	2	Hull	0	r
Telford U	2	Wigan Ath	1	r
Wimbledn	0	N'hamptn	2	r
SECOND ROUND				
Altrinchm	0	Huddersfld	1	
Boston U	1	Sheff Utd	1	
Bristol R	2	Plymouth	2	
Cardiff	2	Weymouth	3	
Gillinghm	1	N'hamptn	1	
Hartlepl	1	York	1	
Manfield	1	Bradford	1	
N.Shields	0	Walsall	3	
Newport	1	Leyton O	0	
Oxford	4	Worthing	0	
Peterboro	5	Doncaster	2	
Portsmth	1	Aldershot	3	
Preston NE	2	Blackpool	1	
Scunthpe	2	Northwich	1	
Slough T	1	Bshp Stor	4	
Southend	3	Yeovil T	0	
Swindon	2	Brentford	2	
Telford U	1	Tranmere	1	
Torquay	4	Carshlton	1	
Worcester	2	Wrexham	1	
Bradford	3	Manfield	2	r
Brentford	1	Swindon	3	re
N'hamptn	3	Gillinghm	2	r
Plymouth	1	Bristol R	0	r
Sheff Utd	5	Boston U	1	r
Tranmere	2	Telford U	1	r
York	4	Hartlepl	0	r
THIRD ROUND				
Arsenal	2	Bolton	1	
Blackburn	1	Liverpool	2	
Bradford	0	Barnsley	1	
Brighton	1	Newcastle	1	
Cambridge	1	Weymouth	0	
Carlisle	2	Burnley	2	
Charlton	2	Ipswich	3	
Coventry	3	Worcester	1	
C.Palace	2	York	1	
Derby	2	Nottm For	0	
Huddersfld	1	Chelsea	1	
Leeds U	3	Preston NE	0	
Leicester	2	Notts Co	3	
Luton	3	Peterboro	0	
Man Utd	2	West Ham	0	
Middlesbro	2	Bshp Stor	2	
Newport	1	Everton	1	
N'hamptn	0	Aston V	1	
Norwich	2	Swansea	1	
Oldham	0	Fulham	2	
Oxford	1	Torquay	1	
Scunthpe	0	Grimsby	0	
Sheff Utd	0	Stoke	0	
Shrewsby	2	Rotherhm	1	
Southend	0	Sheff Wed	0	
Sunderld	0	Man City	0	
Swindon	7	Aldershot	0	
Tottenham	1	Southmptn	0	
Tranmere	0	Wolves	1	
Walsall	0	Birmghm C	0	
Watford	2	Plymouth	0	
West Brom	3	QPR	2	
Birmghm C	1	Walsall	0	re
Bshp Stor	1	Middlesbro	2	r
Burnley	3	Carlisle	1	r
Chelsea	2	Huddersfld	0	r
Everton	2	Newport	1	r
Grimsby	2	Scunthpe	0	r
Man City	2	Sunderld	1	r
Newcastle	0	Brighton	1	r
Sheff Wed	2	Southend	2	re
Stoke	3	Sheff Utd	2	r
Torquay	2	Oxford	1	r
Sheff Wed	2	Southend	1	r2
FOURTH ROUND				
Arsenal	1	Leeds U	1	
Aston V	1	Wolves	0	
Brighton	4	Man City	0	
Burnley	3	Swindon	1	
Cambridge	1	Barnsley	0	
Coventry	2	Norwich	2	
C.Palace	1	Birmghm C	0	
Derby	2	Chelsea	1	
Everton	2	Shrewsby	1	
Ipswich	2	Grimsby	0	
Liverpool	2	Stoke	0	
Luton	0	Man Utd	2	
Middlesbro	2	Notts Co	0	
Torquay	2	Sheff Wed	3	
Tottenham	2	West Brom	1	
Watford	1	Fulham	1	
Fulham	1	Watford	2	r
Leeds U	1	Arsenal	1	re
Norwich	2	Coventry	1	re
Arsenal	2	Leeds U	1	r2
FIFTH ROUND				
Aston V	4	Watford	1	
Cambridge	1	Sheff Wed	2	
C.Palace	0	Burnley	0	
Derby	0	Man Utd	1	
Everton	2	Tottenham	0	
Liverpool	1	Brighton	2	
Middlesbro	1	Arsenal	1	
Norwich	1	Ipswich	0	
Arsenal	3	Middlesbro	2	r
Burnley	1	C.Palace	0	r
SIXTH ROUND				
Arsenal	2	Aston V	0	
Brighton	1	Norwich	0	
Burnley	1	Sheff Wed	1	

Man Utd	1	Everton	0	
Sheff Wed	5	Burnley	0	r
SEMI-FINAL				
Brighton	2	Sheff Wed	1	N
Man Utd	2	Arsenal	1	N
FINAL				
Man Utd	2	Brighton	2	eN
Man Utd	4	Brighton	0	rN

1984

FIRST ROUND				
AP Leamgtn	0	Gillinghm	1	
Aldershot	1	Worcester	1	
Barking	2	Farnborgh	1	
Barnet	0	Bristol R	0	
Boston U	0	Bury	3	
Bournemth	4	Walsall	0	
Bradford	0	Wigan Ath	0	
Burnley	2	Hyde Utd	0	
Burton Al	1	Windsor&E	2	
Chelmsfd	0	Wycombe	0	
Chester	1	Chestrfld	2	
Cor Casls	0	Bristol C	0	
Dagenham	2	Brentford	2	
Darlingtn	5	Mossley	0	
Exeter	1	Maidstone	1	
Frickley	0	Altrinchm	1	
Gainsbrgh	0	Blackpool	2	
Halifax	2	Whitby T	3	
Kettering	0	Swindon	7	
Macclesfd	0	York	0	
Manfield	3	Doncaster	0	
Millwall	2	Dartford	1	
N'hamptn	1	Waterlve	1	
Northwich	1	Bangor C	1	
Oxford	2	Peterboro	0	
Penrith	0	Hull	2	
Poole T	0	Newport	0	
Port Vale	1	Lincoln	2	
Reading	2	Hereford	0	
Rochdale	1	Crewe	0	
Rotherhm	0	Hartlepl	0	
Scunthpe	1	Preston NE	0	
Southend	0	Plymouth	0	
Telford U	3	Stockport	0	
Torquay	1	Colchester	2	
Tranmere	2	Bolton	2	
Wealdstne	1	Enfield	1	
Wimbledn	2	Leyton O	1	
Wrexham	1	Sheff Utd	5	
Yeovil T	0	Harrow B	1	
Bangor C	1	Northwich	0	r
Bolton	4	Tranmere	1	re
Brentford	2	Dagenham	1	r
Bristol C	4	Cor Casls	0	r
Bristol R	3	Barnet	1	r
Enfield	2	Wealdstne	2	re
Hartlepl	0	Rotherhm	1	re
Maidstone	2	Exeter	1	r
Newport	3	Poole T	1	r
Plymouth	2	Southend	0	re
Waterlve	1	N'hamptn	1	re
Wigan Ath	4	Bradford	2	r
Worcester	2	Aldershot	1	r
Wycombe	1	Chelmsfd	2	r
York	2	Macclesfd	0	r
N'hamptn	2	Waterlve	0	r2
Wealdstne	2	Enfield	0	r2
SECOND ROUND				
Bangor C	1	Blackpool	1	
Bolton	2	Manfield	0	
Brentford	3	Wimbledn	2	
Bristol R	1	Bristol C	2	
Chestrfld	2	Burnley	2	
Colchester	4	Wealdstne	0	
Darlingtn	0	Altrinchm	0	
Gillinghm	6	Chelmsfd	1	
Harrow B	1	Newport	3	
Lincoln	0	Sheff Utd	0	
Maidstone	3	Worcester	2	
Millwall	2	Swindon	3	
N'hamptn	1	Telford U	1	
Plymouth	2	Barking	1	
Reading	1	Oxford	1	
Rotherhm	2	Hull	1	
Scunthpe	2	Bury	0	
Wigan Ath	1	Whitby T	0	
Windsor&E	0	Bournemth	0	
York	0	Rochdale	2	
Altrinchm	0	Darlingtn	2	r
Blackpool	2	Bangor C	1	r
Bournemth	2	Windsor&E	0	r
Burnley	3	Chestrfld	2	r
Oxford	3	Reading	0	r
Sheff Utd	1	Lincoln	0	r
Telford U	3	N'hamptn	2	r
THIRD ROUND				
Aston V	1	Norwich	1	
Blackburn	1	Chelsea	0	
Blackpool	2	Man City	1	
Bolton	0	Sunderld	3	
Bournemth	2	Man Utd	0	
Brighton	2	Swansea	0	
Burnley	0	Oxford	0	
Cambridge	0	Derby	3	
Cardiff	0	Ipswich	3	
Carlisle	1	Swindon	1	
Colchester	0	Charlton	1	
Coventry	1	Wolves	1	
C.Palace	1	Leicester	0	
Darlingtn	4	Maidstone	1	
Fulham	0	Tottenham	0	
Gillinghm	5	Brentford	3	
Huddersfld	2	QPR	1	
Leeds U	1	Scunthpe	1	
Liverpool	4	Newcastle	0	
Luton	2	Watford	2	
Middlesbro	3	Arsenal	2	
Nottm For	1	Southmptn	2	
Notts Co	2	Bristol C	2	
Plymouth	2	Newport	2	
Portsmth	2	Grimsby	1	
Rochdale	1	Telford U	4	
Rotherhm	0	West Brom	0	
Sheff Utd	1	Birmghm C	1	
Sheff Wed	1	Barnsley	0	
Shrewsby	3	Oldham	0	
Stoke	0	Everton	2	
West Ham	1	Wigan Ath	0	
Birmghm C	2	Sheff Utd	0	r
Bristol C	0	Notts Co	2	r
Newport	0	Plymouth	1	r
Norwich	3	Aston V	0	r
Oxford	2	Burnley	1	r
Scunthpe	1	Leeds U	1	re
Swindon	3	Carlisle	1	r
Tottenham	2	Fulham	0	r
Watford	4	Luton	3	re
West Brom	3	Rotherhm	0	r
Wolves	1	Coventry	1	re
Coventry	3	Wolves	0	r2
Scunthpe	4	Leeds U	2	r2
FOURTH ROUND				
Brighton	2	Liverpool	0	
Charlton	0	Watford	2	
C.Palace	1	West Ham	1	
Derby	3	Telford U	2	
Everton	0	Gillinghm	0	
Huddersfld	1	Notts Co	2	
Middlesbro	2	Bournemth	0	
Oxford	2	Blackpool	1	
Plymouth	2	Darlingtn	1	
Portsmth	0	Southmptn	1	
Sheff Wed	3	Coventry	2	
Shrewsby	2	Ipswich	0	
Sunderld	1	Birmghm C	2	
Swindon	1	Blackburn	2	
Tottenham	0	Norwich	0	
West Brom	1	Scunthpe	0	
Gillinghm	0	Everton	0	re

Strange but true!

Arsenal skipper Pat Rice became the first - and to date only - player to have appeared in five FA Cup Finals with the same club when he led the Gunners to the 1980 Final. Rice sampled glory in 1971 and 1979 and was left with the bitter taste of defeat in 1972, 1978 and 1980.

Foreign Fields

The only Englishman in Liverpool's winning squad in the 1986 Final was the substitute, Steve McMahon, who did not get on. There were four Scots, three Irish, one Welsh, one Zimbabwean, one South African and a Dane in the Reds' line-up.

Norwich	2	Tottenham	1	r
West Ham	2	C.Palace	0	r
Gillinghm	0	Everton	3	r2
FIFTH ROUND				
Birmghm C	3	West Ham	0	
Blackburn	0	Southmptn	1	
Derby	2	Norwich	1	
Everton	3	Shrewsby	0	
Notts Co	1	Middlesbro	0	
Oxford	0	Sheff Wed	3	
Watford	3	Brighton	1	
West Brom	0	Plymouth	1	
SIXTH ROUND				
Birmghm C	1	Watford	3	
Notts Co	1	Everton	2	
Plymouth	0	Derby	0	
Sheff Wed	0	Southmptn	0	
Derby	0	Plymouth	1	r
Southmptn	5	Sheff Wed	1	r
SEMI-FINAL				
Everton	1	Southmptn	0	eN
Watford	1	Plymouth	0	N
FINAL				
Everton	2	Watford	0	N

1985

FIRST ROUND				
Bangor C	1	Tranmere	1	
Barry T	1	Reading	2	
Blackpool	0	Altrinchm	1	
Bradford	7	Tow Law	2	
Brentford	4	Bshp Stor	0	
Bristol R	2	King's Ln	1	
Buckinghm	0	Leyton O	2	
Burnley	9	Penrith	0	
Burton Al	2	Staines	0	
Cambridge	0	Peterboro	2	
Dagenham	0	Swindon	0	
Darlingtn	3	Chester	2	
Exeter	2	Enfield	2	
Fisher A	0	Bristol C	1	
Frickley	2	Stalyb C	1	
Gillinghm	2	Windsor&E	1	
Halifax	2	Goole T	0	
Hartlepl	2	Derby	1	
Hereford	3	Farnborgh	0	
Hull	2	Bolton	1	
Kettering	0	Bournemth	0	
Lincoln	1	Telford U	1	
Macclesfd	1	Port Vale	2	
Manfield	2	Rotherhm	1	
Met Pol	0	Dartford	3	

Kevin Moran gets his marching orders in 1985

Newport	1	Aldershot	1	
N'hamptn	2	VS Rugby	2	
Northwich	3	Crewe	1	
Nuneaton	1	Scunthpe	1	
Plymouth	3	Barnet	0	
Preston NE	4	Bury	3	
Rochdale	1	Doncaster	2	
Southend	2	Colchester	2	
Stockport	1	Walsall	2	
Swansea	1	Bognor R	1	
Torquay	2	Yeovil T	0	
Weymouth	0	Millwall	3	
Whitby T	1	Chestrfld	3	
Wrexham	0	Wigan Ath	2	
York	2	Newcst BS	0	
Aldershot	4	Newport	0	r
Bognor R	3	Swansea	1	r
Bournemth	3	Kettering	2	r
Colchester	3	Southend	2	re
Enfield	3	Exeter	0	r
Scunthpe	2	Nuneaton	1	re
Swindon	1	Dagenham	2	re
Telford U	2	Lincoln	1	r
Tranmere	7	Bangor C	0	r
VS Rugby	0	N'hamptn	1	r
SECOND ROUND				
Aldershot	0	Burton Al	2	
Altrinchm	1	Doncaster	3	
Bradford	2	Manfield	1	
Brentford	2	N'hamptn	2	
Bristol C	1	Bristol R	3	
Burnley	3	Halifax	1	
Colchester	0	Gillinghm	5	
Dagenham	1	Peterboro	0	
Darlingtn	1	Frickley	0	
Dartford	1	Bournemth	1	
Hartlepl	0	York	2	
Leyton O	3	Torquay	0	
Millwall	1	Enfield	0	
Plymouth	0	Hereford	0	
Port Vale	4	Scunthpe	1	
Preston NE	1	Telford U	4	
Reading	6	Bognor R	2	
Tranmere	0	Hull	3	
Walsall	1	Chestrfld	0	
Wigan Ath	2	Northwich	1	
Bournemth	4	Dartford	1	r
Hereford	2	Plymouth	0	r
N'hamptn	0	Brentford	2	r
THIRD ROUND				
Barnsley	4	Reading	3	
Birmghm C	0	Norwich	0	
Brighton	1	Hull	0	
Bristol R	1	Ipswich	2	
Burton Al	1	Leicester	6	v
Carlisle	1	Dagenham	0	
Chelsea	2	Wigan Ath	2	
Coventry	2	Man City	1	
Doncaster	1	QPR	0	
Fulham	2	Sheff Wed	3	
Gillinghm	2	Cardiff	1	
Hereford	1	Arsenal	1	
Leeds U	0	Everton	2	
Leyton O	2	West Brom	1	
Liverpool	3	Aston V	0	
Luton	1	Stoke	1	
Man Utd	3	Bournemth	0	
Middlesbro	0	Darlingtn	0	

WHAT A STAR ✪ KEITH HOUCHEN

He played for six clubs in 17 years before trying his hand at management, with little success. But big striker Keith Houchen will be remembered for a long time because of his flying header past Ray Clemence in the 1987 Cup Final. That spectacular effort levelled the scores at 2-2 and enabled Coventry's bunch of misfits, mostly cast-offs from other clubs, to go on and inflict Tottenham's first Final defeat, after seven wins. It was City's first trip to Wembley.

GIANTKILLERS

1986 Chorley 3 Wolves 0

Chorley from the Northern Premier caught Wolves at a bad time, for they had been relegated from Division One to Division Four in successive years and were in a terrible state. Even so, Chorley did remarkably well to avoid defeat against such a famous club in three matches: two 'home' games were staged at Bolton with one at Molineux in between, and Wolves managed only one goal in a 0-0, 1-1, 0-3 series.

Millwall	1	C.Palace	1	
Nottm For	1	Newcastle	1	
Notts Co	2	Grimsby	2	
Oldham	2	Brentford	1	
Portsmth	0	Blackburn	0	
Shrewsby	0	Oxford	2	
Southmptn	4	Sunderld	0	
Telford U	2	Bradford	1	
Tottenham	1	Charlton	1	
Watford	5	Sheff Utd	0	
West Ham	4	Port Vale	1	
Wimbledn	3	Burnley	1	
Wolves	1	Huddersfld	1	
York	3	Walsall	0	
Arsenal	7	Hereford	2	r
Blackburn	2	Portsmth	1	r
Burton Al	0	Leicester	1	rN
Charlton	1	Tottenham	2	r
C.Palace	1	Millwall	2	r
Darlingtn	2	Middlesbro	1	r
Grimsby	4	Notts Co	2	r
Huddersfld	3	Wolves	1	r
Newcastle	1	Nottm For	3	re
Norwich	1	Birmghm C	1	re
Stoke	2	Luton	3	r
Wigan Ath	0	Chelsea	5	r
Birmghm C	1	Norwich	1	r2e
Norwich	1	Birmghm C	0	r3
FOURTH ROUND				
Barnsley	2	Brighton	1	
Chelsea	2	Millwall	3	
Darlingtn	1	Telford U	1	
Everton	2	Doncaster	0	
Grimsby	1	Watford	3	
Ipswich	3	Gillinghm	2	
Leicester	1	Carlisle	0	
Leyton O	0	Southmptn	2	
Liverpool	1	Tottenham	0	
Luton	2	Huddersfld	0	
Man Utd	2	Coventry	1	
Nottm For	0	Wimbledn	0	
Oxford	0	Blackburn	1	
Sheff Wed	5	Oldham	1	
West Ham	2	Norwich	1	
York	1	Arsenal	0	
Telford U	3	Darlingtn	0	r
Wimbledn	1	Nottm For	0	r
FIFTH ROUND				
Blackburn	0	Man Utd	2	
Everton	3	Telford U	0	
Ipswich	3	Sheff Wed	2	
Luton	0	Watford	0	
Millwall	2	Leicester	0	
Southmptn	1	Barnsley	2	
Wimbledn	1	West Ham	1	
York	1	Liverpool	1	
Liverpool	7	York	0	r
Watford	2	Luton	2	re
West Ham	5	Wimbledn	1	r
Luton	1	Watford	0	r2
SIXTH ROUND				
Barnsley	0	Liverpool	4	
Everton	2	Ipswich	2	
Luton	1	Millwall	0	
Man Utd	4	West Ham	2	
Ipswich	0	Everton	1	r
SEMI-FINAL				
Everton	2	Luton	1	eN
Man Utd	2	Liverpool	2	eN
Liverpool	1	Man Utd	2	rN
FINAL				
Man Utd	1	Everton	0	eN

1986

FIRST ROUND				
Bournemth	0	Dartford	0	
Brentford	1	Bristol R	3	
Bshp Stor	2	Peterboro	2	
Bury	2	Chester	0	
Chelmsfd	1	Weymouth	0	
Chorley	0	Altrinchm	2	
Dagenham	2	Cambridge	1	
Derby	5	Crewe	1	
Enfield	0	Bognor R	2	
Exeter	2	Cardiff	1	
Fareham T	0	Maidstone	3	
Farnborgh	0	Bath C	4	
Frickley	1	Halesowen	1	
Gillinghm	3	N'hamptn	0	
Halifax	1	Scunthpe	3	
Lincoln	0	Blackpool	1	
Macclesfd	1	Hartlepl	2	
Manfield	1	Port Vale	1	
Notts Co	6	Scarboro	1	
Nuneaton	2	Burnley	3	
Plymouth	1	Aldershot	0	
Reading	1	Wealdstne	0	
Rochdale	2	Darlingtn	1	
Rotherhm	6	Wolves	0	
Runcorn	2	Boston U	2	
Slough T	2	Aylesbury	2	
Southend	0	Newport	1	
Stockport	0	Telford U	1	
Swansea	2	Leyton W	0	
Swindon	0	Bristol C	0	
Tranmere	2	Chestrfld	2	
VS Rugby	2	Leyton O	2	
Walsall	7	Preston NE	3	
Whitby T	1	S.L'pool	0	
Wigan Ath	4	Doncaster	1	
Windsor&E	1	Torquay	1	
Wrexham	3	Bolton	1	
Wycombe	2	Colchester	0	
Yeovil T	2	Hereford	4	
York	0	Morecambe	0	
Aylesbury	2	Slough T	5	rN
Boston U	1	Runcorn	1	re
Bristol C	4	Swindon	2	r
Chestrfld	0	Tranmere	1	r
Dartford	0	Bournemth	2	r
Halesowen	1	Frickley	3	r
Leyton O	4	VS Rugby	1	r
Morecambe	0	York	2	rN
Peterboro	3	Bshp Stor	1	r
Port Vale	1	Manfield	0	r
Torquay	3	Windsor&E	0	r
Runcorn	4	Boston U	1	r2
SECOND ROUND				
Blackpool	1	Altrinchm	2	
Bournemth	4	Dagenham	1	
Bristol C	1	Exeter	2	
Derby	6	Telford U	1	
Gillinghm	6	Bognor R	1	
Hartlepl	0	Frickley	1	
Leyton O	2	Slough T	2	

Ref Justice

Referee Peter Willis, the first official to send off a Final player - Kevin Moran of Manchester United in 1985 - was no stranger to discipline...in day-to-day life he was a policeman.

Pro-File: VINNIE JONES

Vinnie Jones is, without doubt, one of the most controversial characters ever to play professional football.

From the moment the former hod-carrier first walked through the gates of Wimbledon Football Club he has been in the news.

Whether for his early-career ball games with a young Paul Gascoigne, well-publicised threats to the likes of Gary Lineker and Kenny Dalglish or a series of needless bookings and sendings-off, Jones has often had the purists up in arms.

But is he really that bad? After all, he's played for some of the game's major clubs, including Leeds and Chelsea, and has represented Wales at international level.

And no-one can deny that, when you sign Jones, you are signing a player who will give his all and die for the cause.

He will run through a brick wall for you, and if he has to take out a few players on the way through, then so be it.

However, there is obviously more to Jones's game than brute force or he would never have survived at the level he has done for as many years as he has.

And when he finally hangs up his boots, he will have made his mark and he certainly will not be forgotten in a hurry.

Career details

●**Represented:** Wales, Wimbledon (twice), Leeds, Sheffield United, Chelsea ●**Position:** Midfield ●**Born:** Watford, 05.01.65 ●**Height:** 6ft ●**Weight:** 11st 12lbs ●**Club honours:** FA Cup 1988, Division Two Championship 1990 ●**International honours:** Wales 11 full caps

Club League Record

Era	Club	Games	Goals
86/89	Wimbledon	77	9
89/90	Leeds	46	5
90/91	Sheffield United	35	2
91/92	Chelsea	42	4
92/97	Wimbledon	153	12

Cup Highlights

April 9 1988: Wimbledon reach the FA Cup Final just 10 years after joining the Football League. They beat Luton 2-1 at White Hart Lane in the Semi-Final.

May 14 1988: Possibly the greatest FA Cup Final upset in history as Wimbledon stun the world by beating mighty Liverpool 1-0 at Wembley.

Jones On:

●I've already been on the phone to my mate who does all my tattoos and told him to start practising the Welsh dragon. **Jones celebrating his Welsh international call-up in his own inimitable style**

●I really think I've got a lot to offer the game as far as being a manager is concerned. **Jones on his dreams of going into management**

DID YOU KNOW THAT...

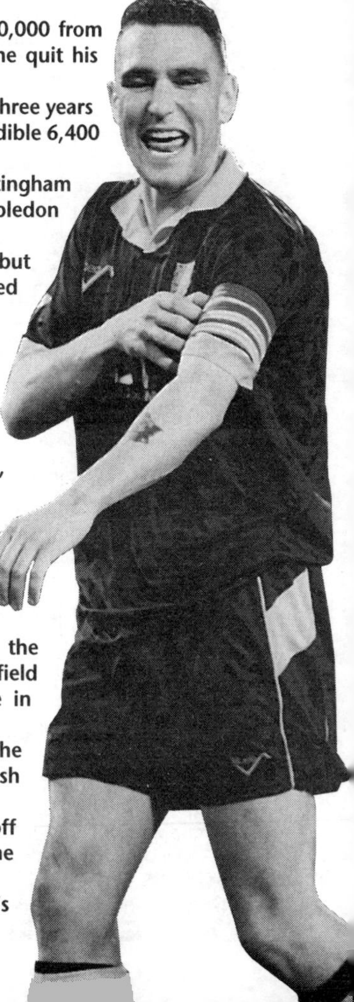

●Vinny Jones cost Wimbledon just £10,000 from non-League Wealdstone in 1986 and he quit his job as a hod-carrier to join them.
●When Wimbledon sold him to Leeds three years later, he cost £650,000. That is an incredible 6,400 per cent profit!
●He made his League debut at Nottingham Forest in November 1986, and Wimbledon lost 3-2.
●A week later he made his home debut against Manchester United...and scored the only goal in a 1-0 win.
●Vinnie shot to fame when he was captured on film grabbing Paul Gascoigne by the testicles during a Wimbledon v Newcastle match.
●Jones was once booked THREE SECONDS into a game against Chelsea, when he was playing for Sheffield United, for a tackle on Dennis Wise. It is believed to be a world record.
●When Wimbledon won the FA Cup in 1988 Jones had a tattoo of the trophy imprinted on his leg to commemorate the occasion. He did the same, on the other leg, when Sheffield United won the Second Division title in 1990.
●When he was called up by Wales, he made a point of learning the Welsh national anthem.
●He once publicly threatened to "tear off Kenny Dalglish's ear and spit in the hole."
●A great lover of the outdoors, Vinny's main hobby is clay pigeon shooting.

Newport	1	Torquay	1	
Notts Co	2	Wrexham	2	
Peterboro	1	Bath C	0	
Plymouth	3	Maidstone	0	
Port Vale	0	Walsall	0	
Reading	2	Hereford	0	
Rotherhm	4	Burnley	1	
Runcorn	1	Wigan Ath	1	
Scunthpe	2	Rochdale	2	
Swansea	1	Bristol R	2	
Tranmere	1	Bury	1	
Wycombe	2	Chelmsfd	0	
York	3	Whitby T	1	
Bury	2	Tranmere	1	r
Rochdale	2	Scunthpe	1	r
Slough T	2	Leyton O	3	r
Torquay	2	Newport	3	re
Walsall	2	Port Vale	1	r
Wigan Ath	4	Runcorn	0	r
Wrexham	0	Notts Co	3	r
THIRD ROUND				
Birmghm C	1	Altrinchm	2	
Bristol R	3	Leicester	1	
Bury	2	Barnsley	0	
Carlisle	1	QPR	0	
Charlton	0	West Ham	1	
Coventry	1	Watford	3	
C.Palace	1	Luton	2	
Everton	1	Exeter	0	
Frickley	1	Rotherhm	3	
Gillinghm	1	Derby	1	
Grimsby	3	Arsenal	4	
Huddersfld	0	Reading	0	
Hull	2	Plymouth	2	
Ipswich	4	Bradford	4	
Liverpool	5	Norwich	0	
Man Utd	2	Rochdale	0	
Middlesbro	1	Southmptn	3	
Millwall	3	Wimbledn	1	
Newcastle	0	Brighton	2	
Nottm For	1	Blackburn	1	
Oldham	1	Leyton O	2	
Oxford	1	Tottenham	1	
Peterboro	1	Leeds U	0	
Portsmth	2	Aston V	2	
Sheff Utd	2	Fulham	0	
Sheff Wed	2	West Brom	2	
Shrewsby	0	Chelsea	1	
Stoke	0	Notts Co	2	
Sunderld	2	Newport	0	
Walsall	1	Man City	3	
Wigan Ath	3	Bournemth	0	
York	2	Wycombe	0	
Aston V	3	Portsmth	2	re
Blackburn	3	Nottm For	2	r
Bradford	0	Ipswich	1	re
Derby	3	Gillinghm	1	re
Plymouth	0	Hull	1	r
Reading	2	Huddersfld	1	re
Tottenham	2	Oxford	1	re
West Brom	2	Sheff Wed	3	r
FOURTH ROUND				
Arsenal	5	Rotherhm	1	
Aston V	1	Millwall	1	
Chelsea	1	Liverpool	2	
Everton	3	Blackburn	1	
Hull	2	Brighton	3	
Luton	4	Bristol R	0	
Man City	1	Watford	1	
Notts Co	1	Tottenham	1	
Peterboro	1	Carlisle	0	
Reading	1	Bury	1	
Sheff Utd	0	Derby	1	
Sheff Wed	5	Leyton O	0	
Southmptn	3	Wigan Ath	0	
Sunderld	0	Man Utd	0	
West Ham	0	Ipswich	0	
York	2	Altrinchm	0	
Bury	3	Reading	0	r
Ipswich	1	West Ham	1	re
Man Utd	3	Sunderld	0	r
Millwall	1	Aston V	0	r
Tottenham	5	Notts Co	0	r
Watford	0	Man City	0	re
Ipswich	0	West Ham	1	r2e
Man City	1	Watford	3	r2
FIFTH ROUND				
Derby	1	Sheff Wed	1	
Luton	2	Arsenal	2	
Peterboro	2	Brighton	2	
Southmptn	0	Millwall	0	
Tottenham	1	Everton	2	
Watford	1	Bury	1	
West Ham	1	Man Utd	1	
York	1	Liverpool	1	
Arsenal	0	Luton	0	re
Brighton	1	Peterboro	0	r
Bury	0	Watford	3	r
Liverpool	3	York	1	re
Man Utd	0	West Ham	2	r
Millwall	0	Southmptn	1	r
Sheff Wed	2	Derby	0	r
Luton	3	Arsenal	0	r2
SIXTH ROUND				
Brighton	0	Southmptn	2	
Liverpool	0	Watford	0	
Luton	2	Everton	2	
Sheff Wed	2	West Ham	1	
Everton	1	Luton	0	r
Watford	1	Liverpool	2	re
SEMI-FINAL				
Everton	2	Sheff Wed	1	eN
Liverpool	2	Southmptn	0	eN
FINAL				
Liverpool	3	Everton	1	N

Strange but true!

Gordon Smith, renowned for his last-minute miss for Brighton in the 1983 Final, played First Division soccer in Switzerland and Austria as well as in England and Scotland. The Scotsman's miss from six yards against Man United in the last minute of extra-time also prompted a Seagulls fanzine to be launched under the name 'And Smith Must Score'. A reference to match commentator John Motson's words as the ball fell to the striker at Wembley.

1987

FIRST ROUND				
Aldershot	1	Torquay	0	
Bath C	3	Aylesbury	2	
Bournemth	7	Fareham T	2	
Bristol C	3	VS Rugby	1	
Bristol R	0	Brentford	0	
Bromsgrv	0	Newport	1	
Bshp Stor	1	Colchester	1	
Caernvn T	1	Stockport	0	
Chester	1	Rotherhm	1	

WHAT A STAR ✪ DAVE BEASANT

The first goalkeeper to captain a Cup Final team. The first 'keeper to save a Cup Final penalty. The first 'keeper to make more than 400 consecutive appearances. That's big Dave Beasant, who led his Wimbledon Crazy Gang to success in one of the Cup's biggest surprises, the 1988 defeat of Liverpool. Things may have not gone too well in recent seasons, but nobody can take that day away from him.

Chorley	1	Wolves	1	N
Darlingtn	2	Manfield	1	
Dartford	1	Enfield	1	
Exeter	1	Cambridge	1	
Frickley	0	Altrinchm	0	
Halifax	1	Bolton	1	
Hereford	3	Fulham	3	
Kettering	0	Gillinghm	3	
Middlesbro	3	Blackpool	0	
N'hamptn	3	Peterboro	0	
Notts Co	1	Carlisle	1	
Nuneaton	0	Rochdale	3	
Port Vale	1	Staffd Rg	0	
Preston NE	5	Bury	1	
Runcorn	1	Boston U	1	
Scunthpe	2	Southport	0	
Slough T	1	Bognor R	1	
Southend	4	Halesowen	1	
Spennym'r	2	Tranmere	3	
Swindon	4	Farnborgh	0	
Telford U	3	Burnley	0	
Ton Pen	1	Cardiff	4	
Walsall	2	Chestrfld	0	
Wealdstne	1	Swansea	1	
Welling U	1	Maidstone	1	
Whitby T	2	Doncaster	2	
Wigan Ath	3	Lincoln	1	
Woking	1	Chelmsfd	1	
Woodfd T	0	Leyton O	1	
Wrexham	2	Hartlepl	1	
York	3	Crewe	1	
Altrinchm	4	Frickley	0	r
Bognor R	0	Slough T	1	r
Bolton	1	Halifax	1	re
Boston U	1	Runcorn	2	re
Brentford	2	Bristol R	0	r
Cambridge	2	Exeter	0	r
Carlisle	0	Notts Co	3	r
Chelmsfd	2	Woking	1	r
Colchester	2	Bshp Stor	0	r
Doncaster	3	Whitby T	2	r
Enfield	3	Dartford	0	r
Fulham	4	Hereford	0	r
Maidstone	4	Welling U	1	r
Rotherhm	1	Chester	1	re
Swansea	4	Wealdstne	1	r
Wolves	1	Chorley	1	re
Chester	1	Rotherhm	0	r2
Chorley	3	Wolves	0	r2N
Halifax	1	Bolton	3	r2
SECOND ROUND				
Aldershot	3	Colchester	2	
Bolton	2	Tranmere	0	
Bournemth	0	Leyton O	1	
Bristol C	1	Bath C	1	
Caernvn T	0	York	0	
Cardiff	2	Brentford	0	
Chester	3	Doncaster	1	
Chorley	0	Preston NE	0	N
Darlingtn	0	Wigan Ath	5	
Fulham	2	Newport	0	
Gillinghm	2	Chelmsfd	0	
Maidstone	1	Cambridge	0	
Notts Co	0	Middlesbro	1	
Rochdale	1	Wrexham	4	
Scunthpe	1	Runcorn	0	
Southend	4	N'hamptn	4	

Keith Houchen does aerial battle for Coventry in 1987

Swansea	3	Slough T	0	
Swindon	3	Enfield	0	
Telford U	1	Altrinchm	0	
Walsall	5	Port Vale	0	
Bristol C	3	Bath C	0	r
N'hamptn	3	Southend	2	r
Preston NE	5	Chorley	0	r
York	1	Caernvn T	2	r
THIRD ROUND				
Aldershot	3	Oxford	0	
Aston V	2	Chelsea	2	
Bristol C	1	Plymouth	1	
Caernvn T	0	Barnsley	0	
Charlton	1	Walsall	2	
Coventry	3	Bolton	0	
C.Palace	1	Nottm For	0	
Everton	2	Southmptn	1	
Fulham	0	Swindon	1	
Grimsby	1	Stoke	1	
Ipswich	0	Birmghm C	1	
Leyton O	1	West Ham	1	
Luton	0	Liverpool	0	
Man Utd	1	Man City	0	
Middlesbro	0	Preston NE	1	
Millwall	0	Cardiff	0	
Newcastle	2	N'hamptn	1	
Norwich	1	Huddersfld	1	
Oldham	1	Bradford	1	
Portsmth	2	Blackburn	0	
QPR	5	Leicester	2	
Reading	1	Arsenal	3	
Sheff Utd	0	Brighton	0	
Sheff Wed	1	Derby	0	
Shrewsby	1	Hull	2	
Swansea	3	West Brom	2	
Telford U	1	Leeds U	2	N
Tottenham	3	Scunthpe	2	
Watford	3	Maidstone	1	
Wigan Ath	2	Gillinghm	1	
Wimbledn	2	Sunderld	1	
Wrexham	1	Chester	2	
Barnsley	1	Caernvn T	0	r
Bradford	5	Oldham	1	r
Brighton	1	Sheff Utd	2	r
Cardiff	2	Millwall	2	re
Chelsea	2	Aston V	1	re

Huddersfld	2	Norwich	4	r
Liverpool	0	Luton	0	re
Plymouth	3	Bristol C	1	re
Stoke	1	Grimsby	1	re
West Ham	4	Leyton O	1	r
Cardiff	1	Millwall	0	r2
Luton	3	Liverpool	0	r2
Stoke	6	Grimsby	0	r2
FOURTH ROUND				
Aldershot	1	Barnsley	1	
Arsenal	6	Plymouth	1	
Bradford	0	Everton	1	
Chester	1	Sheff Wed	1	
Luton	1	QPR	1	
Man Utd	0	Coventry	1	
Newcastle	2	Preston NE	0	
Stoke	2	Cardiff	1	
Swansea	0	Hull	1	
Swindon	1	Leeds U	2	
Tottenham	4	C.Palace	0	
Walsall	1	Birmghm C	0	
Watford	1	Chelsea	0	
West Ham	4	Sheff Utd	0	
Wigan Ath	1	Norwich	0	
Wimbledn	4	Portsmth	0	
Barnsley	3	Aldershot	0	r
QPR	2	Luton	1	r
Sheff Wed	3	Chester	1	r
FIFTH ROUND				
Arsenal	2	Barnsley	0	
Leeds U	2	QPR	1	
Sheff Wed	1	West Ham	1	
Stoke	0	Coventry	1	
Tottenham	1	Newcastle	0	
Walsall	1	Watford	1	
Wigan Ath	3	Hull	0	
Wimbledn	3	Everton	1	
Watford	4	Walsall	4	re
West Ham	0	Sheff Wed	2	r
Walsall	0	Watford	1	r2
SIXTH ROUND				
Arsenal	1	Watford	3	
Sheff Wed	0	Coventry	3	
Wigan Ath	0	Leeds U	2	
Wimbledn	0	Tottenham	2	
SEMI-FINAL				

WHAT A STAR ✪ IAN RUSH

"You're supposed to be a striker," said Bob Paisley. "Be more selfish". Ian Rush, recently bought from Chester, acted on his manager's advice. He went on to smash virtually every Liverpool scoring record as well as those for Wales and for most FA Cup goals (beating Denis Law's 41) and most in FA Cup Finals (five - two in 1986, two in 1989, one in 1992). At the same time he showed himself to be a fine all-round footballer - no other No.9 was ever a better defender in the opposing half of the pitch.

Coventry	3	Leeds U	2	eN
Tottenham	4	Watford	1	N
FINAL				
Coventry	3	Tottenham	2	eN

1988

FIRST ROUND				
Altrinchm	0	Wigan Ath	2	
Barnet	0	Hereford	1	
Billngh S	2	Halifax	4	N
Bognor R	0	Torquay	3	
Brentford	0	Brighton	2	
Bristol C	1	Aylesbury	0	
Bristol R	6	Mert Tyd	0	
Bshk Auck	1	Blackpool	4	
Burnley	0	Bolton	1	
Cambridge	2	Farnborgh	1	
Chelmsfd	1	Bath C	2	
Chester	0	Runcorn	1	
Chorley	0	Hartlepl	2	
Colchester	3	Tamworth	0	
Dagenham	0	Maidstone	2	
Doncaster	1	Rotherhm	1	
Gillinghm	2	Fulham	1	
Halesowen	2	Kiddermst	2	
Hayes	0	Swansea	1	
Leyton O	2	Exeter	0	
Lincoln	2	Crewe	1	
Macclesfd	4	Carlisle	2	
N'hamptn	2	Newport	1	
Northwich	1	Colwyn By	0	
Notts Co	3	Chestrfld	3	
Peterboro	2	Cardiff	1	
Preston NE	1	Manfield	1	
Rochdale	0	Wrexham	2	
Scarboro	1	Grimsby	2	
Scunthpe	3	Bury	1	
Southend	0	Walsall	0	
Sunderld	2	Darlingtn	0	
Sutton U	3	Aldershot	0	
Telford U	1	Stockport	1	
Tranmere	2	Port Vale	2	
VS Rugby	0	Atherstne	0	
Welling U	3	Carshlton	2	
Wolves	5	Chelthnm	1	
Worcester	1	Yeovil T	1	
York	0	Burton Al	0	
Atherstne	0	VS Rugby	2	r
Burton Al	1	York	2	r
Chestrfld	0	Notts Co	1	r
Kiddermst	4	Halesowen	0	r
Manfield	4	Preston NE	2	r
Port Vale	3	Tranmere	1	r
Rotherhm	2	Doncaster	0	r
Stockport	2	Telford U	0	r
Walsall	2	Southend	1	r
Yeovil T	1	Worcester	0	r
SECOND ROUND				
Bristol C	0	Torquay	1	
Cambridge	0	Yeovil T	1	
Colchester	3	Hereford	2	
Gillinghm	2	Walsall	1	
Grimsby	0	Halifax	0	
Leyton O	2	Swansea	0	
Macclesfd	4	Rotherhm	0	
Maidstone	1	Kiddermst	1	
Manfield	4	Lincoln	3	
N'hamptn	1	Brighton	2	
Northwich	0	Blackpool	2	
Peterboro	1	Sutton U	3	
Port Vale	2	Notts Co	0	
Runcorn	0	Stockport	1	
Scunthpe	2	Sunderld	1	
VS Rugby	1	Bristol R	1	
Welling U	0	Bath C	1	
Wigan Ath	1	Wolves	3	
Wrexham	1	Bolton	2	
York	1	Hartlepl	1	
Bristol R	4	VS Rugby	0	r
Halifax	2	Grimsby	0	r
Hartlepl	3	York	1	r
Kiddermst	2	Maidstone	2	re
Kiddermst	0	Maidstone	0	r2e
Maidstone	2	Kiddermst	1	r3
THIRD ROUND				
Arsenal	2	Millwall	0	
Barnsley	3	Bolton	1	
Blackburn	1	Portsmth	2	
Bradford	2	Wolves	1	
Brighton	2	Bournemth	0	
Coventry	2	Torquay	0	
Derby	1	Chelsea	3	
Gillinghm	0	Birmghm C	3	
Halifax	0	Nottm For	4	
Hartlepl	1	Luton	2	
Huddersfld	2	Man City	2	
Ipswich	1	Man Utd	2	
Leeds U	1	Aston V	2	
Manfield	4	Bath C	0	
Newcastle	1	C.Palace	0	
Oldham	2	Tottenham	4	
Oxford	2	Leicester	0	
Plymouth	2	Colchester	0	
Port Vale	1	Macclesfd	0	
Reading	0	Southmptn	1	
Scunthpe	0	Blackpool	0	
Sheff Utd	1	Maidstone	0	
Sheff Wed	1	Everton	1	
Shrewsby	2	Bristol R	1	
Stockport	1	Leyton O	2	

The Crazy Gang conquer Wembley

Stoke	0	Liverpool	0	
Sutton U	1	Middlesbro	1	
Swindon	0	Norwich	0	
Watford	1	Hull	1	
West Ham	2	Charlton	0	
Wimbledn	4	West Brom	1	
Yeovil T	0	QPR	3	
Blackpool	1	Scunthpe	0	r
Everton	1	Sheff Wed	1	re
Hull	2	Watford	2	re
Liverpool	1	Stoke	0	r
Man City	0	Huddersfld	0	re
Middlesbro	1	Sutton U	0	re
Norwich	0	Swindon	2	r
Everton	1	Sheff Wed	1	r2e
Huddersfld	0	Man City	3	r2
Watford	1	Hull	0	r2
Sheff Wed	0	Everton	5	r3
FOURTH ROUND				
Aston V	0	Liverpool	2	
Barnsley	0	Birmghm C	2	
Blackpool	1	Man City	1	
Bradford	4	Oxford	2	
Brighton	1	Arsenal	2	
Coventry	0	Watford	1	
Everton	1	Middlesbro	1	
Leyton O	1	Nottm For	2	
Luton	2	Southmptn	1	
Man Utd	2	Chelsea	0	
Manfield	1	Wimbledn	2	
Newcastle	5	Swindon	0	
Plymouth	1	Shrewsby	0	
Port Vale	2	Tottenham	1	
Portsmth	2	Sheff Utd	1	
QPR	3	West Ham	1	
Man City	2	Blackpool	1	r
Middlesbro	2	Everton	2	re
Everton	2	Middlesbro	1	r2
FIFTH ROUND				
Arsenal	2	Man Utd	1	
Birmghm C	0	Nottm For	1	
Everton	0	Liverpool	1	
Man City	3	Plymouth	1	
Newcastle	1	Wimbledn	3	
Port Vale	0	Watford	0	
Portsmth	3	Bradford	0	
QPR	1	Luton	1	

Norman Invasion

After becoming the youngest-ever Final scorer in 1983, Norman Whiteside of Manchester United became the sixth youngest two years later. He was 18 years 19 days on the first occasion, 20 years 11 days on the second.

Luton	1	QPR	0	r
Watford	2	Port Vale	0	r
SIXTH ROUND				
Arsenal	1	Nottm For	2	
Luton	3	Portsmth	1	
Man City	0	Liverpool	4	
Wimbledn	2	Watford	1	
SEMI-FINAL				
Liverpool	2	Nottm For	1	N
Luton	1	Wimbledn	2	N
FINAL				
Wimbledn	1	Liverpool	0	N

1989

FIRST ROUND				
Aldershot	1	Hayes	0	
Altrinchm	3	Lincoln	2	
Bath C	2	Grays Ath	0	
Blackpool	2	Scunthpe	1	
Bognor R	2	Exeter	1	
Bolton	0	Chestrfld	0	
Brentford	2	Halesowen	0	
Bristol C	3	Southend	1	
Bristol R	3	Fisher A	0	
Burnley	0	Chester	2	
Cardiff	3	Hereford	0	
Dagenham	0	Sutton U	4	
Darlingtn	1	Notts Co	2	
Doncaster	0	Brandon U	0	
Enfield	1	Leyton O	1	
Frickley	0	Northwich	2	
Fulham	0	Colchester	1	
Gillinghm	3	Peterboro	3	
Grimsby	1	Wolves	0	
Guisboro	0	Bury	1	N
Halifax	1	York	0	
Hartlepl	2	Wigan Ath	0	
Huddersfld	1	Rochdale	1	
Kettering	2	Dartford	1	
Manfield	1	Sheff Utd	1	
Newport	1	Maidstone	2	
Preston NE	1	Tranmere	1	
Reading	4	Hendon	2	
Rotherhm	3	Barrow	1	
Runcorn	2	Wrexham	2	
Scarboro	2	Stockport	1	
Southport	0	Port Vale	2	
Staffd Rg	2	Crewe	2	
Swansea	3	N'hamptn	1	
Telford U	1	Carlisle	1	
Torquay	2	Fareham T	2	
Waterlve	1	Aylesbury	4	
Welling U	3	Bromsgrv	0	
Woking	1	Cambridge	4	
Yeovil T	3	Mert Tyd	2	
Carlisle	4	Telford U	1	r
Chestrfld	2	Bolton	3	r
Crewe	3	Staffd Rg	2	r
Doncaster	2	Brandon U	1	r
Fareham T	2	Torquay	3	r
Leyton O	2	Enfield	2	re
Peterboro	1	Gillinghm	0	re
Rochdale	3	Huddersfld	4	r
Sheff Utd	2	Manfield	1	r
Tranmere	3	Preston NE	0	r
Wrexham	2	Runcorn	3	r
Leyton O	0	Enfield	1	r2

Franks a Lot

Irish striker Frank Stapleton set a record by becoming the first player to score for different clubs in different Finals. He scored for Arsenal in 1979, against Manchester United, and for United in 1983, against Brighton.

SECOND ROUND				
Aldershot	1	Bristol C	1	
Altrinchm	0	Halifax	3	
Aylesbury	0	Sutton U	1	
Bath C	0	Welling U	0	
Blackpool	3	Bury	0	
Bognor R	0	Cambridge	1	
Bolton	1	Port Vale	2	
Colchester	2	Swansea	2	
Doncaster	1	Sheff Utd	3	
Enfield	1	Cardiff	4	
Grimsby	3	Rotherhm	2	
Hartlepl	1	Notts Co	0	
Huddersfld	1	Chester	0	
Kettering	2	Bristol R	1	
Northwich	1	Tranmere	2	
Peterboro	0	Brentford	0	
Reading	1	Maidstone	1	
Runcorn	0	Crewe	3	
Scarboro	0	Carlisle	1	
Yeovil T	1	Torquay	1	
Brentford	3	Peterboro	2	r
Bristol C	0	Aldershot	0	re
Maidstone	1	Reading	2	r
Swansea	1	Colchester	3	r
Torquay	1	Yeovil T	0	r
Welling U	3	Bath C	2	r
Aldershot	2	Bristol C	2	r2e
Bristol C	1	Aldershot	0	r3
THIRD ROUND				
Barnsley	4	Chelsea	0	
Birmghm C	0	Wimbledn	1	
Blackpool	0	Bournemth	1	
Bradford	1	Tottenham	0	
Brighton	1	Leeds U	2	
Cardiff	1	Hull	2	
Carlisle	0	Liverpool	3	
Charlton	2	Oldham	1	
Crewe	2	Aston V	3	
Derby	1	Southmptn	1	
Hartlepl	1	Bristol C	0	
Huddersfld	0	Sheff Utd	1	
Kettering	1	Halifax	1	
Man City	1	Leicester	0	
Man Utd	0	QPR	0	
Middlesbro	1	Grimsby	2	
Millwall	3	Luton	2	
Newcastle	0	Watford	0	

Nottm For	3	Ipswich	0	
Plymouth	2	Cambridge	0	
Port Vale	1	Norwich	3	
Portsmth	1	Swindon	1	
Sheff Wed	5	Torquay	1	
Shrewsby	0	Colchester	3	
Stoke	1	C.Palace	0	
Sunderld	1	Oxford	1	
Sutton U	2	Coventry	1	
Tranmere	1	Reading	1	
Walsall	1	Brentford	1	
Welling U	0	Blackburn	1	
West Brom	1	Everton	1	
West Ham	2	Arsenal	2	
Arsenal	0	West Ham	1	r
Brentford	1	Walsall	0	r
Everton	1	West Brom	0	r
Halifax	2	Kettering	3	r
Oxford	2	Sunderld	0	r
QPR	2	Man Utd	2	re
Reading	2	Tranmere	1	r
Southmptn	1	Derby	2	re
Swindon	2	Portsmth	0	r
Watford	2	Newcastle	2	re
Man Utd	3	QPR	0	r2
Newcastle	0	Watford	0	r2e
Watford	1	Newcastle	0	r3e
FOURTH ROUND				
Aston V	0	Wimbledn	1	
Blackburn	2	Sheff Wed	1	
Bradford	1	Hull	2	
Brentford	3	Man City	1	
Charlton	2	Kettering	1	
Grimsby	1	Reading	1	
Hartlepl	1	Bournemth	1	
Man Utd	4	Oxford	0	
Millwall	0	Liverpool	2	
Norwich	8	Sutton U	0	
Nottm For	2	Leeds U	0	
Plymouth	1	Everton	1	
Sheff Utd	3	Colchester	3	
Stoke	3	Barnsley	3	
Swindon	0	West Ham	0	
Watford	2	Derby	1	
Barnsley	2	Stoke	1	r
Bournemth	5	Hartlepl	2	r
Colchester	0	Sheff Utd	2	r
Everton	4	Plymouth	0	r
Reading	1	Grimsby	2	r
West Ham	1	Swindon	0	r
FIFTH ROUND				
Barnsley	0	Everton	1	
Blackburn	0	Brentford	2	
Bournemth	1	Man Utd	1	
Charlton	0	West Ham	1	
Hull	2	Liverpool	3	
Norwich	3	Sheff Utd	2	
Watford	0	Nottm For	3	
Wimbledn	3	Grimsby	1	
Man Utd	1	Bournemth	0	r
SIXTH ROUND				
Everton	1	Wimbledn	0	
Liverpool	4	Brentford	0	
Man Utd	0	Nottm For	1	
West Ham	0	Norwich	0	
Norwich	3	West Ham	1	r
SEMI-FINAL				
Everton	1	Norwich	0	N
Liverpool	3	Nottm For	1	N
FINAL				
Liverpool	3	Everton	2	eN

GIANTKILLERS

1989 Sutton 2 Coventry 1

Coventry had won the Cup in 1987, and eight of their winning squad were still on duty at Sutton's Gander Green Lane when their roof fell in. Sutton, a mid-table Vauxhall Conference side, beat them convincingly and deserved a wider margin. Manager Barrie Williams had done his homework well, and how his team came to concede eight goals at Norwich in the next round remains a mystery. A crowd of 8,000 saw Coventry's humiliation, and Sutton's average gate that season rose to nearly 900 as a result.

Trevor Steven on the ball for Everton in the post-Hillsborough FA Cup Final against Liverpool

1990-1997

UNITED'S HAT-TRICK

The 90s saw a reversal in fortune with the underdogs being forced to take a back seat as the big boys regained control.

There were several memorable Cup moments from the minnows, not least from the likes of Wrexham, Millwall, Luton, Bradford, York and, of course, Chesterfield who went so close in 1997.

But by the time the big day came round in May, it was the big clubs who held centre stage.

And none of those big clubs enjoyed the period more than Manchester United, who helped themselves to the Cup three times in six years.

They beat Crystal Palace in 1990 - to give Bryan Robson his third win as captain - and also won the Cup in 1994 (against Chelsea) and 1996 (against Liverpool) to confirm themselves as the undoubted team of the 90s.

Everton spoiled United's bid to make it three in a row by winning the middle Final in 1995, with a headed goal from Paul Rideout.

The most widely remembered Final of the 90s was the 1991 Final between Tottenham and Nottingham Forest. It should have been a great occasion; Brian Clough's first FA Cup Final as a player or manager; and the chance for a nation to watch England's best player, Paul Gascoigne, do his stuff on the big pitch.

Sadly, Gazza did his stuff all right, but he also did his knee with a reckless challenge on Gary Charles which ended his Cup Final and, some would say, effectively ended his career which has flattered to deceive ever since.

But for all the football played, some good and some bad, the most significant FA Cup event of the 90s took place in an office.

In 1994, the FA decided to allow the competition to be sponsored.

Enter Littlewoods Pools, with a cheque for £14 million, since when the Cup has become known as 'The Football Association Challenge Cup, sponsored by Littlewoods Pools'.

But whatever you call it, it's still the greatest domestic Cup competition in the world.

On the Mark

Mark Hughes scored for Manchester United in the 1994 FA Cup Final against Chelsea. Two years later, he played FOR Chelsea AGAINST United in the 1996 Semi-Final. Again United won, this time 2-1. A year later Sparky became the first player this century to win four Cup winners' medals when he helped Chelsea beat Middlesbrough 2-0.

GIANTKILLERS

1991 West Brom 2 Woking 4

Brian Talbot, twice a Wembley winner as a player, experienced the other side of Cup fortune when he was sacked as West Brom manager three days after a remarkable 4-2 Third Round defeat at home to Isthmian League club Woking. Not that the change made much difference - Albion were relegated to Division Two that season. Tim Buzaglo's hat-trick sent Woking to Everton, where they lost by the only goal but made a lot of friends with the standard of their performance.

1990

FIRST ROUND				
Aldershot	0	Cambridge	1	
Aylesbury	1	Southend	0	
Bas'stokeT	3	Bromsgrv	0	
Bath C	2	Fulham	2	
Blackpool	2	Bolton	1	
Brentford	0	Colchester	1	
Bristol C	2	Barnet	0	
Bristol R	1	Reading	1	
Bshk Auck	2	Tow Law	0	
Burnley	1	Stockport	1	
Cardiff	1	Halesowen	0	
Carlisle	3	Wrexham	0	
Crewe	2	Congleton	0	
Darlingtn	6	Northwich	2	
Dartford	1	Exeter	1	
Doncaster	1	Notts Co	0	
Farnborgh	0	Hereford	1	
Gillinghm	0	Welling U	0	
Gloc City	1	Dorchstr	0	
Hartlepl	0	Huddersfld	2	
Kettering	0	N'hamptn	1	
Kiddermst	2	Swansea	3	
Leyton O	0	Birmghm C	1	
Lincoln	1	Billngh S	0	
Macclesfd	1	Chester	1	
Maidstone	2	Yeovil T	1	
Marine	0	Rochdale	1	N
Peterboro	1	Hayes	1	
Preston NE	1	Tranmere	0	
Redditch	1	Mert Tyd	3	
Rotherhm	0	Bury	0	
Scarboro	0	Whitley B	1	
Scunthpe	4	Matlock T	1	
Shrewsby	2	Chestrfld	3	
Slough T	1	Woking	2	
Staffd Rg	2	Halifax	3	
Sutton U	1	Torquay	1	
Telford U	0	Walsall	3	
Wigan Ath	2	Mansfield	0	
York	1	Grimsby	2	
Bury	1	Rotherhm	2	r
Chester	3	Macclesfd	2	r
Exeter	4	Dartford	1	r
Fulham	2	Bath C	1	r
Hayes	0	Peterboro	1	r
Reading	1	Bristol R	1	re
Stockport	1	Burnley	2	r
Torquay	4	Sutton U	0	r
Welling U	1	Gillinghm	0	r
Bristol R	0	Reading	1	r2
SECOND ROUND				
Bas'stokeT	2	Torquay	3	
Blackpool	3	Chester	0	
Bristol C	2	Fulham	1	
Cambridge	3	Woking	1	
Cardiff	2	Gloc City	2	
Chestrfld	0	Huddersfld	2	
Colchester	0	Birmghm C	2	
Crewe	1	Bshk Auck	1	
Darlingtn	3	Halifax	0	
Grimsby	1	Doncaster	0	
Hereford	3	Mert Tyd	2	
Maidstone	1	Exeter	1	
N'hamptn	0	Aylesbury	0	
Reading	0	Welling U	0	
Rochdale	3	Lincoln	0	
Scunthpe	2	Burnley	2	
Swansea	3	Peterboro	1	
Walsall	1	Rotherhm	0	
Whitley B	2	Preston NE	0	
Wigan Ath	2	Carlisle	0	
Aylesbury	0	N'hamptn	1	r
Bshk Auck	0	Crewe	2	r
Burnley	1	Scunthpe	1	re
Exeter	3	Maidstone	2	r
Gloc City	0	Cardiff	1	r
Welling U	1	Reading	1	re
Burnley	5	Scunthpe	0	r2
Reading	0	Welling U	0	r2e
Welling U	1	Reading	2	r3
THIRD ROUND				
Birmghm C	1	Oldham	1	
Blackburn	2	Aston V	2	
Blackpool	1	Burnley	0	
Brighton	4	Luton	1	
Bristol C	2	Swindon	1	
Cambridge	0	Darlingtn	0	
Cardiff	0	QPR	0	
Charlton	1	Bradford	1	
Chelsea	1	Crewe	1	
C.Palace	2	Portsmth	1	
Exeter	1	Norwich	1	
Hereford	2	Walsall	1	
Huddersfld	3	Grimsby	1	
Hull	0	Newcastle	1	
Leeds U	0	Ipswich	1	
Leicester	1	Barnsley	2	
Man City	0	Millwall	0	
Middlesbro	0	Everton	0	
N'hamptn	1	Coventry	0	
Nottm For	0	Man Utd	1	
Plymouth	0	Oxford	1	
Port Vale	1	Derby	1	
Reading	2	Sunderld	1	
Rochdale	1	Whitley B	0	
Sheff Utd	2	Bournemth	0	
Stoke	0	Arsenal	1	
Swansea	0	Liverpool	0	
Torquay	1	West Ham	0	
Tottenham	1	Southmptn	3	
Watford	2	Wigan Ath	0	
West Brom	2	Wimbledn	0	
Wolves	1	Sheff Wed	2	
Aston V	3	Blackburn	1	r
Bradford	0	Charlton	3	r
Crewe	0	Chelsea	2	r
Darlingtn	1	Cambridge	3	r
Derby	2	Port Vale	3	r
Everton	1	Middlesbro	1	re
Liverpool	8	Swansea	0	r
Millwall	1	Man City	1	re
Norwich	2	Exeter	0	r

Strange but true!

Terry Venables became only the fourth manager to take different clubs to Wembley when he got there with Spurs in 1991, having previously done so with QPR - against Spurs. Billy Walker (Wednesday and Forest) and Tommy Docherty and Dave Sexton (both Manchester United and Chelsea) were the others.

Alan Pardew scores Crystal Palace's winner in their 4-3 Semi-Final win over Liverpool in 1990

Oldham	1	Birmghm C	0	r
QPR	2	Cardiff	0	r
Everton	1	Middlesbro	0	r2
Millwall	3	Man City	1	r2
FOURTH ROUND				
Arsenal	0	QPR	0	
Aston V	6	Port Vale	0	
Barnsley	2	Ipswich	0	
Blackpool	1	Torquay	0	
Bristol C	3	Chelsea	1	
C.Palace	4	Huddersfld	0	
Hereford	0	Man Utd	1	
Millwall	1	Cambridge	1	
Norwich	0	Liverpool	0	
Oldham	2	Brighton	1	
Reading	3	Newcastle	3	
Rochdale	3	N'hamptn	0	
Sheff Utd	1	Watford	1	
Sheff Wed	1	Everton	2	
Southmptn	1	Oxford	0	
West Brom	1	Charlton	0	
Cambridge	1	Millwall	0	re
Liverpool	3	Norwich	1	r
Newcastle	4	Reading	1	r
QPR	2	Arsenal	0	r
Watford	1	Sheff Utd	2	r
FIFTH ROUND				
Blackpool	2	QPR	2	
Bristol C	0	Cambridge	0	
C.Palace	1	Rochdale	0	
Liverpool	3	Southmptn	0	
Newcastle	2	Man Utd	3	
Oldham	2	Everton	2	
Sheff Utd	2	Barnsley	2	
West Brom	0	Aston V	2	
Barnsley	0	Sheff Utd	0	re
Cambridge	1	Bristol C	1	re
Everton	1	Oldham	1	re
QPR	0	Blackpool	0	re
Barnsley	0	Sheff Utd	1	r2e
Cambridge	5	Bristol C	1	r2
Oldham	2	Everton	1	r2
QPR	3	Blackpool	0	r2
SIXTH ROUND				
Cambridge	0	C.Palace	1	
Oldham	3	Aston V	0	
QPR	2	Liverpool	2	
Sheff Utd	0	Man Utd	1	
Liverpool	1	QPR	0	r
SEMI-FINAL				
C.Palace	4	Liverpool	3	eN
Man Utd	3	Oldham	3	eN
Man Utd	2	Oldham	1	reN
FINAL				
Man Utd	3	C.Palace	3	eN
Man Utd	1	C.Palace	0	rN

1991

FIRST ROUND				
Aldershot	6	Tiverton	2	
Altrinchm	1	Huddersfld	2	
Atherstne	3	Fleetwd T	1	
Aylesbury	0	Walsall	1	
Barnet	2	Chelmsfd	2	
Birmghm C	1	Chelthnm	0	
Blackpool	2	Grimsby	0	
Boston U	1	Wycombe	1	
Bournemth	2	Gillinghm	1	
Bradford	0	Shrewsby	0	
Brentford	5	Yeovil T	0	
Bshk Auck	0	Barrow	1	
Cardiff	0	Hayes	0	
Chester	2	Doncaster	2	
Chestrfld	3	Spennym'r	2	
Chorley	2	Bury	1	

WHAT A STAR ✪ PAUL GASCOIGNE

Perhaps the most talented English player of the past decade, but sadly short of the glory that he might have had. His best season - with Spurs in 1990-91 - also ultimately led to his downfall. He took Spurs to Wembley virtually single-handedly that year with some great goals - including a stunning free-kick in the Semis against Arsenal - but the Final was a disaster. He was stretchered off early in the game with ruptured knee ligaments, never played for Spurs again, had a less than successful time with Lazio in Italy, and his spell with Rangers has been less of a test than a player of his type needs.

Pro-File: MARK HUGHES

Mark Hughes made history in May 1997 when he became the first player this century to win four FA Cup winners' medals.

He did so by helping Chelsea beat Middlesbrough 2-0 in the Wembley showpiece to earn him his record haul.

That was added to the three medals he won with Manchester United, in 1985, 1990 and 1994, the latter ironically against Chelsea, and it is a record which any player will find hard to beat.

And perhaps it's fitting that the record should be held by Hughes, a player who has seen and done it all in a career that has seen him play for four of the biggest clubs in the world - Manchester United, Barcelona, Bayern Munich and Chelsea.

Admittedly his spell at Barcelona was not the greatest of successes but no-one can argue about his impact on the domestic scene.

He has won every honour there is to win and even defied the critics by going from strength to strength when he left Old Trafford for Chelsea, a move that many felt signalled the end of his big-time career.

But, in fact, it gave him a new lease of life and he continued to terrorise defences all over the country.

Career details

●**Represented:** Wales, Manchester United (twice), Barcelona, Bayern Munich, Chelsea ●**Position:** Striker ●**Born:** Wrexham, 01.11.63 ●**Height:** 6ft ●**Weight:** 12st 4lbs ●**Club honours:** League Championship 1992-93, 1993-94; FA Cup 1985, 1990, 1994, 1997; League Cup 1992, European Cup-Winners' Cup 1991; PFA Player of the Year 1989, 1991; PFA Young Player of the Year 1985 ●**International honours:** Wales 5 U21, 63 full caps

Club League Record

Era	Club	Games	Goals
80/86	Manchester United	89	37
86/87	Barcelona	28	4
87/88	Bayern Munich	18	6
88/95	Manchester United	256	82
95/97	Chelsea	70	16

Cup Highlights

May 18 1985: Hughes collects his first major honour as ten-man United beat Everton 1-0 after extra-time in the FA Cup Final.

May 12 1990: Hughes scores twice as United draw the FA Cup Final 3-3 with Crystal Palace. They win the replay 1-0.

April 10 1994: Hughes scores a dramatic last gasp equaliser - a stunning volley - to force an FA Cup Semi-Final replay against Oldham, which they win 4-1.

May 14 1994: Hughes collects his third FA Cup winners' medal as United beat Chelsea 4-0 in the Final. He scores the third goal.

April 13 1997: Hughes scores twice as Chelsea beat Wimbledon 3-0 in the FA Cup Semi-Final.

May 17 1997: Hughes becomes the first player this century to win four FA Cup winners' medals as Chelsea beat Middlesbrough 2-0.

On Hughes:

●He is a warrior with whom you could trust your life.
Alex Ferguson

●If I have a problem on the pitch, I just call Marco over and he sorts it out for me. **Gianfranco Zola**

DID YOU KNOW THAT...

●He made his League debut against Southampton on January 21, 1984. United won 3-2.

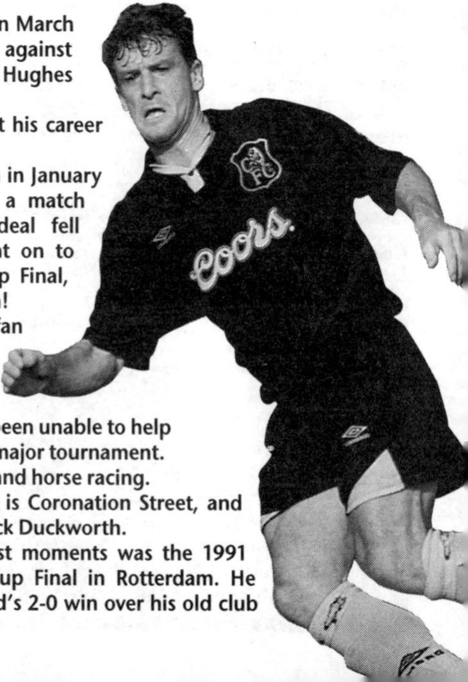

●He scored his first goal on March 10 that year in a 2-0 win against Leicester at Old Trafford. Hughes scored the second.

●His nickname throughout his career has been Sparky.

●He almost joined Everton in January 1995 but was injured in a match against Newcastle. The deal fell through and Hughes went on to help United to the FA Cup Final, where they lost...to Everton!

●Hughes was a Wrexham fan as a youngster.

●His biggest disappointment in football is the fact that he been unable to help Wales reach the finals of a major tournament.

●His hobbies include golf and horse racing.

●His favourite soap opera is Coronation Street, and his favourite character is Jack Duckworth.

●One of Hughes's greatest moments was the 1991 European Cup-Winners' Cup Final in Rotterdam. He scored both goals in United's 2-0 win over his old club Barcelona.

Colchester	2	Reading	1	
Darlingtn	1	York	1	
Exeter	1	Cambridge	2	
Fulham	2	Farnborgh	1	
Halesowen	1	Tranmere	2	
Halifax	3	Wrexham	2	
Hereford	1	Peterboro	1	
Leyton O	3	Southend	2	
Lincoln	1	Crewe	4	
Littlehmp	0	N'hamptn	4	
Maidstone	4	Torquay	1	
Mert Tyd	1	Sutton U	1	
Preston NE	0	Mansfield	1	
Rochdale	1	Scunthpe	1	
Rotherhm	1	Stockport	0	
Runcorn	0	Hartlepl	3	
Scarboro	0	Leek T	2	
Staffd Rg	1	Burnley	3	
Swansea	5	Welling U	2	
Tamworth	4	Whitley B	6	
Telford U	0	Stoke	0	
Wigan Ath	5	Carlisle	0	
Witton Ab	1	Bolton	2	
Woking	0	Kiddermst	0	
Chelmsfd	0	Barnet	2	r
Doncaster	1	Chester	2	re
Hayes	1	Cardiff	0	rN
Kiddermst	1	Woking	1	re
Peterboro	2	Hereford	1	r
Scunthpe	2	Rochdale	1	re
Shrewsby	2	Bradford	1	r
Stoke	1	Telford U	0	r
Sutton U	0	Mert Tyd	1	r
Wycombe	4	Boston U	0	r
York	1	Darlingtn	0	r
Kiddermst	1	Woking	2	r2
SECOND ROUND				
Aldershot	2	Maidstone	1	
Barnet	0	N'hamptn	0	
Birmghm C	1	Brentford	3	
Bournemth	1	Hayes	0	
Burnley	2	Stoke	0	
Chestrfld	3	Bolton	4	
Colchester	0	Leyton O	0	
Crewe	1	Atherstne	0	
Fulham	0	Cambridge	0	
Huddersfld	0	Blackpool	2	
Leek T	1	Chester	1	
Mansfield	2	York	1	
Rotherhm	1	Halifax	1	
Scunthpe	3	Tranmere	2	
Shrewsby	1	Chorley	0	
Swansea	2	Walsall	1	
Whitley B	0	Barrow	1	
Wigan Ath	2	Hartlepl	0	
Woking	5	Mert Tyd	1	
Wycombe	1	Peterboro	1	
Cambridge	2	Fulham	1	r
Chester	4	Leek T	0	r
Halifax	1	Rotherhm	2	r
Leyton O	4	Colchester	1	r
N'hamptn	0	Barnet	1	r
Peterboro	2	Wycombe	0	r
THIRD ROUND				
Arsenal	2	Sunderld	1	
Aston V	1	Wimbledn	1	
Barnet	0	Portsmth	5	
Barnsley	1	Leeds U	1	
Blackburn	1	Liverpool	1	
Blackpool	0	Tottenham	1	
Bolton	1	Barrow	0	
Brighton	3	Scunthpe	2	
Bristol R	0	Crewe	2	
Burnley	0	Man City	1	
Charlton	1	Everton	2	
Chelsea	1	Oxford	3	
Chester	2	Bournemth	3	
Coventry	1	Wigan Ath	1	
C.Palace	0	Nottm For	0	
Hull	2	Notts Co	5	
Leyton O	1	Swindon	1	
Man Utd	2	QPR	1	
Mansfield	0	Sheff Wed	2	
Middlesbro	0	Plymouth	0	
Millwall	2	Leicester	1	
Newcastle	2	Derby	0	
Norwich	2	Bristol C	1	
Oldham	3	Brentford	1	
Port Vale	2	Peterboro	1	
Sheff Utd	1	Luton	3	
Shrewsby	4	Watford	1	
Southmptn	3	Ipswich	2	
Swansea	0	Rotherhm	0	
West Brom	2	Woking	4	
West Ham	0	Aldershot	0	
Wolves	0	Cambridge	1	
Leeds U	4	Barnsley	0	r
Liverpool	3	Blackburn	0	r
Nottm For	2	C.Palace	2	re
Plymouth	1	Middlesbro	2	r
Rotherhm	4	Swansea	0	r
Swindon	1	Leyton O	0	r
West Ham	6	Aldershot	1	r
Wigan Ath	0	Coventry	1	r
Wimbledn	1	Aston V	0	re
Nottm For	3	C.Palace	0	r2
FOURTH ROUND				
Arsenal	0	Leeds U	0	
Cambridge	2	Middlesbro	0	
Coventry	1	Southmptn	1	
Crewe	1	Rotherhm	0	
Everton	1	Woking	0	
Liverpool	2	Brighton	2	
Luton	1	West Ham	1	
Man Utd	1	Bolton	0	
Millwall	4	Sheff Wed	4	
Newcastle	2	Nottm For	2	
Norwich	3	Swindon	1	
Notts Co	2	Oldham	0	
Port Vale	1	Man City	2	
Portsmth	5	Bournemth	1	
Shrewsby	1	Wimbledn	0	
Tottenham	4	Oxford	2	
Brighton	2	Liverpool	3	r
Leeds U	1	Arsenal	1	re
Nottm For	3	Newcastle	0	r
Sheff Wed	2	Millwall	0	r
Southmptn	2	Coventry	0	r
West Ham	5	Luton	0	r
Arsenal	0	Leeds U	0	r2e
Leeds U	1	Arsenal	2	r3
FIFTH ROUND				
Cambridge	4	Sheff Wed	0	
Liverpool	0	Everton	0	
Norwich	2	Man Utd	1	
Notts Co	1	Man City	0	
Portsmth	1	Tottenham	2	
Shrewsby	0	Arsenal	1	
Southmptn	1	Nottm For	1	
West Ham	1	Crewe	0	
Everton	4	Liverpool	4	re
Nottm For	3	Southmptn	1	r
Everton	1	Liverpool	0	r2
SIXTH ROUND				
Arsenal	2	Cambridge	1	
Norwich	0	Nottm For	1	
Tottenham	2	Notts Co	1	
West Ham	2	Everton	1	
SEMI-FINAL				
Nottm For	4	West Ham	0	N

GIANTKILLERS

1992 Wrexham 2 Arsenal 1

Arsenal had won the Championship a few months earlier, while Wrexham had been bottom of Division Four. Arsenal won the Cup in the following season, with eight of the players from the Wrexham debacle still in the side. So it was only a one-off - but one-offs don't come much bigger. The much-travelled Mickey Thomas equalised after an Alan Smith opener, and Steve Watkin got the winner that delighted all Wales - and a large part of England, too.

WHAT A STAR ✪ JOHN BYRNE

A quick, goal-conscious striker who did a great deal to help Sunderland back to Wembley in 1992, scoring in every round of the Cup before the Final, where Liverpool's rigid marking gave him little chance to add to his total. Byrne also played for QPR, then for Le Havre in France, and for Brighton and Millwall, as well as winning 23 caps for the Republic of Ireland.

Tottenham	3	Arsenal	1	N

FINAL

Tottenham	2	Nottm For	1	eN

1992

FIRST ROUND

Aldershot	0	Enfield	1	
Atherstne	0	Hereford	0	
Barnet	5	Tiverton	0	
Blackpool	2	Grimsby	1	
Bournemth	3	Bromsgrv	1	
Brentford	3	Gillinghm	3	
Bridlngtn	1	York	2	
Burnley	1	Doncaster	1	
Bury	0	Bradford	1	
Carlisle	1	Crewe	1	
Chester	1	Guiseley	0	
Colchester	0	Exeter	0	
Crawley T	4	N'hamptn	2	
Darlingtn	2	Chestrfld	1	
Emley	0	Bolton	3	N
Fulham	0	Hayes	2	
Gretna	0	Rochdale	0	
Halesowen	2	Farnborgh	2	
Hartlepl	3	Shrewsby	2	
Huddersfld	7	Lincoln U	0	
Kettering	1	Wycombe	1	
Kiddermst	0	Aylesbury	1	
Leyton O	2	Welling U	1	
Maidstone	1	Sutton U	0	
Mansfield	0	Preston NE	1	
Morecambe	0	Hull	1	
Peterboro	7	Harlow T	0	
Scarboro	0	Wigan Ath	2	
Scunthpe	1	Rotherhm	1	
Slough T	3	Reading	3	
Stockport	3	Lincoln	1	
Stoke	0	Telford U	0	
Swansea	2	Cardiff	1	
Torquay	3	Birmghm C	0	
Tranmere	3	Runcorn	0	
West Brom	6	Marlow	0	
Windsor&E	2	Woking	4	
Witton Ab	1	Halifax	1	
Wrexham	5	Winsford	2	
Yeovil T	1	Walsall	1	
Crewe	5	Carlisle	3	re
Doncaster	1	Burnley	3	r
Exeter	0	Colchester	0	rP
Farnborgh	4	Halesowen	0	r
Gillinghm	1	Brentford	3	r
Halifax	1	Witton Ab	2	re
Hereford	3	Atherstne	0	r
Reading	2	Slough T	1	r
Rochdale	3	Gretna	1	r
Rotherhm	3	Scunthpe	3	rP
Telford U	2	Stoke	1	r
Walsall	0	Yeovil T	1	re
Wycombe	0	Kettering	2	r

SECOND ROUND

Aylesbury	2	Hereford	3	
Blackpool	0	Hull	1	
Bolton	3	Bradford	1	
Bournemth	2	Brentford	1	
Burnley	2	Rotherhm	0	
Crewe	2	Chester	0	
Darlingtn	1	Hartlepl	2	
Enfield	1	Barnet	4	
Exeter	0	Swansea	0	
Hayes	0	Crawley T	2	
Leyton O	2	West Brom	1	
Maidstone	1	Kettering	2	
Peterboro	0	Reading	0	
Preston NE	5	Witton Ab	1	
Rochdale	1	Huddersfld	2	
Torquay	1	Farnborgh	1	
Wigan Ath	2	Stockport	0	
Woking	3	Yeovil T	0	
Wrexham	1	Telford U	0	
York	1	Tranmere	1	
Farnborgh	4	Torquay	3	r
Reading	1	Peterboro	0	r
Swansea	1	Exeter	2	r
Tranmere	2	York	1	r

THIRD ROUND

Aston V	0	Tottenham	0	
Blackburn	4	Kettering	1	
Bolton	2	Reading	0	
Bournemth	0	Newcastle	0	
Brighton	5	Crawley T	0	

Gazza is stretchered off in the 1991 Final

Bristol C	1	Wimbledn	1	
Bristol R	5	Plymouth	0	
Burnley	2	Derby	2	
Charlton	3	Barnet	1	
Coventry	1	Cambridge	1	
Crewe	0	Liverpool	4	
Everton	1	Southend	0	
Exeter	1	Portsmth	2	
Huddersfld	0	Millwall	4	
Hull	0	Chelsea	2	
Ipswich	1	Hartlepl	1	
Leeds U	0	Man Utd	1	
Leicester	1	C.Palace	0	
Middlesbro	2	Man City	1	
Norwich	1	Barnsley	0	
Nottm For	1	Wolves	0	
Notts Co	2	Wigan Ath	0	
Oldham	1	Leyton O	1	
Oxford	3	Tranmere	1	
Preston NE	0	Sheff Wed	2	
Sheff Utd	4	Luton	0	
Southmptn	2	QPR	0	
Sunderld	3	Port Vale	0	
Swindon	3	Watford	2	
West Ham	1	Farnborgh	1	
Woking	0	Hereford	0	
Wrexham	2	Arsenal	1	
Cambridge	1	Coventry	0	r
Derby	2	Burnley	0	r
Hartlepl	0	Ipswich	2	r
Hereford	2	Woking	1	re
Leyton O	4	Oldham	2	re
Newcastle	2	Bournemth	2	rq
Tottenham	0	Aston V	1	r
West Ham	1	Farnborgh	0	r
Wimbledn	0	Bristol C	1	r

FOURTH ROUND

Bolton	2	Brighton	1	
Bristol R	1	Liverpool	1	
Cambridge	0	Swindon	3	
Charlton	0	Sheff Utd	0	
Chelsea	1	Everton	0	
Derby	3	Aston V	4	
Ipswich	3	Bournemth	0	
Leicester	1	Bristol C	2	
Norwich	2	Millwall	1	
Nottm For	2	Hereford	0	
Notts Co	2	Blackburn	1	
Oxford	2	Sunderld	3	
Portsmth	2	Leyton O	0	
Sheff Wed	1	Middlesbro	2	
Southmptn	0	Man Utd	0	
West Ham	2	Wrexham	2	
Liverpool	2	Bristol R	1	r
Man Utd	2	Southmptn	2	rq
Sheff Utd	3	Charlton	1	r
Wrexham	0	West Ham	1	r

FIFTH ROUND

Bolton	2	Southmptn	2	
Chelsea	1	Sheff Utd	0	
Ipswich	0	Liverpool	0	
Norwich	3	Notts Co	0	
Nottm For	4	Bristol C	1	
Portsmth	1	Middlesbro	1	
Sunderld	1	West Ham	1	
Swindon	1	Aston V	2	
Liverpool	3	Ipswich	2	re
Middlesbro	2	Portsmth	4	r
Southmptn	3	Bolton	2	re
West Ham	2	Sunderld	3	r

SIXTH ROUND

Chelsea	1	Sunderld	1	
Liverpool	1	Aston V	0	
Portsmth	1	Nottm For	0	
Southmptn	0	Norwich	0	
Norwich	2	Southmptn	1	re
Sunderld	2	Chelsea	1	r

SEMI-FINAL

Liverpool	1	Portsmth	1	eN
Norwich	0	Sunderld	1	N
Liverpool	0	Portsmth	0	rPN

FINAL

Liverpool	2	Sunderld	0	N

1993

FIRST ROUND

Acctn St	3	Gateshead	2	
Blackpool	1	Rochdale	1	
Blyth S	1	Southport	2	
Bolton	2	Sutton Cd	1	
Bournemth	0	Barnet	0	
Bradford	1	Preston NE	1	
Brighton	2	Hayes	0	
Burnley	2	Scarboro	1	
Bury	2	Witton Ab	0	
Cardiff	2	Bath C	3	
Chester	1	Altrinchm	1	
Colchester	4	Slough T	0	
Crewe	6	Wrexham	1	
Dagenham	4	Leyton O	5	
Darlingtn	1	Hull	2	
Doncaster	1	Hartlepl	2	
Dorking	2	Plymouth	3	
Exeter	1	Kiddermst	0	
Gillinghm	3	Kettering	2	
Kingst'an	1	Peterboro	1	
Lincoln	0	Staffd Rg	0	
Macclesfd	0	Chestrfld	0	
Marine	4	Halifax	1	
Marlow	3	Salisbury	3	
N'hamptn	3	Fulham	1	
Reading	1	Birmghm C	0	
Rotherhm	4	Walsall	0	
Scunthpe	0	Huddersfld	0	
Shrewsby	3	Mansfield	1	
Solihull	2	VS Rugby	2	
St Albns C	1	Chelthnm	2	
Stoke	0	Port Vale	0	
Sutton U	1	Hereford	2	
Swansea	w	Maidstone	s	
Torquay	2	Yeovil T	5	
West Brom	8	Aylesbury	0	
Wigan Ath	3	Carlisle	1	
Woking	3	Nuneaton	2	
Wycombe	3	Mert Tyd	1	
York	1	Stockport	3	
Altrinchm	2	Chester	0	r
Barnet	1	Bournemth	2	r
Chestrfld	2	Macclesfd	2	rq
Huddersfld	2	Scunthpe	1	re
Peterboro	9	Kingst'an	1	rv
Port Vale	3	Stoke	1	r
Preston NE	4	Bradford	5	r
Rochdale	1	Blackpool	0	re
Salisbury	2	Marlow	2	rq

Late, Late Show

Arsenal's David O'Leary was a last-minute Cup-winner against Sheffield Wednesday in 1993 - just as he had been against Manchester United 14 years earlier.

GIANTKILLERS

1994 Liverpool 0 Bristol City 1

The first meeting was abandoned because of a floodlight failure with the score 1-1, and was followed by a draw before City pulled off the victory that led to a change of manager at Anfield - Graeme Souness being replaced by Roy Evans. City were only mid-table in the new Division One, but were by no means the first team to give Liverpool a shock in their own lair during the 90s. Another blow - the old Kop was taken down at the end of the season.

WHAT A STAR ★ ERIC CANTONA

Like him or loathe him, Eric Cantona was a compelling personality in the modern game, a man with a seemingly endless ability to pick up medals for Leagues and Cups, at the same time as upsetting opponents, fans and officialdom. His greatest moments came in recent seasons with Manchester United, who he helped win four Premiership titles and two FA Cups. He scored twice in the 4-0 1994 Final win over Chelsea and, in 1996, grabbed the only goal against Liverpool to clinch the 'double double'. But in May 1997 he stunned the world by retiring at the age of 31. He will be sadly missed.

Staffd Rg	2	Lincoln	1	r
VS Rugby	2	Solihull	1	re
Peterboro	1	Kingst'an	0	r2
SECOND ROUND				
Acctn St	1	Crewe	6	N
Altrinchm	1	Port Vale	4	
Bath C	2	N'hamptn	2	
Bolton	4	Rochdale	0	
Bradford	0	Huddersfld	2	
Brighton	1	Woking	1	
Burnley	1	Shrewsby	1	
Chelthnm	1	Bournemth	1	
Exeter	2	Swansea	5	
Gillinghm	1	Colchester	1	
Hartlepl	4	Southport	0	
Macclesfd	0	Stockport	2	
Marine	3	Staffd Rg	2	
Plymouth	3	Peterboro	2	
Reading	3	Leyton O	0	
Rotherhm	1	Hull	0	
VS Rugby	0	Marlow	0	
Wigan Ath	1	Bury	1	
Wycombe	2	West Brom	2	
Yeovil T	0	Hereford	0	
Bournemth	3	Chelthnm	0	r
Bury	1	Wigan Ath	0	r
Colchester	2	Gillinghm	3	r
Hereford	1	Yeovil T	2	r
Marlow	2	VS Rugby	0	r
N'hamptn	3	Bath C	0	r
Shrewsby	1	Burnley	2	r
West Brom	1	Wycombe	0	r
Woking	1	Brighton	2	r
THIRD ROUND				
Aston V	1	Bristol R	1	
Blackburn	3	Bournemth	1	
Bolton	2	Liverpool	2	
Brentford	0	Grimsby	2	
Brighton	1	Portsmth	0	
Cambridge	1	Sheff Wed	2	
Crewe	3	Marine	1	
Derby	2	Stockport	1	
Gillinghm	0	Huddersfld	0	
Hartlepl	1	C.Palace	0	
Ipswich	3	Plymouth	1	
Leeds U	1	Charlton	1	
Leicester	2	Barnsley	2	
Luton	2	Bristol C	0	
Man City	1	Reading	1	
Man Utd	2	Bury	0	
Middlesbro	2	Chelsea	1	
Newcastle	4	Port Vale	0	
N'hamptn	0	Rotherhm	1	
Norwich	1	Coventry	0	
Nottm For	2	Southmptn	1	
Notts Co	0	Sunderld	2	
Oldham	2	Tranmere	2	
QPR	3	Swindon	0	
Sheff Utd	2	Burnley	2	
Southend	1	Millwall	0	
Swansea	1	Oxford	1	
Tottenham	5	Marlow	1	
Watford	1	Wolves	4	
West Brom	0	West Ham	2	
Wimbledn	0	Everton	0	
Yeovil T	1	Arsenal	3	
Barnsley	1	Leicester	1	rP
Bristol R	0	Aston V	3	r
Burnley	2	Sheff Utd	4	r
Charlton	1	Leeds U	3	r
Everton	1	Wimbledn	2	r
Huddersfld	2	Gillinghm	1	r
Liverpool	0	Bolton	2	r
Oxford	2	Swansea	2	rq
Reading	0	Man City	4	r
Tranmere	3	Oldham	0	r
FOURTH ROUND				
Arsenal	2	Leeds U	2	
Aston V	1	Wimbledn	1	
Barnsley	4	West Ham	1	
Crewe	0	Blackburn	3	
Huddersfld	1	Southend	2	
Luton	1	Derby	5	
Man Utd	1	Brighton	0	
Norwich	0	Tottenham	2	
Nottm For	1	Middlesbro	1	
QPR	1	Man City	2	
Rotherhm	1	Newcastle	1	
Sheff Utd	1	Hartlepl	0	
Sheff Wed	1	Sunderld	0	
Swansea	0	Grimsby	0	
Tranmere	1	Ipswich	2	
Wolves	0	Bolton	2	
Grimsby	2	Swansea	0	r
Leeds U	2	Arsenal	3	re
Middlesbro	0	Nottm For	3	r
Newcastle	2	Rotherhm	0	r
Wimbledn	0	Aston V	0	rP
FIFTH ROUND				
Arsenal	2	Nottm For	0	
Blackburn	1	Newcastle	0	
Derby	3	Bolton	1	
Ipswich	4	Grimsby	0	
Man City	2	Barnsley	0	
Sheff Utd	2	Man Utd	1	
Sheff Wed	2	Southend	0	
Tottenham	3	Wimbledn	2	
SIXTH ROUND				
Blackburn	0	Sheff Utd	0	
Derby	3	Sheff Wed	3	
Ipswich	2	Arsenal	4	
Man City	2	Tottenham	4	
Sheff Utd	2	Blackburn	2	rP
Sheff Wed	1	Derby	0	r
SEMI-FINAL				
Arsenal	1	Tottenham	0	N
Sheff Wed	2	Sheff Utd	1	eN
FINAL				
Arsenal	1	Sheff Wed	1	eN
Arsenal	2	Sheff Wed	1	reN

Strange but true!

The only two players named Rush to appear in a Final did so in the same one - in 1992, when Liverpool's Ian faced Sunderland's David.

1994

FIRST ROUND				
Acctn St	2	Scunthpe	3	N
Barnet	2	Carshlton	1	
Bolton	3	Gretna	2	
Bournemth	4	Brighton	2	
Bradford	0	Chester	0	
Bristol R	1	Wycombe	2	
Burnley	0	York	0	
Cambs C	0	Hereford	1	
Cambridge	0	Reading	0	
Chestrfld	0	Rochdale	1	
Colchester	3	Sutton U	4	

Crewe	4	Darlingtn	2	
Enfield	0	Cardiff	0	
Farnborgh	1	Exeter	3	
Halifax	2	West Brom	1	
Kiddermst	3	Kettering	0	
Knowsley	1	Carlisle	4	N
Leek T	2	Wigan Ath	2	
Leyton O	2	Gravesend	1	
Macclesfd	2	Hartlepl	0	
Mansfield	1	Preston NE	2	
Marlow	0	Plymouth	2	
Met Pol	0	Crawley T	2	
Molesey	0	Bath C	4	
N'hamptn	1	Bromsgrv	2	
Port Vale	2	Blackpool	0	
Rotherhm	1	Stockport	2	
Runcorn	0	Hull	2	N
Scarboro	1	Bury	0	
Shrewsby	1	Doncaster	1	
Slough T	1	Torquay	2	
Stalyb C	1	Marine	1	
Swansea	1	Nuneaton	1	
Telford U	1	Huddersfld	1	
VS Rugby	0	Brentford	3	
Witton Ab	0	Lincoln	2	
Woking	2	Weston SM	2	
Wrexham	1	Walsall	1	
Yeading	0	Gillinghm	0	N
Yeovil T	1	Fulham	0	
Cardiff	1	Enfield	0	r
Chester	1	Bradford	0	r
Doncaster	1	Shrewsby	2	re
Gillinghm	3	Yeading	1	r
Huddersfld	1	Telford U	0	r
Marine	4	Stalyb C	4	rq
Nuneaton	2	Swansea	1	re
Reading	1	Cambridge	2	r
Walsall	2	Wrexham	0	r
Weston SM	0	Woking	1	r
Wigan Ath	3	Leek T	0	r
York	2	Burnley	3	r
SECOND ROUND				
Bath C	2	Hereford	1	
Bournemth	1	Nuneaton	1	
Brentford	1	Cardiff	3	
Burnley	4	Rochdale	1	
Carlisle	3	Stalyb C	1	
Chester	2	Hull	0	
Crawley T	1	Barnet	2	
Crewe	2	Macclesfd	1	
Kiddermst	1	Woking	0	
Leyton O	1	Exeter	1	
Lincoln	1	Bolton	3	
Plymouth	2	Gillinghm	0	
Port Vale	1	Huddersfld	0	
Shrewsby	0	Preston NE	1	
Stockport	5	Halifax	1	
Torquay	0	Sutton U	1	
Walsall	1	Scunthpe	1	
Wigan Ath	1	Scarboro	0	
Wycombe	1	Cambridge	0	
Yeovil T	0	Bromsgrv	2	
Exeter	2	Leyton O	2	rP
Nuneaton	0	Bournemth	1	r
Scunthpe	0	Walsall	0	rP
THIRD ROUND				
Birmghm C	1	Kiddermst	2	
Blackburn	3	Portsmth	3	
Bolton	1	Everton	1	
Bristol C	1	Liverpool	1	
Bromsgrv	1	Barnsley	2	
Cardiff	2	Middlesbro	2	
Charlton	3	Burnley	0	
Chelsea	0	Barnet	0	
Exeter	0	Aston V	1	
Grimsby	1	Wigan Ath	0	
Leeds U	3	Crewe	1	
Luton	1	Southend	0	
Man City	4	Leicester	1	
Millwall	0	Arsenal	1	
Newcastle	2	Coventry	0	
Notts Co	3	Sutton U	2	
Oldham	2	Derby	1	
Oxford	2	Tranmere	0	
Peterboro	1	Tottenham	1	
Plymouth	1	Chester	0	
Preston NE	2	Bournemth	1	
Sheff Utd	0	Man Utd	1	
Sheff Wed	1	Nottm For	1	
Southmptn	1	Port Vale	1	
Stockport	2	QPR	1	
Stoke	0	Bath C	0	
Sunderld	1	Carlisle	1	
Swindon	1	Ipswich	1	
West Ham	2	Watford	1	
Wimbledn	3	Scunthpe	0	
Wolves	1	C.Palace	0	
Wycombe	0	Norwich	2	

Top Draw

There have been 115 FA Cup Finals and only 14 of them have been drawn, but there have been three groups of three in succession - 1884-85-86, 1910-11-12 and 1981-82-83.

Bath C	1	Stoke	4	r
Carlisle	0	Sunderld	1	re
Chelsea	4	Barnet	0	r
Everton	2	Bolton	3	re
Ipswich	2	Swindon	1	re
Liverpool	0	Bristol C	1	r
Middlesbro	1	Cardiff	2	re
Nottm For	0	Sheff Wed	2	r
Port Vale	1	Southmptn	0	r
Portsmth	1	Blackburn	3	r
Tottenham	1	Peterboro	1	rP
FOURTH ROUND				
Bolton	2	Arsenal	2	
Cardiff	1	Man City	0	
Charlton	0	Blackburn	0	
Chelsea	1	Sheff Wed	1	
Grimsby	1	Aston V	2	
Ipswich	3	Tottenham	0	
Kiddermst	1	Preston NE	0	
Newcastle	1	Luton	1	
Norwich	0	Man Utd	2	
Notts Co	1	West Ham	1	
Oldham	0	Stoke	0	
Oxford	2	Leeds U	2	
Plymouth	2	Barnsley	2	
Port Vale	0	Wolves	2	
Stockport	0	Bristol C	4	
Wimbledn	2	Sunderld	1	
Arsenal	1	Bolton	3	re
Barnsley	1	Plymouth	0	r
Blackburn	0	Charlton	1	r
Leeds U	2	Oxford	3	re
Luton	2	Newcastle	0	r
Sheff Wed	1	Chelsea	3	re

WHAT A STAR ✪ IAN WRIGHT

The FA Cup is made for goalscorers...and they don't come any better than Ian Wright. He has scored four goals in Finals and, typically, each has had a major impact. His first two came in the 1990 Final, when he was playing for Crystal Palace against Manchester United, when he climbed off the bench - having recovered from a broken leg - to net twice to force a 3-3 draw and a replay, which Palace lost 1-0. But three years later he was back, with Arsenal against Sheffield Wednesday. Again he scored, again it was a draw. But in the replay he grabbed Arsenal's first goal in their 2-1 win to get a winners' medal at last.

GIANTKILLERS

1994 Arsenal 1 Bolton 3

Arsenal's 1-3 home defeat by Bolton was one of the reasons why manager Bruce Rioch eventually left Burnden Park to take over at Highbury. His First Division team had to begin at Round One and struggled to beat Gretna, even though they were given home advantage for financial reasons after being drawn away. But they eliminated Lincoln and Everton before drawing at home to Arsenal, and surprisingly won the replay. Rioch's side then knocked out Aston Villa, only to fall to Oldham in Round Six when they had a chance to become the first club this century to get to the Final after playing in every round of the competition.

Stoke	0	Oldham	1	r
West Ham	1	Notts Co	0	re
FIFTH ROUND				
Bolton	1	Aston V	0	
Bristol C	1	Charlton	1	
Cardiff	1	Luton	2	
Kiddermst	0	West Ham	1	
Oldham	1	Barnsley	0	
Oxford	1	Chelsea	2	
Wimbledn	0	Man Utd	3	
Wolves	1	Ipswich	1	
Charlton	2	Bristol C	0	r
Ipswich	1	Wolves	2	r
SIXTH ROUND				
Bolton	0	Oldham	1	
Chelsea	1	Wolves	0	
Man Utd	3	Charlton	1	
West Ham	0	Luton	0	
Luton	3	West Ham	2	r
SEMI-FINAL				
Chelsea	2	Luton	0	N
Man Utd	1	Oldham	1	eN
Man Utd	4	Oldham	1	rN
FINAL				
Man Utd	4	Chelsea	0	N

1995

FIRST ROUND				
Altrinchm	3	Southport	2	
Ashford	2	Fulham	2	
Barnet	4	Woking	4	
Bath C	0	Bristol R	5	
Birmghm C	4	Slough T	0	
Bournemth	3	Worthing	1	
Bradford	1	Scunthpe	1	
Bshk Auck	0	Bury	0	
Burnley	2	Shrewsby	1	
Cambs C	2	Brentford	2	
Chesham U	0	Bashley	1	
Chester	2	Witton Ab	0	
Chestrfld	0	Scarboro	0	
Crewe	7	Gresley R	1	
Doncaster	1	Huddersfld	4	
Enfield	1	Cardiff	0	
Exeter	1	Crawley T	0	
Guiseley	1	Carlisle	4	N
Halifax	1	Runcorn	1	
Hereford	2	Hitchin	2	
Heybridge	0	Gillinghm	2	N
Hull	0	Lincoln	1	
Hyde Utd	1	Darlingtn	3	
Kettering	0	Plymouth	1	
Kiddermst	1	Torquay	1	
Kingst'an	2	Brighton	1	
Mansfield	3	Northwich	1	
Marlow	2	Oxford	0	
Nwpt IOW	2	Aylesbury	3	
Peterboro	4	N'hamptn	0	
Port Vale	6	Hartlepl	0	
Preston NE	1	Blackpool	0	
Tiverton	1	Leyton O	3	
Walsall	3	Rochdale	0	
Walton&H	0	Swansea	2	
Wigan Ath	3	Spennym'r	0	
Wrexham	1	Stockport	0	
Wycombe	4	Chelmsfd	0	
Yeading	2	Colchester	2	
York	3	Rotherhm	3	
Brentford	1	Cambs C	2	r
Bury	1	Bshk Auck	1	rP
Colchester	7	Yeading	1	r
Fulham	5	Ashford	3	re
Hitchin	4	Hereford	2	r
Rotherhm	3	York	0	r
Runcorn	1	Halifax	3	re
Scarboro	2	Chestrfld	0	r
Scunthpe	3	Bradford	2	re
Torquay	1	Kiddermst	0	r
Woking	1	Barnet	0	r
SECOND ROUND				
Altrinchm	1	Wigan Ath	0	
Bashley	0	Swansea	1	
Birmghm C	0	Scunthpe	0	
Carlisle	2	Darlingtn	0	
Chester	1	Burnley	2	
Crewe	1	Bury	2	
Enfield	1	Torquay	1	
Exeter	1	Colchester	2	
Gillinghm	1	Fulham	1	
Halifax	0	Mansfield	0	
Hitchin	0	Wycombe	5	
Kingst'an	1	Aylesbury	4	
Leyton O	0	Bristol R	2	
Lincoln	1	Huddersfld	0	
Marlow	2	Woking	1	
Peterboro	0	Cambridge	2	
Plymouth	2	Bournemth	1	
Preston NE	1	Walsall	1	
Scarboro	1	Port Vale	0	
Wrexham	5	Rotherhm	2	
Fulham	1	Gillinghm	2	re
Mansfield	2	Halifax	1	r
Scunthpe	1	Birmghm C	2	r
Torquay	0	Enfield	1	r
Walsall	4	Preston NE	0	r
THIRD ROUND				
Barnsley	0	Aston V	2	
Birmghm C	0	Liverpool	0	
Bristol C	0	Stoke	0	
Bury	2	Tranmere	2	
Cambridge	2	Burnley	4	
Chelsea	3	Charlton	0	
Coventry	1	West Brom	1	
C.Palace	5	Lincoln	1	
Everton	1	Derby	0	
Gillinghm	1	Sheff Wed	2	
Grimsby	0	Norwich	1	
Leicester	2	Enfield	0	
Luton	1	Bristol R	1	
Mansfield	2	Wolves	3	
Millwall	0	Arsenal	0	

Wright On, or Off?

Ian Wright has played in four Cup Finals (two for Palace, two for Arsenal, including a replay with each), scored two goals for both clubs, and has not completed a game, having gone on as sub twice and been taken off twice.

Pro-File: IAN WRIGHT

There is a never a dull moment when Ian Wright is on a football pitch.

And when it comes to the art of goalscoring, there are very few better exponents of the art.

With both Crystal Palace and Arsenal, Wright's career has been a never-ending story of goals, goals and more goals.

He formed one of the most exciting strike partnerships in football with Mark Bright in the late 80s as Palace stormed into the top flight, and he has continued - and bettered - that record at Arsenal.

He is one of the most feared marksmen in the Premiership and it is testimony to his ability that when it looked as though he might leave Highbury there was a queue of clubs waiting to sign him.

And despite his failure to transform his club form onto the international stage, he continues to score goals in club football at an astonishing rate.

Having come into the game at the relatively late age of 22, he is determined to play at the top level for as long as he can, particularly as he is now rapidly closing in on Cliff Bastin's goalscoring record at Highbury.

Wright is desperate to add that record to his list of honours and that is bad news for defenders everywhere.

Career details

●**Represented:** England, Crystal Palace, Arsenal ●**Position:** Striker ●**Born:** Woolwich, 03.11.63 ●**Height:** 5ft 9in ●**Weight:** 11st 8lbs ●**Club honours:** FA Cup 1993; League Cup 1993; Golden Boot winner 1992 ●**International honours:** England 3 B caps, 26 full caps

Club League Record

Era	Club	Games	Goals
85/91	Crystal Palace	225	90
91-97	Arsenal	197	118

Cup Highlights

May 12 1990: Wright comes off the bench - after recovering from a broken leg - to score twice against Manchester United and force an FA Cup Final replay after a 3-3 draw.

May 15 1993: Wright scores another FA Cup Final goal, but again a replay is needed after a 1-1 draw with Sheffield Wednesday.

May 20 1993: Wright breaks the deadlock in the Final replay and Arsenal go on to win 2-1, thanks to a last-minute header from central defender Andy Linighan.

Wright On:

●I've seen other players get away with things that I'd never even contemplate, but people have this perception that I'm some kind of nutcase and I'm not like that at all. **Ian on his reputation.**

On Wright:

●How can Arsenal be boring when you watch players like Wright? I'd love him in my side. **Howard Kendall**

DID YOU KNOW THAT...

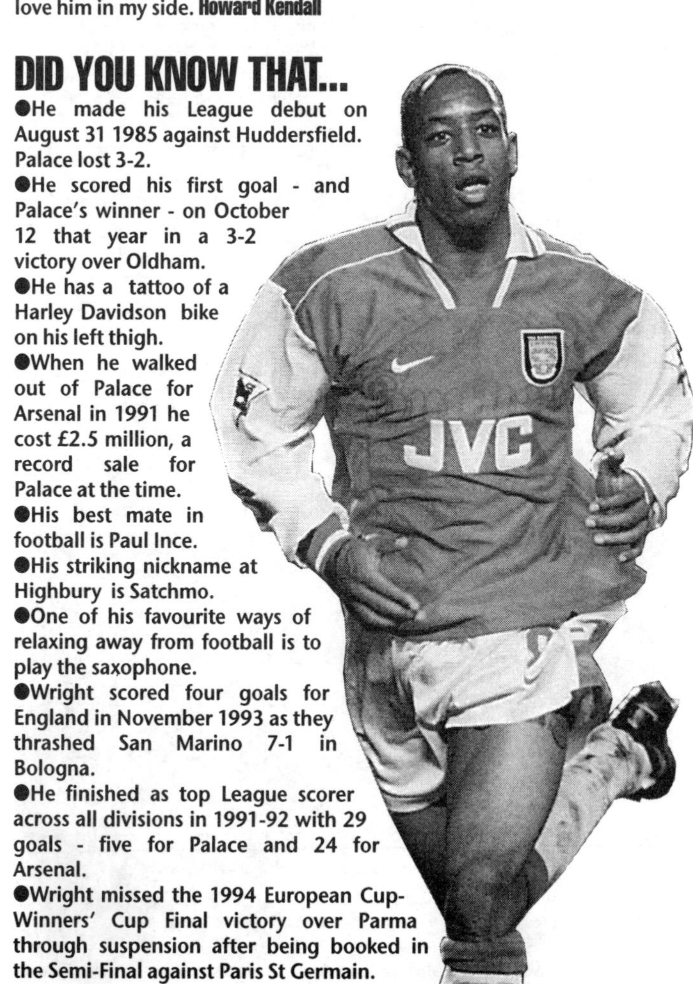

●He made his League debut on August 31 1985 against Huddersfield. Palace lost 3-2.

●He scored his first goal - and Palace's winner - on October 12 that year in a 3-2 victory over Oldham.

●He has a tattoo of a Harley Davidson bike on his left thigh.

●When he walked out of Palace for Arsenal in 1991 he cost £2.5 million, a record sale for Palace at the time.

●His best mate in football is Paul Ince.

●His striking nickname at Highbury is Satchmo.

●One of his favourite ways of relaxing away from football is to play the saxophone.

●Wright scored four goals for England in November 1993 as they thrashed San Marino 7-1 in Bologna.

●He finished as top League scorer across all divisions in 1991-92 with 29 goals - five for Palace and 24 for Arsenal.

●Wright missed the 1994 European Cup-Winners' Cup Final victory over Parma through suspension after being booked in the Semi-Final against Paris St Germain.

Semi Stunners

Manchester United have won their last ten FA Cup Semi-Finals, not having lost one since 1964, when they were beaten by West Ham.

Newcastle	1	Blackburn	1	
Nottm For	2	Plymouth	0	
Notts Co	2	Man City	2	
Portsmth	3	Bolton	1	
QPR	4	Aylesbury	0	
Reading	1	Oldham	3	
Scarboro	0	Watford	0	
Sheff Utd	0	Man Utd	2	
Southmptn	2	Southend	0	
Sunderld	1	Carlisle	1	
Swansea	1	Middlesbro	1	
Swindon	2	Marlow	0	
Tottenham	3	Altrinchm	0	
Walsall	1	Leeds U	1	
Wimbledn	1	Colchester	0	
Wrexham	2	Ipswich	1	
Wycombe	0	West Ham	2	
Arsenal	0	Millwall	2	r
Blackburn	1	Newcastle	2	r
Bristol R	0	Luton	1	r
Carlisle	1	Sunderld	3	r
Leeds U	5	Walsall	2	re
Liverpool	1	Birmghm C	1	rP
Man City	5	Notts Co	2	r
Middlesbro	1	Swansea	2	r
Stoke	1	Bristol C	3	re
Tranmere	3	Bury	0	r
Watford	2	Scarboro	0	r
West Brom	1	Coventry	2	r
FOURTH ROUND				
Bristol C	0	Everton	1	
Burnley	0	Liverpool	0	
Coventry	0	Norwich	0	
Leeds U	3	Oldham	2	
Luton	1	Southmptn	1	
Man City	1	Aston V	0	
Man Utd	5	Wrexham	2	
Millwall	0	Chelsea	0	
Newcastle	3	Swansea	0	
Nottm For	1	C.Palace	2	
Portsmth	0	Leicester	1	
QPR	1	West Ham	0	
Sheff Wed	0	Wolves	0	
Sunderld	1	Tottenham	4	
Tranmere	0	Wimbledn	2	
Watford	1	Swindon	0	
Chelsea	1	Millwall	1	rq
Liverpool	1	Burnley	0	r
Norwich	3	Coventry	1	re
Wolves	1	Sheff Wed	1	rP
FIFTH ROUND				
Everton	5	Norwich	0	
Liverpool	1	Wimbledn	1	
Man Utd	3	Leeds U	1	
Newcastle	3	Man City	1	
QPR	1	Millwall	0	
Tottenham	1	Southmptn	1	
Watford	0	C.Palace	0	
Wolves	1	Leicester	0	
C.Palace	1	Watford	0	re
Southmptn	2	Tottenham	6	re
Wimbledn	0	Liverpool	2	r
SIXTH ROUND				
C.Palace	1	Wolves	1	
Everton	1	Newcastle	0	
Liverpool	1	Tottenham	2	
Man Utd	2	QPR	0	
Wolves	1	C.Palace	4	r
SEMI-FINAL				
Man Utd	2	C.Palace	2	eN
Tottenham	1	Everton	4	N
Man Utd	2	C.Palace	0	rN
FINAL				
Everton	1	Man Utd	0	N

1996

FIRST ROUND				
Altrinchm	0	Crewe	2	
Barnet	2	Woking	2	
Barrow	2	Nuneaton	1	
Blackpool	2	Chester	1	
Bognor R	1	Ashford	1	
Bournemth	0	Bristol C	0	
Bradford	4	Burton Al	3	
Brentford	1	Farnborgh	1	
Burnley	1	Walsall	3	
Bury	0	Blyth S	2	
Canvy Is	2	Brighton	2	
Carlisle	1	Preston NE	2	
Cinderfd	2	Bromsgrv	1	
Exeter	0	Peterboro	1	
Fulham	7	Swansea	0	
Gravesend	2	Colchester	0	
Hartlepl	2	Darlingtn	4	
Hereford	2	Stevenage	1	
Hitchin	2	Bristol R	1	
Hull	0	Wrexham	0	
Kiddermst	2	Sutton U	2	
Kingst'an	5	Wisbech	1	
Mansfield	4	Doncaster	2	
Nwpt IOW	1	Enfield	1	
N'hamptn	1	Hayes	0	
Northwich	1	Scunthpe	3	
Oxford	9	Dorchstr	1	
Rochdale	5	Rotherhm	3	
Runcorn	1	Wigan Ath	1	
Rushden	1	Cardiff	3	
Scarboro	0	Chestrfld	2	
Shrewsby	11	Marine	2	

Eric Cantona celebrates his winning goal against Liverpool in the 1996 Final

WHAT A STAR ✪ GIANFRANCO ZOLA

The little Italian has won the hearts of Englishmen everywhere since joining Chelsea in October 1996. His flair and ability played a major part in The Blues' 1997 success, as they won the FA Cup for the first time in 27 years, and he chipped in with more than his fair share of goals along the way. One in particular will be remembered for ages. It came in the Semi-Final against Wimbledon when his skills in the box opened up the space for him to thunder an unstoppable shot past the helpless Neil Sullivan. And when you see class like that, no-one can deny the value of the foreigners to the English game.

Slough T	0	Plymouth	2	
Spennym'r	0	Colwyn By	1	
Stockport	5	Lincoln	0	
Swindon	4	Cambridge	1	
Telford U	2	Witton Ab	1	
Torquay	1	Leyton O	0	
Wycombe	1	Gillinghm	1	
York	0	Notts Co	1	
Ashford	0	Bognor R	1	r
Brighton	4	Canvy Is	1	r
Bristol C	0	Bournemth	1	r
Enfield	2	Nwpt IOW	1	r
Farnborgh	0	Brentford	4	r
Gillinghm	1	Wycombe	0	r
Sutton U	1	Kiddermst	1	rP
Wigan Ath	4	Runcorn	2	r
Woking	2	Barnet	1	re
Wrexham	0	Hull	0	rP
SECOND ROUND				
Barrow	0	Wigan Ath	4	
Blackpool	2	Colwyn By	0	
Bournemth	0	Brentford	1	
Bradford	2	Preston NE	1	
Cinderfd	1	Gravesend	1	
Crewe	2	Mansfield	0	
Enfield	1	Woking	1	
Fulham	0	Brighton	0	
Gillinghm	3	Hitchin	0	
Hereford	2	Sutton U	0	
Kingst'an	1	Plymouth	2	
Oxford	2	N'hamptn	0	
Peterboro	4	Bognor R	0	
Rochdale	2	Darlingtn	2	
Scunthpe	1	Shrewsby	1	
Stockport	2	Blyth S	0	
Swindon	2	Cardiff	0	
Telford U	0	Notts Co	2	
Torquay	1	Walsall	1	
Wrexham	3	Chestrfld	2	
Brighton	0	Fulham	0	rq
Darlingtn	0	Rochdale	1	r
Gravesend	3	Cinderfd	0	r
Shrewsby	2	Scunthpe	1	r
Walsall	8	Torquay	4	re
Woking	2	Enfield	1	r
THIRD ROUND				
Arsenal	1	Sheff Utd	1	
Aston V	3	Gravesend	0	
Barnsley	0	Oldham	0	

Birmghm C	1	Wolves	1	
Bradford	0	Bolton	3	
Charlton	2	Sheff Wed	0	
Chelsea	1	Newcastle	1	
Crewe	4	West Brom	3	
C.Palace	0	Port Vale	0	
Derby	2	Leeds U	4	
Everton	2	Stockport	2	
Fulham	1	Shrewsby	1	
Grimsby	7	Luton	1	
Hereford	1	Tottenham	1	
Huddersfld	2	Blackpool	1	
Ipswich	0	Blackburn	0	
Leicester	0	Man City	0	
Liverpool	7	Rochdale	0	
Man Utd	2	Sunderld	2	
Millwall	3	Oxford	3	
Norwich	1	Brentford	2	
Notts Co	1	Middlesbro	2	
Peterboro	1	Wrexham	0	
Plymouth	1	Coventry	3	
Reading	3	Gillinghm	1	
Southmptn	3	Portsmth	0	
Stoke	1	Nottm For	1	
Swindon	2	Woking	0	
Tranmere	0	QPR	2	
Walsall	1	Wigan Ath	0	
Watford	1	Wimbledn	1	
West Ham	2	Southend	0	
Blackburn	0	Ipswich	1	re
Man City	5	Leicester	0	r
Newcastle	2	Chelsea	2	rq
Nottm For	2	Stoke	0	r
Oldham	2	Barnsley	1	r
Oxford	1	Millwall	0	r
Port Vale	4	C.Palace	3	re
Sheff Utd	1	Arsenal	0	r
Shrewsby	2	Fulham	1	r
Stockport	2	Everton	3	r
Sunderld	1	Man Utd	2	r
Tottenham	5	Hereford	1	r
FOURTH ROUND				
Bolton	0	Leeds U	1	
Charlton	3	Brentford	2	
Coventry	2	Man City	2	
Everton	2	Port Vale	2	
Huddersfld	2	Peterboro	0	
Ipswich	1	Walsall	0	
Middlesbro	0	Wimbledn	0	

Nottm For	1	Oxford	1	
QPR	1	Chelsea	2	
Reading	0	Man Utd	3	
Sheff Utd	0	Aston V	1	
Shrewsby	0	Liverpool	4	
Southmptn	1	Crewe	1	
Swindon	1	Oldham	0	
Tottenham	1	Wolves	1	
West Ham	1	Grimsby	1	
Crewe	2	Southmptn	3	r
Grimsby	3	West Ham	0	r
Man City	2	Coventry	1	r
Oxford	0	Nottm For	3	r
Port Vale	2	Everton	1	r
Wimbledn	1	Middlesbro	0	r
Wolves	0	Tottenham	2	r
FIFTH ROUND				
Grimsby	0	Chelsea	0	
Huddersfld	2	Wimbledn	2	
Ipswich	1	Aston V	3	
Leeds U	0	Port Vale	0	
Liverpool	2	Charlton	1	
Man Utd	2	Man City	1	
Nottm For	2	Tottenham	2	
Swindon	1	Southmptn	1	
Chelsea	4	Grimsby	1	r
Port Vale	1	Leeds U	2	r
Southmptn	2	Swindon	0	r
Tottenham	1	Nottm For	1	rq
Wimbledn	3	Huddersfld	1	r
SIXTH ROUND				
Chelsea	2	Wimbledn	2	
Leeds U	0	Liverpool	0	
Man Utd	2	Southmptn	0	
Nottm For	0	Aston V	1	
Liverpool	3	Leeds U	0	r
Wimbledn	1	Chelsea	3	r
SEMI-FINAL				
Liverpool	3	Aston V	0	N
Man Utd	2	Chelsea	1	N
FINAL				
Man Utd	1	Liverpool	0	N

1997

FIRST ROUND				
Ashford	2	Dagenham	2	
Blackpool	1	Wigan Ath	0	
Boreham W	1	Rushden	1	
Boston U	3	Morecambe	0	

Brentford	2	Bournemth	0	
Bristol R	1	Exeter	2	
Bromley	1	Enfield	3	
Burnley	2	Lincoln	1	
Cambridge	3	Welling U	0	
Cardiff	2	Hendon	0	
Carlisle	6	Shepshed D	0	
Chester	3	Stalyb C	0	
Chestrfld	1	Bury	0	
Colchester	1	Wycombe	2	
Crewe	4	Kiddermst	1	
Farnborgh	2	Barnet	2	
Gillinghm	1	Hereford	0	
Hartlepl	0	York	0	
Hednesfd	2	Southport	1	
Leyton O	2	Mert Tyd	1	
Macclesfd	0	Rochdale	2	
Mansfield	4	Consett	0	
Newcstl T	0	Notts Co	2	
N'hamptn	0	Watford	1	
Northwich	2	Walsall	2	
Peterboro	0	Chelthnm	0	
Plymouth	5	Fulham	0	
Preston NE	4	Altrinchm	1	
Runcorn	1	Darlingtn	4	
Scunthpe	4	Rotherhm	1	
Shrewsby	1	Scarboro	1	
Stevenage	2	Hayes	2	
Stockport	2	Doncaster	1	
Sudbury T	0	Brighton	0	
Swansea	1	Bristol C	1	
Torquay	0	Luton	1	
Whitby T	0	Hull	0	N
Wisbech	1	St Albns C	2	
Woking	2	Millwall	2	
Wrexham	1	Colwyn By	1	
Barnet	1	Farnborgh	0	r
Brighton	1	Sudbury T	1	rq
Bristol C	1	Swansea	0	r
Chelthnm	1	Peterboro	3	re
Dagenham	1	Ashford	1	rq
Hayes	0	Stevenage	2	r
Hull	8	Whitby T	4	re
Millwall	0	Woking	1	r
Rushden	2	Boreham W	3	r
Scarboro	1	Shrewsby	0	r
Walsall	3	Northwich	1	r
Wrexham	2	Colwyn By	0	r
York	3	Hartlepl	0	r
SECOND ROUND				
Barnet	3	Wycombe	3	
Blackpool	0	Hednesfd	1	
Bristol C	9	St Albns C	2	
Cambridge	0	Woking	2	
Cardiff	0	Gillinghm	2	
Carlisle	1	Darlingtn	0	
Chester	1	Boston U	0	
Chestrfld	2	Scarboro	0	
Enfield	1	Peterboro	1	
Hull	1	Crewe	5	
Leyton O	1	Stevenage	2	
Luton	2	Boreham W	1	
Mansfield	0	Stockport	3	
Notts Co	3	Rochdale	1	
Plymouth	4	Exeter	1	
Preston NE	2	York	3	
Sudbury T	1	Brentford	3	
Walsall	1	Burnley	1	
Watford	5	Ashford	0	
Wrexham	2	Scunthpe	2	
Burnley	1	Walsall	1	rP
Peterboro	4	Enfield	1	r
Scunthpe	2	Wrexham	3	re
Wycombe	3	Barnet	2	r
THIRD ROUND				

Di-namite

Roberto Di Matteo's goal for Chelsea against Middlesbrough after 43 seconds of the 1997 Final is the fastest ever scored in a Cup Final at Wembley.

It was so near, yet so far away for Chesterfield in 1997

GIANTKILLERS

1997 Chesterfield 1 Nott'm Forest 0

A wonderful tonic for fans who feel that the big clubs now buy too much success. Chesterfield, the fourth oldest club in England whose best FA Cup performances had been two trips to the heights of the Fifth Round, got very close to Wembley in 1997 with a series of splendid performances by a bunch of whole-hearted players led by an inspirational manager, former Tottenham and Ipswich forward John Duncan. A Tom Curtis penalty was enough to beat Forest before The Spireites eventually fell at the Semi-Final hurdle to Middlesbrough, although it took the Premiership side two attempts after a thrilling 3-3 draw in the first game.

Arsenal	1	Sunderld	1	
Barnsley	2	Oldham	0	
Birmghm C	2	Stevenage	0	
Blackburn	1	Port Vale	0	
Brentford	0	Man City	1	
Carlisle	1	Tranmere	0	
Charlton	1	Newcastle	1	
Chelsea	3	West Brom	0	
Chestrfld	2	Bristol C	0	
Coventry	1	Woking	1	
Crewe	1	Wimbledn	1	
C.Palace	2	Leeds U	2	
Everton	3	Swindon	0	
Gillinghm	0	Derby	2	
Hednesfd	1	York	0	
Leicester	2	Southend	0	
Liverpool	1	Burnley	0	
Luton	1	Bolton	1	
Man Utd	2	Tottenham	0	
Middlesbro	6	Chester	0	
Norwich	1	Sheff Utd	0	
Nottm For	3	Ipswich	0	
Notts Co	0	Aston V	0	
Plymouth	0	Peterboro	1	
QPR	1	Huddersfld	1	
Reading	3	Southmptn	1	
Sheff Wed	9	Grimsby	9	
Stoke	0	Stockport	2	
Watford	2	Oxford	0	
Wolves	1	Portsmth	2	
Wrexham	1	West Ham	1	
Wycombe	0	Bradford	2	
Aston V	3	Notts Co	0	r
Bolton	6	Luton	2	r
Huddersfld	1	QPR	2	r
Leeds U	1	C.Palace	0	r
Newcastle	2	Charlton	1	re
Sunderld	0	Arsenal	2	r
West Ham	0	Wrexham	1	r
Wimbledn	2	Crewe	0	r
Woking	1	Coventry	2	r
FOURTH ROUND				
Arsenal	0	Leeds U	1	
Birmghm C	3	Stockport	1	
Blackburn	1	Coventry	2	
Bolton	2	Chestrfld	3	
Carlisle	0	Sheff Wed	2	
Chelsea	4	Liverpool	2	
Derby	3	Aston V	1	
Everton	2	Bradford	3	
Leicester	2	Norwich	1	
Man City	3	Watford	1	
Man Utd	1	Wimbledn	1	
Middlesbro	3	Hednesfd	2	
Newcastle	1	Nottm For	2	
Peterboro	2	Wrexham	4	
Portsmth	3	Reading	0	
QPR	3	Barnsley	2	
Wimbledn	1	Man Utd	0	r
FIFTH ROUND				
Birmghm C	1	Wrexham	3	
Bradford	0	Sheff Wed	1	
Chestrfld	1	Nottm For	0	
Derby	3	Coventry	2	
Leeds U	2	Portsmth	3	
Leicester	2	Chelsea	2	
Man City	0	Middlesbro	1	
Wimbledn	2	QPR	1	
Chelsea	1	Leicester	0	re
SIXTH ROUND				
Chestrfld	1	Wrexham	0	
Derby	0	Middlesbro	2	
Portsmth	1	Chelsea	4	
Sheff Wed	0	Wimbledn	2	
SEMI-FINAL				
Chelsea	3	Wimbledn	0	N
Middlesbro	3	Chestrfld	3	eN
Middlesbro	3	Chestrfld	0	rN
FINAL				
Chelsea	2	Middlesbro	0	N

French Fancy

When Eric Cantona collected the FA Cup for Manchester United after their 1-0 win over Liverpool in 1996 - he scored the winner - he became the first Frenchman to captain a winning team in the Final.

Roberto Di Matteo scores the fastest ever FA Cup Final goal, after just 43 seconds against Middlesbrough

1961-1969

SLOW START

The Football League Cup was born in 1961 and was the brainchild of Alan Hardaker, who was the secretary of the Football League for more than 20 years.

It was a competition designed exclusively for the 92 League clubs, with a two-legged Final to be played home and away at the grounds of the Finalists.

But at the outset the competition met with much criticism. It was condemned for adding another burden to the already congested fixture list and six of the big clubs refused to enter.

However, the competition did get off the ground and Aston Villa were the first winners, beating Rotherham 3-2 on aggregate after recovering from a 2-0 deficit from the first game.

Norwich, Birmingham, Leicester, Chelsea and West Brom all won the Cup in its two-legged format, before the face of the competition was changed forever in 1967.

The Final became a one-off affair at Wembley and this, together with the carrot of a place in the Fairs Cup (later the UEFA Cup) for the winners, earned the competition a prominent place in football's priorities.

The first Final at Wembley was between West Brom, of the First Division, and QPR, of the Third, and it turned out to be quite a match.

At half-time, Albion were 2-0 up and cruising but Rangers, inspired by the wonderfully talented Rodney Marsh, stormed back after the break to win 3-2.

Two years later, little Swindon emulated that triumph by beating mighty Arsenal 3-1 in the Final at Wembley, to prove that the FA Cup isn't the only competition where fairytales can come true.

Final Fury

Fixture congestion - as feared by the competition's critics - meant that the first Final was not played until almost a year had passed. The first games were on 26th September 1960 but the two-legged Final did not take place until 22th August and 5th September 1961.

Lights Out

The original plan when the League Cup began in 1961 was for all matches to be on midweek evenings, but some had to be held in the afternoon because not every club had floodlights.

Brum's Rush

Birmingham won their only major trophy, the League Cup, in 1962-63 - in a season in which they just avoided relegation and conceded 103 goals in 53 competitive matches.

KEY League Cup
A = home team won on away goals
a (end of line) = away team won on away goals
a = abandoned
b = bye
B = both teams went through
d = disqualified
D = home team disqualified
d (end of line) = away team disqualifed
e = extra-time
E = both teams were disqualified
N = neutral ground
nr = home team bye to next round
nrd = away team bye to next round
P = home team won on penalties
q = away team won on penalties
r = replay
s = scratched
T = home team went through on a toss of a coin
v = void game, ordered to be replayed
w = walkover

1961

FIRST ROUND				
Bristol R	2	Fulham	1	
Chester	2	Leyton O	2	
Colchester	4	Newcastle	1	
Coventry	4	Barrow	2	
Darlingtn	2	C.Palace	0	
Everton	3	Accringtn	1	
Exeter	1	Man Utd	1	
Hull	0	Bolton	0	
Ipswich	0	Barnsley	2	
Leicester	4	Mansfield	0	
Lincoln	2	Bradfd PA	2	
Middlesbro	3	Cardiff	4	
Millwall	1	Chelsea	7	
Newport	2	Southmptn	2	
Oldham	2	Hartlepl	1	
Plymouth	2	Southport	0	
Preston NE	4	Peterboro	1	
QPR	2	Port Vale	2	
Rochdale	1	Scunthpe	1	
Stockport	2	Carlisle	0	
Watford	2	Derby	5	
West Ham	3	Charlton	1	
York	1	Blackburn	3	
Bolton	5	Hull	1	r
Bradfd PA	1	Lincoln	0	r
Leyton O	1	Chester	0	r
Man Utd	4	Exeter	1	r
Port Vale	3	QPR	1	re
Scunthpe	0	Rochdale	1	r
Southmptn	2	Newport	2	re
Southmptn	5	Newport	3	r2
SECOND ROUND				
Aldershot	1	Bristol C	1	
Aston V	4	Huddersfld	1	
Bolton	6	Grimsby	2	
Bournemth	1	Crewe	1	
Bradford	2	Man Utd	1	
Bradfd PA	0	Birmghm C	1	
Brentford	4	Sunderld	3	
Bury	3	Sheff Utd	1	
Cardiff	0	Burnley	4	
Chelsea	4	Workingtn	2	
Colchester	0	Southmptn	2	
Darlingtn	3	West Ham	2	
Derby	3	Barnsley	0	
Doncaster	3	Stoke	1	
Everton	3	Walsall	1	
Gillinghm	1	Preston NE	1	
Leeds U	0	Blackpool	0	
Leicester	1	Rotherhm	2	
Leyton O	0	Chestrfld	1	
Liverpool	1	Luton	1	
Man City	3	Stockport	0	
N'hamptn	1	Wrexham	1	
Norwich	6	Oldham	2	
Nottm For	2	Halifax	0	
Notts Co	1	Brighton	3	
Plymouth	1	Torquay	1	
Port Vale	0	Tranmere	2	
Portsmth	2	Coventry	0	
Reading	3	Bristol R	5	
Rochdale	5	Southend	2	
Swansea	1	Blackburn	2	
Swindon	1	Shrewsby	1	
Blackpool	1	Leeds U	3	re
Bristol C	3	Aldershot	0	r
Crewe	2	Bournemth	0	re
Luton	2	Liverpool	5	r
Plymouth	2	Torquay	1	r
Preston NE	3	Gillinghm	0	r
Shrewsby	2	Swindon	2	re
Wrexham	2	N'hamptn	0	r
Swindon	0	Shrewsby	2	r2e
THIRD ROUND				
Birmghm C	0	Plymouth	0	
Blackburn	2	Rochdale	1	
Brentford	1	Burnley	1	
Brighton	0	Wrexham	2	
Chestrfld	0	Leeds U	4	
Darlingtn	1	Bolton	2	
Derby	1	Norwich	4	
Doncaster	0	Chelsea	7	
Everton	3	Bury	1	
Liverpool	1	Southmptn	2	
Nottm For	2	Bristol C	1	
Portsmth	2	Man City	0	
Preston NE	3	Aston V	3	
Rotherhm	2	Bristol R	0	
Shrewsby	2	Bradford	1	
Tranmere	2	Crewe	0	
Aston V	3	Preston NE	1	r
Burnley	2	Brentford	1	r
Plymouth	3	Birmghm C	1	r
FOURTH ROUND				
Aston V	3	Plymouth	3	
Blackburn	1	Wrexham	1	
Bolton	0	Rotherhm	2	
Burnley	2	Nottm For	1	
Portsmth	1	Chelsea	0	
Shrewsby	1	Norwich	0	
Southmptn	5	Leeds U	4	
Tranmere	0	Everton	4	
Plymouth	0	Aston V	0	r
Wrexham	3	Blackburn	1	re
Plymouth	3	Aston V	5	r2
FIFTH ROUND				
Aston V	3	Wrexham	0	
Rotherhm	3	Portsmth	0	
Shrewsby	2	Everton	1	
Southmptn	2	Burnley	4	

By George

George Graham played in Finals for three clubs in the 1960s - Aston Villa (lost), Chelsea (won), and Arsenal (lost twice).

WHAT A STAR ✪ PETER McPARLAND

Irish winger Peter McParland usually rose to the big occasion. He scored twice on his debut for Northern Ireland in 1954, equalised for Aston Villa in three FA Cup-ties in 1958 and scored twice in the Final against Manchester United, then hit the extra-time winner when Villa - two down after the first-leg - beat Second Division Rotherham 3-2 in the return to win the first League Cup Final in 1961. He later played for Wolves and Plymouth, and scored 123 League goals in a career total of 352 games.

SEMI-FINAL FIRST-LEG				
Burnley	1	Aston V	1	
Rotherhm	3	Shrewsby	2	
SEMI-FINAL SECOND-LEG				
Aston V	2	Burnley	2	e
agg score Aston V 3 - Burnley 3				
Shrewsby	1	Rotherhm	1	e
Rotherhm win 4-3 on agg				
SEMI-FINAL REPLAY				
Burnley	1	Aston V	2	rN
FINAL FIRST-LEG				
Rotherhm	2	Aston V	0	
FINAL SECOND-LEG				
Aston V	3	Rotherhm	0	e
Aston V win 3-2 on agg				

1962

FIRST ROUND				
Barnsley	3	Southport	2	
Barrow	0	Portsmth	2	
Birmghm C	1	Swindon	1	
Blackpool	2	Port Vale	1	
Bolton	1	Sunderld	1	
Bournemth	2	Torquay	2	
Bradford	3	Aston V	4	
Bristol R	2	Hartlepl	1	
Bury	5	Brighton	1	
Cardiff	2	Wrexham	0	
Carlisle	1	Huddersfld	1	
Chestrfld	2	Norwich	3	
Colchester	1	Crewe	2	
Darlingtn	0	Rotherhm	1	
Doncaster	3	Grimsby	2	
Fulham	1	Sheff Utd	1	
Hull	4	Bradfd PA	2	
Ipswich	4	Man City	2	
Leeds U	4	Brentford	1	
Lincoln	1	Accringtn	0	
Luton	2	N'hamptn	1	
Mansfield	5	Exeter	2	
Millwall	1	Walsall	2	
Newcastle	2	Scunthpe	0	
Newport	0	Shrewsby	0	
Nottm For	4	Gillinghm	1	
Notts Co	2	Derby	2	
Oldham	1	Charlton	4	
Peterboro	1	Blackburn	3	
Preston NE	3	Aldershot	1	

Strange but true!

Although the League Cup was born in 1960-61, the idea of a competition exclusively for Football League members was originally discussed as early as 1892.

QPR	5	C.Palace	2	
Reading	4	Chester	2	
Southmptn	0	Rochdale	0	
Southend	0	Stoke	1	
Stockport	0	Leyton O	1	
Tranmere	3	Middlesbro	6	
Watford	3	Halifax	0	
West Ham	3	Plymouth	2	
Workingtn	3	Coventry	0	
York	3	Bristol C	0	
Derby	3	Notts Co	2	re
Huddersfld	3	Carlisle	0	r
Rochdale	2	Southmptn	1	r
Sheff Utd	4	Fulham	0	r
Shrewsby	3	Newport	1	r
Sunderld	1	Bolton	0	r
Swindon	2	Birmghm C	0	r
Torquay	0	Bournemth	1	r
SECOND ROUND				
Barnsley	1	Workingtn	3	
Bristol R	1	Blackburn	1	
Bury	3	Hull	4	
Charlton	4	Stoke	1	
Leeds U	3	Huddersfld	2	
Leyton O	1	Blackpool	1	
Luton	0	Rotherhm	0	
Mansfield	1	Cardiff	1	
Middlesbro	3	Crewe	1	
Norwich	3	Lincoln	2	
Portsmth	1	Derby	1	
Preston NE	3	Swindon	1	
QPR	1	Nottm For	2	
Rochdale	4	Doncaster	0	

Sheff Utd	2	Newcastle	2	
Shrewsby	1	Bournemth	3	
Sunderld	5	Walsall	2	
Swansea	3	Ipswich	3	
Watford	3	Reading	1	
West Ham	1	Aston V	3	
York	2	Leicester	1	
Blackburn	4	Bristol R	0	r
Blackpool	5	Leyton O	1	r
Cardiff	2	Mansfield	1	r
Derby	2	Portsmth	4	r
Ipswich	3	Swansea	2	r
Newcastle	0	Sheff Utd	2	r
Rotherhm	2	Luton	0	r
THIRD ROUND				
Aston V	2	Ipswich	3	
Bournemth	3	Cardiff	0	
Norwich	3	Middlesbro	2	
Nottm For	1	Blackburn	2	
Preston NE	0	Rotherhm	0	
Rochdale	1	Charlton	0	
Sheff Utd	1	Portsmth	0	
Sunderld	2	Hull	1	
Workingtn	0	Blackpool	1	
York	1	Watford	1	
Rotherhm	3	Preston NE	0	r
Watford	2	York	2	re
York	3	Watford	2	r2
FOURTH ROUND				
Blackburn	4	Ipswich	1	
Rotherhm	1	Leeds U	1	
York	1	Bournemth	0	
Leeds U	1	Rotherhm	2	r
FIFTH ROUND				
Blackpool	0	Sheff Utd	0	
Rochdale	2	York	1	
Rotherhm	0	Blackburn	1	
Sunderld	1	Norwich	4	
Sheff Utd	0	Blackpool	2	r
SEMI-FINAL FIRST-LEG				
Norwich	4	Blackpool	1	
Rochdale	3	Blackburn	1	
SEMI-FINAL SECOND-LEG				
Blackburn	2	Rochdale	1	
Rochdale win 4-3 on agg				
Blackpool	2	Norwich	0	
Norwich win 4-3 on agg				
FINAL FIRST-LEG				

GIANTKILLERS

1965-66 Newcastle 3 Peterborough 4

Peterborough had only a moderate season in the Third Division, finishing mid-table, but surprised everybody by their exploits in the League Cup. After getting a bye in the First Round, manager Gordon Clark's battlers scored four goals in each of four successive ties, beating Newcastle (First Division) 4-3 away, Charlton (Second) 4-3 at home, Third Division runners-up Millwall 4-1 away, and Burnley, who finished third in the First Division, by a remarkable 4-0 at home. Even the eventual winners, West Bromwich, had to battle before knocking Posh out of the two-leg Semi-Final on a 3-6 aggregate.

Rochdale	0	Norwich	3	

FINAL SECOND-LEG

Norwich	1	Rochdale	0	

Norwich win 4-0 on agg

1963

FIRST ROUND

Aldershot	2	Exeter	0	
Barrow	3	Workingtn	2	
Bradford	2	Doncaster	2	
Brentford	3	Wrexham	0	
Chester	2	Stockport	0	
Crewe	2	Oldham	3	
Darlingtn	1	Chestrfld	0	
Halifax	2	Mansfield	3	
Hartlepl	1	Barnsley	1	
Newport	2	Gillinghm	1	
Shrewsby	3	Millwall	1	
Southport	0	Rochdale	0	
Torquay	2	Oxford	0	
Tranmere	2	Carlisle	3	
Watford	1	Colchester	2	
York	2	Lincoln	2	
Barnsley	2	Hartlepl	1	r
Doncaster	2	Bradford	0	r
Lincoln	2	York	0	r
Rochdale	1	Southport	2	re

SECOND ROUND

Aldershot	0	Newport	3	
Aston V	6	Peterboro	1	
Barnsley	3	Grimsby	2	
Barrow	3	Shrewsby	1	
Birmghm C	5	Doncaster	0	
Bradfd PA	3	Huddersfld	1	
Brentford	1	Sheff Utd	4	
Brighton	1	Portsmth	5	
Bristol C	1	Rotherhm	2	
Bristol R	2	Port Vale	0	
Bury	2	Lincoln	2	
Cardiff	5	Reading	1	
Chester	2	Mansfield	2	
Coventry	3	Swansea	2	
Derby	1	Blackburn	1	
Fulham	4	Bournemth	0	
Hull	2	Middlesbro	2	
Leeds U	2	C.Palace	1	
Leicester	4	Charlton	4	
Man City	0	Blackpool	0	
Newcastle	1	Leyton O	1	
N'hamptn	2	Colchester	0	
Norwich	4	Bolton	0	
QPR	1	Preston NE	2	
Southmptn	1	Scunthpe	1	
Southend	2	Notts Co	3	
Southport	1	Luton	3	
Sunderld	7	Oldham	1	
Swindon	4	Darlingtn	0	
Torquay	1	Carlisle	2	
Walsall	1	Stoke	2	
West Ham	6	Plymouth	0	
Blackburn	3	Derby	1	r
Blackpool	3	Man City	3	re
Charlton	2	Leicester	1	r
Leyton O	4	Newcastle	2	re
Lincoln	2	Bury	3	r
Mansfield	0	Chester	1	r
Middlesbro	1	Hull	1	re
Scunthpe	2	Southmptn	2	re
Hull	3	Middlesbro	0	r2e
Man City	4	Blackpool	2	r2N
Southmptn	0	Scunthpe	3	r2N

THIRD ROUND

Aston V	3	Stoke	1	
Barnsley	1	Luton	2	
Barrow	1	Birmghm C	1	
Blackburn	4	Leeds U	0	
Bradfd PA	2	Charlton	2	
Bristol R	2	Cardiff	0	
Bury	3	Sheff Utd	1	
Carlisle	1	Norwich	1	
Hull	1	Fulham	2	
Leyton O	9	Chester	2	
Newport	1	Man City	2	
N'hamptn	1	Preston NE	1	
Notts Co	5	Swindon	0	
Portsmth	5	Coventry	1	
Rotherhm	3	West Ham	1	
Sunderld	2	Scunthpe	0	
Birmghm C	5	Barrow	1	r
Charlton	1	Bradfd PA	0	r
Norwich	5	Carlisle	0	r
Preston NE	2	N'hamptn	1	r

FOURTH ROUND

Aston V	6	Preston NE	2	
Birmghm C	3	Notts Co	2	
Blackburn	4	Rotherhm	1	
Bury	3	Bristol R	1	
Leyton O	3	Charlton	2	
Man City	1	Luton	0	
Norwich	1	Fulham	0	
Portsmth	0	Sunderld	0	
Sunderld	2	Portsmth	1	r

FIFTH ROUND

Aston V	4	Norwich	1	
Birmghm C	6	Man City	0	
Leyton O	0	Bury	2	
Sunderld	3	Blackburn	2	

SEMI-FINAL FIRST-LEG

Birmghm C	3	Bury	2	
Sunderld	1	Aston V	3	

SEMI-FINAL SECOND-LEG

Aston V	0	Sunderld	0	

Aston V win 3-1 on agg

Bury	1	Birmghm C	1	

Birmghm C win 4-3 on agg

FINAL FIRST-LEG

Birmghm C	3	Aston V	1	

FINAL SECOND-LEG

Aston V	0	Birmghm C	0	

Birmghm C win 3-1 on agg

1964

FIRST ROUND

Strange but true!

Maurice Cook scored the first League Cup goal, for Fulham, but his team lost 2-1 to Bristol Rovers.

O's Dear

Leyton Orient beat Chester 9-2 in a League Cup match in 1962-63 - but scored only 37 League goals all season and finished bottom of Division One, in the only season they have spent there.

Aldershot	3	QPR	1	
Bradfd PA	7	Bradford	3	
Carlisle	3	Crewe	2	
Chestrfld	0	Halifax	1	
Darlingtn	2	Barnsley	2	
Doncaster	0	York	0	
Gillinghm	4	Bristol C	2	
Lincoln	3	Hartlepl	2	
Mansfield	2	Watford	1	
Newport	3	Millwall	4	
Oldham	3	Workingtn	5	
Oxford	0	Exeter	1	
Reading	1	Brentford	1	
Rochdale	1	Chester	1	
Shrewsby	1	Bristol R	1	
Southport	2	Barrow	1	
Torquay	1	Brighton	2	
Tranmere	2	Stockport	0	
Barnsley	6	Darlingtn	2	r
Brentford	2	Reading	0	r
Bristol R	6	Shrewsby	2	r
Chester	2	Rochdale	5	r
York	3	Doncaster	0	r

SECOND ROUND

Aston V	3	Barnsley	1	
Blackpool	7	Charlton	1	
Bradfd PA	2	Middlesbro	2	
Brentford	0	Bournemth	0	
Brighton	1	N'hamptn	1	
Bristol R	2	C.Palace	0	
Cardiff	2	Wrexham	2	
Colchester	5	Fulham	3	
Gillinghm	3	Bury	0	
Grimsby	1	Rotherhm	3	
Halifax	4	Rochdale	2	
Hull	1	Exeter	0	
Ipswich	0	Walsall	0	
Leeds U	5	Mansfield	1	
Leicester	2	Aldershot	0	
Luton	3	Coventry	4	
Man City	2	Carlisle	0	
Millwall	3	Peterboro	2	
Newcastle	3	Preston NE	0	
Norwich	2	Birmghm C	0	
Notts Co	2	Blackburn	1	
Plymouth	2	Huddersfld	2	
Portsmth	3	Derby	2	
Scunthpe	2	Stoke	2	
Sheff Utd	1	Bolton	2	
Southend	2	Port Vale	1	
Swansea	3	Sunderld	1	
Swindon	3	Chelsea	0	

Tranmere	2	Southmptn	0	
West Ham	2	Leyton O	1	
Workingtn	3	Southport	0	
York	1	Lincoln	1	
Bournemth	2	Brentford	0	r
Huddersfld	3	Plymouth	3	re
Lincoln	2	York	0	r
Middlesbro	2	Bradfd PA	3	r
N'hamptn	3	Brighton	2	r
Stoke	3	Scunthpe	3	re
Walsall	1	Ipswich	0	r
Wrexham	1	Cardiff	1	re
Plymouth	1	Huddersfld	2	r2N
Stoke	1	Scunthpe	0	r2N
Wrexham	3	Cardiff	0	r2

THIRD ROUND

Aston V	0	West Ham	2	
Bournemth	2	Newcastle	1	
Bristol R	1	Gillinghm	1	
Colchester	4	N'hamptn	1	
Halifax	2	Walsall	0	
Hull	0	Man City	3	
Leeds U	2	Swansea	0	
Millwall	1	Lincoln	1	
Norwich	1	Blackpool	0	
Notts Co	3	Bradfd PA	2	
Rotherhm	4	Coventry	2	
Stoke	3	Bolton	0	
Swindon	3	Southend	0	
Tranmere	1	Leicester	2	
Workingtn	1	Huddersfld	0	
Wrexham	3	Portsmth	5	
Gillinghm	3	Bristol R	1	r
Lincoln	1	Millwall	2	r

FOURTH ROUND

Halifax	1	Norwich	7	
Leicester	3	Gillinghm	1	
Man City	3	Leeds U	1	
Notts Co	3	Portsmth	2	
Rotherhm	5	Millwall	2	
Stoke	2	Bournemth	1	
Swindon	3	West Ham	3	
Workingtn	2	Colchester	1	
West Ham	4	Swindon	1	r

FIFTH ROUND

Norwich	1	Leicester	1	
Notts Co	0	Man City	1	
Stoke	3	Rotherhm	2	
West Ham	6	Workingtn	0	
Leicester	2	Norwich	1	re

SEMI-FINAL FIRST-LEG

Leicester	4	West Ham	3
Stoke	2	Man City	0

SEMI-FINAL SECOND-LEG

Man City	1	Stoke	0

Stoke win 2-1 on agg

West Ham	0	Leicester	2

Leicester win 6-3 on agg

FINAL FIRST-LEG

Stoke	1	Leicester	1

FINAL SECOND-LEG

Leicester	3	Stoke	2

Leicester win 4-3 on agg

1965

FIRST ROUND

Barnsley	2	Lincoln	1	
Bradford	2	York	0	
Brentford	0	Southend	2	
Brighton	2	Millwall	2	
Chester	3	Wrexham	0	
Chestrfld	3	Hartlepl	0	
Colchester	1	Torquay	1	
Doncaster	1	Bradfd PA	0	
Exeter	2	Gillinghm	0	
Halifax	1	Darlingtn	3	
Notts Co	3	Newport	2	
Port Vale	0	Luton	1	
QPR	5	Aldershot	2	
Southport	0	Carlisle	0	
Stockport	1	Rochdale	3	
Tranmere	2	Crewe	0	
Walsall	1	Oxford	1	
Workingtn	9	Barrow	1	
Carlisle	1	Southport	0	r
Millwall	1	Brighton	0	r
Oxford	6	Walsall	1	r
Torquay	3	Colchester	0	r

Terry's All Gold

One of Chelsea's goals when they beat Leicester to win the 1965 Final was scored by Terry Venables - a penalty against Gordon Banks.

SECOND ROUND

Birmghm C	0	Chelsea	3	
Blackpool	3	Newcastle	0	
Bolton	1	Blackburn	5	
Bournemth	0	N'hamptn	2	
Bristol R	0	Chestrfld	2	
Bury	1	Darlingtn	0	
Carlisle	4	Bristol C	1	
Charlton	2	Middlesbro	1	
Chester	5	Derby	4	
Coventry	4	Ipswich	1	
Doncaster	1	Preston NE	0	
Exeter	3	Bradford	5	
Fulham	2	Oxford	0	
Grimsby	3	Oldham	1	
Hull	0	Southend	0	
Leeds U	3	Huddersfld	2	
Leicester	0	Peterboro	0	
Leyton O	3	Barnsley	0	
Luton	0	Aston V	1	
Man City	3	Mansfield	5	
Millwall	1	Norwich	2	
Plymouth	2	Sheff Utd	1	
Reading	4	QPR	0	
Rotherhm	2	Rochdale	0	
Scunthpe	0	Workingtn	1	
Southmptn	3	Cardiff	2	
Stoke	1	Shrewsby	1	
Sunderld	4	West Ham	1	
Swansea	3	Swindon	1	
Torquay	1	Notts Co	2	
Tranmere	0	C.Palace	2	
Watford	2	Portsmth	2	
Peterboro	0	Leicester	2	r
Portsmth	2	Watford	1	r
Shrewsby	0	Stoke	1	r
Southend	3	Hull	1	r

THIRD ROUND

Bury	0	Plymouth	1	
Charlton	2	Leyton O	1	
Chelsea	4	Notts Co	0	
Chestrfld	3	Carlisle	1	
Coventry	3	Mansfield	2	
C.Palace	2	Southmptn	0	
Doncaster	2	Bradford	3	
Grimsby	0	Leicester	5	
Leeds U	2	Aston V	3	
N'hamptn	2	Portsmth	1	
Norwich	5	Chester	3	
Reading	1	Fulham	1	
Rotherhm	2	Swansea	2	
Stoke	3	Southend	1	
Sunderld	4	Blackpool	1	
Workingtn	0	Blackburn	0	
Blackburn	1	Workingtn	5	r
Fulham	1	Reading	3	r
Swansea	2	Rotherhm	0	r

FOURTH ROUND

Aston V	3	Reading	1	
Charlton	0	Bradford	1	
Chelsea	3	Swansea	2	
Coventry	4	Sunderld	2	
Leicester	0	C.Palace	0	
N'hamptn	4	Chestrfld	1	
Stoke	1	Plymouth	1	
Workingtn	3	Norwich	0	
C.Palace	1	Leicester	2	r
Plymouth	3	Stoke	1	r

FIFTH ROUND

Aston V	7	Bradford	1	
Coventry	1	Leicester	8	
Plymouth	1	N'hamptn	0	
Workingtn	2	Chelsea	2	
Chelsea	2	Workingtn	0	r

SEMI-FINAL FIRST-LEG

Aston V	2	Chelsea	3
Leicester	3	Plymouth	2

SEMI-FINAL SECOND-LEG

Chelsea	1	Aston V	1

Chelsea win 4-3 on agg

Plymouth	0	Leicester	1

Leicester win 4-2 on agg

FINAL FIRST-LEG

Chelsea	3	Leicester	2

Strange but true!

Rochdale have, and will keep, one record - they were the only Fourth Division team to play in a League Cup Final, when they were beaten by Norwich in 1962.

GIANTKILLERS

1966-67 QPR 3 West Brom 2

A one-off Wembley Final was now the reward for the last two clubs left in the League Cup, with a place in the UEFA Cup to follow for one. Ironically, the first Wembley winners, QPR, did not go into Europe because they were ineligible, being still in Division Three - although they won the Championship (scoring 103 goals) to go with their League Cup success. Rangers had some luck in the draw, playing only one First Division club, Leicester, before facing holders West Brom at Wembley. But the manner in which they hit back to win after going two down earned great admiration.

FINAL SECOND-LEG

Leicester	0	Chelsea	0	

Chelsea win 3-2 on agg

1966

FIRST ROUND

Barrow	1	Rochdale	1	
Bournemth	0	Aldershot	0	
Bradfd PA	1	Halifax	0	
Colchester	2	Exeter	1	
Crewe	2	Southport	0	
Doncaster	2	Barnsley	2	
Hartlepl	1	Bradford	0	
Lincoln	2	York	2	
Luton	1	Brighton	1	
Newport	2	Southend	2	
Notts Co	0	Chestrfld	0	
Oldham	3	Tranmere	2	
Oxford	0	Millwall	1	
Port Vale	2	Reading	2	
QPR	1	Walsall	1	
Scunthpe	0	Darlingtn	2	
Shrewsby	3	Torquay	0	
Stockport	2	Workingtn	3	
Wrexham	5	Chester	2	
Aldershot	2	Bournemth	1	r
Barnsley	1	Doncaster	2	r
Brighton	2	Luton	0	r
Chestrfld	2	Notts Co	1	r
Reading	1	Port Vale	0	re
Rochdale	3	Barrow	1	r
Southend	3	Newport	1	r
Walsall	3	QPR	2	r
York	4	Lincoln	2	r

SECOND ROUND

Blackburn	0	N'hamptn	1	
Blackpool	5	Gillinghm	2	
Bolton	3	Aldershot	0	
Brighton	1	Ipswich	2	
Bristol R	3	West Ham	3	
Bury	0	Huddersfld	2	
Charlton	4	Carlisle	1	
Chestrfld	3	Bradfd PA	0	
Colchester	2	Middlesbro	4	
Crewe	1	Cardiff	1	
C.Palace	0	Grimsby	1	
Darlingtn	2	Swindon	1	
Doncaster	0	Burnley	4	
Hull	2	Derby	2	
Leeds U	4	Hartlepl	2	
Leyton O	0	Coventry	3	
Man City	3	Leicester	1	
Mansfield	2	Birmghm C	1	
Millwall	4	York	1	
Newcastle	3	Peterboro	4	
Oldham	1	Portsmth	2	
Preston NE	1	Plymouth	0	
Reading	5	Southend	1	
Rotherhm	2	Watford	0	
Shrewsby	1	Bristol C	0	
Southmptn	3	Rochdale	0	
Stoke	2	Norwich	1	
Sunderld	2	Sheff Utd	1	
Swansea	2	Aston V	3	
West Brom	3	Walsall	1	
Workingtn	0	Brentford	0	
Wrexham	1	Fulham	2	
Brentford	1	Workingtn	2	r
Cardiff	3	Crewe	0	r
Derby	4	Hull	3	r
West Ham	3	Bristol R	2	r

THIRD ROUND

Blackpool	1	Darlingtn	2	
Burnley	3	Southmptn	2	
Cardiff	2	Portsmth	0	
Chestrfld	2	Stoke	2	
Derby	1	Reading	1	
Fulham	5	N'hamptn	0	
Grimsby	4	Bolton	2	
Huddersfld	0	Preston NE	1	
Leeds U	2	West Brom	4	
Man City	2	Coventry	3	
Middlesbro	0	Millwall	0	
Peterboro	4	Charlton	3	
Shrewsby	2	Rotherhm	5	
Sunderld	1	Aston V	2	
West Ham	4	Mansfield	0	
Workingtn	1	Ipswich	1	
Ipswich	3	Workingtn	1	r
Millwall	3	Middlesbro	1	re
Reading	2	Derby	0	r
Stoke	2	Chestrfld	1	r

FOURTH ROUND

Cardiff	5	Reading	1	
Coventry	1	West Brom	1	
Fulham	1	Aston V	1	
Grimsby	4	Preston NE	0	
Ipswich	2	Darlingtn	0	
Millwall	1	Peterboro	4	
Rotherhm	1	West Ham	2	
Stoke	0	Burnley	0	
Aston V	2	Fulham	0	r
Burnley	2	Stoke	1	re
West Brom	6	Coventry	1	r

FIFTH ROUND

Cardiff	2	Ipswich	1	
Grimsby	2	West Ham	2	
Peterboro	4	Burnley	0	
West Brom	3	Aston V	1	
West Ham	1	Grimsby	0	r

SEMI-FINAL FIRST-LEG

West Brom	2	Peterboro	1	
West Ham	5	Cardiff	2	

SEMI-FINAL SECOND-LEG

Cardiff	1	West Ham	5	

West Ham win 10-3 on agg

Peterboro	2	West Brom	4	

West Brom win 6-3 on agg

FINAL FIRST-LEG

West Ham	2	West Brom	1	

FINAL SECOND-LEG

West Brom	4	West Ham	1	

West Brom win 5-3 on agg

1967

FIRST ROUND

Aldershot	2	Luton	2	
Barnsley	1	Grimsby	2	
Barrow	2	Oldham	1	
Bradford	1	Doncaster	1	
Bradfd PA	2	Hartlepl	2	
Brentford	0	Millwall	0	
Brighton	1	Leyton O	0	
Bury	2	Rochdale	0	
Cardiff	1	Bristol R	0	
Chester	2	Tranmere	5	
Chestrfld	2	Scunthpe	1	
Crewe	1	Stockport	0	
Exeter	2	Torquay	2	
Halifax	0	Darlingtn	0	
Lincoln	1	Hull	0	

WHAT A STAR ✪ RODNEY MARSH

Only Clive Allen of Spurs, in 1986-87, has passed the individual total of 11 goals in one League Cup season that Rodney Marsh achieved with QPR in 1966-67. 'Rodneeee' was a marvellous entertainer, and in the course of his career, with Fulham, Manchester City and in the USA after leaving Rangers, he made a lot of people feel better just by watching him, even though his highly-individual style did not appeal to England managers. His solo equaliser for QPR against West Brom in 1967 remains one of Wembley's best goals.

Middlesbro	0	York	0	
Newport	1	Swansea	2	
Notts Co	1	Mansfield	1	
Peterboro	2	Oxford	1	
Port Vale	1	Walsall	3	
QPR	5	Colchester	0	
Shrewsby	6	Wrexham	1	
Southend	0	Gillinghm	0	
Southport	0	Workingtn	1	
Swindon	2	Bournemth	1	
Watford	1	Reading	1	
Darlingtn	4	Halifax	0	r
Doncaster	5	Bradford	2	re
Gillinghm	2	Southend	0	re
Hartlepl	1	Bradfd PA	2	r
Luton	1	Aldershot	2	r
Mansfield	3	Notts Co	0	r
Millwall	0	Brentford	1	r
Reading	1	Watford	0	r
Torquay	1	Exeter	2	r
York	2	Middlesbro	1	r

SECOND ROUND

Aldershot	1	QPR	1	
Arsenal	1	Gillinghm	1	
Blackburn	4	Barrow	1	
Blackpool	5	Man Utd	1	
Bradfd PA	0	Grimsby	0	
Brentford	2	Ipswich	4	
Bristol C	1	Swansea	1	
Bury	2	Workingtn	3	
Cardiff	0	Exeter	1	
Carlisle	1	Tranmere	1	
Chelsea	5	Charlton	2	
Coventry	2	Derby	1	
Darlingtn	1	Doncaster	1	
Fulham	2	C.Palace	0	
Leeds U	1	Newcastle	0	
Leicester	5	Reading	0	
Lincoln	2	Huddersfld	1	
Man City	3	Bolton	1	
N'hamptn	2	Peterboro	2	
Norwich	0	Brighton	1	
Nottm For	1	Birmghm C	1	
Preston NE	2	Crewe	0	
Sheff Wed	0	Rotherhm	1	
Shrewsby	1	Burnley	1	
Southmptn	4	Plymouth	3	
Sunderld	1	Sheff Utd	1	
Swindon	4	Portsmth	1	
Walsall	2	Stoke	1	
West Brom	6	Aston V	1	
West Ham	1	Tottenham	0	
Wolves	2	Mansfield	1	
York	3	Chestrfld	2	
Birmghm C	2	Nottm For	1	r
Burnley	5	Shrewsby	0	r
Doncaster	2	Darlingtn	0	r
Gillinghm	1	Arsenal	1	re
Grimsby	3	Bradfd PA	1	r
Peterboro	0	N'hamptn	2	r
QPR	2	Aldershot	0	r
Sheff Utd	1	Sunderld	0	re
Swansea	2	Bristol C	1	re
Tranmere	0	Carlisle	2	r
Arsenal	5	Gillinghm	0	r2

THIRD ROUND

Arsenal	1	West Ham	3	
Birmghm C	2	Ipswich	1	
Blackpool	1	Chelsea	1	
Brighton	1	Coventry	1	
Doncaster	1	Swindon	1	
Exeter	1	Walsall	2	
Fulham	5	Wolves	0	
Grimsby	3	Workingtn	0	
Leicester	5	Lincoln	0	
N'hamptn	2	Rotherhm	1	
Preston NE	1	Leeds U	1	
QPR	2	Swansea	1	
Sheff Utd	2	Burnley	0	
Southmptn	3	Carlisle	3	
West Brom	4	Man City	2	
York	0	Blackburn	2	
Carlisle	2	Southmptn	1	re
Chelsea	1	Blackpool	3	r
Coventry	1	Brighton	3	r
Leeds U	3	Preston NE	0	r
Swindon	4	Doncaster	2	re

FOURTH ROUND

Blackpool	4	Fulham	2	
Brighton	1	N'hamptn	1	
Carlisle	4	Blackburn	0	
Grimsby	2	Birmghm C	4	
QPR	4	Leicester	2	
Sheff Utd	2	Walsall	1	
Swindon	0	West Brom	2	
West Ham	7	Leeds U	0	
N'hamptn	8	Brighton	0	r

FIFTH ROUND

Blackpool	1	West Ham	3	
N'hamptn	1	West Brom	3	
QPR	2	Carlisle	1	
Sheff Utd	2	Birmghm C	3	

SEMI-FINAL FIRST-LEG

Birmghm C	1	QPR	4	
West Brom	4	West Ham	0	

SEMI-FINAL SECOND-LEG

QPR	3	Birmghm C	1	

QPR win 7-2 on agg

West Ham	2	West Brom	2	

West Brom win 6-2 on agg

FINAL

QPR	3	West Brom	2	N

1968

FIRST ROUND

Aldershot	2	Cardiff	3	
Barrow	1	Southport	0	
Bournemth	1	Watford	1	
Brighton	4	Colchester	0	
Crewe	1	Stockport	1	
Darlingtn	1	York	0	
Doncaster	1	Scunthpe	2	
Grimsby	1	Chestrfld	0	
Halifax	5	Bradfd PA	0	
Hartlepl	2	Bradford	0	
Leyton O	1	Gillinghm	3	
Luton	1	Charlton	1	
Mansfield	2	Lincoln	3	
Middlesbro	4	Barnsley	1	
N'hamptn	3	Peterboro	2	
Notts Co	0	Rotherhm	1	
Oxford	3	Swansea	1	
Port Vale	3	Chester	0	
Reading	3	Bristol R	0	
Rochdale	0	Bury	1	
Southend	1	Brentford	0	
Swindon	1	Newport	1	
Torquay	0	Exeter	0	
Tranmere	2	Wrexham	1	

Ell Fire

Leeds won the trophy in the 1967-68 season with a team whose average age was only 24 years and four months.

Walsall	4	Shrewsby	2	
Workingtn	1	Oldham	1	
Charlton	1	Luton	2	re
Exeter	0	Torquay	3	r
Newport	2	Swindon	0	r
Oldham	1	Workingtn	1	re
Stockport	3	Crewe	0	r
Watford	0	Bournemth	0	re
Oldham	1	Workingtn	2	r2N
Watford	2	Bournemth	1	r2N

SECOND ROUND

Barrow	1	C.Palace	0	
Blackburn	3	Brighton	1	
Bristol C	0	Everton	5	
Burnley	2	Cardiff	1	
Carlisle	0	Workingtn	2	
Coventry	1	Arsenal	2	
Derby	4	Hartlepl	0	
Fulham	1	Tranmere	0	
Gillinghm	2	Torquay	2	
Grimsby	2	Bury	2	
Huddersfld	1	Wolves	0	
Ipswich	5	Southmptn	2	
Leeds U	3	Luton	1	
Lincoln	2	Newcastle	1	
Liverpool	1	Bolton	1	
Man City	4	Leicester	0	
Middlesbro	2	Chelsea	1	
Millwall	3	Sheff Utd	2	
Newport	0	Blackpool	1	
N'hamptn	3	Aston V	1	
Norwich	1	Rotherhm	1	
Oxford	2	Preston NE	1	
Plymouth	0	Birmghm C	2	
Portsmth	3	Port Vale	1	
QPR	2	Hull	1	
Reading	3	West Brom	1	
Scunthpe	0	Nottm For	1	
Southend	1	Darlingtn	2	
Stockport	3	Sheff Wed	5	
Stoke	2	Watford	0	
Sunderld	3	Halifax	2	
Walsall	1	West Ham	5	
Bolton	3	Liverpool	2	r
Bury	2	Grimsby	0	r
Rotherhm	0	Norwich	2	r
Torquay	2	Gillinghm	0	r

THIRD ROUND

Arsenal	1	Reading	0	
Blackburn	3	Middlesbro	2	
Burnley	3	Nottm For	0	
Darlingtn	4	Portsmth	1	
Derby	3	Birmghm C	1	
Everton	2	Sunderld	3	
Leeds U	3	Bury	0	
Lincoln	4	Torquay	2	
Man City	1	Blackpool	1	
N'hamptn	0	Millwall	0	
Norwich	0	Huddersfld	1	
QPR	5	Oxford	1	
Sheff Wed	3	Barrow	1	
Stoke	2	Ipswich	1	
West Ham	4	Bolton	1	
Workingtn	2	Fulham	2	
Blackpool	0	Man City	2	r
Fulham	6	Workingtn	2	r
Millwall	5	N'hamptn	1	r

FOURTH ROUND

Arsenal	2	Blackburn	1	
Darlingtn	2	Millwall	0	
Derby	1	Lincoln	1	
Fulham	3	Man City	2	
Huddersfld	2	West Ham	0	
QPR	1	Burnley	2	
Sheff Wed	0	Stoke	0	
Sunderld	0	Leeds U	2	
Lincoln	0	Derby	3	r
Stoke	2	Sheff Wed	1	r

FIFTH ROUND

Burnley	3	Arsenal	3	
Derby	5	Darlingtn	4	
Fulham	1	Huddersfld	1	
Leeds U	2	Stoke	0	
Arsenal	2	Burnley	1	r
Huddersfld	2	Fulham	1	re

SEMI-FINAL FIRST-LEG

Arsenal	3	Huddersfld	2	
Derby	0	Leeds U	1	

SEMI-FINAL SECOND-LEG

Huddersfld	1	Arsenal	3	
Arsenal win 6-3 on agg				
Leeds U	3	Derby	2	
Leeds U win 4-2 on agg				

FINAL

Leeds U	1	Arsenal	0	N

Strange but true!

Arthur Holland of Barnsley was the first referee to handle both major Cup Finals - the League Cup first-leg in 1962 and the FA Cup in 1964.

1969

FIRST ROUND

Aldershot	2	Brentford	4	
Bournemth	1	Southend	6	
Bradford	3	Hartlepl	2	
Bradfd PA	0	Darlingtn	3	
Brighton	2	Oxford	0	
Bristol C	2	Newport	0	
Bristol R	0	Swansea	2	
Bury	1	Stockport	1	
Chester	0	Tranmere	0	
Colchester	2	Reading	0	
Crewe	1	N'hamptn	1	
Derby	3	Chestrfld	0	
Doncaster	0	Peterboro	0	
Gillinghm	2	Leyton O	2	
Grimsby	0	Notts Co	0	
Halifax	0	Hull	3	
Lincoln	2	Mansfield	1	
Luton	3	Watford	0	
Plymouth	0	Exeter	0	
Preston NE	1	Oldham	1	
Scunthpe	2	Rotherhm	1	
Southport	2	Barrow	2	
Swindon	2	Torquay	1	
Walsall	2	Shrewsby	0	
Workingtn	2	Rochdale	1	
Wrexham	2	Port Vale	0	
York	3	Barnsley	4	
Barrow	1	Southport	3	re
Crewe	1	N'hamptn	0	r
Exeter	0	Plymouth	0	re
Leyton O	3	Gillinghm	0	r
Notts Co	0	Grimsby	1	r

GIANTKILLERS

1968-69 Swindon 3 Arsenal 1

A 3-1 defeat of Arsenal at Wembley enabled Swindon to emulate QPR by winning the League Cup and promotion from Division Three in the same season, but theirs was perhaps an even more praiseworthy effort. They had to play 11 matches in getting rid of Torquay, Bradford, Blackburn, Coventry, Derby and Burnley, the latter in a Semi-Final that went to three games. Then they had to face a third successive opponent from the First Division, Arsenal, in the Final, but pulled off probably the biggest surprise in League Cup history by winning 3-1 and being worth an even wider margin.

Swindon stunned football by beating Arsenal in the 1969 Final

Oldham	0	Preston NE	1	r
Peterboro	1	Doncaster	0	r
Stockport	1	Bury	0	r
Tranmere	2	Chester	2	re
Plymouth	0	Exeter	1	r2eN
Tranmere	1	Chester	1	r2e
Chester	1	Tranmere	2	r3
SECOND ROUND				
Arsenal	1	Sunderld	0	
Aston V	1	Tottenham	4	
Barnsley	1	Millwall	1	
Birmghm C	0	Chelsea	1	
Blackburn	1	Stoke	1	
Bradford	1	Swindon	1	
Brentford	3	Hull	0	
Brighton	1	Luton	1	
Bristol C	1	Middlesbro	0	
Carlisle	2	Cardiff	0	
Colchester	0	Workingtn	1	
Coventry	2	Portsmth	0	
C.Palace	3	Preston NE	1	
Darlingtn	1	Leicester	2	
Derby	5	Stockport	1	
Everton	4	Tranmere	0	
Exeter	3	Sheff Wed	1	
Grimsby	1	Burnley	1	
Huddersfld	0	Man City	0	
Ipswich	2	Norwich	4	
Leeds U	1	Charlton	0	
Leyton O	1	Fulham	0	
Liverpool	4	Sheff Utd	0	
Nottm For	2	West Brom	3	
Peterboro	4	QPR	2	
Scunthpe	2	Lincoln	1	
Southmptn	3	Crewe	1	
Southport	0	Newcastle	2	
Walsall	1	Swansea	1	
West Ham	7	Bolton	2	
Wolves	1	Southend	0	
Wrexham	1	Blackpool	1	
Blackpool	3	Wrexham	0	r
Burnley	6	Grimsby	0	r
Luton	4	Brighton	2	r
Man City	4	Huddersfld	0	r
Millwall	3	Barnsley	1	re
Stoke	0	Blackburn	1	r
Swansea	3	Walsall	2	re
Swindon	4	Bradford	3	r
THIRD ROUND				
Blackpool	1	Man City	0	
Brentford	0	Norwich	2	
Carlisle	0	Leicester	3	
Chelsea	0	Derby	0	
Everton	5	Luton	1	
Leeds U	2	Bristol C	1	
Leyton O	0	C.Palace	1	
Liverpool	2	Swansea	0	
Peterboro	2	West Brom	1	
Scunthpe	1	Arsenal	6	
Southmptn	4	Newcastle	1	
Swindon	1	Blackburn	0	
Tottenham	6	Exeter	3	
West Ham	0	Coventry	0	
Wolves	5	Millwall	1	
Workingtn	0	Burnley	1	
Coventry	3	West Ham	2	r
Derby	3	Chelsea	1	r
FOURTH ROUND				
Arsenal	2	Liverpool	1	
Blackpool	2	Wolves	1	
Burnley	4	Leicester	0	
Coventry	2	Swindon	2	
C.Palace	2	Leeds U	1	
Everton	0	Derby	0	
Norwich	0	Southmptn	4	
Tottenham	1	Peterboro	0	
Derby	1	Everton	0	r
Swindon	3	Coventry	0	r
FIFTH ROUND				
Arsenal	5	Blackpool	1	
Burnley	2	C.Palace	0	
Derby	0	Swindon	0	
Tottenham	1	Southmptn	0	
Swindon	1	Derby	0	r
SEMI-FINAL FIRST-LEG				
Arsenal	1	Tottenham	0	
Burnley	1	Swindon	2	
SEMI-FINAL SECOND-LEG				
Swindon	1	Burnley	2	e
agg score Swindon 3 - Burnley 3				
Tottenham	1	Arsenal	1	
Arsenal win 2-1 on agg				
SEMI-FINAL REPLAY				
Burnley	2	Swindon	3	reN
FINAL				
Swindon	3	Arsenal	1	eN

WHAT A STAR ✪ DON ROGERS

Left-winger Don Rogers was a local boy who started young with Swindon, played more than 400 games for the club, and won them the League Cup virtually single-handed by scoring twice in the 1969 Final, when mighty Arsenal unbelievably lost to a Third Division outfit. That earned Rogers a move to big-spending Crystal Palace, but he did not settle there, nor at QPR. So he went back to Swindon to round off his career, and has run a sports shop for over a quarter of a century. Almost every day, a customer asks "Can you tell me about...."

CHAPTER 10 History of the League Cup

1970-1979

FOREST MAKE HISTORY

No Can Do

West Brom midfielder Len Cantello's appearance in the 1970 League Cup Final was only his 12th in the first-team. His team lost. Three days later, his 13th game, in the First Division, he was unlucky again. He was sent-off.

By now, the League Cup was firmly established, and as one of only three routes into Europe it was fiercely contested.

Manchester City won the first Cup of the 70s, beating West Brom 2-1, and Tottenham picked up the trophy in 1971 - well, of course the year ended in a '1' so they had to win something.

Tottenham won it again in 1973, with Stoke triumphing in the middle of those three years.

Aston Villa also won the trophy twice in three years - in 1975 and 1977 - but no-one had been able to win the Cup two years in a row.

No-one, that is, until Brian Clough and his all-conquering Nottingham Forest team in 1978 and 1979.

In '78, they were up against Liverpool, unquestionably the strongest team of the era, but they came through to win 1-0 in the replay after a 0-0 draw in the first game.

And while it was a memorable moment for Clough, it was even more memorable for a young goalkeeper called Chris Woods, who became the youngest 'keeper to play in a Wembley Cup Final aged just 18 years, 125 days.

Woods was in goal for Forest in place of the injured Peter Shilton and kept two clean sheets to keep the mighty Liverpool at bay.

And he did all that before he had even played a League game, which makes his achievement all the more remarkable.

Forest were back at Wembley a year later to become the first team to successfully defend the League Cup, something that they would do again ten years later.

On this occasion, in 1979, their Final opponents at the Twin Towers were Lawrie McMenemy's Southampton and in another thrilling game, Forest came through to win 3-2.

But if Forest went into history as the first team to retain the trophy, their feat was soon to be eclipsed by a team who made Wembley their second home during the 80s.

Not a Bad Ron

Manager Ron Saunders took different teams to the League Cup Final in three successive years - Norwich in 1973, Manchester City in 1974 and Aston Villa in 1975. The first two lost and Villa won - as they did again, still under Saunders, in 1977.

GIANTKILLERS

1970-71 Bristol Rvs 2 Newcastle 1

Bristol City, of the Second Division, got to the League Cup Semi-Final during this season, but much of their glory was stolen by neighbouring Rovers from the Third. Rovers beat a club from a higher division in all their first four rounds - Brighton (Second), Newcastle (First), Norwich (Second) and Birmingham (Second) - before losing to Aston Villa, the eventual beaten Finalists, in a Quarter-Final replay. The unrelated Jones boys, Bobby and Wayne, got most of the headlines, but the run was very much a team effort.

1970

FIRST ROUND

Home		Away		
Aldershot	0	Gillinghm	1	
Barnsley	0	Halifax	1	
Bolton	6	Rochdale	3	
Bournemth	3	Bristol R	0	
Bradford	1	Chestrfld	1	
Bradfd PA	0	Rotherhm	2	
Brighton	1	Portsmth	0	
Chester	1	Aston V	2	
Colchester	1	Reading	1	
Crewe	0	Wrexham	0	
Darlingtn	3	York	0	
Exeter	1	Bristol C	1	
Grimsby	0	Doncaster	2	
Leyton O	0	Fulham	0	
Mansfield	3	Notts Co	1	
Newport	2	Swansea	3	
Oxford	2	N'hamptn	0	
Peterboro	1	Luton	1	
Plymouth	2	Torquay	2	
Port Vale	0	Tranmere	1	
Preston NE	0	Bury	1	
Scunthpe	0	Hartlepl	2	
Shrewsby	1	Walsall	0	
Southend	2	Brentford	2	
Southport	5	Oldham	1	
Stockport	0	Blackburn	2	
Watford	2	Lincoln	1	
Workingtn	0	Barrow	0	
Barrow	3	Workingtn	1	r
Brentford	0	Southend	0	re
Bristol C	3	Exeter	2	r
Chestrfld	0	Bradford	1	r
Fulham	3	Leyton O	1	r
Luton	5	Peterboro	2	r
Reading	0	Colchester	3	r
Torquay	1	Plymouth	0	r
Wrexham	1	Crewe	0	r
Brentford	2	Southend	3	r2e

SECOND ROUND

Home		Away		
Aston V	1	West Brom	2	
Barrow	1	Nottm For	2	
Blackburn	4	Doncaster	2	
Blackpool	3	Gillinghm	1	
Bolton	0	Rotherhm	0	
Brighton	2	Birmghm C	0	
Bristol C	0	Leicester	0	
Carlisle	2	Huddersfld	0	
Charlton	0	Wrexham	2	
Coventry	0	Chelsea	1	
C.Palace	3	Cardiff	1	
Darlingtn	0	Everton	1	
Fulham	0	Leeds U	1	
Hartlepl	1	Derby	3	
Hull	1	Norwich	0	
Ipswich	4	Colchester	0	
Luton	2	Millwall	2	
Man Utd	1	Middlesbro	0	
Mansfield	2	QPR	2	
Oxford	4	Bury	1	
Sheff Utd	2	Newcastle	0	
Sheff Wed	1	Bournemth	1	
Shrewsby	2	Southend	2	
Southmptn	1	Arsenal	1	
Southport	0	Man City	3	
Stoke	0	Burnley	2	
Sunderld	1	Bradford	2	
Swansea	1	Swindon	3	
Tranmere	2	Torquay	1	
Watford	1	Liverpool	2	
West Ham	4	Halifax	2	
Wolves	1	Tottenham	0	
Arsenal	2	Southmptn	0	re
Bournemth	1	Sheff Wed	0	r
Leicester	0	Bristol C	0	re
Millwall	0	Luton	1	re
QPR	4	Mansfield	0	r
Rotherhm	3	Bolton	3	re
Southend	2	Shrewsby	0	r
Leicester	3	Bristol C	1	r2
Rotherhm	1	Bolton	0	r2

THIRD ROUND

Home		Away		
Arsenal	0	Everton	0	
Bournemth	0	Leicester	2	
Bradford	2	Southend	1	
Brighton	2	Wolves	3	
Carlisle	2	Blackburn	1	
C.Palace	2	Blackpool	2	
Derby	3	Hull	1	
Ipswich	1	West Brom	1	
Leeds U	1	Chelsea	1	
Man City	3	Liverpool	2	
Man Utd	2	Wrexham	0	
Nottm For	1	West Ham	0	
Oxford	1	Swindon	0	
QPR	6	Tranmere	0	
Rotherhm	1	Burnley	1	
Sheff Utd	3	Luton	0	
Blackpool	0	C.Palace	1	r
Burnley	2	Rotherhm	0	r
Chelsea	2	Leeds U	0	r
Everton	1	Arsenal	0	r
West Brom	2	Ipswich	0	r

FOURTH ROUND

Home		Away		
Burnley	0	Man Utd	0	
Carlisle	1	Chelsea	0	
C.Palace	1	Derby	1	
Leicester	2	Sheff Utd	0	
Man City	2	Everton	0	
Nottm For	0	Oxford	1	
QPR	3	Wolves	1	
West Brom	4	Bradford	0	
Derby	3	C.Palace	0	r
Man Utd	1	Burnley	0	r

FIFTH ROUND

Home		Away		
Derby	0	Man Utd	0	
Leicester	0	West Brom	0	
Man City	3	QPR	0	
Oxford	0	Carlisle	0	
Carlisle	1	Oxford	0	r
Man Utd	1	Derby	0	r
West Brom	2	Leicester	1	r

SEMI-FINAL FIRST-LEG

Home		Away		
Carlisle	1	West Brom	0	
Man City	2	Man Utd	1	

SEMI-FINAL SECOND-LEG

Home		Away		
Man Utd	2	Man City	2	
Man City win 4-3 on agg				
West Brom	4	Carlisle	1	
West Brom win 4-2 on agg				

FINAL

Home		Away		
Man City	2	West Brom	1	eN

1971

FIRST ROUND

Home		Away		
Aldershot	1	Brentford	0	
Aston V	4	Notts Co	0	
Barnsley	0	Rotherhm	1	
Birmghm C	3	Wrexham	3	
Bristol R	1	Brighton	0	
Bury	1	Oldham	3	
Charlton	3	Southend	0	
Chester	2	Shrewsby	1	
Colchester	5	Cambridge	0	
Crewe	2	Tranmere	2	
Doncaster	1	Darlingtn	1	

Exeter	0	Swansea	0	
Fulham	1	Leyton O	0	
Gillinghm	0	Luton	1	
Halifax	3	Bradford	2	
Hartlepl	2	York	3	
Lincoln	2	Grimsby	1	
Mansfield	6	Chestrfld	2	
Newport	2	Reading	1	
Port Vale	0	Walsall	1	
Portsmth	2	Plymouth	0	
Rochdale	1	Southport	0	
Scunthpe	2	N'hamptn	3	
Stockport	0	Preston NE	1	
Torquay	1	Bournemth	1	
Watford	2	Peterboro	0	
Workingtn	2	Barrow	0	
Bournemth	1	Torquay	2	r
Darlingtn	3	Doncaster	1	r
Swansea	4	Exeter	2	re
Tranmere	4	Crewe	0	r
Wrexham	2	Birmghm C	3	r
SECOND ROUND				
Aldershot	1	Man Utd	3	
Aston V	2	Burnley	0	
Blackpool	4	Newport	1	
Bolton	1	Blackburn	0	
Bristol R	2	Newcastle	1	
Carlisle	2	Man City	1	
Colchester	1	Birmghm C	1	
C.Palace	3	Rochdale	3	
Darlingtn	0	Fulham	4	
Derby	3	Halifax	1	
Huddersfld	0	Nottm For	0	
Ipswich	0	Arsenal	0	
Leicester	3	Southmptn	2	
Lincoln	2	Sunderld	1	
Luton	3	Workingtn	0	
Mansfield	0	Liverpool	0	
Norwich	0	Chester	0	
Oldham	2	Middlesbro	4	
Oxford	1	Wolves	0	
Portsmth	1	Walsall	0	
QPR	4	Cardiff	0	
Rotherhm	0	Bristol C	0	
Sheff Utd	1	Leeds U	0	
Sheff Wed	1	Chelsea	1	
Stoke	0	Millwall	0	
Swindon	4	Watford	2	
Torquay	1	Preston NE	3	
Tottenham	3	Swansea	0	
Tranmere	1	Coventry	1	
West Brom	3	Charlton	1	
West Ham	1	Hull	0	
York	0	N'hamptn	0	
Arsenal	4	Ipswich	0	r
Birmghm C	2	Colchester	1	r
Bristol C	4	Rotherhm	0	r
Chelsea	2	Sheff Wed	1	r
Chester	1	Norwich	2	r
Coventry	2	Tranmere	1	r
Liverpool	3	Mansfield	2	re
Millwall	2	Stoke	1	r
N'hamptn	1	York	1	re
Nottm For	2	Huddersfld	0	r
Rochdale	1	C.Palace	3	r
York	1	N'hamptn	2	r2N
THIRD ROUND				
Birmghm C	2	Nottm For	1	
Blackpool	0	Bristol C	1	
Bolton	1	Leicester	1	
Carlisle	3	Oxford	1	
Chelsea	3	Middlesbro	2	
Coventry	3	West Ham	1	
C.Palace	4	Lincoln	0	
Derby	4	Millwall	2	
Fulham	2	QPR	0	
Luton	0	Arsenal	1	
Man Utd	1	Portsmth	0	
N'hamptn	1	Aston V	1	
Norwich	1	Bristol R	1	
Preston NE	0	West Brom	1	
Swindon	2	Liverpool	0	
Tottenham	2	Sheff Utd	1	
Aston V	3	N'hamptn	0	r
Bristol R	3	Norwich	1	re
Leicester	1	Bolton	0	r
FOURTH ROUND				
Aston V	1	Carlisle	0	
Bristol R	3	Birmghm C	0	
Coventry	1	Derby	0	
C.Palace	0	Arsenal	0	
Fulham	1	Swindon	0	
Leicester	2	Bristol C	2	
Man Utd	2	Chelsea	1	
Tottenham	5	West Brom	0	
Arsenal	0	C.Palace	2	r
Bristol C	2	Leicester	1	r
FIFTH ROUND				
Bristol R	1	Aston V	1	
Fulham	0	Bristol C	0	
Man Utd	4	C.Palace	2	
Tottenham	4	Coventry	1	
Aston V	1	Bristol R	0	r
Bristol C	1	Fulham	0	r
SEMI-FINAL FIRST-LEG				
Bristol C	1	Tottenham	1	
Man Utd	1	Aston V	1	
SEMI-FINAL SECOND-LEG				
Aston V	2	Man Utd	1	
Aston V win 3-2 on agg				
Tottenham	2	Bristol C	0	e
Tottenham win 3-1 on agg				
FINAL				
Tottenham	2	Aston V	0	N

1972

FIRST ROUND				
Aldershot	1	Southend	1	
Aston V	2	Wrexham	2	
Barnsley	0	Hartlepl	0	
Barrow	0	Preston NE	2	
Blackburn	2	Workingtn	0	
Bournemth	2	Portsmth	1	
Bradford	1	Bolton	1	
Charlton	5	Peterboro	1	
Chestrfld	0	Mansfield	0	
Colchester	3	Brentford	1	
Crewe	0	Southport	1	
Darlingtn	0	York	1	
Exeter	0	Bristol R	3	
Fulham	4	Cambridge	0	
Gillinghm	4	Reading	0	
Grimsby	4	Doncaster	3	
Halifax	1	Rochdale	1	
Leyton O	1	Notts Co	1	
Newport	1	Torquay	2	
Oldham	1	Bury	0	
Plymouth	1	Bristol C	0	
Port Vale	0	Shrewsby	2	
Rotherhm	0	Sheff Wed	2	
Scunthpe	0	Lincoln	1	

WHAT A STAR ✪ GEORGE EASTHAM

The oldest player to score in a League Cup Final, he was 35 when he did so for Stoke against Chelsea in 1972, helping his club to their first major trophy, and rounding off a career which had brought him earlier success with Newcastle, Arsenal and England (19 caps), as well as notoriety as the 'wage slave rebel' who helped bring about the abolition of the maximum wage. Eastham claimed that the hold clubs had over players, in terms of contracts, was a restraint of trade and against the law. He was near the end of his career when he picked up his first major medal as part of Stoke's team of veterans...and his goal in their 2-1 Wembley win was his first (and last) of the season.

Stockport	1	Walsall	0	
Swansea	0	Brighton	1	
Tranmere	1	Chester	1	
Watford	2	N'hamptn	0	
Bolton	2	Bradford	1	r
Chester	1	Tranmere	3	r
Hartlepl	0	Barnsley	1	re
Mansfield	0	Chestrfld	5	r
Notts Co	3	Leyton O	1	r
Rochdale	2	Halifax	2	re
Southend	1	Aldershot	2	re
Wrexham	1	Aston V	1	re
Aston V	4	Wrexham	3	r2N
Halifax	2	Rochdale	0	r2
SECOND ROUND				
Arsenal	1	Barnsley	0	
Blackburn	0	Lincoln	0	
Bournemth	0	Blackpool	2	
Bristol R	3	Sunderld	1	
Carlisle	5	Sheff Wed	0	
Charlton	3	Leicester	1	
Chelsea	2	Plymouth	0	
Chestrfld	2	Aston V	3	
Colchester	4	Swindon	1	
Coventry	0	Burnley	1	
C.Palace	2	Luton	0	
Derby	0	Leeds U	0	
Grimsby	2	Shrewsby	1	
Huddersfld	0	Bolton	2	
Ipswich	1	Man Utd	3	
Liverpool	3	Hull	0	
Man City	4	Wolves	3	
Newcastle	2	Halifax	1	
Norwich	2	Brighton	0	
Nottm For	5	Aldershot	1	
Notts Co	1	Gillinghm	2	
Oxford	1	Millwall	0	
QPR	2	Birmghm C	0	
Sheff Utd	3	Fulham	0	
Southmptn	2	Everton	1	
Southport	1	Stoke	2	
Stockport	0	Watford	1	
Torquay	2	Oldham	1	
Tranmere	0	Preston NE	1	
West Brom	0	Tottenham	1	
West Ham	1	Cardiff	1	
York	2	Middlesbro	2	
Cardiff	1	West Ham	2	r
Leeds U	2	Derby	0	r

Strange but true!

No fewer than 15 of the players who played in the Leeds v Arsenal League Cup Final in 1968 played in the 1972 FA Cup Final between the same clubs. Leeds won both, 1-0.

Lincoln	4	Blackburn	1	r
Middlesbro	1	York	2	r
THIRD ROUND				
Arsenal	4	Newcastle	0	
Blackpool	4	Colchester	0	
Bolton	3	Man City	0	
Bristol R	2	Charlton	1	
C.Palace	2	Aston V	2	
Gillinghm	1	Grimsby	1	
Liverpool	1	Southmptn	0	
Man Utd	1	Burnley	1	
Norwich	4	Carlisle	1	
Nottm For	1	Chelsea	1	
Oxford	1	Stoke	1	
QPR	4	Lincoln	2	
Sheff Utd	3	York	2	
Torquay	1	Tottenham	4	
Watford	1	Preston NE	1	
West Ham	0	Leeds U	0	
Aston V	2	C.Palace	0	r
Burnley	0	Man Utd	1	r
Chelsea	2	Nottm For	1	r
Grimsby	1	Gillinghm	0	r
Leeds U	0	West Ham	1	re
Preston NE	2	Watford	1	r
Stoke	2	Oxford	0	r
FOURTH ROUND				
Arsenal	0	Sheff Utd	0	
Blackpool	4	Aston V	1	
Chelsea	1	Bolton	1	
Grimsby	1	Norwich	1	
Man Utd	1	Stoke	1	
QPR	1	Bristol R	1	
Tottenham	1	Preston NE	1	
West Ham	2	Liverpool	1	
Bolton	0	Chelsea	6	r
Bristol R	1	QPR	0	r
Norwich	3	Grimsby	1	r
Preston NE	1	Tottenham	2	re
Sheff Utd	2	Arsenal	0	r
Stoke	0	Man Utd	0	re
Stoke	2	Man Utd	1	r2
FIFTH ROUND				
Bristol R	2	Stoke	4	
Norwich	0	Chelsea	1	
Tottenham	2	Blackpool	0	
West Ham	5	Sheff Utd	0	
SEMI-FINAL FIRST-LEG				
Chelsea	3	Tottenham	2	
Stoke	1	West Ham	2	
SEMI-FINAL SECOND-LEG				
Tottenham	2	Chelsea	2	
Chelsea win 5-4 on agg				
West Ham	0	Stoke	1	e
agg score West Ham 2 - Stoke 2				
SEMI-FINAL REPLAY				
Stoke	0	West Ham	0	reN
Stoke	3	West Ham	2	r2N
FINAL				
Stoke	2	Chelsea	1	N

1973

FIRST ROUND				
Aston V	4	Hereford	1	
Barnsley	0	Grimsby	0	
Blackburn	0	Rochdale	1	
Bolton	3	Oldham	0	
Bradford	1	Stockport	1	
Brentford	1	Cambridge	0	
Brighton	2	Exeter	1	
Cardiff	2	Bristol R	2	
Chester	4	Shrewsby	3	
Darlingtn	0	Rotherhm	1	
Gillinghm	1	Colchester	0	
Halifax	1	Bury	2	
Hartlepl	1	Doncaster	0	
Leyton O	2	Watford	0	
Mansfield	3	Lincoln	1	
N'hamptn	0	Charlton	3	
Notts Co	3	York	1	
Oxford	4	Peterboro	0	
Plymouth	0	Bournemth	2	
Reading	1	Fulham	1	

GIANTKILLERS

1972-73 Southampton 1 Notts Co 3

Notts County manager Jimmy Sirrel had put together one of the most attractive teams in Third Division history, with players such as Don Masson, Dave Needham, Les Bradd and Kevin Randall, and they fully deserved their promotion at the end of a season in which they had held distinct hopes of a first appearance at Wembley before losing 3-1 to Chelsea (Peter Osgood scored for both teams) in the Quarter-Final. On the way they beat York, Southport, and two First Division clubs, Southampton (away) and Stoke.

WHAT A STAR ✪ MARTIN CHIVERS

Tottenham and England striker Martin Chivers was top scorer in the League Cup in successive seasons, with seven goals in both 1970-71 and in 1972-73. He scored both when Spurs won the trophy in the first of those years, beating Aston Villa 2-0, and was a major force in their Final win over Norwich two seasons later, although this time he did not score. Chivers sometimes let himself down by being sloppy on the ball, but his excellent finishing made up for that, and the record fee of £125,000 that he cost Spurs from Southampton in 1968 proved money well spent. He also scored 13 goals in 24 games for England.

Scunthpe	0	Chestrfld	0	
Southend	2	Aldershot	1	
Southport	4	Walsall	1	
Swansea	1	Newport	1	
Torquay	1	Portsmth	2	
Tranmere	0	Port Vale	1	
Workingtn	1	Preston NE	0	
Wrexham	4	Crewe	0	
Bristol R	3	Cardiff	1	r
Chestrfld	5	Scunthpe	0	r
Fulham	1	Reading	1	re
Grimsby	2	Barnsley	0	r
Newport	3	Swansea	0	r
Stockport	1	Bradford	1	re
Bradford	0	Stockport	2	r2N
Reading	0	Fulham	1	r2
SECOND ROUND				
Arsenal	1	Everton	0	
Birmghm C	1	Luton	1	
Bournemth	0	Blackpool	0	
Bristol R	4	Brighton	0	
Bury	1	Grimsby	0	
Carlisle	1	Liverpool	1	
Charlton	4	Mansfield	3	
Coventry	1	Hartlepl	0	
C.Palace	0	Stockport	1	
Gillinghm	0	Millwall	2	
Hull	1	Fulham	0	
Leeds U	4	Burnley	0	
Man City	4	Rochdale	0	
Middlesbro	2	Wrexham	0	
Newport	0	Ipswich	3	
Norwich	2	Leicester	1	
Nottm For	0	Aston V	1	
Notts Co	3	Southport	2	
Oxford	2	Man Utd	2	
Port Vale	1	Newcastle	3	
Portsmth	0	Chestrfld	1	
Rotherhm	2	Brentford	0	
Sheff Wed	2	Bolton	0	
Southmptn	0	Chester	0	
Southend	0	Chelsea	1	
Stoke	3	Sunderld	0	
Swindon	0	Derby	1	
Tottenham	2	Huddersfld	1	
West Brom	2	QPR	1	
West Ham	2	Bristol C	1	
Wolves	2	Leyton O	1	
Workingtn	0	Sheff Utd	1	
Blackpool	1	Bournemth	1	re
Chester	2	Southmptn	2	re
Liverpool	5	Carlisle	1	r
Luton	1	Birmghm C	1	re
Man Utd	3	Oxford	1	r
Birmghm C	1	Luton	0	r2N
Bournemth	1	Blackpool	2	r2eN
Southmptn	2	Chester	0	r2N
THIRD ROUND				
Arsenal	5	Rotherhm	0	
Aston V	1	Leeds U	1	
Birmghm C	2	Coventry	1	
Bristol R	1	Man Utd	1	
Bury	2	Man City	0	
Derby	0	Chelsea	0	
Hull	1	Norwich	2	
Ipswich	1	Stoke	2	
Middlesbro	1	Tottenham	1	
Millwall	2	Chestrfld	0	
Newcastle	0	Blackpool	3	
Sheff Utd	0	Charlton	0	
Southmptn	1	Notts Co	3	
Stockport	2	West Ham	1	
West Brom	1	Liverpool	1	
Wolves	3	Sheff Wed	1	
Charlton	2	Sheff Utd	2	re
Chelsea	3	Derby	2	r
Leeds U	2	Aston V	0	r
Liverpool	2	West Brom	1	re
Man Utd	1	Bristol R	2	r
Tottenham	0	Middlesbro	0	re
Sheff Utd	1	Charlton	0	r2e
Tottenham	2	Middlesbro	1	r2e
FOURTH ROUND				
Blackpool	2	Birmghm C	0	
Bury	0	Chelsea	1	
Liverpool	2	Leeds U	2	
Notts Co	3	Stoke	1	
Sheff Utd	1	Arsenal	2	
Stockport	1	Norwich	5	
Tottenham	2	Millwall	0	
Wolves	4	Bristol R	0	
Leeds U	0	Liverpool	1	r
FIFTH ROUND				
Arsenal	0	Norwich	3	
Chelsea	3	Notts Co	1	
Liverpool	1	Tottenham	1	
Wolves	1	Blackpool	1	
Blackpool	0	Wolves	1	r
Tottenham	3	Liverpool	1	r
SEMI-FINAL FIRST-LEG				
Chelsea	0	Norwich	2	
Wolves	1	Tottenham	2	
SEMI-FINAL SECOND-LEG				
Norwich	1	Chelsea	0	
Norwich win 3-0 on agg				
Tottenham	2	Wolves	2	e
Tottenham win 4-3 on agg				
FINAL				
Tottenham	1	Norwich	0	N

1974

FIRST ROUND				
Aldershot	1	Cambridge	1	
Bolton	1	Preston NE	1	
Bournemth	1	Bristol R	0	
Brentford	1	Leyton O	2	
Brighton	1	Charlton	2	
Bury	0	Oldham	0	
Cardiff	2	Hereford	0	
Carlisle	2	Workingtn	2	
Chester	0	Wrexham	2	
Chestrfld	1	Mansfield	1	
Darlingtn	2	Bradford	1	
Gillinghm	4	Colchester	2	
Grimsby	2	N'hamptn	1	
Halifax	1	Barnsley	1	
Notts Co	3	Doncaster	4	
Peterboro	2	Scunthpe	2	
Portsmth	2	Southend	1	
Reading	2	Watford	2	
Rochdale	5	Hartlepl	3	
Rotherhm	2	Lincoln	1	

Strange but true!

Millwall were drawn at home to Chesterfield in the Third Round of the 1972-73 League Cup - after being drawn away nine times in succession, going back to 1967-68.

WHAT A STAR ✪ KEVIN KEELAN

Goalkeeper Kevin Keelan gained only a fraction of the fame and fortune achieved by his near-namesake, Kevin Keegan, but he was the sort of player football depends on - consistent and loyal, as well as talented. He was born in Calcutta, began at Wrexham, but played over 600 games for Norwich, and his efforts helped to take the club to the League Cup Finals of 1973 - when he had an outstanding match - and 1975. He finished on the losing side both times, as he often did during his long career before he retired and moved to the USA, but his skill and attitude earned him a place among the stars.

Southport	1	Blackburn	1	
Stockport	2	Port Vale	0	
Swansea	1	Exeter	1	
Swindon	3	Newport	3	
Torquay	0	Plymouth	2	
Tranmere	3	Crewe	3	
Walsall	6	Shrewsby	1	
York	1	Huddersfld	0	
Barnsley	0	Halifax	1	r
Blackburn	3	Southport	1	r
Cambridge	3	Aldershot	0	r
Crewe	0	Tranmere	1	r
Exeter	2	Swansea	1	re
Mansfield	0	Chestrfld	1	r
Newport	1	Swindon	2	r
Oldham	2	Bury	3	r
Preston NE	0	Bolton	2	re
Scunthpe	2	Peterboro	1	r
Watford	2	Reading	3	re
Workingtn	0	Carlisle	1	r

SECOND ROUND

Arsenal	0	Tranmere	1	
Blackpool	1	Birmghm C	1	
Bournemth	0	Sheff Wed	0	
Bury	2	Cambridge	0	
Cardiff	2	Burnley	2	
Chestrfld	1	Swindon	0	
Coventry	5	Darlingtn	1	
Derby	2	Sunderld	2	
Everton	1	Reading	0	
Gillinghm	1	Carlisle	2	
Halifax	0	Wolves	3	
Ipswich	2	Leeds U	0	
Leicester	3	Hull	3	
Leyton O	2	Blackburn	0	
Luton	1	Grimsby	1	
Man Utd	0	Middlesbro	1	
Millwall	0	Nottm For	0	
Newcastle	6	Doncaster	0	
Norwich	6	Wrexham	2	
Oxford	1	Fulham	1	
Plymouth	4	Portsmth	0	
QPR	1	Tottenham	0	
Rochdale	0	Bolton	4	
Rotherhm	1	Exeter	4	
Scunthpe	0	Bristol C	0	
Southmptn	3	Charlton	0	
Stockport	1	C.Palace	0	
Stoke	1	Chelsea	0	
Walsall	0	Man City	0	
West Brom	2	Sheff Utd	1	
West Ham	2	Liverpool	2	
York	1	Aston V	0	
Birmghm C	4	Blackpool	2	r
Bristol C	2	Scunthpe	1	r
Burnley	3	Cardiff	2	re
Fulham	3	Oxford	0	r
Grimsby	0	Luton	0	re
Hull	3	Leicester	2	r
Liverpool	1	West Ham	0	r
Man City	0	Walsall	0	re
Nottm For	1	Millwall	3	r
Sheff Wed	2	Bournemth	2	re
Sunderld	1	Derby	1	re
Grimsby	0	Luton	2	r2
Man City	4	Walsall	0	r2N
Sheff Wed	2	Bournemth	1	r2e
Sunderld	3	Derby	0	r2

THIRD ROUND

Birmghm C	2	Newcastle	2	
Bristol C	2	Coventry	2	
Burnley	1	Plymouth	2	
Carlisle	0	Man City	1	
Everton	0	Norwich	1	
Fulham	2	Ipswich	2	
Hull	4	Stockport	1	
Leyton O	1	York	1	
Luton	0	Bury	0	
Millwall	1	Bolton	1	
QPR	8	Sheff Wed	2	
Southmptn	3	Chestrfld	0	
Stoke	1	Middlesbro	1	
Sunderld	0	Liverpool	2	
Tranmere	1	Wolves	1	
West Brom	1	Exeter	3	
Bolton	1	Millwall	2	r
Bury	2	Luton	3	r
Coventry	2	Bristol C	1	r
Ipswich	2	Fulham	1	r
Middlesbro	1	Stoke	2	r
Newcastle	0	Birmghm C	1	re
Wolves	2	Tranmere	1	r
York	2	Leyton O	1	re

FOURTH ROUND

Coventry	2	Stoke	1	
Hull	0	Liverpool	0	
Ipswich	1	Birmghm C	3	
Millwall	3	Luton	1	
QPR	0	Plymouth	3	
Southmptn	0	Norwich	2	
Wolves	5	Exeter	1	
York	0	Man City	0	
Liverpool	3	Hull	1	r
Man City	4	York	1	r

FIFTH ROUND

Birmghm C	1	Plymouth	2	
Coventry	2	Man City	2	
Millwall	1	Norwich	1	
Wolves	1	Liverpool	0	
Man City	4	Coventry	2	r
Norwich	2	Millwall	1	r

SEMI-FINAL FIRST-LEG

Norwich	1	Wolves	1	
Plymouth	1	Man City	1	

SEMI-FINAL SECOND-LEG

Man City	2	Plymouth	0	

Man City win 3-1 on agg

Wolves	1	Norwich	0	

Wolves win 2-1 on agg

FINAL

Wolves	2	Man City	1	N

1975

FIRST ROUND

Barnsley	0	Halifax	1	
Bradford	2	Darlingtn	1	
Brentford	3	Aldershot	0	
Bristol C	2	Cardiff	1	
Bristol R	0	Plymouth	0	
Bury	2	Oldham	0	
Charlton	4	Peterboro	0	
Chester	2	Walsall	1	

Shoot 'Em Up

The first League Cup game settled by penalties was in 1976, when Darlington of the Fourth Division beat Sheffield Wednesday of the Third 5-3, after a 0-0 draw.

Home		Away		
Chestrfld	3	Grimsby	0	
Colchester	1	Oxford	0	
Doncaster	2	Mansfield	1	
Exeter	3	Swansea	1	
Gillinghm	1	Bournemth	1	
Hereford	1	Shrewsby	1	
Newport	1	Torquay	0	
N'hamptn	1	Port Vale	0	
Preston NE	1	Rochdale	0	
Reading	0	Brighton	0	
Rotherhm	1	Lincoln	1	
Scunthpe	1	Sheff Wed	0	
Southend	2	Cambridge	0	
Southport	0	Tranmere	2	
Stockport	0	Blackburn	2	
Swindon	0	Portsmth	1	
Watford	1	C.Palace	1	
Workingtn	1	Hartlepl	2	
Wrexham	1	Crewe	2	
York	0	Huddersfld	2	
Bournemth	1	Gillinghm	1	re
Brighton	2	Reading	2	re
C.Palace	5	Watford	1	r
Lincoln	1	Rotherhm	1	re
Plymouth	0	Bristol R	1	r
Shrewsby	0	Hereford	1	r
Gillinghm	1	Bournmth	2	r2eN
Reading	0	Brighton	0	r2e
Rotherhm	2	Lincoln	1	r2
Brighton	2	Reading	3	r3

SECOND ROUND

Home		Away		
Arsenal	1	Leicester	1	
Aston V	1	Everton	1	
Bolton	0	Norwich	0	
Bournemth	1	Hartlepl	1	
Bradford	0	Carlisle	1	
Bury	2	Doncaster	0	
Chelsea	4	Newport	2	
Chester	3	Blackpool	1	
Coventry	1	Ipswich	2	
Crewe	2	Birmghm C	1	
C.Palace	1	Bristol C	4	
Exeter	0	Hereford	1	
Huddersfld	1	Leeds U	1	
Hull	1	Burnley	2	
Liverpool	2	Brentford	1	
Luton	1	Bristol R	0	
Man City	6	Scunthpe	0	
Man Utd	5	Charlton	1	
N'hamptn	2	Blackburn	2	
Nottm For	1	Newcastle	1	
Portsmth	1	Derby	5	
Preston NE	2	Sunderld	0	
QPR	1	Leyton O	1	
Reading	4	Rotherhm	2	
Sheff Utd	3	Chestrfld	1	
Southmptn	1	Notts Co	0	
Southend	0	Colchester	2	
Stoke	3	Halifax	0	
Tottenham	0	Middlesbro	4	
Tranmere	0	West Ham	0	
West Brom	1	Millwall	0	
Wolves	1	Fulham	3	
Blackburn	1	N'hamptn	0	r
Everton	0	Aston V	3	r
Hartlepl	2	Bournemth	2	re
Leeds U	1	Huddersfld	1	re
Leicester	2	Arsenal	1	r
Leyton O	0	QPR	3	r
Newcastle	3	Nottm For	0	r
Norwich	3	Bolton	1	r
West Ham	6	Tranmere	0	r
Bournemth	1	Hartlepl	1	r2e
Leeds U	2	Huddersfld	1	r2
Hartlepl	1	Bournemth	0	r3

THIRD ROUND

Home		Away		
Bristol C	0	Liverpool	0	
Bury	1	Leeds U	2	
Chelsea	2	Stoke	2	
Chester	1	Preston NE	0	
Colchester	2	Carlisle	0	
Crewe	2	Aston V	2	
Fulham	2	West Ham	1	
Hartlepl	1	Blackburn	1	
Ipswich	4	Hereford	1	
Man Utd	1	Man City	0	
Middlesbro	1	Leicester	0	
QPR	0	Newcastle	4	
Reading	1	Burnley	2	
Sheff Utd	2	Luton	0	
Southmptn	5	Derby	0	
West Brom	1	Norwich	1	
Aston V	1	Crewe	0	r
Blackburn	1	Hartlepl	2	r
Liverpool	4	Bristol C	0	r
Norwich	2	West Brom	0	re
Stoke	1	Chelsea	1	re
Stoke	6	Chelsea	2	r2

FOURTH ROUND

Home		Away		
Chester	3	Leeds U	0	
Colchester	0	Southmptn	0	
Hartlepl	1	Aston V	1	
Ipswich	2	Stoke	1	
Liverpool	0	Middlesbro	1	
Man Utd	3	Burnley	2	
Newcastle	3	Fulham	0	
Sheff Utd	2	Norwich	2	
Aston V	6	Hartlepl	1	r
Norwich	2	Sheff Utd	1	re
Southmptn	0	Colchester	1	r

FIFTH ROUND

Home		Away		
Colchester	1	Aston V	2	
Middlesbro	0	Man Utd	0	
Newcastle	0	Chester	0	
Norwich	1	Ipswich	1	
Chester	1	Newcastle	0	r
Ipswich	1	Norwich	2	r
Man Utd	3	Middlesbro	0	r

SEMI-FINAL FIRST-LEG

Home		Away		
Chester	2	Aston V	2	
Man Utd	2	Norwich	2	

SEMI-FINAL SECOND-LEG

Home		Away		
Aston V	3	Chester	2	

Aston V win 5-4 on agg

Home		Away		
Norwich	1	Man Utd	0	

Norwich win 3-2 on agg

FINAL

Home		Away		
Aston V	1	Norwich	0	N

1976

FIRST ROUND FIRST-LEG

Home		Away		
Aldershot	1	Portsmth	1	
Bradford	2	York	0	
Brentford	2	Brighton	1	
Bury	2	Rochdale	0	
Cambridge	1	Charlton	1	
Cardiff	1	Bristol R	2	
Crewe	2	Tranmere	1	
C.Palace	3	Colchester	0	
Darlingtn	0	Sheff Wed	2	
Doncaster	3	Grimsby	1	
Halifax	4	Hartlepl	1	
Huddersfld	2	Barnsley	1	
Lincoln	4	Chestrfld	2	

GIANTKILLERS

1973-74 QPR 0 Plymouth 3

Britain was affected by an energy crisis and short-time working, but Plymouth sailed breezily on. Although they ended in the lower half of the Third Division, they compiled perhaps the best record of all League Cup giantkillers. They won at nearby Torquay and at home to Second Division Portsmouth, then were drawn away to three teams from Division One and beat them all - Burnley 2-1, QPR 3-0 and Birmingham 2-1, inspired by veteran keeper Jim Furnell and two fine forwards, Steve Davey and Paul Mariner. They also drew the home Semi-Final leg against Manchester City, only to lose 2-0 in the return.

GIANTKILLERS

1974-75 Chester 3 Leeds 0

This was the season when Chester, the only club then in the League never to have won promotion, finally did so. They also reached the League Cup Semi-Final while in Division Four, and lost to eventual Cup winners Villa only on a 4-5 aggregate, having twice come back after being two goals behind. On the way to Wembley they beat Walsall, Blackpool, Preston, star-encrusted Leeds - 3-0, no less - and Newcastle, who could not score in either leg of the Semi-Final. Reg Matthewson, John James and the rest are largely forgotten now...but not in Chester.

Mansfield	4	Scunthpe	0	
Newport	1	Exeter	1	
Oldham	3	Workingtn	0	
Plymouth	2	Bournemth	0	
Port Vale	4	Hereford	2	
Preston NE	2	Blackburn	0	
Reading	0	Gillinghm	1	
Rotherhm	1	Nottm For	2	
Southend	2	Peterboro	0	
Southport	3	Stockport	1	
Swansea	1	Torquay	2	
Swindon	2	Millwall	1	
Walsall	0	Shrewsby	0	
Watford	2	N'hamptn	0	
Wrexham	3	Chester	0	
FIRST ROUND SECOND-LEG				
Barnsley	1	Huddersfld	1	
Huddersfld win 3-2 on agg				
Blackburn	0	Preston NE	0	
Preston NE win 2-0 on agg				
Bournemth	1	Plymouth	2	
Plymouth win 4-1 on agg				
Brighton	1	Brentford	1	
Brentford win 3-2 on agg				
Bristol R	1	Cardiff	1	
Bristol R win 3-2 on agg				
Charlton	3	Cambridge	0	
Charlton win 4-1 on agg				
Chester	0	Wrexham	0	
Wrexham win 3-0 on agg				
Chestrfld	3	Lincoln	2	
Lincoln win 6-5 on agg				
Colchester	3	C.Palace	1	
C.Palace win 4-3 on agg				
Exeter	2	Newport	0	
Exeter win 3-1 on agg				
Gillinghm	1	Reading	1	
Gillinghm win 2-1 on agg				
Grimsby	0	Doncaster	0	
Doncaster win 3-1 on agg				
Hartlepl	2	Halifax	1	
Halifax win 5-3 on agg				
Hereford	2	Port Vale	0	
agg score Hereford 4 - Port Vale 4				
Millwall	0	Swindon	1	
Swindon win 3-1 on agg				
N'hamptn	1	Watford	1	
Watford win 3-1 on agg				
Nottm For	5	Rotherhm	1	
Nottm For win 7-2 on agg				
Peterboro	3	Southend	0	
Peterboro win 3-2 on agg				
Portsmth	2	Aldershot	1	
Portsmth win 3-2 on agg				
Rochdale	0	Bury	2	
Bury win 4-0 on agg				
Scunthpe	0	Mansfield	2	
Mansfield win 6-0 on agg				
Sheff Wed	0	Darlingtn	2	
agg score Sheff W 2 - Darlingtn 2				
Shrewsby	2	Walsall	1	
Shrewsby win 2-1 on agg				
Stockport	1	Southport	2	
Southport win 5-2 on agg				
Torquay	5	Swansea	3	
Torquay win 7-4 on agg				
Tranmere	2	Crewe	1	
agg score Tranmere 3 - Crewe 3				
Workingtn	1	Oldham	3	
Oldham win 6-1 on agg				
York	3	Bradford	0	
York win 3-2 on agg				
FIRST ROUND REPLAYS				
Crewe	2	Tranmere	1	re
Port Vale	0	Hereford	1	rN
Sheff Wed	0	Darlingtn	0	rq
SECOND ROUND				
Aston V	2	Oldham	0	
Birmghm C	4	Leyton O	0	
Bolton	1	Coventry	3	
Bury	1	Middlesbro	2	
Carlisle	2	Gillinghm	0	
Charlton	3	Oxford	3	
Crewe	1	Chelsea	0	
Darlingtn	2	Luton	1	
Derby	2	Huddersfld	1	
Doncaster	2	C.Palace	1	
Everton	2	Arsenal	2	
Halifax	2	Sheff Utd	4	
Hereford	1	Burnley	4	
Hull	4	Preston NE	2	
Leeds U	3	Ipswich	2	
Lincoln	2	Stoke	1	
Man Utd	2	Brentford	1	
Newcastle	6	Southport	0	
Norwich	1	Man City	1	
Nottm For	1	Plymouth	0	
Notts Co	2	Sunderld	1	
Peterboro	2	Blackpool	0	
Portsmth	1	Leicester	1	
Shrewsby	1	QPR	4	
Southmptn	0	Bristol R	1	
Swindon	2	Wolves	2	
Torquay	1	Exeter	1	
Watford	0	Tottenham	1	
West Brom	1	Fulham	1	
West Ham	0	Bristol C	0	
Wrexham	1	Mansfield	2	
York	0	Liverpool	1	
Arsenal	0	Everton	1	r
Bristol C	1	West Ham	3	r
Exeter	1	Torquay	2	r
Fulham	1	West Brom	0	r
Leicester	1	Portsmth	0	re
Man City	2	Norwich	2	re
Oxford	1	Charlton	1	re
Wolves	3	Swindon	2	r
Norwich	1	Man City	6	r2N
Oxford	2	Charlton	3	r2e
THIRD ROUND				
Aston V	1	Man Utd	2	
Birmghm C	0	Wolves	2	
Bristol R	1	Newcastle	1	
Crewe	0	Tottenham	2	
Everton	2	Carlisle	0	
Fulham	0	Peterboro	1	
Hull	2	Sheff Utd	0	
Leeds U	0	Notts Co	1	

Sub Standard

Ralph Coates, who scored the winner for Spurs in the 1973 League Cup Final against Norwich, was and still is the only substitute to score in a Final.

Leicester	2	Lincoln	1	
Liverpool	1	Burnley	1	
Man City	2	Nottm For	1	
Mansfield	2	Coventry	0	
Middlesbro	1	Derby	0	
QPR	1	Charlton	1	
Torquay	1	Doncaster	1	
West Ham	3	Darlingtn	0	
Burnley	1	Liverpool	0	r
Charlton	0	QPR	3	r
Doncaster	3	Torquay	0	r
Newcastle	2	Bristol R	0	r
FOURTH ROUND				
Burnley	2	Leicester	0	
Doncaster	2	Hull	1	
Everton	2	Notts Co	2	
Man City	4	Man Utd	0	
Mansfield	1	Wolves	0	
Middlesbro	3	Peterboro	0	
QPR	1	Newcastle	3	
Tottenham	0	West Ham	0	
Notts Co	2	Everton	0	r
West Ham	0	Tottenham	2	re
FIFTH ROUND				
Burnley	0	Middlesbro	2	
Man City	4	Mansfield	2	
Newcastle	1	Notts Co	0	
Tottenham	7	Doncaster	2	
SEMI-FINAL FIRST-LEG				
Middlesbro	1	Man City	0	
Tottenham	1	Newcastle	0	
SEMI-FINAL SECOND-LEG				
Man City	4	Middlesbro	0	
Man City win 4-1 on agg				
Newcastle	3	Tottenham	1	
Newcastle win 3-2 on agg				
FINAL				
Man City	2	Newcastle	1	N

1977

FIRST ROUND FIRST-LEG				
Aldershot	1	Gillinghm	1	
Bournemth	0	Torquay	0	
Bradford	1	Oldham	1	
Bury	2	Preston NE	1	
Cardiff	2	Bristol R	1	
Chester	2	Hereford	0	
Chestrfld	3	Rotherhm	1	
Crewe	2	Tranmere	1	
C.Palace	2	Portsmth	2	
Doncaster	1	Lincoln	1	
Grimsby	0	Sheff Wed	3	
Halifax	0	Darlingtn	0	
Huddersfld	2	Hartlepl	0	
Mansfield	2	Scunthpe	0	
Millwall	2	Colchester	1	
Oxford	1	Cambridge	0	
Plymouth	0	Exeter	1	
Port Vale	1	Wrexham	1	
Reading	2	Peterboro	3	
Rochdale	0	Blackburn	1	
Shrewsby	0	Walsall	1	
Southend	1	Brighton	1	
Southport	1	Carlisle	2	
Swansea	4	Newport	1	
Swindon	3	N'hamptn	2	
Watford	1	Brentford	1	
Workingtn	0	Stockport	0	
York	0	Barnsley	0	
FIRST ROUND SECOND-LEG				
Barnsley	0	York	0	
Blackburn	4	Rochdale	1	
Blackburn win 5-1 on agg				
Brentford	0	Watford	2	
Watford win 3-1 on agg				
Brighton	2	Southend	1	
Brighton win 3-2 on agg				
Bristol R	4	Cardiff	4	
Cardiff win 6-5 on agg				
Cambridge	2	Oxford	0	
Cambridge win 2-1 on agg				
Carlisle	0	Southport	1	
agg score Carlisle 2 - Southport 2				
Colchester	2	Millwall	1	
agg score Colchester 3 - Millwall 3				
Darlingtn	1	Halifax	1	
agg score Darlingtn 1 - Halifax 1				
Exeter	1	Plymouth	0	
Exeter win 2-0 on agg				
Gillinghm	2	Aldershot	0	
Gillinghm win 3-1 on agg				
Hartlepl	1	Huddersfld	2	
Huddersfld win 4-1 on agg				
Hereford	4	Chester	3	
Chester win 5-4 on agg				
Lincoln	1	Doncaster	1	

Gray Days

Andy Gray, now a SKY TV analyst, won the League Cup with Aston Villa in 1977, against Everton, and the FA Cup in 1984, when playing FOR Everton, against Watford.

agg score Lincoln 2 - Doncaster 2				
Newport	1	Swansea	0	
Swansea win 4-2 on agg				
N'hamptn	2	Swindon	0	
N'hamptn win 4-3 on agg				
Oldham	1	Bradford	3	
Bradford win 4-2 on agg				
Peterboro	0	Reading	1	
agg score Peterboro 3 - Reading 3				
Portsmth	0	C.Palace	1	
C.Palace win 3-2 on agg				
Preston NE	1	Bury	1	
Bury win 3-2 on agg				
Rotherhm	3	Chestrfld	0	
Rotherhm win 4-3 on agg				
Scunthpe	2	Mansfield	0	
agg score Scunthpe 2 - M'sfield 2				
Sheff Wed	0	Grimsby	0	
Sheff Wed win 3-0 on agg				
Stockport	0	Workingtn	0	
Torquay	1	Bournemth	0	
Torquay win 1-0 on agg				
Tranmere	3	Crewe	1	
Tranmere win 4-3 on agg				
Walsall	1	Shrewsby	0	
Walsall win 2-0 on agg				
Wrexham	1	Port Vale	0	
Wrexham win 2-1 on agg				
FIRST ROUND REPLAYS				
Carlisle	3	Southport	2	r
Colchester	4	Millwall	4	rq
Doncaster	2	Lincoln	2	rPN
Halifax	1	Darlingtn	2	re

WHAT A STAR ✪ BRIAN LITTLE

Little had earned a place in Aston Villa's history long before he became manager of the club, during the long battles to win the League Cup in 1974-75 and 1976-77. In the second of those seasons, after four straight victories, Villa had to battle through three matches in both the Semi-Final, against QPR, and the Final, against Everton. Little settled the Semi with a hat-trick at Highbury in the third game, and he won the Cup for his side by scoring a close-range winner in the last minute of the second Final replay, at Old Trafford - his tenth goal in the competition that season. Surely he was worth more to England than the 19 minutes as a sub that made up his international career?

Peterboro	3	Reading	1	re
Scunthpe	2	Mansfield	1	r
Workingtn	0	Stockport	2	rN
York	1	Barnsley	2	re
SECOND ROUND				
Arsenal	3	Carlisle	2	
Aston V	3	Man City	0	
Blackburn	1	Stockport	3	
Blackpool	2	Birmghm C	1	
Bradford	1	Bolton	2	
Bristol C	0	Coventry	1	
Bury	2	Darlingtn	1	
Cardiff	1	QPR	3	
Chelsea	3	Sheff Utd	1	
Chester	2	Swansea	3	
C.Palace	1	Watford	3	
Doncaster	1	Derby	2	
Everton	3	Cambridge	0	
Exeter	1	Norwich	3	
Fulham	1	Peterboro	1	
Gillinghm	1	Newcastle	2	
Ipswich	0	Brighton	0	
Leyton O	1	Hull	0	
Liverpool	1	West Brom	1	
Man Utd	5	Tranmere	0	
Middlesbro	1	Tottenham	2	
N'hamptn	0	Huddersfld	1	
Rotherhm	1	Millwall	2	
Scunthpe	0	Notts Co	2	
Southmptn	1	Charlton	1	
Stoke	2	Leeds U	1	
Sunderld	3	Luton	1	
Torquay	1	Burnley	0	
Walsall	2	Nottm For	4	
West Ham	3	Barnsley	0	
Wolves	1	Sheff Wed	2	
Wrexham	1	Leicester	0	
Brighton	2	Ipswich	1	r
Charlton	2	Southmptn	1	r
Peterboro	1	Fulham	2	r
West Brom	1	Liverpool	0	r
THIRD ROUND				
Aston V	2	Norwich	1	
Blackpool	1	Arsenal	1	
Charlton	0	West Ham	1	
Chelsea	2	Huddersfld	0	
Derby	1	Notts Co	1	
Fulham	2	Bolton	2	
Man Utd	2	Sunderld	2	
Millwall	0	Leyton O	0	
Newcastle	3	Stoke	0	
Nottm For	0	Coventry	3	
QPR	2	Bury	1	
Sheff Wed	3	Watford	1	
Stockport	0	Everton	1	
Torquay	1	Swansea	2	
Tottenham	2	Wrexham	3	
West Brom	0	Brighton	2	
Arsenal	0	Blackpool	0	re
Bolton	2	Fulham	2	re
Leyton O	0	Millwall	0	re
Notts Co	1	Derby	2	r
Sunderld	2	Man Utd	2	re
Arsenal	2	Blackpool	0	r2
Fulham	1	Bolton	2	r2N
Man Utd	1	Sunderld	0	r2
Millwall	3	Leyton O	0	r2N
FOURTH ROUND				
Arsenal	2	Chelsea	1	
Aston V	5	Wrexham	1	
Brighton	1	Derby	1	
Everton	3	Coventry	0	
Man Utd	7	Newcastle	2	
Millwall	3	Sheff Wed	0	
Swansea	1	Bolton	1	
West Ham	0	QPR	2	
Bolton	5	Swansea	1	r
Derby	2	Brighton	1	r
FIFTH ROUND				
Aston V	2	Millwall	0	
Derby	1	Bolton	2	
Man Utd	0	Everton	3	
QPR	2	Arsenal	1	
SEMI-FINAL FIRST-LEG				
Everton	1	Bolton	1	
QPR	0	Aston V	0	
SEMI-FINAL SECOND-LEG				
Aston V	2	QPR	2	e
agg score Aston V 2 - QPR 2				
Bolton	0	Everton	1	
Everton win 2-1 on agg				
SEMI-FINAL REPLAY				
QPR	0	Aston V	3	rN
FINAL				
Aston V	0	Everton	0	N
Aston V	1	Everton	1	reN
Aston V	3	Everton	2	r2eN

1978

FIRST ROUND FIRST-LEG				
Aldershot	1	Colchester	1	
Brentford	2	C.Palace	1	
Bristol R	1	Walsall	2	
Burnley	2	Chester	0	
Bury	3	Crewe	0	
Cambridge	0	Brighton	0	
Chestrfld	4	Barnsley	1	
Darlingtn	0	Scunthpe	0	
Exeter	2	Plymouth	2	
Fulham	0	Leyton O	2	
Gillinghm	1	Wimbledn	1	
Grimsby	3	Hartlepl	0	
Hereford	2	Bournemth	0	
Huddersfld	1	Carlisle	1	
Mansfield	0	Lincoln	1	
Oxford	3	Shrewsby	0	
Peterboro	4	Bradford	1	
Port Vale	2	Preston NE	1	
Portsmth	3	Newport	1	
Rochdale	1	Halifax	1	
Rotherhm	3	York	0	
Sheff Wed	5	Doncaster	2	
Southend	2	N'hamptn	3	
Swansea	1	Swindon	3	
Torquay	1	Cardiff	0	
Tranmere	0	Southport	1	
Watford	2	Reading	1	
Wrexham	1	Stockport	0	
FIRST ROUND SECOND-LEG				
Barnsley	3	Chestrfld	0	
agg score Barnsley 4 - Chestrfld 4				
Bournemth	4	Hereford	2	
agg score B'nemth 4 - Hereford 4				
Bradford	1	Peterboro	1	
Peterboro win 5-2 on agg				
Brighton	0	Cambridge	0	
Cardiff	3	Torquay	2	
agg score Cardiff 3 - Torquay 3				
Carlisle	2	Huddersfld	2	
agg score Carlisle 3 - Huddersfld 3				
Chester	1	Burnley	0	
Burnley win 2-1 on agg				
Colchester	4	Aldershot	1	
Colchester win 5-2 on agg				
Crewe	1	Bury	1	
Bury win 4-1 on agg				
C.Palace	5	Brentford	1	
C.Palace win 6-3 on agg				
Doncaster	0	Sheff Wed	3	
Sheff Wed win 8-2 on agg				

WHAT A STAR ✪ JOHN ROBERTSON

This short, dumpy, moderate-to-slow outside-left was one of the outstanding performers in the excellent Nottingham Forest team of the late 70s and 80s, when they won the Championship, the European Cup twice and the League Cup twice, as well as losing in their third successive Final. Robertson, with his 100 per cent control, vision and accurate passing, earned his medals. He scored the only goal in two Finals - the 1978 League Cup, keeping icy cool as a row raged over a penalty award, and the 1980 European Cup.

Ground Swell

The first 100,000 attendance for a League Cup game was at the 1971 Final between Spurs and Aston Villa. Receipts came to £132,000.

Fulham	2	Leyton O	1	
Leyton O win 3-2 on agg				
Halifax	1	Rochdale	2	
Rochdale win 3-2 on agg				
Hartlepl	1	Grimsby	2	
Grimsby win 5-1 on agg				
Lincoln	0	Mansfield	0	
Lincoln win 1-0 on agg				
Newport	3	Portsmth	2	
Portsmth win 5-4 on agg				
N'hamptn	2	Southend	1	
N'hamptn win 5-3 on agg				
Plymouth	0	Exeter	0	
agg score Plymouth 2 - Exeter 2				
Preston NE	2	Port Vale	1	
agg score Preston NE 3 - P Vale 3				
Reading	1	Watford	0	
agg score Reading 2 - Watford 2				
Scunthpe	3	Darlingtn	1	
Scunthpe win 3-1 on agg				
Shrewsby	2	Oxford	2	
Oxford win 5-2 on agg				
Southport	2	Tranmere	2	
Southport win 3-2 on agg				
Stockport	1	Wrexham	1	
Wrexham win 2-1 on agg				
Swindon	2	Swansea	1	
Swindon win 5-2 on agg				
Walsall	1	Bristol R	0	
Walsall win 3-1 on agg				
Wimbledn	3	Gillinghm	1	
Wimbledn win 4-2 on agg				
York	3	Rotherhm	0	
agg score York 3 - Rotherhm 3				

FIRST ROUND REPLAYS

Barnsley	0	Chestrfld	2	re
Brighton	3	Cambridge	1	r
Cardiff	2	Torquay	1	r
Hereford	1	Bournemth	2	re
Huddersfld	2	Carlisle	1	r
Plymouth	0	Exeter	1	r
Port Vale	1	Preston NE	2	rN
Watford	5	Reading	0	r
York	1	Rotherhm	1	rq

SECOND ROUND

Arsenal	3	Man Utd	2	
Birmghm C	0	Notts Co	2	
Blackburn	1	Colchester	1	
Blackpool	2	Sheff Wed	2	
Bolton	1	Lincoln	0	
Brighton	0	Oldham	0	
Bristol C	1	Stoke	0	
Burnley	3	Norwich	1	
Charlton	1	Wrexham	2	
Chestrfld	0	Man City	1	
C.Palace	0	Southmptn	0	
Derby	3	Leyton O	1	
Exeter	1	Aston V	3	
Grimsby	1	Watford	2	
Huddersfld	0	Coventry	2	
Ipswich	5	N'hamptn	0	
Liverpool	2	Chelsea	0	
Newcastle	0	Millwall	2	
Nottm For	5	West Ham	0	
Oxford	1	Bury	1	
Peterboro	1	Scunthpe	1	
Portsmth	2	Leicester	0	
QPR	2	Bournemth	0	
Rochdale	0	Leeds U	3	
Sheff Utd	0	Everton	3	
Southport	2	Hull	2	
Sunderld	2	Middlesbro	2	
Swindon	5	Cardiff	1	
Tottenham	4	Wimbledn	0	
Walsall	0	Preston NE	0	
West Brom	4	Rotherhm	0	
Wolves	1	Luton	3	
Bury	1	Oxford	0	re
Colchester	4	Blackburn	0	r
Hull	1	Southport	0	r
Middlesbro	1	Sunderld	0	r
Oldham	2	Brighton	2	re
Preston NE	0	Walsall	1	re
Scunthpe	0	Peterboro	1	r
Sheff Wed	3	Blackpool	1	r
Southmptn	2	C.Palace	1	re
Brighton	1	Oldham	2	r2eN

THIRD ROUND

Arsenal	2	Southmptn	0	
Aston V	1	QPR	0	
Bolton	3	Peterboro	1	
Burnley	1	Ipswich	2	
Everton	2	Middlesbro	2	
Hull	2	Oldham	0	
Leeds U	4	Colchester	0	
Liverpool	2	Derby	0	
Luton	1	Man City	1	
Millwall	1	Bury	1	
Nottm For	4	Notts Co	0	
Portsmth	1	Swindon	1	
Sheff Wed	2	Walsall	1	
Tottenham	2	Coventry	3	
West Brom	1	Watford	0	

Magnificent Seven

Seven Chelsea players appeared in the FA Cup Final of 1970, the Cup-Winners' Cup Final of 1971, and the League Cup Final of '72 - Bonetti, Dempsey, Webb, Harris, Hollins, Osgood and Houseman.

Wrexham	1	Bristol C	0	
Bury	2	Millwall	0	r
Man City	0	Luton	0	re
Middlesbro	1	Everton	2	r
Swindon	4	Portsmth	3	r
Luton	2	Man City	3	r2eN

FOURTH ROUND

Arsenal	5	Hull	1	
Bolton	1	Leeds U	3	
Bury	1	West Brom	0	
Ipswich	1	Man City	2	
Liverpool	2	Coventry	2	
Nottm For	4	Aston V	2	
Sheff Wed	1	Everton	3	
Wrexham	2	Swindon	0	
Coventry	0	Liverpool	2	r

FIFTH ROUND

Bury	0	Nottm For	3	
Leeds U	4	Everton	1	
Man City	0	Arsenal	0	
Wrexham	1	Liverpool	3	
Arsenal	1	Man City	0	r

SEMI-FINAL FIRST-LEG

Leeds U	1	Nottm For	3	
Liverpool	2	Arsenal	1	

SEMI-FINAL SECOND-LEG

Arsenal	0	Liverpool	0	
Liverpool win 2-1 on agg				
Nottm For	4	Leeds U	2	
Nottm For win 7-3 on agg				

FINAL

Nottm For	0	Liverpool	0	eN
Nottm For	1	Liverpool	0	rN

1979

FIRST ROUND FIRST-LEG

Aldershot	0	Millwall	1	
Barnsley	1	Chestrfld	2	
Bournemth	0	Exeter	1	
Bradford	2	Lincoln	0	
Bristol R	2	Hereford	1	
Cambridge	2	N'hamptn	2	
Cardiff	1	Oxford	2	
Carlisle	2	Blackpool	2	
Colchester	2	Charlton	3	
Crewe	1	Rochdale	0	
Doncaster	0	Sheff Wed	1	
Grimsby	2	York	0	
Hull	0	Peterboro	1	
Mansfield	0	Darlingtn	1	
Newport	2	Swansea	1	
Plymouth	1	Torquay	1	
Port Vale	0	Chester	3	
Portsmth	0	Swindon	0	
Preston NE	3	Huddersfld	0	
Reading	3	Gillinghm	1	
Rotherhm	5	Hartlepl	0	
Scunthpe	0	Notts Co	1	
Shrewsby	1	Stockport	0	
Southend	1	Wimbledn	0	
Tranmere	1	Wigan Ath	1	
Walsall	2	Halifax	1	
Watford	4	Brentford	0	
Wrexham	2	Bury	0	

FIRST ROUND SECOND-LEG

Blackpool	2	Carlisle	1	
Blackpool win 4-3 on agg				

GIANTKILLERS

1978-79 Man Utd 1 Watford 2

Graham Taylor took his Third Division Watford team very close to the Final after being drawn to play through a succession of clubs from Divisions 3,2,1,3,2,1. The clubs were Brentford, Newcastle, Manchester United (beaten 2-1 at Old Trafford after they had gone in front), Exeter, Stoke and, in the Semi-Final, Nottingham Forest. They proved two goals too strong over two legs, but Watford had earned a lot of tributes, as well as promotion. Ross Jenkins scored 37 goals during the season, Luther Blissett 28.

Brentford	**1**	**Watford**	**3**	
Watford win 7-1 on agg				
Bury	**1**	**Wrexham**	**2**	
Wrexham win 4-1 on agg				
Charlton	**0**	**Colchester**	**0**	
Charlton win 3-2 on agg				
Chester	**1**	**Port Vale**	**1**	
Chester win 4-1 on agg				
Chestrfld	**0**	**Barnsley**	**0**	
Chestrfld win 2-1 on agg				
Darlingtn	**2**	**Mansfield**	**2**	
Darlingtn win 3-2 on agg				
Exeter	**1**	**Bournemth**	**1**	
Exeter win 2-1 on agg				
Gillinghm	**1**	**Reading**	**2**	
Reading win 5-2 on agg				
Halifax	**0**	**Walsall**	**2**	
Walsall win 4-1 on agg				
Hartlepl	**1**	**Rotherhm**	**1**	
Rotherhm win 6-1 on agg				
Hereford	**4**	**Bristol R**	**0**	
Hereford win 5-2 on agg				
Huddersfld	**2**	**Preston NE**	**2**	
Preston NE win 5-2 on agg				
Lincoln	**1**	**Bradford**	**1**	
Bradford win 3-1 on agg				
Millwall	**1**	**Aldershot**	**0**	
Millwall win 2-0 on agg				
N'hamptn	**2**	**Cambridge**	**1**	
N'hamptn win 4-3 on agg				
Notts Co	**3**	**Scunthpe**	**0**	
Notts Co win 4-0 on agg				
Oxford	**2**	**Cardiff**	**1**	
Oxford win 4-2 on agg				
Peterboro	**1**	**Hull**	**2**	
agg score Peterboro 2 - Hull 2				
Rochdale	**2**	**Crewe**	**4**	
Crewe win 5-2 on agg				
Sheff Wed	**0**	**Doncaster**	**1**	
agg score Sheff W 1 - Doncaster 1				
Stockport	**3**	**Shrewsby**	**1**	
Stockport win 3-2 on agg				
Swansea	**5**	**Newport**	**0**	
Swansea win 6-2 on agg				
Swindon	**4**	**Portsmth**	**2**	
Swindon win 4-2 on agg				
Torquay	**1**	**Plymouth**	**2**	
Plymouth win 3-2 on agg				
Wigan Ath	**2**	**Tranmere**	**1**	
Wigan Ath win 3-2 on agg				
Wimbledn	**4**	**Southend**	**1**	
Wimbledn win 4-2 on agg				
York	**0**	**Grimsby**	**3**	
Grimsby win 5-0 on agg				
FIRST ROUND REPLAYS				
Doncaster	**0**	**Sheff Wed**	**1**	**r**
Hull	**0**	**Peterboro**	**1**	**r**
SECOND ROUND				
Aston V	**1**	**Sheff Wed**	**0**	
Birmghm C	**2**	**Southmptn**	**5**	
Blackpool	**2**	**Ipswich**	**0**	
Bolton	**2**	**Chelsea**	**1**	
Brighton	**1**	**Millwall**	**0**	
Bristol C	**1**	**C.Palace**	**2**	
Burnley	**1**	**Bradford**	**1**	
Chester	**2**	**Coventry**	**1**	
Crewe	**2**	**Notts Co**	**0**	
Everton	**8**	**Wimbledn**	**0**	
Exeter	**2**	**Blackburn**	**1**	
Fulham	**2**	**Darlingtn**	**2**	
Leicester	**0**	**Derby**	**1**	
Leyton O	**1**	**Chestrfld**	**2**	
Luton	**2**	**Wigan Ath**	**0**	
Man City	**2**	**Grimsby**	**0**	
Man Utd	**3**	**Stockport**	**2**	
Middlesbro	**0**	**Peterboro**	**0**	
N'hamptn	**0**	**Hereford**	**0**	
Oldham	**0**	**Nottm For**	**0**	
Oxford	**1**	**Plymouth**	**1**	
Preston NE	**1**	**QPR**	**3**	
Reading	**1**	**Wolves**	**0**	
Rotherhm	**3**	**Arsenal**	**1**	
Sheff Utd	**1**	**Liverpool**	**0**	
Sunderld	**0**	**Stoke**	**2**	
Swansea	**2**	**Tottenham**	**2**	
Walsall	**1**	**Charlton**	**2**	
Watford	**2**	**Newcastle**	**1**	
West Brom	**0**	**Leeds U**	**0**	
West Ham	**1**	**Swindon**	**2**	
Wrexham	**1**	**Norwich**	**3**	
Bradford	**2**	**Burnley**	**3**	**r**
Darlingtn	**1**	**Fulham**	**0**	**r**
Hereford	**0**	**N'hamptn**	**1**	**r**
Leeds U	**0**	**West Brom**	**0**	**re**
Nottm For	**4**	**Oldham**	**2**	**r**
Peterboro	**1**	**Middlesbro**	**0**	**re**
Plymouth	**1**	**Oxford**	**2**	**re**
Tottenham	**1**	**Swansea**	**3**	**r**
West Brom	**0**	**Leeds U**	**1**	**r2N**
THIRD ROUND				
Aston V	**1**	**C.Palace**	**1**	
Blackpool	**1**	**Man City**	**1**	
Burnley	**1**	**Brighton**	**3**	
Chester	**0**	**Norwich**	**2**	
Chestrfld	**4**	**Charlton**	**5**	
Everton	**1**	**Darlingtn**	**0**	
Exeter	**2**	**Bolton**	**1**	
Luton	**2**	**Crewe**	**1**	
Man Utd	**1**	**Watford**	**2**	
N'hamptn	**1**	**Stoke**	**3**	
Oxford	**0**	**Nottm For**	**5**	
Peterboro	**1**	**Swindon**	**1**	
QPR	**2**	**Swansea**	**0**	
Rotherhm	**2**	**Reading**	**2**	
Sheff Utd	**1**	**Leeds U**	**4**	
Southmptn	**1**	**Derby**	**0**	
C.Palace	**0**	**Aston V**	**0**	**re**
Man City	**3**	**Blackpool**	**0**	**r**
Reading	**1**	**Rotherhm**	**0**	**r**
Swindon	**0**	**Peterboro**	**2**	**re**
Aston V	**3**	**C.Palace**	**0**	**r2N**
FOURTH ROUND				
Aston V	**0**	**Luton**	**2**	
Brighton	**1**	**Peterboro**	**0**	
Charlton	**2**	**Stoke**	**3**	
Everton	**2**	**Nottm For**	**3**	
Exeter	**0**	**Watford**	**2**	
Norwich	**1**	**Man City**	**3**	
QPR	**0**	**Leeds U**	**2**	
Reading	**0**	**Southmptn**	**0**	
Southmptn	**2**	**Reading**	**0**	**r**
FIFTH ROUND				
Leeds U	**4**	**Luton**	**1**	
Nottm For	**3**	**Brighton**	**1**	
Southmptn	**2**	**Man City**	**1**	
Stoke	**0**	**Watford**	**0**	
Watford	**3**	**Stoke**	**1**	**re**
SEMI-FINAL FIRST-LEG				
Leeds U	**2**	**Southmptn**	**2**	
Nottm For	**3**	**Watford**	**1**	
SEMI-FINAL SECOND-LEG				
Southmptn	**1**	**Leeds U**	**0**	
Southmptn win 3-2 on agg				
Watford	**0**	**Nottm For**	**0**	
Nottm For win 3-1 on agg				
FINAL				
Nottm For	**3**	**Southmptn**	**2**	**N**

1980-1989

ROCKIN' REDS

Six Hitters

Six Liverpool players appeared on the winning side in all their four successive League Cup Final victories from 1980-84 - Phil Neal, Alan Kennedy, Alan Hansen, Kenny Dalglish, Sammy Lee and Ian Rush.

Not content with completely dominating the League Championship race, Liverpool also made the League Cup the sole property of Anfield during the early 80s.

Wolves won the first trophy of the 80s, beating Forest 1-0 in the Final and so preventing them from completing a hat-trick of wins, but that was the last time anyone else would get their hands on the Cup for five years as Liverpool took over.

The Reds won the League Cup in 1981, 1982, 1983 and 1984, an astonishing sequence that no-one has come near to matching since.

They beat West Ham in '81, although they needed a replay to see off the Londoners, and then defeated Tottenham, Manchester United and Everton, in the first ever all-Merseyside Wembley Final.

The 1983 Final against United was a memorable occasion, particularly for a young Irishman called Norman Whiteside.

The Belfast-born forward was aged just 17 years, 324 days when he took the field for United at Wembley that day.

That didn't make him Wembley's youngest ever player, but when he crashed home the game's first goal from the edge of the Liverpool penalty area he earned his place in history as Wembley's youngest ever scorer - a record that still stands today.

Unfortunately it wasn't enough to earn Whiteside his first winner's medal because Liverpool recovered to win 2-1 and retain their stranglehold on the League Cup.

That stranglehold was finally broken in 1985 when Norwich won the Cup for the first time since 1962, defeating Sunderland by the only goal of the game.

Oxford proved again that the little clubs could have their day by winning the trophy in 1986, and Luton emulated that feat in 1988, when they recovered from 1-2 down with just nine minutes to go to beat Arsenal 3-2.

But by the end of the 80s, the competition had a familiar feel to it with Forest claiming the Cup in both 1989 and 1990.

Winning Pool

Liverpool did not lose a League Cup-tie between February 1980 and October 1985 -a record for any Football League club in any competition.

WHAT A STAR ✪ ALAN KENNEDY

He played 349 games for Liverpool in various competitions, and his 21 goals included three in Cup Finals. He scored against West Ham in the League Cup in 1981, and equalised against Manchester United in the same competition two years later. In between, he scored the only goal of the 1981 European Cup Final against Real Madrid, and added another in a penalty shoot-out against Roma in the same competition in 1984. The Kop called him 'Barney' after the Flintstones character, and loved him dearly. With a record like his, that's hardly surprising.

1980

FIRST ROUND FIRST-LEG				
Blackpool	1	Rochdale	1	
Bradford	0	Darlingtn	2	
Bury	0	Blackburn	3	
Chester	2	Walsall	1	
Chestrfld	5	Hartlepl	1	
Colchester	2	Watford	0	
Gillinghm	3	Luton	0	
Grimsby	2	Scunthpe	0	
Halifax	2	Shrewsby	2	
Hereford	1	Exeter	3	
Huddersfld	2	Crewe	1	
Leicester	1	Rotherhm	2	
Lincoln	2	Barnsley	1	
Mansfield	1	York	0	
Newport	1	Plymouth	0	
N'hamptn	2	Millwall	1	
Oxford	1	Reading	5	
Peterboro	3	Charlton	1	
Port Vale	1	Tranmere	2	
Portsmth	1	Swindon	1	
Sheff Utd	1	Doncaster	1	
Sheff Wed	1	Hull	1	
Southend	2	Brentford	1	
Stockport	2	Wigan Ath	1	
Swansea	4	Bournemth	1	
Torquay	1	Bristol R	2	
Wimbledn	4	Aldershot	1	
Wrexham	1	Carlisle	1	
FIRST ROUND SECOND-LEG				
Aldershot	1	Wimbledn	2	
Wimbledn win 6-2 on agg				
Barnsley	2	Lincoln	1	P
agg score Barnsley 3 - Lincoln 3				
Blackburn	3	Bury	2	
Blackburn win 6-2 on agg				
Bournemth	0	Swansea	0	
Swansea win 4-1 on agg				
Brentford	1	Southend	4	
Southend win 6-2 on agg				
Bristol R	1	Torquay	3	e
Torquay win 4-3 on agg				
Carlisle	1	Wrexham	2	
Wrexham win 3-2 on agg				
Charlton	1	Peterboro	1	
Peterboro win 4-2 on agg				
Crewe	1	Huddersfld	3	
Huddersfld win 5-2 on agg				
Darlingtn	0	Bradford	3	
Bradford win 3-2 on agg				
Doncaster	3	Sheff Utd	1	
Doncaster win 4-2 on agg				
Exeter	2	Hereford	1	
Exeter win 5-2 on agg				
Hartlepl	2	Chestrfld	1	
Chestrfld win 6-3 on agg				
Hull	1	Sheff Wed	2	
Sheff Wed win 3-2 on agg				
Luton	1	Gillinghm	1	
Gillinghm win 4-1 on agg				
Millwall	2	N'hamptn	2	
N'hamptn win 4-3 on agg				
Plymouth	2	Newport	0	
Plymouth win 2-1 on agg				
Reading	2	Oxford	1	
Reading win 7-2 on agg				
Rochdale	0	Blackpool	1	
Blackpool win 2-1 on agg				
Rotherhm	3	Leicester	0	
Rotherhm win 5-1 on agg				
Scunthpe	0	Grimsby	0	
Grimsby win 2-0 on agg				
Shrewsby	1	Halifax	0	
Shrewsby win 3-2 on agg				
Swindon	2	Portsmth	0	
Swindon win 3-1 on agg				
Tranmere	1	Port Vale	0	
Tranmere win 3-1 on agg				
Walsall	0	Chester	0	
Chester win 2-1 on agg				
Watford	2	Colchester	1	
Colchester win 3-2 on agg				
Wigan Ath	0	Stockport	0	
Stockport win 2-1 on agg				
York	3	Mansfield	2	a
agg score York 3 - Mansfield 3				
SECOND ROUND FIRST-LEG				
Birmghm C	2	Preston NE	1	e
Blackburn	1	Nottm For	1	
Bolton	1	Southend	2	
Brighton	2	Cambridge	0	
Bristol C	1	Rotherhm	0	
Burnley	1	Wolves	1	
Chestrfld	3	Shrewsby	0	
Colchester	0	Aston V	2	
Derby	0	Middlesbro	1	
Doncaster	3	Exeter	1	
Everton	2	Cardiff	0	
Gillinghm	1	Norwich	1	
Grimsby	1	Huddersfld	0	
Ipswich	0	Coventry	1	
Leeds U	1	Arsenal	1	
Leyton O	2	Wimbledn	2	
N'hamptn	3	Oldham	0	
Notts Co	0	Torquay	0	
Peterboro	0	Blackpool	0	
Plymouth	2	Chelsea	2	
QPR	2	Bradford	1	
Reading	4	Mansfield	3	
Sheff Wed	1	Man City	1	
Southmptn	5	Wrexham	0	
Stockport	1	C.Palace	1	
Stoke	1	Swansea	1	
Sunderld	2	Newcastle	2	
Swindon	1	Chester	0	
Tottenham	2	Man Utd	1	
Tranmere	0	Liverpool	0	
West Brom	1	Fulham	1	
West Ham	3	Barnsley	1	
SECOND ROUND SECOND-LEG				
Arsenal	7	Leeds U	0	
Arsenal win 8-1 on agg				
Aston V	0	Colchester	2	P
agg score Aston V 2 - Colchester 2				
Barnsley	0	West Ham	2	
West Ham win 5-1 on agg				
Blackpool	0	Peterboro	1	
Peterboro win 1-0 on agg				
Bradford	0	QPR	2	
QPR win 4-1 on agg				
Cambridge	1	Brighton	2	
Brighton win 4-1 on agg				
Cardiff	1	Everton	0	
Everton win 2-1 on agg				
Chelsea	1	Plymouth	2	
Plymouth win 4-3 on agg				
Chester	1	Swindon	1	
Swindon win 2-1 on agg				
Coventry	0	Ipswich	0	
Coventry win 1-0 on agg				
C.Palace	7	Stockport	0	
C.Palace win 8-1 on agg				
Exeter	5	Doncaster	1	e
Exeter win 6-4 on agg				
Fulham	0	West Brom	1	
West Brom win 2-1 on agg				
Huddersfld	1	Grimsby	4	
Grimsby win 5-1 on agg				
Liverpool	4	Tranmere	0	

Liverpool win 4-0 on agg
Man City 2 Sheff Wed 1
Man City win 3-2 on agg
Man Utd 3 Tottenham 1
Man Utd win 4-3 on agg
Mansfield 4 Reading 2 e
Mansfield win 7-6 on agg
Middlesbro 1 Derby 1 e
Middlesbro win 2-1 on agg
Newcastle 2 Sunderld 2 q
agg score N'castle 4 - Sunderld 4
Norwich 4 Gillinghm 2
Norwich win 5-3 on agg
Nottm For 6 Blackburn 1
Nottm For win 7-2 on agg
Oldham 3 N'hamptn 1
N'hamptn win 4-3 on agg
Preston NE 0 Birmghm C 1
Birmghm C win 3-1 on agg
Rotherhm 1 Bristol C 1
Bristol C win 2-1 on agg
Shrewsby 0 Chestrfld 0
Chestrfld win 3-0 on agg
Southend 0 Bolton 0
Southend win 2-1 on agg
Swansea 1 Stoke 3 e
Stoke win 4-2 on agg
Torquay 0 Notts Co 1
Notts Co win 1-0 on agg
Wimbledn 2 Leyton O 2 P
agg score W'bledn 4 - Leyton O 4
Wolves 2 Burnley 0
Wolves win 3-1 on agg
Wrexham 0 Southmptn 3
Southmptn win 8-0 on agg

THIRD ROUND

Arsenal 2 Southmptn 1
Aston V 0 Everton 0
Birmghm C 1 Exeter 2
C.Palace 1 Wolves 2
Grimsby 3 Notts Co 1
Liverpool 3 Chestrfld 1
Man City 1 Sunderld 1
Mansfield 0 QPR 3
Middlesbro 1 Nottm For 3
N'hamptn 0 Brighton 1
Norwich 4 Man Utd 1
Peterboro 1 Bristol C 1
Plymouth 0 Wimbledn 0
Stoke 2 Swindon 2
West Brom 2 Coventry 1
West Ham 1 Southend 1
Bristol C 4 Peterboro 0 r
Everton 4 Aston V 1 r
Southend 0 West Ham 0 re
Sunderld 1 Man City 0 r
Swindon 2 Stoke 1 r
Wimbledn 1 Plymouth 0 re
West Ham 5 Southend 1 r2

FOURTH ROUND

Brighton 0 Arsenal 0
Bristol C 1 Nottm For 1
Grimsby 2 Everton 1
Liverpool 2 Exeter 0
QPR 1 Wolves 1
Sunderld 1 West Ham 1
West Brom 0 Norwich 0
Wimbledn 1 Swindon 2
Arsenal 4 Brighton 0 r
Norwich 3 West Brom 0 r
Nottm For 3 Bristol C 0 r
West Ham 2 Sunderld 1 r
Wolves 1 QPR 0 r

FIFTH ROUND

Arsenal 1 Swindon 1
Grimsby 0 Wolves 0
Norwich 1 Liverpool 3
West Ham 0 Nottm For 0
Nottm For 3 West Ham 0 re
Swindon 4 Arsenal 3 re
Wolves 1 Grimsby 1 re
Grimsby 0 Wolves 2 r2N

SEMI-FINAL FIRST-LEG

Nottm For 1 Liverpool 0
Swindon 2 Wolves 1

SEMI-FINAL SECOND-LEG

Liverpool 1 Nottm For 1
Nottm For win 2-1 on agg
Wolves 3 Swindon 1
Wolves win 4-3 on agg

FINAL

Wolves 1 Nottm For 0 N

1981

FIRST ROUND FIRST-LEG

Aldershot 2 Wimbledn 0
Blackburn 0 Huddersfld 0
Bournemth 1 Swindon 1
Brentford 3 Charlton 1
Bury 2 Halifax 2
Carlisle 2 Rochdale 0
Chester 1 Stockport 1
Chestrfld 1 Darlingtn 0
Colchester 0 Gillinghm 2
Doncaster 1 Mansfield 1
Exeter 1 Bristol R 1
Grimsby 1 Notts Co 0
Hereford 1 Newport 0
Lincoln 5 Hull 0
N'hamptn 0 Reading 2
Peterboro 3 Fulham 2
Plymouth 0 Portsmth 1
Port Vale 2 Tranmere 3
Rotherhm 1 Bradford 3
Scunthpe 0 Barnsley 1
Sheff Wed 2 Sheff Utd 0
Southend 1 Oxford 0
Torquay 0 Cardiff 0
Walsall 2 Blackpool 3
Watford 2 Millwall 1
Wigan Ath 2 Crewe 1
Wrexham 1 Burnley 3
York 2 Hartlepl 1

FIRST ROUND SECOND-LEG

Barnsley 2 Scunthpe 1
Barnsley win 3-1 on agg
Blackpool 3 Walsall 1
Blackpool win 6-3 on agg
Bradford 0 Rotherhm 0
Bradford win 3-1 on agg
Bristol R 1 Exeter 1 P
agg score Bristol R 2 - Exeter 2
Burnley 2 Wrexham 1
Burnley win 5-2 on agg
Cardiff 2 Torquay 1
Cardiff win 2-1 on agg
Charlton 5 Brentford 0
Charlton win 6-3 on agg
Crewe 2 Wigan Ath 2 e
Wigan Ath win 4-3 on agg
Darlingtn 1 Chestrfld 2
Chestrfld win 3-1 on agg
Fulham 1 Peterboro 1 e
Peterboro win 4-3 on agg
Gillinghm 2 Colchester 1
Gillinghm win 4-1 on agg
Halifax 0 Bury 1

GIANTKILLERS

1980-81 Sunderland 1 Stockport 2

Stockport finished 88th out of the 92 League clubs in 1980-81, but by then they had become the first team from Division Four to beat a First Division outfit over two legs in the League Cup. After defeating Chester after extra-time in Round One, they drew 1-1 at home to Sunderland and then caused an upset by winning 2-1 away. The decider was a penalty by Tommy Sword, a headline-writer's dream in those circumstances, and shaken Sunderland only just avoided relegation after it.

Home		Away		
Bury win 3-2 on agg				
Hartlepl	**0**	**York**	**0**	
York win 2-1 on agg				
Huddersfld	**1**	**Blackburn**	**1**	a
agg score Huddersfld 1 - Blackburn 1				
Hull	**0**	**Lincoln**	**2**	
Lincoln win 7-0 on agg				
Mansfield	**2**	**Doncaster**	**1**	e
Mansfield win 3-2 on agg				
Millwall	**0**	**Watford**	**2**	
Watford win 4-1 on agg				
Newport	**5**	**Hereford**	**0**	
Newport win 5-1 on agg				
Notts Co	**3**	**Grimsby**	**0**	
Notts Co win 3-1 on agg				
Oxford	**2**	**Southend**	**0**	
Oxford win 2-1 on agg				
Portsmth	**2**	**Plymouth**	**1**	
Portsmth win 3-1 on agg				
Reading	**2**	**N'hamptn**	**3**	
Reading win 4-3 on agg				
Rochdale	**1**	**Carlisle**	**1**	
Carlisle win 3-1 on agg				
Sheff Utd	**1**	**Sheff Wed**	**1**	
Sheff Wed win 3-1 on agg				
Stockport	**1**	**Chester**	**0**	e
Stockport win 2-1 on agg				
Swindon	**2**	**Bournemth**	**0**	e
Swindon win 3-1 on agg				
Tranmere	**0**	**Port Vale**	**1**	
agg score Tranmere 3 - Port Vale 3				
Wimbledn	**4**	**Aldershot**	**1**	
Wimbledn win 4-3 on agg				
SECOND ROUND FIRST-LEG				
Aston V	**1**	**Leeds U**	**0**	
Birmghm C	**2**	**Bristol C**	**1**	
Blackburn	**0**	**Gillinghm**	**0**	
Bolton	**0**	**C.Palace**	**3**	
Bradford	**1**	**Liverpool**	**0**	
Brighton	**3**	**Tranmere**	**1**	
Burnley	**0**	**West Ham**	**2**	
Cambridge	**3**	**Wolves**	**1**	
Cardiff	**1**	**Chelsea**	**0**	
Carlisle	**1**	**Charlton**	**2**	
Chestrfld	**3**	**Oxford**	**1**	
Everton	**3**	**Blackpool**	**0**	
Leyton O	**0**	**Tottenham**	**1**	
Lincoln	**1**	**Swindon**	**1**	
Man Utd	**0**	**Coventry**	**1**	
Mansfield	**0**	**Barnsley**	**0**	
Middlesbro	**3**	**Ipswich**	**1**	
Newcastle	**3**	**Bury**	**2**	
Newport	**1**	**Notts Co**	**1**	
Nottm For	**3**	**Peterboro**	**0**	
Oldham	**3**	**Portsmth**	**2**	
Preston NE	**1**	**Wigan Ath**	**0**	
QPR	**0**	**Derby**	**0**	
Reading	**0**	**Luton**	**2**	
Shrewsby	**1**	**Norwich**	**1**	
Southmptn	**4**	**Watford**	**0**	
Stockport	**1**	**Sunderld**	**1**	
Stoke	**1**	**Man City**	**1**	
Swansea	**1**	**Arsenal**	**1**	
West Brom	**1**	**Leicester**	**0**	
Wimbledn	**2**	**Sheff Wed**	**1**	
York	**2**	**Bristol R**	**1**	
SECOND ROUND SECOND-LEG				
Arsenal	**3**	**Swansea**	**1**	
Arsenal win 4-2 on agg				
Barnsley	**4**	**Mansfield**	**2**	e
Barnsley win 4-2 on agg				
Blackpool	**2**	**Everton**	**2**	
Everton win 5-2 on agg				
Bristol C	**0**	**Birmghm C**	**0**	
Birmghm C win 2-1 on agg				
Bristol R	**1**	**York**	**0**	
agg score Bristol R 2 - York 2				
Bury	**1**	**Newcastle**	**0**	
agg score Bury 3 - Newcastle 3				
Charlton	**2**	**Carlisle**	**1**	
Charlton win 4-2 on agg				
Chelsea	**1**	**Cardiff**	**1**	
Cardiff win 2-1 on agg				
Coventry	**1**	**Man Utd**	**0**	
Coventry win 2-0 on agg				
C.Palace	**2**	**Bolton**	**1**	
C.Palace win 5-1 on agg				
Derby	**0**	**QPR**	**0**	q
Gillinghm	**1**	**Blackburn**	**2**	e
Blackburn win 2-1 on agg				
Ipswich	**3**	**Middlesbro**	**0**	
Ipswich win 4-3 on agg				
Leeds U	**1**	**Aston V**	**3**	
Aston V win 4-1 on agg				
Leicester	**0**	**West Brom**	**1**	
West Brom win 2-0 on agg				
Liverpool	**4**	**Bradford**	**0**	
Liverpool win 4-1 on agg				
Luton	**1**	**Reading**	**1**	
Luton win 3-1 on agg				
Man City	**3**	**Stoke**	**0**	
Man City win 4-1 on agg				
Norwich	**2**	**Shrewsby**	**0**	e
Norwich win 3-1 on agg				
Notts Co	**2**	**Newport**	**0**	
Notts Co win 3-1 on agg				
Oxford	**3**	**Chestrfld**	**0**	
Oxford win 4-3 on agg				
Peterboro	**1**	**Nottm For**	**1**	
Nottm For win 4-1 on agg				
Portsmth	**1**	**Oldham**	**0**	
agg score Portsmth 3 - Oldham 3				
Sheff Wed	**3**	**Wimbledn**	**1**	
Sheff Wed win 4-3 on agg				
Sunderld	**1**	**Stockport**	**2**	
Stockport win 3-2 on agg				
Swindon	**2**	**Lincoln**	**0**	
Swindon win 3-1 on agg				
Tottenham	**3**	**Leyton O**	**1**	
Tottenham win 4-1 on agg				
Tranmere	**2**	**Brighton**	**4**	
Brighton win 7-3 on agg				
Watford	**7**	**Southmptn**	**1**	e
Watford win 7-5 on agg				
West Ham	**4**	**Burnley**	**0**	
West Ham win 6-0 on agg				
Wigan Ath	**1**	**Preston NE**	**2**	
Preston NE win 3-1 on agg				
Wolves	**0**	**Cambridge**	**1**	
Cambridge win 3-1 on agg				
THIRD ROUND				
Barnsley	**3**	**Cardiff**	**2**	
Birmghm C	**1**	**Blackburn**	**0**	
Brighton	**1**	**Coventry**	**2**	
Bristol R	**0**	**Portsmth**	**0**	
Bury	**0**	**Nottm For**	**7**	
Cambridge	**2**	**Aston V**	**1**	
Charlton	**1**	**West Ham**	**2**	
Everton	**1**	**West Brom**	**2**	
Ipswich	**1**	**Norwich**	**1**	
Liverpool	**5**	**Swindon**	**0**	
Luton	**1**	**Man City**	**2**	
Notts Co	**4**	**QPR**	**1**	
Preston NE	**1**	**Oxford**	**0**	
Sheff Wed	**1**	**Watford**	**2**	
Stockport	**1**	**Arsenal**	**3**	

WHAT A STAR ✪ CLIVE ALLEN

Allen set a scoring record for the League Cup without even getting to the Final. His 12 goals in 1986-87 beat the previous individual best by one, even though Spurs lost to Arsenal in a Semi-Final that went to a third match. Even more impressively, Allen scored in all nine games his club played in the competition that season. He also scored 33 League goals and four in the FA Cup, when Spurs lost in the Final to Coventry, for a seasonal total of 49. Not many people were surprised when Allen, a member of one of soccer's biggest 'tribes', was voted Footballer of the Year.

GIANTKILLERS

1980-81 Watford 7 Southampton 1

A run to the Fifth Round by a club in Division Two, including victories over two sides in the top division, is a creditable achievement, although not all that unusual. This one takes on an air of fantasy though, because Watford overturned the biggest deficit in League Cup history by winning 7-1 in extra-time after losing the first leg 4-0 away to Southampton, a team including four internationals. They also beat Nottingham Forest 4-1 and held Coventry 2-2 in the Quarter-Final, but lost the replay 5-0.

Tottenham	0	C.Palace	0	
C.Palace	1	Tottenham	3	re
Norwich	1	Ipswich	3	r
Portsmth	2	Bristol R	0	r
FOURTH ROUND				
Birmghm C	2	Ipswich	1	
Coventry	1	Cambridge	1	
Liverpool	4	Portsmth	1	
Man City	5	Notts Co	1	
Tottenham	1	Arsenal	0	
Watford	4	Nottm For	1	
West Brom	0	Preston NE	0	
West Ham	2	Barnsley	1	
Cambridge	0	Coventry	1	r
Preston NE	1	West Brom	1	re
West Brom	2	Preston NE	1	r2e
FIFTH ROUND				
Liverpool	3	Birmghm C	1	
Man City	2	West Brom	1	
Watford	2	Coventry	2	
West Ham	1	Tottenham	0	
Coventry	5	Watford	0	r
SEMI-FINAL FIRST-LEG				
Coventry	3	West Ham	2	
Man City	0	Liverpool	1	
SEMI-FINAL SECOND-LEG				
Liverpool	1	Man City	1	
Liverpool win 2-1 on agg				
West Ham	2	Coventry	0	
West Ham win 4-3 on agg				
FINAL				
Liverpool	1	West Ham	1	eN
Liverpool	2	West Ham	1	rN

1982

FIRST ROUND FIRST-LEG				
Aldershot	0	Wimbledn	0	
Bolton	2	Oldham	1	
Bournemth	0	Fulham	1	
Bradford	3	Blackpool	1	
Bristol C	2	Walsall	0	
Bury	3	Carlisle	3	
Cardiff	2	Exeter	1	
Chester	1	Plymouth	1	
Colchester	2	Gillinghm	0	
Crewe	1	Bristol R	1	
Darlingtn	1	Rotherhm	3	
Doncaster	0	Chestrfld	0	
Halifax	1	Preston NE	2	
Hereford	1	Port Vale	1	
Huddersfld	3	Rochdale	1	
Leyton O	1	Millwall	1	
Lincoln	3	Hull	0	
N'hamptn	2	Hartlepl	0	
Oxford	1	Brentford	0	
Peterboro	2	Barnsley	3	
Reading	2	Charlton	2	
Scunthpe	0	Mansfield	0	
Sheff Utd	1	York	0	
Southend	0	Portsmth	0	
Torquay	2	Newport	3	
Tranmere	4	Burnley	2	
Wigan Ath	3	Stockport	0	
Wrexham	3	Swindon	2	
FIRST ROUND SECOND-LEG				
Barnsley	6	Peterboro	0	
Barnsley win 9-2 on agg				
Blackpool	0	Bradford	0	
Bradford win 3-1 on agg				
Brentford	0	Oxford	2	
Oxford win 3-0 on agg				
Bristol R	1	Crewe	0	e
Bristol R win 2-1 on agg				
Burnley	3	Tranmere	3	
Tranmere win 7-5 on agg				
Carlisle	2	Bury	1	e
Carlisle win 5-4 on agg				
Charlton	3	Reading	1	e
Charlton win 5-3 on agg				
Chestrfld	1	Doncaster	1	a
agg score Chestrfld 1 - D'caster 1				
Exeter	3	Cardiff	1	e
Exeter win 4-3 on agg				
Fulham	2	Bournemth	0	
Fulham win 3-0 on agg				
Gillinghm	1	Colchester	1	
Colchester win 3-1 on agg				
Hartlepl	2	N'hamptn	1	
N'hamptn win 3-2 on agg				
Hull	1	Lincoln	1	
Lincoln win 4-1 on agg				
Mansfield	2	Scunthpe	0	
Mansfield win 2-0 on agg				
Millwall	3	Leyton O	2	
Millwall win 4-3 on agg				
Newport	0	Torquay	0	
Newport win 3-2 on agg				
Oldham	4	Bolton	2	e
Oldham win 5-4 on agg				
Plymouth	1	Chester	0	
Plymouth win 2-1 on agg				
Port Vale	2	Hereford	0	
Port Vale win 3-1 on agg				
Portsmth	4	Southend	1	
Portsmth win 4-1 on agg				
Preston NE	0	Halifax	0	
Preston NE win 2-1 on agg				
Rochdale	2	Huddersfld	4	
Huddersfld win 7-3 on agg				
Rotherhm	2	Darlingtn	1	
Rotherhm win 5-2 on agg				
Stockport	1	Wigan Ath	2	
Wigan Ath win 5-1 on agg				
Swindon	0	Wrexham	2	
Wrexham win 5-2 on agg				
Walsall	1	Bristol C	0	
Bristol C win 2-1 on agg				
Wimbledn	1	Aldershot	3	
Aldershot win 3-1 on agg				
York	1	Sheff Utd	1	
Sheff Utd win 2-1 on agg				
SECOND ROUND FIRST-LEG				
Aldershot	2	Wigan Ath	2	
Aston V	3	Wolves	2	
Barnsley	2	Swansea	0	
Birmghm C	2	Nottm For	3	
Blackburn	1	Sheff Wed	1	
Bradford	3	Mansfield	4	
Bristol R	1	N'hamptn	2	
Carlisle	0	Bristol C	0	
Colchester	3	Cambridge	1	
Derby	2	West Ham	3	

Treble Chance

Oxford's 3-0 defeat of QPR in 1986 set a record for a winning League Cup Final margin in a single match, equalled by Aston Villa when they beat Leeds in 1996.

Pro-File: CHARLIE NICHOLAS

Charlie Nicholas was a pop star footballer long before the days of Giggs, Beckham and the like.

The former Celtic and Arsenal striker was arguably the first player since George Best to be as famous off the field as he was on it.

During his days in London he earned the nickname 'Champagne Charlie' and, on occasions at least, he appeared to be more than happy to live up to that reputation.

But unfortunately for both him and Arsenal, the form that prompted The Gunners to buy him from Celtic in the first place largely deserted him during his four-year stay in England.

When he left Parkhead in 1983, he was one of the hottest striking properties in Europe, having notched 29 goals in just 35 League games. He could have taken his pick from the biggest clubs around.

Liverpool and Manchester Unted both wanted him but he chose the bright lights of London, and ultimately that proved to be his downfall.

He had his moments at Arsenal but they were too few and far between and he eventually quit London to return to Scotland, with Aberdeen, in 1987.

He later returned to Celtic and also had a brief spell at Clyde before quitting the game to take up a career in TV and radio.

Career details

●**Represented:** Scotland, Celtic (twice), Arsenal, Aberdeen, Clyde ●**Position:** Striker ●**Born:** 30.12.61. ●**Height:** 5ft 10in ●**Weight:** 11st ●**Club honours:** Scottish League Championship 1980-81, 1981-82; Scottish Cup 1990; Scottish League Cup 1983, 1990; League Cup 1987; PFA Player of the Year 1982-83 ●**International honours:** Scotland Youth, 6 U21, 20 full caps

Club League Record

Era	Club	Games	Goals
80/83	Celtic	74	48
83/87	Arsenal	151	34
87/90	Aberdeen	78	30
90/95	Celtic	114	37
95/96	Clyde	31	5

Cup Highlights

Jan 21 1987: Nicholas scores the first goal as Arsenal beat Nottingham Forest 2-0 in the League Cup Quarter-Final at Highbury.

April 5 1987: Charlie's finest hour in an Arsenal shirt. He scores both goals as The Gunners beat Liverpool 2-1 in the League Cup Final at Wembley. It was the first match Ian Rush had scored in that Liverpool had lost.

Nicholas On:

●It had reached the stage where I had made up my mind to return to Celtic. Only a few well chosen words from George Graham changed my mind. **Nicholas on his decision to stay at Arsenal for one more year.**

●He was the man who made me into the player I was. **Nicholas on his old Celtic boss Billy McNeill.**

DID YOU KNOW THAT...

●He was the first winner of the Daily Record Golden Shot award in 1982-83, as the first player to reach 30 League goals that season.
●He scored 51 goals that season in all competitions.
●He grew up next door to Hibernian manager Jim Duffy. Nicholas describes him as his first ever minder.
●He had trials at Wolves as a teenager but was chased by a gang one night and decided not to sign.
●He scored a hat-trick on his debut for Celtic against Stirling Albion in 1980.
●His last act before returning to Celtic was to deny them the Scottish Cup with Aberdeen in a penalty shoot-out in 1990.
●Nicholas was one of four rebel players at Celtic who took on the board on behalf of the fans and threatened to strike. The others were Paul McStay, Pat Bonner and Peter Grant.
●He scored on his full Scotland debut in a 2-2 draw against the Swiss in 1983.

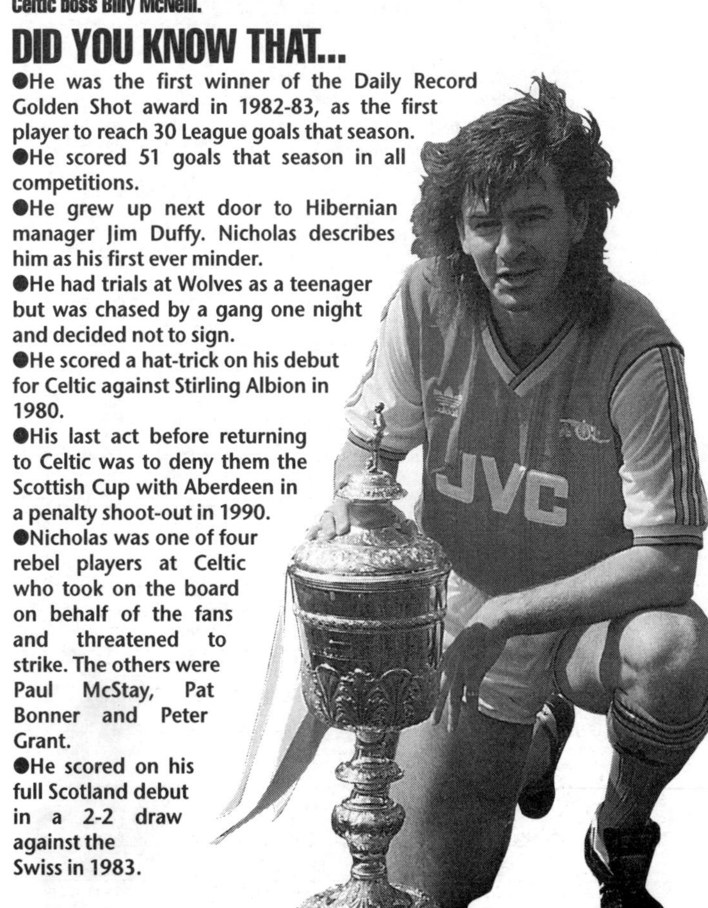

Doncaster 1 C.Palace 0
Everton 1 Coventry 1
Grimsby 1 Watford 0
Huddersfld 1 Brighton 0
Leeds U 0 Ipswich 1
Lincoln 1 Notts Co 1
Liverpool 5 Exeter 0
Luton 0 Wrexham 2
Man City 2 Stoke 0
Middlesbro 2 Plymouth 1
Millwall 3 Oxford 3
Newcastle 1 Fulham 2
Norwich 1 Charlton 0
Oldham 1 Newport 0
Preston NE 1 Leicester 0
QPR 5 Portsmth 0
Sheff Utd 1 Arsenal 0
Shrewsby 3 West Brom 3
Southmptn 1 Chelsea 1
Sunderld 2 Rotherhm 0
Tottenham 1 Man Utd 0
Tranmere 2 Port Vale 0

SECOND ROUND SECOND-LEG

Arsenal 2 Sheff Utd 0 e
Arsenal win 2-1 on agg
Brighton 2 Huddersfld 0
Brighton win 2-1 on agg
Bristol C 2 Carlisle 1
Bristol C win 2-1 on agg
Cambridge 3 Colchester 2 e
Colchester win 5-4 on agg
Charlton 0 Norwich 1
Norwich win 2-0 on agg
Chelsea 2 Southmptn 1 e
Chelsea win 3-2 on agg
Coventry 0 Everton 1
Everton win 2-1 on agg
C.Palace 2 Doncaster 0
C.Palace win 2-1 on agg
Exeter 0 Liverpool 6
Liverpool win 11-0 on agg
Fulham 2 Newcastle 0
Fulham win 4-1 on agg
Ipswich 3 Leeds U 0
Ipswich win 4-0 on agg
Leicester 4 Preston NE 0
Leicester win 4-1 on agg
Man Utd 0 Tottenham 1
Tottenham win 2-0 on agg
Mansfield 0 Bradford 2
Bradford win 5-4 on agg
Newport 0 Oldham 0
Oldham win 1-0 on agg
N'hamptn 3 Bristol R 1
N'hamptn win 5-2 on agg
Nottm For 2 Birmghm C 1
Nottm For win 5-3 on agg
Notts Co 2 Lincoln 3
Lincoln win 4-3 on agg
Oxford 1 Millwall 0
Oxford win 4-3 on agg
Plymouth 0 Middlesbro 0
Middlesbro win 2-1 on agg
Port Vale 1 Tranmere 2
Tranmere win 4-1 on agg
Portsmth 2 QPR 2
QPR win 7-2 on agg

Strange but true!

Sponsorship of the League Cup began in 1982, when it became the Milk Cup. Sponsors since then have been Littlewoods (1987-90), Rumbelows (1991-92) and Coca-Cola (1993 to date).

Rotherhm 3 Sunderld 3
Sunderld win 5-3 on agg
Sheff Wed 1 Blackburn 2
Blackburn win 3-2 on agg
Stoke 2 Man City 0 q
agg score Stoke 2 - Man City 2
Swansea 3 Barnsley 2 e
Barnsley win 4-3 on agg
Watford 3 Grimsby 1
Watford win 3-2 on agg
West Brom 2 Shrewsby 1
West Brom win 5-4 on agg
West Ham 2 Derby 0
West Ham win 5-2 on agg
Wigan Ath 1 Aldershot 0
Wigan Ath win 3-2 on agg
Wolves 1 Aston V 2
Aston V win 5-3 on agg
Wrexham 0 Luton 1
Wrexham win 2-1 on agg

THIRD ROUND

Arsenal 1 Norwich 0
Barnsley 4 Brighton 1
Blackburn 0 Nottm For 1
Everton 1 Oxford 0
Ipswich 1 Bradford 1
Leicester 0 Aston V 0
Liverpool 4 Middlesbro 1
Man City 3 N'hamptn 1
Oldham 1 Fulham 1
QPR 3 Bristol C 0
Sunderld 0 C.Palace 1
Tottenham 2 Wrexham 0
Tranmere 1 Colchester 0
Watford 2 Lincoln 2
West Ham 2 West Brom 2
Wigan Ath 4 Chelsea 2
Aston V 2 Leicester 0 r
Bradford 2 Ipswich 3 re
Fulham 3 Oldham 0 r
Lincoln 2 Watford 3 r
West Brom 1 West Ham 1 re
West Ham 0 West Brom 1 r2

FOURTH ROUND

Arsenal 0 Liverpool 0
Barnsley 1 Man City 0
C.Palace 1 West Brom 3
Everton 2 Ipswich 3
Nottm For 2 Tranmere 0
Tottenham 1 Fulham 0
Watford 4 QPR 1
Wigan Ath 1 Aston V 2
Liverpool 3 Arsenal 0 re

FIFTH ROUND

Aston V 0 West Brom 1
Ipswich 2 Watford 1
Liverpool 0 Barnsley 0
Tottenham 1 Nottm For 0
Barnsley 1 Liverpool 3 r

SEMI-FINAL FIRST-LEG

Ipswich 0 Liverpool 2
West Brom 0 Tottenham 0

SEMI-FINAL SECOND-LEG

Liverpool 2 Ipswich 2
Liverpool win 4-2 on agg
Tottenham 1 West Brom 0
Tottenham win 1-0 on agg

FINAL

Liverpool 3 Tottenham 1 eN

1983

FIRST ROUND FIRST-LEG

Bradford 1 Mansfield 0
Bristol R 2 Torquay 2
Bury 3 Burnley 5
Cardiff 2 Hereford 1
Carlisle 3 Bolton 3
Chester 1 Blackpool 2
Chestrfld 2 Hartlepl 1
Colchester 2 Aldershot 0
Crewe 1 Tranmere 1
C.Palace 2 Portsmth 0
Darlingtn 0 Peterboro 2
Exeter 1 Newport 2
Gillinghm 3 Leyton O 0
Halifax 2 Derby 1
Huddersfld 1 Doncaster 1
Millwall 0 N'hamptn 2
Plymouth 2 Bournemth 0
Port Vale 1 Rochdale 0
Reading 0 Oxford 2
Scunthpe 1 Grimsby 2
Sheff Utd 3 Hull 1
Southend 1 Fulham 0
Stockport 1 Wigan Ath 1
Swindon 2 Bristol C 1
Walsall 0 Preston NE 1
Wimbledn 1 Brentford 1
Wrexham 1 Shrewsby 0
York 2 Lincoln 1

FIRST ROUND SECOND-LEG

Aldershot 0 Colchester 1
Colchester win 3-0 on agg
Blackpool 5 Chester 1
Blackpool win 7-2 on agg
Bolton 4 Carlisle 0
Bolton win 7-3 on agg
Bournemth 3 Plymouth 0 e
Bournemth win 3-2 on agg
Brentford 2 Wimbledn 0
Brentford win 3-1 on agg
Bristol C 2 Swindon 0
Bristol C win 3-2 on agg
Burnley 3 Bury 1
Burnley win 8-4 on agg
Derby 5 Halifax 2 e
Derby win 6-4 on agg

Doncaster 0 Huddersfld 1
Huddersfld win 2-1 on agg
Fulham 4 Southend 2
Fulham win 4-3 on agg
Grimsby 0 Scunthpe 0
Grimsby win 2-1 on agg
Hartlepl 2 Chestrfld 0 e
Hartlepl win 3-2 on agg
Hereford 1 Cardiff 2
Cardiff win 4-2 on agg
Hull 1 Sheff Utd 0
Sheff Utd win 3-2 on agg
Leyton O 2 Gillinghm 0
Gillinghm win 3-2 on agg
Lincoln 3 York 1
Lincoln win 4-3 on agg
Mansfield 0 Bradford 2
Bradford win 3-0 on agg
Newport 6 Exeter 0
Newport win 8-1 on agg
N'hamptn 2 Millwall 2
N'hamptn win 4-2 on agg
Oxford 2 Reading 0
Oxford win 4-0 on agg
Peterboro 4 Darlingtn 2
Peterboro win 6-2 on agg
Portsmth 1 C.Palace 1
C.Palace win 3-1 on agg
Preston NE 1 Walsall 1
Preston NE win 2-1 on agg
Rochdale 2 Port Vale 0
Rochdale win 2-1 on agg
Shrewsby 2 Wrexham 0
Shrewsby win 2-1 on agg
Torquay 0 Bristol R 4
Bristol R win 6-0 on agg
Tranmere 0 Crewe 0
agg score Tranmere 1 - Crewe 1
Wigan Ath 1 Stockport 1 P
agg score Wigan 2 - Stockport 2

SECOND ROUND FIRST-LEG

Arsenal 2 Cardiff 1
Aston V 1 Notts Co 2
Barnsley 2 Cambridge 1
Bolton 1 Watford 2
Brentford 3 Blackburn 2
Bristol C 1 Sheff Wed 2
Bristol R 1 Swansea 0
Burnley 3 Middlesbro 2

Ronnie Whelan holds aloft the Milk Cup

Chelsea 3 Tranmere 1
Colchester 0 Southmptn 0
Derby 2 Hartlepl 0
Fulham 2 Coventry 2
Gillinghm 2 Oldham 0
Grimsby 3 Sheff Utd 3
Huddersfld 2 Oxford 0
Ipswich 1 Liverpool 2
Leeds U 0 Newcastle 1
Lincoln 2 Leicester 0
Luton 3 Charlton 0
Man Utd 2 Bournemth 0
Newport 0 Everton 2
N'hamptn 1 Blackpool 1
Norwich 2 Preston NE 1
Nottm For 6 West Brom 1
Peterboro 0 C.Palace 2
Rochdale 0 Bradford 1
Rotherhm 2 QPR 1
Shrewsby 1 Birmghm C 1
Stoke 1 West Ham 1
Tottenham 1 Brighton 1
Wigan Ath 1 Man City 1
Wolves 1 Sunderld 1

SECOND ROUND SECOND-LEG

Birmghm C 4 Shrewsby 1
Birmghm C win 5-2 on agg
Blackburn 0 Brentford 0
Brentford win 3-2 on agg
Blackpool 2 N'hamptn 1 e
Blackpool win 3-2 on agg
Bournemth 2 Man Utd 2
Man Utd win 4-2 on agg
Bradford 4 Rochdale 0
Bradford win 5-0 on agg
Brighton 0 Tottenham 1
Tottenham win 2-1 on agg
Cambridge 1 Barnsley 3
Barnsley win 5-2 on agg
Cardiff 1 Arsenal 3
Arsenal win 5-2 on agg
Charlton 2 Luton 0
Luton win 3-2 on agg
Coventry 0 Fulham 0
agg score Coventry 2 - Fulham 2
C.Palace 2 Peterboro 1
C.Palace win 4-1 on agg
Everton 2 Newport 2
Everton win 4-2 on agg
Hartlepl 4 Derby 2 a
agg score Hartlepl 4 - Derby 4
Leicester 0 Lincoln 1
Lincoln win 3-0 on agg
Liverpool 2 Ipswich 0
Liverpool win 4-1 on agg
Man City 2 Wigan Ath 0
Man City win 3-1 on agg
Middlesbro 1 Burnley 1
Burnley win 4-3 on agg
Newcastle 1 Leeds U 4 e

WHAT A STAR ✪ RONNIE WHELAN

Whelan was not renowned as a heavy scorer for Liverpool, but his goals won them two of their five League Cups. In 1982, he netted twice as they came back from a goal down to beat Spurs 3-1 in extra-time. A year later, after his team had seemed down and out against Manchester United before Alan Kennedy's equaliser, Whelan hit a perfectly-judged curler for a glorious winner, again in the extra period. Oddly enough, Whelan's goals equalled the Final record set by Clive Clark of West Brom (one in 1966, two in 1967) and no player since has done better.

Leeds U win 4-2 on agg				
Notts Co	**1**	**Aston V**	**0**	
Notts Co win 3-1 on agg				
Oldham	**1**	**Gillinghm**	**0**	
Gillinghm win 2-1 on agg				
Oxford	**1**	**Huddersfld**	**0**	
Huddersfld win 2-1 on agg				
Preston NE	**1**	**Norwich**	**2**	
Norwich win 4-2 on agg				
QPR	**0**	**Rotherhm**	**0**	
Rotherhm win 2-1 on agg				
Sheff Utd	**5**	**Grimsby**	**1**	
Sheff Utd win 8-4 on agg				
Sheff Wed	**1**	**Bristol C**	**1**	e
Sheff Wed win 3-2 on agg				
Southmptn	**4**	**Colchester**	**2**	
Southmptn win 4-2 on agg				
Sunderld	**5**	**Wolves**	**0**	
Sunderld win 6-1 on agg				
Swansea	**3**	**Bristol R**	**0**	
Swansea win 3-1 on agg				
Tranmere	**1**	**Chelsea**	**2**	
Chelsea win 5-2 on agg				
Watford	**2**	**Bolton**	**1**	e
Watford win 4-2 on agg				
West Brom	**3**	**Nottm For**	**1**	
Nottm For win 7-4 on agg				
West Ham	**2**	**Stoke**	**1**	
West Ham win 3-2 on agg				

THIRD ROUND

Birmghm C	**3**	**Derby**	**1**	
Bradford	**0**	**Man Utd**	**0**	
Brentford	**1**	**Swansea**	**1**	
Coventry	**1**	**Burnley**	**2**	
C.Palace	**1**	**Sheff Wed**	**2**	
Everton	**1**	**Arsenal**	**1**	
Gillinghm	**2**	**Tottenham**	**4**	
Leeds U	**0**	**Huddersfld**	**1**	
Lincoln	**1**	**West Ham**	**1**	
Liverpool	**1**	**Rotherhm**	**0**	
Luton	**4**	**Blackpool**	**2**	
Man City	**1**	**Southmptn**	**1**	
Nottm For	**7**	**Watford**	**3**	
Notts Co	**2**	**Chelsea**	**0**	
Sheff Utd	**1**	**Barnsley**	**3**	
Sunderld	**0**	**Norwich**	**0**	
Arsenal	**3**	**Everton**	**0**	r
Man Utd	**4**	**Bradford**	**1**	r
Norwich	**3**	**Sunderld**	**1**	r
Southmptn	**4**	**Man City**	**0**	r
Swansea	**1**	**Brentford**	**2**	r
West Ham	**2**	**Lincoln**	**1**	r

FOURTH ROUND

Arsenal	**1**	**Huddersfld**	**0**	
Burnley	**3**	**Birmghm C**	**2**	
Liverpool	**2**	**Norwich**	**0**	
Man Utd	**2**	**Southmptn**	**0**	
Nottm For	**2**	**Brentford**	**0**	
Notts Co	**3**	**West Ham**	**3**	
Sheff Wed	**1**	**Barnsley**	**0**	
Tottenham	**1**	**Luton**	**0**	
West Ham	**3**	**Notts Co**	**0**	r

FIFTH ROUND

Arsenal	**1**	**Sheff Wed**	**0**	
Liverpool	**2**	**West Ham**	**1**	
Man Utd	**4**	**Nottm For**	**0**	
Tottenham	**1**	**Burnley**	**4**	

SEMI-FINAL FIRST-LEG

Arsenal	**2**	**Man Utd**	**4**	
Liverpool	**3**	**Burnley**	**0**	

SEMI-FINAL SECOND-LEG

Burnley	**1**	**Liverpool**	**0**	
Liverpool win 3-1 on agg				
Man Utd	**2**	**Arsenal**	**1**	
Man Utd win 6-3 on agg				

FINAL

Liverpool	**2**	**Man Utd**	**1**	eN

1984

FIRST ROUND FIRST-LEG

Aldershot	**3**	**Leyton O**	**1**	
Blackpool	**2**	**Walsall**	**1**	
Bolton	**3**	**Chester**	**0**	
Bournemth	**1**	**Bristol R**	**2**	
Bradford	**0**	**Sheff Utd**	**1**	
Brentford	**3**	**Charlton**	**0**	
Colchester	**3**	**Reading**	**2**	
Crewe	**1**	**Burnley**	**0**	
C.Palace	**3**	**Peterboro**	**0**	
Exeter	**2**	**Cardiff**	**3**	
Gillinghm	**1**	**Chelsea**	**2**	
Halifax	**0**	**Darlingtn**	**1**	
Hereford	**3**	**Portsmth**	**2**	
Hull	**0**	**Lincoln**	**0**	
Mansfield	**1**	**Huddersfld**	**2**	
Middlesbro	**0**	**Chestrfld**	**1**	
Millwall	**3**	**N'hamptn**	**0**	
Newport	**2**	**Torquay**	**3**	
Oxford	**1**	**Bristol C**	**1**	
Port Vale	**3**	**Wrexham**	**1**	
Preston NE	**1**	**Tranmere**	**0**	
Rochdale	**0**	**Stockport**	**3**	
Rotherhm	**0**	**Hartlepl**	**0**	
Scunthpe	**1**	**Doncaster**	**1**	
Southend	**1**	**Wimbledn**	**0**	
Swindon	**1**	**Plymouth**	**0**	
Wigan Ath	**1**	**Bury**	**2**	
York	**2**	**Grimsby**	**1**	

FIRST ROUND SECOND-LEG

Bristol C	**0**	**Oxford**	**1**	
Oxford win 2-1 on agg				
Bristol R	**2**	**Bournemth**	**2**	
Bristol R win 4-3 on agg				
Burnley	**3**	**Crewe**	**4**	
Crewe win 5-3 on agg				
Bury	**2**	**Wigan Ath**	**0**	
Bury win 4-1 on agg				
Cardiff	**2**	**Exeter**	**1**	
Cardiff win 5-3 on agg				
Charlton	**2**	**Brentford**	**1**	
Brentford win 4-2 on agg				
Chelsea	**4**	**Gillinghm**	**0**	
Chelsea win 6-1 on agg				
Chester	**3**	**Bolton**	**0**	P
agg score Chester 3 - Bolton 3				
Chestrfld	**0**	**Middlesbro**	**1**	P
agg score Chestrfld 1 -Mid'sbro 1				
Darlingtn	**3**	**Halifax**	**2**	
Darlingtn win 4-2 on agg				
Doncaster	**3**	**Scunthpe**	**0**	
Doncaster win 4-1 on agg				
Grimsby	**2**	**York**	**0**	e
Grimsby win 3-2 on agg				
Hartlepl	**0**	**Rotherhm**	**1**	
Rotherhm win 1-0 on agg				
Huddersfld	**5**	**Mansfield**	**1**	
Huddersfld win 7-2 on agg				
Leyton O	**3**	**Aldershot**	**3**	
Aldershot win 6-4 on agg				
Lincoln	**3**	**Hull**	**1**	e
Lincoln win 3-1 on agg				
N'hamptn	**1**	**Millwall**	**2**	
Millwall win 5-1 on agg				
Peterboro	**3**	**C.Palace**	**0**	P
agg score Peterboro 3 - C.Palace 3				
Plymouth	**4**	**Swindon**	**1**	
Plymouth win 4-2 on agg				
Portsmth	**3**	**Hereford**	**1**	
Portsmth win 5-4 on agg				
Reading	**4**	**Colchester**	**3**	a
agg score Reading 6 - Colchester 6				
Sheff Utd	**1**	**Bradford**	**1**	
Sheff Utd win 2-1 on agg				
Stockport	**2**	**Rochdale**	**2**	
Stockport win 5-2 on agg				
Torquay	**1**	**Newport**	**0**	
Torquay win 4-2 on agg				
Tranmere	**0**	**Preston NE**	**0**	
Preston NE win 1-0 on agg				
Walsall	**3**	**Blackpool**	**1**	
Walsall win 4-3 on agg				
Wimbledn	**6**	**Southend**	**4**	e
Wimbledn win 6-5 on agg				
Wrexham	**1**	**Port Vale**	**5**	
Port Vale win 8-2 on agg				

SECOND ROUND FIRST-LEG

Aldershot	**2**	**Notts Co**	**4**	
Brentford	**1**	**Liverpool**	**4**	
Brighton	**4**	**Bristol R**	**2**	
Bury	**1**	**West Ham**	**2**	
Cambridge	**2**	**Sunderld**	**3**	
Cardiff	**0**	**Norwich**	**0**	
Carlisle	**2**	**Southmptn**	**0**	
Chestrfld	**0**	**Everton**	**1**	
Derby	**0**	**Birmghm C**	**3**	
Doncaster	**1**	**Fulham**	**3**	
Grimsby	**0**	**Coventry**	**0**	
Huddersfld	**2**	**Watford**	**1**	
Ipswich	**4**	**Blackburn**	**3**	
Leeds U	**0**	**Chester**	**1**	
Leicester	**0**	**Chelsea**	**2**	
Millwall	**3**	**West Brom**	**0**	

Shot Away

Aldershot held Sheffield Wednesday to a 0-0 draw in the Second Round of the League Cup in 1989-90, only to lose the second-leg 0-8 - at home. Both clubs finished third from bottom of their respective Divisions, Fourth and First.

GIANTKILLERS

1985-86 Swindon 3 Sunderland 1

A great season for Swindon, Fourth Division title-winners with a record 102 points and League Cup victors over two famous names, Sunderland of the Second Division and Sheffield Wednesday of the First. Swindon lost the first-leg of the Second Round, 2-3 at Roker Park, only to pull through 3-1 at home, and a goal by Peter Coyne saw off Wednesday in a thrilling match at the County Ground. Not even a 1-6 crash at Ipswich next time out could take away the memories.

Newcastle	1	Oxford	1	
Plymouth	1	Arsenal	1	
Port Vale	0	Man Utd	1	
Portsmth	2	Aston V	2	
QPR	8	Crewe	1	
Rotherhm	2	Luton	3	
Sheff Wed	3	Darlingtn	0	
Shrewsby	2	Sheff Utd	1	
Stockport	0	Oldham	2	
Stoke	0	Peterboro	0	
Swansea	1	Colchester	1	
Torquay	0	Man City	0	
Tottenham	3	Lincoln	1	
Walsall	1	Barnsley	0	
Wimbledn	2	Nottm For	0	
Wolves	2	Preston NE	3	
SECOND ROUND SECOND-LEG				
Arsenal	1	Plymouth	0	
Arsenal win 2-1 on agg				
Aston V	3	Portsmth	2	e
Aston V win 5-4 on agg				
Barnsley	0	Walsall	2	
Walsall win 3-0 on agg				
Birmghm C	4	Derby	0	
Birmghm C win 7-0 on agg				
Blackburn	1	Ipswich	2	
Ipswich win 6-4 on agg				
Bristol R	2	Brighton	1	e
Brighton win 5-4 on agg				
Chelsea	0	Leicester	2	P
agg score Chelsea 2 - Leicester 2				
Chester	1	Leeds U	4	
Leeds U win 4-2 on agg				
Colchester	1	Swansea	0	
Colchester win 2-1 on agg				
Coventry	2	Grimsby	1	
Coventry win 2-1 on agg				
Crewe	3	QPR	0	
QPR win 8-4 on agg				
Darlingtn	2	Sheff Wed	4	
Sheff Wed win 7-2 on agg				
Everton	2	Chestrfld	2	
Everton win 3-2 on agg				
Fulham	3	Doncaster	1	
Fulham win 6-2 on agg				
Lincoln	2	Tottenham	1	
Tottenham win 4-3 on agg				
Liverpool	4	Brentford	0	
Liverpool win 8-1 on agg				
Luton	0	Rotherhm	2	e
Rotherhm win 4-3 on agg				
Man City	6	Torquay	0	
Man City win 6-0 on agg				
Man Utd	2	Port Vale	0	
Man Utd win 3-0 on agg				
Norwich	3	Cardiff	0	
Norwich win 3-0 on agg				
Nottm For	1	Wimbledn	1	
Wimbledn win 3-1 on agg				
Notts Co	4	Aldershot	1	
Notts Co win 8-3 on agg				
Oldham	2	Stockport	2	
Oldham win 4-2 on agg				
Oxford	2	Newcastle	1	
Oxford win 3-2 on agg				
Peterboro	1	Stoke	2	
Stoke win 2-1 on agg				
Preston NE	1	Wolves	0	
Preston NE win 4-2 on agg				
Sheff Utd	2	Shrewsby	2	
Shrewsby win 4-3 on agg				
Southmptn	3	Carlisle	0	e
Southmptn win 3-2 on agg				
Sunderld	4	Cambridge	3	
Sunderld win 7-5 on agg				
Watford	2	Huddersfld	2	
Huddersfld win 4-3 on agg				
West Brom	5	Millwall	1	
West Brom win 5-4 on agg				
West Ham	10	Bury	0	
West Ham win 12-1 on agg				
THIRD ROUND				
Aston V	3	Man City	0	
Birmghm C	2	Notts Co	2	
Chelsea	0	West Brom	1	
Colchester	0	Man Utd	2	
Everton	2	Coventry	1	
Fulham	1	Liverpool	1	
Ipswich	3	QPR	2	
Leeds U	1	Oxford	1	
Norwich	0	Sunderld	0	
Preston NE	0	Sheff Wed	2	
Rotherhm	2	Southmptn	1	
Stoke	0	Huddersfld	0	
Tottenham	1	Arsenal	2	
Walsall	2	Shrewsby	1	
West Ham	1	Brighton	0	
Wimbledn	3	Oldham	1	
Huddersfld	0	Stoke	2	r
Liverpool	1	Fulham	1	re
Notts Co	0	Birmghm C	0	re
Oxford	4	Leeds U	1	r
Sunderld	1	Norwich	2	r
Birmghm C	0	Notts Co	0	r2e
Fulham	0	Liverpool	1	r2e
Notts Co	1	Birmghm C	3	r3
FOURTH ROUND				
Arsenal	1	Walsall	2	
Birmghm C	1	Liverpool	1	
Ipswich	0	Norwich	1	
Oxford	1	Man Utd	1	
Rotherhm	1	Wimbledn	0	
Stoke	0	Sheff Wed	1	
West Brom	1	Aston V	2	
West Ham	2	Everton	2	
Everton	2	West Ham	0	re
Liverpool	3	Birmghm C	0	r
Man Utd	1	Oxford	1	re
Oxford	2	Man Utd	1	r2e
FIFTH ROUND				
Norwich	0	Aston V	2	
Oxford	1	Everton	1	
Rotherhm	2	Walsall	4	
Sheff Wed	2	Liverpool	2	
Everton	4	Oxford	1	r
Liverpool	3	Sheff Wed	0	r
SEMI-FINAL FIRST-LEG				
Everton	2	Aston V	0	
Liverpool	2	Walsall	2	
SEMI-FINAL SECOND-LEG				
Aston V	1	Everton	0	
Everton win 2-1 on agg				
Walsall	0	Liverpool	2	
Liverpool win 4-2 on agg				
FINAL				
Liverpool	0	Everton	0	eN
Liverpool	1	Everton	0	rN

King Ray

Ray Clemence kept goal in successive League Cup Finals for different clubs - for Liverpool against West Ham in 1981 and for Spurs against Liverpool in 1982.

WHAT A STAR ✪ ANDY DIBBLE

You would have put your mortgage on an Arsenal victory in the 1988 League Cup Final, to go with their win the previous year. With 12 minutes left they were 2-1 up and the ball was on the spot in the Luton box for a penalty. But although Nigel Winterburn's shot was by no means the worst you would see, Andy Dibble dived into the headlines by making the save that turned the match. Luton, given new inspiration, scored twice to snatch victory, and although Welsh lad Dibble did little else of note during his time with the club, you only have to mention his name to see a Luton fan's eyes light up.

1985

FIRST ROUND FIRST-LEG

Aldershot	4	Bournemth	0	
Blackpool	1	Chester	0	
Bolton	2	Oldham	1	
Bradford	2	Middlesbro	0	
Brentford	2	Cambridge	0	
Bristol C	2	Newport	1	
Burnley	1	Crewe	2	
C.Palace	1	N'hamptn	0	
Darlingtn	1	Rotherhm	2	
Derby	5	Hartlepl	1	
Doncaster	2	York	3	
Exeter	1	Cardiff	0	
Gillinghm	3	Colchester	2	
Halifax	1	Chestrfld	1	
Hereford	2	Oxford	2	
Leyton O	2	Southend	1	
Lincoln	0	Hull	2	
Plymouth	1	Torquay	0	
Port Vale	1	Bury	0	
Portsmth	3	Wimbledn	0	
Reading	1	Millwall	1	
Scunthpe	0	Mansfield	1	
Sheff Utd	1	Peterboro	0	
Stockport	3	Rochdale	1	
Swansea	0	Walsall	2	
Swindon	1	Bristol R	5	
Tranmere	2	Preston NE	3	
Wrexham	0	Wigan Ath	3	

FIRST ROUND SECOND-LEG

Bournemth	0	Aldershot	1	
Aldershot win 5-0 on agg				
Bristol R	0	Swindon	1	
Bristol R win 5-2 on agg				
Bury	2	Port Vale	1	a
agg score Bury 2 - Port Vale 2				
Cambridge	1	Brentford	0	
Brentford win 2-1 on agg				
Cardiff	2	Exeter	0	
Cardiff win 2-1 on agg				
Chester	0	Blackpool	3	
Blackpool win 4-0 on agg				
Chestrfld	1	Halifax	2	
Halifax win 3-2 on agg				
Colchester	0	Gillinghm	2	
Gillinghm win 5-2 on agg				
Crewe	0	Burnley	3	
Burnley win 4-2 on agg				
Hartlepl	0	Derby	1	
Derby win 6-1 on agg				
Hull	4	Lincoln	1	
Hull win 6-1 on agg				
Mansfield	1	Scunthpe	2	a
agg score Mansf'ld 2 - Scunthpe 2				
Middlesbro	2	Bradford	2	
Bradford win 4-2 on agg				
Millwall	4	Reading	3	
Millwall win 5-4 on agg				
Newport	0	Bristol C	3	
Bristol C win 5-1 on agg				
N'hamptn	0	C.Palace	0	
C.Palace win 1-0 on agg				
Oldham	4	Bolton	4	e
Bolton win 6-5 on agg				
Oxford	5	Hereford	3	
Oxford win 7-5 on agg				
Peterboro	2	Sheff Utd	2	e
Sheff Utd win 3-2 on agg				
Preston NE	2	Tranmere	2	e
Preston NE win 5-4 on agg				
Rochdale	1	Stockport	2	
Stockport win 5-2 on agg				
Rotherhm	4	Darlingtn	0	
Rotherhm win 6-1 on agg				
Southend	0	Leyton O	0	
Leyton O win 2-1 on agg				
Torquay	0	Plymouth	1	
Plymouth win 2-0 on agg				
Walsall	3	Swansea	1	
Walsall win 5-1 on agg				
Wigan Ath	2	Wrexham	0	
Wigan Ath win 5-0 on agg				
Wimbledn	1	Portsmth	0	
Portsmth win 3-1 on agg				
York	5	Doncaster	0	
York win 8-2 on agg				

SECOND ROUND FIRST-LEG

Arsenal	4	Bristol R	0	
Birmghm C	4	Plymouth	1	
Blackburn	1	Oxford	1	
Brighton	3	Aldershot	1	
Bristol C	2	West Ham	2	
Charlton	0	Notts Co	1	
Chelsea	3	Millwall	1	
Fulham	2	Carlisle	0	
Gillinghm	1	Leeds U	2	
Grimsby	3	Barnsley	0	
Halifax	1	Tottenham	5	
Ipswich	4	Derby	2	
Leicester	4	Brentford	2	
Leyton O	1	Luton	4	
Man City	4	Blackpool	2	
Man Utd	4	Burnley	0	
Newcastle	3	Bradford	1	
Port Vale	1	Wolves	2	
Portsmth	1	Nottm For	0	
Preston NE	3	Norwich	3	
Scunthpe	2	Aston V	3	
Sheff Utd	2	Everton	2	
Sheff Wed	3	Huddersfld	0	
Shrewsby	2	Bolton	2	
Southmptn	3	Hull	2	
Stockport	0	Liverpool	0	
Stoke	1	Rotherhm	2	
Sunderld	2	C.Palace	1	
Walsall	1	Coventry	2	
Watford	3	Cardiff	1	
Wigan Ath	0	West Brom	0	
York	2	QPR	4	

SECOND ROUND SECOND-LEG

Aldershot	3	Brighton	0	e
Aldershot win 4-3 on agg				
Aston V	3	Scunthpe	1	
Aston V win 6-3 on agg				
Barnsley	1	Grimsby	1	
Grimsby win 4-1 on agg				
Blackpool	1	Man City	3	
Man City win 7-3 on agg				
Bolton	2	Shrewsby	1	
Bolton win 4-3 on agg				
Bradford	0	Newcastle	1	
Newcastle win 4-1 on agg				
Brentford	0	Leicester	2	
Leicester win 6-2 on agg				
Bristol R	1	Arsenal	1	
Arsenal win 5-1 on agg				
Burnley	0	Man Utd	3	
Man Utd win 7-0 on agg				
Cardiff	1	Watford	0	
Watford win 3-2 on agg				
Carlisle	1	Fulham	2	
Fulham win 4-1 on agg				
Coventry	0	Walsall	3	
Walsall win 4-2 on agg				
C.Palace	0	Sunderld	0	
Sunderld win 2-1 on agg				

Derby	**1**	**Ipswich**	**1**	
Ipswich win 5-3 on agg				
Everton	**4**	**Sheff Utd**	**0**	
Everton win 6-2 on agg				
Huddersfld	**2**	**Sheff Wed**	**1**	
Sheff Wed win 4-2 on agg				
Hull	**2**	**Southmptn**	**2**	
Southmptn win 5-4 on agg				
Leeds U	**3**	**Gillinghm**	**2**	
Leeds U win 5-3 on agg				
Liverpool	**2**	**Stockport**	**0**	e
Liverpool win 2-0 on agg				
Luton	**3**	**Leyton O**	**1**	
Luton win 7-2 on agg				
Millwall	**1**	**Chelsea**	**1**	
Chelsea win 4-2 on agg				
Norwich	**6**	**Preston NE**	**1**	
Norwich win 9-4 on agg				
Nottm For	**3**	**Portsmth**	**0**	e
Nottm For win 3-1 on agg				
Notts Co	**2**	**Charlton**	**0**	
Notts Co win 3-0 on agg				
Oxford	**3**	**Blackburn**	**1**	e
Oxford win 4-2 on agg				
Plymouth	**0**	**Birmghm C**	**1**	
Birmghm C win 5-1 on agg				
QPR	**4**	**York**	**1**	
QPR win 8-3 on agg				
Rotherhm	**1**	**Stoke**	**1**	
Rotherhm win 3-2 on agg				
Tottenham	**4**	**Halifax**	**0**	
Tottenham win 9-1 on agg				
West Brom	**3**	**Wigan Ath**	**1**	
West Brom win 3-1 on agg				
West Ham	**6**	**Bristol C**	**1**	
West Ham win 8-3 on agg				
Wolves	**0**	**Port Vale**	**0**	
Wolves win 2-1 on agg				
THIRD ROUND				
Birmghm C	**0**	**West Brom**	**0**	
Ipswich	**1**	**Newcastle**	**1**	
Leeds U	**0**	**Watford**	**4**	
Luton	**3**	**Leicester**	**1**	
Man City	**0**	**West Ham**	**0**	
Man Utd	**1**	**Everton**	**2**	
Norwich	**0**	**Aldershot**	**0**	
Nottm For	**1**	**Sunderld**	**1**	
Notts Co	**6**	**Bolton**	**1**	
Oxford	**3**	**Arsenal**	**2**	
QPR	**1**	**Aston V**	**0**	
Rotherhm	**0**	**Grimsby**	**0**	
Sheff Wed	**3**	**Fulham**	**2**	
Southmptn	**2**	**Wolves**	**2**	
Tottenham	**1**	**Liverpool**	**0**	
Walsall	**2**	**Chelsea**	**2**	
Aldershot	**0**	**Norwich**	**4**	r
Chelsea	**3**	**Walsall**	**0**	r
Grimsby	**6**	**Rotherhm**	**1**	r
Newcastle	**1**	**Ipswich**	**2**	r
Sunderld	**1**	**Nottm For**	**0**	re
West Brom	**3**	**Birmghm C**	**1**	r
West Ham	**1**	**Man City**	**2**	r
Wolves	**0**	**Southmptn**	**2**	r
FOURTH ROUND				
Chelsea	**4**	**Man City**	**1**	
Everton	**0**	**Grimsby**	**1**	
Ipswich	**2**	**Oxford**	**1**	
Norwich	**3**	**Notts Co**	**0**	
Sheff Wed	**4**	**Luton**	**2**	
Southmptn	**1**	**QPR**	**1**	
Sunderld	**0**	**Tottenham**	**0**	
Watford	**4**	**West Brom**	**1**	
QPR	**0**	**Southmptn**	**0**	re
Tottenham	**1**	**Sunderld**	**2**	r
QPR	**4**	**Southmptn**	**0**	r2
FIFTH ROUND				
Chelsea	**1**	**Sheff Wed**	**1**	
Grimsby	**0**	**Norwich**	**1**	
Ipswich	**0**	**QPR**	**0**	
Watford	**0**	**Sunderld**	**1**	
QPR	**1**	**Ipswich**	**2**	r
Sheff Wed	**4**	**Chelsea**	**4**	re
Chelsea	**2**	**Sheff Wed**	**1**	r2
SEMI-FINAL FIRST-LEG				
Ipswich	**1**	**Norwich**	**0**	
Sunderld	**2**	**Chelsea**	**0**	
SEMI-FINAL SECOND-LEG				
Chelsea	**2**	**Sunderld**	**3**	
Sunderld win 5-2 on agg				
Norwich	**2**	**Ipswich**	**0**	
Norwich win 2-1 on agg				
FINAL				
Norwich	**1**	**Sunderld**	**0**	N

Norwich take the League Cup in 1985

Baby Barry

Sunderland's Barry Venison became the youngest captain in any major Cup Final when he led his team against Norwich in the 1985 League Cup Final at the age of 20 years, seven months and eight days.

1986

FIRST ROUND FIRST-LEG				
Aldershot	**1**	**Leyton O**	**3**	
Bolton	**4**	**Stockport**	**1**	
Bradford	**2**	**Chestrfld**	**2**	
Bristol R	**2**	**Newport**	**0**	
Burnley	**2**	**Bury**	**1**	
Cambridge	**1**	**Brentford**	**1**	
Cardiff	**2**	**Swansea**	**1**	
Charlton	**1**	**C.Palace**	**2**	
Colchester	**2**	**Millwall**	**3**	
Crewe	**3**	**Carlisle**	**3**	
Darlingtn	**3**	**Scunthpe**	**2**	
Derby	**3**	**Hartlepl**	**0**	
Halifax	**1**	**Hull**	**1**	
Hereford	**5**	**Bristol C**	**1**	
Mansfield	**2**	**Middlesbro**	**0**	
Notts Co	**1**	**Doncaster**	**0**	
Peterboro	**0**	**N'hamptn**	**0**	
Plymouth	**2**	**Exeter**	**1**	
Preston NE	**2**	**Blackpool**	**1**	
Reading	**1**	**Bournemth**	**3**	
Rotherhm	**1**	**Sheff Utd**	**3**	
Southend	**1**	**Gillinghm**	**1**	
Torquay	**1**	**Swindon**	**2**	
Tranmere	**1**	**Chester**	**3**	
Walsall	**1**	**Wolves**	**1**	
Wigan Ath	**2**	**Port Vale**	**1**	
Wrexham	**4**	**Rochdale**	**0**	
York	**2**	**Lincoln**	**1**	
FIRST ROUND SECOND-LEG				
Blackpool	**1**	**Preston NE**	**3**	
Preston NE win 5-2 on agg				
Bolton	**1**	**Stockport**	**1**	
Bolton win 5-2 on agg				
Bournemth	**2**	**Reading**	**0**	
Bournemth win 5-1 on agg				
Brentford	**2**	**Cambridge**	**0**	
Brentford win 3-1 on agg				
Bristol C	**2**	**Hereford**	**0**	
Hereford win 5-3 on agg				
Bury	**5**	**Burnley**	**3**	
Bury win 6-5 on agg				
Carlisle	**3**	**Crewe**	**4**	
Crewe win 7-6 on agg				
Chester	**0**	**Tranmere**	**0**	
Chester win 3-1 on agg				
Chestrfld	**3**	**Bradford**	**4**	e

Bradford win 6-5 on agg
C.Palace 1 Charlton 1
C.Palace win 3-2 on agg
Doncaster 2 Notts Co 1 a
agg score Doncaster 2 - Notts Co 2
Exeter 2 Plymouth 0
Exeter win 3-2 on agg
Gillinghm 2 Southend 0
Gillinghm win 3-1 on agg
Hartlepl 2 Derby 0
Derby win 3-2 on agg
Hull 3 Halifax 0
Hull win 4-1 on agg
Leyton O 2 Aldershot 2
Leyton O win 5-3 on agg
Lincoln 1 York 2
York win 4-2 on agg
Middlesbro 4 Mansfield 4
Mansfield win 6-4 on agg
Millwall 4 Colchester 1
Millwall win 7-3 on agg
Newport 1 Bristol R 0
Bristol R win 2-1 on agg
N'hamptn 2 Peterboro 0
N'hamptn win 2-0 on agg
Port Vale 2 Wigan Ath 0
Port Vale win 3-2 on agg
Rochdale 2 Wrexham 1
Wrexham win 5-2 on agg
Scunthpe 0 Darlingtn 0
Darlingtn win 3-2 on agg
Sheff Utd 5 Rotherhm 1
Sheff Utd win 8-2 on agg
Swansea 3 Cardiff 1
Swansea win 4-3 on agg
Swindon 2 Torquay 2
Swindon win 4-3 on agg
Wolves 0 Walsall 1
Walsall win 2-1 on agg

SECOND ROUND FIRST-LEG

Brentford 2 Sheff Wed 2
Brighton 5 Bradford 2
Bristol R 2 Birmghm C 3
Bury 1 Man City 2
Chester 1 Coventry 2
Crewe 1 Watford 3
C.Palace 0 Man Utd 1
Derby 2 Leicester 0
Everton 3 Bournemth 2
Exeter 1 Aston V 4
Fulham 1 Notts Co 1
Gillinghm 1 Portsmth 3
Grimsby 1 York 1
Hereford 0 Arsenal 0
Ipswich 3 Darlingtn 1
Leeds U 0 Walsall 0
Leyton O 2 Tottenham 0
Liverpool 3 Oldham 0
Mansfield 2 Chelsea 2
Millwall 0 Southmptn 0
Newcastle 0 Barnsley 0
Nottm For 4 Bolton 0
Oxford 2 N'hamptn 1
Preston NE 1 Norwich 1
QPR 3 Hull 0
Sheff Utd 1 Luton 2
Shrewsby 2 Huddersfld 3
Sunderld 3 Swindon 2
West Brom 1 Port Vale 0
West Ham 3 Swansea 0
Wimbledn 5 Blackburn 0
Wrexham 0 Stoke 1

SECOND ROUND SECOND-LEG

Arsenal 2 Hereford 1 e
Arsenal win 2-1 on agg
Aston V 8 Exeter 1
Aston V win 12-2 on agg
Barnsley 1 Newcastle 1 a
agg score Barnsley 1 - Newcastle 1
Birmghm C 2 Bristol R 1
Birmghm C win 5-3 on agg
Blackburn 2 Wimbledn 1
Wimbledn win 6-2 on agg
Bolton 0 Nottm For 3
Nottm For win 7-0 on agg
Bournemth 0 Everton 2
Everton win 5-2 on agg
Bradford 0 Brighton 2
Brighton win 7-2 on agg
Chelsea 2 Mansfield 0
Chelsea win 4-2 on agg
Coventry 7 Chester 2
Coventry win 9-3 on agg
Darlingtn 1 Ipswich 4
Ipswich win 7-2 on agg
Huddersfld 0 Shrewsby 2
Shrewsby win 4-3 on agg
Hull 1 QPR 5
QPR win 8-1 on agg
Leicester 1 Derby 1
Derby win 3-1 on agg
Luton 3 Sheff Utd 1
Luton win 5-2 on agg
Man City 2 Bury 1
Man City win 4-2 on agg
Man Utd 1 C.Palace 0
Man Utd win 2-0 on agg
N'hamptn 0 Oxford 2
Oxford win 4-1 on agg
Norwich 2 Preston NE 1
Norwich win 3-2 on agg
Notts Co 2 Fulham 4 e
Fulham win 5-3 on agg
Oldham 2 Liverpool 5
Liverpool win 8-2 on agg
Port Vale 2 West Brom 2
West Brom win 3-2 on agg
Portsmth 2 Gillinghm 1
Portsmth win 5-2 on agg
Sheff Wed 2 Brentford 0
Sheff Wed win 4-2 on agg
Southmptn 0 Millwall 0 P
Stoke 1 Wrexham 0
Stoke win 2-0 on agg
Swansea 2 West Ham 3
West Ham win 6-2 on agg
Swindon 3 Sunderld 1 e
Swindon win 5-4 on agg
Tottenham 4 Leyton O 0
Tottenham win 4-2 on agg
Walsall 0 Leeds U 3
Leeds U win 3-0 on agg
Watford 3 Crewe 2
Watford win 6-3 on agg
York 2 Grimsby 3
Grimsby win 4-3 on agg

THIRD ROUND

Birmghm C 1 Southmptn 1
Chelsea 1 Fulham 1
Coventry 0 West Brom 0
Derby 1 Nottm For 2
Grimsby 0 Ipswich 2
Leeds U 0 Aston V 3
Liverpool 4 Brighton 0
Luton 0 Norwich 2
Man City 1 Arsenal 2
Man Utd 1 West Ham 0
Oxford 3 Newcastle 1
Portsmth 2 Stoke 0
Shrewsby 1 Everton 4

GIANTKILLERS

1988-89 Tranmere 1 Middlesbrough 0

Middlesbrough were a struggling First Division outfit, not long free from the bailiffs, at the time when fate unleashed Tranmere Rovers on them in the Second Round of the League Cup. Even with players such as Tony Mowbray, Gary Pallister and Bernie Slaven on board, they were held 0-0 at home and beaten at Prenton Park by the only goal, scored by the other Mark Hughes. Rovers went on to beat Blackpool, then lost to Bristol City, but had consolation with promotion.

GIANTKILLERS

1986-87 Cardiff 2 Chelsea 1

A real oddity, even among Cup runs by lowly clubs. Cardiff, midway in the Fourth, were 1-4 down at one stage at home to Second Division Plymouth in the two-legged First Round, but won 6-4 on aggregate. Then they were given a walkover in the next round, because Luton had withdrawn during a wrangle with the League over the banning of away supporters in an effort to combat hooliganism. Cardiff then beat First Division Chelsea 2-1, both goals coming from the well-travelled Nicky Platnauer, only to come unstuck against Shrewsbury, another Second Division side.

Swindon	1	Sheff Wed	0	
Tottenham	2	Wimbledn	0	
Watford	0	QPR	1	
Fulham	0	Chelsea	1	r
Southmptn	3	Birmghm C	0	r
West Brom	4	Coventry	3	r

FOURTH ROUND

Arsenal	0	Southmptn	0	
Aston V	2	West Brom	2	
Chelsea	2	Everton	2	
Ipswich	6	Swindon	1	
Liverpool	2	Man Utd	1	
Oxford	3	Norwich	1	
QPR	3	Nottm For	1	
Tottenham	0	Portsmth	0	
Everton	1	Chelsea	2	r
Portsmth	0	Tottenham	0	re
Southmptn	1	Arsenal	3	r
West Brom	1	Aston V	2	r
Portsmth	1	Tottenham	0	r2

FIFTH ROUND

Aston V	1	Arsenal	1	
Liverpool	3	Ipswich	0	
Oxford	3	Portsmth	1	
QPR	1	Chelsea	1	
Arsenal	1	Aston V	2	r
Chelsea	0	QPR	2	re

SEMI-FINAL FIRST-LEG

Aston V	2	Oxford	2	
QPR	1	Liverpool	0	

SEMI-FINAL SECOND-LEG

Liverpool	2	QPR	2	
QPR win 3-2 on agg				
Oxford	2	Aston V	1	
Oxford win 4-3 on agg				

FINAL

Oxford	3	QPR	0	N

1987

FIRST ROUND FIRST-LEG

Aldershot	1	Fulham	3	
Blackpool	0	Preston NE	0	
Bournemth	0	Bristol C	1	
Bristol R	1	Reading	2	
Bury	2	Bolton	1	
Cardiff	5	Plymouth	4	
Carlisle	1	Grimsby	0	
Chestrfld	0	Wrexham	2	
Colchester	0	Peterboro	0	
Derby	0	Chester	1	
Doncaster	1	Rotherhm	1	
Exeter	0	Newport	0	
Gillinghm	1	N'hamptn	0	
Hartlepl	1	Middlesbro	1	
Hereford	3	Swansea	3	
Huddersfld	3	Halifax	1	
Leyton O	2	Cambridge	2	
Notts Co	1	Port Vale	3	
Rochdale	1	Burnley	1	
Scunthpe	2	Darlingtn	0	
Shrewsby	0	Crewe	0	
Southend	1	Brentford	0	
Stockport	2	Tranmere	1	
Sunderld	2	York	4	
Swindon	3	Torquay	0	
Walsall	1	Mansfield	0	
Wigan Ath	1	Blackburn	3	
Wolves	1	Lincoln	2	

FIRST ROUND SECOND-LEG

Blackburn	2	Wigan Ath	0	
Blackburn win 5-1 on agg				
Bolton	0	Bury	0	
Bury win 2-1 on agg				
Brentford	2	Southend	3	
Southend win 4-2 on agg				
Bristol C	1	Bournemth	1	e
Bristol C win 2-1 on agg				
Burnley	1	Rochdale	3	
Burnley win 4-2 on agg				
Cambridge	1	Leyton O	0	
Cambridge win 3-2 on agg				
Chester	1	Derby	2	a
agg score Chester 2 - Derby 2				
Crewe	0	Shrewsby	4	
Shrewsby win 4-0 on agg				
Darlingtn	1	Scunthpe	2	
Scunthpe win 4-1 on agg				
Fulham	2	Aldershot	0	
Fulham win 5-1 on agg				
Grimsby	2	Carlisle	0	
Grimsby win 2-1 on agg				
Halifax	2	Huddersfld	2	e
Huddersfld win 5-3 on agg				
Lincoln	0	Wolves	1	
agg score Lincoln 2 - Wolves 2				
Mansfield	2	Walsall	4	
Walsall win 5-2 on agg				
Middlesbro	2	Hartlepl	0	
Middlesbro win 3-1 on agg				
Newport	1	Exeter	0	
Newport win 1-0 on agg				
N'hamptn	2	Gillinghm	2	
Gillinghm win 3-2 on agg				
Peterboro	2	Colchester	0	
Peterboro win 2-0 on agg				
Plymouth	0	Cardiff	1	
Cardiff win 6-4 on agg				
Port Vale	4	Notts Co	1	
Port Vale win 7-2 on agg				
Preston NE	2	Blackpool	1	
Preston NE win 2-1 on agg				
Reading	4	Bristol R	0	
Reading win 6-1 on agg				
Rotherhm	4	Doncaster	1	
Rotherhm win 5-2 on agg				
Swansea	5	Hereford	1	
Swansea win 8-4 on agg				
Torquay	2	Swindon	3	
Swindon win 6-2 on agg				
Tranmere	3	Stockport	3	
Stockport win 5-4 on agg				
Wrexham	2	Chestrfld	2	
Wrexham win 4-2 on agg				
York	1	Sunderld	3	
agg score York 5 - Sunderld 5				

SECOND ROUND FIRST-LEG

Arsenal	2	Huddersfld	0	
Barnsley	2	Tottenham	3	
Bradford	2	Newcastle	0	
Brighton	0	Nottm For	0	
Bristol C	2	Sheff Utd	2	
Cambridge	1	Wimbledn	1	
Charlton	3	Lincoln	1	
Coventry	3	Rotherhm	2	
C.Palace	0	Bury	0	
Derby	4	West Brom	1	
Everton	4	Newport	0	
Hull	1	Grimsby	0	
Liverpool	10	Fulham	0	
Man Utd	2	Port Vale	0	
Middlesbro	2	Birmghm C	2	

Oldham 3 Leeds U 2
Oxford 6 Gillinghm 0
Peterboro 0 Norwich 0
Preston NE 1 West Ham 1
QPR 2 Blackburn 1
Reading 1 Aston V 1
Scunthpe 1 Ipswich 2
Sheff Wed 3 Stockport 0
Shrewsby 2 Stoke 1
Southmptn 3 Swindon 0
Southend 0 Man City 0
Swansea 0 Leicester 2
Walsall 0 Millwall 1
Watford 1 Rochdale 1
Wrexham 1 Portsmth 2
York 1 Chelsea 0

SECOND ROUND SECOND-LEG

Aston V 4 Reading 1
Aston V win 5-2 on agg
Birmghm C 3 Middlesbro 2 e
Birmghm C win 5-4 on agg
Blackburn 2 QPR 2
QPR win 4-3 on agg
Bury 0 C.Palace 1
C.Palace win 1-0 on agg
Chelsea 3 York 0
Chelsea win 3-1 on agg
Fulham 2 Liverpool 3
Liverpool win 13-2 on agg
Gillinghm 1 Oxford 1
Oxford win 7-1 on agg
Grimsby 1 Hull 1
Hull win 2-1 on agg
Huddersfld 1 Arsenal 1
Arsenal win 3-1 on agg
Ipswich 2 Scunthpe 0
Ipswich win 4-1 on agg
Leeds U 0 Oldham 1
Oldham win 4-2 on agg
Leicester 4 Swansea 2
Leicester win 6-2 on agg
Lincoln 0 Charlton 1
Charlton win 4-1 on agg
Man City 2 Southend 1
Man City win 2-1 on agg
Millwall 3 Walsall 2
Millwall win 4-2 on agg
Newcastle 1 Bradford 0
Bradford win 2-1 on agg
Newport 1 Everton 5
Everton win 9-1 on agg
Norwich 1 Peterboro 0
Norwich win 1-0 on agg
Nottm For 3 Brighton 0
Nottm For win 3-0 on agg
Port Vale 2 Man Utd 5
Man Utd win 7-2 on agg
Portsmth 2 Wrexham 0
Portsmth win 4-1 on agg
Rochdale 1 Watford 2
Watford win 3-2 on agg
Rotherhm 0 Coventry 1
Coventry win 4-2 on agg
Sheff Utd 3 Bristol C 0
Sheff Utd win 5-2 on agg
Stockport 0 Sheff Wed 7
Sheff Wed win 10-0 on agg

Strange but true!
Luton Town went almost three seasons without losing a League Cup-tie in the late 80s. They withdrew from the competition in 1986-87, won it in 87-88 and got to the Final in 88-89, losing 3-1 to Nottingham Forest.

Stoke 0 Shrewsby 0
Shrewsby win 2-1 on agg
Swindon 0 Southmptn 0
Southmptn win 3-0 on agg
Tottenham 5 Barnsley 3
Tottenham win 8-5 on agg
West Brom 0 Derby 1
Derby win 5-1 on agg
West Ham 4 Preston NE 1
West Ham win 5-2 on agg
Wimbledn 2 Cambridge 2 a
agg score W'bledn 3 - Cambdge 3

THIRD ROUND

Arsenal 3 Man City 1
Bradford 3 Portsmth 1
Cambridge 1 Ipswich 0
Cardiff 2 Chelsea 1
Charlton 1 QPR 0
Coventry 2 Oldham 1
C.Palace 2 Nottm For 2
Derby 1 Aston V 1
Everton 4 Sheff Wed 0
Liverpool 4 Leicester 1
Man Utd 0 Southmptn 0
Norwich 4 Millwall 1
Oxford 3 Sheff Utd 1
Shrewsby 1 Hull 0
Tottenham 5 Birmghm C 0
Watford 2 West Ham 3
Aston V 2 Derby 1 r
Nottm For 1 C.Palace 0 r
Southmptn 4 Man Utd 1 r

FOURTH ROUND

Arsenal 2 Charlton 0
Bradford 0 Nottm For 5
Cambridge 1 Tottenham 3
Coventry 0 Liverpool 0
Norwich 1 Everton 4
Shrewsby 1 Cardiff 0
Southmptn 2 Aston V 1
West Ham 1 Oxford 0
Liverpool 3 Coventry 1 r

FIFTH ROUND

Arsenal 2 Nottm For 0
Everton 0 Liverpool 1
Southmptn 1 Shrewsby 0
West Ham 1 Tottenham 1
Tottenham 5 West Ham 0 r

SEMI-FINAL FIRST-LEG

Arsenal 0 Tottenham 1
Southmptn 0 Liverpool 0

SEMI-FINAL SECOND-LEG

Liverpool 3 Southmptn 0
Liverpool win 3-0 on agg
Tottenham 1 Arsenal 2 e
agg score Tottenham 2 - Arsenal 2

SEMI-FINAL REPLAY

Tottenham 1 Arsenal 2 r

FINAL

Arsenal 2 Liverpool 1 N

1988

FIRST ROUND FIRST-LEG

Blackpool 2 Chester 0
Bournemth 1 Exeter 1
Brentford 2 Southend 1
Bristol R 1 Hereford 0
Bury 2 Preston NE 2
Cambridge 1 Aldershot 1
Cardiff 1 Newport 2
Chestrfld 2 Peterboro 1
Crewe 3 Shrewsby 3
Fulham 3 Colchester 1
Gillinghm 1 Brighton 0
Grimsby 3 Darlingtn 2
Halifax 1 York 1
Leyton O 1 Millwall 1
Mansfield 2 Birmghm C 2
Port Vale 0 N'hamptn 1
Rochdale 3 Tranmere 1
Rotherhm 4 Huddersfld 4
Scarboro 1 Doncaster 0
Scunthpe 3 Hartlepl 1
Stockport 0 Carlisle 1
Sunderld 1 Middlesbro 0
Swindon 3 Bristol C 0
Torquay 2 Swansea 1
West Brom 2 Walsall 3
Wigan Ath 2 Bolton 3
Wolves 3 Notts Co 0
Wrexham 1 Burnley 0

FIRST ROUND SECOND-LEG

Aldershot 1 Cambridge 4
Cambridge win 5-2 on agg
Birmghm C 0 Mansfield 1
Mansfield win 3-2 on agg
Bolton 1 Wigan Ath 3
Wigan Ath win 5-4 on agg

Strange but true!
Gordon Chisholm played in two League Cup Finals in different countries in the same year, 1985, and lost both. He was with Sunderland against Norwich in March, and with Hibs against Aberdeen in October.

Home		Away		
Brighton	1	Gillinghm	0	q
agg score Brighton 1 - Gillinghm 1				
Bristol C	3	Swindon	2	
Swindon win 5-3 on agg				
Burnley	3	Wrexham	0	
Burnley win 3-1 on agg				
Cardiff	2	Newport	2	
Newport win 4-3 on agg				
Carlisle	3	Stockport	0	
Carlisle win 4-0 on agg				
Chester	1	Blackpool	0	
Blackpool win 2-1 on agg				
Colchester	0	Fulham	2	
Fulham win 5-1 on agg				
Darlingtn	2	Grimsby	1	
agg score Darlingtn 4 - Grimsby 4				
Doncaster	3	Scarboro	1	
Doncaster win 3-2 on agg				
Exeter	1	Bournemth	3	e
Bournemth win 4-2 on agg				
Hartlepl	0	Scunthpe	1	
Scunthpe win 4-1 on agg				
Hereford	2	Bristol R	0	
Hereford win 2-1 on agg				
Huddersfld	1	Rotherhm	3	
Rotherhm win 7-5 on agg				
Middlesbro	2	Sunderld	0	
Middlesbro win 2-1 on agg				
Millwall	1	Leyton O	0	
Millwall win 2-1 on agg				
N'hamptn	4	Port Vale	0	
N'hamptn win 5-0 on agg				
Notts Co	1	Wolves	2	
Wolves win 5-1 on agg				
Peterboro	2	Chestrfld	0	
Peterboro win 3-2 on agg				
Preston NE	2	Bury	3	e
Bury win 5-4 on agg				
Shrewsby	4	Crewe	1	
Shrewsby win 7-4 on agg				
Southend	4	Brentford	2	
Southend win 5-4 on agg				
Swansea	1	Torquay	1	
Torquay win 3-2 on agg				
Tranmere	1	Rochdale	0	
Rochdale win 3-2 on agg				
Walsall	0	West Brom	0	
Walsall win 3-2 on agg				
York	1	Halifax	0	e
York win 2-1 on agg				
SECOND ROUND FIRST-LEG				
Barnsley	0	West Ham	0	
Blackburn	1	Liverpool	1	
Blackpool	1	Newcastle	0	
Bournemth	1	Southmptn	0	
Burnley	1	Norwich	1	
Bury	2	Sheff Utd	1	
Cambridge	0	Coventry	1	
Carlisle	4	Oldham	3	
Charlton	3	Walsall	0	
C.Palace	4	Newport	0	
Darlingtn	0	Watford	3	
Doncaster	0	Arsenal	3	
Everton	3	Rotherhm	2	
Fulham	1	Bradford	5	
Ipswich	1	N'hamptn	1	
Leeds U	1	York	1	
Leicester	2	Scunthpe	1	
Man City	1	Wolves	2	
Man Utd	5	Hull	0	
Middlesbro	0	Aston V	1	
Nottm For	5	Hereford	0	
Oxford	1	Mansfield	1	
Peterboro	4	Plymouth	1	
QPR	2	Millwall	1	
Reading	3	Chelsea	1	
Rochdale	1	Wimbledn	1	
Shrewsby	1	Sheff Wed	1	
Southend	1	Derby	0	
Stoke	2	Gillinghm	0	
Swindon	3	Portsmth	1	
Torquay	1	Tottenham	0	
Wigan Ath	0	Luton	1	
SECOND ROUND SECOND-LEG				
Arsenal	1	Doncaster	0	
Arsenal win 4-0 on agg				
Aston V	1	Middlesbro	0	
Aston V win 2-0 on agg				
Bradford	2	Fulham	1	
Bradford win 7-2 on agg				
Chelsea	3	Reading	2	
Reading win 5-4 on agg				
Coventry	2	Cambridge	1	
Coventry win 3-1 on agg				
Derby	0	Southend	0	
Southend win 1-0 on agg				
Gillinghm	0	Stoke	1	
Stoke win 3-0 on agg				
Hereford	1	Nottm For	1	
Nottm For win 6-1 on agg				
Hull	0	Man Utd	1	
Man Utd win 6-0 on agg				
Liverpool	1	Blackburn	0	
Liverpool win 2-1 on agg				
Luton	4	Wigan Ath	2	
Luton win 5-2 on agg				
Mansfield	0	Oxford	2	
Oxford win 3-1 on agg				
Millwall	0	QPR	0	
QPR win 2-1 on agg				
Newcastle	4	Blackpool	1	
Newcastle win 4-2 on agg				
Newport	0	C.Palace	2	
C.Palace win 6-0 on agg				
N'hamptn	2	Ipswich	4	e
Ipswich win 5-3 on agg				
Norwich	1	Burnley	0	
Norwich win 2-1 on agg				
Oldham	4	Carlisle	1	e
Oldham win 7-5 on agg				
Plymouth	1	Peterboro	1	
Peterboro win 5-2 on agg				
Portsmth	1	Swindon	3	
Swindon win 6-2 on agg				
Rotherhm	0	Everton	0	
Everton win 3-2 on agg				
Scunthpe	1	Leicester	2	
Leicester win 4-2 on agg				
Sheff Utd	1	Bury	1	
Bury win 3-2 on agg				
Sheff Wed	2	Shrewsby	1	
Sheff Wed win 3-2 on agg				
Southmptn	2	Bournemth	2	
Bournemth win 3-2 on agg				

Strange but true!

A Bolton v Swindon saga in 1989 will remain the longest in League Cup history now that penalty deciders are used. Swindon won 2-1 after draws of 3-3, 1-1 and 1-1 again, and a total of 450 minutes.

Home		Away		
Tottenham	3	Torquay	0	
Tottenham win 3-1 on agg				
Walsall	2	Charlton	0	
Charlton win 3-2 on agg				
Watford	8	Darlingtn	0	
Watford win 11-0 on agg				
West Ham	2	Barnsley	5	e
Barnsley win 5-2 on agg				
Wimbledn	2	Rochdale	1	
Wimbledn win 3-2 on agg				
Wolves	0	Man City	2	
Man City win 3-2 on agg				
York	0	Leeds U	4	
Leeds U win 5-1 on agg				
THIRD ROUND				
Arsenal	3	Bournemth	0	
Aston V	2	Tottenham	1	
Barnsley	1	Sheff Wed	2	
Bury	1	QPR	0	
Charlton	0	Bradford	1	
Ipswich	1	Southend	0	
Leeds U	2	Oldham	2	
Liverpool	0	Everton	1	
Luton	3	Coventry	1	
Man City	3	Nottm For	0	
Man Utd	2	C.Palace	1	
Oxford	0	Leicester	0	
Peterboro	0	Reading	0	
Stoke	2	Norwich	1	
Swindon	1	Watford	1	
Wimbledn	2	Newcastle	1	
Leicester	2	Oxford	3	r
Oldham	4	Leeds U	2	re
Reading	1	Peterboro	0	r
Watford	4	Swindon	2	r
FOURTH ROUND				
Arsenal	3	Stoke	0	
Aston V	1	Sheff Wed	2	
Bury	1	Man Utd	2	
Everton	2	Oldham	1	
Ipswich	0	Luton	1	
Man City	3	Watford	1	
Oxford	2	Wimbledn	1	
Reading	0	Bradford	0	
Bradford	1	Reading	0	r
FIFTH ROUND				
Everton	2	Man City	0	
Luton	2	Bradford	0	
Oxford	2	Man Utd	0	

Sheff Wed	**0**	**Arsenal**	**1**	
SEMI-FINAL FIRST-LEG				
Everton	**0**	**Arsenal**	**1**	
Oxford	**1**	**Luton**	**1**	
SEMI-FINAL SECOND-LEG				
Arsenal	**3**	**Everton**	**1**	
Arsenal win 4-1 on agg				
Luton	**2**	**Oxford**	**0**	
Luton win 3-1 on agg				
FINAL				
Luton	**3**	**Arsenal**	**2**	**N**

1989

FIRST ROUND FIRST-LEG				
Bolton	**1**	**Chester**	**0**	
Bournemth	**1**	**Bristol R**	**0**	
Bristol C	**1**	**Exeter**	**0**	
Bury	**2**	**Wrexham**	**1**	
Cambridge	**1**	**Gillinghm**	**2**	
Cardiff	**0**	**Swansea**	**1**	
Carlisle	**1**	**Blackpool**	**1**	
Colchester	**0**	**N'hamptn**	**0**	
Crewe	**1**	**Lincoln**	**1**	
Doncaster	**1**	**Darlingtn**	**1**	
Fulham	**2**	**Brentford**	**2**	
Grimsby	**0**	**Rotherhm**	**1**	
Hartlepl	**2**	**Sheff Utd**	**2**	
Hereford	**0**	**Plymouth**	**3**	
Leyton O	**2**	**Aldershot**	**0**	
Notts Co	**5**	**Mansfield**	**0**	
Port Vale	**3**	**Chestrfld**	**2**	
Rochdale	**3**	**Burnley**	**3**	
Scarboro	**1**	**Halifax**	**1**	
Scunthpe	**3**	**Huddersfld**	**2**	
Shrewsby	**2**	**Walsall**	**2**	
Southend	**2**	**Brighton**	**0**	
Stockport	**0**	**Tranmere**	**1**	
Torquay	**0**	**Reading**	**1**	
West Brom	**0**	**Peterboro**	**3**	
Wigan Ath	**0**	**Preston NE**	**0**	
Wolves	**3**	**Birmghm C**	**2**	
York	**0**	**Sunderld**	**0**	
FIRST ROUND SECOND-LEG				
Aldershot	**0**	**Leyton O**	**0**	
Leyton O win 2-0 on agg				
Birmghm C	**1**	**Wolves**	**0**	
agg score Birmghm C 3 - Wolves 3				
Blackpool	**3**	**Carlisle**	**0**	
Blackpool win 4-1 on agg				
Brentford	**1**	**Fulham**	**0**	**e**
Brentford win 3-2 on agg				
Brighton	**0**	**Southend**	**1**	

Strange but true!

When Nottingham Forest won the League Cup in both 1989 and 1990, it was the second time they had retained the trophy, having done the same in 1978 and 1979. The only other side ever to retain the Cup are Liverpool.

Southend win 3-0 on agg				
Bristol R	**0**	**Bournemth**	**0**	
Bournemth win 1-0 on agg				
Burnley	**2**	**Rochdale**	**1**	
Burnley win 5-4 on agg				
Chester	**3**	**Bolton**	**1**	
Chester win 3-2 on agg				
Chestrfld	**1**	**Port Vale**	**1**	
Port Vale win 4-3 on agg				
Darlingtn	**2**	**Doncaster**	**0**	
Darlingtn win 3-1 on agg				
Exeter	**0**	**Bristol C**	**1**	
Bristol C win 2-0 on agg				
Gillinghm	**3**	**Cambridge**	**1**	
Gillinghm win 5-2 on agg				
Halifax	**2**	**Scarboro**	**2**	**a**
agg score Halifax 3 - Scarboro 3				
Huddersfld	**2**	**Scunthpe**	**2**	**e**
Scunthpe win 5-4 on agg				
Lincoln	**2**	**Crewe**	**1**	
Lincoln win 3-2 on agg				
Mansfield	**1**	**Notts Co**	**0**	
Notts Co win 5-1 on agg				
N'hamptn	**5**	**Colchester**	**0**	
N'hamptn win 5-0 on agg				
Peterboro	**0**	**West Brom**	**2**	
Peterboro win 3-2 on agg				
Plymouth	**3**	**Hereford**	**2**	
Plymouth win 6-2 on agg				
Preston NE	**1**	**Wigan Ath**	**0**	
Preston NE win 1-0 on agg				
Reading	**3**	**Torquay**	**1**	
Reading win 4-1 on agg				
Rotherhm	**1**	**Grimsby**	**0**	

Rotherhm win 2-0 on agg				
Sheff Utd	**2**	**Hartlepl**	**0**	**e**
Sheff Utd win 4-2 on agg				
Sunderld	**4**	**York**	**0**	
Sunderld win 4-0 on agg				
Swansea	**0**	**Cardiff**	**2**	
Cardiff win 2-1 on agg				
Tranmere	**1**	**Stockport**	**1**	
Tranmere win 2-1 on agg				
Walsall	**3**	**Shrewsby**	**0**	
Walsall win 5-2 on agg				
Wrexham	**2**	**Bury**	**2**	**e**
Bury win 4-3 on agg				
SECOND ROUND FIRST-LEG				
Barnsley	**0**	**Wimbledn**	**2**	
Birmghm C	**0**	**Aston V**	**2**	
Blackburn	**3**	**Brentford**	**1**	
Blackpool	**2**	**Sheff Wed**	**0**	
Bournemth	**0**	**Coventry**	**4**	
Darlingtn	**2**	**Oldham**	**0**	
Derby	**1**	**Southend**	**0**	
Everton	**3**	**Bury**	**0**	
Hull	**1**	**Arsenal**	**2**	
Leicester	**4**	**Watford**	**1**	
Leyton O	**1**	**Stoke**	**2**	
Lincoln	**1**	**Southmptn**	**1**	
Liverpool	**1**	**Walsall**	**0**	
Luton	**1**	**Burnley**	**1**	
Man City	**1**	**Plymouth**	**0**	
Middlesbro	**0**	**Tranmere**	**0**	
Millwall	**3**	**Gillinghm**	**0**	
N'hamptn	**1**	**Charlton**	**1**	
Norwich	**2**	**Preston NE**	**0**	
Nottm For	**6**	**Chester**	**0**	
Notts Co	**1**	**Tottenham**	**1**	
Oxford	**2**	**Bristol C**	**4**	
Peterboro	**1**	**Leeds U**	**2**	
Port Vale	**1**	**Ipswich**	**0**	
Portsmth	**2**	**Scarboro**	**2**	
QPR	**3**	**Cardiff**	**0**	
Reading	**1**	**Bradford**	**1**	
Rotherhm	**0**	**Man Utd**	**1**	
Scunthpe	**4**	**Chelsea**	**1**	
Sheff Utd	**3**	**Newcastle**	**0**	
Sunderld	**0**	**West Ham**	**3**	
Swindon	**1**	**C.Palace**	**2**	
SECOND ROUND SECOND-LEG				
Arsenal	**3**	**Hull**	**0**	
Arsenal win 5-1 on agg				
Aston V	**5**	**Birmghm C**	**0**	
Aston V win 7-0 on agg				
Bradford	**2**	**Reading**	**1**	**e**

WHAT A STAR ✪ FRANKIE BUNN

Frankie Bunn missed a lot of Oldham's 64-game 1989-90 season because of injuries, and scored only 13 goals - but six of them came in one game, to set a League Cup record likely to stand for ages. Bunn hit his six against a goalkeeper named Ironside, of Scarborough, in a 7-0 victory early in a march to Wembley that included defeats of Arsenal, Southampton and West Ham before an unlucky Final defeat by Forest.

Forest wrestled the Cup from Luton in 1989

Bradford win 3-2 on agg				
Brentford	**4**	**Blackburn**	**3**	
Blackburn win 6-5 on agg				
Bristol C	**2**	**Oxford**	**0**	
Bristol C win 6-2 on agg				
Burnley	**0**	**Luton**	**1**	
Luton win 2-1 on agg				
Bury	**2**	**Everton**	**2**	
Everton win 5-2 on agg				
Cardiff	**1**	**QPR**	**4**	
QPR win 7-1 on agg				
Charlton	**2**	**N'hamptn**	**1**	
Charlton win 3-2 on agg				
Chelsea	**2**	**Scunthpe**	**2**	
Scunthpe win 6-3 on agg				
Chester	**0**	**Nottm For**	**4**	
Nottm For win 10-0 on agg				
Coventry	**3**	**Bournemth**	**1**	
Coventry win 7-1 on agg				
C.Palace	**2**	**Swindon**	**0**	
C.Palace win 4-1 on agg				
Gillinghm	**1**	**Millwall**	**3**	
Millwall win 6-1 on agg				
Ipswich	**3**	**Port Vale**	**0**	
Ipswich win 3-1 on agg				
Leeds U	**3**	**Peterboro**	**1**	
Leeds U win 5-2 on agg				
Man Utd	**5**	**Rotherhm**	**0**	
Man Utd win 6-0 on agg				
Newcastle	**2**	**Sheff Utd**	**0**	
Sheff Utd win 3-2 on agg				
Oldham	**4**	**Darlingtn**	**0**	**e**
Oldham win 4-2 on agg				
Plymouth	**3**	**Man City**	**6**	
Man City win 7-3 on agg				
Preston NE	**0**	**Norwich**	**3**	
Norwich win 5-0 on agg				
Scarboro	**3**	**Portsmth**	**1**	
Scarboro win 5-3 on agg				
Sheff Wed	**3**	**Blackpool**	**1**	**a**
agg score Sheff W 3 - Blackpool 3				
Southmptn	**3**	**Lincoln**	**1**	
Southmptn win 4-2 on agg				
Southend	**1**	**Derby**	**2**	
Derby win 3-1 on agg				
Stoke	**1**	**Leyton O**	**2**	**q**
agg score Stoke 3 - Leyton O 3				
Tottenham	**2**	**Notts Co**	**1**	
Tottenham win 3-2 on agg				
Tranmere	**1**	**Middlesbro**	**0**	
Tranmere win 1-0 on agg				
Walsall	**1**	**Liverpool**	**3**	
Liverpool win 4-1 on agg				
Watford	**2**	**Leicester**	**2**	
Leicester win 6-3 on agg				
West Ham	**2**	**Sunderld**	**1**	
West Ham win 5-1 on agg				
Wimbledn	**0**	**Barnsley**	**1**	
Wimbledn win 2-1 on agg				
THIRD ROUND				
Aston V	**3**	**Millwall**	**1**	
Bradford	**1**	**Scunthpe**	**1**	
Bristol C	**4**	**C.Palace**	**1**	
Everton	**1**	**Oldham**	**1**	
Ipswich	**2**	**Leyton O**	**0**	
Leeds U	**0**	**Luton**	**2**	
Leicester	**2**	**Norwich**	**0**	
Liverpool	**1**	**Arsenal**	**1**	
Man City	**4**	**Sheff Utd**	**2**	
Nottm For	**3**	**Coventry**	**2**	
QPR	**2**	**Charlton**	**1**	
Scarboro	**2**	**Southmptn**	**2**	
Tottenham	**0**	**Blackburn**	**0**	
Tranmere	**1**	**Blackpool**	**0**	
West Ham	**5**	**Derby**	**0**	
Wimbledn	**2**	**Man Utd**	**1**	
Arsenal	**0**	**Liverpool**	**0**	**re**
Blackburn	**1**	**Tottenham**	**2**	**re**
Oldham	**0**	**Everton**	**2**	**r**
Scunthpe	**0**	**Bradford**	**1**	**r**
Southmptn	**1**	**Scarboro**	**0**	**r**
Liverpool	**2**	**Arsenal**	**1**	**r2N**
FOURTH ROUND				
Aston V	**6**	**Ipswich**	**2**	
Bradford	**3**	**Everton**	**1**	
Bristol C	**1**	**Tranmere**	**0**	
Leicester	**0**	**Nottm For**	**0**	
Luton	**3**	**Man City**	**1**	
QPR	**0**	**Wimbledn**	**0**	
Southmptn	**2**	**Tottenham**	**1**	
West Ham	**4**	**Liverpool**	**1**	
Nottm For	**2**	**Leicester**	**1**	**r**
Wimbledn	**0**	**QPR**	**1**	**r**
FIFTH ROUND				
Bradford	**0**	**Bristol C**	**1**	
Luton	**1**	**Southmptn**	**1**	
Nottm For	**5**	**QPR**	**2**	
West Ham	**2**	**Aston V**	**1**	
Southmptn	**1**	**Luton**	**2**	**re**
SEMI-FINAL FIRST-LEG				
Nottm For	**1**	**Bristol C**	**1**	
West Ham	**0**	**Luton**	**3**	
SEMI-FINAL SECOND-LEG				
Bristol C	**0**	**Nottm For**	**1**	**e**
Nottm For win 2-1 on agg				
Luton	**2**	**West Ham**	**0**	
Luton win 5-0 on agg				
FINAL				
Nottm For	**3**	**Luton**	**1**	**N**

CHAPTER 12 History of the League Cup

1990-1997

VILLA VICTORS

By now the League Cup had a new name. We had had the Milk Cup and the Littlewoods Cup and in 1991 the competition became known as the Rumbelows Cup.

Sheffield Wednesday were the first winners of the new trophy in 1991, beating Manchester United 1-0 thanks to a goal from midfielder John Sheridan.

But United were back a year later, and this time they emerged triumphant with Brian McClair scoring the only goal of the game to defeat Nottingham Forest.

Incredibly, that was the first time United had won the League Cup in any of its various guises, and they haven't won it since then either.

Aston Aces

When Villa won the Cup in 1996, they set two records along the way. Their Semi-Final appearance was their tenth - a new record - and by reaching the Final they equalled Liverpool's record of seven appearances in the showpiece match.

No team has dominated the competition in the 90s in the way that Liverpool, and to a lesser extent, Forest did during the 80s.

The closest anyone has come has been Aston Villa, who have won the trophy - now called the Coca-Cola Cup - twice in this decade.

They won it in 1994 against Manchester United and again in 1996, when they beat Leeds 3-0 in one of Wembley's most one-sided Finals of all-time.

But in 1997 it was back to fairytale stuff as Leicester claimed the trophy for the first time since 1964.

They were expected to show up and roll over for Middlesbrough's expensive imports from Brazil and Italy - Juninho, Emerson and Ravanelli - but Martin O'Neill's side had other ideas and, after snatching a last-gasp equaliser in the first match, they then won the replay thanks to a goal from one of football's journeymen.

Strange but true!

The 24 players who appeared in the 1996 League Cup Final between Aston Villa and Leeds came from ten countries.

Steve Claridge, socks rolled down to his ankles, has taken the scenic route to the top but he was The Foxes hero as his goal shattered Boro's dreams.

The competition still has its critics in today's overcrowded schedule - indeed England's European representatives now receive a bye to the Third Round - but in whatever format, the League Cup looks to be here to stay.

1990

FIRST ROUND FIRST-LEG

Home		Away		
Birmghm C	2	Chestrfld	1	
Blackpool	2	Burnley	2	
Brighton	0	Brentford	3	
Bristol C	2	Reading	3	
Bristol R	1	Portsmth	0	
Cambridge	3	Maidstone	1	
Cardiff	0	Plymouth	3	
Colchester	3	Southend	4	
Crewe	4	Chester	0	
Exeter	3	Swansea	0	
Fulham	0	Oxford	1	
Gillinghm	1	Leyton O	4	
Halifax	3	Carlisle	1	
Hartlepl	3	York	3	
Huddersfld	1	Doncaster	1	
Hull	1	Grimsby	0	
Mansfield	1	N'hamptn	1	
Peterboro	2	Aldershot	0	
Preston NE	3	Tranmere	4	
Rochdale	2	Bolton	1	
Scarboro	2	Scunthpe	0	
Sheff Utd	1	Rotherhm	1	
Shrewsby	3	Notts Co	0	
Stockport	1	Bury	0	
Torquay	0	Hereford	1	
Walsall	1	Port Vale	2	
Wolves	1	Lincoln	0	
Wrexham	0	Wigan Ath	0	

FIRST ROUND SECOND-LEG

Home		Away		
Aldershot	6	Peterboro	2	e
Aldershot win 6-4 on agg				
Bolton	5	Rochdale	1	
Bolton win 6-3 on agg				
Brentford	1	Brighton	1	
Brentford win 4-1 on agg				
Burnley	0	Blackpool	1	
Blackpool win 3-2 on agg				
Bury	1	Stockport	1	
Stockport win 2-1 on agg				
Carlisle	1	Halifax	0	
Halifax win 3-2 on agg				
Chester	0	Crewe	2	
Crewe win 6-0 on agg				
Chestrfld	1	Birmghm C	1	
Birmghm C win 3-2 on agg				
Doncaster	1	Huddersfld	2	
Huddersfld win 3-2 on agg				
Grimsby	2	Hull	0	e
Grimsby win 2-1 on agg				
Hereford	3	Torquay	0	
Hereford win 4-0 on agg				
Leyton O	3	Gillinghm	0	
Leyton O win 7-1 on agg				
Lincoln	0	Wolves	2	
Wolves win 3-0 on agg				
Maidstone	0	Cambridge	1	
Cambridge win 4-1 on agg				
N'hamptn	0	Mansfield	2	
Mansfield win 3-1 on agg				
Notts Co	3	Shrewsby	1	
Shrewsby win 4-3 on agg				
Oxford	3	Fulham	5	
Fulham win 5-4 on agg				
Plymouth	0	Cardiff	2	
Plymouth win 3-2 on agg				
Port Vale	1	Walsall	0	
Port Vale win 3-1 on agg				
Portsmth	2	Bristol R	0	
Portsmth win 2-1 on agg				
Reading	2	Bristol C	2	
Reading win 5-4 on agg				
Rotherhm	1	Sheff Utd	0	
Rotherhm win 2-1 on agg				
Scunthpe	1	Scarboro	1	
Scarboro win 3-1 on agg				
Southend	2	Colchester	1	
Southend win 6-4 on agg				
Swansea	1	Exeter	1	
Exeter win 4-1 on agg				
Tranmere	3	Preston NE	1	
Tranmere win 7-4 on agg				
Wigan Ath	5	Wrexham	0	
Wigan Ath win 5-0 on agg				
York	4	Hartlepl	1	
York win 7-4 on agg				

SECOND ROUND FIRST-LEG

Home		Away		
Arsenal	2	Plymouth	0	
Aston V	2	Wolves	1	
Barnsley	1	Blackpool	1	
Birmghm C	1	West Ham	2	
Bolton	2	Watford	1	
Brentford	2	Man City	1	
Cambridge	2	Derby	1	
Charlton	3	Hereford	1	
Chelsea	1	Scarboro	1	
Crewe	0	Bournemth	1	
C.Palace	1	Leicester	2	
Exeter	3	Blackburn	0	
Grimsby	3	Coventry	1	
Ipswich	0	Tranmere	1	
Leyton O	0	Everton	2	
Liverpool	5	Wigan Ath	2	
Mansfield	3	Luton	4	
Middlesbro	4	Halifax	0	
Norwich	1	Rotherhm	1	
Nottm For	1	Huddersfld	1	
Oldham	2	Leeds U	1	
Port Vale	1	Wimbledn	2	
Portsmth	2	Man Utd	3	
QPR	2	Stockport	1	
Reading	3	Newcastle	1	
Sheff Wed	0	Aldershot	0	
Shrewsby	0	Swindon	3	
Stoke	1	Millwall	0	
Sunderld	1	Fulham	1	
Tottenham	1	Southend	0	
West Brom	1	Bradford	3	
York	0	Southmptn	1	

SECOND ROUND SECOND-LEG

Home		Away		
Aldershot	0	Sheff Wed	8	
Sheff Wed win 8-0 on agg				
Blackburn	2	Exeter	1	
Exeter win 4-2 on agg				
Blackpool	1	Barnsley	1	P
agg score Blackpool 2 - Barnsley 2				
Bournemth	0	Crewe	0	
Bournemth win 1-0 on agg				
Bradford	3	West Brom	5	a
agg score Bradford 6 - W Brom 6				
Coventry	3	Grimsby	0	
Coventry win 4-3 on agg				
Derby	5	Cambridge	0	
Derby win 6-2 on agg				
Everton	2	Leyton O	2	
Everton win 4-2 on agg				
Fulham	0	Sunderld	3	
Sunderld win 4-1 on agg				
Halifax	0	Middlesbro	1	
Middlesbro win 5-0 on agg				

GIANTKILLERS

1991-92 Peterborough 1 Liverpool 0

Peterborough have done quite a lot of giantkilling in their comparatively brief League existence, but 1991-92 was perhaps their best season in that line, for although still in Division Three they beat three clubs from higher groups - Wimbledon 4-3 over two legs, Newcastle 1-0 and Liverpool 1-0, before losing by that same margin to Middlesbrough in a Quarter-Final replay. Promotion via a last-minute goal in a Wembley play-off was deserved reward for Posh, but their victory over Liverpool was the first major setback for Graeme Souness as manager at Anfield.

Home		Away		
Hereford	0	Charlton	1	
Charlton win 4-1 on agg				
Huddersfld	3	Nottm For	3	a
agg score Huddersfld 4 - N For 4				
Leeds U	1	Oldham	2	
Oldham win 4-2 on agg				
Leicester	2	C.Palace	3	a
agg score Leicester 4 - C.Palace 4				
Luton	7	Mansfield	2	
Luton win 11-5 on agg				
Man City	4	Brentford	1	
Man City win 5-3 on agg				
Man Utd	0	Portsmth	0	
Man Utd win 3-2 on agg				
Millwall	2	Stoke	0	e
Millwall win 2-1 on agg				
Newcastle	4	Reading	0	
Newcastle win 5-3 on agg				
Plymouth	1	Arsenal	6	
Arsenal win 8-1 on agg				
Rotherhm	0	Norwich	2	
Norwich win 3-1 on agg				
Scarboro	3	Chelsea	2	
Scarboro win 4-3 on agg				
Southmptn	2	York	0	
Southmptn win 3-0 on agg				
Southend	3	Tottenham	2	a
agg score S'thend 3 - Tottenham 3				
Stockport	0	QPR	0	
QPR win 2-1 on agg				
Swindon	3	Shrewsby	1	
Swindon win 6-1 on agg				
Tranmere	1	Ipswich	0	
Tranmere win 2-0 on agg				
Watford	1	Bolton	1	
Bolton win 3-2 on agg				
West Ham	1	Birmghm C	1	
West Ham win 3-2 on agg				
Wigan Ath	0	Liverpool	3	
Liverpool win 8-2 on agg				
Wimbledn	3	Port Vale	0	
Wimbledn win 5-1 on agg				
Wolves	1	Aston V	1	
Aston V win 3-2 on agg				
THIRD ROUND				
Arsenal	1	Liverpool	0	
Aston V	0	West Ham	0	
C.Palace	0	Nottm For	0	
Derby	2	Sheff Wed	1	
Everton	3	Luton	0	
Exeter	3	Blackpool	0	
Man City	3	Norwich	1	
Man Utd	0	Tottenham	3	
Middlesbro	1	Wimbledn	1	
Newcastle	0	West Brom	1	
Oldham	7	Scarboro	0	
QPR	1	Coventry	2	
Southmptn	1	Charlton	0	
Sunderld	1	Bournemth	1	
Swindon	3	Bolton	3	
Tranmere	3	Millwall	2	
Bolton	1	Swindon	1	re
Bournemth	0	Sunderld	1	r
Nottm For	5	C.Palace	0	r
West Ham	1	Aston V	0	r
Wimbledn	1	Middlesbro	0	r
Bolton	1	Swindon	1	r2e

Strange but true!

Jones is a common surname, but when Rob Jones played for Liverpool in the 1995 League Cup Final he was the first player of that name to do so since 1977, when David Jones played for Everton.

Home		Away		
Swindon	2	Bolton	1	r3e
FOURTH ROUND				
Derby	2	West Brom	0	
Exeter	2	Sunderld	2	
Man City	0	Coventry	1	
Nottm For	1	Everton	0	
Oldham	3	Arsenal	1	
Swindon	0	Southmptn	0	
Tranmere	2	Tottenham	2	
West Ham	1	Wimbledn	0	
Southmptn	4	Swindon	2	re
Sunderld	5	Exeter	2	r
Tottenham	4	Tranmere	0	r
FIFTH ROUND				
Nottm For	2	Tottenham	2	
Southmptn	2	Oldham	2	
Sunderld	0	Coventry	0	
West Ham	1	Derby	1	
Coventry	5	Sunderld	0	r
Derby	0	West Ham	0	re
Oldham	2	Southmptn	0	r
Tottenham	2	Nottm For	3	r
West Ham	2	Derby	1	r2
SEMI-FINAL FIRST-LEG				
Nottm For	2	Coventry	1	
Oldham	6	West Ham	0	
SEMI-FINAL SECOND-LEG				
Coventry	0	Nottm For	0	
Nottm For win 2-1 on agg				
West Ham	3	Oldham	0	
Oldham win 6-3 on agg				
FINAL				
Nottm For	1	Oldham	0	N

1991

Home		Away		
FIRST ROUND FIRST-LEG				
Birmghm C	0	Bournemth	1	
Bradford	2	Bury	0	
Brentford	2	Hereford	0	
Brighton	0	N'hamptn	2	
Bristol R	1	Torquay	2	
Carlisle	1	Scunthpe	0	
Chestrfld	1	Hartlepl	2	
Darlingtn	0	Blackpool	0	
Doncaster	2	Rotherhm	6	
Exeter	1	Notts Co	1	
Fulham	1	Peterboro	2	
Gillinghm	1	Shrewsby	0	
Grimsby	2	Crewe	1	
Halifax	2	Lincoln	0	
Huddersfld	0	Bolton	3	
Maidstone	2	Leyton O	2	
Mansfield	1	Cardiff	1	
Middlesbro	1	Tranmere	1	
Preston NE	2	Chester	0	
Reading	0	Oxford	1	
Rochdale	4	Scarboro	0	
Southend	2	Aldershot	1	
Stockport	0	Burnley	2	
Stoke	0	Swansea	0	
Walsall	4	Cambridge	2	
West Brom	2	Bristol C	2	
Wigan Ath	0	Barnsley	1	
York	0	Wrexham	1	
FIRST ROUND SECOND-LEG				
Aldershot	2	Southend	2	
Southend win 4-3 on agg				
Barnsley	0	Wigan Ath	1	P
agg score Barnsley 1 - Wigan 1				
Blackpool	1	Darlingtn	1	a
agg score Blackp'l 1 - Darlingtn 1				
Bolton	2	Huddersfld	1	
Bolton win 5-1 on agg				
Bournemth	1	Birmghm C	1	
Bournemth win 2-1 on agg				
Bristol C	1	West Brom	0	e
Bristol C win 3-2 on agg				
Burnley	0	Stockport	1	
Burnley win 2-1 on agg				
Bury	3	Bradford	2	e
Bradford win 4-3 on agg				
Cambridge	2	Walsall	1	
Walsall win 5-4 on agg				
Cardiff	3	Mansfield	0	
Cardiff win 4-1 on agg				
Chester	5	Preston NE	1	e
Chester win 5-3 on agg				
Crewe	1	Grimsby	0	
agg score Crewe 2 - Grimsby 2				
Hartlepl	2	Chestrfld	2	
Hartlepl win 4-3 on agg				
Hereford	1	Brentford	0	
Brentford win 2-1 on agg				
Leyton O	4	Maidstone	1	
Leyton O win 6-3 on agg				
Lincoln	1	Halifax	0	
Halifax win 2-1 on agg				
N'hamptn	1	Brighton	1	
N'hamptn win 3-1 on agg				
Notts Co	1	Exeter	0	
Notts Co win 2-1 on agg				
Oxford	2	Reading	1	
Oxford win 3-1 on agg				
Peterboro	2	Fulham	0	
Peterboro win 4-1 on agg				
Rotherhm	2	Doncaster	1	
Rotherhm win 8-3 on agg				
Scarboro	3	Rochdale	3	
Rochdale win 7-3 on agg				
Scunthpe	1	Carlisle	1	
Carlisle win 2-1 on agg				
Shrewsby	2	Gillinghm	0	
Shrewsby win 2-1 on agg				
Swansea	0	Stoke	1	
Stoke win 1-0 on agg				
Torquay	1	Bristol R	1	
Torquay win 3-2 on agg				

Tranmere	1	Middlesbro	2	
Middlesbro win 3-2 on agg				
Wrexham	2	York	0	
Wrexham win 3-0 on agg				
SECOND ROUND FIRST-LEG				
Aston V	1	Barnsley	0	
Bournemth	0	Millwall	0	
Cardiff	1	Portsmth	1	
Carlisle	1	Derby	1	
Charlton	2	Leyton O	2	
Chester	0	Arsenal	1	
Coventry	4	Bolton	2	
C.Palace	8	Southend	0	
Darlingtn	3	Swindon	0	
Halifax	1	Man Utd	3	
Hull	0	Wolves	0	
Leicester	1	Leeds U	0	
Liverpool	5	Crewe	1	
Luton	1	Bradford	1	
Middlesbro	2	Newcastle	0	
N'hamptn	0	Sheff Utd	1	
Norwich	2	Watford	0	
Nottm For	4	Burnley	1	
Notts Co	1	Oldham	0	
Plymouth	1	Wimbledn	0	
Port Vale	0	Oxford	2	
QPR	3	Peterboro	1	
Rochdale	0	Southmptn	5	
Rotherhm	1	Blackburn	1	
Sheff Wed	2	Brentford	1	
Shrewsby	1	Ipswich	1	
Sunderld	0	Bristol C	1	
Torquay	0	Man City	4	
Tottenham	5	Hartlepl	0	
Walsall	0	Chelsea	5	
West Ham	3	Stoke	0	
Wrexham	0	Everton	5	
SECOND ROUND SECOND-LEG				
Arsenal	5	Chester	0	
Arsenal win 6-0 on agg				
Barnsley	0	Aston V	1	
Aston V win 2-0 on agg				

United Front

Ron Atkinson led Manchester United to the 1983 League Cup Final, where they were beaten by Liverpool. He then managed Sheffield Wednesday to victory over United in the 1991 competition and followed that up with another success in the League Cup Final in 1994 with Aston Villa. The beaten Finalists were United again.

Blackburn	1	Rotherhm	0	
Blackburn win 2-1 on agg				
Bolton	2	Coventry	3	
Coventry win 7-4 on agg				
Bradford	1	Luton	1	P
agg score Bradford 2 - Luton 2				
Brentford	1	Sheff Wed	2	
Sheff Wed win 4-2 on agg				
Bristol C	1	Sunderld	6	
Sunderld win 6-2 on agg				
Burnley	0	Nottm For	1	
Nottm For win 5-1 on agg				
Chelsea	4	Walsall	1	
Chelsea win 9-1 on agg				
Crewe	1	Liverpool	4	
Liverpool win 9-2 on agg				
Derby	1	Carlisle	0	
Derby win 2-1 on agg				
Everton	6	Wrexham	0	
Everton win 11-0 on agg				
Hartlepl	1	Tottenham	2	
Tottenham win 7-1 on agg				
Ipswich	3	Shrewsby	0	
Ipswich win 4-1 on agg				
Leeds U	3	Leicester	0	
Leeds U win 3-1 on agg				
Leyton O	1	Charlton	0	
Leyton O win 3-2 on agg				
Man City	0	Torquay	0	
Man City win 4-0 on agg				
Man Utd	2	Halifax	1	
Man Utd win 5-2 on agg				
Millwall	2	Bournemth	1	
Millwall win 2-1 on agg				
Newcastle	1	Middlesbro	0	
Middlesbro win 2-1 on agg				
Oldham	5	Notts Co	2	e
Oldham win 5-3 on agg				
Oxford	0	Port Vale	0	
Oxford win 2-0 on agg				
Peterboro	1	QPR	1	
QPR win 4-2 on agg				
Portsmth	3	Cardiff	1	e
Portsmth win 4-2 on agg				
Sheff Utd	2	N'hamptn	1	
Sheff Utd win 3-1 on agg				
Southmptn	3	Rochdale	0	
Southmptn win 8-0 on agg				
Southend	1	C.Palace	2	
C.Palace win 10-1 on agg				
Stoke	1	West Ham	2	
West Ham win 5-1 on agg				
Swindon	4	Darlingtn	0	
Swindon win 4-3 on agg				
Watford	0	Norwich	3	
Norwich win 5-0 on agg				
Wimbledn	0	Plymouth	2	
Plymouth win 3-0 on agg				
Wolves	1	Hull	1	a
agg score Wolves 1 - Hull 1				
THIRD ROUND				
Aston V	2	Millwall	0	
Chelsea	0	Portsmth	0	
Coventry	3	Hull	0	
C.Palace	0	Leyton O	0	
Derby	6	Sunderld	0	
Ipswich	0	Southmptn	2	

Leeds U	2	Oldham	0	
Man City	1	Arsenal	2	
Man Utd	3	Liverpool	1	
Middlesbro	2	Norwich	0	
Oxford	2	West Ham	1	
Plymouth	1	Nottm For	2	
QPR	2	Blackburn	1	
Sheff Utd	2	Everton	1	
Sheff Wed	0	Swindon	0	
Tottenham	2	Bradford	1	
Leyton O	0	C.Palace	1	r
Portsmth	2	Chelsea	3	r
Swindon	0	Sheff Wed	1	r
FOURTH ROUND				
Arsenal	2	Man Utd	6	
Aston V	3	Middlesbro	2	
Coventry	5	Nottm For	4	
Oxford	1	Chelsea	2	
QPR	0	Leeds U	3	
Sheff Utd	0	Tottenham	2	
Sheff Wed	1	Derby	1	
Southmptn	2	C.Palace	0	
Derby	1	Sheff Wed	2	r
FIFTH ROUND				
Chelsea	0	Tottenham	0	
Coventry	0	Sheff Wed	1	
Leeds U	4	Aston V	1	
Southmptn	1	Man Utd	1	
Man Utd	3	Southmptn	2	r
Tottenham	0	Chelsea	3	r
SEMI-FINAL FIRST-LEG				
Chelsea	0	Sheff Wed	2	
Man Utd	2	Leeds U	1	
SEMI-FINAL SECOND-LEG				
Leeds U	0	Man Utd	1	
Man Utd win 3-1 on agg				
Sheff Wed	3	Chelsea	1	
Sheff Wed win 5-1 on agg				
FINAL				
Sheff Wed	1	Man Utd	0	N

1992

FIRST ROUND FIRST-LEG				
Barnet	5	Brentford	5	
Blackburn	1	Hull	1	
Bolton	2	York	2	
Cambridge	1	Reading	0	
Cardiff	3	Bournemth	2	
Charlton	4	Fulham	2	
Chester	1	Lincoln	0	
Crewe	5	Doncaster	2	
Darlingtn	1	Huddersfld	0	
Exeter	0	Birmghm C	1	
Halifax	3	Tranmere	4	
Hartlepl	1	Bury	0	
Leicester	3	Maidstone	0	
Leyton O	5	N'hamptn	0	
Mansfield	0	Blackpool	3	
Peterboro	3	Aldershot	1	
Portsmth	2	Gillinghm	1	
Preston NE	5	Scarboro	4	
Rochdale	5	Carlisle	1	
Rotherhm	1	Grimsby	3	
Shrewsby	1	Plymouth	1	
Stockport	1	Bradford	1	
Stoke	1	Chestrfld	0	
Swansea	2	Walsall	2	

Home		Away		
Swindon	**2**	**West Brom**	**0**	
Torquay	**2**	**Hereford**	**0**	
Watford	**2**	**Southend**	**0**	
Wigan Ath	**3**	**Burnley**	**1**	
Wrexham	**1**	**Scunthpe**	**0**	
FIRST ROUND SECOND-LEG				
Aldershot	**1**	**Peterboro**	**2**	
Peterboro win 5-2 on agg				
Birmghm C	**4**	**Exeter**	**0**	
Birmghm C win 5-0 on agg				
Blackpool	**4**	**Mansfield**	**2**	
Blackpool win 7-2 on agg				
Bournemth	**4**	**Cardiff**	**1**	
Bournemth win 6-4 on agg				
Bradford	**3**	**Stockport**	**1**	e
Bradford win 4-2 on agg				
Brentford	**3**	**Barnet**	**1**	
Brentford win 8-6 on agg				
Burnley	**2**	**Wigan Ath**	**3**	
Wigan Ath win 6-3 on agg				
Bury	**2**	**Hartlepl**	**2**	
Hartlepl win 3-2 on agg				
Carlisle	**1**	**Rochdale**	**1**	
Rochdale win 6-2 on agg				
Chestrfld	**1**	**Stoke**	**2**	
Stoke win 3-1 on agg				
Doncaster	**2**	**Crewe**	**4**	
Crewe win 9-4 on agg				
Fulham	**1**	**Charlton**	**1**	
Charlton win 5-3 on agg				
Gillinghm	**3**	**Portsmth**	**4**	
Portsmth win 6-4 on agg				
Grimsby	**1**	**Rotherhm**	**0**	
Grimsby win 4-1 on agg				
Hereford	**2**	**Torquay**	**1**	
Torquay win 3-2 on agg				
Huddersfld	**4**	**Darlingtn**	**0**	
Huddersfld win 4-1 on agg				
Hull	**1**	**Blackburn**	**0**	
Hull win 2-1 on agg				
Lincoln	**4**	**Chester**	**3**	a
agg score Lincoln 4 - Chester 4				
Maidstone	**0**	**Leicester**	**1**	
Leicester win 4-0 on agg				
N'hamptn	**2**	**Leyton O**	**0**	
Leyton O win 5-2 on agg				
Plymouth	**2**	**Shrewsby**	**2**	a
agg score Plym'th 3 - Shrewsby 3				
Reading	**0**	**Cambridge**	**3**	
Cambridge win 4-0 on agg				
Scarboro	**3**	**Preston NE**	**1**	e
Scarboro win 7-6 on agg				
Scunthpe	**3**	**Wrexham**	**0**	
Scunthpe win 3-1 on agg				
Southend	**1**	**Watford**	**1**	
Watford win 3-1 on agg				
Tranmere	**4**	**Halifax**	**3**	e
Tranmere win 8-6 on agg				
Walsall	**0**	**Swansea**	**1**	
Swansea win 3-2 on agg				
West Brom	**2**	**Swindon**	**2**	
Swindon win 4-2 on agg				
York	**1**	**Bolton**	**2**	
Bolton win 4-3 on agg				
SECOND ROUND FIRST-LEG				
Blackpool	**1**	**Barnsley**	**0**	
Bradford	**1**	**West Ham**	**1**	
Brentford	**4**	**Brighton**	**1**	
Bristol R	**1**	**Bristol C**	**3**	
Charlton	**0**	**Norwich**	**2**	
Chelsea	**1**	**Tranmere**	**1**	
Coventry	**4**	**Rochdale**	**0**	
Crewe	**3**	**Newcastle**	**4**	
Derby	**0**	**Ipswich**	**0**	
Everton	**1**	**Watford**	**0**	
Grimsby	**0**	**Aston V**	**0**	
Hartlepl	**1**	**C.Palace**	**1**	
Hull	**0**	**QPR**	**3**	
Leicester	**1**	**Arsenal**	**1**	
Leyton O	**0**	**Sheff Wed**	**0**	
Liverpool	**2**	**Stoke**	**2**	
Luton	**2**	**Birmghm C**	**2**	
Man City	**3**	**Chester**	**1**	
Man Utd	**3**	**Cambridge**	**0**	
Middlesbro	**1**	**Bournemth**	**1**	
Millwall	**2**	**Swindon**	**2**	
Nottm For	**4**	**Bolton**	**0**	
Oldham	**7**	**Torquay**	**1**	
Port Vale	**2**	**Notts Co**	**1**	
Portsmth	**0**	**Oxford**	**0**	
Scarboro	**1**	**Southmptn**	**3**	
Scunthpe	**0**	**Leeds U**	**0**	
Sunderld	**1**	**Huddersfld**	**2**	
Swansea	**1**	**Tottenham**	**0**	
Wigan Ath	**2**	**Sheff Utd**	**2**	
Wimbledn	**1**	**Peterboro**	**2**	
Wolves	**6**	**Shrewsby**	**1**	
SECOND ROUND SECOND-LEG				
Arsenal	**2**	**Leicester**	**0**	
Arsenal win 3-1 on agg				
Aston V	**1**	**Grimsby**	**1**	a
agg score Aston V 1 - Grimsby 1				
Barnsley	**2**	**Blackpool**	**0**	e
Barnsley win 2-1 on agg				
Birmghm C	**3**	**Luton**	**2**	
Birmghm C win 5-4 on agg				
Bolton	**2**	**Nottm For**	**5**	
Nottm For win 9-2 on agg				
Bournemth	**1**	**Middlesbro**	**2**	e
Middlesbro win 3-2 on agg				
Brighton	**4**	**Brentford**	**2**	e
Brentford win 6-5 on agg				
Bristol C	**2**	**Bristol R**	**4**	a
agg score Bristol C 5 - Bristol R 5				
Cambridge	**1**	**Man Utd**	**1**	
Man Utd win 4-1 on agg				
Chester	**0**	**Man City**	**3**	
Man City win 6-1 on agg				
C.Palace	**6**	**Hartlepl**	**1**	
C.Palace win 7-2 on agg				
Huddersfld	**4**	**Sunderld**	**0**	
Huddersfld win 6-1 on agg				
Ipswich	**0**	**Derby**	**2**	
Derby win 2-0 on agg				
Leeds U	**3**	**Scunthpe**	**0**	
Leeds U win 3-0 on agg				
Newcastle	**1**	**Crewe**	**0**	
Newcastle win 5-3 on agg				
Norwich	**3**	**Charlton**	**0**	
Norwich win 5-0 on agg				
Notts Co	**3**	**Port Vale**	**2**	a
agg score Notts Co 4 - Port Vale 4				
Oxford	**0**	**Portsmth**	**1**	
Portsmth win 1-0 on agg				
Peterboro	**2**	**Wimbledn**	**2**	
Peterboro win 4-3 on agg				
QPR	**5**	**Hull**	**1**	
QPR win 8-1 on agg				
Rochdale	**1**	**Coventry**	**0**	
Coventry win 4-1 on agg				
Sheff Utd	**1**	**Wigan Ath**	**0**	
Sheff Utd win 3-2 on agg				
Sheff Wed	**4**	**Leyton O**	**1**	
Sheff Wed win 4-1 on agg				
Shrewsby	**3**	**Wolves**	**1**	
Wolves win 7-4 on agg				
Southmptn	**2**	**Scarboro**	**2**	

GIANTKILLERS

1992-93 Scarborough 3 Coventry 0

Scarborough's brief League career has contained few moments of great joy. Most of them came in 1992-93, when their League Cup campaign was one long thrill, the sort anyone would envy. Defeat of Bradford City 8-3 on aggregate preceded a victory over Coventry, who had been two up from the first-leg, and still one up with only two minutes to go, and was followed by a 4-3 aggregate disposal of Plymouth, despite Peter Shilton. Arsenal ended it with a 1-0 win before a near 7,000 crowd, who paid a record £37,609. And 50 pence.

WHAT A STAR ✪ PAUL MERSON

Merson has had his problems, with drinking, gambling and drugs, but even at the height of those problems he was still a handful for any defence, as he showed in the 1993 League Cup Final against Sheffield Wednesday. He scored a memorable first goal for Arsenal in The Gunners' 2-1 win and also emerged clutching the Man of the Match award. The scenes of his famous 'Let's all have a lager' celebration probably haunt him now, but the fact that he faced his problems, conquered them, and came back better than ever, should be applauded throughout the land.

Southmptn win 5-3 on agg				
Stoke	**2**	**Liverpool**	**3**	
Liverpool win 5-4 on agg				
Swindon	**3**	**Millwall**	**1**	
Swindon win 5-3 on agg				
Torquay	**0**	**Oldham**	**2**	
Oldham win 9-1 on agg				
Tottenham	**5**	**Swansea**	**1**	
Tottenham win 5-2 on agg				
Tranmere	**3**	**Chelsea**	**1**	**e**
Tranmere win 4-2 on agg				
Watford	**1**	**Everton**	**2**	
Everton win 3-1 on agg				
West Ham	**4**	**Bradford**	**0**	
West Ham win 5-1 on agg				
THIRD ROUND				
Birmghm C	**1**	**C.Palace**	**1**	
Coventry	**1**	**Arsenal**	**0**	
Everton	**4**	**Wolves**	**1**	
Grimsby	**0**	**Tottenham**	**3**	
Huddersfld	**1**	**Swindon**	**4**	
Leeds U	**3**	**Tranmere**	**1**	
Liverpool	**2**	**Port Vale**	**2**	
Man City	**0**	**QPR**	**0**	
Man Utd	**3**	**Portsmth**	**1**	
Middlesbro	**1**	**Barnsley**	**0**	
Norwich	**4**	**Brentford**	**1**	
Nottm For	**2**	**Bristol R**	**0**	
Oldham	**2**	**Derby**	**1**	
Peterboro	**1**	**Newcastle**	**0**	
Sheff Utd	**0**	**West Ham**	**2**	
Sheff Wed	**1**	**Southmptn**	**1**	
C.Palace	**1**	**Birmghm C**	**1**	**re**
Port Vale	**1**	**Liverpool**	**4**	**r**
QPR	**1**	**Man City**	**3**	**r**
Southmptn	**1**	**Sheff Wed**	**0**	**r**
C.Palace	**2**	**Birmghm C**	**1**	**r2**
FOURTH ROUND				
Coventry	**1**	**Tottenham**	**2**	
Everton	**1**	**Leeds U**	**4**	
Man Utd	**2**	**Oldham**	**0**	
Middlesbro	**2**	**Man City**	**1**	
Norwich	**2**	**West Ham**	**1**	
Nottm For	**0**	**Southmptn**	**0**	
Peterboro	**1**	**Liverpool**	**0**	
Swindon	**0**	**C.Palace**	**1**	
Southmptn	**0**	**Nottm For**	**1**	**r**
FIFTH ROUND				
C.Palace	**1**	**Nottm For**	**1**	
Leeds U	**1**	**Man Utd**	**3**	
Peterboro	**0**	**Middlesbro**	**0**	
Tottenham	**2**	**Norwich**	**1**	
Middlesbro	**1**	**Peterboro**	**0**	**r**
Nottm For	**4**	**C.Palace**	**2**	**r**
SEMI-FINAL FIRST-LEG				
Middlesbro	**0**	**Man Utd**	**0**	
Nottm For	**1**	**Tottenham**	**1**	
SEMI-FINAL SECOND-LEG				
Man Utd	**2**	**Middlesbro**	**1**	**e**
Man Utd win 2-1 on agg				
Tottenham	**1**	**Nottm For**	**2**	**e**
Nottm For win 3-2 on agg				
FINAL				
Man Utd	**1**	**Nottm For**	**0**	**N**

1993

FIRST ROUND FIRST-LEG				
Bolton	**2**	**Port Vale**	**1**	
Cardiff	**1**	**Bristol C**	**0**	

Paul Merson's had plenty to shout about during his Arsenal career

Pro-File: DWIGHT YORKE

Dwight Yorke plays football the way it should be played...with a smile on his face.

Aston Villa's Trinidad international striker is one of football's genuine nice guys and nothing seems to ruffle him.

Mind you, he has had quite a bit to smile about in the past few seasons.

Yorke has been one of the main men as Villa have emerged from the doldrums to become one of the Premiership's major forces, and they now have genuine title ambitons.

They have been constantly in the hunt for honours in recent years and Yorke has more than played his part in that.

He has developed from an exciting, but raw, young striker into one of English football's most dangerous and clinical marksman, and he is a feared opponent at Premiership grounds everywhere.

His movement is second to none and he has a range of tricks and skills that any Brazilian would be proud of.

Throw in a fair smattering of goals and you are well on the way to building the complete striker.

And if he continues his development in the same way then Villa will have a truly exceptional talent on their hands, and will rightly expect to continue to challenge for the game's top honours.

And that will really give Yorke something to smile about!

Career details

●**Represented:** Trinidad & Tobago, Aston Villa ●**Position:** Striker ●**Born:** 3.11.71. ●**Height:** 5ft 11in ●**Weight:** 11st 13lbs ●**Club honours:** Coca-Cola Cup 1996 ●**International honours:** Trinidad & Tobago 35 full caps

Club League Record

Era	Club	Games	Goals
89/97	Aston Villa	200	61

Cup Highlights

Sep 20 1995: Yorke scores twice, both penalties, as Villa crush Peterborough 6-0 in the Coca-Cola Cup Second Round.

Feb 14 1996: Dwight grabs two more goals as Villa recover from 2-0 down to draw 2-2 in the Coca-Cola Cup Semi-Final first-leg at Highbury. A 0-0 draw a week later earns them a place in the Final.

Mar 24 1996: Yorke stars as Villa win the Cup in style with a 3-0 win over Leeds. He has a hand in the first two goals, and scores the third himself.

Yorke On:

●Sometimes I'd have to go next door to get fed. I've seen people starving and I know that side of life. **Yorke on growing up in Trinidad**

On Yorke:

●Dwight is a great footballer and I'm hoping the two of us can provide as good an understanding and as many goals as myself and Robbie Fowler. **Stan Collymore after signing for Aston Villa**

DID YOU KNOW THAT...

●His best mate in football is Newcastle goalkeeper Shaka Hislop. The two grew up together in Trinidad.

●Yorke and Hislop regularly have bets with each other when they come face-to-face. Yorke bets he'll score, Hislop bets he'll stop him.

●He is also close friends with West Indies cricketing superstar Brian Lara.

●He joined Aston Villa from St Clair's in Tobago in November 1989. He cost just £120,000.

●Villa discovered him when they were on a pre-season tour of the West Indies.

●Yorke made his Villa debut on March 24, 1989 in a 1-0 defeat at Crystal Palace.

●Dwight scored his first goal for Villa in a 3-2 win over Derby on February 2, 1991. And just to make it a bit more special it was the winner.

●One of his biggest disappointments in football was being left out of the Villa side to play in the 1994 Coca-Cola Cup Final against Manchester United.

●Dwight jointly holds the record for the fastest Premiership goal, with Blackburn's Chris Sutton. Both men struck after just 13 seconds, Yorke at Coventry on September 30, 1995.

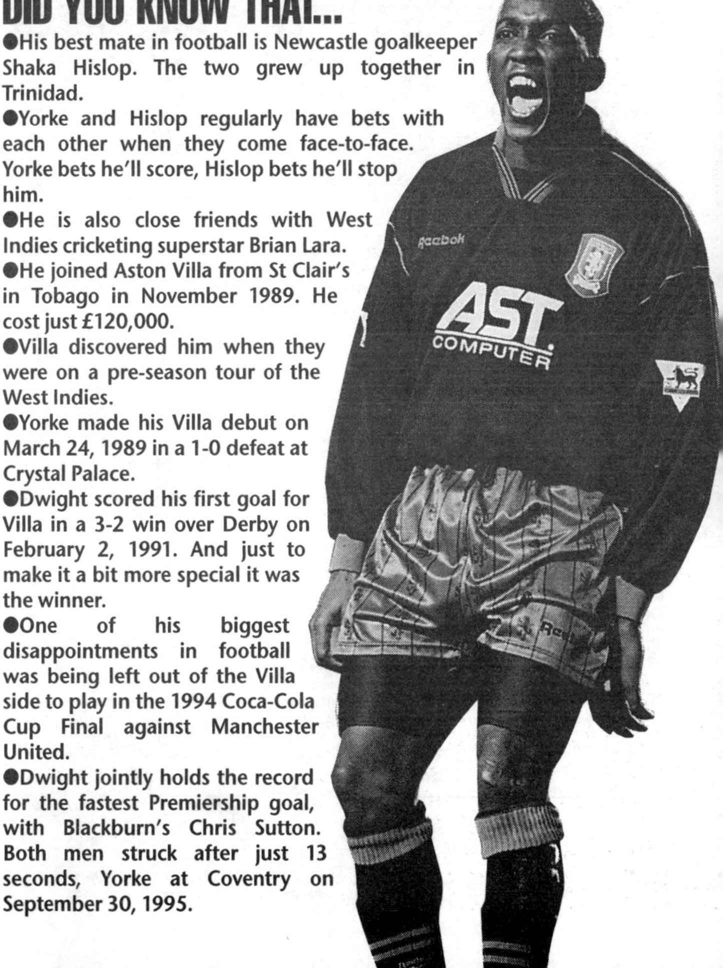

GIANTKILLERS

1993-94 Tranmere 2 Nottm For 0

Tranmere, in 1993-94, were the first giantkillers to have a Cup run ended on penalties after getting to a Semi-Final, and after they had not just won four ties, but won them with something to spare. Their margins of goals in the previous rounds were 4, 3, 3 and 2, against Oxford, Grimsby, Oldham and Nottingham Forest respectively. Eventually they went out to Aston Villa after each side had won the home Semi-Final 3-1. Tranmere's luck stayed out - they missed promotion by losing in the play-offs.

Carlisle 4 Burnley 1
Chestrfld 2 York 0
Colchester 1 Brighton 1
Crewe 4 Rochdale 1
Darlingtn 1 Scunthpe 1
Doncaster 0 Lincoln 3
Exeter 0 Birmghm C 0
Fulham 0 Brentford 2
Gillinghm 2 N'hamptn 1
Grimsby 1 Barnsley 1
Halifax 1 Hartlepl 2
Hereford 2 Torquay 2
Hull 2 Rotherhm 2
Leyton O 2 Millwall 2
Newcastle 2 Mansfield 1
Oxford 3 Swansea 0
Peterboro 4 Barnet 0
Preston NE 2 Stoke 1
Scarboro 3 Bradford 0
Shrewsby 1 Wigan Ath 2
Stockport 1 Chester 1
Sunderld 2 Huddersfld 3
Tranmere 3 Blackpool 0
Walsall 1 Bournemth 1
West Brom 1 Plymouth 0
Wrexham 1 Bury 1

FIRST ROUND SECOND-LEG

Barnet 2 Peterboro 2
Peterboro win 6-2 on agg
Barnsley 1 Grimsby 1 q
agg score Barnsley 2 - Grimsby 2
Birmghm C 1 Exeter 4
Exeter win 4-1 on agg
Blackpool 4 Tranmere 0
Blackpool win 4-3 on agg
Bournemth 0 Walsall 1
Walsall win 2-1 on agg
Bradford 3 Scarboro 5
Scarboro win 8-3 on agg
Brentford 2 Fulham 0
Brentford win 4-0 on agg
Brighton 1 Colchester 0
Brighton win 2-1 on agg
Bristol C 5 Cardiff 1
Bristol C win 5-2 on agg
Burnley 1 Carlisle 1
Carlisle win 5-2 on agg
Bury 4 Wrexham 3
Bury win 5-4 on agg
Chester 1 Stockport 2
Stockport win 3-2 on agg
Hartlepl 3 Halifax 2
Hartlepl win 5-3 on agg
Huddersfld 0 Sunderld 1
agg score Huddersfld 3 - S'derld 3
Lincoln 1 Doncaster 1
Lincoln win 4-1 on agg
Mansfield 0 Newcastle 0
Newcastle win 2-1 on agg
Millwall 3 Leyton O 0
Millwall win 5-2 on agg
N'hamptn 0 Gillinghm 2
Gillinghm win 4-1 on agg
Plymouth 2 West Brom 0
Plymouth win 2-1 on agg
Port Vale 1 Bolton 1
Bolton win 3-2 on agg
Rochdale 1 Crewe 2
Crewe win 6-2 on agg
Rotherhm 1 Hull 0
Rotherhm win 3-2 on agg
Scunthpe 2 Darlingtn 0
Scunthpe win 3-1 on agg
Stoke 4 Preston NE 0
Stoke win 5-2 on agg
Swansea 1 Oxford 0
Oxford win 3-1 on agg
Torquay 5 Hereford 0
Torquay win 7-2 on agg
Wigan Ath 0 Shrewsby 1
agg score Wigan 2 - Shrewsby 2
York 0 Chestrfld 0
Chestrfld win 2-0 on agg

SECOND ROUND FIRST-LEG

Arsenal 1 Millwall 1
Blackpool 0 Portsmth 4
Bolton 1 Wimbledn 3
Brighton 1 Man Utd 1
Bristol C 2 Sheff Utd 1
Bury 0 Charlton 0
Cambridge 2 Stoke 2
Carlisle 2 Norwich 2
Coventry 2 Scarboro 0
C.Palace 3 Lincoln 1
Exeter 0 Oldham 1
Gillinghm 0 Southmptn 0
Huddersfld 1 Blackburn 1
Leeds U 4 Scunthpe 1
Leicester 2 Peterboro 0
Liverpool 4 Chestrfld 4
Luton 2 Plymouth 2
Man City 0 Bristol R 0
Newcastle 0 Middlesbro 0
Notts Co 3 Wolves 2
Oxford 1 Aston V 2
QPR 2 Grimsby 1
Rotherhm 1 Everton 0
Sheff Wed 3 Hartlepl 0
Southend 1 Derby 0
Stockport 2 Nottm For 3
Torquay 0 Swindon 6
Tottenham 3 Brentford 1
Walsall 0 Chelsea 3
Watford 2 Reading 2
West Ham 0 Crewe 0
Wigan Ath 2 Ipswich 2

SECOND ROUND SECOND-LEG

Aston V 2 Oxford 1
Aston V win 4-2 on agg
Blackburn 4 Huddersfld 3 e
Blackburn win 5-4 on agg
Brentford 2 Tottenham 4
Tottenham win 7-3 on agg
Bristol R 1 Man City 2 e
Man City win 2-1 on agg
Charlton 0 Bury 1
Bury win 1-0 on agg
Chelsea 1 Walsall 0
Chelsea win 4-0 on agg
Chestrfld 1 Liverpool 4
Liverpool win 8-5 on agg
Crewe 2 West Ham 0
Crewe win 2-0 on agg
Derby 7 Southend 0
Derby win 7-1 on agg
Everton 3 Rotherhm 0
Everton win 3-1 on agg
Grimsby 2 QPR 1 q
agg score Grimsby 3 - QPR 3
Hartlepl 2 Sheff Wed 2
Sheff Wed win 5-2 on agg
Ipswich 4 Wigan Ath 0
Ipswich win 6-2 on agg
Lincoln 1 C.Palace 1
C.Palace win 4-2 on agg
Man Utd 1 Brighton 0
Man Utd win 2-1 on agg

Middlesbro	**1**	**Newcastle**	**3**	
Newcastle win 3-1 on agg				
Millwall	**1**	**Arsenal**	**1**	q
agg score Millwall 2 - Arsenal 2				
Norwich	**2**	**Carlisle**	**0**	
Norwich win 4-2 on agg				
Nottm For	**2**	**Stockport**	**1**	
Nottm For win 5-3 on agg				
Oldham	**0**	**Exeter**	**0**	
Oldham win 1-0 on agg				
Peterboro	**2**	**Leicester**	**1**	
Leicester win 3-2 on agg				
Plymouth	**3**	**Luton**	**2**	
Plymouth win 5-4 on agg				
Portsmth	**2**	**Blackpool**	**0**	
Portsmth win 6-0 on agg				
Reading	**0**	**Watford**	**2**	
Watford win 4-2 on agg				
Scarboro	**3**	**Coventry**	**0**	
Scarboro win 3-2 on agg				
Scunthpe	**2**	**Leeds U**	**2**	
Leeds U win 6-3 on agg				
Sheff Utd	**4**	**Bristol C**	**1**	
Sheff Utd win 5-3 on agg				
Southmptn	**3**	**Gillinghm**	**0**	
Southmptn win 3-0 on agg				
Stoke	**1**	**Cambridge**	**2**	
Cambridge win 4-3 on agg				
Swindon	**3**	**Torquay**	**2**	
Swindon win 9-2 on agg				
Wimbledn	**0**	**Bolton**	**1**	
Wimbledn win 3-2 on agg				
Wolves	**0**	**Notts Co**	**1**	
Notts Co win 4-2 on agg				
THIRD ROUND				
Aston V	**1**	**Man Utd**	**0**	
Blackburn	**2**	**Norwich**	**0**	
Bury	**0**	**QPR**	**2**	
Chelsea	**2**	**Newcastle**	**1**	
Crewe	**0**	**Nottm For**	**1**	
Derby	**1**	**Arsenal**	**1**	
Everton	**0**	**Wimbledn**	**0**	
Man City	**0**	**Tottenham**	**1**	
Notts Co	**2**	**Cambridge**	**3**	
Plymouth	**3**	**Scarboro**	**3**	
Portsmth	**0**	**Ipswich**	**1**	
Sheff Utd	**0**	**Liverpool**	**0**	
Sheff Wed	**7**	**Leicester**	**1**	
Southmptn	**0**	**C.Palace**	**2**	
Swindon	**0**	**Oldham**	**1**	
Watford	**2**	**Leeds U**	**1**	
Arsenal	**2**	**Derby**	**1**	r
Liverpool	**3**	**Sheff Utd**	**0**	r
Scarboro	**2**	**Plymouth**	**1**	r
Wimbledn	**0**	**Everton**	**1**	r
FOURTH ROUND				
Aston V	**2**	**Ipswich**	**2**	
Blackburn	**6**	**Watford**	**1**	
Cambridge	**1**	**Oldham**	**0**	
Everton	**2**	**Chelsea**	**2**	
Liverpool	**1**	**C.Palace**	**1**	
Nottm For	**2**	**Tottenham**	**0**	
Scarboro	**0**	**Arsenal**	**1**	
Sheff Wed	**4**	**QPR**	**0**	
Chelsea	**1**	**Everton**	**0**	r
C.Palace	**2**	**Liverpool**	**1**	re
Ipswich	**1**	**Aston V**	**0**	r
FIFTH ROUND				
Arsenal	**2**	**Nottm For**	**0**	
Blackburn	**3**	**Cambridge**	**2**	
C.Palace	**3**	**Chelsea**	**1**	
Ipswich	**1**	**Sheff Wed**	**1**	
Sheff Wed	**1**	**Ipswich**	**0**	r
SEMI-FINAL FIRST-LEG				
Blackburn	**2**	**Sheff Wed**	**4**	
C.Palace	**1**	**Arsenal**	**3**	
SEMI-FINAL SECOND-LEG				
Arsenal	**2**	**C.Palace**	**0**	
Arsenal win 5-1 on agg				
Sheff Wed	**2**	**Blackburn**	**1**	
Sheff Wed win 6-3 on agg				
FINAL				
Arsenal	**2**	**Sheff Wed**	**1**	N

1994

FIRST ROUND FIRST-LEG				
Birmghm C	**3**	**Plymouth**	**0**	
Bolton	**0**	**Bury**	**2**	
Bournemth	**3**	**Cardiff**	**1**	
Brentford	**2**	**Watford**	**2**	
Bristol R	**1**	**West Brom**	**4**	
Cambridge	**1**	**Luton**	**0**	
Chestrfld	**3**	**Carlisle**	**1**	
Crewe	**0**	**Wrexham**	**1**	
Darlingtn	**1**	**Bradford**	**5**	
Doncaster	**0**	**Blackpool**	**1**	
Fulham	**2**	**Colchester**	**1**	
Gillinghm	**1**	**Brighton**	**0**	
Hereford	**0**	**Torquay**	**2**	
Huddersfld	**0**	**Scarboro**	**0**	
Leyton O	**0**	**Wycombe**	**2**	
Notts Co	**2**	**Hull**	**0**	
Port Vale	**2**	**Lincoln**	**2**	
Preston NE	**1**	**Burnley**	**2**	
Reading	**3**	**N'hamptn**	**0**	
Rochdale	**2**	**York**	**0**	
Shrewsby	**1**	**Scunthpe**	**0**	
Southend	**0**	**Barnet**	**2**	
Stockport	**1**	**Hartlepl**	**1**	
Stoke	**2**	**Mansfield**	**2**	
Sunderld	**3**	**Chester**	**1**	
Swansea	**0**	**Bristol C**	**1**	
Walsall	**0**	**Exeter**	**0**	
Wigan Ath	**0**	**Rotherhm**	**1**	
FIRST ROUND SECOND-LEG				
Barnet	**1**	**Southend**	**1**	
Barnet win 3-1 on agg				
Blackpool	**3**	**Doncaster**	**3**	
Blackpool win 4-3 on agg				
Bradford	**6**	**Darlingtn**	**0**	
Bradford win 11-1 on agg				
Brighton	**2**	**Gillinghm**	**0**	
Brighton win 2-1 on agg				
Bristol C	**0**	**Swansea**	**2**	
Swansea win 2-1 on agg				
Burnley	**4**	**Preston NE**	**1**	
Burnley win 6-2 on agg				
Bury	**0**	**Bolton**	**2**	q
agg score Bury 2 - Bolton 2				
Cardiff	**1**	**Bournemth**	**1**	
Bournemth win 4-2 on agg				
Carlisle	**1**	**Chestrfld**	**1**	
Chestrfld win 4-2 on agg				
Chester	**0**	**Sunderld**	**0**	
Sunderld win 3-1 on agg				
Colchester	**1**	**Fulham**	**2**	
Fulham win 4-2 on agg				
Exeter	**2**	**Walsall**	**1**	
Exeter win 2-1 on agg				

United they Stand

Three Manchester United players have scored in the Finals of both the FA Cup and the League Cup, with Mark Hughes and Brian McClair of the 90s following Norman Whiteside of the 80s.

WHAT A STAR ✪ SAVO MILOSEVIC

The Yugoslavian striker had his critics, but on his day he was a joy to watch. His touch and skills were sensational for such a big man, but for a striker he did have a tendency to miss when it seemed easier to score, hence his nickname 'Savo Missalotovic'. But when it mattered most, he delivered the goods. He scored a stunner in the League Cup Final as Aston Villa crushed Leeds 3-0 at Wembley in 1996, to prove once and for all, that he could also 'score a lot' too.

Hartlepl 1 Stockport 2
Stockport win 3-2 on agg
Hull 3 Notts Co 1 a
agg score Hull 3 - Notts Co 3
Lincoln 0 Port Vale 0
agg score Lincoln 2 - Port Vale 2
Luton 0 Cambridge 1
Cambridge win 2-0 on agg
Mansfield 3 Stoke 1
Mansfield win 5-3 on agg
N'hamptn 0 Reading 2
Reading win 5-0 on agg
Plymouth 2 Birmghm C 0
Birmghm C win 3-2 on agg
Rotherhm 4 Wigan Ath 2
Rotherhm win 5-2 on agg
Scarboro 0 Huddersfld 3
Huddersfld win 3-0 on agg
Scunthpe 1 Shrewsby 1
Shrewsby win 2-1 on agg
Torquay 0 Hereford 2 q
agg score Torquay 2 - Hereford 2
Watford 3 Brentford 1
Watford win 5-3 on agg
West Brom 0 Bristol R 0
West Brom win 4-1 on agg
Wrexham 3 Crewe 3
Wrexham win 4-3 on agg
Wycombe 1 Leyton O 0
Wycombe win 3-0 on agg
York 0 Rochdale 0
Rochdale win 2-0 on agg

SECOND ROUND FIRST-LEG

Barnet 1 QPR 2
Barnsley 1 Peterboro 1
Birmghm C 0 Aston V 1
Blackburn 1 Bournemth 0
Blackpool 3 Sheff Utd 0
Bolton 1 Sheff Wed 1
Bradford 2 Norwich 1
Burnley 0 Tottenham 0
Coventry 3 Wycombe 0
C.Palace 3 Charlton 1
Exeter 1 Derby 3
Fulham 1 Liverpool 3
Grimsby 3 Hartlepl 0
Hereford 0 Wimbledn 1
Huddersfld 0 Arsenal 5
Ipswich 2 Cambridge 1
Lincoln 3 Everton 4
Man City 1 Reading 1
Middlesbro 5 Brighton 0
Newcastle 4 Notts Co 1
Rochdale 1 Leicester 6
Rotherhm 0 Portsmth 0
Southmptn 1 Shrewsby 0
Stoke 2 Man Utd 1
Sunderld 2 Leeds U 1
Swansea 2 Oldham 1
Swindon 2 Wolves 0
Tranmere 5 Oxford 1
Watford 0 Millwall 0
West Brom 1 Chelsea 1
West Ham 5 Chestrfld 1
Wrexham 3 Nottm For 3

SECOND ROUND SECOND-LEG

Arsenal 1 Huddersfld 1
Arsenal win 6-1 on agg
Aston V 1 Birmghm C 0
Aston V win 2-0 on agg
Bournemth 0 Blackburn 0
Blackburn win 1-0 on agg
Brighton 1 Middlesbro 3
Middlesbro win 8-1 on agg
Cambridge 0 Ipswich 2
Ipswich win 4-1 on agg
Charlton 0 C.Palace 1
C.Palace win 4-1 on agg
Chelsea 2 West Brom 1
Chelsea win 3-2 on agg
Chestrfld 0 West Ham 2
West Ham win 7-1 on agg
Derby 2 Exeter 0
Derby win 5-1 on agg
Everton 4 Lincoln 2
Everton win 8-5 on agg
Hartlepl 0 Grimsby 2
Grimsby win 5-0 on agg
Leeds U 1 Sunderld 2
Sunderld win 4-2 on agg
Leicester 2 Rochdale 1
Leicester win 8-2 on agg
Liverpool 5 Fulham 0
Liverpool win 8-1 on agg
Man Utd 2 Stoke 0
Man Utd win 3-2 on agg
Millwall 4 Watford 3 e
Millwall win 4-3 on agg
Norwich 3 Bradford 0
Norwich win 4-2 on agg
Nottm For 3 Wrexham 1
Nottm For win 6-4 on agg
Notts Co 1 Newcastle 7
Newcastle win 11-2 on agg
Oldham 2 Swansea 0
Oldham win 3-2 on agg
Oxford 1 Tranmere 1
Tranmere win 6-2 on agg
Peterboro 3 Barnsley 1 e
Peterboro win 4-2 on agg
Portsmth 5 Rotherhm 0
Portsmth win 5-0 on agg
QPR 4 Barnet 0
QPR win 6-1 on agg

Villa crushed Leeds in the 1996 Final

GIANTKILLERS

1995-96 Man United 0 York 3

York had to wait until the last match of the 1995-96 season to make sure of avoiding relegation to the Third Division, but some months earlier they had achieved a marvellous success against mighty Manchester United. York, fielding a team without a single household name (even in York) won 3-0 at Old Trafford against somewhat under-strength opponents, then managed to lose only 1-3 in the second-leg against Fergie's finest to go through.

Reading	**1**	**Man City**	**2**	
Man City win 3-2 on agg				
Sheff Utd	**2**	**Blackpool**	**0**	
Blackpool win 3-2 on agg				
Sheff Wed	**1**	**Bolton**	**0**	
Sheff Wed win 2-1 on agg				
Shrewsby	**2**	**Southmptn**	**0**	
Shrewsby win 2-1 on agg				
Tottenham	**3**	**Burnley**	**1**	
Tottenham win 3-1 on agg				
Wimbledn	**4**	**Hereford**	**1**	
Wimbledn win 5-1 on agg				
Wolves	**2**	**Swindon**	**1**	
Swindon win 3-2 on agg				
Wycombe	**4**	**Coventry**	**2**	**e**
Coventry win 5-4 on agg				
THIRD ROUND				
Arsenal	**1**	**Norwich**	**1**	
Blackburn	**0**	**Shrewsby**	**0**	
Blackpool	**2**	**Peterboro**	**2**	
Derby	**0**	**Tottenham**	**1**	
Everton	**2**	**C.Palace**	**2**	
Liverpool	**3**	**Ipswich**	**2**	
Man City	**1**	**Chelsea**	**0**	
Man Utd	**5**	**Leicester**	**1**	
Middlesbro	**1**	**Sheff Wed**	**1**	
Nottm For	**2**	**West Ham**	**1**	
Oldham	**2**	**Coventry**	**0**	
Portsmth	**2**	**Swindon**	**0**	
QPR	**3**	**Millwall**	**0**	
Sunderld	**1**	**Aston V**	**4**	
Tranmere	**4**	**Grimsby**	**1**	
Wimbledn	**2**	**Newcastle**	**1**	
C.Palace	**1**	**Everton**	**4**	**r**
Norwich	**0**	**Arsenal**	**3**	**r**
Peterboro	**2**	**Blackpool**	**1**	**r**
Sheff Wed	**2**	**Middlesbro**	**1**	**re**
Shrewsby	**3**	**Blackburn**	**4**	**re**
FOURTH ROUND				
Arsenal	**0**	**Aston V**	**1**	
Everton	**0**	**Man Utd**	**2**	
Liverpool	**1**	**Wimbledn**	**1**	
Nottm For	**0**	**Man City**	**0**	
Peterboro	**0**	**Portsmth**	**0**	
QPR	**1**	**Sheff Wed**	**2**	
Tottenham	**1**	**Blackburn**	**0**	
Tranmere	**3**	**Oldham**	**0**	
Man City	**1**	**Nottm For**	**2**	**r**
Portsmth	**1**	**Peterboro**	**0**	**re**
Wimbledn	**2**	**Liverpool**	**2**	**rP**
FIFTH ROUND				
Man Utd	**2**	**Portsmth**	**2**	
Nottm For	**1**	**Tranmere**	**1**	
Tottenham	**1**	**Aston V**	**2**	
Wimbledn	**1**	**Sheff Wed**	**2**	
Portsmth	**0**	**Man Utd**	**1**	**r**
Tranmere	**2**	**Nottm For**	**0**	**r**
SEMI-FINAL FIRST-LEG				
Man Utd	**1**	**Sheff Wed**	**0**	
Tranmere	**3**	**Aston V**	**1**	
SEMI-FINAL SECOND-LEG				
Aston V	**3**	**Tranmere**	**1**	**P**
agg score Aston V 4 - Tranmere 4				
Sheff Wed	**1**	**Man Utd**	**4**	
Man Utd win 5-1 on agg				
FINAL				
Aston V	**3**	**Man Utd**	**1**	**N**

1995

FIRST ROUND FIRST-LEG				
Barnet	**4**	**Leyton O**	**0**	
Blackpool	**1**	**Chestrfld**	**2**	
Bournemth	**2**	**N'hamptn**	**0**	
Bradford	**2**	**Grimsby**	**1**	
Brighton	**2**	**Wycombe**	**1**	
Bristol R	**1**	**Port Vale**	**3**	
Burnley	**1**	**York**	**0**	
Bury	**2**	**Hartlepl**	**0**	
Cardiff	**1**	**Torquay**	**0**	
Colchester	**0**	**Brentford**	**2**	
Crewe	**2**	**Wigan Ath**	**1**	
Darlingtn	**2**	**Barnsley**	**2**	
Doncaster	**2**	**Wrexham**	**4**	
Exeter	**2**	**Swansea**	**2**	
Gillinghm	**0**	**Reading**	**1**	
Hereford	**0**	**West Brom**	**0**	
Hull	**2**	**Scarboro**	**1**	
Lincoln	**2**	**Chester**	**0**	
Luton	**1**	**Fulham**	**1**	
Oxford	**3**	**Peterboro**	**1**	
Portsmth	**2**	**Cambridge**	**0**	
Preston NE	**1**	**Stockport**	**1**	**N**
Rochdale	**1**	**Mansfield**	**2**	
Rotherhm	**1**	**Carlisle**	**0**	
Scunthpe	**2**	**Huddersfld**	**1**	
Shrewsby	**2**	**Birmghm C**	**1**	
Southend	**0**	**Watford**	**0**	
Walsall	**4**	**Plymouth**	**0**	
FIRST ROUND SECOND-LEG				
Barnsley	**0**	**Darlingtn**	**0**	
agg score Barnsley 2 - Darlingtn 2				
Birmghm C	**2**	**Shrewsby**	**0**	
Birmghm C win 3-2 on agg				
Brentford	**2**	**Colchester**	**0**	
Brentford win 4-0 on agg				
Cambridge	**2**	**Portsmth**	**3**	
Portsmth win 5-2 on agg				
Carlisle	**3**	**Rotherhm**	**1**	
Carlisle win 3-2 on agg				
Chester	**2**	**Lincoln**	**3**	
Lincoln win 5-2 on agg				
Chestrfld	**4**	**Blackpool**	**2**	
Chestrfld win 6-3 on agg				
Fulham	**1**	**Luton**	**1**	**P**
agg score Fulham 2 - Luton 2				
Grimsby	**1**	**Bradford**	**2**	
Bradford win 4-2 on agg				
Hartlepl	**5**	**Bury**	**1**	
Hartlepl win 5-3 on agg				
Huddersfld	**3**	**Scunthpe**	**0**	
Huddersfld win 4-2 on agg				
Leyton O	**1**	**Barnet**	**1**	
Barnet win 5-1 on agg				
Mansfield	**1**	**Rochdale**	**0**	
Mansfield win 3-1 on agg				
N'hamptn	**0**	**Bournemth**	**1**	
Bournemth win 3-0 on agg				
Peterboro	**0**	**Oxford**	**1**	
Oxford win 4-1 on agg				
Plymouth	**2**	**Walsall**	**1**	
Walsall win 5-2 on agg				
Port Vale	**1**	**Bristol R**	**1**	
Port Vale win 4-2 on agg				
Reading	**3**	**Gillinghm**	**0**	
Reading win 4-0 on agg				
Scarboro	**2**	**Hull**	**0**	
Scarboro win 3-2 on agg				
Stockport	**4**	**Preston NE**	**1**	
Stockport win 5-2 on agg				
Swansea	**2**	**Exeter**	**0**	
Swansea win 4-2 on agg				
Torquay	**4**	**Cardiff**	**2**	
Torquay win 4-3 on agg				
Watford	**1**	**Southend**	**0**	
Watford win 1-0 on agg				
West Brom	**0**	**Hereford**	**1**	
Hereford win 1-0 on agg				
Wigan Ath	**3**	**Crewe**	**0**	
Wigan Ath win 4-2 on agg				
Wrexham	**1**	**Doncaster**	**1**	

Pro-File: STEVE McMANAMAN

Liverpool's Steve McManaman has the potential to become one of the best players in the world. Who says so? None other than Pele.

The Brazilian legend was so impressed with McManaman during Euro 96 that he tipped him to be one of the stars of the World Cup in France in 1998.

That is high praise indeed but there is little doubt that Macca possesses all the qualities to take him to the very top, both at domestic and international levels.

He is already an established member of the England squad and is one of the most feared players in the Premiership.

Opponents hate playing against him, and opposition managers hate trying to plan ways to stop him.

His rangey running style and his fantastic close control make him a near-on impossible player to stop when he is at full pace with the ball at his feet, but he's a great sight to watch, unless of course you are the person charged with the responsibility of trying to to stop him.

The one criticism of him is that his finishing doesn't match his approach play, but if he could add goals to his overall game he would be very nearly the finished article.

And then he would be well on the way to proving Pele exactly right.

Career details

●**Represented:** England, Liverpool ●**Position:** Winger ●**Born:** Bootle, 11.02.72 ●**Height:** 6ft ●**Weight:** 10st 6lbs ●**Club honours:** FA Cup 1992, Coca-Cola Cup 1995 ●**International honours:** England 7 U21, 15 full caps

Club League Record

Era	Club	Games	Goals
90/97	Liverpool	208	31

Cup Highlights

May 9 1992: He wins his first major honour, at the age of 20, as he helps Liverpool win the 1992 FA Cup Final with a 2-0 win over Sunderland.

April 2 1995: McManaman wins the Man of the Match award as his two goals help Liverpool beat Bolton 2-1 in the Final of the 1995 Coca-Cola Cup.

Macca On:

●Clearly we still have a little way to go to become Champions. There can be no excuses now. **McManaman on Liverpool's title failure in 1996-97**

On Macca:

●He is a terrific player and can go on to become one of the best in the world. **Pele on Macca during Euro 96**

DID YOU KNOW THAT..

●McManaman made his League debut on December 15, 1990 against Sheffield United at Anfield. Liverpool won 2-0.

●He scored his first goal on October 9, 1991 in a Rumbelows Cup Second Round, second-leg match at Stoke as Liverpool won 3-2 to complete a 5-4 aggregate victory.

●His first League goal came ten days later when he notched Liverpool's first in a 2-2 draw at Chelsea.

●His best mate at Anfield is Robbie Fowler and the pair regularly hang out together away from the club.

●He doesn't fit the popular profile of the uneducated footballer. Indeed, he writes a weekly column for The Times newspaper.

●As a schoolboy, he was a local athletics star in Liverpool.

●He was actually an Everton supporter as a youngster and used to go and watch his heroes in action at Goodison.

●Steve's nickname at Liverpool is Macca.

●McManaman made his England debut on November 16, 1994 as a substitute against Nigeria at Wembley.

Wrexham win 5-3 on agg
Wycombe 1 Brighton 3
Brighton win 5-2 on agg
York 2 Burnley 2
Burnley win 3-2 on agg

SECOND ROUND FIRST-LEG

Aston V	5	Wigan Ath	0
Barnet	1	Man City	0
Blackburn	2	Birmghm C	0
Brighton	1	Leicester	0
Bristol C	0	Notts Co	1
Carlisle	0	QPR	1
Chelsea	1	Bournemth	0
Chestrfld	1	Wolves	3
Everton	2	Portsmth	3
Fulham	3	Stoke	2
Hartlepl	0	Arsenal	5
Huddersfld	0	Southmptn	1
Ipswich	0	Bolton	3
Leeds U	0	Mansfield	1
Lincoln	1	C.Palace	0
Liverpool	2	Burnley	0
Millwall	2	Sunderld	1
Newcastle	2	Barnsley	1
Norwich	3	Swansea	0
Nottm For	2	Hereford	1
Oxford	1	Oldham	1
Port Vale	1	Man Utd	2
Reading	3	Derby	1
Scarboro	1	Middlesbro	4
Sheff Wed	2	Bradford	1
Stockport	1	Sheff Utd	5
Swindon	1	Charlton	3
Tranmere	1	Brentford	0
Walsall	2	West Ham	1
Watford	3	Tottenham	6
Wimbledn	2	Torquay	0
Wrexham	1	Coventry	2

SECOND ROUND SECOND-LEG

Arsenal 2 Hartlepl 0
Arsenal win 7-0 on agg
Barnsley 0 Newcastle 1
Newcastle win 3-1 on agg
Birmghm C 1 Blackburn 1
Blackburn win 3-1 on agg
Bolton 1 Ipswich 0
Bolton win 4-0 on agg
Bournemth 0 Chelsea 1
Chelsea win 2-0 on agg
Bradford 1 Sheff Wed 1
Sheff Wed win 3-2 on agg
Brentford 0 Tranmere 0
Tranmere win 1-0 on agg
Burnley 1 Liverpool 4
Liverpool win 6-1 on agg

Denis the Manace

Denis Irwin has played in four League Cup Finals during the 1990s, one for Oldham and three for Manchester United.

Charlton 1 Swindon 4 e
Swindon win 5-4 on agg
Coventry 3 Wrexham 2
Coventry win 5-3 on agg
C.Palace 3 Lincoln 0 e
C.Palace win 3-1 on agg
Derby 2 Reading 0
agg score Derby 3 - Reading 3
Hereford 0 Nottm For 0
Nottm For win 2-1 on agg
Leicester 0 Brighton 2
Brighton win 3-0 on agg
Man City 4 Barnet 1
Man City win 4-2 on agg
Man Utd 2 Port Vale 0
Man Utd win 4-1 on agg
Mansfield 0 Leeds U 0
Mansfield win 1-0 on agg
Middlesbro 4 Scarboro 1
Middlesbro win 8-2 on agg
Notts Co 3 Bristol C 0
Notts Co win 4-0 on agg
Oldham 1 Oxford 0
Oldham win 2-1 on agg
Portsmth 1 Everton 1
Portsmth win 4-3 on agg
QPR 2 Carlisle 0
QPR win 3-0 on agg
Sheff Utd 1 Stockport 0
Sheff Utd win 6-1 on agg
Southmptn 4 Huddersfld 0
Southmptn win 5-0 on agg
Stoke 1 Fulham 0
agg score Stoke 3 - Fulham 3
Sunderld 1 Millwall 1
Millwall win 3-2 on agg
Swansea 1 Norwich 0
Norwich win 3-1 on agg
Torquay 0 Wimbledn 1
Wimbledn win 3-0 on agg
Tottenham 2 Watford 3
Tottenham win 8-6 on agg
West Ham 2 Walsall 0 e
West Ham win 3-2 on agg
Wigan Ath 0 Aston V 3
Wolves 1 Chestrfld 1
Wolves win 4-2 on agg

THIRD ROUND

Aston V	1	Middlesbro	0	
Blackburn	2	Coventry	0	
Brighton	1	Swindon	1	
Liverpool	2	Stoke	1	
Mansfield	0	Millwall	2	
Newcastle	2	Man Utd	0	
Notts Co	3	Tottenham	0	
Oldham	0	Arsenal	0	
Portsmth	0	Derby	1	
QPR	3	Man City	4	
Sheff Utd	1	Bolton	2	
Sheff Wed	1	Southmptn	0	
Tranmere	1	Norwich	1	
West Ham	1	Chelsea	0	
Wimbledn	0	C.Palace	1	
Wolves	2	Nottm For	3	
Arsenal	2	Oldham	0	r
Norwich	4	Tranmere	2	r
Swindon	4	Brighton	1	r

Strange but true!

Michael Thomas, a Liverpool substitute in the 1995 League Cup Final against Bolton, had been an Arsenal substitute in the 1987 Final...against Liverpool.

FOURTH ROUND

Arsenal	2	Sheff Wed	0	
Blackburn	1	Liverpool	3	
C.Palace	4	Aston V	1	
Man City	1	Newcastle	1	
Norwich	1	Notts Co	0	
Nottm For	0	Millwall	2	
Swindon	2	Derby	1	
West Ham	1	Bolton	3	
Newcastle	0	Man City	2	r

FIFTH ROUND

Bolton	1	Norwich	0
C.Palace	4	Man City	0
Liverpool	1	Arsenal	0
Swindon	3	Millwall	1

SEMI-FINAL FIRST-LEG

Liverpool 1 C.Palace 0
Swindon 2 Bolton 1

SEMI-FINAL SECOND-LEG

Bolton 3 Swindon 1
Bolton win 4-3 on agg
C.Palace 0 Liverpool 1
Liverpool win 2-0 on agg

FINAL

Liverpool 2 Bolton 1 N

1996

FIRST ROUND FIRST-LEG

Barnet	0	Charlton	0
Birmghm C	1	Plymouth	0
Bradford	2	Blackpool	1
Cambridge	2	Swindon	1
Chester	4	Wigan Ath	1
Chestrfld	0	Bury	1
Colchester	2	Bristol C	1
Crewe	4	Darlingtn	0
Doncaster	1	Shrewsby	1
Fulham	3	Brighton	0
Gillinghm	1	Bristol R	1
Hereford	0	Oxford	2
Huddersfld	1	Port Vale	2
Hull	1	Carlisle	2
Luton	1	Bournemth	1
Mansfield	0	Burnley	1
Notts Co	2	Lincoln	0
Portsmth	0	Cardiff	2
Preston NE	1	Sunderld	1
Rochdale	2	York	1
Scarboro	1	Hartlepl	0
Scunthpe	4	Rotherhm	1
Stockport	1	Wrexham	0

Swansea	**4**	**Peterboro**	**1**	
Torquay	**0**	**Exeter**	**0**	
Walsall	**2**	**Brentford**	**2**	
West Brom	**1**	**N'hamptn**	**1**	
Wycombe	**3**	**Leyton O**	**0**	
FIRST ROUND SECOND-LEG				
Blackpool	**2**	**Bradford**	**3**	
Bradford win 5-3 on agg				
Bournemth	**2**	**Luton**	**1**	e
Bournemth win 3-2 on agg				
Brentford	**3**	**Walsall**	**2**	
Brentford win 5-4 on agg				
Brighton	**0**	**Fulham**	**2**	
Fulham win 5-0 on agg				
Bristol C	**2**	**Colchester**	**1**	P
agg score Bristol C 3 - Colchester 3				
Bristol R	**4**	**Gillinghm**	**2**	
Bristol R win 5-3 on agg				
Burnley	**3**	**Mansfield**	**1**	
Burnley win 4-1 on agg				
Bury	**2**	**Chestrfld**	**1**	
Bury win 3-1 on agg				
Cardiff	**1**	**Portsmth**	**0**	
Cardiff win 3-0 on agg				
Carlisle	**2**	**Hull**	**4**	
Hull win 5-4 on agg				
Charlton	**2**	**Barnet**	**0**	
Charlton win 2-0 on agg				
Darlingtn	**1**	**Crewe**	**1**	
Crewe win 5-1 on agg				
Exeter	**1**	**Torquay**	**1**	a
agg score Exeter 1 - Torquay 1				
Hartlepl	**1**	**Scarboro**	**0**	P
agg score Hartlepl 1 - Scarboro 1				
Leyton O	**2**	**Wycombe**	**0**	
Wycombe win 3-2 on agg				
Lincoln	**0**	**Notts Co**	**2**	
Notts Co win 4-0 on agg				
N'hamptn	**2**	**West Brom**	**4**	
West Brom win 5-3 on agg				
Oxford	**3**	**Hereford**	**2**	
Oxford win 5-2 on agg				
Peterboro	**3**	**Swansea**	**0**	
agg score Peterboro 4 - Swansea 4				
Plymouth	**1**	**Birmghm C**	**2**	
Birmghm C win 3-1 on agg				
Port Vale	**1**	**Huddersfld**	**3**	
Huddersfld win 4-3 on agg				
Rotherhm	**5**	**Scunthpe**	**0**	e
Rotherhm win 6-4 on agg				
Shrewsby	**0**	**Doncaster**	**0**	
agg score Shrewsby 1 - D'caster 1				
Sunderld	**3**	**Preston NE**	**2**	
Sunderld win 4-3 on agg				
Swindon	**2**	**Cambridge**	**0**	
Swindon win 3-2 on agg				
Wigan Ath	**1**	**Chester**	**3**	
Chester win 7-2 on agg				
Wrexham	**2**	**Stockport**	**2**	
Stockport win 3-2 on agg				
York	**5**	**Rochdale**	**1**	e
York win 6-3 on agg				
SECOND ROUND FIRST-LEG				
Aston V	**6**	**Peterboro**	**0**	
Birmghm C	**3**	**Grimsby**	**1**	
Bolton	**1**	**Brentford**	**0**	
Bradford	**3**	**Nottm For**	**2**	
Bristol C	**0**	**Newcastle**	**5**	
Bristol R	**0**	**West Ham**	**1**	
Cardiff	**0**	**Southmptn**	**3**	
Coventry	**2**	**Hull**	**0**	
Crewe	**2**	**Sheff Wed**	**2**	
Hartlepl	**0**	**Arsenal**	**3**	
Huddersfld	**2**	**Barnsley**	**0**	
Leeds U	**0**	**Notts Co**	**0**	
Leicester	**2**	**Burnley**	**0**	
Liverpool	**2**	**Sunderld**	**0**	
Man Utd	**0**	**York**	**3**	
Middlesbro	**2**	**Rotherhm**	**1**	
Millwall	**0**	**Everton**	**0**	
Norwich	**6**	**Torquay**	**1**	
Oxford	**1**	**QPR**	**1**	
Reading	**1**	**West Brom**	**1**	
Sheff Utd	**2**	**Bury**	**1**	
Shrewsby	**1**	**Derby**	**3**	
Southend	**2**	**C.Palace**	**2**	
Stockport	**1**	**Ipswich**	**1**	
Stoke	**0**	**Chelsea**	**0**	
Swindon	**2**	**Blackburn**	**3**	
Tottenham	**4**	**Chester**	**0**	
Tranmere	**1**	**Oldham**	**0**	
Watford	**1**	**Bournemth**	**1**	
Wimbledn	**4**	**Charlton**	**5**	
Wolves	**2**	**Fulham**	**0**	
Wycombe	**0**	**Man City**	**0**	
SECOND ROUND SECOND-LEG				
Arsenal	**5**	**Hartlepl**	**0**	
Arsenal win 8-0 on agg				
Barnsley	**4**	**Huddersfld**	**0**	
Barnsley win 4-2 on agg				
Blackburn	**2**	**Swindon**	**0**	
Blackburn win 5-2 on agg				
Bournemth	**1**	**Watford**	**1**	q
agg score B'nemth 2 - Watford 2				
Brentford	**2**	**Bolton**	**3**	
Bolton win 4-2 on agg				
Burnley	**0**	**Leicester**	**2**	
Leicester win 4-0 on agg				
Bury	**4**	**Sheff Utd**	**2**	
Bury win 5-4 on agg				
Charlton	**3**	**Wimbledn**	**3**	e
Charlton win 8-7 on agg				
Chelsea	**0**	**Stoke**	**1**	
Stoke win 1-0 on agg				
Chester	**1**	**Tottenham**	**3**	
Tottenham win 7-1 on agg				
C.Palace	**2**	**Southend**	**0**	
C.Palace win 4-2 on agg				
Derby	**1**	**Shrewsby**	**1**	
Derby win 4-2 on agg				
Everton	**2**	**Millwall**	**4**	e
Millwall win 4-2 on agg				
Fulham	**1**	**Wolves**	**5**	
Wolves win 7-1 on agg				
Grimsby	**1**	**Birmghm C**	**1**	
Birmghm C win 4-2 on agg				
Hull	**0**	**Coventry**	**1**	
Coventry win 3-0 on agg				
Ipswich	**1**	**Stockport**	**2**	e
Stockport win 3-2 on agg				
Man City	**4**	**Wycombe**	**0**	
Man City win 4-0 on agg				
Newcastle	**3**	**Bristol C**	**1**	
Newcastle win 8-1 on agg				
Nottm For	**2**	**Bradford**	**2**	
Bradford win 5-4 on agg				
Notts Co	**2**	**Leeds U**	**3**	
Leeds U win 3-2 on agg				
Oldham	**1**	**Tranmere**	**3**	
Tranmere win 4-1 on agg				
Peterboro	**1**	**Aston V**	**1**	
Aston V win 7-1 on agg				
QPR	**2**	**Oxford**	**1**	e
QPR win 3-2 on agg				
Rotherhm	**0**	**Middlesbro**	**1**	
Middlesbro win 3-1 on agg				
Sheff Wed	**5**	**Crewe**	**2**	
Sheff Wed win 7-4 on agg				
Southmptn	**2**	**Cardiff**	**1**	
Southmptn win 5-1 on agg				
Sunderld	**0**	**Liverpool**	**1**	
Liverpool win 3-0 on agg				
Torquay	**2**	**Norwich**	**3**	
Norwich win 9-3 on agg				
West Brom	**2**	**Reading**	**4**	
Reading win 5-3 on agg				

WHAT A STAR ✪ FABRIZIO RAVANELLI

He helped Middlesbrough reach their first major Final - the Coca-Cola Cup - in 1997, scoring eight goals along the way. Sadly for the big Italian, the day didn't have a fairytale ending. Although he scored the first goal against Leicester, The Foxes equalised with virtually the last kick of the game through Emile Heskey, and then won the replay 1-0 with a goal from Steve Claridge. To add insult to injury, Boro also lost the FA Cup Final to Chelsea and Ravanelli was injured early on.

West Ham	3	Bristol R	0	
West Ham win 4-0 on agg				
York	1	Man Utd	3	
York win 4-3 on agg				
THIRD ROUND				
Aston V	2	Stockport	0	
Barnsley	0	Arsenal	3	
Birmghm C	1	Tranmere	1	
Bolton	0	Leicester	0	
Coventry	3	Tottenham	2	
C.Palace	2	Middlesbro	2	
Derby	0	Leeds U	1	
Liverpool	4	Man City	0	
Millwall	0	Sheff Wed	2	
Norwich	0	Bradford	0	
QPR	3	York	1	
Reading	0	Bury	2	
Reading	2	Bury	1	
Southmptn	2	West Ham	1	
Stoke	0	Newcastle	4	
Watford	1	Blackburn	2	
Bradford	3	Norwich	5	re
Charlton	1	Wolves	2	re
Leicester	2	Bolton	3	r
Middlesbro	2	C.Palace	0	r
Tranmere	1	Birmghm C	3	re
FOURTH ROUND				
Arsenal	2	Sheff Wed	1	
Aston V	1	QPR	0	
Leeds U	2	Blackburn	1	
Liverpool	0	Newcastle	1	
Middlesbro	0	Birmghm C	0	
Norwich	0	Bolton	0	
Reading	2	Southmptn	1	
Wolves	2	Coventry	1	
Birmghm C	2	Middlesbro	0	r
Bolton	0	Norwich	0	rq
FIFTH ROUND				
Arsenal	2	Newcastle	0	
Aston V	1	Wolves	0	
Leeds U	2	Reading	1	
Norwich	1	Birmghm C	1	
Birmghm C	2	Norwich	1	r
SEMI-FINAL FIRST-LEG				
Arsenal	2	Aston V	2	
Birmghm C	1	Leeds U	2	
SEMI-FINAL SECOND-LEG				
Aston V	0	Arsenal	0	
agg score Aston V 2 - Arsenal 2				
Leeds U	3	Birmghm C	0	
Leeds U win 5-1 on agg				
FINAL				
Aston V	3	Leeds U	0	N

Dynamic Duo

Chris Woods and Viv Anderson played in the Sheffield Wednesday team in the 1993 League Cup Final - 15 years after they had appeared together in Forest's Final line-up.

Juninho and Boro had to settle for second best in '97

1997

FIRST ROUND FIRST-LEG			
Brentford	1	Plymouth	0
Brighton	0	Birmghm C	1
Cardiff	1	N'hamptn	0
Carlisle	1	Chester	0
Darlingtn	1	Rotherhm	0
Doncaster	1	York	1
Exeter	0	Barnet	4
Hartlepl	2	Lincoln	2
Huddersfld	3	Wrexham	0
Hull	2	Scarboro	2
Ipswich	2	Bournemth	1
Luton	3	Bristol R	0
Mansfield	0	Burnley	3
Millwall	1	Peterboro	0
Notts Co	1	Bury	1
Oldham	0	Grimsby	1
Oxford	1	Norwich	1
Port Vale	1	Crewe	0
Portsmth	2	Leyton O	0
Reading	1	Wycombe	1
Rochdale	2	Barnsley	1
Scunthpe	2	Blackpool	1
Sheff Utd	3	Bradford	0
Shrewsby	0	Tranmere	2
Southend	0	Fulham	2
Stockport	2	Chestrfld	1
Swansea	0	Gillinghm	1
Swindon	2	Wolves	0
Torquay	3	Bristol C	3
Walsall	1	Watford	0
Wigan Ath	2	Preston NE	3
FIRST ROUND SECOND-LEG			
Barnet	2	Exeter	0
Barnet win 6-0 on agg			
Barnsley	2	Rochdale	0
Barnsley win 3-2 on agg			
Birmghm C	2	Brighton	0
Birmghm C win 3-0 on agg			
Blackpool	2	Scunthpe	0
Blackpool win 3-2 on agg			
Bournemth	0	Ipswich	3
Ipswich win 5-1 on agg			
Bradford	1	Sheff Utd	2
Sheff Utd win 5-1 on agg			
Bristol C	1	Torquay	0
Bristol C win 4-3 on agg			
Bristol R	2	Luton	1
Luton win 4-2 on agg			
Burnley	2	Mansfield	0
Burnley win 5-0 on agg			
Bury	1	Notts Co	0
Bury win 2-1 on agg			
Chester	1	Carlisle	3
Carlisle win 4-1 on agg			
Chestrfld	1	Stockport	2
Stockport win 4-2 on agg			
Crewe	1	Port Vale	5
Port Vale win 6-1 on agg			
Fulham	1	Southend	2
Fulham win 3-2 on agg			

Gillinghm	2	Swansea	0	
Gillinghm win 3-0 on agg				
Grimsby	0	Oldham	1	q
agg score Grimsby 1 - Oldham 1				
Leyton O	1	Portsmth	0	
Portsmth win 2-1 on agg				
Lincoln	3	Hartlepl	2	
Lincoln win 5-4 on agg				
N'hamptn	2	Cardiff	0	
N'hamptn win 2-1 on agg				
Norwich	2	Oxford	3	e
Oxford win 4-3 on agg				
Peterboro	2	Millwall	0	e
Peterboro win 2-1 on agg				
Plymouth	0	Brentford	0	
Brentford win 1-0 on agg				
Preston NE	4	Wigan Ath	4	e
Preston NE win 7-6 on agg				
Rotherhm	0	Darlingtn	1	
Darlingtn win 2-0 on agg				
Scarboro	3	Hull	2	
Scarboro win 5-4 on agg				
Tranmere	1	Shrewsby	1	
Tranmere win 3-1 on agg				
Watford	2	Walsall	0	
Watford win 2-1 on agg				
Wolves	1	Swindon	0	
Swindon win 2-1 on agg				
Wrexham	1	Huddersfld	2	
Huddersfld win 5-1 on agg				
Wycombe	2	Reading	0	
Wycombe win 3-1 on agg				
York	2	Doncaster	0	
York win 3-1 on agg				
SECOND ROUND FIRST-LEG				
Barnet	1	West Ham	1	
Barnsley	1	Gillinghm	1	
Blackpool	1	Chelsea	4	
Brentford	1	Blackburn	2	
Bristol C	0	Bolton	0	
Bury	1	C.Palace	3	
Charlton	4	Burnley	1	
Coventry	1	Birmghm C	1	
Everton	1	York	1	
Fulham	1	Ipswich	1	
Huddersfld	1	Colchester	1	
Leeds U	2	Darlingtn	2	
Lincoln	4	Man City	1	
Luton	1	Derby	0	
Middlesbro	7	Hereford	0	
Nottm For	1	Wycombe	0	
Oldham	2	Tranmere	2	
Port Vale	1	Carlisle	0	
Preston NE	1	Tottenham	1	
Scarboro	0	Leicester	2	
Sheff Wed	1	Oxford	1	
Southmptn	2	Peterboro	0	
Stockport	2	Sheff Utd	1	
Stoke	1	N'hamptn	0	
Swindon	1	QPR	2	
Watford	0	Sunderld	2	
Wimbledn	1	Portsmth	0	
SECOND ROUND SECOND-LEG				
Birmghm C	0	Coventry	1	
Coventry win 2-1 on agg				
Blackburn	2	Brentford	0	
Blackburn win 4-1 on agg				
Bolton	3	Bristol C	1	e
Bolton win 3-1 on agg				
Burnley	1	Charlton	2	
Charlton win 6-2 on agg				
Carlisle	9	Port Vale	0	
Carlisle win 9-1 on agg				
Chelsea	1	Blackpool	3	
Chelsea win 5-4 on agg				
Colchester	0	Huddersfld	2	e
Huddersfld win 3-1 on agg				
C.Palace	4	Bury	0	
C.Palace win 7-1 on agg				
Darlingtn	0	Leeds U	2	
Leeds U win 4-2 on agg				
Derby	2	Luton	2	
Luton win 3-2 on agg				
Gillinghm	1	Barnsley	0	
Gillinghm win 2-1 on agg				
Hereford	0	Middlesbro	3	
Middlesbro win 10-0 on agg				
Ipswich	4	Fulham	2	
Ipswich win 5-3 on agg				
Leicester	2	Scarboro	1	
Leicester win 4-1 on agg				
Man City	0	Lincoln	1	
Lincoln win 5-1 on agg				
N'hamptn	1	Stoke	2	e
Stoke win 3-1 on agg				
Oxford	1	Sheff Wed	0	
Oxford win 2-1 on agg				
Peterboro	1	Southmptn	4	
Southmptn win 6-1 on agg				

Yankee Doodle

Sheffield Wednesday's John Harkes became the first American to play in a major Final at Wembley when he faced Arsenal in 1993. He also scored, but Wednesday lost 2-1.

Steve Claridge wins the League Cup for Leicester

WHAT A STAR ✪ STEVE CLARIDGE

Juninho, Ravanelli, Emerson, all great names and all great players. But they were all upstaged in the 1997 Coca-Cola Cup Final by a scruffy Englishman who used to sell fruit and veg on a market stall. Leicester striker Steve Claridge is one of football's unfashionable heroes, with his ungainly style and his socks rolled down to his ankles. But one thing he is smart at is putting the ball in the net. He scored the goal that rocketed Leicester into the Premiership in the play-off Final against Crystal Palace in May 1996, and almost a year later he grabbed the winner in the Final replay to beat Middlesbrough and earn Leicester a place in Europe, and him a place in history.

Portsmth	**1**	**Wimbledn**	**1**	
Wimbledn win 2-1 on agg				
QPR	**1**	**Swindon**	**3**	e
Swindon win 4-3 on agg				
Sheff Utd	**2**	**Stockport**	**5**	
Stockport win 7-3 on agg				
Sunderld	**1**	**Watford**	**0**	
Sunderld win 3-0 on agg				
Tottenham	**3**	**Preston NE**	**0**	
Tottenham win 4-1 on agg				
Tranmere	**0**	**Oldham**	**1**	
Oldham win 3-2 on agg				
West Ham	**1**	**Barnet**	**0**	
West Ham win 2-1 on agg				
Wycombe	**1**	**Nottm For**	**1**	e
Nottm For win 2-1 on agg				
York	**3**	**Everton**	**2**	
York win 4-3 on agg				

Claridge's greatest moment as he lifts the Coca-Cola Cup

THIRD ROUND				
Blackburn	**0**	**Stockport**	**1**	
Bolton	**2**	**Chelsea**	**1**	
Charlton	**1**	**Liverpool**	**1**	
Gillinghm	**2**	**Coventry**	**2**	
Ipswich	**4**	**C.Palace**	**1**	
Leeds U	**1**	**Aston V**	**2**	
Man Utd	**2**	**Swindon**	**1**	
Middlesbro	**5**	**Huddersfld**	**1**	
Newcastle	**1**	**Oldham**	**0**	
Port Vale	**0**	**Oxford**	**0**	
Southmptn	**2**	**Lincoln**	**2**	
Stoke	**1**	**Arsenal**	**1**	
Tottenham	**2**	**Sunderld**	**1**	
West Ham	**4**	**Nottm For**	**1**	
Wimbledn	**1**	**Luton**	**1**	
York	**0**	**Leicester**	**2**	
Lincoln	**1**	**Southmptn**	**3**	r
Luton	**1**	**Wimbledn**	**2**	re
Oxford	**2**	**Port Vale**	**0**	r
FOURTH ROUND				
Bolton	**6**	**Tottenham**	**1**	
Ipswich	**1**	**Gillinghm**	**0**	
Leicester	**2**	**Man Utd**	**0**	
Liverpool	**4**	**Arsenal**	**2**	
Middlesbro	**3**	**Newcastle**	**1**	
Oxford	**1**	**Southmptn**	**1**	
West Ham	**1**	**Stockport**	**1**	
Wimbledn	**1**	**Aston V**	**0**	
Southmptn	**3**	**Oxford**	**2**	r
Stockport	**2**	**West Ham**	**1**	r
FIFTH ROUND				
Bolton	**0**	**Wimbledn**	**2**	
Ipswich	**0**	**Leicester**	**1**	
Middlesbro	**2**	**Liverpool**	**1**	
Stockport	**2**	**Southmptn**	**2**	
Southmptn	**1**	**Stockport**	**2**	r
SEMI-FINAL FIRST-LEG				
Leicester	**0**	**Wimbledn**	**0**	
Stockport	**0**	**Middlesbro**	**2**	
SEMI-FINAL SECOND-LEG				
Middlesbro	**0**	**Stockport**	**1**	
Middlesbro win 2-1 on agg				
Wimbledn	**1**	**Leicester**	**1**	a
agg score W'bledn 1 - Leicester 1				
FINAL				
Leicester	**1**	**Middlesbro**	**1**	eN
Leicester	**1**	**Middlesbro**	**0**	reN

FOR THE RECORD

ROLL OF HONOUR

FA CUP

WINNERS:

9	Man Utd
8	Tottenham Hotspur
7	Aston Villa
6	Arsenal, Blackburn Rovers, Newcastle Utd
5	Everton, Liverpool, The Wanderers, West Bromwich Albion
4	Bolton Wanderers, Man City, Sheff Utd, Wolves
3	Sheff Wed, West Ham
2	Bury, Chelsea, Nottm Forest, Old Etonians, Preston NE, Sunderland
1	Barnsley, Blackburn Olympic, Blackpool, Bradford City, Burnley, Cardiff City, Charlton Athletic, Clapham Rovers, Coventry City, Derby County, Huddersfield Town, Ipswich Town, Leeds United, Notts Co, Old Carthusians, Oxford University, Portsmouth, Royal Engineers, Southampton, Wimbledon

APPEARANCES IN FINALS (FIGURES DO NOT INCLUDE REPLAYS):

14	Man Utd
12	Arsenal, Everton
11	Liverpool, Newcastle Utd
10	West Bromwich Albion
9	Aston Villa, Tottenham Hotspur
8	Blackburn Rovers, Man City, Wolves
7	Bolton Wanderers, Preston North End
6	Old Etonians, Sheff Utd, Sheff Wed
5	Huddersfield, The Wanderers*, Chelsea
4	Derby County, Leeds Utd, Leicester City, Oxford University, Royal Engineers, Sunderland, West Ham United
3	Blackpool, Burnley, Nottm Forest, Portsmouth, Southampton
2	Barnsley, Birmingham City, Bury*, Cardiff City, Charlton Athletic,

Clapham Rovers, Notts Co, Queen's Park (Glasgow)

1 Blackburn Olympic*, Bradford City*, Brighton & HA, Bristol City, Coventry City*, Crystal Palace, Fulham, Ipswich Town*, Luton Town, Middlesbrough, Old Carthusians*, Queens Park Rangers, Watford, Wimbledon*

(Denotes: Undefeated)*

APPEARANCES IN SEMI-FINALS (FIGURES DO NOT INCLUDE REPLAYS):

23 Everton

21 Man Utd

20 Liverpool

19 West Bromwich Albion

18 Arsenal, Aston Villa

16 Blackburn Rovers, Sheff Wed

15 Tottenham Hotspur

13 Chelsea, Derby Co, Newcastle Utd, Wolves

12 Bolton Wanderers, Nottm Forest

11 Sheff Utd, Sunderland

10 Man City, Preston NE, Southampton

9 Birmingham City

8 Burnley, Leeds United

7 Huddersfield Town, Leicester City

6 Old Etonians, Oxford University, West Ham Utd

5 Fulham, Notts Co, Portsmouth, The Wanderers

4 Luton Town, Queens Park (Glasgow), Royal Engineers

3 Blackpool, Cardiff City, Clapham Rovers, Crystal Palace*, Ipswich Town, Millwall, Norwich City, Old Carthusians, Oldham Athletic, Stoke City, The Swifts, Watford

2 Barnsley, Blackburn Olympic, Bristol City, Bury, Charlton Athletic, Grimsby Town, Swansea Town, Swindon Town, Wimbledon

1 Bradford City, Brighton & HA, Cambridge University, Chesterfield United, Coventry City, Crewe Alexandra, Darwen, Derby Junction, Hull City, Marlow, Middlesbrough, Old Harrovians, Orient, Plymouth Argyle, Port Vale, QPR, Rangers (Glasgow), Reading, Shropshire Wanderers, York City

(Denotes: A previous, and different, Crystal Palace club reached the FA Cup Semi-Final in 1871-72)*

LEAGUE CUP

WINNERS:

5 Aston Villa, Liverpool

4 Nottm Forest

2 Arsenal, Leicester City, Man City, Norwich City, Tottenham Hotspur, Wolves

1 Birmingham City, Chelsea, Leeds Utd, Luton Town, Man Utd,

	Oxford Utd, QPR, Sheff Wed, Stoke City, Swindon Town, West Bromwich Albion

APPEARANCES IN FINALS (FIGURES DO NOT INCLUDE REPLAYS):

7	Aston Villa, Liverpool
6	Nottm Forest
5	Arsenal
4	Man Utd, Norwich City
3	Leicester City, Man City, Tottenham Hotspur, West Bromwich Albion
2	Chelsea, Everton, Leeds United, Luton Town, QPR, Sheff Wed, Stoke City, West Ham Utd, Wolves
1	Birmingham City, Bolton Wanderers, Middlesbrough, Newcastle Utd, Oldham Athletic, Oxford Utd, Rochdale, Rotherham, Southampton, Sunderland, Swindon.

APPEARANCES IN SEMI-FINALS (FIGURES DO NOT INCLUDE REPLAYS):

10	Aston Villa
9	Liverpool
8	Arsenal, Tottenham Hotspur
7	Man Utd, West Ham Utd
6	Nottm Forest
5	Chelsea, Leeds Utd, Man City, Norwich City
4	West Bromwich Albion
3	Birmingham City, Burnley, Everton, Leicester City, Middlesbrough, QPR, Sheff Wed, Swindon, Wolves
2	Blackburn Rovers, Bolton Wanderers, Bristol City, Coventry City, Crystal Palace, Ipswich Town, Luton Town, Oxford Utd, Plymouth Argyle, Southampton, Stoke City, Sunderland
1	Blackpool, Bury, Cardiff City, Carlisle Utd, Chester City, Derby Co, Huddersfield Town, Newcastle Utd, Oldham Athletic, Peterborough Utd, Rochdale, Rotherham Utd, Shrewsbury Town, Stockport Co, Tranmere Rovers, Walsall, Watford, Wimbledon

THE LEAGUE CUP IN ALL ITS GUISES:

1961 to 1981	The League Cup
1982 to 1986	The Milk Cup
1987 to 1990	The Littlewoods Cup
1991 to 1992	The Rumbelows League Cup
1993 to 1997	The Coca-Cola Cup

OTHER COMPETITIONS

The FULL MEMBERS' CUP FINALS (1986 to 1992. At Wembley)

AS FULL MEMBERS' CUP

1985-86 Chelsea 5, Man City 4

1986-87 Blackburn Rovers 1, Charlton Athletic 0

AS SIMOD CUP

1987-88 Reading 4, Luton Town 1

1988-89 Nottingham Forest 4, Everton 3

AS ZENITH DATA SYSTEMS CUP

1989-90 Chelsea 1, Middlesbrough 0

1990-91 Crystal Palace 4, Everton 1

1991-92 Nottingham Forest 3, Southampton 2

The ASSOCIATE MEMBERS' CUP FINALS
(1984 to Present. At Wembley unless stated)

AS ASSOCIATE MEMBERS' CUP

1984 Bournemouth 2, Hull City 1 (at Hull)

AS FREIGHT ROVER TROPHY

1985 Wigan Athletic 3, Brentford 1

1986 Bristol City 3, Bolton Wanderers 0

1987 Mansfield Town 1, Bristol City 1
(aet: Mansfield won 5-4 on penalties)

AS SHERPA VAN TROPHY

1988 Wolves 2, Burnley 0

1989 Bolton Wanderers 4, Torquay United 1

AS LEYLAND DAF CUP

1990 Tranmere Rovers 2, Bristol Rovers 1

1991 Birmingham City 3, Tranmere Rovers 2

AS AUTOGLASS TROPHY

1992 Stoke City 1, Stockport County 0

1993 Port Vale 2, Stockport County 1

1994 Huddersfield Town 1, Swansea City 1
(aet: Swansea won 3-1 on penalties)

AS AUTO WINDSCREENS SHIELD

1995 Birmingham City 1, Carlise United 0
(After 90 minutes 0-0. Birmingham won in sudden-death overtime)

1996	Rotherham United 2, Shrewsbury Town 1
1997	Carlisle United 0, Colchester United 0

(aet: Carlisle won 4-3 on penalties)

ANGLO-ITALIAN CUP FINALS (1970 to 1973 and 1993 to 1996)

1970	*Napoli 0, Swindon Town 3
1971	*Bologna 1, Blackpool 2 (aet)
1972	*AS Roma 3, Blackpool 1
1973	*Fiorentina 1, Newcastle United 2
1993	Derby County 1, Cremonese 3 (at Wembley)
1994	Notts County 0, Brescia 1 (at Wembley)
1995	Ascoli 1, Notts County 2 (at Wembley)
1996	Port Vale 2, Genoa 5 (at Wembley)

(* Denotes: home team)

SCREEN SPORT SUPER CUP

1985/86	Liverpool 3, Everton 1
	Everton 1, Liverpool 4

Liverpool won the tournament 7-2 on aggregate. Although the competition was mainly staged in 1985/86, the two-leg Final wasn't contested until early the following season.

Carlisle lift the 1997 Auto Windscreens Shield

AND FINALLY

AN A-Z OF THE FA CUP

A is for Aldridge, an early scorer against Everton in 1989 - the only goal Liverpool have managed in the first half in ANY of their 11 FA Cup Finals.

B is for bursting. The ball went pop in both the 1946 and 1947 Finals.

C is for Coventry, who won one of the Cup's great Finals when they beat Tottenham 3-2 in 1987.

D is Derek Dougan of Blackburn, who played in the 1960 Final which Rovers lost 3-0 to Wolves. On the morning of the game he had broken the usual pre-match routine by asking for a transfer.

E is for Everton, still the only side to come back from 0-2 down to win the Cup. They did it when they beat Sheffield Wednesday 3-2 in 1966

F is for Finney, who achieved much in the game but played in only one FA Cup Final, for Preston against West Brom in 1954. His team lost 3-2.

A familiar sight as Liverpool parade the FA Cup

G is for gate receipts. Now megabucks, but the 123,000 who officially attended the 1923 Final paid a total of just £2,776.

H is for hat-trick. There has been only one in a Wembley FA Cup Final, by Stan Mortensen for Blackpool v Bolton in 1953.

I is for Irwin, Denis, who played in seven Wembley Finals in seven years between 1990 and 1996. He played for Oldham in the League Cup in 1990, and then with Manchester United he played in the League Cup in 1991, 1992 and 1994, and in the FA Cup in 1994, 1995 and 1996.

J is for Jones, unlucky Mick of Leeds. He scored against Chelsea in the 1970 Final draw. He scored in the replay. His team were level or in front for all but six minutes of the two games spread over four hours. And he still finished on the losing side.

K is Kevin Keegan, who turned in a Wembley wonder-show, and scored two goals, when Liverpool beat Newcastle 3-0 in the 1974 Final.

L is Leicester's lousy luck. They have played in four FA Cup Finals and lost the lot. And in 1969, when they lost to Manchester City, they were relegated as well!

M is for misprints, or so it seemed. In 1993, Viv Anderson of Sheffield Wednesday wore Anderson on his back and Sanderson (Wednesday's sponsor) on his front.

N is for numbers, first worn from 1-22 as an experiment in the 1933 Final.

O is for Osgood, the last player to score in every round of the Cup in one season. He did so for Chelsea in 1970.

P is for penalty. There have been 11 in Wembley finals and only two players have missed - John Aldridge in 1988 and Gary Lineker in 1991.

Q is for Quigley (Forest 1959), Quixall (Man United 1963) and Quinn (Sheff Wed 1966). They are the only Wembley FA Cup Finalists whose surnames began with a Q.

R is for Rice, Arsenal full-back Pat, the only man to play in five post-war Wembley FA Cup Finals, with a replay. He won two and lost three.

S is for Stan, as in Matthews and Mortensen, the heroes of Blackpool's 4-3 win over Bolton in 1953.

T is for Tottenham, who will be looking forward to the FA Cup in 2001. They won the Cup in 1901, 1921, 1961, 1981 and 1991.

U is for unbeaten, as in Arsenal's post-war record run of 21 FA Cup-ties (11 won, 10 drawn) between January 1979 and May 1980.

V is for vicar, the Reverend Kenneth Hunt, who scored one of the goals when Wolves beat Newcastle 3-1 in the 1909 Final.

W is for Wembley, which has been the home of the FA Cup Final since 1923.

X is for draw. There have been only six out of 68 Wembley Finals. They came in 1970, 1981, 1982, 1983, 1990 and 1993.

Y is for Young, Arsenal defender Willie, who became Public Enemy No.1 for pulling down West Ham's Paul Allen, Wembley's youngest ever Finalist, as he was going through on goal in 1980. Incredibly, Young was not sent-off.

Z is for Zimbabwe, as represented by Bruce Grobbelaar, who is only the second goalkeeper, after Dick Pym of Bolton in the 1920s, to play in three FA Cup-winning teams.

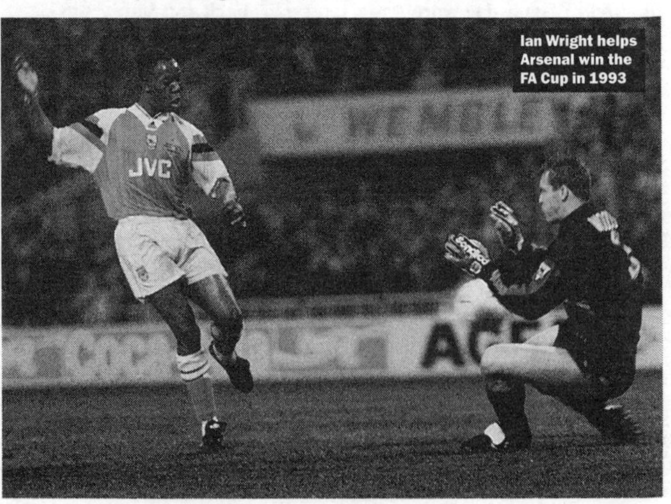

Ian Wright helps Arsenal win the FA Cup in 1993